Bill Lahni

Letters
of the
Master

Volume I

Dr. K.C. Varadachari, Shri Ram Chandraji, and Shri Ishwar Sahai

Letters
of the
Master

Volume I

Letters between Shri Ram Chandraji
and Dr. K.C. Varadachari — 1954 to 1959

Edited by
Mr. Thomas J. Whitlam

First Edition   1992 : 1,000 Copies

All rights reserved

© Shri Ram Chandra Mission
North American Publishing Committee
Pacific Grove, CA, USA, 1992

No part of this book may be reproduced in any form or by any means without permission in writing from Shri Ram Chandra Mission.

Printed in U.S.A.

ISBN 0-945242-20-4 (Vol. I)
ISBN 0-945242-19-0 (Set)

Table of Contents

Publishers' Notes vii

1954 1

1955 5

1956 39

1957 81

1958 179

1959 323

Glossary 443

Dr. K.C. Varadachari

Publishers' Notes

Volume I of *Letters of the Master* is the first of two volumes containing all the existing correspondence between the divine Master, Shri Ram Chandra Maharaj of Shahjahanpur, U.P., Founder-President of Shri Ram Chandra Mission, and one of his foremost disciples from South India, Dr. K.C. Varadachari of Tirupati, Andhra Pradesh.

Dr. K.C. Varadachari was a renowned scholar and philosopher, an expert especially in the Visishtadvaita philosophy. He was a reputed academician and the last post he held was as Professor of the Vivekananda Chair of Philosophy at Madras University. Apart from being one of the first abhyasis of the Mission in South India, he was also one of the first preceptors, and brought the lustre of his intellectual acumen and devotion to the Mission's work, ever since he came to the feet of the Master in 1954. He passed away in 1971 after a brief illness. He rendered signal service to Babuji Maharaj in furthering the aims and objectives of the Mission.

The publishers hope to release in due course further volumes of the Master's correspondence with other preceptors and abhyasis.

Please note that the photos in these two volumes are not in any chronological order.

This correspondence was kindly made available to us by the family of the late Dr. K.C. Varadachari and to them we shall be ever grateful.

1954

No. 1066/SRCM **Shahjahanpur, U.P.**
Dated 20th December, 1954

Dear brother,

Reference to your letter dated 2nd December, 1954 to Shri N. Kumaraswamy of Vijayawada. I have the pleasure in forwarding herewith a copy of *Efficacy of Raja Yoga* as desired by you.

Yours brotherly,
Ram Chandra
President

1955

No. 200/SRCM Shahjahanpur, U.P.
Dated 1st February, 1955

Dear brother,

Your kind letter of the 22nd January, 1955. Thanks for your pains for reviewing the book *Reality at Dawn*. In other words you have joined hands with me in the right cause of humanity, and may God bless you for it.

I am glad to find in you a craving for spirituality which is the birth right of everybody. As for the guru of the type mentioned in the book, I pray that you may have such a one. You too must pray for it, for "More things are wrought by prayer than the world dreams of." I am glad to know that you have made a close study of the books presented to you. I regret I could not understand what you meant by saying, 'I was genuinely interested in the localisation'. So I reserve my comments on it till you clear it to me.

Yours brotherly,
Ram Chandra
President

No. 2045/SRCM Shahjahanpur, U.P.
Dated 4th March, 1955

Dear brother,

I am very thankful to you for the pains you have taken in writing the nice review which appeared in the "Hindu" of the 20th February, 1955. Since then I have received several letters from Southern India in which people have enquired a good deal about the

Mission and its teachings and demanded the books for themselves. I have sent the books to them and also answered all the queries. You have thus rendered valuable service to the Mission and to humanity in general. I am deeply touched by your selfless service and wish you divine blessings for the same. In return I shall be serving you spiritually (the only service I can render to my fellow being) if you stand in need of it, not minding the distance that is between us at present.

With best wishes. Hoping to hear from you soon.

Yours brotherly,
Ram Chandra
President

No. 2078/SRCM **Shahjahanpur, U.P.**
Dated 23rd March, 1955

My dear brother,

Received your kind letter dated 17th March, 1955. Read the contents therein which gave me a good deal of pleasure. When my Master made me his representative, he demanded the *Guru Dakshina* from me which is prevalent among the Hindus from the time immemorial so as to spread spiritualism throughout, because the method of transmission is fading away from amidst the Hindus. I solemnly affirmed that throughout my life I shall devote myself for this sort of service. As such all my spiritual energy is secured for the service of you all. So often I become restless to impart spiritualism to my fellow beings. The work I did in the short tenure of power, the world will remember after me when those things would come to light that I have so far reserved. So if any body comes to me for the spiritual service I think myself indebted to him. I do not stand as a guru to impart training, but as a servant of humanity; consequently, to be more frank I shall spare no pains in giving you every possible approach to a higher vision. The attraction of the transitory world of course is predominant in every mind, because we have been attracted towards it, by our own force. If that force be directed towards Almighty we will naturally be relieved of the things mentioned in your letter. You please leave all these things to me because this is my work and not the business of an abhyasi. There are practices too, which we all do in Mission. I am writing to you these practices to do for some time in the morning and in the evening. If you do them, you will soon develop your *anubhava shakti* and will be able to notice the condition of your mind very soon. In this way you will be helping me also in my task. If you have no time to do the practices even then your progress is sure and I am now taking your case in my hand from the night of 23rd March 1955. But I will request you not to avoid prayer, given hereinafter; that you must do at bed times in the way I am writing to you. I promise you for full support but please make it a point to inform me your condition fortnightly. I will take some time no doubt in removing the complexities, darkness and other impediments from your system, which I am reading from this place, infusing at the same time the godly effulgence. You will begin to feel light heartedness by the grace of God in a very short time.

A few of my associates are again attracting me to South India and I am sure that I shall have to go there. If such opportunity presents itself I shall come to you.

Prayer

"O Master ye are the real goal of human life. We are yet, but slaves of wishes putting bar to our advancement. Ye are the only God and power to bring me up to that stage."

Repeat the words once or twice in your mind and begin to meditate over its true sense and then try to get lost in it. This is real method of prayer and greatly beneficial.

Sit for meditation in the morning, say for half an hour in the beginning and think that divine light is present in your heart. Do this in quite simple and natural way, without forcing your mind to it. Never mind if you do not actually see the light there. Start with a mere supposition so to say and remain sitting in a meditative mood (in one posture as far as possible) with your inward eye turned towards the heart, in the most natural way, without trying to force yourself to concentrate. In the evening sit in the same manner for the same duration and think that all inner complexities and grossness are going out from your back side in the form of smoke or vapours.

For your information, I may point out though with human grief that my prediction given at page 138 in *Reality at Dawn* is coming true. The Gulf Stream is changing its course vide Sunday 'Pioneer' magazine section a prominent daily of Lucknow dated the 6th March, 1955.

With best wishes, Yours affectionately,

Ram Chandra

President

No. 2104/SRCM   **Shahjahanpur, U.P.**
                         Dated 5th April, 1955

My dear brother,

Many thanks for your letter of the 31st March, 1955 which gave me great pleasure. It seems that you are sensitive to spiritual influences. Those who devote themselves to work under proper guidance must succeed.

Faith and love are sure medicines for all kinds of diseases of the mind and its weaknesses. It is the brave who conquer battles of life as well as attain bliss.

You have begun well, may you tread the path with steady feet and a stout heart. Rest assured my services are always at your disposal.

I hope by the Grace of God you will develop capacity to endure worldly disappointments etc. to an appreciable extent by the end of this month.

Please inform me when you feel so.

With best wishes,
Yours brotherly,
Ram Chandra

No. 2126/SRCM   **Shahjahanpur, U.P.**
                         18th April, 1955

My dear brother,

Received your letter of the 6th instant, which I presume must have been dispatched before the delivery of my reply to your previous letter. I look with grave concern to your disturbed condition which I am confident shall definitely end by the close of this month as I already wrote to you in my last letter. By that time your internal troubles and obstructions shall considerably be reduced along with an increase in your power of endurance.

Weaknesses and shortcomings, there are no doubt in everyone but I find no reason why he should take the pessimistic view of them. We should never be disheartened. Dejections and disappointments are the worst poison for a spiritual life. Will, faith and confidence are the essential factors of spirituality. They dispel clouds of dejections and disappointment which surround our mind.

You should watch your day to day condition and write it in a notebook datewise in the form of a spiritual diary. I advise this process to all my associates. It will be very helpful for speedy progress. If you do it you will soon begin to feel a general improvement in your condition.

I am sure that there will come a time when you will see the light of the day. But it will take some time. However, decidedly you will feel something of the sort in a few months by the Grace of God.

Please continue your abhyas by which I will be helped a good deal.

With best wishes,

Yours affectionately,
Ram Chandra

No. 2149/SRCM **Shahjahanpur, U.P.**
Dated 4th May, 1955

My dear brother,

Your letter dated 21st April, 1955. It is but a month since you have been doing the abhyas. I may now ask you (because you are sensitive enough to feel and realise) whether or not the peace of mind in greater degree has developed in you or confusing thoughts are losing their density. Do you feel that your mind when at leisure is automatically absorbed in same inner condition of the heart? For myself I feel perfectly satisfied with the result of my labour, done so far. I find your system clearer and purer. There is no doubt some thing still but only a very little which too will soon disappear.

It is a great fortune to have *darshan* of such big saints. Now happily or unhappily you came in contact with this insignificant fellow who himself does not know what he is. I shall however be pleased to serve you and will continue doing so till your problem of life is solved provided you keep on knocking at me frequently. I do not think it costs you anything.

You asked for my date of birth and of some important events of my life. This is the first time that any one has ever asked me about it. I have not revealed them publicly as yet for, as I think, it might do no good to any body; besides no body will probably be prepared to believe it. Some may even think it to be only a mind's play however I am writing to you as desired for I find a touch of sincerity in your request.

I was born on Sunday the 30th April at Shahjahanpur in the year 1899 at 7:26 A.M. morning (Baisakh badi Panchami Janm Samai (time of birth) 4 Ghari 55 Pal, Bikrmi Sambat 1956). My father was late Rai Bahadur Shri Badri Prasad, pleader and Hon'y Magistrate I Class.

As for important events of spiritual life which you want to know, I treat most of them as confidential. But thinking you as one of us for my affectionate feeling towards you (not knowing why?) I write to you some of my private notes which I believe you will keep strictly to yourself. I kept them reserved for one who writes my life.

From the age of nine I felt a kind of thirst for Reality and I remained extremely confused and perplexed just like a man who is drowned in water. It continued for some time but finding no solution I fixed my mind upon making myself deserving. I went on with this idea till the age of 14 praying at the same time for getting a good and capable master. I also made up my mind that I shall not seek for a master and if I went at all with this idea to some one I shall definitely accept him as my Master. My fortune favoured me and I reached at the holy feet of my Master Samarth Guru Mahatma Ram Chandra Ji of Fatehgarh, U.P. on 3rd June, 1922. That was to me one of the most important events which contributed to solve my problem of life. I commenced abhyas under his guidance and gave up *pranayama* which I had been practising for the last seven years or so. A feeling of perfect satisfaction prevailed upon me when his first glance fell upon me.

Since my Master had bestowed upon me his blessings and favoured me with perfection, I felt an automatic tendency to take up some important working which was the imminent need of the time, of material as well as the spiritual character.

June 1924 (relating to my condition during the period of abhyas) I felt an ubiquitous force present in every animate or inanimate object and particle. I felt God pervading all over like a broad day light. I was drowned in a sea of wonder. I find that the intensity of devotion grew to such a degree of excellence that I often felt unconscious. Had not my reins been in the hand of my worthy Master I would probably have gone down in the state of an *avadhuta gati*.

15th August, 1931 (early morning) I found a great flow of power within and outside me which my inner voice assured me to have been bestowed by my Master. My Master had gone into *mahasamadhi* on the night of 14th August, 1931. This was a usual system of transferring of power adopted by saints of calibre for his representative. It was in fact the merging of the Master into me. The next evening when I heard of the shocking news I felt like a hard blow at my stomach. Strange to tell you that the same pain persists even to this day. I fell ill with diarrhoea which subsequently developed into cholera on 30th March, 1931. After recovery I felt a new spiritual life in me.

12th October, 1932. I felt my Master transmitting to me in dream. I felt two jerks of very strong force. In the first I found my body overflowing with spiritual energy from top to toe. In the second I felt that my heart having over full was almost on the point of breaking down. The third jerk might have ended my life but I prayed to him expressing my inability to bear any more. He consequently stopped.

April 1944. I prayed to my Master (in the brighter world) for several days continuously to show me the light which Moses is said to have felt on Mount Touras. He was kind enough to accept my prayer and showed it to me. It happened in the night at about 2:30 A.M., in a waking state. The light was enveloping me up to a distance of several feet all round.

Under order from above I undertook to tour Southern India from 18th December, 1944 to 28th January, 1945, for the purpose of charging and illumining the whole country with spiritual force together with the temples of Rameshwaram and Dwarka.

I visited a number of places during my tour. I was directed to go to Hyderabad too, not for the above purpose but for blowing up the Nizam Government. I did it by creating circumstances there, which might naturally result in the same in course of time, as it really did come to pass later.

14th August, 1944 I devoted several days in praying to Lord Krishna to reveal to me the Vision of Virat Rup as shown to Arjuna during Mahabharat. The prayer was granted and he appeared to me in my vision showing the full view of Virat.

18th October, 1944 The Over Ruling Providence entrusted to me the task of over-throwing the British rule in India and winning for her independence. I meditated for it for a time when in the end I was ordered to proceed to Delhi to give a finishing jerk to British rule. I did so and completed my work on 16th

April, 1945. Even at present I am not at leisure even for a moment. I am doing working of similar nature still which in reality is my real job, for which I am at present in my material form (the spiritual training being only secondary).

Some of points noted herein are strictly confidential and should be kept as such by you too. I exercised my will in accordance with Divine Command on wars and also on activities of Mr. Bose and numerous other events. I have in notes a good deal about what is to come, about mines recently formed or under formation in the country and about destructive elements found here. But still my knowledge, experience and working is for the Nature's work and I apply myself to it strictly in accordance with the Divine will revealed to me through direction from above.

I have opened my self to you much beyond I ordinarily do. I do not know how will you take all these but facts they are, without doubt and the results are appearing before us in some form or the other continuously.

Some of the dates are missing although the year and month is noted. This is due to the fact that I could not go through my old notes which cover about 1200 pages of the manuscript as it was a very tedious task. All the events are entered in my notes with dates and time of actual direction or working. I have written only a few which I did remember or could easily collect.

With best wishes.

Yours affectionately,
Ram Chandra

No. 2163/SRCM   Shahjahanpur, U.P.
                             Dated 11th May, 1955

My dear brother,

I was simply shocked to learn about the accident. It appears from your letter that you have been hurt in hand. I may assure you that this injury of yours might have put you in physical agony while to me this news itself has brought mental worry. I pray for an early recovery and expect from you that you will stand patiently the trial of hardship which has come before you from God. For the present I close with the prayers and will reply in detail later on.

Your affectionately,
Ram Chandra

No. 2180/SRCM   Shahjahanpur, U.P.
                             Dated 20th May, 1955

My dear Brother,

I am glad to know that you feel the effect I wanted to bring about, though so far only to some extent, but I am sure it will develop if you keep your tendencies directed to it as far as you can.

Numerous forces are no doubt at work in Nature, which affect us diversely causing joy or sorrow. It is beyond human power to eliminate any of them permanently. All that a man can do is to mould himself so as to be free from their effect. Now so long as you think yourself responsible, the effect is bound to come upon you. But if you dedicate every thing to the Master, you will be rid of the responsibility and shall then be doing it in the sense of duty. Their effect will then be minimized and the question of dejection, frustration and distress will not rise at all. I have written enough about it in *Reality at Dawn*.

I presume you did not follow the real sense of my sentence (Now happily or unhappily...). I merely meant to express my actual condition to you which may in other words be expressed as the Changeless condition following the forgetful state of ignorance.

Your feeling of a sense of freedom and nearness in respect to my humble self may ultimately prove to be a fortunate sign. I, for reasons not known even to myself, feel special interest in your training. It may be perhaps because of your having accepted my services so kindly. I may be frank to say that I like and love the southerners much for their being religious minded, and I am confident that there shall be more of spiritual awakening in south India than elsewhere. I hope you must have recovered from your injuries by this time.

Just after closing the above letter I received your next letter of 15th May, 1955. I am greatly pained to know of your feelings of distress and misery. If the actual circumstances which caused those feelings are intimated to me, I may perhaps be in a better position to advise or guide you through. I shall be anxiously waiting your reply to it. Do not think of me as a stranger but as one of your own, closely related to you with bonds of affection and always at your service as a brother. Meanwhile I may suggest to you to read a few pages of the *Reality at Dawn* from 30 onwards which deal with the same topic.

As far as my vision goes I can confidently assert that you have definitely improved and internal peace (*shanti*) prevails remarkably within you.

Shri S.K. Rajagopalan has gone to Badri-Narain along with the Deputy Minister. With best wishes,

Yours affectionately
Ram Chandra
President

No. 2211/SRCM Shahjahanpur, U.P.
Dated 11th June, 1955

Dear brother,

Your letter of 31st May, 1955 to hand. I was very glad to note the contents. You say that in your lectures on Religion you were confronted with your own special problems. That is generally the case with philosophers who take a practical view of the subject. Our ancient philosophers generally tried to arrive at the bottom of things, through practical experience and fortunately the same is the case with you.

A man's problems comprise chiefly of things of his own making. Just as God, through Divine will brought into effect this vast creation, so did the man bring into effect his own tiny creation by his own will. The result was that his Real self got completely enwrapped within the thick covering of grossness. Now the agencies working for it are mainly *manas* (psyche), *chit* (consciousness), *buddhi* (intellect) and *ahankar* (ego). They lead to the formation of samskaras and all these things collectively form a sort of network, round the Real self. That is the true picture of our tiny creation. The only solution is to bring this creation to a state of dissolution (*pralaya*). When this covering is shattered off and the Real self emerges out of it, the real life of spirit (*atman*) begins. That is what spirituality must be taken to mean. This is what I wanted to denote by the sentence 'Give up all thy belongings!' But if a man goes on developing the activities of agencies mentioned above, he continues adding to his material existence in the form of his tiny creation. Thus instead of dissolving, he makes it all the more solid. The only method is to give up or surrender every thing to the Supreme Master. This will end the working of the agencies and the formation of the samskaras will cease altogether. If this is achieved, you can yourself imagine, how far you have advanced towards Realisation. You wish to see the light within and peace which I find in you. You do not seem to feel it at present. For this, I may suggest to you to compare your present condition with that of some time ago. Minute observation is essential. For this very reason I generally advise the maintenance of regular date-wise diary.

Your dream is significant. The demise of your own self indicates the end of grosser existence. It means the beginning of a new finer life (more *suksham*). The royal buffalo must be the visionary form of grossest samskaras of the past. The absence of fear and anxiety shows that they have lost their disturbing character and are now passing away smoothly without much weight upon your mind. Being busy with my own share of the work for you, I expect to hear in reply to my letters, something about your new life of spirituality with definite features exhibiting your steady progress on the path.

With best wishes,

Yours affectionately
Ram Chandra

P.S. It gave me real joy to learn that you are doing great service to the country through your series of lectures on religion. I appreciate it from the bottom of my heart.

No. 2232/SRCM   Shahjahanpur, U.P.
Dated 20th June, 1955

My dear brother,

Received your kind letters of the 6th and the 14th instant. I was greatly pleased to read in the former letter that you realise some growth in you, internally, which you think to be due to the 'subtle and deep spiritual influence'. Your second letter was specially encouraging to me in respect that you have now begun to feel the effect of my labour.

The feeling of my presence near about your self indicates the development of devotional feelings. The only solution of all the miseries of life is resignation to the will of the Master. I am glad to know that you now find it developing in you. Do not please mind if you had not been as co-operative as you should have been. You will, however, I hope, now try to make up the deficiency, if you realise it. I serve all to my best, but everyone receives his due share according to the capacity he develops and the extent to which he creates a vacuum within him for the Divine Current to flow in. In other words the more one co-operates with me and my efforts, the greater the benefit he will derive. I hope to receive further encouragement to my efforts in this respect. With best wishes,

Yours affectionately,
Ram Chandra

No. 2264/SRCM　　　　　**Shahjahanpur, U.P.**
　　　　　　　　　　　　　　　　Dated 6th July, 1955

My dear brother,

Your letter of the 28th June, 1955. I am glad to note that you are hopeful of change in your inner life. It is, of course, unnatural to expect everything to correspond with your tendencies and liking, and so far, none, including even the great saints or avatars, have ever had that in his life. Every one is faced with adversities alike. The only difference is that some take them joyfully as a gift from the Lord, while others grudge them, lament over them, and create a feeling of resentment against them. This adds to our miseries and brings us to a state of distraction. The best and perhaps the only solution is to try to mould ourselves so as to fit in with the circumstances and the environments. Adversity will then lose its pinching effect. That is the true implication of our 7th Commandment of Sahaj Marg, to which I draw your special attention. The inspiring example of saint Mirabai offers a lively picture of devotion and surrender. She joyfully took the poison merely on being told that it was sent for her by Lord Krishna.

However under exceptional circumstances, causing uncontrollable disturbances, one may resort to prayer for the restoration of the peace of mind.

Your resolve to resign and surrender to the Will of the Master is encouraging and goes to show that you are now co-operating with me to a greater degree.

On the inducement of Miss Z.A. Taylor, Asstt. Editor 'General Welfare' Bulletin (England) to advocate the cause of World-peace, I have written a message for the peace loving people of the world and have sent it for publication in the above Bulletin and also in several Indian papers. I send a copy to you as well, with a hope that you will send it for publication in the 'Hindu' under your own covering letter.

If I am informed in detail of your day to day condition, during the meditation time and at other hours of the day separately, I may be in a better position to understand your inner state and may perhaps be more helpful to you.

With best wishes,

Yours affectionately,
Ram Chandra

No. 2295/SRCM   Shahjahanpur, U.P.
Dated 26th July, 1955

My dear brother,

I had posted you a letter No. 2264/SRCM on 6th July, 1955 but have heard nothing so far from you and it created an anxiety about your welfare. I am sure some of your preoccupations might have refrained from writing to me, but please do write to me forthwith.

With best wishes,

Yours affectionately,
Ram Chandra
President

No. 2325/SRCM   **Shahjahanpur, U.P.**
Dated 11th August, 1955

My dear brother,

Received your letter of the 28th July, 1955 and the post card of 29th July, 1955 the same day. I am thankful to you for recommending my appeal for publication in the 'Hindu'. Never mind they have not published it. I had a severe attack of stomach pain which lasted for about 10 days. Even now it sometimes becomes a bit severe. During the intensity of pain I could not serve my associates and you have rightly remarked your condition to be on a standstill during this period. I have now resumed my duty, though weakness hampers its efficient discharge sometimes.

The law of karma referred to in your letter is an established theory of the Hindu philosophy supported by almost all the great sages of the past. But that does not mean we should be an idle spectator of things that befall to our lot, and suffer things tamely and passively. God has bestowed us with reason, intelligence and vigour. We must judge and understand things rightly and apply our vigour and strength in accomplishing what stands fair and just in our sound and unbiased judgement. We must not be lead away by our old set prejudices, nor by our sense of liking or attraction. But we must take things on their merit and stick to that which is just and fair, not minding whether it suits to our liking or not. When this is achieved all our thoughts and actions assume the form of duty and we are considerably relieved of the responsibilities of the result. Thus it shall be all the same to us whether we meet with success or failure in our endeavours. Suffering and worries come (in the form as we understand them) only when we think ourselves to be the actual doer of things. But this idea falls grossly short of the mark of real devotion, not to speak of surrender. I may as well say that worries and sufferings arise only when there is a conflict between our will and the God's will. Such a conflict, if it does exist, is a sufficient proof of the want of true devotion. In fact sufferings in their absolute form as they come to us from Nature are the least painful. It is really we who make them so. We aggravate their effect by making additions to them through our indiscriminate thoughts and actions. Thus most of our sufferings are of our own creation. If we stop this aggravation and give up adding force to them through our will or thought, we will find that they almost disappear from sight altogether. I have sufficiently dealt with this topic in the *Reality at Dawn* on pages 28-34.

Your interpretation of the word 'wishes' as to be referring to sufferings may be a far fetched implication of the word. 'Wishes' is here used in its simplest sense meaning all that we wish for or desire in life. Our desires are to a great extent the cause of miseries. So we pray to God to bestow upon us the state of desirelessness, or freedom from wishes. It is almost certain that unless it is achieved we can never acquire a balanced state of mind. Desirelessness means we stop further formation of samskaras. What remains then is only to undergo the effect of the previous samskaras which when exhausted lead us to the level of liberation. Thus under the system of spiritual training prescribed by my Master, the purging of mind and the clearing of samskaras are the essentials. I am accordingly serving you to the best of my capacity, trying all the while to bring you as early as possible to the state of harmony and peace. Thus I think you are not merely wasting your time with me. I am confident that you will surely see the light of the day even within this very life.

May I be sure that you are cooperating with me as best as you can, which I understand from your letter of 20th July, 1955, in which you stated, 'The idea of surrender has begun to work within me.' I am very grateful to you for all your endeavours in this respect and sincerely wish you to acquire soon a balanced state of mind unaffected by circumstances or occasional outbursts of inner feelings and emotions. I firmly believe that by the Master's grace it may not be a far off thing to you. To quote my Master's words, we are to adopt the life of the waterfowl in as much as its wings never get wet although it remains in water all the time. It corresponds with the example of a lotus which though in water is always dry. Thus, being merged within the water of worldliness we may like lotus or waterfowl be absolutely dry and unaffected by it. It is possible only when we transform our life of body into life of spirit. The life of spirit can be attained by submitting ourselves to the Superior Power or divine force.

Evidently the process thereof can only be as I have often expressed to other associates, 'Deposit every thing in the Master's treasure, having no concern with it.' One might say that I am speaking of lofty things which are unattainable... One can begin it even from the first day of a spiritual life. We will soon begin to realise it as his condition improves, and finally feel himself relieved of every thing of his belongings. The real need of the time for you is to remain absorbed within yourself as far as possible. This is in other words the real form of the Master's remembrance, of which you speak in your last letter of the 6th instant which I received after I had almost finished the above reply. I am exceedingly glad to know that the flow of events seems likely to offer me a chance of having your *darshan* at my humble dwelling here. For your convenience's sake I give below detailed information relating to my house. It is in Mohalla Dewan Jograj which is situated near Carew Ganj, a place well known to every rikshaw driver or tongawala. My father's name late Rai Bahadur Shri Badri Prasad Vakil and special Magistrate may also be helpful to you in tracing out my address. If you inform me the date and time of your arrival I may be able to offer you greater facilities by sending someone to receive you at the station. Moreover it may also avoid the possibility of my being out of station at that time.

    I felt somewhat encouraged by the contents of your last letter, for which I thank you warmly.

    With best wishes.

Yours affectionately,
Ram Chandra

Shahjahanpur, U.P.
29th August, 1955

Dear brother,

Received your kind letter of the 16th August, 1955. I regret delay in reply but I have not been unmindful of my office in respect of you at any time. Your letter which was greatly encouraging gave me a sigh of relief. I had been busy with you from the time you took up my Master's method. I am very hopeful of your case now, time it may take, but it is as certain as death that your resignation and devotion will bear desired fruit. So long I was busy with the double duty, that of clearing off the sinuations from your astral body (due to the effect of samskaras) as well as that of keeping you calm to some extent at least if not more. May I now request you to give me a free scope of work in removing inwardly the things which bar higher approach and not engaging myself alongside in giving you palliative medicine, in order to keep you convinced. Correct training depends upon the thorough purging of the mind which ultimately causes the seed to germinate and flourish.

You should not bother yourself with my stomach ache or other troubles. Let them do their own business and let me remain alive to my duties. For your affectionate attachment with me it is but natural that you should feel vexed over my ailment and I appreciate your love and sympathy. I will try as best as I can to follow your advice for maintaining my health and I am taking care of it already. I shall be very happy if you grace my humble dwelling with your auspicious presence whenever opportunity presents itself.

With best wishes,

Yours affectionately,
Ram Chandra

No. 2386/SRCM **Shahjahanpur, U.P.**
Dated 13th September, 1955

My dear brother,

Your kind letter dated 2nd September, 1955 to hand. I am very glad to note that submission to the Lord's will is gaining ground in your heart. The renowned Sage Mirabai of Mewar offers a remarkable instance of it when she joyfully drank the cup of poison offered to her with the words that it was the Lord's gift for her. And lo! the poison when it reached her body lost all its harmful effect and turned into the very nectar. Such is the effect of Devotion and Surrender. Petty adverse circumstances of our daily life count nothing in comparison to the incident related above. Your acknowledgement of some improvement in your condition offered me a bit of satisfaction and encouragement. I am persistent in my endeavour to help you spiritually as best as I can (that being my primary duty). I am never disheartened in the least because it is the Master's will that is operating through my medium and so it is bound to bring success in the long run.

Hoping to witness further improvement.

With best wishes,

Yours affectionately,
Ram Chandra

P.S. I am sending you a copy of prayer printed in Madras.

No. 2400/SRCM   **Shahjahanpur, U.P.**
Dated 22nd September, 1955

My dear brother,

Your kind letter dated 18th September, 1955 to hand. When there is no end of the difficulties we have no other alternative but to bear them up patiently. There were saints in that past who had courted miseries and afflictions; and there are such spiritual hearts even now who will willingly submit to these miseries. If you think proper and consider me as one near to your heart (and I believe the feeling is reciprocal) you may narrate them by all means. I cannot neglect you in any way, my dear, as long as you welcome my service.

It is surprising to note that my prayers and concentration for your spiritual uplift are having little effect. My Master's power never failed. If you want to test your spiritual power gained in such a short period, howsoever insignificant it may be, please take one or two virtuous persons and transmit them as a trial. If they find bliss under your transmission then it is a healthy sign of your own improvement.

With best wishes.

Yours affectionately,
Ram Chandra

No. 2435/SRCM Shahjahanpur, U.P.
Dated 12th October, 1955

My dear brother,

Received your kind letter dated 26th September, 1955. The delay is regretted. I was greatly pleased to note that you seem to take an impressive effect of my views regarding miseries. I believe and experience that none of the mortals is free from them. In fact they are our most faithful companions who never desert us in an hour of need. But it is really we who make miseries miserable, by the action of our thoughts and will. Joy and sorrow are the two ends of a thing or the two poles of a magnet. As in case of magnet poles unlike attract each other, so does joy attract sorrow and vice versa. When this is the case how can it be possible to ignore either. The only solution in my view is to divert our attention from them, stop giving them strength by the action of our thought and will, and let them wither away like the unwatered plants. This can easily be achieved if we dedicate every thing to the Master and resign to His will. Our job is to remain firm and sincere to our duty and the result rests with God. To feel resentment for what He gives or what He does not give is against the principle of true love and devotion.

I feel and realise the difficulties of the people in this respect and I assure you most sincerely that that is the foremost item taken up by me in most of the cases. My efforts to bring in this elementary progress will be more fruitful if co-operation from the other side is also prompt and active. Without active co-operation the results may considerably be delayed. But I mean no delay on my part so I insist upon it again and again. I am always impatient to see every one on the pinnacle of glory in the minimum possible time. The same I long for you. May you soon rise up to my expectations, Amen.

In my humble opinion the feelings of friendliness or opposition are more often mutual and reciprocal. As such our share in it corresponds to a great extent with that of the others. May God help us all to do our part of the duty in this respect.

With best wishes.

Yours affectionately,
Ram Chandra

No. 2453/SRCM   **Shahjahanpur, U.P.**
Dated 20th October, 1955

My dear brother,

Your affectionate letter of the 8th October, 1955 was no doubt encouraging to me in the sense that my labour has at least come to bear some fruit and silent resignation is growing in you. You say that you are looking forward to experiencing the guru in the heart. That is in itself an abhyas which most of my associates here practice in many ways. Some think him to be in the heart, others think him to be near them or before their mental vision and so on. The process needs no comments. If you think this abhyas to be useful, you may supplement it with your own efforts and try to retain the thought for as long as possible. This is a form of constant remembrance and one who remains in this state with unbroken chain of thought, will find no time to attend to things other than those suited to his sacred purpose.

You say that 'life is a vale of sorrow to those who are ungifted with spiritual light.' Truly it is so. Spiritual light is needed to awaken a man to the consciousness of self and so far as the real self is concerned there is none high and low or great and small.

The occasional feelings of agitation may also be due, to some extent, to the effect of previous habit. It will disappear when you are absorbed more and more in sacred thoughts with an unbroken chain. That is the most effective method of getting over all such ugly things and the surest means of securing close relationship with the Master.

I hope this may be enough for your adjustment. I am very glad to learn that you feel some progress and wish you more and more of it in the shortest possible time. A cup, full of tea, cannot contain pure milk at the same time. One thing must necessarily be thrown out in order to contain the other. So if your heart is occupied in Godly thoughts all the while, there will be no room left for undesirable things and you will automatically be drifted to resignation and surrender. Hoping to receive more encouraging report on your spiritual condition.

With best wishes,

Yours affectionately,
Ram Chandra

P.S. I shall be outstation from 23rd October to 29th October, 1955.

No. 2479/SRCM   Shahjahanpur, U.P.
                                 Dated 16th November, 1955

My dear brother,

Your kind letter of the 6th November, 1955, to hand. Though you write you have nothing to report yet I find many encouraging things reported in it. Really there is no mystery regarding Reality. Complications arise only when we take things in the light of our own knowledge and understanding and build our path based on our particular convictions and prejudices. In other words we become practically individualistic, sticking closely to our own sense of morality, self-interest, superstition and other similar ways, taking it to be the path of righteousness. This brings us to a chaotic state of mind creating trouble and difficulties in our path.

My interpretation of the dream which you related may also be equally peculiar. The tunnel through which you descended may be narrower views of the individualistic mind. The landscape you entered into may be the broader field of spirituality which has been the final resting place of so many. The view of the golden-hued person at a distance may be the representation of some supernatural power towards which you are being led by some superior force appearing to you in the form of a lady. The dark figures in the way are the past samskars which are being silenced and made ineffective. So I infer this to be a fortunate dream which reflects the true state you are at present passing through.

I am very glad to find your chaotic state having subsided to a greater extent and your mind coming up to the normal level from which march towards peace and calmness begins.

I shall be out to Mathura during the last week of November to participate in the marriage of one of my relations.

With best wishes to you,

Yours affectionately,
Ram Chandra

No. 2521/SRCM   Shahjahanpur, U.P.
Dated 14th December, 1955

My dear brother,

Received your kind letter of 2nd December, 1955. I am glad to see your condition improving though the speed has not yet come up to the required level. Growing resignation is a healthy sign. I think it will be greatly helpful to your progress if you devote a few minutes at intervals several times during the day to study your state of mind at the time and note it down so that it may not slip out of your memory and write to me datewise if you can spare time for it. The method is very beneficial and increases the speed of progress. It will help you a good deal to dispel all disturbing elements from your mind.

I quite agree with you that you are sure to achieve that peace of illumination rather I can assert with full faith and confidence that you shall and must realise the true significance of Eternity which is the very basis of the Divine life, provided you remain firm on the path.

It is good on your part to avoid struggling with the circumstances judging them adversely. The outer circumstances in that case will lose their intensity and cease troubling you. To be unmindful of them is the surest remedy of all such evils and I believe you are now slowly advancing towards it.

With best wishes.

Yours affectionately,
Ram Chandra

No. 2523/SRCM   **Shahjahanpur, U.P.**
Dated 20th December, 1955

My dear brother,

Your affectionate letter dated 9th December, 1955 and 15th December, 1955 to hand. Shri Raghavendra Rao of Gulbarga is a man of devotional turn of mind, that is why he was impressed with this insignificant being. It was due to his crystal heart that he held a good opinion about myself, so really he is to be praised for his sincere love. On my part I consider myself to be a servant of humanity and I pray that I may be able to play my part faithfully with our Master's.

I am sorry that I could not give you so much affection as you deserve, for which I can only pray that the blessings of the Almighty may be pouring in every fibre of your being. My affectionate heart is open to everybody and you are not an exception to it. I shall be very happy if the problem of your life be solved by the grace of my Master. I have every hope that you will reach your cherished goal provided your thirst for knowledge increases day by day. I have never met with despondency in spiritual field so far by the grace of my Master. I always pray that you may be one of the best figures in South India and people may be benefited by your spiritual attainments. The frustration and despondency that stand out as a test of sterling qualities, I hope will not last long. There will be an end to them as well.

I eagerly wish to see you and my other associates of South India and I try to seek the opportunity for it. But I meet with dejection as my mother, aged about eighty-seven, is suffering from cardiac asthma and she constantly requires my services.

We are two brothers, the younger one after taking some degree in medicine is established in London and has given up the idea of coming back. This thing is naturally shocking to my mother and she does not brook the idea that I may remain away from her for some time. If I go anywhere she does not allow me to remain out for more than a week. If I go to South India, it will take at least a month and a half, because I have to see all my associates at different stations, devoting at least some days in their company for their satisfaction.

With best wishes,

Yours affectionately,
Ram Chandra

P.S. I think you must have received my letter No. 2521/SRCM dated 14th December, 1955.

1956

No. A33/SRCM   Shahjahanpur, U.P.
Dated 12th January, 1956

My dear brother,

    Your kind letter dated 2nd January, 1956 to hand. I am doing my duty towards you as much as I can and I am confident that you must be progressing. If you study yourself a little you will find the marked difference internally. Your system is greatly purified and inner peace, I witness, is developing.

    I could not get the Homeo medicines Kali Carb 30X and Carb. Veg. 30X here for my mother. I have requested a friend of mine to get them from Lucknow. It will be very kind of you if you send the address where reliable medicines can be had. For the time being I am giving her the Ayurvedic pearl preparation as her asthma is pertaining to heart. Attack of asthma is accompanied with palpitation of heart. Please give detailed instructions about the administration of the medicine.

    I celebrate the birthday function of our Master on Vasant Panchami day, which falls this year on 16th February, 1956. The function will last from 15th February to 17th February. I give you my personal invitation for the function.

    With best wishes to you and love to children.

                              Yours affectionately,
                                  Ram Chandra
                                      President

No. A69/SRCM   Shahjahanpur, U.P.
                             Dated 5th February, 1956

Dear brother,

Your kind letter to hand. My mother is taking the Homeopathic medicines as instructed by you. She is feeling relief, although she is not quite free from the trouble. On the 30th Jan. she had an attack of asthma but it was not very serious. It might have been due to her fast on that day which she had observed for the sake of her children's welfare. I only give her Carb Veg in the morning and Kali Carb once in the night. I want to know whether Kali Carb can be repeated only when the attack is in full swing or at the time when there is breathlessness which generally remains constant to some extent. Kali Carb of course gives her relief but it does not stop breathlessness altogether. I hope you will give further directions on the above points. I shall be trying to give the medicine regularly for some time according to your directions at times. She is also suffering from cough which troubles her more in the night but a little in the day too.

I hope that you shall be free from depression by now. If so please inform me so that I may be again with the regular course of your spiritual training.

With best wishes to you and love to children.

                             Yours affectionately,
                             Ram Chandra

No. A81/SRCM   Shahjahanpur, U.P.
                            Dated 21st February, 1956

My dear brother,

I feel greatly encouraged to hear from you that you are aware of my spiritual influence during these days. I shall all the time be conscious of my duty towards you, and it is all due to your co-operation which makes progress more speedy. Everything no doubt depends on the divine grace but our job is to make room for it within ourselves. That is all the purport of our practice or abhyas to which we should all try to remain alive every moment.

As for my mother's condition, I may inform you that I gave her the medicine No.1. It relieved her to a great extent. But breathlessness persisted. On the fourth day I gave her another dose and now the breathlessness is much decreased. I shall give other doses when required. Now please give me further directions whether I should give the doses which are still with me, at times when the trouble is aggravated. Also whether Carb Veg and Kali Carb also are to be given, when the present medicine is finished. Any other direction which you deem necessary. I thank you for your greetings for the birthday celebrations of my Master. My mother wishes you a long blissful life.

With best wishes to you and love to children.

Yours affectionately,
Ram Chandra
President

No. A124/SRCM   Shahjahanpur, U.P.
                        Dated 17th March, 1956

My dear brother,

Your kind letter dated 3rd and 13th March, 1956 to hand. Read the contents thereof, which gave me a good deal of pleasure. I am feeling the signs that you are co-operating with me and have now begun to develop faith in the Master. So what you have written about your condition, the credit goes to you. I am really speaking the helper in serving the humanity to the best of my ability. You require a good of labour upon my part and I am doing it very gladly. What I eagerly desire from you is that you prove yourself useful spiritually *pro bono publico*, when so many things you are doing for the public good.

I am now appraising you of my mother's condition as desired. I gave your dose No.1 and the other ones. At first some relief was noticed in breathlessness and that too for a short period, and thereafter the trouble reappeared with greater force. I then prolonged the duration of administering the medicines and waited for its result and at last when I found that the trouble in spite of decreasing was assuming critical dimensions, I had to resume the Ayurvedic treatment for her immediate relief. She does not ordinarily take Allopathic medicines. She will take them only when she is convinced by me and the doctor that the medicine does not contain anything forbidden by the religion. The disease seven or eight years back started from cough. The condition at present is that she is still suffering from cough accompanied by breathlessness. The sputum does not come out easily but when it comes out even in small quantity it gives her relief. During the attack she feels dryness a good deal. She finds a little relief while sitting. The trouble increases during after midnight and specially in the gray of the morning.

Doctors of this place are of opinion that it is cardiac asthma and the opinion of the heart specialist is the same. I was under the impression that during the attack her heart begins to palpitate but as she says and I too notice that the first part of belly which begins from the end of ribs, i.e. midway between liver and spleen, begins to move to and fro. I do not know the technical word of this part and so you will try to gather the sense. Her blood pressure is also a bit higher.

If you prescribe any medicine for her, please write the name of the medicine to me and I shall purchase it here. If it will not be available here I shall send for it from you. She has grown sufficiently weak and has lost the wonderful memory which she once possessed. The winter season is practically out and at present it is like that of Madras and Trivandrum in winter season. It sometimes becomes cloudy and gives showers which makes the atmosphere cold which is short lived.

I am enclosing herewith a copy of message for you and for your friend. With best wishes to you and love to children.

Yours affectionately,
Ram Chandra

No. A 149/SRCM Shahjahanpur, U.P.
Dated 28th March, 1956

My dear brother,

Received your kind letter of 21st March, 1956. I thank you for your appreciation of my humble appeal.

I am glad to note that you feel more recollected and peaceful internally. That is a sign of progress. In fact, that is the very thing which we all strive for in the beginning.

As for the inner vision which you say has not developed in you so far, I think it will grow clearer and as you advance with internal peace and calmness and develop the habit of remaining absorbed in divine thoughts all the while. But I do not understand what you mean by saying, 'The meditation has always been on my lips'. Please explain it further.

I shall try the medicines suggested by you for my mother. The medicines shall be available here in the market. If not I shall write to you for them.

With best wishes to you and love to children,

Yours affectionately,
Ram Chandra
President

No. A 149/SRCM Shahjahanpur, U.P.
March 30, 1956

My dear brother,

Received your kind letter of 27th March, 1956, from camp Waltair. Your thirst for speedy progress is highly encouraging. I feel greatly elevated to hear that you feel greatly relieved of materiality and the effect of reverses. It is all due to the benevolent grace of the Great Master. I do not actually know exact nature of your worries, though I am able to guess some, from the general state of affairs and circumstances prevailing in that part of the country, revealed to me by my associates in South India.

You say, you always think of me alone. That may probably be due to your own feeling of love and attachment towards this humble self. If it continues, it shall be greatly beneficial to you as thereby you shall be knocking at my heart continuously. You say you are now in my hands. I rather feel myself to be in your hands, as you seem to have captured my heart by your sincere love and devotion. However be it as it may, probably you shall not be a loser either way. I wish you to be another Vivekananda but my expectations waver with the thought that I am no Ramakrishna Paramhansa. It is however up to you and your efforts to be 'He' if you desire to be so, earnestly. In fact to transmit Power is a matter of but a second. But power without proper moulding is of no avail, rather it is detrimental and even dangerous. The making of a man involves the purging of the mind of all darkness, physical and mental grossness and the unbalancing conditions of senses and *indriyas*. Thus it is not an easy job. It is a long and tedious process which requires continued strenuous labour and combined efforts on the part of both the teacher and the taught.

The book *Ten Commandments of Sahaj Marg** is in Urdu and I am afraid you might not be acquainted with the language. It is no doubt a wonderful book, dealing with the dynamical relation with man and God. One of our South Indian associates has just completed its English translation which will be sent to the press after I have gone through it myself. But that may perhaps take several months.

I am very glad to find that you now seem to be fully alive to your own sense of duty in this respect and it shall be of great help to me in my work.

With best wishes and love to children,

Affectionately yours,
Ram Chandra
President

No. A 185/SRCM **Shahjahanpur, U.P.**
Dated 20th April, 1956

My dear brother,

Your kind letter of 10th April, 1956 to hand. Humility, so far as it serves as a safeguard against pride and vanity, is a virtue. But when it leads us to underrate our talents and inner capacity, it is harmful. The Master can without doubt do any and everything, by his own unlimited power. So one who is attached to Him in true sense can never entertain any idea of weakness or inefficiency because the great Master's power begins to work through when there is need for it.

---

* Editor's Note: "Ten Commandments" refers to the "Ten Maxims" of Sahaj Marg.

You say that you know yourself to be most unfit and unprepared but I seriously differ with you on that point. We are so, only so long as we think ourselves to be so. That is probably the only hindrance in our path. 'A man can do what a man has done,' is a common saying. If Swami Vivekananda could attain that high level of spiritual elevation, why can't we, who are endowed with all the powers of body, mind and soul like him. Despondency is the real stumbling block. If it is removed our march becomes smooth and easy, and we soon begin to develop the feeling of resignation and surrender. In fact we are the real makers of our destiny, hence much of our future depends upon us. There is no limit of time and age to it. Spirit is never old, hence spirituality is not affected in the least by old age. Spiritually a man feels himself always young, at all stages of human life. It is therefore never too late to attain anything in the spiritual field.

I am very sorry to learn that you had some trouble caused by the excessive heat. Thanks to the Great Master for your recovery therefrom. Your mother's condition too has put me to great anxiety. May she recover soon. As for my mother, I have again started Ayurvedic treatment and it is giving her some relief. I have a mind to wait and see the effect of this treatment. If I do not get the medicines you have suggested locally, I shall request you for the same without any hesitation.

With best wishes,

Yours most affectionately,
Ram Chandra
President

No. A 189/SRCM   Shahjahanpur, U.P.
                              Dated 23rd April, 1956

My dear brother,

Your kind letter dated 20th April, 1956 to hand. I am happy to note that you are feeling mental peace. Before replying your letter I must confess that I want to take some spiritual work from you. I am fully convinced of your ability and spiritual capacity so during this age you take up the spiritual work, of course you are doing a little. I was also holding a Govt. job and retired from service on 24th February, 1956. I did not request for my extension in service because I wanted to spend the remaining part of my life to the spiritual service of mankind. Although there were circumstances that I could very easily get extension for a year or two but I neglected it. As regards my present income I have only to feed upon miserably because unhappily the abolition of Zamindari adversely affected my financial position. I have got some agricultural fields no doubt, but owing to the work of the Mission I personally can not attend to them with the result that the profit is not very much.

Now I come to the point on which you invited my opinion. I pondered over the question and came to the conclusion that you must not try for the Directorship of the Oriental Institute in which you worked previously. This will also keep you aloof from further humiliations. Depend upon God and do your duty.

May God give your mother speedy recovery. My mother is a bit better by the present Ayurvedic treatment.

With best wishes to you and love to children.

Yours affectionately,
Ram Chandra
President

Shahjahanpur, U.P.
Dated 28th May, 1956

My dear brother,

I received your two letters and the book *Aspects of Bhakti* for which I am very thankful to you. I shall go through it after some time as I am overbusy with the marriage arrangements of my elder daughter, Maya Devi, which is to be held on the 9th June. Please accept my humble invitation for your participation on the occasion.

I regret that during this time I shall not be able to attend to correspondence, except of an important nature.

With best wishes,

Yours affectionately,
Ram Chandra
President

P.S. Shri Raghavendra Rao of Gulburga (Hyderabad State) who was staying with me since 17th May is now leaving for Gulburga tomorrow. Please accept his *pranam*. He is now going back as a preceptor, to work at the Mission branch newly opened at Gulburga.

No. A262/SRCM   Shahjahanpur, U.P.
                 Dated 6th July, 1956

My dear brother,

Received your affectionate letter of 29th June, 1956. Shri Raghavendra Rao is a man of talents with a great devotional mind. It was due to his own merits and the Master's blessings that he was able so soon to rise up to the required level so as to represent the Mission's branch at Gulburga. I feel convinced that he will put up well with the work of the Mission, helping the associates in south India through Transmission. It is true I propose to undertake a tour of south India in the coming winter. I have also a mind to establish branches at different places there provided proper hands are available to work as preceptors. It shall however be a matter of great regret to me if Tirupati remains lagging behind in this respect. I can not express the feeling of affection for you which I find present in my heart and which is all due to the reaction of your thoughts. So in fact the credit is due to you alone. It may be true that you sometimes feel the torture of the past memories but if you judge minutely, you will find their weight considerably reduced.

I earnestly wish for your transformation through Divine Grace, which you crave for so eagerly. I am ceaselessly busy with my job for you, expecting closer co-operation from your side, to ensure the desired result. The words 'Divine Grace' used in your letter reminded me of the Supramental of Shri Aurobindo, for which his disciples are still waiting with eager expectations. To my mind that which he meant by Supramental, has already descended on earth with the advent of the Special Personality in existence today. You are sensitive enough and intellectually advanced too. Please try to feel whether the huge tidal wave of Divine Grace is overflowing the atmosphere or not, filling every nook and corner of the world. What one needs under the circumstances is only to prepare himself to receive the Divine Grace, so lavishly available all over.

I have only gone through half of the book as yet but I feel quite convinced of its merits and the noble ideas contained therein.

For your good wishes and the Master's blessings my daughter's marriage has been celebrated in the most graceful manner. I thank you for the same.

With good wishes,   Yours affectionately,
    Ram Chandra

No. A300/SRCM   **Shahjahanpur, U.P.**
    Dated 27th July, 1956

My dear brother,

Received your kind letter of 11th July, 1956. I am glad to note that one of my boys, admitted in your college, is interested in philosophy. He will do still better if help from within is available to him in a greater degree. I was also greatly interested in philosophy since my very boyhood. But when I reached the holy feet of my Master, I closed the book and opened my heart to Him. That was my only study then (the reading of the Book of Heart). It continued for full 22 years, after which I found myself satisfied with my lot and completely settled at heart.

You had invited my opinion about the job, so I was obliged to do so in good faith, as far as my poor understanding could allow me. I still feel confident that you did well in not applying for the post. God is Great. We must have faith in Him and He will help us all through.

I appreciate highly your grandfather's remarks, which is a great truth. Nothingness is the very nectar of the Real Life, which I earnestly wish you to have a full taste of. Your eager craving for it offers me a bright hope of your success in this regard.

I am very glad to learn that you follow Shri Vaishnavism. Here in Northern India too most of the high class persons follow it. Shaivism comes next to it. My mother, sisters and other members of the family also follow the same course. Saints must in all cases be duly respected. Shri Aurobindo Ji and Maharishi Raman were the dynamic personalities and we must all bow to them in full respect.

I do not, my dearest brother, claim in any way to be the messenger of God nor the special personality, but only as one of the humblest servants of humanity. May God grant me strength and means to play my part well in this respect. I say only what I feel and believe when it comes to me automatically. Trusting my associates full well I open my heart to them without any reserve. The same was the basis of my last letter to you. You are perfectly justified in disbelieving it unless you have experienced it personally. I am, after all a human being, liable to mistakes and errors and the same can sometimes be the basis of my views and expressions. If they have, however, injured your sentiment in any way, I feel repentant for the same and apologise to you for it.

As for my spiritual services it is and shall always be at your disposal, so long as you may be pleased to welcome it.

I only try to invoke God's blessings by means of prayer through the medium of my Master. In case I apply my own insignificant force for the purpose, my thought gets connected with the Main Channel in prayer for the accomplishment of all that is needed in the aspirant. Thus I can in no way be called a Master in this respect. I may however be only a helping factor in the spiritual growth. But after all, my dear brother, it is but a bare truth that one can be successful only when the good Gracious God by His own Divine Grace pulls him up, out of the mire of worldliness.

I am however, deeply impressed by your extreme eagerness for an experience of the presence of the Supreme Personality who has already descended. It is of course very difficult to recognise him, amid so many claimants to the title. The difficulty becomes greater when we try to judge and recognise him in his outward form, according to our own conception of him as an avatar. But that does not at all concern him nor does it affect his presence in any way. He is, as he may be, busy all the time with his own programme of the Nature's work, unknown and unnoticed by almost all, especially by those drowned in absolute materialism. His authentic Voice may be resounding in every heart, though it may not be audible to any one of them on account of the clamour of innumerable voices within. All these voices, my dear brother, must necessarily be silenced in order to catch the vibrations of the Voice of Silence, and that, in fact is all that we are to endeavour for during the course of our spiritual march, in order to gain a direct experience of the Eternal Ultimate. With kind regards and best wishes,

Yours most affectionately,

Ram Chandra

No. A 328/SRCM   Shahjahanpur, U.P.
Dated 10th August, 1956

Dear brother,

Your most affectionate letter of 1st August, 1956. I appreciate highly your firm faith and devoted resignation to Divine Will, which is the surest means of Realisation.

Shri Ramanuja and Shri Aurobindo have no doubt been great personalities who have done immense work for the welfare of the people on the Divine path. I have a great regard for them and think highly of their services. My humble help is always available without any reserve to all those who are needful of it without any regard to class or sect. Spirituality pertains only to Infinite Reality devoid of all differentiations and complexities. For that, it is but essential to have complexities removed as early as possible. The philosophy at the root of the system is simple. We try to dissolve the tiny creation of our own making. Our individual existence in the form of a tiny creation is in fact the miniature copy of the God's creation. So like *mahapralaya*, the final phase of the God's creation, *pralaya* of our individual creation is essential for our return to the Origin. The method too is quite simple. Negation of everything is the only process to bring about dissolution. This is what we do throughout.

My oft-repeated words, "Give up all your belongings," convey the same sense and for this we have to discover means. That is our only pursuit.

As regards your ignorance of philosophic conditions, as you call it, I may say that some of the thinkers hold that doubt is the basis of philosophy. But I would prefer to put in the word 'wonder' for 'doubt'. Doubt implies a latent sense of knowledge, whereas wonder implies ignorance. We doubt when anything appears contrary to our knowledge but we wonder when anything appears to be un-understandable to us. That indirectly indicates our ignorance of the thing, and inwardly induces us to try for its realisation. **We start from total ignorance and end in complete ignorance.** Will you, my dear brother, like to agree with me on this point? This stage of complete ignorance is almost the last state we have necessarily to achieve, and blessed are those who acquire it in this very life time.

I am glad to note your earnest craving for the knowledge (which is beyond knowledge) and vision of the Divine Personality incarnate in the world today. May you soon be blessed with it.

With best wishes and love to children.

We would be observing complete fast on 28th August, the auspicious Janma Ashtami day, in honour of Lord Krishna's birthday and would be devoting ourselves entirely to prayer and meditation for the whole day, as usual.

Yours affectionately,
Ram Chandra
President

No. A 340/SRCM Shahjahanpur, U.P.
Dated 21st August, 1956
My dear brother,

Received your kind letter of 18th August, 1956. The news of your son's fracture at the elbow created anxiety. May he recover soon.

I shall reply your letter after sometime as my mother has had a severe heart attack a week ago and is almost confined to bed. The attack has almost subsided, but her vitality is not developing which is causing great anxiety. I am therefore busy in attending her.

With best wishes to you and love to children.

Yours affectionately,
Ram Chandra

No. A 349/SRCM Shahjahanpur, U.P.
Dated 28th August, 1956
Dear brother,

Your affectionate letter of the 18th August, 1956. I am glad to note that you seem to agree with my views regarding the liberation process. But it is not all we aspire for. We take into view the farthest point, which can but be where every thing ends. As such it must be the point wherefrom everything had started at the time of creation. For expression's sake let us call it the Zero point or the Origin. This is our destination as it must be of every one who aspires for the highest.

Liberation is but a far lower level as compared to it. Now whatever the nirvana of the Buddhist may be taken to mean, I do not feel contented with anything short of this highest mark. I no doubt agree with you that theories are useless. Blind philosophy too is of no avail in this respect. The solution lies only in the direct experience of things and for that the only process is the total negation of all things of our creation.

I am glad to learn about your experiences of growing peace for which the Lord is to be thanked. It is but a preliminary stage. I wish you to be blessed with higher experiences.

My mother though out of danger now has grown extremely weak and asthma too still persists.

With best wishes to you and love to children,

Yours affectionately,
Ram Chandra
President

No. A 369/SRCM   Shahjahanpur, U.P.
Dated 9th September, 1956

My dear brother,

Received your kind letter dated 28th August, 1956. You must have received my letter No. A 349/SRCM dated 28th August, 1956. My mother has now recovered from the shock of heart attack, but she is extremely weak and cannot move by herself. Please pray for her recovery. It is a matter of pleasure to me that you witness peace. I hope it is not long before that you will be able to win up the disturbances. I am after all at your service.

I appreciate your idea of surrendering to the Master. The easy method of doing it is to acquire the state of submission to the great Master which will ultimately develop to self-surrender. I do not want to discuss its philosophy before my learned brother but only add a sentence that in this way you make yourself negative for the Divine power to rush in torrent.

I am writing below a meditation which has proved efficacious. If you do it it will help you a good deal in your spiritual progress. This is my tried meditation and recently I made it compulsory to all my associates.

Meditation

Think that you are drowned in the shoreless ocean of bliss and the waves of the ocean are passing from the front through your entire body (which should be supposed as transparent at that time) towards back side, carrying along with them, darkness, grossness, dirt and all the ills of the body which are impediment to spiritual progress. It should be done 10 or 15 minutes in the morning and then start the meditation of light on heart.

With best wishes to you and love to children,

Yours affectionately,
Ram Chandra

No. A 394/SRCM Shahjahanpur, U.P.
Dated 25th September, 1956

My dear brother,

Received your kind letter dated 17th September, 1956. I am glad to inform you that my mother is improving and I think I shall be able to visit South India by the grace of God. You are really a true seeker and I think it a pride to serve you spiritually what my poor self can do. There is a Persian saying that even the leaves of the tree do not move without the Divine dictate so you are perfectly right in saying that without His grace peace cannot reign, and one cannot sway over *indriyas*. We always try to invoke His blessings through our Master.

I am always hopeful to your case due to your eager desire to attain the goal.

May the day dawn when you taste the nectar of life that is real.

With best wishes to you and love to children.

Yours affectionately,
Ram Chandra
President

No. A 403/SRCM Shahjahanpur, U.P.
Dated 1st October, 1956

My dear brother,

Your kind letter dated 27th September, 1956 to hand. I am happy to note that you have begun our new meditation. You may adjust it according to your own convenience, either in the night hours after *japa* or in the morning.

Reality dawns on him, who proceeds steering, away to the main goal. Goal, of course, is within you, but the thoughts are travelling at a long distance. Now the distance you have created yourself; and that you have to cross with the help of the same force which has created the distance. Now to cover that visionary distance we take some methods which seem to be artificial in comparison to Reality. But how can we leave them? The meditation I have written to you is not to gain anything so that you may develop idolatory but it is for the cleaning of the different forms of idolatory which have entered into being. We do not conceive it as a paraphernalia of *shanti* or bliss so that it may bring artificial trend, but we make it a source to bring the standard of Reality which is yet to dawn. It is not the case here. We are only setting up an equation having X as the value to solve the problem of life. You have expressed in your letter your revolting nature against imagination etc. I have taken all these points into consideration, before prescribing the meditation to our associates. Sometimes a peculiar meditation, prescribed under the avowed authority, becomes dangerous and my revered Master had strictly warned not to prescribe such meditations unless one has become capable of hitting at the root or the Divine wisdom has developed. I have taken all these precautions while laying down the prescription.

I do not take a single step, my dear brother, unless I get light from my Master and a representative of a great saint must have that faculty. So by this method even the sleepy idolatory will dig its own grave and grossness will bid farewell. I assure you, brother, I do not take childish steps in these matters.

The effulgence you have expressed at the base of the brain is real and I congratulate you for this. Please do not think it to be an hallucination. The love you are developing accounts to your own merit. I assure you for good that I take it as a pleasure if you ask me for anything; and the more I am delighted, when you depict in your letter the true picture of your thoughts.

Before writing the reply to Dr. Nicoll's statement I must go to hundreds of years back to tally the statement of the Western thinkers, who are yet to learn spiritualism from India. Scientifically they have dealt with our thoughts as far as it was possible within the limits of the mind. The Western thinkers stop where the mind ends. It is we the Hindus, warm salutations to our sages, who start where they end. Dr. Nicoll, whom I will study, has according to you described Sahaj Marg as fourth way. I have not been able to make out as to what was his actual notion about the fourth way. Whether he had laid it down in order of preference or he mentions it as one of the numerous ways. However you name it as zero or X, the efficacy remains the same. The word *sahaj samadhi* has occurred in the songs of Saint Kabir praising it thoroughly well. Guru Nanak has also written it as *sahaj avastha.* As far as I remember Swami Shankaracharya adopted this word in his commentary of Vedanta philosophy. My Master used to call this method as 'Sant Mat'. Afterwards he named it as sahaj marga (Natural Way — for God realisation) because we proceed side by side with nature. I agree with the opinion of Dr. Nicoll that the nature of consciousness must be changed. I have dealt with this thing in *Efficacy of Raja Yoga*.

After proceeding a long way in spirituality, consciousness grows subtle and subtle till it turns into potentiality itself and as soon as we get rid of it we reach the Reality — pure and simple. We go far above the elements and the nature of transmission depends upon the calibre of the guide. The pure sort of transmission is free from all these *mayavic* character which ultimately develops in elements.

I agree with Dr. Nicoll that Hydrogen 6 is the highest because the subtler potency of the elements works more effectively in the system, which as a Homeopath you can understand very well. To tell you the truth the highest form of transmission is **its** subtlest state which the Guru of high calibre does at one's deathbed when he wants to make him perfect in the shortest possible time. It sometimes can shatter the nerves so the saints reserve it for the last moment. I have gone so far to say that we have to become zero where number is gone and the wreath is broken. If you add zero to any number it becomes tenfold. So the value of zero is greater than all the numbers. I have tried to express myself as much as this poor self could afford.

With best wishes to you and love to children.

Yours affectionately,
Ram Chandra
President

No. A 432/SRCM   **Shahjahanpur, U.P.**
Dated 20th October, 1956

My dear brother,

Received your kind letter of 4th October, 1956. I was greatly moved by what you have written about yourself and it shall be highly gratifying to me if even patches of my heart are applied to cure up your wounds in the form of numerous complexities and afflictions received during the course of your search for Reality. My very flesh and blood is meant for the service of my fellow beings and you are no exception to it.

I want to be a bit frank in writing on the points raised in your recent letter. I hope you will not please mind if there is anything disagreeable to your taste or feelings, as it is all meant in good faith for your guidance for the transformation of your being. Being yourself a great intellectual, you apply the same instrument for the search of Him, and believe in, where this thing is common, because that serves as food for your brain. But this is not the sure cure of the evil. Considering it deeply, I come to the conclusion that it may be justifiable in so far as it has been generally the weighing instrument for a Mahatma. The literature and books satisfied the mathematical cult of realisation, where the digits increase the number and each one becomes, in itself, a knot to complete the chain. To gain knowledge is, of course, commendable but to apply it in its own way for spiritual development is, many a times, wrong in my humble opinion. Wisdom works only when we take into consideration individuality, and so long as individuality is in our view we are away from the real point. Simple faith earned by devotion will carry you far. But while moving towards faith, great difficulty arises when we find so many seemingly deserving, to claim faith from our side. We or most of us fall into error (and this is but human nature) because one is generally inclined to repose faith in whatever seems relatively closer to him in the knowledge which he himself possesses. Where there is no knowledge but complete barrenness, there rests the thing. This barrenness or bankruptcy of thought brings a man on the right path. If one is rich in letters and has it as his sole hobby, he will be attracted towards the same rich but unauxiliary state. My dear brother, if you find any man totally bankrupt or entirely done away with, think that the state of barrenness — the real goal — prevails full fledged in him. Sages have expressed Reality as light because no other word seems to be more appropriate for the expression of the state. But it is not the luminous condition as we understand from the word. The light generally carries the sense of something pleasant which in itself becomes the quality and not the Reality. No doubt, we observe light during our march to freedom but its value in real sense is nothing but that which invades the eye. If you think deeply you come to the conclusion that it is only reactionary because it has its own results. The mystery deepens when we apply our mind to it. When we go deeper we rest upon its cause which is unchangeable. The amalgamation of matter with spirit gives spark, which is fanned up by abhyas and invasion is the result. It is no doubt commendable because it reminds the abhyasi that there is something behind it, in which we have to be absorbed. The state of absorbency is the same as expressed by, 'a drop of water in the ocean.' Lord Buddha is said to have seen the 'light' which had transformed him all over. To my mind, it was in fact the unfoldment of the very Being, as the outcome of his deep meditation with sincere devotion, and not the luminous sight of bright and dazzling light.

With good wishes to you and love to children.

Yours affectionately,
Ram Chandra
President

No. A 451/SRCM Shahjahanpur, U.P.
Dated 29th October, 1956

My dear brother,

Received your letters dated 17th October and 23rd October, 1956. I had already replied your letter dated 4th October, 1956 under this Office letter No. A 432/SRCM dated 20th October, 1956. I presume that it has not been received by you so I will send its duplicate copy with the reply of your letters referred to above.

You are free to write me any thing you like about yourself. Be it far from me that I get annoyed in any way. Such things help me for my proper adjustment.

With best wishes to you and love to children.

Yours affectionately,
Ram Chandra
President

No. A 460/SRCM Shahjahanpur, U.P.
Dated 4th November, 1956

My dear brother,

Received your kind letters of the 23rd and 26th October, 1956. The contents of the letters indicate, to my great joy, more hopeful signs of your better and higher approach in spirituality. You, whom people consider to be a great intellectual, do not think yourself to be so. This is in fact the real sign of greatness and learning. I crave for such men all over the country. It is said of Raja Bhoja that once a man came to him for an employment. The Raja told him that there was no vacancy but he still insisted upon his request. At last the Raja asked him to go about the whole kingdom and find out a person unsufficiently educated, so that he might be replaced. But he could find none such. The fact was that even parrots in his kingdom recited *Veda mantrams*. This was the condition of the country which I wish for once again. It is on account of your being an intellectual in true sense, that you sincerely want to understand things fully. But Divine Reality not being a thing to be understood only by means of intellect, you naturally feel thirst for Divine insight which finally leads you to practicality. I greatly appreciate your sincerity and earnestness in this respect which in my opinion can never go unrewarded. The frank expression of your mind cannot in any way be attributed to impertinence. It is just what I want and it is necessary too for the right direction of the spiritual training. As such it has been greatly helpful to me in my work for your betterment.

From your letter I feel you have strong craving for a more abiding experience of self for which as you say you are ready to bear the loss of intellect even. The process and practices which you have undertaken, all tend only that way and are sure to bear fruit in no distant future. That is my sincere wish for you and for all my associates. I feel that you are daily having some internal change which you yourself will understand in due course, the signs of which you mention in your letters in different ways.

As for your expected experiences during the period from December 2nd to 19th. I too may luckily be there to witness them as I propose to have your *darshan* at Tirupati during that time.

Your feeling of the descending flow from the cerebellum to the mid-back indicates divine touch.

Our system of spiritual training proceeds in the most natural way. We start from the 'heart'. There are five points in the heart as shown in the rough diagram enclosed herewith. We start from point no.1 (which we call as 'heart'). When our spiritual state improves we come to the next step which is marked as point no.2. From this place we travel on diagonally to point 3 and then to 4 and 5. These are the main points of the lower region known as *pind desh*. There is a reference to three of these points in the *Rig Veda* which I accidentally happened to come across. Now crossing of these five points means the end of our march through *pind desh*. There are numerous conditions which an abhyasi goes through in this region. But four of them are very important.

An abhyasi passes through all these, though they may understand them or not. Those who are sensitive enough do feel them. The first condition brings him to a consciousness that all animate and inanimate beings in the world seem to be ejecting a lovely divine influence everywhere with the result that sometimes the abhyasi is inwardly aroused to embrace even thorns and thistles. The next condition brings him to a feeling of 'everything as God'. In the third state he does not feel the existence of any object animate or inanimate. The fourth state rouses in him the feeling of the One and only One, reigning all over. As we go through these major states we grow more and more subtle. When we acquire *avyakta gati* (or undifferentiated state) all these conditions fade away. We lose contact with *maya* or elements. The entire structure now falls and we begin to proceed by the state of Bliss which can only be felt in a practical way. Thus we enter the godly kingdom. There are still very many things after it which I wish you all to witness and experience for yourselves having your own share in the Nature's work. This is in short the usual line of process, followed under our system. I have touched only the elementary steps. Further on we proceed in almost the same way through other regions, e.g. *brahmand* and *para brahmand mandal*, etc. In the end I would add that your problem of life will be solved without doubt, the signs of which are distinct and clear. The following quotation from Shri Aurobindoji also supports my above view, 'The time of your turning to the spiritual life depends upon your own aspiration. A sincere aspiration brings always its response and if there is continuity in the will, the result cannot fail.'

With best wishes to you and love to children.

Yours affectionately,
Ram Chandra
President

No. A 483/SRCM **Shahjahanpur, U.P.**
Dated 21st November, 1956

My dear brother,

Your kind letter of 9th November, 1956. I appreciate highly your view that God's Will is supreme. Man has no other alternative but to submit to it whether he likes it or not. I am glad to note that you have taken the wisest course of dedication which is the preliminary stage of resignation and surrender. Self-surrender is undoubtedly the gateway of Divine realm.

I used the word *darshan* in respect of you, simply because I respect you for your vast learning and extensive knowledge, which I myself sadly miss. I believe I may be able to gain something from you in this respect, when I am with you during the coming tour. In my early age I felt an inner aversion to the idea of borrowing knowledge from the experiences of others. I, therefore, devoted every moment of my life to experiencing things practically. But now I feel that learning too has its own merits and counts much in our set up. I have therefore great regard for all such personalities. Now I often try to read and study books but unfortunately I am unable to retain anything in my mind.

Though there is, as you say, nothing fresh to report yet I see encouraging signs of progress in your spiritual condition.

With best wishes to you and love to children.

Yours affectionately,
Ram Chandra
President

P.S. I am just in receipt of your kind letter of 18th November, 1956. Reply to each of your points is given below as desired.

1. I shall start from here in the night of 10th December, 1956 and shall drop at Jhansi for about 24 hours. I will leave Jhansi on 12th December, 1956 and am expected to reach Tirupati on 14th December, 1956. I intend to stay at Tirupati for 3 days.

2. Only two persons are coming, i.e., myself along with Syt. Ishwar Sahai, Preceptor in charge Shri Ram Chandra Mission Branch, Lakhimpur-Kheri, U.P.

3. I always feel homely with my brothers and I would be very glad to stay with you as one of your family members. No special arrangements are to be made for our stay there.

4. I intend to start from Tirupati on 17th December, 1956 for Madras. Thus you will be able to start from there on the 18th December, 1956, for attending the Phil. Congress Session from 19th to 23rd December.

The current Southern Railway Timetable is not available here at present and as such I am not definite about the actual time of my arrival there. I am trying to get it from Lucknow or somewhere else and I shall then inform you the exact train and time of my arrival there. If, however, I am not able to do so for want of the Timetable, I shall inform you by wire from Jhansi about the exact train of my arrival there. My mother's condition is much better now and I will be able to start for South India provided her condition remains as it is at present.

I am also in receipt of your kind letter dated 13th November, 1956 which will be replied later on.

Yours affectionately,
Ram Chandra

Please let me know your telegraphic address and also that whether I should get down at Tirupati East or Tirupati West.

Ram Chandra

No. A 502/SRCM　　　　**Shahjahanpur, U.P.**
Dated 4th December, 1956

My dear brother,

Your affectionate letter of 13th November, 1956, the contents of which offered me encouraging hopes of your capacity. It reveals the real worth required in an aspirant of spirituality. How humbly and meekly you have expressed your inner feelings. I cannot say what more ability can there be expected in a true seeker. There may be a few things which might be capturing your mind for the present but they shall all disappear in due course. Your very aspiration for Reality shall wipe off all dirt and rubbish from the way. If it does not or if you do not improve spiritually I must confess it to be due to my own weakness.

I thank you for your kind suggestions about the Patrika. I have already written about it to Shri Kashi Ramji. The difficulty is that all of them are Hindi-knowing persons except one who is only High School. Shri Kashi Ram knows 5 or 6 languages but his knowledge of English is not much. I have entrusted this work to the Assam branch only to reduce the pressure of work here. Every branch of the Mission is almost overbusy with its particular work. The Gulburga branch too contributes its own part and the pressure of work there is likely to increase shortly. Shri Ishwar Sahai, a very capable man, in charge of the Lakhimpur branch has been entrusted with the work of spreading the Mission's ideology in foreign countries. His articles are invited by the Japanese saint, Rev. Yonosuke Nakano and are put up at the World Religion Conferences held every year in Japan. I only peruse them and then they are sent. On my own part I too remain ever busy with **doing nothing**.

I have recently written a book in Hindi, in which I have also discussed the spiritual as well as material powers gained at the different points mentioned in my last letter to you, and also how they can be utilised. It deals with all the various conditions from the beginnings of our march to the end.

Very recently, while I was getting *Rig Veda* read over to me by one of my associates, I was greatly surprised to discover a mysterious power flowing through the sound caused by the correct pronunciation and proper recitation of the *mantrams*. The vibrations created by the rise and fall of sound, automatically affect the vital points of our chakras, thereby affecting a spiritual awakening in them. By and by all the spiritual stages are revealed and crossed over by mere recitation of the *mantrams*. Thus I can now boldly assert that it is the only book of which mere recitation or *swadhyaya* can bring a man to perfection. The meter and rhyme of the *mantrams* is so wonderfully set, as to help our march (*yatra*) through the various points of the chakras. This is quite a unique thing untraceable anywhere else. As for example, the *mantrams* in praise of Indra have a direct relation with point No. 3 and their recitation directly affects the spiritual state at the point. Similar is the case with Vayu. It touches point No. 4. The *mantrams* of Agni affect the *kantha chakra* (Point 5) which if recited for some time will bring *kantha chakra* to a state of awakening. The hymns in praise of Saraswati affect a particular point of the head with which it is directly connected and in course of time it is awakened by the effect (though of course with a little help through transmission). The recitation of the *mantrams* relating to Usha (dawn) Minerva Latin, Athene Greek, affect the left-side portion of Trikuti where the state of super-consciousness abides as stated in the *Efficacy of Raja Yoga*. There are thus very many wonderful things in them. Though I do not know Sanskrit still I fully grasp the effect of the rise and fall of the *mantrams* and I am quite sure and definite about it on the basis of my personal experience.

My Master had also written much about different topics of Vedanta and on his own researches in the spiritual field. But as he was a scholar of Urdu, Persian and Arabic, though he knew English as well, all his writings are in high class classical Urdu for the translation of which equivalent Hindi words are hardly available. He too did not know a word of Sanskrit but it was most wonderful of him that he could easily translate and explain the Sanskrit slokas and Hindi verses. The points mentioned in my last letter are all connected with all such powers which gods possess.

With best wishes and love to children,

Affectionately yours,

Ram Chandra

P.S.- I also received your letter dated 26th November, 1956. I am grateful for your kind offer of hospitality. I could not get the South Indian railway timetable as yet, so it is difficult to let you know the time of our arrival. Of this much I am sure, that I shall start from Jhansi on 12th December, 1956 at 1 A.M. by Grand Trunk Express, and will take the very first available train, wherever there is a change for Tirupati. I will very easily search out your house, if I fail to let you know the time of our arrival. However, if I get the timings at Jhansi, I shall inform you by telegram. You have written to me that you felt in meditation as if the mind entered the heart. I could not grasp the sense. So I could not reply.

My mother's condition is much better these days. It is due to our South Indian brothers, who are offering prayers for my mother's health, in order to enable me to be in their midst.

Ram Chandra

After the close of the postscript I received the South Indian railway timetable from Delhi. Now I find that the G.T. express by which I will be travelling, reaches Gudur junction at 10:08 A.M. on 14th December, 1956. Therefrom I shall catch 11:53 Gudur-Katpadi passenger at 11:40 A.M. and reach Tirupati East at 5:26 P.M. on 14th December, 1956. Now I hope this information will suffice and there remains no need of sending the telegram to you.

Ram Chandra

No. A 547/SRCM   **Madras Camp**
Dated 23rd December, 1956

My dear brother,

It gives me immense pleasure to offer my heartfelt gratitude for all the entertainments we had during our stay at Tirupati. Though this, being a common form of etiquette, may also be treated as such, still I find it based on love and devotion.

For myself, if I were to translate my feelings of heart I would say that I feel rather captivated in such a manner that in spite of all my flutterings I am unable to get out of the snare of love and remembrance. Can you offer me any explanation of this? I fail to understand what charm you have pronounced on me so as to keep me spellbound in this way. Your words, 'I am yours,' and 'My services are at your disposal,' are constantly ringing in my ears, producing an echo of "I am Thine" in my heart. Unable to restrain my feelings I must frankly confess that "I am Thine — I am Thine."

After all I am one of the human beings and not a sage in any respect. For in my term a sage can be only one who has established himself firmly in the changeless state and who may not require another second to bring a man up to Perfection, as was the case with my great Master whom I now represent in my own humble way. I am very glad to find you gone up, to the point no.2 at 8:45 P.M. on 19th December, 1956.

With best wishes and love to children.

Yours affectionately,
Ram Chandra

No. A 549/SRCM Trichy
Dated 26th December, 1956

My dear brother,

I have received information from my son, that my mother had fallen down and had hurt herself in the ribs. She wants me to be there earlier. So I have decided to cut short our tour programme. Consequently I propose to leave Trichy on 29th December, 1956 at 21:50 P.M. reaching Madras at 6 A.M. on the 30th. I shall immediately leave for Renigunta at 8:40 A.M. reaching there at 13:58 on 30th. I may stop at Renigunta for a few hours before leaving for Tirupati. I propose to reach your place by any train till evening. I shall leave Tirupati on 1st January, 1957 at 9:12 A.M. and shall catch Bombay Express at Renigunta at 10:36 A.M. Please inform the people at Renigunta of my programme as they were very eager to detain me there at least for a few hours. I do not know why I am unable to forego meeting you again under any circumstances.

I could easily curtail my programme at other places but not at yours. May God bless you for all this — for keeping me bound to you as one, your own. With best wishes and love to children.

Yours affectionately,
Ram Chandra

You must have by this time received my previous letter No. 547/... from Madras.

1957

No. B 57/SRCM   **Shahjahanpur, U.P.**
Dated 14th January, 1957

My dear Varadachari,

I arrived here on 12th January, 1957. I had stopped at Kanpur and Lucknow for a day only. I got your most affectionate letter on my return. It disclosed the true picture of your devotional heart. I find no words to express my feelings, created by your own self. Not being paradoxical as I had been before I can safely say that I think myself as you. And that is the reaction of your feelings, so it is you who deserve the credit.

The highly commendable terms used for this humble self may possibly be justified only when I find myself successful in making you like that. May the Master's power bring you up to it.

While at Gulburga I happened to notice several times that you were trying to communicate your heart's feelings to me through prayer. You may be doing this consciously or in a subconscious state, that I cannot say. But I understood the sense though the words were not quite clear, and I did reply to you in the like manner. This denotes that you are proceeding towards Intercommunication stage. I think I should now be more plain about myself without any likelihood of being taken as an arrogant fellow. I often talk, when need be, to some distant sages in the like manner.

You say you find me sitting before you in meditation time. Yes. I do come (in astral form) at your call and sometimes of my own accord too.

The conditions which an aspirant usually goes through are changing, and it must be, change being essential to bring in the state of Changelessness.

I like all my associates to have a full experience of all the states so that they may be well fitted for the task of helping others by their own experience. To tell you frankly I have a burning desire to see at least one in every house, capable of coaching others spiritually. That is in fact a moment's work with the Master's power at the back. But I want you to have a full view of the inner life which in the words of Swami Vivekanandaji means 'Man behind man!'

You talk of the merging of the lover with the Beloved. That does come by ultimately. You should never think even for a while, that your progress is slow. I know best how to regulate and where to make the speed slow or fast. The *brahmand mandal* is a very vast region. The rishis of old have often taken years to go through all the numerous phases in order to acquire sufficient power for further approaches. I have devoted about one and a half years in cleaning your entire system, not minding whether you feel satisfied with it or not. The result thereof is now before you. I am at present busy with your inner making in addition to the usual job of preparing you for approach to upper regions. Rest assured that I shall detain you at points only so long as it be absolutely essential for your own good. I am taking your emotional and intellectual centres also alongside, which I explain to you by the diagram, enclosed herewith, to give you a knowledge of them.

Point A is the centre of Desires and B of Thoughts. I discovered them when I was at Madras and immediately tested them on Shri I. Sahai. But at present I do not think it advisable to touch them in your case. I am taking your points X_1, X_2, Y_1, Y_2, Z_1, Z_2 devoting a week on each. I have omitted X_3, Y_3, Z_3 because they are related to Kundalini and other powers. They may be taken up when it is proper. You should inform me of your condition regularly, leaving the rest to my judgement and discretion.

I have also taken up the case of sister. Please direct her to practise meditation at any time when she is free from the household work, in the usual manner as you do, thinking of the Divine Light in the heart.

Will you please write to me the full particulars of my children regarding name, age, class in which reading etc. Also please warn Narayana on my behalf not to be negligent with his studies as he had been during these few days.

I have left the book *In Search of the Miraculous* with Shri Raghavendra Rao for his study. He may be able to pick up things better as he is a student of science and mathematics.

When I left Tirupati I had discovered that a new state (i.e., seeing everything coloured in Divinity personified) was developing in you. Is my observation correct?

It is extremely cold here nowadays on account of frequent hailstorms all over and heavy snowfall in the Himalayan regions. I think it might be almost unbearable to the people of the South who may better choose warmer months for their trip to this place.

I remember Mr. Balasubramaniam often. I have started my work for him. Please tell him to practise regularly and report his condition. Frequent association with you will also be helpful to him. During the Annual Function Days i.e., 4th and 5th February both of you must sit for meditation (morning and evening from 6:30 to 7:30) and on the 6th in the morning only. This must be observed strictly by all associates to view the Divine current act in motion during these days.

Shri I. Sahai is leaving for Lakhimpur today. He conveys his *pranam* to you and father.

My mother is now better.

With best wishes and love to children. Convey my humble *pranam* to Rev. Appaji.

Yours,
Ram Chandra

No. B 65/SRCM   **Shahjahanpur, U.P.**
Dated 20/21 January, 1957

My dear Varadachari,

Your affectionate letter dated 15th January, 1957 to hand. My previous letter no. B-57 dated 14th January, 1957 in response to your last letter must have reached you by now.

I am glad to hear that all my children are deeply interested in me and I pray for their long life, prosperity and spiritual well-being. I wish you all glittering prospects in spiritual life, by the grace of the Master, with Divine Wisdom dawning upon them ultimately, imperceptible though it may be at present. I cannot open my mind to show how much devotion you all have created in me. I again raise my hands in prayer for you all. Now you are entirely mine. Believe me that you shall taste the nectar of the real life. I am cocksure that you can never miss it. I can confidently say that you are on a higher level, there is no doubt about it. But since you are entirely mine I do not mind whether you are calm at times or disturbed at others. These are all the various states which an abhyasi must pass through. Change being essential to bring in the state of changelessness as stated in my previous letter. You must not care if bliss prevails or not, as bliss itself becomes a bondage in the end. However I shall give you doses of Bliss at times to relieve you of the disgust.

Your doubts as regards your approach are but natural as you have not fully undergone the experiences of the various states. In this respect I may present the examples of Shri Ishwar Sahai and Kumari Kasturi, the two personalities of whom the Mission may well be proud of. Shri Ishwar Sahai was brought up to *brahmand mandal* within six months of his approach to me. What induced me to it was that I required hands for the Mission's work. Further on his selfless services compelled me to give him stages after stages in quick succession with the result that he has now entered the 12th circle (as described in the *Reality at Dawn*). He is now in a position to pull on the Mission's work with his efficacious training. He remains almost thoughtless, and enjoys the state where even Bliss has departed. He has not the slightest tinge of *maya* in his Transmissions. But in spite of this he has no experiential knowledge of all the various states in detail. In the case of Kumari Kasturi I did the same up to the *brahmand mandal*. But then I realised that experiential knowledge too must be acquired by the abhyasis for their own satisfaction. So I took her step by step. She has therefore a fair knowledge of all the states, major or minor, which she has passed through. She has so far gone through points counting from A to Z and again from A_1 to M_1. Her experiences together with my explanatory comments over them forms a unique record of the spiritual march.

You wish to remain steady in the state of Bliss and I too pray for it, rather I am taking you towards the point where Bliss even, fades away. I assure you that there is no likelihood of a 'Fall' when so much of the Master's power is at our back. Your reading about the centres is correct. I am taking several things all together for the sake of your speedy progress, as intimated in my previous letter. I am happy to note that you are going deep into the *brahmand mandal* with good speed. All the powers of Nature (pleasant or unpleasant) are stored up here. I want you to contact them all. Please have patience and let me have a chance to play my part well. I want, rather Nature wants you to be useful for the practical purposes. For that you must have practical experience and that is the true internal knowledge. Practical experience is necessary for a good trainer, so I wish you to have it full fledged, not minding the time, which I may assure you, shall not be longer than necessary. As for a hint of your present state I may say that one who has crossed the *pind desh* can in no case return to this world after death.

I feel an uncontrollable inward inducement to be with you again and again and this is due to strong attraction from your side. This evening at 8:15 P.M. (20th January, 1957) I felt you were telling me something. Please verify if it is true or it is only my fancy.

All that Shri Raghavendra Rao wrote to you is due to his own devotion and that of the associates there, that they felt so much pleasure in the company of this Handful of bones.

As for the children they are required only to hear the vibrations of the heart, resounding with 'Om' or 'Rama' for 15 minutes only and not to go in deep meditation. Their duty at present is to look to character-building and their studies to which they must devote themselves entirely.

With best wishes and love to children. Please convey my humble *pranama* to revered Appaji.

Yours,
Ram Chandra

No. B 68/SRCM Shahjahanpur, U.P.
Dated 21st January, 1957

My dear Varadachari,

After closing the last letter, I received yours of 17th January, 1957, full of promising hopes of brighter prospects. The point of Brahamarindra is not yet open, but you were led to believe it so, because while going deep into the *brahmand mandal* you had come across glimpses of it. Every cell contains the essence of all the foregoing states.

I am taking up the purification of your centre X_1, hence there may have been slight sex trouble but it shall soon come round. I shall not be able to continue this work from 4th to 8th Feb. but due to my making by the Master's grace when and wherever help is needed, my thought is automatically there though I may be as busy as possible.

I am glad that you felt our Master's power rushing in though slowly. It is so, but it is very deep acting like a homeopathic dose of high potency. This is very essential for the inner making and you will realise its effect when time matures for it.

By the way I may quote from the letter of Kumari Kasturi the wonderful description of her state on the point M_1 as intimated to me by her recent letter. She says, 'I feel that *puja*, meditation, love and devotion were all like dirt which has been washed away.' What a high state it is no doubt.

Narayana should give up his lethargic habits and should be more smart and active like a young boy as he is.

Yours,
Ram Chandra

P.S. As for a piece of advice to my dear Arvinda I may say that he should have courage to work with a will of confidence. He should be regular with his studies and finish his day's work without fail. He should devote Sundays for the revision of the week's work. That is all what is required for easy and sure success in the examination. The same will be useful for all other children.

Ram Chandra

No. B 88/SRCM   Shahjahanpur, U.P.
Dated 7th February, 1957

My dear Varadachari,

Received your affectionate letter of 23rd, 28th and 30th January. The function is now over. My Tamilian friend, Shri S.K. Rajagopalan and two associates from Assam were among the participants. The Master's grace prevailed bountifully all over during the period.

On the 22nd night I had practically no sleep except for about an hour. I remained busy all night with the work lying in arrears on account of S.I. tour. At midnight I watched you to be sleeping, with the same idea of "I" (as related to me) present in your heart. I was very glad and began transmitting to you strongly. Your experiences the next morning may probably be due to that effect.

The bluish grey colour witnessed by you is the colour of *brahmand*. As such it is but natural to experience it as we pass through.

The eleven circles of Egoism (and not ten as you stated) have no connection with five points of *pancha agni*. It is very difficult to locate them physically in the human body as they are extremely fine and subtle. They are really the different states of Ego or *ahankar* in the purified form. The circles end in an almost extinction of Egoism.

As for your uplift it is needless to say that it is continuous from day to day in a supernormal way but it is very difficult to explain the daily changes which are so minute that they can hardly be distinguished from each other.

You had been, as you say, accustomed to communicate to God. But mind this capacity (to communicate with Souls) develops automatically when a certain spiritual state is arrived at. Attempts to acquire it before that by artificial means or force of practice is often dangerous and is likely to lead to false conceptions.

As regards the spirit message you sent to me I think it needs no comments from my side. However since the matter has been moved by your uncle you may with due respect offer him your advice on the points if it is at all necessary. But I shall for good reasons advise you not to get yourself entangled in it or even take an active part in the affairs.

I thank you for your devotion to the Mission. I am sending herewith the books. Please give *Efficacy of Raja Yoga* to Mr. A. Balasubramaniam and the Urdu book to Mr. A.K. Moorti of Renigunta.

With best wishes and love to children. Convey my due respect to your father.

Yours,

Ram Chandra

P.S. The spirit message is returned herewith, as desired.

No. B 96/SRCM **Shahjahanpur, U.P.**
Dated 9th February, 1957

My dear Varadachari,

I received your letter dated 6th February, 1957, just now. I am deeply perplexed to know about your serious illness. I am praying for your speedy recovery and I hope my prayer will be granted. On 1st and 2nd February I felt myself disturbed to know the welfare of yourself and children. I wanted to ask you the reason of the same but I could not do so. My dear, your illness, no doubt, how painful it is to me, will bring excellent result in your spiritual life. You will gain strength very soon. You need not do any meditation during illness. Really speaking you are all the time in meditation inwardly. So please start the meditation when you recover. Please tell Mr. Balasubramaniam to write to me about your health because I do not want to keep on you this strain as well or any of my boys may inform me about it.

With best wishes to you and love to children.

Yours,
Ram Chandra

No. B 141/SRCM   **Shahjahanpur, U.P.**
Dated 2nd March, 1957

My dear Varadachari,

Received your affectionate letters dated 11th February, 1957 and 23rd February, 1957. I did not reply these letters earlier with a view to avoid mental strain upon you during the previous illness. I am overjoyed to know that you are now free from sufferings. May you live long to irrigate the minds of the people morally, intellectually and spiritually! The time is not now far off for it. I speak highly of you that you could stand patiently such a painful disease. You are perfectly right that the disease was a boon to you and an anxiety to me. You have really been purified to a great extent, swimming at the higher pitch of *pind pradesh*.

You have begun to become the part and parcel of the condition of the *pind pradesh* which we call *laya avastha* in that region. Think it deeply and you will find that there is a change in your inner life. You must be feeling a kind of spiritual fragrance.

You have surpassed me in love to my Master. I think I must write with tears that I could not love my Master as he deserved. I do not want to keep in myself the spiritual treasure bestowed to me by my Master for you all. Please relieve me of the pressure of this responsibility as soon as possible.

When I read your lovely letters I often think, 'Am I a fit man to be loved?'

Papita (papaya) is very useful for stomach, liver and removes the constipation. This is a fruit from which the English medicine papain is obtained. The juice of the different vegetables boiled without water is beneficial to health.

The second issue of the "Sahaj Marg Patrika" has been received after publication. The manager of the press did not send the proof to Shri Kashi Ramji at Tinsukia (Assam), so the mistakes are there like that of the first issue. His charges too are very high. He charges Rs. 375/-. You will get your copy direct from Tinsukia.

With best wishes to you and love to children. Please convey my respect to Appaji.

Yours,
Ram Chandra

No. B 153/SRCM Shahjahanpur, U.P.
Dated 7th March, 1957

My dear Varadachari,

Your most affectionate letter dated 28th February, 1957 to hand. I will reply this letter a week after clearing everything which you want to know. You must not feel yourself distressed at all. God is great. I believe you must have received my letter No. B 141/SRCM dated 2nd March, 1957.

With best wishes to you and with love to children. Please convey my respect to Appaji.

Yours,
Ram Chandra

No. B 166/SRCM Shahjahanpur, U.P.
Dated 17th March, 1957

My dear Brother,

Received your most affectionate letters of the 28th February, 8th March and 11th March. I am replying all of them. Events at Allahabad seem to have distressed you much. I came to know of it from Shri Ishwar Sahai too. He had informed you of all incident. I too on my part do not want to keep any secret from you, who is developing to be a part and parcel of my own self. I shall always be free to you henceforth.

Now I come to the point. My heart has already melted to an extent that when vibrations of thoughts enter in it, they form their own shape. Bewailings of the mother and the patient's children moved my heart to pity to an extent that I underwent the process, which I did not even know a minute before. Once I had requested my Master to reveal the process to me, but he refused saying that he did not trust me in this respect. But when time came, the process was clear to me within a moment's concentration and in an instant the action was done, so suddenly of course, that even my Master found no time to check me from doing so. I had even acted in an unnatural way in this case. I wiped off the evil influence of the stars at the time and directed with full force, the good effect of the favourable stars. This was being verified at each step by one of my associates who is an astronomer. Soon after I observed heavy frowns on the Master's face and he scolded me much saying that the part of life I had transferred did not belong to me entirely, but to the world which had full claim over it. You will be surprised to know that the thing came to the knowledge of Saint Kasturi, the very instant it was done at Allahabad and she told about it to her mother and others. When I returned to Lakhimpur she verified it from me.

When the doctors saw that the tuberculosis glands had burst spreading the poison throughout the body they entirely gave up hopes and stopped further treatment. When I watched her system I too found the poison there. I pulled it out, though the process is generally disallowed, as the poison, being very powerful, acts upon the doer. So I got it. Afterwards I liquidated about 60% of it as I felt that my brain was not working as soundly as before. But when I resumed its normal working I left the rest at its place as that much time could better be utilised for the good of others. This is but my nature which may be attributed to lethargy. One of my associates has prescribed Natrum Mur 6X for me which I sometimes take. The blackness is still there although considerably reduced. The acute pain, soon after, has also eaten away much of the poison. When the disease is taken out it is not brought on one's own self but is thrown aside. Whereas in poison cases it does affect the doer to some extent. For this very reason the process is generally disallowed in pthsis, snake-bite and syphillis or like cases. It may be a wonder to note that in case of a disciple, so closely attached to the Master as to feel almost one with him, his samskaras pass on to the Master for bhoga, though of course a greater part of it is fried up by itself. You may thereby naturally conclude that loving the Master means torture to him but so is not the case. Suppose there is no such disciple of that capacity, the Master, being himself free from all samskaras past and present, shall then begin to contract samskaras from unknown source to keep up his physical existence. Such a question was once asked by Shri Ganesan of Trichy. It will appear in the next issue of the magazine along with my answer to it. It is thus the Nature's Boon to the Master who cannot otherwise attain the state of Liberation in life. But these are the things reserved only for personalities of my Master's calibre. One thing more in this connection. The abhyasi too after a time begins to stop the formation of samskaras. I pray and hope that you may come up to it soon and I shall inform you when you are there. I think you are right in saying that my life is more useful to the Mission and the world in general. There are men in India, (occident may mourn for such ones) who have not the least regard for their life if they find some good coming out by sacrificing it. Take the case of Gandhiji. He was once fasting for 21 days and his condition had at a time fallen down so much as to compel the doctor to declare, 'Nothing but the immediate ending of fast or some miracle can save his life.' At that critical moment a saint of India did transfer his whole life to him. He also left a note stating that Gandhiji's life is more precious than his and he was immediately dead. It was published in the papers the cutting of which was preserved by one of my brother disciples.

So has it happened again now in my case. At 7:55 pm on (date unavailable) I was intercommuned by a sage of Ceylon who stated that he has been ordered from above that he should transfer to me from his life, the portion which I have lost. My Master directed me to be attentive to him. I did so and in an instant the action was over and the gap was filled in. This sage was the disciple of one who was in communion with me sometime ago and was in my personal attendance (in astral form) at the time of my first tour to South India. He also used to draw impulse from me and was under my training. He attended me for all the time I remained on tour. He kept me informed of all things necessary and helped me at every step. He had also requested me to blow up Colombo as it was the place of grossest debauchery due to the influence of the foreigners. I consulted the Master and he disallowed it. He also promised to offer me his full support if I started my Master's Mission in S.I. He is now in the Brighter World. The present sage is his disciple. He has made this great sacrifice in compliance with his Master's order. On 7th March some more sages made the same offer which I declined to accept as I do not mean to stay for more than the allotted period. Saint Kasturi knew of it the very moment and she reported to me all about it for verification. This is due to her devotion that now nothing can remain as secret from her. Shri Ishwar Sahai also verified it by his own insight. Thus your worry over the incident should now be over. I am highly indebted to the sage for this sacrifice and I am thinking how it is to be repaid.

Now your letter of the 8th March, 1957. Believe me my dear Varadachari that you deserve more than you understand. My heart is like a piece of iron which is easily attracted by a magnet. Your devotional attitude has made your heart a magnet to attract mine, for which you deserve my congratulations. It is now a pretty hard task for me to restrain myself from giving you further approaches earlier than necessary for the sake of proper training and internal knowledge of experiences. Experiences however subtle they might be, add to the store of internal knowledge. There are different kinds of bliss which an abhyasi can well understand by comparing them with one another. What you have finally to gain is neither bliss nor otherwise — a changeless state. I remember to have asked my Master whether this is the very bliss reigning in me, for which your gracious self has laboured so long. I feel but Nothing and Nothing. He replied to me that if your present state is for a moment pulled off from you, would you like it or not. I submitted respectfully that I would prefer death to parting from it even for a moment. What charm is there, no words can describe. Regarding your idea that my every word and action displays Negation I may say that I feel nothing of the kind in me. Similar may be the case with you. You too may not be feeling the state which I do in you. Surely enough if any one having a keen eye studies you he will definitely arrive at the conclusion that my Varadachari is born newly again. Think my heart to be your playground. Mr. Subramaniam has written me that you have unbounden love for me (i.e. for one who is totally gone in true sense). Now you can yourself imagine where your devotion rests. I think where everything ends. What that place can be? Nothing but that where we are to rest — the main goal of life. In other words you are where you want to reach finally. What else now you want to acquire? Nothing but experiences of the path and the unfoldment of self for the guidance of others.

Now your letter of 11th March, 1957. I am elated with joy to read the contents. How fortunate I am to see such a good condition displaying in you. I think that thousands of kingdoms can be sacrificed even for a tiny grain of it. You write, 'I was feeling indrawn throughout yesterday and getting a state of inactivity or quietness of mind.' This state of quietness remains inwardly all along your day's work. It means you have embraced the soul in all its corners and you are now proceeding with it. This is a kind of *laya avastha*. This is the fragrance of the soul which I meant in my last letter. It is not felt by the sense organs as it is not a material thing. A man having an open internal vision will be soothed if he peeps into your internal condition. This very moment as I am attentive to you I am feeling the same thing and find myself soothed, by the mere touch.

Mr. Subramaniam has written to me that there are a few persons who are interested in our system and wants to organise a group of satsanghis including all such persons. I have replied to him that they can start the practice and I may be informed of it so that I may adjust myself accordingly. Your group if so formed will be a nice one. I shall be waiting for an opportunity for the same.

I have sent you a parcel of books. It contained one Urdu book for Mr. A. Krishnamurti of Renigunta. Have you received the second issue of the magazine from Assam? I have sent one to Mr. Subramaniam. Children are all well except my second son, Dinesh Chandra (appearing at the coming H.S. examination next week) who has been spitting blood for about two months due to the after effects of typhoid. He has been X-rayed and the report stands as below:

"Both sides of the chest move well in respiration. Both costophrenic and cardiophrenic angles clear. Hilar shadow grossly exaggerated. Peribronchial markings prominent in both upper zones. There are no signs of any active disease of lung or pleura."

I am deeply concerned with my children there and pray for their success at every stage of life. Amen.

I believe sister might by now be relieved of the sciatic pain. Massaging in my opinion will be useful. In my case too I feel considerably relieved from respiratory troubles by the effect of the massaging of the whole body.

My respects to dear Appaji and loving good wishes to children.

With best wishes,

Yours,

Ram Chandra

Tirupati
25th March 1957

My dear Revered and loving Gurudev,

Please accept my pranams and love. I have been able to meditate for some time all these days and yesterday morning I did extend the time for half an hour, though in the evening it was much less. So also this morning. I have not yet got back the strength or is it due to something else? I do not know.

I am deeply moved by the letter from Shri Ishwar Sahai that you have been speaking highly of my love and devotion. I do not feel that I have merited this praise yet, for yet there are waves of depression on and off which makes me feel utterly helpless and a sense of nothingness. I am impatient in a sense for the full experience and I do not know that I have already been taken over many of the hurdles. Further whilst one has crossed over the *pind pradesh* how can he be yet swimming or becoming part and parcel of the *laya avastha* of the *pind pradesh*? This was one of my problems. But I have taken it that it is no longer my concern whether I go past the *pind pradesh* or swim in the *brahmanda mandal* or attain the state that has to be achieved and all that remains is to know each and every step in between so that I could be of use to all and perform my humble service to Thee who art the Incarnate Guru, the Personality sent by the Divine for our salvation and evolution. I am thine and that is that. As Thou hast said when the conditions are ready all will be shewn and made known.

Shri Ishwar Sahai also wrote to me that I should attend to Thee more and more. I am trying my best thanks to Thy grace. Certain past bondages, both spiritual and physical and otherwise, come again and again for solution and discussion. I get into certain states of being which reflect the disturbance. I hope that I could get over the same by Thy grace. It is as I have felt truly, Thy love that drags me to Thee and I have felt that though there are all types of interfering thoughts and dreams, Thy will will prevail ultimately so that I may be able to reconcile and recognize all the facets of Reality or how the many could be reconciled by the One Knowledge of Changeless Reality; I do not wish to limit the Nature of Reality to any one particular experience or creed or dogma of speculation or seer even.

I only sincerely pray that all my doubts will be soon resolved and I will be Thine without reserve and know Thee to be the summit awareness, the fulfillment of all that is to be known and loved.

Thou hast written to me that Thou canst not wait longer for giving me further steps on the Path. I am deeply looking forward for thy blessing and open my self to thee without any reserve.

Please accept again my self as thy Body and Be Thou my Self.

All are well.

Yours
KCV

No. B 197/SRCM Shahjahanpur, U.P.
Dated 30th March, 1957

My dear Varadachari,

Received your affectionate letters dated 19, 20 and 21st March, 1957. I could not go to Lakhimpur on 18th instant because Dinesh was down with fever and the examination was at hand. Changes are being undoubtedly made subtly and I hope and pray that in near future you will feel yourself my very being. You have strongly linked up with me so you feel peace all the time. I am now clearing the point regarding your *laya avastha* of the *pind pradesh*. *Pind* is regarded as body so I use this word in term of yoga denoting the forgetfulness of the body. It remains continued for a longer time, of course with so many changes. *Laya avastha* in *brahmand mandal* means to be absorbed in the condition what one has there. You cross region after region getting force for this very thing. The spirituality works in bringing *laya avastha* of the body first and the soul afterwards. When the body idea is gone the idea of soul creeps in, when that too is gone then *laya avastha* is admirably high. What you feel today must be gone tomorrow for something higher. Am I now clear on this point? I have finished the work of the centres x, y and soon and you are relating the condition as their outcome. The centres which follow after them will be taken up when you proceed high above the level required for the taking up of the subtler ones. My dear Varadachari I promise that I will leave no stone unturned what is possible for me for your approach. May God help me.

Of course we are all indebted to the sage for his great sacrifice. My Master has ordered me to help him in the spiritual pursuit. Just after this order he had intercommuned that he had been given under my teaching by his Master so I am doing it. With all the respect to the sage I cannot help saying that the idea of cleaning the system prevails only in your *sanstha*. It is of course a very tedious job but it has grown into mania to me.

I am attracted to your sentence as you say, 'I am experiencing profound calm and indrawn condition.' Nothing in the world can give me more pleasure than to see my associates progressing spiritually. When I viewed the other sentence of the letter that you feel yourself to be my body I was reminded to write a sentence more in connection with *laya avastha* of *pind pradesh*. I have mentioned somewhere in *Efficacy of Raja Yoga* that an abhyasi after some practice begins to feel his body to be of his master. This is the symptom of *laya avastha* which exhausts the feeling of the body to be his own. I must congratulate you for it.

May I ask you if you feel your *indriyas* regulated as the result of touching the centres x, y and so on. Personally I feel a thin layer over them for which I am pondering if it should be torn off at present. I have not yet come to the definite conclusion but it will be done decidedly if not this time.

When you mentioned Kasturi in your letter I began to feel that there is certainty of producing another Kasturi at Tirupati. The starting point of her love was almost the same as you do. From her very childhood she was of religious mind, devoting herself in her own ways to the realisation. Once I went through a few pages of her autobiography. I found in it written that in her tender age whenever any crawling creature ended its life by crushing under her foot she used to take out blood from her body with the sharp knife as the atonement for the loss of the life of the creature. She has a very good knowledge of scriptures, a very good Hindi writer and a poetess. She has passed the High School examination and is a very good speaker. In spite of all this there is one thing touching to me in respect of her health that she has suffered from intestinal T.B., esonophelia and bad digestion. She is about 25 years old and her weight is nearly 30 seers or so. She often gets relapses of her former diseases and I apply myself to relieve her by prayer and she does the same for me. That is why her father in consonance with her will did not marry her. She is so conjoined with me that there remains nothing to her as a secret about myself, but she has yet to go a long way off to reach near about the centre. I am thinking of connecting your link to the spot where you have to jump ultimately as I have done in a few cases. In this state your progress cannot be retarded even if I am gone from this world. This is one of the reasons why curvature cannot form in my *sanstha* according to Ouspensky's thought, and Shri Ram Chandra Mission can never come into decay. There are other reasons too which cannot give rise to curvature. I will explain them to you by means of diagrams relating their dynamics during my next visit to Tirupati. I will call saint Kasturi to this place when you visit this poor cottage. She has expressed her willingness to go along with me to South India during this happy tour; but I refused permission as she could have not borne the strain of the journey.

While I was dictating the above letter your letter dated 25th March reached me. I think the point which you wanted to know is covered in the above reply of the letter. Remember — you cannot come down, there is absolutely no fear of a fall. Regarding Shri Ishwar Sahai's writing that you should attend to me more and more, I would say in this respect that may God give me strength to attend to you more and more. I shall be happy only when I see my Varadachari in all forms and colours. I have reserved this week for your inner evolution understanding at the same time that more such weeks will have to be reserved for it. I am glad that my sister is improving in health. Her spiritual condition is that her heart is full of light, and regarding yourself your whole body is flooded with it. A few days back I was sitting before my Master receiving His grace. I diverted it a little to you to make you also the co-sharer.

I found, a minute after, the glow of light in your entire body. I was elated with joy to see this scene.

My son Dinesh Chandra is running the course of injections and bleeding is stopped. I will give your medicine (Calc. Phos.) which I have got with me, after the course of injection is over.

My elder daughter Maya, who is married, is appearing in Intermediate Examination. She is suffering from whooping cough. Her younger sister Chhaya will appear in B.A.(Pt.1). The examination will be held from 5th April.

I hope my children of Tirupati must be doing their papers satisfactorily.

With best wishes to you and love to children. Convey my *pranam* to Appaji,

Yours,
Ram Chandra

No. B 229/SRCM   **Shahjahanpur, U.P.**
Dated 10th April, 1957

My dear Varadachari,

Your affectionate letters dated 29th March, 1957 and 4th April, 1957 to hand. Your experiences of the inflow of spiritual energy are highly encouraging.

"The joy in being Nothing in me" is of course a thing of great merit and must be grasped in true sense by a real seeker. But my view goes further on over the ideas of 'joyless joy in being nothing as mine or mine as nothing'. Now what does my Varadachari say to it? Does the living dead (in your sense as being 'in the Master or dead to ourself') convey anything else? The question whether I have captivated you or you have captivated me remains pending still. How is it to be solved? I leave it to your arbitration. But mind! Please do not be partial in your judgement.

In reply to your next letter I may say that a man takes up residence in a house only when it is thoroughly cleaned and furnished. So I have devoted the week to the similar type of service to my Master who has been showering blessings incessantly. This is all for the duty of a servant. The rest depends upon the

Master's sweet will. The result though not clearly perceptible to you at present may come to your knowledge after some time.

Keshava Chandra Sen's view quoted in your letter as to 'wait to hear the voice of God,' implies indirectly to meditation or prayer which of course is essential.

As for clairvoyance and clairaudience do not bother yourself with it. Let it come automatically. It really develops when one is reduced to 'Nothing as me' as referred to in the preceding para of this letter.

I shall pray for peace to mother on her *shradha* day, i.e., 15th, 16th.

With best wishes and love to children. Please convey my *pranam* to Appaji.

Yours,

Ram Chandra

P.S. I am very glad to inform you that Shri Raghavendra Rao of Gulburga is coming over here in the next month when his summer vacation begins.

Ram Chandra

No. B 247/SRCM   **Shahjahanpur, U.P.**
Dated 20/23 April, 1957

My dear Varadachari,

Received your affectionate letters dated 13th and 18th April 1957. Since I went to Tirupati, I find that I have begun to live with you. There is certainly the inflow of spiritual energy nearly all the time because you remain mostly in pious thoughts of eternity. I have every hope from you that you will turn to be a spiritual giant and the people will be benefitted by you. All you desire about the merging of senses will ultimately come to pass and the joyless joy for which you are endeavouring will be the outcome of your spiritual activities. The condition of being a living dead has been started. The vacuity which you have felt is due to the fact that senses are now being affected to come in the state of suspension. It will not be a long time before you will feel the effect.

I have written to you probably in the last letter that all your body is flooded with light and that you have experienced yourself. You have felt me in yourself and the feeling is correct.

You have mentioned in your letter dated 18th April 57 that you feel yourself sinful and so the feeling of depression arises. I remember I had written the same to my Master. He replied that this sort of feeling shows the complete gentlemanliness required in a man. So we should not submit to depression. This is the spiritual condition for which I must be happy.

I am happy to feel that the *yatra* of *pind pradesh* is over about a week ago. Now comes the turn to pull you to the *para brahmanda mandal* where the nature of bliss will be changed. I have not pulled you to that region so far because I have to correct several other things and also to make you powerful to reach the *para brahmanda mandal* yourself. But you have no concern with these things. I am doing what is best for you. Will you please inform me that you feel yourself restless to go above your present state? Do you feel yourself vexed sometimes when your thought fails to take the higher jump. If so, do you feel any limitations in giving your thought a free access to the next higher region?

Mr. Balasubramaniam seems to be a man of very devotional mind; as such I pray to my Master to give me sufficient strength to render services to him.

My dear Varadachari, *moksha* is not a difficult job but we should see what are the factors in nature that may be utilised for the good of a man.

I feel that your mother has not taken birth as yet. So I feel that liberation is possible for that pious lady if earnestly prayed. This is our duty too.

With best wishes to you and love to children. Please convey my *pranams* to Appaji.

Yours,

Ram Chandra

P.S. I found your letters kept in the book presented by you and I am sending them back. I did not read these letters.

As a precaution I must inform you that you must not utter any harmful word (what we call *shrap* in Sanskrit) to others because if you are deeply absorbed in the Being at that time it may come to pass.

Ram Chandra

Tirupati

25th April 1957

My dear revered and beloved Gurudev,

Pranams and greetings. I believe you are in receipt of my letter of last week. Since last week I have nothing to report except to say that I had tried to comprehend the meaning of what you wrote regarding 'dying in me'. It had been an obsession with me to experience this for a long time. To live in God is life, to live outside him is death. The experience of the utter nothingness of 'I' is perhaps the other death which is significant. I should like to have the latter for I die in God and God alone IS. That obviously was what I believe was meant by the laya-state. My ego merged in Thee, my mind merged in Thy Mind, my senses merged in Thy Senses and the organs of action (*karma indriyas*) merged in Thy *karma indriyas*. I do not know whether this *nyasa* or dedication or offering will not lead to that ecstasy of *laya* which will also be peace.

In any case I found myself constantly thinking of this mergence in Thee.

However I have another thing to report. Why is it that I am worried about my future employment etc., for it is imminent and I have too many commitments which without further employment or extension of service I cannot see any way to discharge, not to speak of living. Again and again during the past two days I was forced up from my sleep about midnight to appeal to Thee and seek shelter about this future. You have written a few months ago that I need not worry and that things seem to be clear in the future and the problem of life is solved. I am only sorry that I have to be forced to think of it again and again, and not give up myself entirely to God and the Master for things to turn up without distress. I also feel that it is indeed not quite good form to be writing about my economic and other situations to the Master and yet I could not help writing about them to You who knowest all. It grieves me much but I do not know to whom else I could turn except you. Please forgive me. Things are not all right with me however in that direction.

I also observed that though I am in continuous meditation the duration of my meditation period in the evenings and mornings hardly exceeds 15 minutes for I find the experience of breaking off. Can I have an explanation from the Master. This also gives me some anxiety. My health is almost restored and I am not having any worry about the matter.

I am sure that my peace will not be disturbed and the abhyas will go on triumphantly to its glorious conclusion.

All children and my father are all right in health.

Please accept my loving pranams.

Yours,
KCV

No. B 264/SRCM   **Shahjahanpur, U.P.**
Dated 9th May, 1957

My dear Varadachari,

Received your affectionate letters dated 25th April, 1957, 26th April, 1957 and 5th May, 1957.

It is not your thought that awakened you from the sleep for pondering over the future problems. I often considered it and prayed for the better prospects in your life. Even now this problem often comes to my mind, and I pray to God for His grace. In our parts Allahabad and Lucknow Universities have fixed 62 years as the maximum age for service; while Agra University has fixed the age limit at 60. I do not know as to what is the age of superannuation fixed by your university. You are about 52 years of age, and I think after the maximum period, some university will most probably engage you if the extension is not allowed in your university. You have revealed all these facts to me because you regard me as one of the members of your own family. It denotes your affection.

I do not mind if the duration of meditation in the morning and evening is 15 minutes, for you remain engrossed in the Being for the most part of the day and night. You have defined the ultimate *laya avastha* correctly. But *laya avasthas* come at each step; and when you emerge out of it a kind of life according to the step taken, begins to prevail, till the turn of the other higher one (*laya avastha*) comes. I give you a true indication of *laya avastha*, which ultimately comes after a toilsome journey. Where 'I' is totally gone, and when you speak that word it refers to none… i.e., neither to the soul nor to the body and nor to God. There is something after it as well, which is not at all possible to be expressed in words. However, it can only be said that this is the stage where you make *laya* of *laya avastha* itself. Now you are benumbed and senseless, and at the same time the knower of almost everything. My dear, if I say anything further, people may call me a dunce. So my prayer is, 'May the day dawn when the living souls may come to know of it.'

How anxious I am to give you approach as much as is possible for me; and am always encouraged in your case because my Master's grace is there. During my next visit to Tirupati, I will pray to Him to connect you with the main source, with the result that you will remain connected permanently. It is a very happy sign that you are yearning to go beyond the present stage; and you will have it without doubt. Really speaking the whole of the continent belongs to you, but it is ruled by the foreigners.

You have written to me in the letter dated May 5 that you are experiencing transmission power during the past few days. Your feeling is correct, but I have not been unmindful with certain important things of the system. I will do what I am doing at least for a few days more. Afterwards you will have glad tidings of reaching *brahmand mandal*. But look here, Varadachari, this is not the goal. You have to travel a far off distance. The true seeker of knowledge must not rest at any place, but should always be on the march.

Since my children are enjoying summer vacation after a good deal of labour in studies they must get something soothing and exhilarating. I shall give some time to them because they are the future hopes of the nation.

Convey my respects to Appaji. With best wishes to you and love to children,

Yours,
Ram Chandra

No. B 268/SRCM   **Shahjahanpur, U.P.**
Dated 17th May, 1957

My dear Varadachari,

Received your affectionate letters dated 9th, 11th and 13th May, 1957. You are nearly all the time in meditation. So if the duration has not increased it matters little. But if you increase the meditation then you will have the knowledge and experience of your spiritual elevation. You are really very sensitive and you are right in judging that the centres on the right back are being purified. I have touched them a little and have purified them greatly.

Here is a happy news for you that on 14th May, 1957 at 3:15 p.m. you reached the border of *para brahmanda mandal*. I heartily congratulate you for the same. Specially because you reached out of your own effort for which I was eagerly waiting.

I am very glad to hear from you that the Tamil translation of the book is complete. I agree with you to give the diagram No.5 from *Efficacy of Raja Yoga* in *Reality at Dawn*; but the number of the diagram which is 5 is engraved in the block we have got. So I think you will have to insert a few words more in the translation as "... the diagram is taken from the *Efficacy of Raja Yoga.*" If you find any necessity to add a sentence or two about it you may do so. Regarding the Telugu rendering of the book I think it more proper to watch the response of the people towards it before we start the other translation. I am really moved by the services of Shri A. Balasubrahmaniam to the Mission and the credit goes to you also for introducing the book to him. I shall refer his case to my Master earlier and I hope His grace may shape his final destiny. But I do not know why I am so strict on you — can you give me any reason for it? I think it may be due to the fact that the Reward is waiting for you, not you for the reward.

I find the grace of the Master in abundance towards our Mission that He has moulded His teachings in a way as to quicken the approach.

Throbbing at *Brahmarindhra* and at many other places, I find here among my associates also. I recall my period of abhyas and my fellow disciples, who did not experience such sensations so early.

I am going to participate in the marriage ceremony of Shri Ishwar Sahai's son along with my Gulbarga associates who are also invited in this marriage on 18th, direct at Lucknow. This is yet to be considered whether we should return to Shahjahanpur or go to Lakhimpur from Lucknow for a day or two. One of our associates near Lakhimpur Kheri wants to arrange a picnic in the Terai forest for our associates. It is yet to be decided by us.

With best wishes to you and love to children. Please convey my respect and *pranams* to Appaji,

Yours,

Ram Chandra

P.S. Will you please throw some light on the question I am pondering over these days? In the case of intentions, *manas* (individual mind) follows the intention. Wherefrom does this intention arise? Is it the work of the individual mind to arouse the intention with its deeper aspect and then to follow it by its outer aspect? Or the soul grasps what we see and hear and then it causes waves in the mind-lake (*chitta*) to be followed by the mind?

No. B 287/SRCM **Shahjahanpur, U.P.**
Dated 27th May, 1957

My dear Varadachari,

Received your affectionate letter dated 21st May, 1957. Shri Raghavendra Rao along with his two associates has gone back to Gulburga on 25th May. They will break their journey at Agra to see Taj Mahal and some other historical places.

I am very glad to see my boy Ch. Aravinda coming out successful in the examination. I heartily congratulate for the same.

I agree with your solution about the 'intention' and the 'individual mind'. You have written to me a new thing to be considered, that in the stage of ignorance intention comes first and then mind and the soul attains the object. The circles I have given in the *Reality at Dawn* covers the wider range of spirituality. Regarding it I can say you have crossed the first circle. You need not bother yourself with these things. This is my business and duty.

The man who crosses two or three circles is no less than a sage. I will rather call him and respect him as one of the great sages. Will you please study how nature of bliss changes and ultimately it comes to naught.

I am moved to read your sentence, "I have not found any reason in me so far for my worthiness. Even so is the case with thy interest or strictness with me." This shows your submissiveness and devotion towards the Master. Really speaking if my Master is kind to me his eyes are there on me. If he is strict even then his eyes fall upon me. We succeed in turning his attention on ourselves. What else does a servant require?

The service of the Mission is always rewarded because it is the pious work for the general good. That is why Mr. Balasubramanian feels himself improved. I shall write about the reward nearly after a fortnight or so. Let us see what falls in his lot. I have got block of diagrams denoting the circles and also what is given on the title page of the book already. The other diagram will be prepared in Madras when the time comes for its publication. I am glad that you are free from trouble caused by going to Bangalore.

With best wishes to you and love to children. Please convey my *pranams* to Appaji.

Yours,
Ram Chandra

31st May 1957

My dear revered and beloved Gurudev,

Please accept my pranams. Your kind letter dated 27th was thankfully received by me today. I am grateful for the loving words of encouragement.

I was wondering about the matter of correspondence or relationship between the circles and the *pradeshas* — whether there was any relation between the first five circles and the *pind pradesh*, the second 11 circles and the *brahmanda* and so on. Therefore my question about my being at what circle. I am deeply thankful to you for the information. As you have said it is none of my business. All that is relevant is to intimate to you my present condition.

I felt I was almost experiencing living death during the past five days. Indeed today I had to leave for Mysore but cancelled it as I was feeling physically unfit for the journey, the left side hernia seems to be giving some difficulty. Further I was somehow overpowered by a kind of dejection though it is different from the usual kind of worry and so on.

Again another curiosity or rather doubt arose in my mind about the relationship between the Vasu, Dhrua, Dhruadhipa and the Vasu, Rudra and Aditya of the Vedas which equate these with the ancestors the dead father, dead grandfather and dead great-grandfather of the *tarpanas*. I was wondering whether the word Dhrua was a play on Rudra (reversing the word in Sanskrit). This was an interesting thing also. But these pertain to the view that such ancestors are those who have gone beyound the *pind pradesh* and not to all, though it is being used otherwise these days.

I shall be glad to have your replies to these.

The state of bliss has passed away leaving a kind of vacuity or naught. But the old samskaras yet invade. Anxiety is less present, but a kind of numbness of the mind is present except when some work has to be done. I merely sit on and on without any activity for hours except for some old and sometimes unwelcome reflections. But thanks to my thinking of Thee soon they pass. Resentment and anger also slowly pass away leading to the sense of resignation on my part waiting for the Master's will to do as He pleases.

I have told Shri Balasubramaniam about your kind thoughts and expectations. He told me that he had a fine meditation this morning and he was throbbing in all his body also till about 10 o'clock.

I am trying to keep up my spirits high in the knowledge that my Master is with me all the time and nothing untoward can happen to me. I am aspiring and looking forward to the day when I might do my humble best for my Master and God.

Have I merged in Thee and God in all my parts then I would feel free from all the experience of unhappiness, humiliation and all? When I cease to be then perhaps all will be well.

With humblest pranams to my Self,

Yours,
KCV

No. B 304/SRCM   **Shahjahanpur, U.P.**
                           Dated 8th June, 1957

My dear Varadachari,

Received your affectionate letter dated 31st May, 1957. The experience of the feeling of the 'living dead' supplemented by a sense of vacuity reflects signs of vanishing of Ego and this is on account of the process you have undertaken. The dream state mentioned in the first letter also relates to the same condition.

In response to your query about the merging of self, all that I can say is that when I look to myself I find myself to be Varadachari. That may be sufficient to give you an idea of the thing. Complete merging means no difference between the two, and that is an end of all activities. There is no training of any kind after it. It may in a sense be regarded as full-fledged 'Perfection'. You are no doubt proceeding towards it and with a wonderfully rapid pace too, but it is still a long course and may yet take a good time.

May you be pleased to know that at 10-30 A.M. on 4/6/57 you advanced a pretty good distance into *para brahmanda mandal* with one sudden leap. My congratulations to you for this.

The Godly functionaries termed as Vasu, Dhruva etc. are meant for nature's work. These stages are possible only when one goes beyond *pind desh*. In that case the point in the Hylem Shadow is awakened through the medium of a saint of calibre or in certain cases automatically by nature herself. In *pind desh* there is of course one petty post, the Sanskrit name of which is given by the Master somewhere but which I do not remember at present. No special point is fixed for it. The state is awakened by energising the five points of *pind desh*, and strengthening the condition at their back.

The throbbing at certain points in the body shows that action has started on those points. It is thus a fortunate sign.

Shri Ishwar Sahai is with me and has induced me to accompany him to Lakhimpur for a brief stay in the Tarai forests with a view to recoup health. For some time past I had been suffering from stomach troubles of diarrhoea and dysentery. Though relieved of these troubles now I feel some weakness still. I therefore hope to be out for about a fortnight. Please communicate with me by Shri Ishwar Sahai's address.

Just now I received a long letter from Shri Seshadri stating his eagerness to take up our practices and guidance. I am replying to him accordingly.

With best wishes to you and love to children. Please convey my respect and *pranams* to Appaji.

Yours,
Ram Chandra

27th June 1957

My Dear Revered Gurudev,

Please accept my loving pranams, I trust you are now restored to health after your stay in the forests near Lakhimpur.

Shri Raghavendra Rao wrote to me a long letter about his problems and I replied to him to the best of my knowledge in these matters. I believe he would be communicating his reactions to your good self.

I believe Shri Ishwar Sahai and his family and children are all well at Lakhimpur.

During the past one week, from about the 24th I have been experiencing great restlessness.

I do not know any reason for the same except perhaps my anxiety about my future at this place of which I have hardly any definite information yet. I have obviously no plans too about the future. I have placed myself at the feet of the Divine Master and only pray for guidance and help in all things. But I also felt that it was not merely due to this anxiety. Something much deeper seems to be taking place. The throbbing at the crown of the head (*brahmarandra*) the back and pressure on the chest region, now on the right and now on the left, seems to suggest that Nature's processes are going on deep in the being. I feel myself several times as having no work and no energy.

I pray that I may be enlightened and I may be able to see with what vision that the Master deigns to grant. I am feeling restless all the time.

The colleges will be reopening soon and the children are all getting ready to go to their respective studies after the vacation. The flu of course did make some advances on all but I am glad to write that almost all have since recovered.

My father's health is fairly all right.

Please accept my pranams and love.

Yours,
KCV

No. B 329/SRCM   **Shahjahanpur, U.P.**
Dated 30th June, 1957
1st July, 1957

My dear Varadachari,

Received your affectionate letters dated 7th June, 1957 and 14th June, 1957. I am sorry I could not reply them earlier. I sincerely apologise for it. If Ch. Arvinda is desirous for further studies he should not be checked. I am deeply interested in learning. As such I always want that our children may take the higher education which opens the mind.

I am very thankful to you to receive your speech delivered in connection with Shri Aurobindo Jayanti. It is really displaying your learning. I am writing a little for your understanding about the description of real Reality given in the *Reality at Dawn*. I experienced it after 22 years of continuous abhyas when the charm of life was lost and I was nowhere in myself. "The true nature of Zero or Centre which one must crave for if he is really earnest about achieving the Ultimate, is neither unreal nor elusive. It however, appears so only when we apply the wrong medium of senses to enclose it within the fold of human language for the sake of expression. That is the main difficulty in the path and the philosophy is to a great deal responsible for it. To realise 'Him as He be' must therefore be the real pursuit of life. I have said something about that ultimate state in a recently written Hindi book under the name *Anant Ki Or (Towards Infinity)* which could not be yet sent to the press for want of funds."

On your march to freedom you will cross innumerable kinds of blisses and conditions. When you acquire the changeless state then the problem of life is thoroughly solved and that is the perfect realisation, the air of which you may be feeling sometimes though momentary. I cannot rest unless I am able to bring you to that state of realisation. If the thoughts torment you during meditation then it is a sure sign that the poisonous matter is coming out to the surface to be removed. Since we have to gain liberation in this very life we are obliged to take up the earlier course. It generally happens that one does not remember the thoughts flowing during meditation. The system is being cleaned in this way so that the field may be free from roughness.

Now I am replying your letter dated June 14, 1957. I have improved my health by going to the suburb of the Tarai forest. I thank you very much for your kind invitation. I will surely come to you if God affords me the opportunity of reaching Gulbarga. These days the question of extension for your further term of service is drawing my attention mostly. I am praying for it. I am doing my duty but the success depends upon God. The U.P. Government has recently fixed the age of retirement as 58 instead of 55 for all the departments here. My prayer for you is that you may lead a happy life both worldly and spiritually. The colour you feel at the present stage is really dark blue. As you proceed on bluish colour gradually diminishes and dark follows which also grows faint in your further march. I assure you once more that the whole of your body is illumined which you witnessed sometimes.

Regarding the idea of merging I can only say that you are welcoming me and I am coming to you. We are the followers of Shri Vaishnavism but personally I have only one thought of my Master. Now I have begun to love Shri Ramanujacharya appreciating him in all respects and I often automatically think of him during day and night. It shows that you are giving to me your own belongings and that is a step towards merging. I have seen you twice in this week in dreams. Last time I saw you giving me food.

Shri Ishwar Sahai, along with his four children, was suffering from influenza raging in epidemic form in many places. Now they are getting better. Similar is the case with Saint Kasturi, her sisters, mother and niece.

With best wishes to you and love to children. Please convey my respects to Appaji.

Yours,
Ram Chandra

Tirupati
30th June 1957

My dear Revered and beloved Gurudev,

Please accept my pranams. I was shown your kind letter to Shri Balasubramaniam yesterday. I am glad you have returned to Shahjahanpur having recouped your health. I shall be happy to receive your letter in reply to mine after you have finished with earlier and urgent matters.

This is just to let me know whether on Saturday evening at about 4:30 P.M. you had entered my being as I felt myself so. It continued for about a couple of minutes or may be more when I had just begun meeting a student after sending away Shri Balasubramaniam.

Of course I had experienced this some time before.

The other things continue.

Chi. Srivatsa failed to get through his examination in F.L. As I wrote to you the other children are well and will begin to attend the college from tomorrow.

Please accept my loving pranams to Thyself and praying for guidance and increase of love and all.

Yours,
KCV

No. B 350/SRCM   Shahjahanpur, U.P.
                    Dated 13th July, 1957

My Varadachari,

Received your affectionate letter of 27th June, 1957. I had gone to Lakhimpur for three days on account of some important work. Shri Ishwar Sahai and all his family members are now quite well. They have all now recovered from the effects of flu.

I am glad to hear of the intense restlessness which you feel these days. It is a very happy sign which I wish everybody to be blessed with. The other symptoms appearing as throbbing and pressure all indicate that the effect of the processes undertaken, is growing stronger and deeper. I remained in that state of restlessness for a pretty long period. But now it is all over and there is no trace of it at all, unless it is revived by the persistent restlessness of my associates. The nature of this restlessness now is different too. Now I feel restless for giving higher approaches to those who feel restlessness in themselves, their restlessness being for the realisation of the Goal, conscious or unconscious it may be. But I keep myself under check to a great extent waiting for orders from above.

The feeling of 'no work and no energy' denotes some progress towards inactiveness of mind. In fact to march from our present state of activity to our primitive state of Inactiveness is the gist of all our spiritual pursuit. But this must not be misinterpreted as idleness or dullness of mind.

With best wishes, love to children and my humble *pranams* to Appaji,

Yours,
Ram Chandra

No. B 351/SRCM   **Shahjahanpur, U.P.**
Dated 13th July, 1957

My dear Varadachari,

Received your affectionate letter dated 30th June, 1957. I am sorry to learn that Ch. Srivatsa got plucked this year. One of my sons Dinesh Chandra appeared in High School Examination, elder daughter in Intermediate and the younger in B.A.(Part I). All of them got plucked. The younger daughter got IInd division marks in all subjects but failed in General English by 10 marks. She will appear in the supplementary examination in that subject on 2nd August, 1957.

You have asked me to let you know whether I entered your being on Saturday at 4:30 p.m. I cannot say the exact date of occurrence. But I did the process of carrying unto you my subtle body (*suksham sharir*). Once my Master had told me this process to work out on the taught who develops unflinching faith and devotion to the Master. In such cases *sukshama sharir* is made to enter in the body of the taught which effects greatly in spiritual advancement. I have no words to express in appreciation to your *anubhava*. This very thing will help you greatly in the divine pursuit even if I am gone from this world. I am serving you as best as I can and hope my labour will bring fruit someday.

Shri Raghavendra Raoji sent a copy of your excellent letter dated 23rd June, 1957, in response to his own. The heart is the nucleus of the body; plants and flowers have their own nucleus on which their lives depend as the Botany tells us. It is like a seed which grows full-fledged when properly moulded to the congenial atmosphere of spirituality. If the abhyasi observes minutely he will see that the idea of heart is gone and he is meditating internally on some higher plane. Sometimes he is so much internally connected that he feels the pure divine touch. I think I have hinted down about it in my previous letter. If the heart remains in view all along your march that means you are not worshipping God but idol. We should not try to forget the heart but let this condition prevail automatically. It is only the start for your unfoldment. These things cannot be scaled down by the stride of human wisdom.

I shall write to Shri Raghavendra Rao to write one by one the questions which occur to him in connection with abhyas. He has often asked me a number of questions and I have replied them all to his satisfaction. I am sorry to know through his letter that he could not clear his doubts because he fell in spiritual delirium when he was here.

I think, Doctor, I have become contagious.

I am sending the copies of 'Sahaj Marg Patrika' for you and others from this very place as that was managed to publish here. It would have taken a long time if it would have been sent from Assam.

There is a section in U.N.O. for World Peace. They want to have separate army well equipped to crush the power which attacks any country and uses the modern weapons. They have sent to me a form for membership and to help them in this cause. I have sent them a letter by air expressing my views to this point. I am sending you a copy of the letter so poorly drawn up for your perusal.

After drafting the above letter I received your affectionate card dated 9th July 1957. I shall write to Shri Raghavendra Raoji to request his friends that they should not waste your valuable time by interrogations. They are free to question me and Shri Raghavendra Raoji. When you are satisfied with the Tamil translation of the book you may call for the estimate of printing.

With best wishes to you and love to children. Please convey my respect to Appaji.

Yours,
Ram Chandra

(Letter to U.N.O.)
No. B 349/SRCM **Shahjahanpur, U.P.**
Dated 8th July, 1957

Dear Sir,

I am glad to receive your bulletin and I pour forth my warm thanks for the awakening for peace created among our brethren of the World. The idea of peace common in all minds, though shattered by the self of the individual mind, is working on individualistic basis to gain one's own end on account of the narrow mindedness of people. To dissipate the idea of individual self and to work harmoniously for the common good is the demand of the time. The conferences and meetings held for the purpose, may only be like a spark to offer a temporary glow to the scattered fragment of peace. Their cries in the wilderness will not carry far on the path of success because of the material agony of faith working at the bottom.

What we, therefore, require at present is only to improve the morals and to discipline the mind. We must learn how to create within the heart a feeling of universal love which is the surest remedy of all evils and can help to free us from the horrors of war. I perfectly agree with our friend late Mr. Bernard Malan when he expresses his faith to unite in the common search for happiness. Happiness, of course, is necessary to end all griefs. But it is like the Black Wall of the scientists which does not allow them to proceed further towards universal love. To come up to the level of real happiness we must necessarily rise above ourselves which is essential for the creation of atmosphere of universal love. That is the primary factor in the solution of the problem. India has ever since been in search of it. She did not encroach upon other countries for war and bloodshed not for reason of her cowardice but because she realised her pious duty towards humanity. They were happy in their own homes in spite of the torturous incursions of other nations. These tortures were to them nothing but flowers sent by the Divine Master to coach them to proper steps necessary for the uplift of mankind individually and collectively. The seed of it is so deeply laid that still its branches bear blossoms filling the air with the sweet fragrance of peace and happiness. It is so firmly rooted that even the worst tempest cannot uproot it. Such are the things necessary for the uplift of mankind, which every one, occidental or oriental must treat as a part of his duty. Unless the foundation of peace is made to rest on spiritual basis no better prospects can be expected. It is but definite and certain that sooner or later we will have to adopt spiritual principles if we want to maintain our existence. If the incursions and attacks can be averted by the material force, bloodshed cannot be avoided because even then we have to apply force causing thereby bloodshed on either side. Arrogance cannot be stopped by material force. It is only the spiritual force which can remove the causes of war from the minds of people.

How to introduce these things among the masses who are yet unfamiliar with the accuracy of the mark is the next problem and is equally intricate. If my opinion were to be invited I would lay down the simplest possible method as given below.

Let us all brothers and sisters sit daily at a fixed hour individually at our respective places and meditate for about an hour thinking that all people of the World are growing peace- loving and pious.

This process, suggested not with exclusively spiritual motives, is highly efficacious in bringing about the desired result and weaving the destiny of the miserable millions.

With prayer for the success of your noble mission.

Yours sincerely,
Ram Chandra
President,
Shri Ram Chandra Mission
Shahjahanpur, U.P., India.

No. B 374/SRCM Shahjahanpur, U.P.
Dated 23rd July, 1957

My dear Varadachari,

On receipt of your affectionate letter dt. 17th July I deeply studied your inner system and came to the definite conclusion that the samskaras have cropped up. When I see with the eye of actual training, I leap with joy and when I see your torturous condition, I want to shed tears. My dearest Varadachari, it is my fault and I admit it in broad daylight, that I have given you very deep acting doses due to which the samskaras which were lying dormant for future *bhogam*, have become manifest to finish their course, in the earliest possible time. Samskaras, when they crop up, associate themselves, with the ideas which are nearest to them and it is due to this that the abhyasi feels that past and present in a little aggravated form. Since we have to attain liberation in this very life, it is necessary to end the foreign matter. If one life is spent in tortures to save the hundreds of such births, then I think this sacrifice is not much. I do not want to suppress these things, but to minimise the intensity. I will call it a Nature's boon, though everyone will get angry to hear such words. I will try my level best to fry up such things if I am assured that it will not be against the Nature.

I have begun my work from the night of 22nd July 1957 and will continue it till 28th i.e. I have given this week exclusively to you. I will not attend to any other work besides, unless it is extra-ordinarily important. You will please write to me on 29th July 57 the condition which you then feel.

I want to add in the Tamil translation of the book, the Publisher's Note, which I have sent to Shri Ishwar Sahai for his perusal. Please take the estimate of the printing charges etc. of the book and intimate to me so that I may make necessary arrangement of its finance.

These days I am badly suffering from acidity, due to taking food twice a day for the last about one week. I am again coming to having normally one meal daily and I hope that this will relieve me of the trouble. You have not written anything since long about the sister i.e., your wife. Kindly convey my best respects to Appaji.

With best wishes to you and love to children,

Yours,

Ram Chandra

Tirupati
29th July 1957

My dear Revered and Beloved Gurudev,

Please accept my sincerest and loving pranams. I received your kind letter dated 23rd instant on the 26th. I am grateful to Thee for the removal of the samskaras of all lifetimes within the period of this single lifetime. It is Nature's boon as you say. I have come to the conclusion that my sins should have been so great that God hath not been able to remove them as it has to be 'enjoyed' (*bhogam*). You have asked me to report to you about my condition on the 29th after a week of training from the 22nd so to speak at Thy divine hands. I am sure that I should have been immensely purified.

I shall record what I had written in my diary. On the 22nd: nothing significant — mind has been roving about all and sundry. 23rd: same as previous day. 24th: Throbbing all over. Meditation in the morning has increased to 45 minutes; feeling of presence; evening meditation disturbed and restless. 25th: morning (5:05 to 5:50 A.M.) bathing in light: a type of *ajapa* experience. Throbbing at the heart region. Head region, *Bhrumadhya*, back right, throbbing. Again at 7:00 to 7:30 A.M. same. Evening short meditation. 26th: 6-45 to 7-30 A.M. feeling of *ajapa*. Feel very much controlled and peaceful, looking on at things as inevitable and 'must be gone through'. The state of living dead not yet fully established. 27th: (5:05 to 5:45, 7:45 to 8:10, and evening 7:00 to 7:30) attempt to settle down at the Heart centre. But it is seen that the mind goes up to the overhead. 28th: (5:15 to 5:50 A.M., 7:15 to 8:10 and this has been usual. Throbbing sensation all over immediately after getting up from meditation is the usual phenomenon all these days. Evening meditation disturbed owing to mind movements on all things. 29th: (5:15 to 6:00 A.M. and 7:15 to 7:30 A.M.) Whole being is as it were experiencing tension. I was able to feel I believe that *sarvam khalvidam Brahma*. Illumination of the bluish moonlight not very bright. I am unable to express the type of feeling I have or experience. I am hoping that soon I shall be able to recognize all these.

I believe that the original arrangement up to May 1958 for my services stands as I have not heard from authorities regarding my retirement age. It is owing to Thy blessings.

Thou hast asked about my wife's condition. I believe she is having peace in spite of all the pressing situation. This again is consciously or unconsciously due to her receiving Thy Blessings. My father was disturbed about his eyesight very badly and wished to go to Madras for further consultation. He has however postponed the trip.

I have sent the medicines to Capt. Srivastava and by Thy grace I believe He would be better soon. I am deeply thankful for making use of me in this work.

I intended to go to Madras regarding the estimates for the publication of the Tamil translation. But I have not been able to do so.

I am daily praying to My Gurudev to lead me to that state which will help me to verify the ancients, be able to speak with knowledge on transcendent things. I am not so much oppressed by the suffering — though it is intense and even driving me to thoughts of suicide many times even in recent months — as the colossal ignorance that reigns everywhere defeating truth. Truth is never sweet and I believe not Being even. Strangely Negation attracts all.

I crave for Realisation and freedom from these. But it is all God's and Guru's grace.

With loving pranams and deeming myself to be Thy Body

I remain, Yours
KCV

No. B 406/SRCM Shahjahanpur, U.P.
Dated 9th August, 1957

My dear Varadachari,

Received your affectionate letter dated 22nd and 29th July, 1957. You have felt the glow and throbbing sensations all over. This is a very good condition and for some reason or other I stop to throw light on the experiences till they are matured. This is of course a wonderful experience to feel that you are seeing the things from the back part of the head. I had also felt this sort of experience during my abhyas period. I believe that the real eye which is an instrument of God is being attended to. God is really called Omniscient the refuse of which you have already experienced. Regarding the condition of living dead it is but a start.

I am very glad to see in your letter that you are increasing the duration of the meditation. You have tremendous contact with me even if you do not increase the time you will improve, but if you do so you will gain experience and knowledge. When you sit in meditation the things coming within your purview are polarized as you meditate with the idea of tranquillity and realisation. You will be surprised to know that my associates Dr. P. Sen of Calcutta Medical College meditates for six to eight hours daily. Recently he meditated for 10 hours together with the idea of sacrificing his life and to become one with Brahm. He felt sensations at *sahasra dal kamal* and wanted to give up his life through that centre. The result was that he suffered from paralysis of the left hand. He will recover soon. I have written to him not to commit such blunder in future. Although he writes, "My ideal was not achieved and I am still living."

I had written to you in my previous letter probably that if the heart remains in view all the time then it becomes the idol worship so the abhyasi must travel on. The heart is only a via media. Although we must not try to be away from the heart but let it take its natural course. You felt the tension on 28th July '57. Your feeling regarding it is correct because I transmitted to the very core of your being. Regarding the illumination of the bluish moonlight I would say that it would gradually fade away to have its real colour. Your feeling about *Servam Khalvidam Brahma* is correct. It is also a condition felt by an abhyasi in almost all the higher stages. But it grows subtle as he proceeds on.

I shall be very thankful to God if you get the extension for the further term of service. Capt. Srivastava must have written to you about his condition as he says that the first medicine subsides the pain and the other aggravates. In the Ayurvedic system of medicine (Saunph) Anise is recommended to keep up the eyesight. It is a medicine for stomach and acidity too. It is also used for spices in our part and the bitter gourd is roasted with anise in it. It is not in any way harmful. The powdered anise about half an ounce with as much sugar if taken twice a day will be helpful in preserving the eyesight. I have heard the Telugu speaking person to call it Saunph.

Please do not feel oppressed to see the ignorance reigning all over. I had the same feeling for some time during my abhyas period and I had written to my Master like that. These things will go away in course of time and please try to absorb in you and not to absorb yourself, this time, in the uncivilized and unbalanced state of humanity so to say. It speaks of your noble heart no doubt but please try to remain unmindful of all these things.

Now I am writing a few words concerning you, for the last few days I often felt the mood of weeping in your remembrance although it did not actually happen. It is the reaction of love which you have for this poor being. Do not think about the sins that they have not been condoned by God. When you are mine your sins are my own and they should be shared out by me also. The sins to some extent are fried up also by the fire of love and devotion and the rest come out for *bhogam*.

Your sentence that you have learnt the art of enjoying physical pain reminded me of my Master. In his last days he was suffering from liver abscess, and the pain was acute in nature and unbearable. During that time he used to sing *bhajan* (the song sung in the praise of our God) instead of wasting time in crying. He was one of the best singers. He knew the art of singing with the help of chakras. This seems to be his own discovery. I also consulted a few famous singers about it but they were silent saying that only the higher saints can sing in this way. He used to sing sometimes with Brahmandi Sur and the result was that all of us were in the state of trance.

If superfluous thoughts come when you transmit others, you should not worry about. Mostly they are not yours. But they appear like that on account of the push from behind. Sometimes the thoughts of the abhyasis strike when you are transmitting them.

The environment brings about these things because the yogi begins to be super-sensuous and sensitive and cleaned. Even a little darkness appears to him like a heap. I give you an example as to what the environment affects. A few years ago I was at Mathura and meditated at the place where Lord Krishna was born. There the mosque stands; the thoughts of theft began to resound while sitting in meditation on the platform of the mosque. I opened my eyes for a little while and then again went into the meditation. To my utter despair the same thoughts crept again. I studied the situation and came to know that this is the den of thieves which after enquiry found to be correct.

I give you another example of the same type. I was at Hardwar some time back and put up in a *choultry*. I meditated in the room allotted to me and found that a woman appeared before me with her throat lanced. When this scene remained for sometime I opened my eyes and stopped meditation for a few minutes. When I meditated again the same appearance and the scene was coming to my view. I then studied the case and found that the same woman was assassinated there and buried on the spot where I was sitting in meditation. I could not guess as how much time elapsed before she was killed. I cleaned the spot affected and transmitted the dead lady for the peace of her soul. After doing this I found that everything was calm and quiet and dead lady was coming no more to my view. There are so many other examples connected with me and my Master.

I am exceedingly happy to note that you want to spend your time in spiritual work so dear to me. I am very thankful to you that you are ready to write the foreword of the book. Shri Ishwar Sahai will send you the book when the threatened danger of strike of postal staff is over. Registrations, money orders and parcels have been stopped by the Government for the time being. Only this morning I have heard that it has been postponed. Shri Raghavendra Rao has agreed to go along with me to Tirupati from Gulburga during my next visit as he says in his recent letter.

With best wishes to you and love to children. And my sincere *pranams* to Appaji. I remember Engineer Sahib, who met me at your place, very often.

Yours,

Ram Chandra

President

P.S. My son Prakash Chandra lawyer has a daughter born on 1st August, 1957 just at 1 o'clock at night.

Ram Chandra

No. B 422/SRCM **Shahjahanpur, U.P.**
Dated 17th August, 1957

My dear Varadachari,

Received your affectionate letter dated 6th August, 1957. I have already replied your letters dated 22nd and 29th July, 1957 under this office No. B 406/SRCM dated 9th August, 1957. I believe it must have reached you by now. I am overjoyed at the prospects that you are going by leaps and bounds in the spiritual field. I feel that you have nearly finished the journey of the *para brahmanda mandal*. I am praying that you may get power to proceed further yourself as you have done previously. May I know whether these throbbing sensations prove burdensome to you or they give happiness. If you feel them troublesome, I will minimise them a little. These throbs are almost felt by all my associates. St. Kasturi has gone so far to say that she feels as if the whole body is being eaten away by the white ants. The powers which have grown blunt are being sharpened. The pressure is due to the fact that I had infused the transcendental energy vehemently on 22nd or 23rd July and my working lasted all night long because I was rather confounded with your letter which compelled me to do so. I do not want pressure on any of the organs or the parts of the body. Please write to me if the pressure is still there. The glow of light you feel very often is a fact your whole body is luminous. These are all preparations for the Union.

After dictating the reply of the said letters I received your letter of the 13th instant.

I am elated to hear from you that the state of blankness has now begun to dawn upon you though momentarily. This is the condition which we so heartily crave. This is really the divine touch which falls to the share of abhyasi by His Grace. Probably I had written to you in some letter that five points of the heart have their peculiar colours. The same conditions and the same colours come again and again in refined form as we march on although they differ in nature. On reaching *avyakta gati*, they all die out and *maya* is left far behind. The several colours sometimes come within the short interval of meditation. The colour greyish blue shows that you get hint of the refuse of Reality. I used this word for the sake of expression which means the beginning of Reality more or less to its unadulterated state. I hope that you will get into some state which may be a bit of higher sort of consciousness before the letter reaches you.

How beautifully Saint Kasturi expresses the idea of devotion which runs, "I attempted to bind you with the thread of love but when I regained consciousness I found nothing — neither thread nor myself."

So please observe it and then write to me, I will mention it in my next letter, waiting response.

Cholera has broken out at Shahjahanpur in epidemic form. Municipal authorities are taking precautions. All are well here. With best wishes to you and the sister. LOVE to children and respect to Appaji.

Yours,
Ram Chandra

22nd August 1957

My dear revered and beloved Gurudev,

Please accept my pranams. Your kind letter dated August 17th was received by me today. I am deeply moved by Thy divine love for my humble self. Thy grace it is that is taking me to the centre and the Union.

The throbbing continues now off and on. It has not been troublesome though it was unusual to have it and as such looked rather so. Now the calm condition prevails, though the value and existence of the calm is felt when one gets into another state. There was pressure on all the organs but now it persists at the cerebellum.

My diary runs thus: 31st: agitation all over the body from head downwards feeling of a dynamo working within.

3rd August: All light — whole body flooded. All these I have written in my letter dated 6th August.

I returned to Tirupati after my trip to Mysore on the 18th night.

The experience of blankness continues always — the only disturbance is the samskaras or thoughts of every day.

13th August: 2:25 A.M. got up for meditation as if called by Gurudev. Blankness. The usual feature is there. When one gets disturbed from meditation or after meditation there is throbbing all over.

20th Morning I accompanied a relation to Tirumalai. When returning I experienced as it were that Gurudev was with me.

The other condition continues.

I have sent the manuscript to Madras for quotations. I expect to hear about it in a couple of days. I am praying that I should be able to completely cross over the *para brahmanda mandal* and enter the blissful experience of the Highest Being which the Gurudev is granting me through His grace.

I am praying that my real love be manifest and grow in strength and knowledge for the Master and the Highest. I shall try to observe the consciousness and write to you. I am leaving for Mysore again on the 24th and will be back on the 28th night.

I am so sorry that cholera has broken out there. I trust all will be well. By thy grace all of us are well. I am going to Mysore with my wife. My father is fairly keeping well.

With loving pranams,
yours in all things.
KCV

No. B 453/SRCM   **Shahjahanpur, U.P.**
Dated 3rd September, 1957

My dear Varadachari,

Received your affectionate letter dated 22nd August, 1957. I am very late in replying the letter due to the strong headache continuing for several days. The pain has now subsided but the heaviness is still there. There is nothing to worry about. Cholera has now subsided at Shahjahanpur and its sister cities. You are perfectly right in guessing about yourself that a dynamo is working within. I had written to you some time back that my *sookshma sharir* has been grafted in you. In other words, I exist in you in subtle form, so to say. I hope it will help you greatly in your transformation. It is the discovery of my revered Master to be weighed in gold. There are so many discoveries of my Lord which help a good deal in making man a real one. When I will come to Tirupati, I will tell you many such things regarding the methods of teaching because I want now to take work from you and that will be the wages of my services which you will like to pay. Now I reveal the mystery about your state flourishing at present. You have read in your book, *Efficacy of Raja Yoga* dealing with the different sorts of super-conscious states. The elementary stage starts from the heart and that has been awakened on the birthday of Lord Krishna. We have observed fast on that day as he is the head of the *sanstha*. It is the system of the ancients to connect the link of the *sansthas* with the last avatar. Moreover, we get light from Him for the work directly. If you ask me the function of this elementary state of super-consciousness, I will quote Justice M.L. Chaturvedi of Allahabad. He had written to me that when he was bestowed with it, he could give better judgements. When he was here with me, on 8th July, he was telling me that one of his friends, who is the judge of Supreme Court was praising him very much for his balance in judgement. What I understand is that it is the gate of the Divine wisdom. One begins to rise above the human consciousness speedily if this state is awakened. Suppose the different sorts of super-conscious states be not taken up by the teacher, they will develop out of themselves in the long run. If the teacher is aware of these things and takes them up, the time is greatly saved.

I am glad that the pressure on the organs is now over. If it persists at cerebellum you will find it minimised now. This part of the head remains at work. So the pressure is sometimes felt by the abhyasis, and especially those who try to remain engrossed in the Real Being. It cannot harm you or anybody in any way. My Master once told me that it is necessary for the abhyasis, if God provides, to have good diet.

When you receive the estimate of the book, please inform me so that I may arrange for its finances.

All are well here.

With best wishes to you and love to children. Please convey my respects to Appaji.

Yours,
Ram Chandra

9th September 1957

My dear beloved revered Gurudev,

Please accept my humble pranams. I received thy kind letter. I am deeply grateful for the awakening of the elementary super-consciousness in my humble self. I have been having quite a blank and mixed with all kinds of perseverating thoughts and experiences, so much so I even felt that I have lost all that previously came to me. I believe that it is all an intimation of a change. Further I had dreams of all sorts but none so vivid as to be reported or even recorded. I believe it is all dross samskaras being thrown up. I believe you received my report after my return from Mysore. From the letter you had written to Shri Balasubramaniam I learnt that you have had severe headaches and that it had prevented you from attending to letters. I am glad to learn now that you have recovered almost completely.

I had the manuscript of *Anant Ki Or* (Towards Infinity) read and translated to me by Shri Somesvara Sarma. It is very grand and beyond most of us. The knots could hold us away from the final destiny but for the Master. Shri Balasubramaniam also was present. I do not know what exactly I have to write as a foreword but I trust in Thy granting me inspiration, for I have not yet become aware of the steps Thou hast led me through clearly. I await Thy arrival here. When Thou dost come here please make it convenient to stay here for a week at least. I believe it will be in December or earlier.

Shri Tyagarajah came here last week on the 5th and spent with me a couple of hours. Things seem to be not quite all right at that end. But what is there to worry about. Master knows all.

I have been deeply moved by Thy grace and Thy love. I do not know what I could do. I only pray for that dynamic experience that will dissolve all doubts and make me plunge in 'Ignorance' into the Ocean of Bliss and then move to the stage of *tam* and so on. The Master alone can take me. I had experienced swimming with the Master within me as my self and I as His body (which I now perceive the Master has stated in the work as the reconciliation of both *dvaita* and *advaita* and their transcendence).

...during my sickness. It was an ecstatic experience. I had experienced the Master descending into me as light, and now the Master has said that He had grafted His *sookshma sharir* into me. I am blessed, but can I crave for the great plunge into the Ocean of Divine Bliss and feel myself transformed in all my parts? Is it supra-mentalisation? and supra-mental descent or ascent? Maybe I am not blessed to be the verifier of that experience. But possibly my intuition would clearly perceive the One that has achieved it and be His co-worker through life, through death, through eternity. I only pray that my Master would carry me through all these without the slightest taint or smear of ego, for I believe so far the Master had carried me through the several *avasthas*, through *laya* and *sarupyata*, which does not focus the ego, but abolishes it or dissolves the forming ego ere it forms itself. That is why I am not even conscious of passing through all the *pradesas, pind, brahmanda* and *para brahmanda*. Am I right?

Here all of us are otherwise well. I indeed observed that I am terribly hungry. I shall try to take care of my diet. Chi. Padmini has gone to Mysore along with the College excursion party yesterday and would return on Thursday. Chi. Srivatsa has his F.L. examination on the 25th and will go to Madras on the 16th or the 19th. I also mean to take father for a couple of days to Madras on the 20th. My wife is all right. Owing to lot of guests she is having strain of home work. My uncle the Postmaster was here and was anxious that Thy grace should help his sons and inquired when Thou wouldst be here. Shri Subramaniam (Engineer) came to me twice and told me that he was praying to the Master.

I do not know what Shri Balasubramaniam would have written about a proposal of his to purchase a place for the forthcoming Shri Ram Chandra Mission Branch. I told him that nothing can be finalised till Thy visit over to this place.

Some have constructive ideas: I have only transformative ideas of the individual. Not until one is free can one try to free others for one may bind all otherwise.

With loving pranams.

Yours ever and thy body.
KCV

No. B 465/SRCM   **Shahjahanpur, U.P.**
Dated: 11th September, 1957

My dear Varadachari,

Received your affectionate letter dated 7th September, 1957. When I look to your letter, I naturally rebound to myself to see if the conditions you are feeling are due to myself or to yourself. If we examine this thing at the surface, we are happy to write my pet sentence that the merit goes to you. But if we go deep into the matter, the conscience calls up to the glory of the Master. Anyhow, you deserve congratulations. Your progress is so rapid that I hope to see with my own eyes at least a few personalities proving themselves to be the shining stars of the Mission. I have every hope from you as well that my dreams would be a reality. But when I write this thing to you, my thoughts reflect to Shri Raghavendra Rao also. The sentences above are the downpour of my love issuing forth from the very core of my heart.

Now I come to your letter, giving you a happy news that you have crossed the region of *para brahmanda mandal* on 6th September at 10:35 P.M. I congratulate you for such a speedy improvement and pray that your step may go on and on without a break. There are so many regions after it that I hesitate to write lest you should be confused. Although the power of the Master is behind your back. It has been a custom of the guides generally in the past not to tell the abhyasis beforehand the conditions they were to experience lest they might create them artificially by exercising their developed will-force; but I don't expect this thing from you, hence telling you a little about the region which you have stepped in. This is the region where the greatness of God is established and the wonder begins. What is the wonder? The idea of the greatness of God is in itself so great that we think ourselves a drop of the ocean. Surrender begins in that region. Those who are sensitive feel these things, but the conditions prevail in all. I will ask you sometime later about the immobilisation of desire. It has taken its root now.

We should try to remain unmindful of the ideas and thoughts and not to allow ourselves to the suggestiveness of the surroundings. In other words, we should be unmindful and not to fight with them. If somehow or other they arise, think them as mine because you are mine. In this way the breeding ground of thought is my heart and not yours. For your sentence about imagination of events, I give below the English translation of a couplet by a Persian poet:

"The Creator has every care of His creatures; to care for one's own needs is the cause of all worries."

I am glad that you are restless to go beyond what is at present under your grip. You have risen a little beyond the human consciousness which is developing more and more. The white grey colour speaks of something akin to real one, but the condition of the faint reflection of the colourlessness is being expected. This thing is the dawn of Reality.

You have experienced my presence in the Shiva temple. I hope further on to see me everywhere. Doctor, have you observed that I remain with you like the shadow with the body.

Did Shri Thyagarajan meet you at Tirupathi? I had also been at Mysore in the year 1945, but I am sorry that I could not visit the sacred shrine of Shri Ramanuja because I was not knowing that it exists there. I received a letter from Shri A. Balasubramaniam that he is arranging to transfer a plot of land to the Mission which he will take on lease. This is a very good idea and I agree with your view. I shall write to him also.

With best wishes to you and love to children. Convey my respects to Appaji.

Yours,
Ram Chandra

16th September, 1957

My dear Revered and beloved Gurudev,

Please accept my sincerest pranams. Your kind letter dated 11th September to hand. I have been deeply moved by the sentiments expressed by your good self. All glory to the Master.

It is so good to have been led beyond the *para brahmanda mandal* and to enter into super-conscious regions. I believe you would have by now received my letter dated 9th or 10th instant.

I have been trying to verify the experience (i) of Thyself as always with me, (ii) as having grafted Thy *karana sharir* in me, and (iii) the immobilization of desire. These few days I have been earnestly seeking to explore myself in meditation. I found that the meditation was somehow different and even a feeling of dejection took possession of me.

I have been the day before yesterday almost all the night in the endeavour to catch myself in that state of which Thou hast spoken, but I became tired. But I cannot complain, for there are perhaps knots which have yet to be untied before I could experience all that Thou hast written to me about.

I only pray that the dejection will not be long lasting and all that I feel would be but steps in the ascent. Can you make clear to me when the supramental consciousness or super-mind arises and becomes the knot of a higher type of being? Have you any verification of the Aurobindonian experience of the Super-mind? Of course this is because of the curiosity to verify and fix the planes of the divine evolutionism of which He speaks.

I am glad that Shri Raghavendra Rao is also progressing rapidly and has earned Thy blessing in fullest measure.

I gave the preface to Shri Somesvara Sarma last Wednesday and until now he did not meet me. I learn that his family has returned after confinement with twins last Thursday or Friday. Perhaps he is busy with it. In the meanwhile I am posting today the manuscript of *Anant Ki Or* and my English preface which perhaps could be got translated by Shri Ishwar Sahai. I do not know whether it is adequate for the purpose of introducing the Master's work.

I have not yet received the quotation about printing. But I believe it will be about 600 Rs. (22 Rs. per forme of 16 pages and about 12 formes, plus cost of paper for 1000 copies and binding as per the original). Today I received a letter from the Madras man asking me to meet him.

I expect to take my father to Madras on the 19th or 20th and be back on the 23rd.

All children are well as also my wife.

Please inform Shri Ishwar Sahai about the receipt of the manuscript and my preface. I will also be writing to him. I shall send the translation of Shri Somesvara Sarma to him as soon as I receive it.

With loving pranams.

Yours,
KCV

Shri Somesvara Sarma could not make out the meanings of the following terms: 1) *taldhat*, 2) *bhamuk*, 3) *thas*, 4) *kuredan*. He has also pointed out some transcriptional mistakes in pencil in the manuscript.

No. B 480/SRCM   **Shahjahanpur, U.P.**
Dated 21st September, 1957

My dear Varadachari,

Received your affectionate letter dt. 9th September, 1957. The blankness is the seed-bed for the stage of 'Ignorance'. The thoughts you feel are not yours. They come from the things round about us, and from other persons. Thoughts swimming in the atmosphere also affect the abhyasis who have their approaches in *brahmanda mandal*. In such case they will not be anchored to the attention. If they persist then it means that the drifting thoughts have found their relatives sleeping in your mind and has awakened them to activity and the result is that you find yourself taking the personal interest and some irritation, disappointment or anxiety has arisen. Pay no heed to them is the remedy.

When the devotion is developed in the heart of the abhyasi for his Master, the samskaras are thrown up in dreams. I had written to you in one of my letters that samskaras which have become manifest will be minimised. They are now being thrown out in different ways, trying always as far as possible that they may not burst out into some disease. You are undergoing their *bhog* unknowingly and unnoticed.

Re. approach: You have already crossed 8 knots as given in the book, *Anant Ki Or.* You are now on ninth one from 6.9.57 as I had written to you previously in my last letter. I have taken the major knots and discussed them in the book and left out the minor ones. We take generally in training the master cell of the knot which illumines all other minor cells in its sphere. You get power thereby to complete the course of the journey in that sphere.

I assure you that you will enter the region of 'Ignorance' by the grace of God. I am hurrying up in your case but at the same time I want that you may have the experiences of the way. The training of my Master is of course, unlike others, a peculiar one that an abhyasi does not know his strength for some time for fear of being overtaken by egoism. The will of Master is at work continually for digging the grave of egoism to its last run. Regarding your question of supramental, I would submit that it is in flow. I have a mind to let you know the very thing practically by the grace of my Master when I come to you. Last time when I was with you I thought about how to warm yourself with it by *anubhava* but it was too early at that time. I hope my prayers will be granted and I will succeed in what I have said above. I am now entirely open-hearted to you because you have already mortgaged me. I will also give you a hint of *tam* as far as your nervous system allows and it rests upon you to understand it.

Shri Thyagarajan has written to me a letter from Trichy that he was greatly moved by your devotion to the Master and he praises you highly for it. He enjoyed your company well and felt charged with divine force which has now become natural to you.

You have correctly guessed that the things are otherwise at Trichy. I have a mind to take your opinion about it when I get to Tirupati. Since my return from south I am regularly having bloodless operations from Shri Ganesan. The bone of contention was that being his guest I did not observe the etiquette of informing him directly about my safe arrival at Shahjahanpur blaming my position in the letter. I sincerely apologised for it. He had written in reply that S. India is a land of etiquette and I must observe that if I want to spread the cult of the Mission there. After that he had written the same thing to Shri Ishwar Sahai at Lakhimpuri-Kheri that he had not informed his arrival to him but to Shri Krishnamoorti like myself. The reason for writing to Shri Krishnamoorti for both of us was that we got his letters at our own places when we arrived. With no idea of any kind we have replied his letters saying to inform all concerned of our safe arrival. Shri Ishwar Sahai also apologized for the wrong. In reply to his letter he had written to Shri Ishwar Sahai that if he was under the impression that Shri

Krishnamoorti loved him much then his duty of the Mission ends. I took this view seriously and informed Mr. Ganesan that his correspondence was being sent to Shri Raghavendra Rao under whom the training centre of Trichy is working and if he so advises I would close down the Centre. Shri Raghavendra Rao had written to me not to stop functioning the Centre but to give him a chance to improve. I agreed to his proposal. If I ever wrote to him anything it was for his own good. The bloody knife was always presented to me in the form of words. I now regret that I knowingly committed the blunder.

When I was before Mr. Ganesan I had told him clearly that he was neither fit for initiation nor for spiritual training. He promised to mend himself and Shri Ishwar Sahai recommended his case. Really I have committed the Himalayan blunder that I initiated him in Sahaj Marg to smoothen his way (as I discussed in *Reality at Dawn*). I keep this thing reserved for a chosen few but I don't keep any difference in training between the initiated and non-initiated ones. After initiation I become powerless to break one off. If the circumstances demand of breaking the initiated the permission of the Master is sought and the power obtained for it. The initiated one can leave me at any time. To tell you the truth, I have been bestowed with special powers from my Master for breaking any initiation of any *sanstha* if the opportunity presents itself. But I don't mean to act upon it unless some extraordinary urgency presents itself. I am now in a fix what to do. I will consult you in the matter when I come to you along with Shri Raghavendra Rao.

I shall try best to devote a week with you. The difficulty is that my ailing mother feels my separation very much.

I am deeply concerned with my children and I pray that they may lead a happy and prosperous life. Amen. My sincere love to them.

With best wishes to you and the sister. Convey my respects to Appaji.

Yours,
Ram Chandra

P.S. I am intending to start for South in the 1st week of December.

26th September 1957

My dear Revered and beloved Gurudev,

Please accept my humble pranams and forgive me if I have in any sense committed any folly. Your kind letter dated 21st instant reached me yesterday. I had sent you the manuscript and other material on the 19th which must have reached you by now.

I returned from Madras with my father on the 23rd evening. All went off well. The doctor has not tampered further with the eye as nothing more could be done to make the vision better.

My friend at Madras has decided to bring out the book before the end of next month and I have left him all discretion about the types, paper etc., and said that the get-up should be like the original.

Could you kindly send to his address given below, the blocks of yourself and Samartha Guruji, and the crest of the Mission, and the block regarding the

Efficacy of Raja Yoga which you said were with you. That would facilitate quick work.

Address to which the blocks etc., have to be sent:

Sri S. Rajam
Murry & Co. Auctioners
S Thambu Chetty Street. G.T. Madras

I shall also be happy if you could bring with you some copies of the *Reality at Dawn* and the *Efficacy of Raja Yoga* as I have left mine with my friends at Madras.

I am glad to be told that I am at the 9th knot. Though the distance to be travelled is great yet thanks to the interest which the Master has bestowed on this unworthy creature, he will reach the goal promised. I should of course confess to you that I have during these two weeks and more not anything more to report. I am feeling utterly helpless and tired about all the impressions, incidents and so on. Again and again I have felt that I am no better than a stone and all strength and knowledge that I can get are from the Divine Master alone. Should I say that it is all my karma and fate. It is true that when one's possession, such as ego, goes and nothing else has yet taken its place, when the true Ruler is yet not apprehended and felt consciously or otherwise within, then one suffers a feeling of loss. I believe I am in such a condition of restlessness and helplessness. How can I have awareness of my devotion? I feel I have had no devotion so far and all devotion has been on Thy side alone. It is a veriest truth that I am saying. God knows when my humiliations would end and the light shine brightest in me so that I may lift the burden of sorrow away from so many of our innocent victims here.

Regarding Shri Ganesan, I had been appraised of all the facts which thou hast stated in the letter. I am so unhappy that he should have hurt you of all persons. Yet I do not know why in heaven he should have been chosen to this work before his ego has suffered eclipse, as it seems that it is the cause. Shri Krishna speaks of *anasuyatmaka buddhi* as the most important qualification for yoga. I have a holy horror of all egoism, and I have prayed throughout that that should be extinguished. I can fully remember why I had been unfit for so long because of this *asuya* which corrupts all understanding. No wonder I have been tested, and am indeed even now being tested, till the roots of ego are completely uprooted. May my Master be pleased to bestow on me the boon of egolessness and *anasuya*. I have already been told that in the meditations it is felt that power passes from the others around him to him rather than the other way about and so many are avoiding him. It may be so. In any case it is better to be firm at the beginning itself. As for the etiquettes of South India I believe South India knows how to honour saints than Shri Ganesan knows.

At least it does not know Shri Ganesan's etiquette. That is enough. I only pray that you will be pleased to look at it from your internal supra-mental vision rather than rely on our opinions. I should even feel that that should be the only natural method of selection. Personally I should invite your kind attention to the fact that a centre should naturally function with its spiritual members and possibly the preceptor or whoever is to look after the centre, should not be one who claims any privileges or has any. A natural functioning unit is the desideratum. I do not know how you will organize it. I have been really seriously thinking with my friend Shri Balasubramaniam about the composition and function and working of the same, and would very much like to remain utterly incognito in work. I realise that Thy greatest hope is in getting the best men fitted for the huge task of transformation. Men's minds and hearts have to be changed and a new outlook has to come into being, a supra-mental force must operate in and outside every institution of whatever kind so as to help in the regeneration of all. This I am sure is so very serious a work that it requires perfect spiritual organisms through which the Divine force of thine works and even unconsciously to the world and the organisms till the fullest possibility is attained. I do not know whether I have expressed myself correctly. But I shall abide by Thy will.

I am feeling again and again despondent about external things, though it is very much like a sting and a pang, albeit short-lived.

I am not even concerned with the distinction between initiated and uninitiated. I do not know the difference. I am hopeful that by the grace of God and the Master I shall deserve to be His wholly and enjoy Him wholly too if that is possible.

I am glad that the programme is being finalised.

All of us are doing well.

With loving pranams,

Yours,
KCV

No. B 513/SRCM   Shahjahanpur, U.P.
Dated 5th October, 1957

My dear Varadachari,

Received your affectionate letters dated September 19, 26, 27 and 29, 1957. I am very grateful to you for the trouble you took in writing the foreword of the Hindi book. It is all inspired and unparalleled. I had already written to Shri Balasubramaniam to insert Justice Chaturvedi's Preface as it is in the book. He was of opinion that the same should be incorporated in the Tamil translation and its Tamil translation is not necessary. So it can go with the book in English as he wishes. I have dispatched the blocks of photos of myself and the Master with emblem of the Mission and diagrams to Shri S. Rajam. I agree with your opinion to include the photo in the book. I have directed Shri Ishwar Sahai, the Superintendent of the Publication Department, to correct the mistakes pointed out by Shri Sameshur Sharma.

I shall reply your question about the super-mind practically, if possible by His grace, when I will be with you. Your view is correct that when one loses his possessions such as ego etc., whatever remains after it is the Master's and is the true form of dedication. In such a state, the feelings of suffering humiliation or helplessness vanish automatically. If you remember Him constantly, it becomes then sufficient for your awareness of devotion. I appreciate the idea that as you say, you feel no devotion to the Master. It shows that you are relieved of a part of egoism.

I appreciate what you have written in reference to Shri Ganesan for the cause of the Mission. I shall take care of your golden advice in this connection. The power both inside and outside is there in the Mission. If anybody takes up this work, he will feel the truth of what I have said.

Your letter of 27th September, 1957. I felt with concern your feeling of distress over certain facts and events of life. Prayer of course, as you agree, is the best solution. It is no doubt painful to swallow the poison but if the poison is freed of its poisonous effect, it shall no longer be unpalatable. To avoid controversies is not cowardice but a virtue. It means you are inwardly more attached to higher pursuits and do not want to waste your time and energy fruitlessly. With regard to your sleepless night, referred to in the letter, I think, so far as I can recollect, it may possibly be the same night on which I too could not sleep till 3:30 remaining all the while in your thought. I do not remember the date. After 3:30 I had an hour's sleep only.

Please let me know the number of copies of *Efficacy of Raja Yoga* and *Reality at Dawn* I should bring with me. I am sending you the Bank Draft for Rs.600/- for the printing expenses.

With best wishes to you and Sister and love to children. Convey my respect to Appaji.

Yours,
Ram Chandra

Tirupati
6th October, 1957

My dear Revered and beloved Gurudev,

Please accept my humble and loving pranams. I cannot express my fullest faith in Thy wisdom. Thou hast given me so much of thyself that I feel very moved. I cannot say more. During the past fortnight I was almost every day waiting for Thy word. But all through meditations and otherwise all other kinds of thoughts ideas and dreams had interfered with me. With all these as thou hast written I had begun to feel that they are thine and the test or working out of karma and samskaras is vigorously on.

In the meanwhile I had to answer to important points regarding my work.

A sadhaka from the Shri Aurobindo Ashram came about 10 days ago with a request that I should collaborate in the completion of the work begun by Shri Aurobindo on the *Veda* — the completion of the translation of the *Rig Veda* on the lines laid down by Shri Aurobindo. I replied that unless I achieved His consciousness I could not possibly do it.

There is a function taking place in the University here. The Shri Aurobindo Study Circle has presented Shri Aurobindo's portrait to the University College Philosophy Association. Presumably taking advantage of the fact that I am held to be affiliated with that great teacher. This is to be on the 9th. I had to do the preliminary and I also wrote to the Mother of the Ashram for a message today.

All these undoubtedly created and continue to create some peculiar mental movements. Why are the Aurobindonians interested in me? Could the Master explain. I only pray to the Master to lead me. I have entirely surrendered myself to Thee.

During the past three days I have been praying that I may be drowned in Thee who art my Ocean of Bliss and Grace and *Narayana*.

7th October, 1957. I waited for Thy kind letter today. As I did not get the same I am concluding my letter.

I request you not to worry about the finance for the publication. I have arranged that it will be paid at our convenience. In the meanwhile my friend wrote to me that he is waiting for the blocks etc. Kindly send them early. I am anxious that the publication should come out about the time you go over here.

I have not heard from you also about the foreword I had written. I trust it is all right but if Thou thinkest that it should be modified I shall do so. I am afraid the same looks to be the work of an ignorant man in yoga.

All of us are well.

I believe you are now completely restored in health and all children at home are keeping fit.

With loving pranams,

Yours as body and instrument,

KCV

No. B 527/SRCM   Shahjahanpur, U.P.
                        Dated 19th October, 1957

My dear Varadachari,

Received your affectionate letter dated 16th October, 1957 just now. I shall reply your previous letters after two or three days. I am very grateful to the gentleman who is presenting a plot to the Mission. I agree to your proposal and you may get the gift deed executed. But it will take time before this Mission succeeds in constructing the building over the plot as it depends mostly on natural rains for its crop. I don't think the gentleman will be in hurry for it. With best wishes to you and love to children. Respect to Appaji.

Yours
Ram Chandra

No. B 539/SRCM   Shahjahanpur, U.P.
                        Dated 25th October, 1957

My dear Varadachari,

Received your affectionate letters of the 6th, 10th and 16th October. Since you wanted an early reply in connection with the gift deed, I communicated to you telegraphically followed by a post card.

Asthma is troubling me for the last two weeks. It was very intense on the 20th, but today I feel a bit relieved. Weakness, however, persists which hampers proper expression of thoughts.

You find Aurobindonians interested in you. The reason is clear. You are a talented man of vast learning and noble characteristics. They want to utilise your merits, acquired by your self efforts, for their cause, in the interest of the people. The same is the case with me though in a slightly different way. I too mean to utilise your services for the Mission, but with the instrument sharpened by my humble services and prayers for your approach up to the level where learning assumes the trend of forgetfulness. That means the dawn of real knowledge, which by itself makes other hearts charged with divine influence.

You want to absorb in this poor being which is dead and gone. That may be fortunate for me. To tell you the truth I also did the same. With me the only object in view was to realise my revered Master. God was a distant thing for me to conceive of. It was on a Dipawali day that I happened to find the beloved Master himself absorbed in me and it was later verified by him. In this respect Dipawali is a very significant occasion in my life. I did all this because my Master was worthy of it and I know Him and HIM alone.

I may also intimate to you that since you have stepped into the region beyond *para brahmanda mandal*, the kundalini also seems to be affected in a way. I do not mean to touch this latent power except a little cleaning thereof. Ouspensky is very critical as regards this Serpent Power, but I see in you a natural trend towards it though it may yet take sufficient time for its awakening. Do you feel some tension or pain in the region between the navel point and the *swadhistan chakra*, though I do not expect it so soon. I received a very bad letter from Mr. Ganesan in view of which I had to close down the Centre at Trichy. Copies of letters to this effect are enclosed for information.

I am greatly remembering one of my boys there for about a month. He may probably be Ch. Narayan. This may perhaps be of some good to him. My affection for the sister too is developing. Please ask my children to tell me if they want anything from this place. I am going to Delhi on the 15th stopping at several places en route. I shall return by the 30th. I shall leave for South India on the 5th of December. The tour programme is sent herewith.

With best wishes and love to children. Respect to Appaji.

Yours,
Ram Chandra

9th November, 1957

My dear Revered and beloved Gurudev,

Please accept my humble pranams. I believe that you are all keeping well. My previous letter must have reached you and obviously your time is taken up with arranging things before you start for Delhi and the South. I am sure by the time this letter reaches you you would have received a letter from Shri Balasubramaniam.

I think your programme stands and you would be arriving at Tirupati on the 19th December from Gulbarga. I trust also that you would be accompanied by Brother Ishwar Sahaiji and Brother Raghavendra Rao. My warm welcome to all of you at my humble residence.

I have not received from Thyself a detailed letter as stated in thy previous letter about points raised. But I am hopeful that they will be solved when You come over here next month.

In the meanwhile I have not perceived any further progress or change. I feel that though the meditation lasts yet the invading impressions from outside is yet disturbing. I yearn for the plunge into the Ocean of Bliss which thou hast prescribed for cleaning the body so that I might feel myself beyond the pleasure-pain principle and delight in the glory of the Supreme Master and drink deep both within and without that real being which keeps me going.

Indeed I now find that I sleep longer hours than I used to do, though once or twice the dreams about which I wrote come vividly.

I trust this letter would reach you before you leave for Delhi on the 15th.

Please let me know what I can do. I have not yet got the final proofs of the book given for printing. I have reminded the printer at Madras and hope to have the books ready by the end of this month.

I am so sorry that things do not get moving quickly and something or other comes in the way.

All of us including my father and wife and children are keeping fit.

With loving pranams,

Yours,
KCV

No. B 573/SRCM   Shahjahanpur, U.P.
Dated 11th November, 1957

My dear Varadachari,

Received your affectionate letter dated 27th October, 1957. It does not matter if Swamiji did not agree to the gift. Let us wait for His grace. My asthma is now subsided. I think I am having the natural cure because I was affected by this disease after ten months. I shall travel under all conditions of health. But please pray that my mother's condition may remain satisfactory. She had a very strong attack of asthma which has since subsided. The same thing happened last year, but as the days of my journey were nearing she began to recover. The same thing is happening this time also and she is gradually improving. This is the effect of the prayers of my associates.

I am happy to find that you are feeling neither happiness nor unhappiness. When we travel we meet the different sorts of surroundings and environment. Some are pleasing and some unpleasant. But the journey continues in spite of all these things. The same is the case with our march towards Reality. While travelling we get different impressions in different parts of the regions. They rise for the sake of fall because we have to be free from all these things for merging in Reality. But everything dwindles into nothing in the last reach. We acquire the state of balance but not perfectly because in that case the life will be extinct. Before the world was born everything was in a perfect balanced state. The balance was disturbed and the world came into being. The saints are generally said to have the thoughtless state, but my experience and theory show that they can become almost thoughtless and can never enjoy the perfect state of thoughtlessness, because in that case they will return to the state where life is extinct. They are of course not perturbed with the different musings and if the thoughts come they can remove them instantly, and can remain for any length of time without the presence of thoughts. In other words they can command over the musings and are not their slaves. What happens generally, these thoughts are replaced by divine thoughts and they are not to be checked, but should be cordially welcomed. Their tongues become the tongue of Nature, their hearts become the playground of divine thoughts, their minds become the abode of pure consciousness.

Now I come to your condition. You write, "I am neither happy nor unhappy." When you feel neither happy nor unhappy, think it to be the seed, and it is decidedly so, of that condition which will grow and develop, resulting in the condition depicted above. This is the condition which generally the abhyasis do not like, but I am elated to know it. The condition you have written is only in the seed form. It will have the different squall of winds which will be fanning the seed to grow into a perennial tree. I remember once I said to my Master, "I feel myself permanently in one condition which is neither bliss nor otherwise. No change happens even if every bone of my body be hacked off with an iron weapon. In other words the taste is like that of 'stone without salt'." He very beautifully replied "If I take out this condition from you for a while, will you like it?"

After pondering a while I replied, "I shall prefer death rather than to be away from it."

The pressure you feel in the chest is due to transmission, although I take care to insert the required amount of power only as much as may be needed. In such case you should always inform me, although there is no danger of any kind. Throbbing in several parts means the awakening of different things which are in sleepy condition.

When I say for any condition to be far off, you must not be confused. All the stages are for human beings and specially for a person like you. My idea of perfection is a peculiar one and almost none will agree to it. My own experience has brought me to think it like that. A man should have complete *laya avastha* with Brahma, as far as is possible for the soul, resulting in the Knowledge of the Real and also the knowledge of all the sciences and elements for which people are trying. If one has no awareness of these things on concentration, *laya avastha* is not complete in the Knower.

The dream you saw is good. The Godly *shaktis* are arising to co-operate with you. The dreams also come according to the tendencies of a man and his attitude in life. I had many such dreams during my abhyas period.

I received a letter from Shri A. Balarama Reddy who had seen you at Tirupati asking me to send a copy of *Reality at Dawn* which I am sending.

With best wishes to you and love to children, please convey my respect to Appaji.

Yours,
Ram Chandra

No. B 593/SRCM   **Shahjahanpur, U.P.**
Dated 15th November, 1957

My dear Varadachari,

Received your affectionate letter dated 9th November, 1957. I have replied your previous letter under No. B 573/SRCM dated 11th November, 1957. I believe that it must have reached you.

Shri Ishwar Sahai will accompany me from Shahjahanpur. Regarding Shri Raghavendra Rao I will inform you from Gulbarga. My mother's condition is satisfactory and my programme stands by His grace. I shall write to you from Hyderabad when I reach there. The address is given below.

It is, of course, right that you are not perceiving your inner condition nowadays. But when I peep into you, I am overjoyed. My thought seems to have wings when I study the efficacious teaching of my Master coming to you direct. I write to you a few lines for your information and can boldly say that curvature will never form in our *sanstha*. Please go through my letter where I have written the word 'echo'. You and Shri Raghavendra Rao both are undergoing the course of Nature herself which will weave transformation ultimately. Pure consciousness is descending infusing the regions below. It is absorbing in the blood and flesh. The course of Nature is now about to complete and yesterday at about 11 in the night I observed that it will take only a few days more. I kept quiet but only engaged myself in cleaning the points and the system according to my habit. It is really a great thing which I will call a boon of Nature. Now I can entirely rely upon the Shastric injunctions that an abhyasi can only gain the object when God Himself wants it. The symptom is now apparent. The *yatra* of the region you get after crossing the *para brahmanda mandal* has not yet commenced because the Nature was having her own course. So please do not think that you have not improved.

My Master once talked of the echo and I was thinking and thinking but the matter was not clear to me. Now the cases are before me. You have left yourself under my care, so the disturbing elements are mine and you are free from them. If such disturbing things come unto you think that they are mine and I trust that they will immediately bid farewell.

You have done well to remind the Manager of the Press for the final proof. If they are not available yet please issue another reminder. I remember when the book *Reality at Dawn* was in the Press the final proof reached me after about a month when Justice Chaturvedi had strongly written to the Manager who for fear of legal steps sent the proof.

I am starting for Mathura tomorrow morning. Please convey my respects to Appaji. With best wishes to you and love to children,

Yours,
Ram Chandra

<u>Hyderabad address:</u>
C/o Shri P. Madhava Rao, M.Sc.,
Lecturer, Nizam's College,
No. 3-4-512/18 Barkatpura,
Hyderabad (Deccan).

No. B 607/SRCM Shahjahanpur, U.P.
Dated 4th December, 1957

My dear Varadachari,

Your affectionate letters of 19th and 22nd. I am glad to learn about your recent experiences given in the first letter. It is not mere imagination but has a real basis. The experiences stated in the next letter confirm the view. Your love and devotion has put me under a spell, so to say, and I eagerly wish to be closer and closer to your heart, viewing my Varadachari everywhere, in and out. When I was on tour to Delhi, my third son got a crack in the wrist bone, on account of fall from the cycle. It has been plastered and there is nothing to worry about. My programme stands as it is.

With best wishes and love to children and respects to Appaji,

Yours,
Ram Chandra

No. B 618/SRCM Shahjahanpur, U.P.
Dated 14th December, 1957

My dear Varadachari,

Received your affectionate card of 9th December, 1957. I shall reach Tirupati on the 19th evening at 17:35 according to programme. By this time you must have received my letter from Hyderabad. Shri Raghavendra Rao shall reach Tirupati on 24th evening. My impatience to see you the earliest, cannot be translated in words. This is the reaction of your own devotional feelings.

I regret the sad result of the boy who was under your treatment. Mysterious are the ways of God who alone can know what is best in every particular case. Our dreams and visions may or may not have any bearing with them. The appearance of saints in dreams is often usual in the course of the automatic run of spiritual development. They tend to help the abhyasi. They work from higher spheres and their actions and words are all divine.

With best wishes and love to children. My respects to Appaji.

Yours,
Ram Chandra

Trichy
Dated 28th December, 1957

My dear brother,

I shall reach Madras at 6 A.M. on the 30th and I think I shall be able to catch the Bombay Express leaving Madras at 7:35. If so I shall arrive at Renigunta at about 10:30 A.M. If I find your disciples there at the time I shall stay with them for a few hours otherwise I shall take the first train for Tirupati. If possible please inform them accordingly. I eagerly wish for the earliest meeting with you and I am very restless for it.

With best wishes,

Yours affectionately,
Ram Chandra

P.S. Our associates will be at the Madras Station to see me and it is possible they might like me to be with them for an hour more. In that case I may leave by the next passenger train at 8:40. M.K. Ganesan will accompany me to Madras.

No. B 650(41)/SRCM **Shahjahanpur, U.P.**
Dated 30th December, 1957

My dear Varadachari,

We arrived here quite safely. I am now relieved of all troubles. Cough has almost subsided, weakness is also reduced much. I shall be expecting you at Madras on my return. I hope to reach Madras on 4th morning.

With best wishes,

Yours,
Ram Chandra

1958

Madras
Dated 9th January, 1958

My dear Varadachari,

Received your affectionate letter dated 7th January, 1958. Mr. S. Vedantam gave us a pleasant drive in his car. We went to Adiyar, visiting several places on the way. He also took me to his house and offered us nice refreshment. I also saw your room.

We should be thankful to the Great Master for bestowing upon our mother the luminous state of liberation which she rightly deserved.

If sister feels uncomfortable on account of *anahat*, I may make the effect go deeper. Throbbings shall no doubt remain to some extent, due to the force of energy descending.

As for yourself you are right in doing with your samskaras as you do. For your craving to discover and see the states, I suggest the following but it must be done only once or at the most twice.

'Lie down flat on the bed and begin to meditate on your soul.' By the process may you begin to discover the states. But it is rather difficult to understand the finer states of subtle existence.

I have cleaned your entire system. The *suksham* dots there, have all been dissolved. Your system is now made quite pure. All limitations have been removed from the point 1 & 2 which now possess unlimited powers. You are full of energy for the work which I wanted to have from you.

Shri S.P. Srivastava has been very thankful for the kind hospitality he met with at your house. He has been busy with his own programme and he will write to you from his place.

Now I have decided to leave for Shahjahanpur on the 10th January (i.e., a day earlier) so as to accompany Shri S.P. Srivastava in the journey.

I had been down with cough all the time and it still persists to some extent. I am however much better than before and shall be quite well when I reach my place.

With good wishes to you and all brethren and respects to Appaji.

Shri I. Sahai and all associates here want me to convey their *pranam* to you.

Yours,
Ram Chandra

No. C 49/SRCM Shahjahanpur
14th January, 1958

My dear Varadachari,

We got here safely on the 13th January, after a brief halt at Lucknow. I am exceedingly glad to inform you that during my stay at your place I felt unbroken peace which even my physical illness could not disturb. That was the best hospitality you had offered me and which is usually very rare.

At Madras I found that the problem there is somewhat difficult as speeches and lectures are the only means that can attract the mind of the people there to our thought. But I find myself to be incapable for this kind of work as I am not a speaker.

Just now I received your affectionate letter of the 10th January, 1958 together with the copies of photograph and the prayer cards. Shri Vedantam took me to his house and I saw his wife too. I did not make a close study of them but they seemed to be good souls with loving hearts. I could not see Mr. S. Rajan at the time for he was not at home.

I appreciate your work as a preceptor, finding the people of your satsangh improving in almost all cases. I am glad to tell you a very fortunate incident on the 12th January at about 1:30 P.M. while in train at the time, I found a trail of samskaras descending upon your heart. Though I took them out for the most part, in order to avoid their *bhogam*, still some effect thereof could not be avoided and a subtle state of it remains which may likely be disturbing to you for some time. I am doing my best in this connection.

I had once written to you that the divine instrument is at work for putting down desires and you will have clear knowledge of it when it comes in full swing. Uneasiness (for that reason), may however remain for some time. I shall be looking to it according to needs, though I am very weak at present. But the work cannot suffer on that account.

I am glad to note that my sister is feeling better. Really speaking my task in this connection is mostly over because her direct relation with God is established. I had told you about it at the time. What remains for me to do is to purify the different centres and make her more and more receptive to divine influence.

I hope you must be attending to Appaji at your leisure. I am anxious to see him relieved of opacity.

I shall try to gather information you wanted in connection with my first son. But I think it may be a difficult task to collect this old record.

With best wishes and love to my disciplined children, my respects to Appaji.

Yours,
Ram Chandra

P.S.- I did some spiritual good to Mr. Vedantam. Let us hope it gives turning.

No. C 53/SRCM   **Shahjahanpur**
21st January, 1958

My dear Varadachari,

Recd. your letter of dt. 15th January, 1958 on 20th January, 1958. I also received the diaries of the *satsanghi* sent by you, in a separate cover. I shall write to you in short, about the diaries, when our *utsav* will be over.

I was much grieved to learn that sister is suffering from some 'toothache'. I consulted Dr. P. Sen of Calcutta, a satsanghi of our Mission, about the cause of 'headache'. He told me that headache is due to the pain referred from the toothache. Please see if it is cured by this time, by ordinary treatment, and inform me accordingly. I am also sending a reply paid telegram, to know about her health.

The spiritual state of my sister is of course remarkably good, but I have suspended the direct descent for the time being, and in that case, I was obliged to sever her direct connection, because you are much confused. But I assure you that the pain is not due to direct descent of divine influence but is due to some external material causes.

When I did the process for direct descent, I kept a bondage there, so that the divine wave may descend according to her capacity. And it was our duty to develop her capacity.

Regarding your state of contact, I am happy to note that you get absorbancy in the 'Real' for sometime.

With best wishes to both of you, and my love to your children.

My respect to Appaji also.

Yours,
Ram Chandra

P.S.- I believe you must have received my letter No. C 49/SRCM dated 14th September, 1957. I am almost free from cough but the weakness still persists.

Ram Chandra

No. C 65/SRCM   **Shahjahanpur, U.P.**
Dated 30th January, 1958

My dear Varadachari,

Received your affectionate letters of January 22 & 24 and also the telegram. You seem to be anxious about my health. In this connection I relate to you two of the recent incidents, which show clearly enough that ill health does not hamper work which God wants to have from us. You know of my illness at Salem during the recent tour. The acute pain about the loins had completely confined me to bed. Shri Rajagopal and Sahai advised me to postpone departure for some days till I had recovered. But I did not like any change and was resolute that leave I must for Madras at any cost. About two hours before the departure time I suddenly felt a heavy jerk in the diseased portion of the body which shook me all over. Wonder of wonders, the pain was at once reduced by 90%. I could take up the journey with comfort and ease which otherwise was almost impossible. While I was in the train I felt another similar jerk and the pain was gone altogether.

The other incident happened on the 24th Jan. Before that date I was so weak and feeble that I could not give even one sitting without having several hours rest after that. I was anxiously thinking how shall I be able to transmit continuously for 3 days without a break, though to be away from it was out of question for me. I would and must have done it even at the cost of my life. At 6:25 when I came out of bath I felt surprised to find myself absolutely diseaseless and full of energy like a young healthy man and even till now I feel myself so. Do not these incidents teach us a great lesson that we must be carefree, trying to abide by the Nature's will. Health must no doubt be cared for and that is our duty but at the same time we must be confident that no work can suffer on that account.

Please do not fear that I shall leave you all some day. That happens only when time comes, but my case is different. As I have expressed in many of my letters, I shall be more useful when I leave my physical form. As long as I am in this world I shall be serving you all and my services will continue even after that. Moreover before leaving the body I shall not take away even a grain of power or spirituality with me. All that will be transferred to you all, those deeply attached getting the greater share therefrom. Besides, another one, the best from amongst you all shall be there in my place. When my Master entrusted the work to me, proclaiming me as his representative, I did not set to work for about a year (with His permission no doubt). All this period I devoted to the study of the various types of systems of the people and the proper methods for their spiritual elevation. For several years after I had begun working I sought for hints from above, in all matters relating to the training work. Afterwards when I had studied and experienced everything thoroughly I discovered and practised the method of giving higher approaches in a short time without causing any harm. When I put before the Master my method of bringing a man to Perfection even at a glance without any risk of life, He appreciated it in high terms. There is one drawback in it still which I could not remove. It is that in such cases the real condition will be revealed to him gradually in course of time and not instantly, in which case death is certain. I shall be very glad if anybody helps me in the solution. During our next meeting I shall tell you how the power of transmission can be moulded so as to bring about the desired result without any strain or harm to the nervous system.

The centres of light seen in you by Dr. Kuppuswami are correct though in a different way. You are illumined all over that is a fact beyond doubt. I perfectly believe that you have thrown your responsibility on me and I am fully conscious of it.

You often say you have no love for me. The same I feel in respect of my Master. Once I had asked my

Master about it and he replied that it is the greatest love. But this does not relate to persons who are really devoid of true love. For example take the case of sister. She is smouldering in the thought of love without knowing anything of it. Her case is peculiar.

For some good reasons I do not mean to touch you for about a week or so and I do not mind whether you feel *shanti* or the otherwise. I have filled you with spiritual energy to your utmost capacity and it requires to be digested. The process has already started from 8:35 A.M. on 23rd January, 1958.

I know your anxiety and have already started praying for it even before I received your letter. Our job is only to pray, and the rest with the Master.

My card-size photo which you had sent to me is demanded by many of the associates. So please manage to get the negative from the photographer if possible. Otherwise ask him to keep it safe for further copies, and settle with him the price of prints on superior paper. Please let me know about the rates immediately.

You told me that you shall be going to Calcutta in February 1958. Please let me know the exact dates so that I may inform the associates there. They may also have the opportunity of seeing you and being benefitted by your association. Also your address at Calcutta. I shall send you their addresses later on.

I received a letter from your uncle. My reply to it is enclosed herewith. There is much of grossness in his system which can go only if he takes up the practices in the right spirit. I have tried to explain to him as clearly as I could. It is very fortunate that our Appaji is getting devoid of grossness. You have succeeded mostly in his case.

One of my friends at Trichy, who practices yoga and had come to see me on 30th December, 1957 for about 5 minutes, has sent to me the following message of love. I do not know what he meant, neither do I understand my own reply.

"Dear Love,

With love.

Lovingly His

R. Radhakrishnan"

(He who was with Him only for 5 minutes on 30th December, 1957.)

I replied to him as given below:

"Dear love's Love,

With naught beyond

Beingless His

Ram Chandra"

You asked me once about the colours at the points which I give below:

Point No. 1   Yellow
"   2   Red
"   3   White
"   4   Black
"   5   Green

Note: These colours can be utilised in curing diseases. Whatever colour is required for curing a particular disease, the same colour is transmitted to him. The effect of these colours is explained in the system of treatment through solar colours.

With best wishes and love to children and *pranam* to Appaji.

Yours,
Ram Chandra

P.S.- I have gone through the diaries, sent by you and I have given my views in brief. One thing which I specially want to point out is that I want the diaries in a form which might help me or you to understand the spiritual state of the abhyasi or about his difficulties or entanglements. For this purpose it is better to have it under the following heads:

1. Date and time.

2. Hour and duration of meditation.

3. Experiences and condition at the time of meditation.

4. General condition of mind at other hours of the day with any other thing he specially wants to mention.

With reference to your remark about Shri Raghavendra Raoji I find that both of you are quite good persons and the future hopes of the Mission. That is why I told you when he was at your place that I am now going back leaving the Mission's work on both of you.

Ram Chandra

No. C 73/SRCM **Shahjahanpur, U.P.**
Dated 3rd February, 1958

My dear Varadachari,

Received your affectionate letter dt. 27th January, 1958.

As far as I see and understand, 'pure consciousness' was at work among you all during the Utsav — the celebration days.

I have also replied to Dr. Kuppuswami. He is a very good man, and he deserves close attention. His inner system is a bit gross. If this grossness is removed, it will give him 'bliss'. I presume he must be doing the meditation — of ocean of bliss. That will help him a good deal in cleansing the system. He is a man of devotional mind.

I have already written to you that *satsanghis* at your place are all improving and your work is really second to none of the preceptors of the mission. You are getting your own share along with it.

About sister's ailment, I consulted Dr. P. Sen of Calcutta, who is now here. He prescribes 'Listerine' gargle. (Take 1/2 a teaspoonful of Listerine, and pour it over a cup of tepid water, and then, wash the mouth with it, several times.) I think, it will not meddle with the homeopathic medicine.

I am overjoyed to learn of your impatience for 'Realisation'. It reminds me of my own tale of the past. It is the only instrument which speeds up our march to realisation. You are being moulded by the Nature, for the real service, which you are already attending to.

Regarding your question of 'real consciousness', I would add that I am ready to infuse you with my very blood, if it can be of any use to it. I think, I did not get you, but I searched and found out my own being in the form of Varadachari. Real consciousness is your share and you will have it decidedly, but I must wait for some time, so that you may get the experiences of all stages you are going into, and your capacity may become so great that you may impart this very thing to others, so dear to you and myself.

I have promised you in several letters; if I pull on to that stage instantly, even that, you will take time for its revelation, because sudden transformation means sure death of your mortal being. You will have everything speedily. I, of course, admire your impatience in this respect.

I believe you must have received my letter No. C 65/SRCM 16 dated 29th January. Mr. Rajagopalan of Delhi, had recommended a medicine for asthma. The name was given in Tamil language. You may ask that to Shri Subramanian, to find it out, but I forgot to ask him about it. If it is available there, Mr. Balasubramanian who suffers from asthma, may try that medicine, after consulting some proper physician.

With best wishes to you and to sister, and love to children. My respect to Appaji.

Yours,
Ram Chandra

3rd February 1958

My dear Revered and beloved Gurudev,

Please accept my humble pranams. I am in receipt of the letter which thou hast sent on the 30th Jan. I am happy to know that you are now absolutely all right. I did not doubt at all about Thy great powers but prayed that as it has become my business for the Master's welfare all the while.

I am equally deeply grateful for the unique opportunity of being related to you in this life and may I be thy humble servant doing my work humbly, with God-given light and strength.

I had been to Madras on the 1st and returned last evening. The printing of the book has been taken up and the proofs are regularly coming. It is expected that the work will be completed by the 15th if not earlier.

I have asked them to put up a plain yellow outer wrapper with the title and author's name and the crest of the Mission and the name of the Publisher.

The price of the book is proposed to be Rs. 1/8 as in the case of the original. The cost may go up to Rs. 900/- for thousand copies, though my friend is trying to bring it down. If you would like it to be priced higher please let me know immediately.

As soon as the books are ready please let me know where they have to be kept. My friend S. Rajam suggested that he would keep them and dispatch the required number to the various destinations as and when you advise.

The extra number of 100 copies of the pictures of Samartha Guru and Thyself will be dispatched to whichever address you advice.

2. Regarding the Photo, I have the negative. I shall try to get cheap rate for the printing of copies. We have been supplying each copy at Rs. 1/8 as the price of the printing paper has gone up. The photo dealer is quoting this price. Some concession can be got if we take a large number. Please let me know how many copies you would like to have. We got 36 copies already distributed.

3. Two gentlemen: 1) C.R. Krishnamurthi, De Silva House, Renigunta; 2) V. Venkatapathi, Poonimangadu Village (via Tiruttani) had come and wanted to take up meditations according to Thy instructions. I gave them 2 sittings thanks to the Master's grace.

4. I am scheduled to leave for Calcutta on the 18th night and return on the 23rd evening by Madras Mail. The address is 15 College Square, Calcutta, the headquarters of the Shri Aurobindo pathamandir. I shall be very happy to get from you the addresses of our associates there meeting with whom would be immensely profitable to me.

5. One of our associates Shri Velu Mudaliar, has offered to print Telugu translation of the *Reality at Dawn* **free** of printing charges, only the paper cost has to be supplied. I think it can be done after we finish this work. I am myself looking out to get a competent abhyasi among us to undertake a Telugu translation. But it has to wait.

6. The plot assigned for the Mission is likely to materialise today. I told Mr. Balasubramania Aiyar

that on receipt of Thy consent and blessing we can inspect the site to be taken over.

I am glad to receive Thy observations on the dairies. I am yet quite a novice in this matter and very incompetent in the perceptions about the other abhyasis. With thy ever present presence in me I hope to be able to witness and help the abhyasis. Of course it is Thy supreme work. I feel myself just an instrument. Sometimes I am not even aware of the transmission taking place.

I now understand why I am not able to know my condition myself. But I am assured that all will be well. I have resigned myself completely to Thee, and in fact I was even feeling why I was accepting invitations to speak of Shri Aurobindo. But in a way that too may by thy blessing help the cause.

Shri Vedantam is already feeling the effects of Thy work on him; he has started on the path as he was saying that he saw brilliant light but through mesh. I asked him to follow The method of the Master.

I am thankful for the letter to my uncle. I hope he will take up this method without any hesitation. I shall if he inclines to it permit him to join the satsangh.

Your reply to Shri Radhakrishnan of Trichy is indeed worth pondering over. It is a clear proof of the Love of the Master to any one who seeks Him fully.

I am deeply aware of the colour problem. I shall try to use the analysis in my work.

All is Thy work. It is Thou who workest through every one of us and I am praying that this consciousness should never forsake me.

I am sure with Thy blessings it will be possible for me to more and more be Thine alone and in thy own language 'dead and gone'.

With most loving pranams,

Your body,
KCV

No. C 78/SRCM   **Shahjahanpur, U.P.**
Dated 6th February, 1958

My dear Varadachari,

Received your affectionate letter dt. 3rd February. According to your suggestions the price of the book as fixed Rs. 1/8 is just what I wanted. I am glad to note that the plot sanctioned for our Mission is approved by you all. My consent and blessings for the plot to be taken over is always with you all.

Please inform me when the publication charges are finalised so that I may send it. The reply of the other part of the letter will be given later on.

With best wishes to both of you and love to children. Respect to Appaji.

Yours,
Ram Chandra

No. C 93/SRCM   Shahjahanpur, U.P.
                                  Dated 9th February, 1958

My dear Varadachari,

Received your affectionate letter dated 3rd February, 1958. You must have received my letter No. C 73/SRCM dt. 3rd February, 1958 and also a letter No. C 78/SRCM dt. 6th February, 1958. I have already informed you that if you approve the plot my consent is there.

I have improved my health much under the proper care of Dr. P. Sen of Calcutta. He specialized in Europe in heart, abdomen and infectious diseases and attended the Thysis cases in Germany and Switzerland. He met the wife of Subhash Chandra Bose and his daughter at Weine and enquired about him. She confirmed that he was dead. He was professor in Medical College, Calcutta but now he has resigned the service and has given up his own profession too. He now remains in meditation and constant remembrance. I had written about him some time back in the letter. He will live with me for some months.

You are God given gift for me and I will spare no pains in serving you thoroughly. I think all the chains have been broken out by our Master, but there is only one, that is, I remain fast bound in the trammels of affections which you or anybody have for me.

As soon as the work of publication is complete and the charges are settled, please inform me to send the rest of the amount. The price of the book must not be more than one eighth. (Rs. 1/8).

I am very grateful to Mr. S. Rajan that he would keep the books in stock and will send the copies required anywhere. This is also a kind of service to the Mission. May he be awarded for it.

I have informed Shri Kashi Ram of Tinsukia and to Ishwar Sahai at Lakhimpur to write to you the number of photos required by them.

I am glad that a few more persons have joined the Mission. There are so many others waiting.

Very soon you will be able to read the inner conditions of the abhyasis. The work will teach you all these things. It depends upon the practice also. When you transmit any abhyasi concentrate a little over him with the idea of perception then you will know whether the place is stony or dark or otherwise. If there is light in any abhyasi whether he belongs to the Mission or any other *sanstha* you will be able to know by the above method. It is not at all difficult. Only a little confidence in yourself will reveal the mystery. When you transmit anybody you are not aware if it is taking place. The same condition is mine, when the preceptor gets subtle and gains absorbency in the inner being he does not feel that he is transmitting because the power itself becomes free from matter and it touches the very core of the being. I am very glad to hear this thing from you.

Since my last visit to Madras, I began to develop automatically affection for Shri Vedantam. I think this is the reaction. I have taken him up along with others to render spiritual service.

Shri Radha Krishnan is the disciple of his father who is a yogi. He came to see me and wanted to judge me, but I found that it would be difficult for him, so I gave a little clue. After that I told him that your *agya chakra* is glowing with light but there is darkness in *sahasra dal kamal* and you are not able to get into it. I also asked him if he wanted that the darkness be removed. He said, "Let us wait for some time." I did not tell him some other things about him because a few other *satsanghis* were present there. He admitted that there is darkness in his *sahasra dal kamal* and he could not yet remove it.

That was the only talk between us. He is very good man and I enjoyed his company. I am releasing below the address of Mr. P.A. Krishna and Mr. P.N. Midyil, the satsanghis of Calcutta at present.

1. Shri P.A. Krishna,
   General Agent
   1, Madan Street,
   Suite 6, P.B. 2482,
   Calcutta-13 (Telephone Bank 2980).

2. Shri P.N. Midyil,
   Opposite Express Dairy Co. Ltd.,
   198, Bhupinroy Road,
   Behala,
   Calcutta-34.

With best wishes to you and love to children. Respect to Appaji.

Yours,
Ram Chandra

Tirupati
11th Feb. 1958

My dear Revered and Beloved Gurudev,

Please accept my humble pranams. I believe you would have received my letter intimating the entry with the brother associates on the land assigned to the Mission. I believe it is a good piece of land.

The copies of papers are herewith being sent to you for file. There is a clause saying that we have to develop that piece of land soon. I trust by the Master's grace it will be done. Some persons are offering to do help putting up a shed, etc. We hope that by the time you will be coming here some progress would have been made.

I received your kind P.C. confirming the price fixed for the book. I believe you approve the get up with paper wrapper of yellow colour, without any design as in the original as that would mean making a block. If you have the block of the wrapper cover that could be sent to Mr. Rajam Madras.

I am going to Calcutta by the 19th Mail and reach Calcutta on the 21st instead of 20th as thought of originally. As I have no casual leave I spare a day by this arrangement. I return by AIR to Madras on the 24th and reach the same night Tirupati. I am almost free I believe on the 22nd morning till about 3 P.M. and might be able to meet our associates there.

I have been going through a lot of depression. I cannot express my intense sorrows sometimes at my inability to perceive anything of the higher consciousness within me. I feel myself so gross and even incapable of ascent. The work of the preceptor even seems to be obstructed by my opacity. I do not always find the condition of the abhyasi before me, though I must inform you that many of them feel better. Where am I and how am I these questions crop up again and again. I am in a sense ashamed of this condition, as the Master has constantly been telling me to be otherwise. Of course the Master knows what bhog to give and to remove. The dream state has been very confusing of late. My wife also was speaking of the same condition in her experiences. Sometimes she had trembling and saw all light descending.

As I wrote to Thee last time I do not know anything. I feel myself (or do I?) not even as a conduit pipe of the Master's energy. I have been trying to transmit the love of the Master which like energy will remove all dirt. I have not been particularly instructed to do the transmission in any way so I am using my ingenuity to the best of Thy will. I am Thine. This Thou knowest. But I may not be up to the mark or even advanced enough. The visions seem to be just several passing stages but granting neither the intuitive direct knowledge of the Veda or the Ultimate which entails so many consequences. But I am yet 'craving' rather than going beyond all desires or wishes. I pray for the higher energy that will make nought all these and I pray for the entire abolition of my ignorance and ego.

Thou hast done so much for me and it would be sheer ingratitude if I do not praise Thee for all that Thou hast been doing. But I love more for more, to be really able to do and do more, for the Glory of the Master.

Please accept my humble pranams again. Forgive me these reflections arising out of a heart bruised and pained and loving the Ultimate Master.

I am yours as body,

KCV

Tirupati
15th February, 1958

My dear revered and beloved Gurudev,

Please accept my humble pranams. I am in receipt of Thy affectionate letter dated the 9th inst. I am so happy to learn that under the loving care of Dr. Sen of Calcutta Thy health is improving steadily. I pray that you would be completely free from asthma.

I am happy to inform Thee that two more have taken up the abhyas. They are

1. T.V. Gopalachari, Assistant Librarian, Dept of Archaeology, Fort St George, Madras - 9.

2. M.P. Moothadath, Railway Contractor, Shoranur, Kerala State.

The work is going on. By Thy Grace I believe that the abhyasis are improving. I am indeed deeply happy to learn that the very feeling of absence of transmission is a very good sign of naturalness and that the power of the Master flows unobstructed by my awareness, which is perhaps itself a heaviness. I shall try to observe more closely. I intend to keep a separate diary of what I observe for each abhyasi who chooses to come for special or individual sitting. I am of late encouraging the abhyasis to come for individual sitting. I gave today a sitting to Bro.

Annayya Naidu and he felt exactly as he said he felt when the Master was here and gave him a sitting. That really helped much and I have asked him to come every Saturday fortnight or weekly so that he may grow in the anubhava.

I am in my own condition as I wrote last week. But Thy letter has somehow produced in me a very good effect. I have dedicated myself to Thee and may yet grow to love thee as my very Self and all and give up myself to Thee to do as Thou willest. Only I pray that it may be soon.

Chi. Narayan has been down with fever with 105 and now it has come down to 99.6 thanks to the Master's grace. I believe he will be well in a couple of days.

I have noted down the names of our satsanghis at Calcutta and shall endeavour to meet them during my stay there on the 22nd.

Thy meeting with Shri Radhakrishnan is very interesting. Thou art unfathomable and Thy power is omniscient and omnipotent.

Bro. Balasubramaniam has been moving forward towards drawing a plan for building on the site. There seems to be some promise of material assistance and in the meanwhile I am writing to request the Master's guidance and blessings and consent regarding the manner of erecting a structure. The need for a pucca building of the dimensions noted and the need for having a bore well or another water source seems to be urgent. With the blessings of the Master and without any monetary assistance from the Mission, we hope to be able to erect the structures.

I hope to be back at Tirupati on the 26th morning as I have now a meeting at Madras on the 25th.

All children are keeping fit. My wife is also feeling better. My father is also keeping better health.

I trust all there are well and Mataji's health is good.

My humble pranams and love to Thee.

Yours ever,
KCV

No. C 107/SRCM **Shahjahanpur, U.P.**
Dated 25th February, 1958

My dear Varadachari,

Received your affectionate letters dt. 9th February, 1958, 11th February, 1958, 15th February, 1958. I sincerely apologise for the delay in keeping the letters unanswered. The reason of the silence is, that I had to go to Etah and Delhi, for some good reason. I am now again going to Lakhimpur-Kheri, along with Dr. P. Sen, probably on 28th February, 1958, and may stay there for about a week or so.

You are doing good to the Mission, and the associates are helping you also. I am very grateful to them. The plan of the plot at Tirupati is a very nice one. I and Dr. Sen also, approve the plan.

You have written in your letter dt. 9th February, 1958, (I have felt myself entirely as possessed by thee, and felt, thou art all for me). How happy I am to write the reply of the sentences of yours. The *laya avastha* (absorbancy state), has now commenced in you; which is of course, a very difficult thing to attain for those who do not adopt the real method you have adopted. I do not want to say to other abhyasis openly these things. I have written the same thing in the *Efficacy of Raja Yoga* but in a different way, so that the people may not hold opinion that I want to be worshipped by them.

My Master once told me in private that he had got so many disciples, but hardly any one of them had attained the *laya avastha*. Spiritually, they are quite good, but this is a very special thing, in the spiritual life, which when it shines out brings up a man to a very high state soon. But Dr. you are being absorbed in me. I do not know whether I am a fit man for it. But I tell you that Shri Ishwar Sahai, when attaining high elevation, came to know of this method, he began to say it to the Lovers of the Mission. The result is that those who are following it are directed towards the object.

I tell you my Varadachari, to be specially guarded with yourself with the thoughts mentioned in your letter dt. 11.2.58. You must not think yourself weak or the grossed one, because in that case your own will-power, will bring up all your thoughts to be real-one sometime. What you feel you can write out whether it may be grossness or opacity, but please do not go into it deeply. Please remove the idea of depression, because in that case, since you have started the *laya avastha*, it will have its effect in maturing your grossness. I remain open hearted with you so I want to write something about myself in this connection. During the period of my *abhyas* I devoted myself wholly to consume myself with my Master. How far I have succeeded, that only is known to my Master. But I can boldly say, that I am perfectly confident in myself to bring about the desired result in the spirituality within no time.

So, my dear Dr. Varadachari, you will excuse me, if I go beyond the human limitations to say, that I now feel the Realisation as child's play, because it is the easiest and no time is required for it. I am also writing these things for your encouragement, that you are attempting a very simple thing and is growing simpler day by day for its achievement. Truly speaking the real faith comes only when you absorb yourself only to the Real Being. There the will works as the command in the spiritual matter.

I have not told you the method of transmission, because in any way what you do now is all correct, as your force will be working for the spiritual uplift of others. During my next visit, I shall tell you a few masterly things, which you can do perfectly well. Meanwhile you please gain some experience yourself. I keep watch over your works also and help is bestowed upon you always and all of them are proving and the system is clarified thereby.

It is better, if you keep a separate diary of what you observe in each abhyasi, and if you doubt on any point you can seek my advice.

As I approved the suggestion about the get-up of the book with paper wrapped up in yellow colour, without any impression on the wrapper block, I did not write anything about it to Mr. Rajan.

I shall write about the diaries sent by you, in my next letter. I trust Chi. Narayan must have recovered from his illness.

With best wishes to you and love to children. Pay my respects to Appaji.

Yours,
Ram Chandra

P.S. I have noted down the names of the *satsanghis* who have newly joined the Mission. Shri T.V. Gopalachari be directed to have sittings with Shri N. Kumaraswamy when he goes to Madras. Mr. M.P. Moothadath had asked me to send the English books which I did. He had also sent me a letter along with the order which I also replied.

No. C 112/SRCM **Shahjahanpur**
Dated 28th February, 1958

My dear Varadachari,

Received your affectionate letter dated 25th February, 1958, sent by you from Madras. I am sending a copy of the photograph of my Master for block today. I do not want the block of my photo taken at Tirupati because I have been shown there in garlanded. Since the book is written by me, it will not be proper for me to be depicted in the book, in a decorated form. I, therefore, have requested him to get a block prepared out of the impression of the photoblock used in the book *Reality at Dawn*, if the block which is already there, is not at all serviceable. As I have no copy of my photo here, nor any of my associates here have it, I am writing to Shri I. Sahai at Lakhimpur Kheri to supply him with a copy of photo which was taken two years hence and sent to Japan, in the world religious conference, on demand.

As soon as the cost of printing etc. of the book is settled, please inform me to enable me to send the balance of the same. I would like to send it, for the sake of economy, by Bank Draft of the State Bank of India, but I find that the branch of the State Bank is in Chittur district and not at Tirupati; so, if you like, I may send the balance, in the name of Shri S. Rajan, as State Bank is there at Madras and it will be convenient for him to draw the amount. Please inform Mr. S. Rajan to obtain a bill for the whole cost of printing etc. of the book and send it to me for audit purpose.

I wanted to start for Lakhimpur Kheri on the 28th February but I postponed it because my mother did not like the idea of my going to Lakhimpur during the Holi festival. So, most probably, I will now be able to go there, a day or two after the festival.

I hope you must have received a letter from Mr. P.N. Midayal from Calcutta informing me that he felt much elevated in the sitting given by you. When a man is charged with the spiritual force, then follows the automatic run of its display. Moreover, you will find this effect developing day by day. There may come a time when the audience may go into a state of trance, while hearing you. I found in my Master that whenever he spoke or read anything, all of us felt suspended. The transmission by voice is very strong. When you ever speak on our system of Sahaj Marg, then observe how much power is gushing out from you towards the audience. I have yet to give power to speech when you really require it. My experience tells me one thing more — that there are certain limitations in one's system which prevent a man in coming up to the Nature's harmony. Our voice should be in conformity with the silent voice of Nature and this condition begins from the very first stage and ends in the last one. That is why I often say that nobody can go out of the platform of the Mission, without having some spiritual food dissolved in him, if one gets the chance of hearing the preceptors of the Mission.

Mr. Vedantam seems to me a man of the type who is naturally in-drawn devotionally and if the heaviness of his system is cleaned, which you and I will do, he will shine out. I am waiting for your 'amazing experiences' you felt at Calcutta, as written in your letter to which this is a reply.

With best wishes to you and love to children. My respects to Appaji.

Yours,
Ram Chandra

No. C 123/SRCM   **Shahjahanpur, U.P.**
Dated 6th March, 1958

My dear Varadachari,

Received your letter dated Tirupati 26th February, 1958 by Lakhimpur address. I have replied almost all points previously in my last letter, which might have been received by you. Both the photographs have been sent as required.

I was happy to know of the vision you felt at Calcutta. This is due to your state of progress. I have already written about this in my previous letter and there is nothing to add now.

The audience at Calcutta, according to the tendencies of their fashioned minds, felt the presence of

'Mother' and who knows it might be so, but that, at the root, must I think, be a tongueless power working through the agency. You have prepared field for it, though mostly by self-effort, which goes to your own credit. This is why Nature works its own way through you as in the case of atom, ions and electrons. There is but one energy working through all the universe. What we are therefore to do is to become the medium for the utilisation of its power for proper use. There is the example of the rishis of the Vedic time who were in conformity with Nature. The result of it was *sruti*. This can happen even now but only if we become blind and deaf. Realisation comes only when we become blind and *sruti* follows only when we turn deaf, the words 'deaf' and 'blind' not being used in physical sense. So these things are neither difficult nor impossible at any time. Nature which once set into action through human medium, can do so again through similar medium, and this may be the time as Nature is evidently attracting humanity towards itself. That is why religious awakening, crude or subtle as it may be, is found everywhere in one or the other form.

I tell you, Doctor, that the long forgotten Transmission will be the subject of attention for all human beings in existence. We have got that which seemed to have been lost, and now we have it and work with it, thanks to my Great Master. My dear Varadachari, I am sure you will be sorry to hear our tale of woe. Since U.P. has long been under Mohammedan influence, Hinduism here underwent changes, creating knots to separate each other. It may be surprising to note that Mohammedans here claim it as their own originality, which though far from being a fact, I do not dispute, with a view that it may work for the betterment of humanity at large, not minding whoever may be its originator. All the different sects of Mohammedanism (72 in all) have Transmission as their base, directly or indirectly, and every one of them is acquainted with it and acknowledges it. But among Hindus a few perhaps might even believe its genuineness. They are mostly incredulous about it and prefer to interpret it as hypnotism or similar baser science. We must pray to God that His will be done and the down-trodden masses may wake up to the Real Life. Now it is our lookout to improve it as best as possible for the benefit of humanity irrespective of caste or creed.

I am over-joyed to inform you that you have crossed the region and have come to the Point A (as I call it) on 1st March, 1958 at 9:42 A.M. I do not find names for these regions so I take them by numbers.

You write that disturbance often occurs in meditation, sleep and dream, but when you seek refuge in me they disappear. I tell you a prescription for it and it is perhaps the best. It is this, 'Make room for me to take refuge in you permanently.' In that case all things will settle down in a permanent way. I think, Doctor, you will like this prescription very much because it can very easily be taken.

The reading of other's condition depends upon practice also. For example I give you my experience. Once when I gave a sitting to a gentleman I found in his heart huge piles of bricks. I cleaned it off. Then I saw heaps of coal in its place. I asked him whether he ever had a business of bricks and coal to which he replied in the affirmative. Now look here Doctor, intuition brought all these things to my knowledge, but it was experience and intelligence that helped me to come to the right conclusion.

It is the Holi today. Let us all of us colour ourselves with colourless-ness.

My mother has been suffering from fever for the last five days besides her asthma troubles. She is completely confined to bed and has grown so weak that she cannot even get up without help. She is however showing signs of some improvement.

Appaji must have by now recovered by the Master's grace. My best respects to him.

With best wishes and love to children,

Yours,

Ram Chandra

Comments on diaries enclosed.

After closing the letter I received Mr. Thyagarajan's letter. He had met you at Tirupati some time back. I am sending you a copy of it for perusal for your experience. Please try to study his system and write to me your findings. I do not like to give any hint at present.

Ram Chandra

Trichinopoly-8
2nd/4th March, 1958

(Copy of letter)

Beloved Babuji,

My hearty namaskarams to you--- In enclosing herewith the diary from 6th January. I like to express the latest experience on 23rd February which was a peculiar one. In the beginning started the abhyas as usual, but finding no power or no mood to meditate on the heart, I had to divert my thought otherwise to meditate; I thought you are in my place and practice on your heart. Immediately felt that heart was spreading to an endless atmosphere like a shoreless ocean. I like a flame of a candle was swimming deep in the ocean. Swimming, swimming in that endless ocean came to a spot where it was more brighter (no darkness anywhere, only light was found) a huger fire was burning. The candle-like flame seeing the huge fire wanted to join that huge fire, slowly moved towards that. Coming to a distance the candle-like flame was attracted by the huge fire as if a magnet attracts a piece of iron. The small flame entered the huge fire. At the time of entering it was felt that it was only CHILL instead of extreme heat (to my wonder). The whole body was felt as if in the air-conditioned room. The whole body was in a kind of BLISS, which continued for ten minutes. All the nerves were in extreme pleasure not felt so far. All the hair holes were feeling that condition, a condition which I could not express. It is all yours. You have given all these which I can't get from others. I am at your feet always.

Poor being,
N. Thyagarajan

No. C 141/SRCM **Shahjahanpur, U.P.**
Dated 21st March, 1958

My dear Varadachari,

Received your loving letters dated 3rd March, 1958 and 14th March, 1958. Thanks to God that my mother is out of danger and is slowly recovering.

She has grown so weak that she cannot even sit without help. Mind does not work properly on account of extreme weakness and old age. It so happens sometimes that she will call any one of us for hours with no work of her own. In that case, specially during the night, I have to make her mind calm by transmission. Then she gets sleep. My presence on this account has become completely necessary for her attendance.

I am happy to note that your experiences are genuine and not the concocted ones. Due to the efficacious teachings of my Master, very high conditions begin to reign sometimes, though momentary, so that the abhyasi may get the real substance for his approach to the Ultimate. Now I come to the question of Realisation. I can safely say that you have realised to the extent of your approach. But my conception, as I have expressed in some of my letters, is the simplest and the nearest. When you begin to live in Brahma permanently with changeless condition as its characteristics then it is the complete Realisation, as much as reserved for the human beings. I am taking you to that stage of the real life and I hope I will succeed by God's grace. The thing is not at all difficult but it looks like that because there is still field to cross over. I give you my idea because you are mine and you will ever remain mine. I do not generally hanker that my associates may get liberation because it is the cheapest thing to acquire and no time is needed for it. What I want is that you may have your share of work in the Nature and the mystery be revealed to you like an open book. If I could create one such man even, my Mission is over but I will not rest a while unless such many personalities may come in existence. But that is my desire only and its fulfillment depends solely upon God.

Now comes your another question regarding your being in harmony with nature. I think I have sufficiently expressed in the above lines, but to make it more clear on this point concerning you, I would add as I said in one of my letters that I have dissolved the creases or the dots which find place when the river shifts its bed from one place to another. This is an example only. My vision has been degenerated so much that I always see the defects to be removed and the minutest things are coming to my view. I assure you one thing more, which you have said in one of your previous letters that you are not at all gross. But subtle and gross are two different things. Where exists subtleness, the idea of grossness is there. Now it becomes my duty that I may keep you off with both of these things so that you may become beyond the relative terms. Then will come the Nature's harmony. You have entered the sandy desert but you are still affected by the *simooms* coming from the other side. Proceed on and on which you are doing. Then you will be free from the effects of these winds. I have every hope from you.

I am very thankful to you that you are doing the work of satsangh effectively. The strength is there in you and it works. I prefer individual sittings besides congregational satsangh because in that case you get time to give him satsangh according to his needs. I have noted down the names of new satsanghis with great delight. Regarding Shri A. Balasubramaniam he is to be attended to.

Your reading about Shri Thyagarajan is correct. I have every hope from him to reach the state of self-surrender. Now I tell you all about him which you will also try to see by yourself. When I went to Trichy and saw him for the first time I remarked that in spite of the fact that he loves me, he had darkness in all his system and stiffness in the heart. As long as I was there, I tried to disperse the darkness and remove the grossness of the heart. Since Shri Raghavendra Rao was with me, I handed over his charge along with others with certain hints to him. I find that he is successful and his present inner condition is that there is a very little stiffness in his heart and the stray light is there in the major part of the chest. If you study deep you will find a few arcs of darkness in which the light is hemmed in. Now I shall pray and will write to Shri Raghavendra Rao also to remove this thing. You may also do it because it is common concern for us all. He has not yet gone beyond the heart region, to the extent of *pind pradesh*. There is a good deal of work still left regarding his heart, for us to do. Regarding the work of publication and photos, blocks and so on, I agree with you on all points. I am happy to note that our Appaji's health has much improved. I pray that all my children be successful in the examination.

With best wishes to you, love to children and respects to Appaji.

Yours,
Ram Chandra

P.S.- Comments on diaries are enclosed. A letter for Shri A. Balasubramaniam is also kept herewith.

It may please be handed over to him. This is done for the sake of economy in postage.

Ram Chandra

No. C 145/SRCM   **Shahjahanpur, U.P.**
Dated 22nd March, 1958

My dear Varadachari,

Received your affectionate letter dt. 17th March, 1958. My mother is slowly recovering and she is nursed like an infant. I am anxious since I have heard that my boy Narayana is down with high fever. We must pray for his speedy recovery, because his examination must be near.

I am happy to note that Shri V.K. Narasimhan has joined you and has started the meditation. I remember him fully and I pray that he may advance in spirituality. I also pray that he may successfully complete his American tour and return safely, but let us wait for the time when one prepares himself to go to America and elsewhere to preach the ideology of the Mission for the good of the mankind. If Shri Narasimhan so prefers, he can take along with him as many books (*Reality at Dawn*) he likes, for distribution to interested Americans and others. If you like the idea and he agrees to the proposal, please write to me the number of copies required, along with his address, so that I may send these to him.

Regarding Tamil publication, Shri Kumaraswamy will require some books and he will take them from Shri S. Rajan direct and I am writing to him as well for it. The emblem which is in the press, should also be given to Shri N. Kumaraswamy, when done with. Shri S.K. Rajagopalan of Delhi will require ten copies of the book, which may kindly be dispatched to the address given below. I will require ten copies for the present. I am also writing to Trichy if they require some books.

You are writing in your letter that you are unable to say anything about your present condition adding that whoever sits in your satsangh, feels *anand*. This in itself is depictive of your own condition. I have now taken your case again which I had left, as I had told you in one of my letters, for some time so that the power imparted by the Master at Tirupati, may be digested. Now you have come to the standard that my task is growing easier. Though I do not know the reason but I find it very easy to work when a man comes to the higher regions. But I again say to the contrary to what I have said that my work remains as it is, to bring the abhyasi into harmony with Nature. The higher region works very much in this cause but there is still a place left for me to work into. Please study your condition minutely and you will find decidedly a change.

I have dispatched a letter with comments and diaries under this office No. C 141/SRCM dated 21st March, 1958 which I believe, must reach you.

The address of Shri Rajagopalan is:

Shri S.K. Rajagopalan, Divisional Engineer (Ministry of Home Department), A.20/25, Lodhi Colony, New Delhi.

With best wishes to you, love to children and respects to Appaji.

Yours,
Ram Chandra

No. C 176/SRCM   **Shahjahanpur, U.P.**
                       Dated 5th April, 1958

My dear Varadachari,

Received your affectionate letter dated 25th and 29th March, 1958. Mother though free from ailment is bed-ridden. She cannot get up without other's help and one of her legs seems to be paralysed. Smallpox broke out here as well in epidemic form. I am sending you tinned pineapple which I received from Assam for Chiranjeev Narayan. It is the product of Terai area and is best produced in Assam. It is very useful for heart and brain and will remove the heat caused by pox. I also enclose therein the receipts to be issued for the subscribers, as I came to know through Shri A. Balasubramaniam that you have to issue receipts for payments. As a preceptor of the branch you are fully authorized to deposit money in the Bank and Post Offices and to draw the amount whenever needed. I am writing to you a separate authority slip to show in the Bank if needed. Mr. A. Balasubramaniam should be given the required copies of the book. I am grateful to Shri S. Rajan for the pains he has taken in the publication. The get up and finish of the book is very fine and I liked it. The printing also is very good. I am fully satisfied with the work and congratulate you and Shri S. Rajan for the interest he took in getting the work done in such a manner. Of course Shri Balasubramaniam who took great pains in translating the book on your suggestion deserves no lesser thanks. I am also sending the form signed by me. Three copies of the constitution and the bye-laws of the Mission have already been sent by post, which I trust you must have received them. You can utilize the books in any way you like. I am thankful to the brothers of Mission of Tirupati that they are keen to build ashram.

Your dream has no spiritual significance. It is neither for nor against it. Such dreams come due to dietic error and physiological disturbances.

I do not know whether I should express in the book written by Shri Ishwar Sahai about my conception of Kundalini when it does not tally with the scriptures. But I do not know my dear Varadachari, why I am always sure of my revelation. I also tally my own readings sometimes from my Master then only I pen it down. When I concentrate a little on any point its character begins to reveal and the heart becomes contented.

I am writing to you the circumstances which led me to believe about my right conception. When Shri Raghavendra Rao met me for the first time, about three years ago, he being a science student put me some questions about electrons and ions. I gave him my own research in the matter but not in scientific terms. When I met him at Gulbarga this time, he told me that a Chinese philosopher, six months ago, gave out the same research as you did, about three years before. Divisional Forest Officer is my friend and he put me to trial by questioning me about some botanical matters. I gave him my own findings which were not so far known. He was already researching something about it and wrote down the points and later the research was found correct. There are so many other things. Now I again come to Shri Raghavendra Rao, who said this time in

Gulbarga that there is a theory in science of 'indiscrimination' which hampers the further research regarding electrons and ions. I told him the way if research be made by this method then the theory of indiscrimination will not work. Having regard to this matter, I gave him the further research and also told him that there is one atom near about. If you concentrate on it to reveal the character of the electrons and ions, then you will be saved from the theory of indiscrimination. We were walking on the street of Gulbarga, when he told me such a thing. Dr. I always praise you and myself.

I find in Shri Thyagarajan the signs of higher improvements. I am sending to you his latest diary for your perusal and you need not send it back to me. The stage you are enjoying at present is the pretty realisation for others. But to me it is only a glimpse. Having this idea I have written to you that you have realised to the extent of your approach.

I received a letter direct from Shri Y.K. Narasimhan on 31st to send him the six copies of *Reality at Dawn*. I have dispatched the required copies the same day.

You are perfectly right that you have no separate existence but let it flourish to its full length. I hope there will come a time when neither you will be there nor God Himself. That is the merging point. I don't think I am using the heathen language in the expression of the condition. You have written something about Kam etc. They will all come to moderation.

How happy am I to inform you that you are coming to the state of *turiya*.

The time was about 11 P.M. but I hesitate to give date that it was the 1st April, 1958. Let us see how much time you take in coming to its full fledged state.

Appaji should be given some tonic to regain his health if doctor prescribes. My sincere *pranam* to him. Love to children. With best wishes.

Yours,
Ram Chandra

No. C 207/SRCM **Shahjahanpur, U.P.**
Dated 21st April, 1958

My dear Varadachari,

Received your affectionate letter dated 11th April, 1958. I am praying already for the continuance of your service and am also very anxious about it. Let us see what the Divinity holds in store for us. We must pray, abiding by His will.

As you have got the printed receipts with you already, you may use them. The receipt books sent by me will remain with you till I come next time. You need not send them back to avoid unnecessary postal charges.

Shri Raghavendra Rao had written to me that he read Brahma Sutra translated in Hindi by the editor of *Kalyan*, but he couldn't follow much. I replied that I do not like the translation made by the Gita Press. So I will like that he may read the Bhashya of Shri Ramanuja or Shri Shankaracharya and for this I asked him to consult you whichever commentary you suggest. I will order that for him. What do you think about the English translation of the commentary of Brahm Sutra by Thibqut. It has become Shri Rao's habit to read the books. I also allowed him to see the books on religious literature so that they may help him in writing and understanding the things as they are.

Your work as a preceptor is excellent. I find that all the abhyasis are improving in the very depth of being and its effect is coming from the depth to the surface. I have to learn this method. You have written that you are unable to read fully the mental and the physical condition of the abhyasi which is a very easy thing in comparison to your great work. Please read the abhyasi with confidence in yourself and you will see that it will be correct. You have got the capacity of reading. I assure you, but you are not sure that you can read it. That is the only difficulty in the way. Please take two or three cases of your satsanghis, read them internally whether they have darkness, grossness and so on and write me for the sake of verification. I shall devote some time so that you may develop this character also, although you are not wanting in it. This is a very easy thing.

My affection towards Shri Vedantam is growing day by day and I find that he is being purged of heaviness. The effect of your transmission is proceeding firmly and happily from the root to the surface.

I was elated to see the words of your sentence that you will not rest till the Ultimate condition is arrived at. It is for you and you will decidedly realise it. I do not remember what I have written in the book regarding the state given under each *granthis* and the book is at Lakhimpur, but I remember that on your question in one of your letters I had written to you that your approach is on the ninth knot. After the ninth or tenth *granthi* I took the major ones because the difference between the minor knots was inexpressible. So I took the broader steps regarding these *granthis* and I finished the run of spiritual life on thirteen *granthis*. I conclude from these things that you are on the tenth knot.

I think I have given you my conception of realisation. When saint Kasturi reached the point of X Y she was in the state of *jivan moksha*. Now she has to cross sixteen points more. She is now on the point P-1 where the circumstances are being created for forgetting the soul consciousness. But I cannot call her the full realised soul, but to others she is a perfectly realised one. My Dr. if I think of any point or approach as ultimate, my thought will not travel further. Of course when an abhyasi creates *laya avastha* in Brahma my thought will automatically cease, because there is no programme of work for further approach.

You have crossed the richer regions and now you have entered the dry ones. The conditions of these spheres are mostly inexpressible, but you can relish the state and see its effects in yourself. I used to write to my Master my condition by way of diary, but the time came when even metaphorical language failed to express that. I hope your body idea will soon depart and please write to me to what extent it has faded out. I have touched upon this thing in *Efficacy of Raja Yoga*.

When Master's blessings are pouring in you what not you will have.

Shri Raghavendra Rao is reaching here on 13th May or near about it along with a few of his associates. He is not sure of the date and time which he will intimate to me later on. As the examination has begun and you are busy with it, you can have your own time in replying the letter. There is no hurry about it. You have done well to send the book for review in different Tamil papers.

I hope Ch. Narayan must be feeling better. If you find any after-effects of the illness, please write to me. I trust that Appaji must have regained his health by now.

I have posted the names of new satsanghis in the register.

With best wishes to you. Love to children and my profound respect to Appaji.

Yours,
Ram Chandra

April 28th 1958

My dear Revered and beloved Gurudev,

Please accept my sincere and loving pranams. I am in receipt of your kind letter dated 21 inst. It is all due to thy grace that I am able to do the preceptorial work efficiently. If the work is of the kind you have described the method also is due to thee. I do not know whether I know the roots from the stem or branches.

Since thy wish is that I should not say that I am gross or ignorant, subtle or intelligent, I shall stop thinking about my condition, and let it go on.

The whole system has been in a state of peculiar excitement, which I am unable to describe. I had prayed for the fullness of this humble being by the Master so that I could experience the supersensuous states of sabda, sparsa, tejas, rasa and gandha. My internal condition then is one of excitement over the next step. Sometimes I feel almost that I should cease to be — so trying are the outer conditions — but I am looking out for the signs of Thee in me — of the merging of the Isvara in me and me in the Isvara. Even consciousness seems to be a burden. How I wish I could dive into the Ocean of Bliss.

Nothing is known about my service here. Hope there is of continuation. Only I do not know how the forces will work. Should one be precarious in spirituality.

Master so far as I know I tried to read the internal conditions. Sometimes I am successful after five or ten minutes. In the meanwhile my absorption in myself comes up and then again I revert to my work of cleaning the abhyasi. They do not feel anything except improvement and calm, and in some cases I find that the abhyasis are getting into a state of absorption, unable to get up — it happened in the case of Somesvara Sarma who told me that he felt a great flare up of energy within him when I called a halt to the meditation. In another case, of V. Seetaramayya there was the descending flood of light removing all dirt. In the case of Dhond Rao, there was a sense of being absorbed. He seems to be developing extreme love.

I tried to read the condition of Shri Mother of the Shri Aurobindo Ashram, a few days ago. I found her condition to be 'Azure Blue'. So too I have been attempting to read some others, including idols (*archavataras*). Should I do it? or not?

The work of digging the well is progressing satisfactorily. Shri Balasubramaniam would have written to Thee about it. By Thy grace alone can the work come to any conclusion.

I am enclosing the final receipt (stamped) from Sadhu Press.

A new abhyasi came. His name is P.S. Sundaram Ayyar, Pensioner, 118 Theertha Katta Street, Tirupati.

He has already taken two sittings and attended the satsangh yesterday.

I agree with Thy suggestion to Bro. Raghavendra Rao. I have also written the same. Thibaut's is the best. I shall try to help him if he wants my clarification of the points.

Master, this is my prayer: Let me experience the Ultimate permanently in me. Be thou with me permanently.

I cannot express my feelings regarding the body idea. I shall write to you about it as soon as I see that fading out.

I had Thy article in the latest issue of Sahajmarg translated and read at the satsangh yesterday. Thy last words that Nature has taken up the work of purging the world of 'bhaktas' has been most encouraging news.

I am sometimes thinking whether Master the *avyakta* state of *prakrti* of Nature is working in the abhyasis when I transmit Thy Power and Light as it is suggested that it is *samatva* by the Samartha

Guru in his latest publication in the *Sahaj Marg*. Perhaps that might be the reason why Thou suggestest that I work from the roots to the surface.

Whatever is happening and will happen are in Thy hands. I can only surrender and abide by Thy will.

Chi. Narayana is all right. All other children are keeping fit. My father has completely recovered. I am giving hoemeo tonic pills. He is finding improvement.

I am happy that you find Shri Vedantam's condition is getting better.

With loving pranams, I am yours,

KCV

Please convey my respects to Saint Kasturi. I have asked the next article to be read at the next meeting of the satsangh to be hers.

No. C 246/SRCM **Shahjahanpur, U.P.**
Dated 5th May, 1958

My dear Varadachari,

Received your loving letter dt. 16th April, 1958 together with the diary and the bill for publication charges. I am really very thankful to Mr. S. Rajan who succeeded in reducing the publication charges considerably. Dr. Kuppuswami is really improving and I have written a letter to him in reply to his own which you will please read it and give it to him. Mr. Thyagarajan is almost free from heaviness and darkness too and Appaji too. Dr. I tell you my experience of satsangh that those who are intellectual, having full faith on our cult and God advance soon. Devotion of course counts much in the field.

I always desire that you remain happy in every way — worldly and spiritually and I am glad to hear from you that the difficulties of life do not touch you so painfully. Your experience on Sunday the 13th April was correct and you have done well in removing the darkness. If it remains anything of the sort, I will play my own part.

I am glad that you have sent Chi. Srivatsa to Madras to join the firm and carry along with it his studies too. May he prosper. My mother's condition is almost the same.

I have also informed Shri Ishwar Sahai for the shortage of money in sinking the well.

With best wishes to you and love to children. Respect to Appaji.

Yours,
Ram Chandra

No. C 247/SRCM   **Shahjahanpur, U.P.**
Dated 5th May, 1958

My dear Varadachari,

After closing the above letter I received your affectionate letter dt. 28th April, 1958. I have written to you previously that you should not think or consider yourself as gross. I think there is a difference, between thinking and feeling. If you feel a thing, that means that there is the revelation of a certain thing. Thinking also has the idea of the thing which may be not there. There are two such powers which are awakened automatically in a yogi. One of them is that he can bring about the desired results by mere imagination. The other thing that comes in a yogi is attraction. This is all due to the fact that you practise like that. You meditate on the heart waiting for His grace, that means you get into practice in inviting His grace. When this power develops to the highest degree of eminence, the greatest souls can appear before him at his bid. The next thing is when you meditate on light, for reality, the very attribute of God which you have made the point of meditation, brings the real thing at the bottom. So, please, if you feel anything, it must be written to me because feeling will continue. Feeling cannot deceive you. On the contrary, thinking if unwisely directed may bring the bad results.

You have depicted very good condition in your letter regarding your excitement. Really we should be devoted to the Divine Master and this thing will help you in merging. Kabir has written very beautifully that, "The drop enters the ocean, is known to all and the ocean enters the drop is known to a few only." Now, I refer to your condition. I would like just to give you a hint. You have proceeded with the thought of Divine Master. Now the condition changes. The Divine Master is Himself in your own thought. The same condition is surely there in you, but let us see whether you feel like that or not. Kabir says, "I can only get rest, if Ram thinks of me." I remember that I have read in some of the Sufi literature, saying so, but the author has given only one word, "Mahboobiat" — "Object of love". How I wish, that all our associates may get into this condition. Those who are marching with faith and devotion, they come across all such conditions, a few feel and the other do not, but they all pass through these conditions.

How beautifully you have put in, that consciousness has become the burden to you. Dr., I think I am very fortunate to find such conditions among my associates. If you observe anything there in your system as consciousness, think that you have to go further off. I shall be elated if I see your approach above the consciousness which is the basis of the existence. All our inner activities should be faded out to observe super-sensuous states. The occidental philosophers may not believe it, because they have probably no such word as super-consciousness in their dictionary. Am I right doctor? We add the word state after the conscious or super-conscious, which is itself a proof that these are mere conditions and we have to go far above them. It may be the essence of all these consciousnesses. If we reach that stage, that means we are abiding in Ishwar, but the journey or *yatra* is not finished as yet. I would stop here.

You have asked me, "If one should be precarious in spirituality." I think this is the question to be solved by men of your calibre. I can, however, give my own view. As long as we have the idea of our own existence, the Master is there and service becomes obligatory to us. We abide by His Will praying at the same time for our good, because it becomes our duty as a devotee to lay before our Master the shortcomings and difficulties. When anyhow, we are aware of the idea of our existence and also of God then the Master and the servant both almost converge themselves into one unity that is 'Real'. I tell you Doctor, my idea that there always remains a bondage as long as we exist in physical form. There are of course, the stages, which one shall have to cross i.e., all the circles mentioned in *Reality at Dawn*. But if the bondage is not kept on the last circle, the soul will leave the body to its original Existence.

When the bondage is there, the idea of our existence is also there. The idea of course remains in a sleeping condition i.e., in a 'nascent state'. Our duty too comes in consonance with it.

You are successful in reading the internal condition of abhyasi but your absorption puts a check to it. This will occur with every reader, if he proceeds in your way. When you want to know a thing, concentrate on the abhyasi, but do not increase the depth of concentration. If there is the depth, the God will begin to charge you with His grace, and absorption will be the result. The effect of your transmission is so powerful that the abhyasi becomes absorbed in the inner power and the different senses do not work in that case. So they do not get up. I tell you one more thing, the abhyasis who easily go into that condition are good media. When the sun shines, the darkness dispels and when you shine in the heart of abhyasi the dirt finds its exit.

I always remained silent whenever the question of the approach of Shri Aurobindoji came in. But, now, this is the question about mother only. I tell you that your reading is correct. Shri Aurobindoji has pulled the mother to his own standard of spirituality. If you go deeply comparing the pious personalities, you will find that Shri Aurobindoji had immense power in comparison to the mother. In other words mother is not so powerful in her sphere, as Shri Aurobindoji was. You should not give up this practice, as that will be helpful in knowing others. If you doubt on any point you may consult me. Regarding the mother's condition as "azure blue" I would like to say that you try to find out the cause of it, yourself, then I will write to you.

What I have written in my previous letter means that (your power acts at the very root from which we grow), that it influences the outer coverings to be torn off. It is really *samatva* by the Samartha Guru of Fatehgarh, which works through us. When we did not come in contact with the Master, we could do nothing. If you want to ask anything further in this connection, please write to me. It is very pleasing to me that you are taking a great pain in serving the associates spiritually for which, I can only pray, that your services may be counted. I am glad to hear from you that Chi. Narayan is all right and Appaji is now completely recovered.

Shall I give the homeo-tonic pills (alfalfa) to my ailing mother, because she is bed-ridden, on account of extreme weakness? Although she is mostly free from the disease, she had got also bed sores which are now healing up and Dr. P. Sen has taken the pains to treat her, so that they may not develop further. He has given back-rest to support her. Her condition is so low that Dr. P. Sen does not advise us to give any allopathic medicine. Herbo-mineral and homeopathic medicines are being given to her.

With best wishes to you and love to children. My respect to Appaji.

Yours,
Ram Chandra

5th May 1958

My dear Gurudev,

Please accept my loving pranams. All of us are keeping fit. I have not yet heard from the University about myself. I have placed myself at the hands of the Master and am having a quiet resignation.

The work of the digging of the well is proceeding. Of course we are not having as speedy a help from those who promised as desired. Master alone can help us to complete it without interruption.

Shri Balasubramaniam has his way of doing things with an eye to future. So he got the local photographer to enlarge a picture of the Samarth Guru. I saw it only last Thursday. He had painted the chaddar red and the white band as yellow. I have asked him to restore the white for the shirt to which he agreed, but it will be difficult to change the red colour. How do you suggest? Please let me have a line as soon as possible.

I have an old request about the date of birth and so on of your eldest born — my astrologer friend who had written about that Sitadevi who remembered her previous life is anxious to carry on his researches on that point. I shall be glad if you could ransack your old papers and let me have the details at an early date.

I have been full of Thy energy these days. Indeed I have been trying to bring down the spiritual energy from the Central Region to play more and more on the *adhars* of the abhyasis. I believe that is thy will. I found that Shri C.R. Krishnamurti telling me that he had begun to experience the *ajap* for a couple of minutes last week. I indeed did that transmission last week. I am almost all the time anxious to merge myself, to dive into the depths of the Infinite Bhuma.

I believe that by the grace of the Master, Mataji is getting better and her paralytic condition is being relieved.

All children are keeping fit. The heat has become unbearable. But that is but Nature. Regarding the loss of body consciousness, I have to report that the other day when I was meditating, it seems I scratched myself (my wife reported that), but I was utterly unaware of that action. I believe this is mentioned in Thy book in the very manner. I do not know whether that means loss of body consciousness.

I am glad that Shri Raghavendra Rao is going over there.

My best compliments for his speedy attainment.

With love,

Yours,
KCV

No. C 251/SRCM **Shahjahanpur, U.P.**
Dated 8th May, 1958

My dear Varadachari,

Received your loving letter dated 5th May, 1958. How I wish that your service may remain continued and I pray for that. That is the only remedy open to us; the result remains with Him and Him alone. We should adjust ourselves abiding by His will. If He closes one door, He opens some other.

As regards the enlarged photograph of my Master Samarth Guru Shri Ram Chandraji of Fategarh, I agree with your suggestion that the colour of garments should better be the same as in the original photograph. But if the photographer has finished the job, there is no help, and let it rest at that.

With best wishes to you and love to children. Respects to Appaji.

Yours,
Ram Chandra

19th May 1958

My dear Revered and beloved Gurudev,

Please accept my humble pranams. I believe you are in receipt of my previous letter and have administered Alfalfa tonic to Mataji. May I know the results?

I received the affectionate letter addressed by Thee in regard to the enlargement of Samartha Gurudev's picture.

I have been getting along with the work and experienced the dry condition all through. Last night I seriously took up over again the business of looking at the saintly souls today. Confidentially perhaps I can state that I looked at Swami Sivananda (who as thou knowest has been in touch with me for the past four years) and Shri Aurobindo also since thou hast stated that the Mother of the Ashram Pondy was lifted up by him, and since as you know I have been tenderly attached to him for quite a long time. I could not get any results in the first sitting (11-30 P.M. to 12- 30 A.M.); I once again attempted the same at 2 A.M. I found that with Swami Sivananda there was transmission going from Thee (through me) as also with Shri Aurobindo. How far is this correct I am unable to state. But I again tried to see between 4 and 4-50 A.M. with the same result. I am unable to understand this. What is this experience? I found that my whole being is of course filled by Thy force and I am all the time thinking of thee, though the pressure of mundane work is on.

I found that almost a majority of the abhyasis are moving steadily and I must request thee to let me know whether they are ready for the onward journey. Shri A. Balasubramaniam has not been keeping fit and yet he is looking after the digging of the well, which is over, only the upper construction has to be gone through. He is worried about some black-magician poking into his house affairs thanks to his son who has brought him in for consultations. I assured him that the Master's power will remove all apprehensions.

A new abhyasi, a resident of Ambattur near Madras, practising raja yoga under a gentleman came the other day and wanted to be taken in by the Master. He showed earnestness and I gave him two sittings and he felt cleared. He wished to surrender to Thee. He is a teacher in a school at Villivakkam (Madras): A.V. Rangachari, 2/34 Old Post Office Street, Vendatapuram, Ambattur P.O. I have also asked him to contact Sri Kumaraswamy.

I am sending the diaries of the abhyasis.

Please convey my best regards and pranams to all satsanghis there and my love to Shri Raghavendra Rao and Ishwar Sahaiji who would by now have gone over to Thee.

All children are keeping fit as also my father.

With loving pranams,

Yours,
KCV

2nd June 1958

My dear revered and beloved Gurudev,

Please accept my humble pranams. I believe that the ceremonies in connection with Mataji are over and you are having some rest.

I am sending herewith the diaries of the abhyasis here. The well has been almost completed and in a couple of days it may be over.

Here children are all keeping fit and I trust the same of you there.

The fortnight has been mainly uneventful. I cannot clearly describe my condition. It is a kind of quiet, sometimes I am deeply aware of Thy power and grace — one day I felt myself full of fire and energy. I pray that my consciousness of thee may be permanent and Thou reside in me permanently.

My wife's health has been somewhat indifferent and she feels very weak. I believe thou hast received my previous letters and will be writing to me on the points raised. Not that it matters. Anyhow I wanted to know about Shri Aurobindo, though I fully respect Thy reticence in this matter and such others.

Please convey my respects and pranams to Ishwar Sahaiji and others there,

With humble pranams,

Yours,
KCV

I have arranged to take back the books from Sri Kumaraswami at Madras by Murrays.

No. C 273/SRCM   **Shahjahanpur, U.P.**
Dated 5th June, 1958

My dear Varadachari,

Received all your loving letters. I feel it a matter of pride to find that most of the members there improving and a few having begun to experience *ajapa*. I wish that by the time this letter reaches you *ajapa* may have started in every satsanghi there. I appreciate your idea of merging into the depth of the Infinite Bhuma. The very craving for it brings the goal nearer.

I have given in the *Efficacy of Raja Yoga* that a sleeping man being stung by the mosquitoes begins to rub or scratch the spot involuntarily and unconsciously. I thereby mean to say that all our worldly actions also should be done in the same way so that they might produce no impression upon the mind. If the impressions are there you are the doer of all things and the formation of samskaras is there. Forgetting of the body-idea means that your mind does not feel in any way that you are embodied. I think the condition is there. When you forget the body-idea in toto you come to the regime of soul. When you forget the soul-idea then you have entered into

Reality. When that too is gone you are nearest to Bhuma.

You have written that some disembodied souls seem to receive transmission from you. It often happens with other preceptors too. The souls do come to receive benefit from the effect of transmission. I think I had told you about it when I was there with you.

When you feel yourself there you are full of energy and when you are not there the Divine Master shines in you.

If you see the shadow you feel some material thing behind, or the smoke, giving clue of the fire. Similarly vacant-ness (using the word in the unusual sense for vacuity) reflects signs of Divinity. When a man begins to absorb in Brahm, the first symptom of it is that he feels himself vacuumised and at its highest limit *laya avastha* begins. If at times you feel vacant- ness that means Brahm has begun to give Its own clue. Like ultraviolet rays which are used for curing physical diseases, vacant-ness too is a means for removing defilements. Now Nature is helping you and as you proceed on, her work becomes stronger and that is the idea of Dry region. Maya begins to melt away and dryness begins to follow, as you become poorer by losing sight of enrichment. In short you begin to get free from the moisture of the world as you proceed on.

Regarding your latest experience about Swami Sivananda and Shri Aurobindoji I may say that high tide rises only in the deep sea under the direct influence of the moon. It sweeps far on over the shore filling the ditches with the water. If you make a deep study of Swami Sivananda you will find the effect of your transmission there in him. As for the mother of Pondy, the azure blue colour witnessed in her by you, denotes that she has developed some occult powers as the colour referred to above is closely related with *vishudha chakra*, which is also known as *durga chakra* and is the centre of *maya* in *pind desh*. Her thought seems to be more within the state of fluttering than of soaring.

I have written a letter to Shri Balasubramaniam about the black magic. A copy of it is attached herewith along with my observations on the diaries. Shri Raghavendra Rao and his nephew Shri Ramakrishna Rao came here on the 25th May. They shall leave for Haridwar on the 10th instant. I shall also accompany them to Haridwar. They offer you their humble *pranam*.

With best wishes to you and love to children and respects to Appaji.

Yours,
Ram Chandra

CONFIDENTIAL
No. C 285/SRCM   **Shahjahanpur, U.P.**
                           Dated 8th June, 1958

My dear Varadachari,

Received your affectionate letter of 2nd June, 1958. I am sure I replied all your points in my letter No.C.273/SRCM dated 5th June, 1958 which I trust must have reached you by now. I do not want to keep anything secret from one who is so close to my bosom except that which is absolutely essential.

Moreover when you seem to be so earnest about knowing facts it is my duty to express my views frankly.

The greatness of Hindu nation lies in the fact that it entertains feelings of respect towards all religions and every saint, be he of high calibre or low, and it is our pious duty to do so, for charity begins at home. If we neglect them it will then be very difficult to present to the world the picture of highest spiritual culture attained by great saintly souls of India which predominates the world in this respect. Here you will find one greater than the other, so much so that it may almost be impossible to determine who is the greatest. Still every one of whatever calibre he might be has contributed his own share to the development of the Hindu supremacy in the spiritual field. Moreover the true reading of the inner capabilities of a saint can only be made by him who has eyes for it. Common folk will only judge him by his character and the teachings put forth by him. The intelligentsia will judge him by his noble thoughts and by the impressive way of putting them up. But here too I may say that their opinion about the calibre of saint depends to a considerable extent upon the lofty character and elevated feelings of the readers themselves.

As for Shri Aurobindoji, with all due respect to him, I think it shall be more advantageous to the growth of your power of observation if you apply yourself to study his approach. The way to do it is as follows: Take his astral body (*sookshma sharir*) into conception and observe to find out to what extent you find it illumined. That will reveal the limit of his ultimate approach. Before reading further try to observe him as directed.

His approach was up to *brahmanda mandal* but he had acquired an onward position in it, having secured command over the electric rays present there. This is no doubt a very great achievement not commonly attainable to every saint. The Mohammedan saints at this level of attainment are mostly considered to be worshipable Masters. *Brahmanda mandal* is the storehouse of power and energy. But in Sahaj Marg system, which aims at the super-highest point of possible human approach, it is but an attainment of an ordinary level in comparison to the ultimate point. I have discussed this thing in the book *Anant-Ki-Or (Towards Infinity)* to be published soon. Of the five points of *pind desh* about which I wrote to you sometime ago, some of them were yet dark. Only the points number 1, 2 & 5 were illumined. The right and left corners of the *brahmand* too were dark. There is an episode connected with it which I have kept confidential so far. Now I tell you about it. Two or three years prior to his death I was ordered by my Master to help him in overcoming a certain point in *brahmanda mandal* where he had been staying for some time past. I complied and the stop was removed. Nature always helps saints through her agency. Again after a year or so when I peeped into his inner state, I found there a knot which checked his further flight. I consulted my Master for instructions to help him clear it up. But he disallowed saying that it was the Nature's punishment awarded to him for some gross mistake. I meditated to discover it out with an intention to serve as a safeguard for the preceptors working in the Mission. I found out that it was due to some work in connection with Tibet affairs, which he brought into action by his own will-force against the wish of Nature. He had no doubt a very strong will and often he used to exercise his material will for the apparent good of the people (as is common with saints) irrespective of the demand of Nature. Saddest of all, he derived conclusions for determining his course of action through the medium of intellectual understandings and not on the basis of spiritual light coming from above. On the basis of these very facts I had come to the conclusion that he shall soon be passing away. A friend of mine, a Deputy Collector here wanted to go to him for *darshan* during that very period. I told him frankly to hurry up if he desires for his *darshan* earnestly. Of course I did not openly disclose that his days were numbered. I must not keep secret in this connection. Without further comments I may tell you that all that you suspected in connection with Shri Aurobindo's state, is true but not being sure of your own capability of observation you referred it to me.

Maharishi Raman was far higher than Aurobindo. He was not boastful of his intellectual or spiritual advancement. The other day I asked Shri Raghavendra Rao to read the spiritual condition of Maharishi Raman, and his final approach. He did it and his findings were mostly correct. His points no. 1, 2 & 5 were all glowing and his approach was up to near about *brahmarindhra*.

A few days after Shri Aurobindoji's death two of my associates one of whom was a District Judge and the other a Deputy Collector enquired from me about spiritual state and about his liberation. In reply I requested them to read for themselves the effect of his presence in astral form. The District Judge being very sensitive watched it and discovered that the atmosphere of the room we were sitting in had grown considerably heavier in comparison to that before. He thereby concluded that it was an antisign of liberation. Now please recall to your mind the instance of your holy Mother. How calm and light the atmosphere had grown when you meditated upon her soul. That is a sure sign of liberation.

For the rest of your letter, about your own spiritual condition I may say that I am grateful to my Master who has bestowed upon you such a nice spiritual state. I feel that your *yatra* of point 'A' is now over. I wish you may step on to the next point by yourself for which I am trying and I think it will be so within a few days. I feel anxious about sister's health. Please give her some tonic. Doctor P. Sen prescribes for her the following tonics:

Metatone (P.D. & Co.)
or Minadex (Glaxo).

Shri Raghavendra Rao will leave for Haridwar on the 10th. I wanted to accompany him but I am suffering from low blood pressure and dry cough so I think I shall not be able to go but since it is a new place for him I shall send Ishwar Sahai with him in case I do not go, as there is no associate at Haridwar. At all other places he will find our associates there to help him and be benefited by him. My second son Dinesh suffered from fever and due to that he developed pleurisy. This was detected by Doctor P. Sen two days after his illness. He is being treated for it. There is no cause of anxiety.

I have completely recovered from boil but Shri Raghavendra Rao developed a similar one at the same spot. He too is now recovered. See, this is the benefit he derived from me by coming over to this place. Saint Kasturi is here. She has been called by me as Shri Raghavendra Rao wanted to see her. She offers *namaskaram* to you. You have done well to make arrangement for taking back the Tamil books from Shri N. Kumaraswami.

With best wishes to you and love to children and respects to Appaji, Yours,

Ram Chandra

P.S.- Shri Swami Sewa Nand is no doubt a saintly man.

In addition to that I have already stated about Shri Aurobindo. I may say that he was no doubt a highly learned man and a philosopher too. He had done great service to humanity. He had laid down hints for further development of thought. This is a great thing but the spiritual approach in each individual case always differs and I can safely say that you have gone far ahead.

Ram Chandra

June 14th 1958

My dear beloved and revered Gurudev,

Please accept my humble pranams. I am in receipt of thy affectionate letter. I am so very sorry that you are suffering from dry cough as you had it at Tirupati and also from boil. I am however relieved of anxiety thanks to your writing to me as also Shri Sahaiji that it is under control.

Thy wonderful letter regarding Shri Aurobindoji throws a clear light on many facts. It explains why as early as 1944 one sufi who had come to Tirupati told that he was not as high as I thought of him. His name was Abdul Ahmed (babaji). In 1945 I was prevented by mysterious spiritual forces from going for darshans. I thought that it was done by Shri Venkatesvara our patron deity. The last time that I went there was in 1947 when I also visited Shri Ramana (the first and last time). I had no inclination thereafter of going to Pondy even on the date of his demise. Though I was invited to their functions.

But for thy grace I do not think that I could have gone forward to a stage from where I could observe these undoubtedly great souls. Indeed I predicted astrologically that he was bound to pass away before 1950 in 1936-7. Of course they could not believe me. I also in another paper wrote that there was an egoistic assertion and the result was mortality.

Now I need not worry about them but push forward to the goal. I got a book yesterday for review *Swami Vivekananda in America* published by Almora people. It is interesting. How high Swami Vivekananda was Thou has thyself spoken.

I am deeply sensible of the love and affection that the Master has for my humble self and pray to Him of all wisdom and light and glory to lead me to the Ultimate. I have only one idea now, that of attaining the Ultimate and by Thy grace and I hope that my love for thee may grow more and more intense and concentrated as to be constant remembrance.

Shri Balasubramaniam has gone to Madura and is expected back in a couple of days. The college reopens on Monday and the work will start in right earnest.

Our satsangh is doing well. The individual sittings also are fairly good.

Three new satsanghis had come for sittings today, their names are as follows:

1. M. Sreeramulu B.A., Assistant Secretary to Government of Andhra Pradesh, Agriculture Secretariat Dept. Hyderabad

2. D. Damodaran B.A., (Upper Division Clerk, Health & Local Administration Dept., Government of Andhra Pradesh, Hyderabad), No.1 C-2 Erram Manzil, Khairtabad, P.O. Hyderabad.

3. Sri Y.K. Srinivasan B.A., Upper Division Clerk. Acct. General's Office, Bangalore City

My wife's health is due to the recurrence of an old complaint sciatic type. The children are keeping fit as also my father.

By the time this letter reaches thee I presume that Chiranjeevi Dinesh Chandra will have got rid of pluerisy.

Indeed I believe I wrote to Thee about the title of my address at Calcutta — Shri Aurobindo as the father of future philosophy and insisted that the final word on the subject is not his but the beginning.

I do not know when I would have the opportunity of paying my humble respects to thee at Shahajahanpur and also to Saint Kasturi. My deep pranams to her. My love to all.

With all my soul and being yours,

KCV

Tirupati
23rd June 1958

My dear and beloved Gurudev,

Please accept my humble pranams. I am hoping that by now you will be free from cough and etc., and are restored to health. Shri Balasubramaniam had been to Madhurai and Trichy and returned to station day before yesterday. He had met Shri Tyagarajan and others at Trichy.

I have a matter to place before you. Shri Balasubramaniam feels that sittings with me aggravate his piles etc, even when he sits for the satsangh. This is rather odd inference. It is a matter of great concern. None others feels like this here. I can only pray for him.

We have at present only a dozen regular abhyasis, the rest are indifferent and even absent. This is another phenomenon.

A new satsanghi or abhyasi came in at the instance of Shri Balasubramaniam, who belongs to Madhurai district. He took a sitting on the 19th. His name is: A. Audimoorthy, T. Kallupatty S.O. via Tirumangalam (Madhurai Dist. Madras S.).

I have not been able to express myself clearly about many things. It may well be asked when is the clear reading of a person made possible? In some cases it has been seen that my own light is reflected from the others? What is the possible explanation seeing recently almost all as coloured by the blue lighting?

Recently many persons, worshipers of Saibaba and Meher Baba, had come. I do not wish to probe into their status but that is for my own guidance. I am sorry I have begun to be inquisitive.

Regarding my experience of the present state or stage I have to submit that it is very dry. Infrequently I have the experience of fullness as in the last satsangh yesterday. Master, how can I say that I have gone beyond or far ahead of the gentlemen you had mentioned in your last letter?

Things here are in the outer world much the same and indeed nothing has been clarified. I am attending the College from the 26th instant as no contrary order had been passed. Further the new set up does not promise any good work to be done. I cannot of course get reconciled to this except by feeling that All is for the best in the long run. It is this that continues to cause anguish and depression. Yet one finds that one has to carry on the running of the family and employment seems to be the only way. **To make ends meet.** Resignation to God is the only way as far as I can see, and I believe I have done it to God and Thee.

In the meanwhile I am praying that light be granted to me to be able to do my work for thee and be able to serve the Master, I know that but for thy grace the work could not be done and further I am aware that though I am not perfect thou makest it appear all the work as perfect. Transmission is by thee alone and I seem to be just an imperfect conduit pipe, unconscious of the flow of Thy energy. I pray for more and more illumination of the path and the highest achievement of union with Thee — the ultimate.

Children are busy joining the colleges and my father is progressing well. Please convey my regards to Ishwar Sahaiji and other associates,

With loving pranams,

yours
KCV

[Editor's Note: the following was hand written by Dr. KCV on this letter:] This letter not sent, as I received a letter from Shahjahanpur that Dinesh Chandra shot himself dead on the 20th of June.

STRICTLY PRIVATE
No. C 295/SRCM   **Shahjahanpur, U.P.**
Dated 30th June, 1958

My dear Varadachari,

Received your affectionate letter of 14th June, 1958. I could not reply earlier due to the unhappy incident of Dinesh's death. He was a young man of character and firm will, possessing a sound physique. He was bold and courageous but at the same time obedient and respectful towards the elders. By nature he was silent type with firm determination. He was not excited by the news of failure but remained perfectly calm and peaceful, busy with his own plans, perhaps. His death has opened for me a new chapter to think over. I put down the same to you for the correct solution.

We must have faith in God and the Divine Will, which is the last resort of us all. But being a free thinker, I feel induced to trace out the real cause of the incident on the basis of my experience and whether it could be averted or not.

A few days after his examination was over an idea flashed across my mind that he may likely shoot himself if he fails in the examination. But the thought disappeared the very moment it arose. Again on the day of occurrence, the same idea came in several times, but I paid no heed to it. Why? I do not know. Nature's Will over-rules everything, but I feel bold enough to assert, irreligious though it might be, that it could be stopped or averted if I had attended to the thought arising within my mind. Usually in all such cases related to my associates, I am always alert and do my best to remove the effect of shock instantly. Why I failed to attend in this particular case is a mystery to me! His suicidal tendencies were known to my mind and could very easily be removed by the exercise of spiritual force or by administering some Homeopathic medicines for the purpose. I failed to do anything and he went off uncared for in this respect. Was it the Divine will or the result of my careless inattentiveness?

For some instances of the kind I may say that once one of my associates (a man of very ordinary standing of only a few months) chanced to meet two of his friends who had resolved firmly to commit suicide and were going to bring their plan into action. He talked to them for some time, inwardly meditating on the thought that my power was working through him to change their minds. After a few minutes they confessed that they had given up the idea of suicide.

Shri Kashi Ram of Tinsukia once resolved to end his life by striking his head against the wall in a fit of devotional madness. But the moment he stood up for it, he saw me in a vision, pulling him aside and rebuking him for it.

Another incident happened two years ago when he was leaving this place for Assam. Finding him to be very sad and remorseful, I told him that I shall accompany him during the entire journey. He realised my presence all along. During the course of journey he had to cross the Brahmaputra by steamer. But as no steamer was available at the time he preferred to take up a boat in order to avoid delay. But unfortunately the boat began to capsize in the middle of the river. All of a sudden my mind echoed that Kashi Ram's boat was in danger. Instantly I rushed to the spot in the astral form and carried him safely to the other bank. Kashi Ram felt that he saw my form in the river supporting the boat right and left till it got safely to the bank.

As for Dinesh just before committing suicide, he offered the last moment homage with real faith to my Master and then thinking of me he pulled the trigger. He had great faith in me and my Master, this I did not know before. Regarding his inner state he was all light within, having a very pure heart. As the result he was already in a state of elevation at which the formation of samskaras ceases. After his death I studied his case and found very few samskaras of the past life in him, which could be very easily exhausted within this very life. The suicidal ideas were of course there in heaps which I cleared off and burnt down. Soon after, the soul appeared to me and fell down at my feet saying that he was very sorry for all that had been done and apologised for it, stating that he could not gain liberation unless I pardoned him. I pardoned him and he is now in the Brighter World.

Now the mystery for you to solve. If it is taken as a Divine Will, no question arises at all. But if it is weighed philosophically, the theory of determination and indetermination comes in.

Let me come to your letter referred to above. It is good, what I had written to you about Shri Aurobindoji tallies with your astrological perceptions also. If you want anything further about the inner history of his spiritual pursuit it can also be given to you in a nutshell. I tell you one thing in this connection. Before he regularly started spiritual practice blue light appeared in his heart which he took to be from Lord Krishna. It is not a new thing. It can occur in different ways to individuals who have got pious heart. The amalgamation of thought according to its tendency with the matter, produces light according to it. Since he was highly intellectual the same colour he noticed in the form of light. Our method is systematic and we allow the different colours to come in the natural way. To those who take up the coloured light, it also changes in its different stages, but the process to get the right thing is prolonged.

I tried to find out the gist of your speech at Calcutta in the Amrit Bazar Patrika but I could not get it. If it is published, please send to me a copy of it, if possible. You are perfectly correct in saying that the final word in philosophy is yet to be said. He has dealt with the different stages of consciousness with minute divisions in them, and it was on account of his vast knowledge and ability. His expression too is very clear. To my view too they are as clear as daylight but I have neither words nor ability to differentiate them. I have given in the *Efficacy of Raja Yoga* that consciousness is not our goal. The time is soon at hand when you will actually realise it yourself, because you have already crossed the major portion of consciousness. When you cross all these states of consciousness you will come to a dormant stage or the silent type of consciousness. When you go farther into it, you will have immense power at your command. I think it may not be a vain assertion to say that the rotation of earth can be stopped for some moments if that power is utilised. It can be utilised for general good of the world; change of season can be affected by it; rain can be brought in at any time. But however we may proceed on we have to remain dependent to the Divine. I tell you one thing more which may seem to be contradictory to the above view. When Nature gives sole charge of a work to any one, She does not then meddle with what he does in that respect.

Let me tell you that Atri Rishi who is still alive and resides in Himalayan region is as handsome as you are and your features resemble his to a great extent. He is in charge of the adjustment of seasons. If he does anything nature will not interfere in it. He does what is needed. Only if any commanding authority orders him to have showers, he is bound to do that. He can do it himself if it is within the range of his programme. I have written all this simply for the sake of your general information.

The money preceding from the sales of the books should be kept with you in the Mission's account to be used for the further publications.

I shall also go through the book *Swami Vivekanand in America* which you are going to review.

But that will be possible only when I am there in my next tour. Swami Vivekanand was indeed a very high personality. His master once revealed to me that he could make only one man and he had transferred all his powers to him, while on death bed, just as my Master had done in my case. I have previously pointed out to you that when a saint of calibre leaves the world the power he possessed is left for the disciples. If there is no disciple able to digest it he has then to wait for the purpose or transfer it to another capable man without any regard to *sanstha*. By his Master's order he did transfer his power to me claiming me to be his representative. I had to accept it under instructions from my Master. Two more saints have done likewise. I find a similar example among Sufis where a great saint had nominated his representative after a lapse of 150 years. My Master has instructed me to take Swami Vivekanand also as master and that his orders require no confirmation from him. He has severed his connection from his own *sanstha* in 1949 when I was on tour to Gaya along with Ishwar Sahai. Since then the curvature has started in that *sanstha* and it is now going down towards degeneration, as Shri Krishnamurti of Madras has already guessed. Under directions from Swamiji I had intimated this fact to the President of Ram Krishna Mission Calcutta requesting him to connect his dynamo with me to receive spiritual help. There was no reply. Probably he took me to be a man of insane mind.

After writing the above, I received your condolence letter of 23rd June, 1958. I am very grateful to you for having consoled me so lovingly. In my earlier days I had lost two sons and one daughter, one son aged 9, the other aged 4 and the daughter aged about a year. Their death did not affect me more than that of a tame bird. But the case of Dinesh is different. The horrible scene I witnessed at the time, together with an idea of my own negligence in the matter as stated above often makes my heart heavy. According to my nature I would have felt alike if I had witnessed such a scene elsewhere. My tender heart is unable to bear such afflictions and that is the main puzzle.

With good wishes and love to children, and due respects to Appaji.

Yours,

Ram Chandra

P.S.- A copy of the horoscope of dear Dinesh is enclosed herewith with a view that it may help you to study the reason of his sad passing away and other related factors.

Ram Chandra

Tirupati
undated

My dear Beloved Master,

Please accept my salutations and pranams. I received your loving letter. I can well appreciate the deep distress that has been caused by the death of Dinesh. Indeed for men other than thy calibre it would have been terrible. But the distress in Thy case is not merely love but the peculiar hand of fate. I remember challenging Aurobindonites who said that though astrology is true yet the Yogi transcends the laws and determinations of the stars. All that can be done is that we can utilise the forces of the stars for the higher purposes of higher evolution. Indeed this death is an opening to Ch. Dinesh quicker to the liberation he asked for free from the maddening crises of examinations, which examine nothing at all really. Even so the death of Aurobindoji must be an opener to new frontiers to him, frontiers he would not recognize as he was committed gravely to a different view. The problem of determinism and freedom of will or the power to change the natural law or change over to another law is indeed beyond most of us. I cannot say that there was dereliction or non-alertness something deep in Thy Being must have prompted the neglect to take precaution. That is the Divine Will, with which Thou art indeed identified. That shows thy transcendence. We have not been able to explain why there should be this neglect to take warnings at home. There must have been a deep feeling of the Master taking care of one's own. The secret meaning of this the Master alone can say. It is exactly a similar situation to what Naciketas foreboded when he asked what happens to one on release: does he exist or does he not? However I must pray to the Master to bear with this calamity and protect His heart which is very tender and sensitive to this. Our philosophy has no answer to this except to say that man hopes he is free and deeply feels that he ought to be free to change all natural laws. Hence all our effort.

I felt that this news may not be distributed to all but since it has been done I pray to God that all satsanghis will pray for the Master's Health and the welfare of the departed soul, however misguided. I personally do not like mystery but things do happen that lead us beyond the level of ordinary perception.

I should very much like to know more about the personalities spoken by thee in the last letter.

Master when I had been trying to observe thee of late frequently I discovered that in Thee there was hardly any stir or movement but the calm plenitude of the dusky dawn — colourless but sometimes glowing with subdued light. Then I knew that thou art indeed the supreme Personality. This has been very constant and I prayed that I may perceive thy form also.

Thou sayest that very soon I shall reach the silent consciousness which is beyond all consciousness. I am eagerly looking forward to that stage when I shall drown myself in Thee. Digested by Thee I shall discover the true poise of being I hope.

Though I find myself incompetent to console Thee yet I know that it is most difficult to console the children and Mataji at home. The mystery of death is indeed the profoundest mystery and if our yoga can open up the frontiers of this would beyond it would perhaps remove the terrors and agonies of death. It has to be some thing that comes with the vividness of a real experience and that is one of the many yearnings in my humble heart.

I shall send a copy of my speech at Calcutta as soon as I receive it.

Thy kindness and love to me are such that thou attributest achievements to me when really it is the Master's. All progress in this place is due to Thy Grace and presence within me and with me permanently.

All children are keeping fit. They have deeply been moved by the tragedy suffered by Thee. My father also is keeping fit.

With love,
Yours,
KCV

No. C 302/SRCM   **Shahjahanpur, U.P.**
Dated 8th July, 1958

My dear Varadachari,

I acknowledge the receipt of your affectionate letter dt. nil. I will reply it a few days after.

Of course my letter No. C 295/SRCM dt. 30th June, 1958 was private and it should be treated as such. Dinesh's mother had already passed away in 1949. Had she been alive it would have been the hard task for her to bear the shock.

Respect to Appaji. Love to children.

With best wishes,

Yours,
Ram Chandra

11th July 1958

My dear Revered and beloved Gurudev,

Please accept my loving pranams. I received very gratefully your letter of the 30th as well as the p.c. which reached me yesterday. Yes. I fully appreciate the point and as you have already stated it I shall keep its contents private.

I find that the time of birth of Dinesh is not in the horoscope enclosed. It is stated that it is *tulalagna* and that is not enough for our purposes. However I found that some of the most important planets are on 'suicidal' degrees and that has been the tendency all along. I once remember to have read the wise saying of a Greek Satyr: "The first best is not to be born: the second best is to die at once." Such a purified soul as Dinesh must have felt this call. Thou hast thyself told me not to give sittings to students and boys who are yet studying and that is presumably because they discover that there are more things than study can give.

The Samartha Guru Mahatma Ramachandraji's oil painting was completed and was installed in the hall in the house on Monday evening.

I have been feeling thy presence and full force during the sittings at the satsangh on Sunday mornings. I have also been perceiving pressure in different parts of the head. I perceive continuously 'Thee' as a firm light — colourless. I do not perceive Thy Form but the formless and indeed this seems to be for me the only way of perception of the rest of the sadhakas too. I pray Master that thou mayest grant me the prayer to be able to see, hear and mind all through thy divine vision, audition and mentation, so that I may cross over this ignorance. It is true that for the first time during the past few weeks I have been finding myself to be all light — more like the moonlight than the sunlight. Surely I think one reflects the Divine light.

The love for thee may it grow every day till I can be drowned in Thee or more fully get digested in thee.

The abhyasis are, some of them at least, like Dhond Rao and Someswara Sarma, experiencing elevation during their abhyasa and satsangh and individual sitting. Dr. G. Kuppuswami is certainly progressing, his inner system is more and more clean and clear though he says that he has nothing special to report. Indeed there is more and more quiet. Y.K. Laksmanan is progressing satisfactorily though he has been going through the colour experiences, but the colour that grants him peace is red and disquiet is blue. Otherwise he is quite all right, he has had the ajapa experience also.

By thy grace the affairs regarding village which was worrying my father for the past eight years has been squared up last week and we have sold away the lands. I believe my father's mental condition will improve considerably and he will be able to grow spiritually. I am praying for thy grace.

My wife's health was causing anxiety but now it has subsided and there is yet some difficulty which by Thy grace will go away in a few days.

All children have joined the college and by Thy blessings will have a successful time.

I learnt from Shri Thyagarajan that Shri Raghavendra Rao wrote to him that the Master will be touring the South during November and December as usual. It goes without saying that we shall be most happy if you could spend as much time as you can spare for this place, not less than 10 days.

In case I have to go to Ahmedabad during December after 18th the programme can be had either before or after 27th December when I hope to be back. But otherwise it will be all right.

Praying that I may attain the Ultimate and know all by thy grace and for thy work, I offer my loving pranams to you,

yours as body,
KCV

No. C 310/SRCM   **Shahjahanpur, U.P.**
Dated 15th July, 1958

My dear Varadachari,

Received your affectionate letter as referred to in my previous card. I was really waiting for your injunction regarding the settlement of the cause of Dinesh's death. I do not keep any secret and want to stand before you as naked as I was when I was born for the first time. It will be revealed to you sooner or later because you are gradually coming in conformity with me. I remember that if I find anything substantial in me, Kasturi's thought was there to reveal it. There are one or two such examples more. There is no mystery in Nature herself. It is our complex thinking alone that has made it such. Believe me, my dear Varadachari, that at the time of Dinesh's death, I was perfectly well-balanced, and still I do not lose it even for a moment. When I study myself I do not find any feeling of grief or sorrow within, but as my heart is tender and habituated to feel the pangs of others it sometimes plays its part momentarily in this case too. The horrible sight of his deformed figure, sometimes coming to my mental view, leaves a little pressure on the heart. But in spite of it all, my spiritual services towards my brothers continued as usual, except with a gap of two or three days, which I devoted exclusively to

Dinesh. My daily routine including regular meals, physical exercises and everything goes on as usual.

As you say in your letter that you have not been able to explain why there should be the neglect to take warnings at home. The other day my revered Master, verifying all that you have written about the Divine Will, said to me that the happening was bound to come and when the idea of his suicidal tendency came to my mind, it was He who had made me forget it instantly, so that I may not exercise the powers bestowed by Him for averting the incident. Look here, my Varadachari we cannot meddle with what is ordained. Regarding the change in natural laws, Lord Krishna will have to come down again, if needed.

Doctor! You say that you fall short of reading others, I find that you have got a very good *anubhava shakti*, and the few lines that you have written about me offer ample proof of it. You have rightly depicted my inner state so far as I understand it myself. When the consciousness grows dull and assumes the form of silent type, the reading of such things becomes easier and you are coming to that level. Please recall to your mind the incident I wrote to you about some time ago, concerning Shri Radhakrishnan at Trichy. He wanted to judge me, but as he was not internally so deep to be able to know what I am really bestowed with, I got down to the elementary stage and made the vibrations stronger to give him the clue. It is really wonderful for you to come to know of my position, and this shows that you are so deeply connected with my inner being. If a saint tries to judge me internally, he will come to the conclusion that either I am a dunce or only a simple-minded fellow (if he takes a favourable view). When a man reaches the final state of Negation, his actual depth can hardly be fathomed. I tell you plainly that I am still unable to know the real depth of my great Master.

You want to know about the other personalities, hinted at in my last letter. They are Chaitanya Mahaprabhu and Mahatma Buddha. Besides these great personalities, I was offered field for work by Christ himself during the war time, giving the result of war beforehand and also by Guru Nanak. But I offered my apology to them for thrusting myself into it of my own accord, promising to do my best if one required my services of his own free will. There are so many other saints, whom I do not even know have also transmitted to me in dreams and allowed me to take up their work. This had also been the case with my Master too. Lord Krishna is the Head and Supreme Patron of our *sanstha* and the name Sahaj Marg came direct from Him. The very words echoed distinctly through the vibrations received direct from Him.

Regarding the mystery of death, I can only say (but that of course requires practical experience) that when an abhyasi is favoured by God to have a jump into the everlasting peace and unbroken silence, he does not then like to stay in the body even for a moment. But he is made to live till the time matures for his death, by means of bondage kept in it. When a man having body goes beyond the sixteenth circle he does not like to live a material life. I prayed long to my Master to let me stay in that condition permanently without any bondage, so that I may have enough experience to bring that thing to common view. He was kind enough to grant my request and had kept me in that state for twenty-four hours and His will instead of bondage was working to keep up the material existence. The experience I got was that I grew dumb. But I can give this experience to those only whose inner state warrants it.

The agony of death becomes bitter only when the idea of body sense is present. When that is gone there remains then the soul-idea to be forgotten. When that too is gone for good, you have secured the Union and the idea of existence is extinct.

So long as we recognise the world as it is, we hatch in the difference between this and the world beyond. When this difference disappears the whole Universe seems alike, rather it turns into Wilderness, which is a real pitch felt in the Brighter World. We then get into conformity with the real spirit, marking both the worlds, the material and the Brighter. There remains then no difference and no barrier and we feel the same air everywhere, in the material world or in higher planes. That may in a way be expressed as the drowning state in real spirit where everything abandons us. The condition is not so difficult as it seems to be and it comes by itself through practice under the system of Sahaj Marg. It is the easiest because it has no material base. There remains then no difference between life and death, both appearing in true sense to be mere relative terms. This is what I meant by the phrase, "the structure falls off," used in the *Efficacy of Raja Yoga*.

After dictating the above I received your next letter of 11th July, 1958. Your Intense devotion gives me such immense happiness that I am sometimes led to think that with all my spiritual services to you I am still wanting in giving you due return of it.

The light becomes 'The Light' when its glow or lustre fades away, The Dawn colour being the material exposition of it. I wanted to give you some practical experiences last year during my visit there, but on account of my indisposition at the time I could not do so. I wish I may not fall short of it this time and pray to my Master for it. I shall keep in mind your programme during the coming December, while fixing mine for the South India tour and shall consult you on the point. I propose to devote more time with you at Tirupati because there are so many satsanghis there. The abhyasis in your charge are all improving. Mr. Kuppuswami is improving in devotion and has made a definite progress. Regarding Mr. Y.K. Lakshman's feeling of a soothing sensation in the red colour I may say that that being the colour of the point No.2 known as the seat of Atman, gives him peace. As for the feeling of disquietness in the blue colour, I think that he has practised some *yog-*like things previously, which if he reveals them to me I may be in better position to explain. Meanwhile I shall however see that the discomfort thereby is removed.

I am glad to know that your worry about the village land is now over and that Appaji now feels more satisfied. Your working in connection with his inner system has been wonderful, though I too have transmitted to him three or four times. Now I shall try to take him in my usual routine. I sometimes get anxious about sister's health. She has to pull on all the burden of the household work with little time to rest.

I may here put before you my latest experience about one of my associates. When he came to me for the first time about three years ago he was extremely gross. I removed the grossness to my best capacity. When this year he came for the second time, I found him full again, but with the subtle form of grossness and it becomes the hardest task to correct the subtle state of grossness. By the Master's grace I traced out the cause with great difficulty. It was, he relied more upon his own labours than upon the grace of God. This is a new experience to me. You will please impress upon every satsanghi to rely upon God's grace, doing his duty faithfully.

I am glad to inform you that you have stepped into the next region (i.e., Point B) at 12:50 in the night following the 16th July. You will please observe the difference in the condition at the points A & B. I hope the yatra of this region will also start soon.

The date and time of birth of Dinesh, according to his horoscope is 13th (Krishna Paksh) of the month of Kartik (i.e., 29th October, 1940) at 59/52 (59 Ghari & 52 Palas) or 6:12 morning, calculating the day to commence from sunrise as usual in the Hindi system. But as it was the morning time (6:12 A.M.), according to the current English system of calculation of dates, the day is changed and it is then 30th October, Wednesday and not as given in the horoscope. The time of sunrise on that day is given as 6:27 and the time of birth is 6:12 i.e., about 15 minutes before sunrise. So according to Hindi calculation it is the 29th October (Tuesday) but according to the English calculation it is the 30th October (Wednesday). I hope you will adjust yourself accordingly.

Saint Kasturi is also here and she offers you *pranam*.

Please convey my respects to Appaji.

With best wishes and love to children,

Yours,
Ram Chandra

P.S.- I have made certain investigations relating to Dinesh's death. Now I want to see how far they tally with your reading of the horoscope. I shall afterwards release the findings to the preceptors for their knowledge and experience for public good.

Ram Chandra

Tirupati
July 24th 1958

My dear and beloved Gurudev,

Please accept my humble pranams of love. I do not know how to express myself before such love as thine. But for thy Grace I do not think that I could have been able to perceive thy condition at all, for it is something so high. I do not know why I am unable always to keep up that vision, which only means it is due to thy grace. I have hardly any views on many matters since I find that no distinction can be drawn between living and the dead. I do not know whether this is the nature of point B. I suffered exquisitely from herpes zoster for twelve days on the left shoulder and left scapula. I have somehow learnt the art of enjoying physical pain. You have asked me to note my condition. I have been rather in a difficulty about this being untrained in self-observation in the sense you want. By thy grace I think I will be able to do it. Anyhow I found that my superficial and surface thoughts have a knack of obtruding whenever I begin to give sittings and it used to require an act of prayer and will to proceed with the sitting. However in the meanwhile the abhyasis did feel nothing of this but experienced thy presence etc.../ I pray to thee to grant me the capacity to throw out all such interferences of my superficial life. Secondly I found that I wish to spend my time in doing thy work — spiritual — rather than seek to attain the Ultimate myself. Today I found that I want to reach the Ultimate alone. This difference in attitudes is rather funny. I know that it is thy wish that each one of us should experience the Ultimate and the path of Return rather than try to see what the Master previously states about it, as that would lead to prejudgment. Individual judgment has to be developed and cultivated. I pray that this new faculty may develop in me steadily. Master alone can grant me this.

I was thinking of some personalities as Meher Baba, Sai Baba and others. Last week I got a journal entitled Mother from Calcutta, about one Shri Mataramdas Omkarnath who used to initiate by rousing the Kundalini, very much like one C.V.V. many years ago at Kumbhakonam. I could not find much time for the study of these persons. Though I have the *amurta* or formless experience of persons I have not been able to get the *murta* form-experiences so that I may be able to fix the points about which you have spoken and written. I am wondering sometimes whether I am perceiving the previous lives of the abhyasis when some incidents occur in the course of the sittings. I can only pray that these may become clearer and clearer.

I am happy that you will be spending more time with us and at Trichy. I am due to go to Trivandran on the 9th August. If I can find time I shall get down there and proceed to Tirupati. I am going to Bezwada on the 28th. I have written to Shri Bro. Kumaraswamy and hope to meet him and spend some time with him.

Please forgive me as I seem to be taking much of your time on these personal problems. I sometimes wonder when I would reach the 16th circle so that one may experience the here and the hereafter and be able to communicate with the two at the same time.

It is so very kind of the Samartha Guru to 'verify' but there is surely a vast difference between my ignorance and His Omniscience. Thy affection for me is surely very deep and I do not know how I am fit to receive thy Grace at all. This is a mystery for me. Could you explain this. Every day I feel I am in the Kingdom of Grace. Is this the passing beyond to the points A, B .....? There are so many things that I wish to write and discuss and know and experience. I am looking forward to the experience and understanding of the different centres and points by thy grace. I am so happy that the abhyasis are moving towards the real experience by thy Grace.

Children have all joined the College. My wife's health is better. I am trying my very best to help my father. But thy grace is all effective and by that I hope to live and move and have my being.

With loving pranams, Yours as body,
KCV

No. C 339/SRCM **Shahjahanpur, U.P.**
Dated 29th July, 1958

My dear Varadachari,

Received your affectionate letter dt. 24th July and you will get the reply of the letter in detail, when you return back from Trivandrum.

I had also been at Trivandrum in 1945. If you find time, please get down at Trichy so that the satsanghis of the place be benefitted by your company.

I received a letter from Shri Thyagarajan, informing me that you will visit Trichy on the way to Trivandrum.

All my children at Tirupati will take the spiritual trend in due course. My prayer for them at this time is that they may prosper in life.

I am exceedingly happy that my boy Chi. Aravind has attained his 23rd birthday. May he live long and prove himself worthy of the soil of India, where many great men were born and rose to the eminence. I suffered also from herpes zoster in the scapular region three times in my life which are very painful. I wish that you may not suffer for the second time.

With best wishes to you and love to children and respects to Appaji. Yours,
Ram Chandra

Tirupati
8th August 1958

My Beloved and Revered Gurudev,

Please accept my humble pranams. I believe you would have received my letter with enclosures by now. I finally decided not to go to Trivandrum. I have been feeling very sad and agitated for no reason except of unfounded imaginations but not quite unfounded also. By the grace of the Master I think that all the fears etc., will pass away. I am so sorry not to be able to go to Trichy also. I am afraid that Shri Balasubramaniam has rather misunderstood me completely. I of course do not discourage him in his ambitions even for the Mission. I am not made his way. I am sorry he raised many points in his letter to you, which was not shown to me (for I infer that from your reply to him) and to Shri Raghavendra Rao. I am not of course thinking in terms of enthusiasms. I believe the Master knows everything about me. The Mission's work is the work of the Master, and every preceptor is responsible to the Master who may direct him to do work in any area. Surely your orders are final to me. But I do not like to be committed to programmes which I may not be able to fulfill. As thou art aware my father's health has been giving me some worry whenever I leave station, and as I wrote to Thee I am finding it very trying with heavy work at the College and journeys do not help me to recoup my health. Anyway I leave it to the Master to decide everything for me.

The condition represented in my previous letters has not altered at all. The influx of my own thoughts seems not to abate. But the abhyasis are feeling improved.

I am regular in my work I believe and am trying my best to deserve Thy grace more fully.

I do not know when I would gain complete confidence in myself regarding the perception of other's condition. Indeed some of these days I was quite unable to find it. Today I saw a person in meditation during the sitting given to Dhond Rao, and could not recognize him. But after the sitting the abhyasi told me that he saw the Master seated before him, and at the end of the sitting as if an electric current passed through his lower limbs.

Master, please do not think me amiss. I am praying to be dissolved and drowned in the Ultimate — Thee. Without that deep and abiding Experience I do not feel at all anywhere. I am but putting my condition as it is prevailing in me. I am afraid of going about also and lack the confidence which Shri Balasubramaniam has. Thou self alone can explain these things to me. I mean nothing about my Brother Balasubramaniam. Indeed though my foes abound and are anxious to do their worst, it is all Thy grace and whatever happens may be for the very best and a blessing. Permit me to seek forgiveness if I have written anything. My apologies to all about whom I have thought ill and above all permit me to be Thine more consciously and fully and permanently within me.

With affectionate pranams,

One dissolved in thee,

KCV

No. C 377/SRCM   **Shahjahanpur**
                                           Dated 9th August, 1958

My dear brother Varadachari,

Received your loving letter dated 24th July, 1958. It is good that you have perceived my inner condition. It really shows how much tenderly you are connected with me.

I have often written to you whatever good and virtue you feel in yourself is all your merit. I would like to quote a Persian poet, "Love takes its abode in the heart of a beloved before it brings lover to him. It is the candle that kindles first before the moth comes to it."

When Saint Kasturi was on point B, I had described the condition laid in the letter, but my memory is not sharp. I forgot it, what I read from your condition and described by you also is surely the condition of point B. The consciousness with which you are connected with the material world is growing dull and void. The condition if you study deeply, you will find that there is some feeling what one feels in the grey of the morning. At the time of dictating letter I found that there is something which prevents you in feeling it. I will devote myself hereinafter to remove it.

Your sentence that you have learnt the art of enjoying physical pain reminded me of my Master. In his last days he was suffering from liver abscess, and the pain was acute in nature and unbearable. During that time he used to sing *bhajan* (the song sung in the praise of God) instead of wasting time in crying. He was one of the best singers. He knew the art of singing with the help of chakras. This seems to be his own discovery. I also consulted a few famous singers about it but they were silent saying that only the higher saints can sing in this way. He used to sing sometimes from *brahmandi sur* and the result was that all of us were in the state of trance.

If superflous thoughts come when you transmit others, you should not worry about. Mostly they are not yours. But they appear like that on account of the push from behind. Sometimes the thoughts of the abhyasis strike when you are transmitting them. The environment brings about these things because the yogi begins to be super-conscious and sensitive and cleaned. Even a little darkness appears to him like a heap. I give you an example as to what the environment affects. A few years ago I was at Mathura and meditated at the place where Lord Krishna was born. There the mosque stands; the thoughts of theft began to resound while sitting in meditation on the platform of the mosque. I opened my eyes for a little while and then again went into the meditation. To my utter despair the same thoughts crept again. I studied the situation and came to know that this is the den of thieves which after enquiry found to be correct.

I give you another example of the same type. I was at Hardwar sometimes back and put up in a *chaultry*. I meditated in the room allotted to me and found that a woman appeared before me with her throat lanced. When this scene remained for sometime I opened my eyes and stopped meditation for a few minutes. When I meditated again the same appearance and the scene was coming to my view. I then studied the case and found that the same woman was assasinated there and buried on the spot where I was sitting in meditation. I could not guess as how much time elapsed before she was killed. I cleaned the spot affected and transmitted the dead lady for the peace of her soul. After doing this I found that every thing was calm and quiet and dead lady was coming no more to my view. There are so many examples connected with me and my Master.

I am exceedingly happy to note that you want to spend your time in spiritual work so dear to me and Master for the good of the mankind in preference to your own advancement. It shows how broader heart you have got. In such cases God helps with both hands enriching one spiritually. On the contrary you felt that you yourself want to reach the goal. This is of course funny, but since you have the idea of realising the Ultimate in the bottom of your heart, it clings to achieve the One-Ultimate.

My Master used to say that I brought the *anubhava shakti* from the past life, but still to develop it. I used to remember my Master constantly, linking at the same time to the condition which I used to have in the flight. I got accustomed to do two things together. If you take care a little your practice will bring the desired result. I assure you that you are not wanting in *anubhava shakti* but the way by which it is brought out requires improvement.

Shri Sitaramdas Onkar Math is a great scholar of Sanskrit learning. He is a pious and a religious man. Dr. P. Sen knows him well. He is a Vaishnav saint. He teaches meditation.

May our Appaji live for hundreds of years, but as there is limit to it also, so it becomes our sacred duty as his children to send him free when the time matures for it. If we fail in this duty we are not free from parental debt.

I hope Appaji must be feeling calm as you have done his spiritual service. I must tell you one thing about it that the outer surface of the heart is quite clean, but there is grossness in the inner layers, for which please be attentive. Please take the cleaning of the whole system which includes *sookshma* body. I will also help you in this matter.

The thought of marrying my daughters Chaya here and Km. Padmini and Chitra there resound very often and we must try to have a good match for each of them.

Dr. P. Sen has gone to Nagpur on 4th August spending a few days with my associates at Lucknow, Kanpur, Agra and Allahabad. After staying sometime at Nagpur with his brother and cousin he will go to Calcutta.

Has Shri V.K. Narsimhan come back from America? I remember Shri S. Vedantam very much. He also seems to be the embodiment of love.

With best wishes to you and love to children. Respect to Appaji.

Yours,
Ram Chandra

P.S.- Dr. P. Sen of Calcutta has taken *sanyas* as I came to know through Chaturvediji.

His yoga pat (Christened name) is something plus Atmanand.

Shri Ishwar Sahai arrived here just this morning. He is on two weeks leave and will stay with me till 22nd August.

I am sending herewith seeds of a creeper. Since it is the rainy season they may all be sown in one bed. When the plants are about 6" in height they may be transplanted to suitable places in the Ashram, temples and houses. Its flower resembles a snake's hood with coils below. It is very efficacious in snake bite and in all rabid bite cases. In Burma it is known as Isarwal. But I have after great difficulty traced out its ancient name as 'Ishwarmul' which is so highly spoken of in Ayurvedic books. It has long been unknown in this country. My father got it from Burma.

In case of snake bite 5 leaves with 5 peppers thoroughly powdered and mixed with one ounce of water is to be given to the patient. It may be repeated after 5 or 10 minutes, if its effect is not traceable. If it bears good effect the repetition may be after longer duration.

Rains are very here these days. Most of the rivers are in spate. The Ganga and the Yamuna have crossed the danger point at several places.

No. C 385/SRCM **Shahjahanpur, U.P.**
                    Dated 14th August, 1958

My dear Varadachari,

Received your affectionate letters dated 5th August, 1958 and 8th August, 1958. Since second one is confidential I replied in my own hand. I hope you must have received my last letter along with comments on diaries.

Your frank disclosure of private difficulties is a remarkable sign of affection. I too disclosed everything to my Master. Thus the question of troubling me on this account does not arise. I feel your difficulties much and I am ready to extend every possible help. Accordingly I pray for it.

If I put up the atrocities of your opponents before God for justice, I fear the faulty persons will be duly dealt with. But I have never done such a thing so far, in spite of the fact that often in my life I had to pass through such circumstances.

I tell you an episode from my life. After my father's death on 7th January, 1933 one of my uncles (distantly related) wanted to have in charge of the management of our estate, so that he may have a chance of deriving all possible advantage by fair or foul means. I and my brother both did not accept his offer and this turned him into an opponent. For years together he remained so, creating difficulties for me at every step by underhand means up till his very death in 1956 he went on with his activities setting up causes of worry, harassments and loss for me. He excited persons against me, tried to involve me in law cases or other entanglements. He even did not restrain from gangsterism in order to harm me in any possible way. Though I too, being in possession of a state had every means to pay him in his own coins, I never made up my mind for it. I bore everything patiently and calmly remaining ever on the defensive side with no intention to retaliate. During his last days his own policy turned against him.

Another incident is connected with Shri Kashi Ram of Tinsukia (Assam). His brother-in-law (i.e., sister's husband) who was also a partner to his business was somehow kidnapped and murdered. His dead body was found lying on the back of his house after five months and it showed signs that murder had taken place about a month ago. At that time Shri Kashi Ram was here. When he went back the Superintendent of Police came to him for enquiry suspecting him to be a culprit. Shri Kashi Ram's thought took a strange turn. He began to see S.P. who was interrogating him in my form with extreme love. A few minutes after the S.P. was moved to tears and embraced Shri Kashi Ram warmly assuring him that he was convinced of his innocence. He further promised to trace out the real culprits soon and since then he is ardently busy with it and has made several arrests. All the time he was calm and fearless in complete resignation.

So far it replies the confidential portion of your letter. For the rest please see the enclosed letter.

Yours,
Ram Chandra

No. C 386/SRCM   **Shahjahanpur, U.P.**
Dated 14th August, 1958

My dear Varadachari,

In your letter dated 2nd August, 1958, you write that your anxiety about the condition of a patient often troubles you. If you entrust the patient to the care of God, doing your own part of the duty, the anxiety will be reduced. I have advised Shri Munjanatha Iyer of Mysore to approach you for contact and satsangh. He has also expressed his desire to see me here in September. He says that he has begun practising. You will yourself find out, when he is before you, whether he is gross or subtle. He is a coffee planter. Will you please write to me whether your sadness and agitation has disappeared or not.

You rightly conclude that the work of the Mission is the work of the Master. It is for this reason that a preceptor can take up work, according to need in any area, without consulting me. The divisions are only for the purpose of regulating the activities of the individuals and making them feel their respective responsibilities for the spiritual good of the abhyasis.

I have great consideration for your health. The thoughts flashing across a trainer's mind do not affect an abhyasi, because it is the Divine current, which after descending upon the trainer passes on through him to the abhyasi. Besides the impulse imparted to the abhyasi is regulated in accordance with the suggestions you offer.

I wonder how you say that you are lacking in perception. Your reading of the inner state of Appaji and of others, so far, has been quite correct. It is, in my opinion, not the lack of perception but of confidence. It can be removed if you only apply your insight and feel satisfied with what comes to your view internally.

Shri Sitaramaiah gives in his report that he saw a boy holding a chart in front. The boy must be Dinesh who, as he told me, visits the centres of the Mission in fulfilment of his pledge. He is frequently at your place during the time of satsangh. He demands for spiritual work but I have so far been silent in the matter. He, being bestowed with liberation, can help the members of his own accord. During his life time too he felt greatly interested in hearing about you, although he had not seen you. He knew only Kumaraswami and Raghavendra Rao, who had been here.

I wonder why Shri Balasubramaniam does not come to you for individual satsangh when he lives so close by. This I inferred from the fact that you never mentioned his name among those coming up for satsangh individually.

It gives me great joy to speak something relating to my children at Tirupati. When I look to my heart, I find that they are all connected with me. As the result prayer for better prospects of life in all its phases, gushes out from my mind unintentionally. They love me dearly and I too take them to be my own. May they all prosper, both worldly and spiritually. Your responsibility is reduced when they are settled in life. I expect Mission's work from them and I have a right to it. Recently I saw a funny dream. Shri Jawaharlal Nehru, the Prime Minister appeared to me in several different aspects. I remember only one. It is this. He was holding a court, seated in a chair. He wanted to deliver a judgement and he asked me the meaning of the Quranic phrase of the Mohammedans "La ilah il-lil-lah" (There is no God but the One — Allah). I turned towards his clerk who was a Mohammedan, and he gave the meaning. I awoke. What may be the interpretation of it I do not understand. Perhaps it may be that he might be growing somewhat religious minded.

With best wishes and love to children. My respects to Appaji.

Yours,
Ram Chandra

No. C 441/SRCM **Shahjahanpur, U.P.**
Dated 29th August/1st September, 1958

My dear Varadachari,

Received your loving letter of 17th August. I am happy to learn that you got the extension of service, for one year. Extension as a rule is always given for a period of one year, let us trust in God; when He has heard our prayer this year He will hear us next year also.

You see yourself in everything, that is a good spiritual state. It will be rarefied as you proceed till everything goes away. It is no doubt a remarkable *anubhava* that you saw me entering your body, it shows a *laya avastha* in a good state. If you search deep in you, you will find my abode in you. I put you to the point 'C' along with point 'B' near about 15th of August. Now the yatra of both the points is running side by side. I want that, when I get the opportunity of meeting you, you may be able to cross the 5 or 6 points out of your own endeavour and let us pray for it. The levitation you felt is the seedling for the reality, it will end in negation ultimately. I hope the reality is soon to dawn on you. Everybody will call your present state a good presence of reality, but this is not the end of our efforts, I have yet to take you further along. The light as luminous grey is a sign of real light.

I received a letter from Mr. Manjunath on 28th August, 1958 saying that he will reach you on this date.

I have received a letter from Mr. V.K.P. Nathan, the editor of 'Thinakaran' 'Sakuralai', Navaly, North Manipay, Ceylon, asking me to send him 2 copies of *Sathyodayam* for review in his esteemed journal 'Thinakaran' a daily paper. I am sending him 2 copies, as desired, out of those received by me from Madras. I am asking him to please send the paper containing his review direct to you for your perusal.

I received a letter from a Book & News Agent at Madurai asking me to send him 50 copies of *Sathyodayam* along with a Railway Receipt and a bill for the price by post. He also asks me to let him know about our other publications. His post card is enclosed herewith. I am writing to him that he would receive the required copies direct from you; please settle with him if R.R. may be sent per V.P.P. or only a bill for payment, as I do not know the party. Regarding other publications I am writing to him the name of the English book, *Efficacy of Raja Yoga*, which will be supplied to him if desired, although we have in hand a very limited number of copies of the book with us.

I received a letter from Mr. M. Ramulu enquiring certain things about abhyas. I am enclosing herewith a copy of his letter along with a copy of my reply to him for your perusal.

Shri N. Thyagarajan of Trichy has sent me his diary I am herewith sending it along with a copy of my reply to the same for your perusal. In the other letter, as he writes, he was told by me to proceed to Rameswaram and the poor fellow went there. I also made a remark in this very letter that this letter includes the reply of the other letter with the direction to consult me beforehand if such a thing occurs in future. These things speak of his faith and obedience no doubt, and in such cases consultation is always necessary because it is very difficult to understand if it is the echo of the individual mind or the real being. You need not send back the diary or other letters sent herewith.

I have studied the case of Appaji and I am very thankful to you that his inner layer has been cleaned to a very great extent. In a few days you will find him free from this.

All the associates under your guidance are decidedly improving and I am entirely satisfied with your work. I have a mind to give more time to Mr. Vedantam. I shall write to you when I hear anything from Mr. V.K. Narasimham.

With best respects to Appaji and love to you and the children,

Yours,

Ram Chandra

P.S. The food stuff is very dear in U.P. on account of failure of wheat crop in March last and the untimely rains. In many places granaries have been looted.

R.C.

6th September 1958

My dear Beloved and revered Gurudev,

Please accept my humble pranams. I received your affectionate letter with enclosures and greatly appreciated them.

It is true that the Master has not yet begun to use me for the work ahead. I read that 5th February 1962 will be the beginning of a new epoch as seven planets have a conjunction, so to speak, in one house and a solar eclipse. A student of Ouspensky, late Rodney Collin, has spoken about it. Of course that is a long way yet.

Personally I am yet going through the double movement — my outer self and Thy supreme power in transmission — when these two get to be one I believe it will mean a great advance. When it would be that my dissolution in Thee or God will mean that perception of all Reality and in Reality and for Reality?

Shri Manjunath had been here and I wrote to you about him. Shri Thyagarajan sent me your note about him, but I proceeded independently. About Shri Thyagarajan it is really a case requiring immediate attention. I can say that even Shri Balasubramaniam was somewhat carried away by his romantic imagination. I am glad you have written to him clearly. I am going to Trivandrum on the 2nd October and hope to break at Trichy on the 3rd morning, and start at 10:30 A.M. there and reach Trivandrum on the 4th morning. I have business at the University in the afternoon there. Mostly I will return that night itself and get down at Trichy if necessary on the 5th evening and after four hours entrain at 9:30 p.m. for Madras.

This programme would stand unless I am followed by my wife, in which case I may go to Madura also and extend my leave by one more day. I shall write to Shri Thyagarajan early enough.

I believe your health is much improved. I am glad to inform you that the work of the well has been completed and it has cost us Rs.715 or so.

I am happy to learn that my father's condition is improved thanks to Thy grace. So also am I happy that Shri Vedantam is in your thoughts.

I shall be indeed very grateful if I can move forward more quickly and realise the essence and feel it and drink it and drown myself in it and lose myself. There is a peculiar sense of vacuity in me which I am unable to explain.

Lacking siddhis, one at least prays for a fuller experience of God and Master. Thou hast asked me to let thee know where thou art in me? I have not been able to locate thee, but I feel that it is at the central region marked in the diagram. Is it so? If not please reveal that secret to me. I believe it will work no harm.

All children are well. Today is Shri Krishna's Janmasthami and May His blessings be on us all.

With loving pranams,

Yours,
KCV

No. C 472/SRCM   **Shahjahanpur, U.P.**
Dated 14th September, 1958

My dear Varadachari,

Received your affectionate letter dated 2nd September, 1958 and 6th September, 1958. I am happy to note that Shri Manjanath Ayer attended the satsangh and reaped benefit of it. He is really a sincere man and will turn out a good member of the Mission if he regularly practices on devotional basis. It is correct that I have taken his case from 9th August, 1958 and engaged myself in his inner cleaning which I felt necessary. He feels heat in the evening and I cannot say whether it is due to some mistake in *pranayam* or to some other cause. I have written to him to perform *sheethali* and the way to do it which proved beneficial to him. I have not yet received any letter since he left Tirupati. I had replied his previous letter saying that the doctor had appreciated him greatly.

When I look into you I found my presence in your body. The feeling of vacuity is a happy sign and will work as a foundation stone of negation. When you arrive at the depth of vacuity, the condition becomes remarkably good. When that state too bids farewell, God is nearest.

I remember I had written to you in one of my letters that you are coming to *turiya avastha*. How happy am I to see the same state in you and in Shri Raghavendra Rao almost simultaneously.

Your presence in Trichy will be very beneficial to the satsanghis and the people will be attracted towards you if they hear your speech. There are two persons at Madura also whose particulars are with Shri A. Balasubramanium Ayer. There are a few men at Madura who want to start the practice as Shri Thyagarajan writes. He knows those men.

There is a magazine 'Film of India' in which predictions by an astronomer are given. He has drawn up the horoscope of India and Pakistan. He says there will be famine beginning from 1959 and getting worst in 1962. In 1965 Portuguese will attack Bombay with the help of Pakistan. The big people of Bombay will flee away to Gujarat and Maharashtra. With the help of Maharashtrians Bombay will be conquered back. During this struggle Pakistan Govt. will vanish, East Pakistan and West Pakistan coming over to India, and western frontier province becoming Pakhtunistan will go over to Afghanistan. The ministry is likely to change and another ministry will come in. Thereafter the condition of India is likely to improve. The next elections will be won by the congress no doubt, but it would be hell of a job to succeed in the election. But the circumstances will demand a coalition ministry and no party will be in extreme majority.

Captain Laxmi Narain Srivastava of New Delhi conveys his best respects to you. He is staying with me and will live with me for about 2 months. He is now almost free from neuralgic pain after a year and a quarter. I gave him an Indian drug which brought sufficient relief. The medicine is *asafoetida talabi* and *musabbar* in equal quantity. Pills are to be prepared in the size of green gram. Two pills in the morning and two pills in the evening are to be taken with hot water. The medicine is also useful in sciatica pain. I do not know the English name of *mussabbar*. The Hindi word for it is *ailwa*.

I forgot to mention a few facts in connection with the prophecy. Recently one of my advanced associates has written to me that the wave of Almighty has begun to descend for the change of the world. About seven years ago one of my associates had written to me that he saw in the vision, while meditating, that the map of India is before him having a curtain over it with the word danger written on it, and I entered the danger zone. Afterwards he saw the same thing in the dream. Swami Vivekanand in some of his lectures said that the Godly energy was set in motion and he was dead sure that a personality had come into existence somewhere in Asia who will work for the good of the world. I also pondered over it and found the gradual descent of divine energy for the change. It is coming with some check, because as I understand if it may be brought in full swing the special personality's work will be over and he will have to leave the world immediately. Work he has completed but there is a check for the above reason because, who knows, he may be thinking of doing some spiritual work, too, side by side for the benefit of the human race.

We have all kept fast on 5th September on Shri Krishna's Janmashtami and I myself have transmitted the men keeping fast on 5th and 6th September. Shri Vedantam is attracting me too much nowadays. Shri A. Balasubramanium's case requires labour.

With best wishes to you and love to children and respect to Appaji.

Yours,

Ram Chandra

P.S.- I am still waiting the reply of the queries about Dinesh to arrive at the correct solution about timely and untimely death. He failed in Biology by one mark and in Hindi by 3 marks although he was a good student in Hindi.

Ram Chandra

15th September, 1958

My dear Revered and beloved Gurudev,

Please accept my humble pranams. I received today a letter from Shri Ishwar Sahaiji about Dr. Sen with enclosures of your letters to him. It is a sad thing and I only pray that these events do not occur again and again to cause mental worry to you in your present state of health. I shall take good care of myself in respect of such gentlemen as Dr. Sen. Please permit me to say that I do not know why I did not have a good opinion of him even when you had written to me about him in your letters.

I am more concerned with the report that your health is not good and you are in fact not improving at all owing to one reason or another. I am taking this opportunity of imploring you to take care of the physical as it is very necessary for some time to come, though you may yourself think that you would be more efficient when you give up this body than when in it. I for one must plead that till a particular state of verification of the infinite possibility of the Spirit is had here and now our Mission may be one more hope and not a realisation. I wonder whether it is not the attractiveness of Shri Aurobindo. By the by, I have to bring to your kind notice that the Aurobindonites have not published my address at Calcutta nor my contribution invited by them in America. That is how the wind is blowing. This throws on me the burden of having to prove that our path is higher and fuller and more dynamic than that of Shri Aurobindo. I do not know how I could do it. Indeed I have been more than feeling worried about the constant invasions of my private thoughts and anxieties etc., even during the transmissions, though again I verified and found that the abhyasis are not interfered with by them. This is the general condition. I am praying as to when I would be in that condition of 'Tam', and when I would distinctly be able to verify the so called centres etc. and appreciate the progress made to that ultimate state. I am so sorry to pester thee with these problems of mine. Shri Manjunath Iyer wrote to me today that he has been feeling lighter and calmer in mind and that he would go over here in the beginning of October or the end of September. All other things are going on fairly well.

I found that I could not write much these days for I feel that a real and fully authentic work must come from realisation and investigation. How it will be possible to 'compete' with Shri Aurobindo or others so that a higher note and authentic experiences and directions and laws can be presented I do not know. I do not know whether I have at all a part to play in that regard. I tried to read Dr. Radhakrishnan — I found at first difficulty — at another point I found it rather dark all over. Yet is he not today at the very top — from where does he get his power? even as Shri Aurobindo?

You wrote to me about Nehruji once recently. Yes I had a funny dream a few years ago (3 yrs) and that was when we were as if old friends. Yet we have not even met, not to speak of being known. If he believes in higher spirituality it is only when he finds the barrenness of socialism and Radhakrishnan's humanism or Buddhism Hinduised.

All children are keeping fit. May I pray that the unconscious influence of Sri Dinesh's death will not affect your health any more and that Thou wilt regain perfect Health. The Mission has need for Thy presence and physically and all through. Please assure me that Thou wilt regain the precious health.

With loving pranams,

Yours,

KCV

No. C 506/SRCM   **Shahjahanpur, U.P.**
Dated 25/26th September, 1958

My dear Varadachari,

Received your affectionate letters dated 15th September and 18th September, 1958.

My health no doubt has gone down these days on account of stomach-ache of acute nature due to acidity. In the rainy weather it generally happens, but it is subsiding now. There is one thing more responsible for my ill health, and it is my sedentary habit, I like to rest more than to walk. I will somehow try to leave it. Due to this trouble I suffer from low blood pressure also.

I am perfectly sure that the attractiveness of our Mission will prove real and will not remain simply a hope and I feel that it will be proved so through you. When you will begin to bring up the real thing I have strong hopes that the super-conscious state will work as is also the experience of a few of my advanced associates. Before writing the above I studied a little about your inner system and I came to the conclusion that the points of *saraswati* is in awakening state. If any one of us recites the *mantrams* of Rig Veda pertaining to *saraswati* the stress effects the points described hereafter, as verified by my conclusions:-

It will become more glittering if a little more attention is paid to it for which I pray.

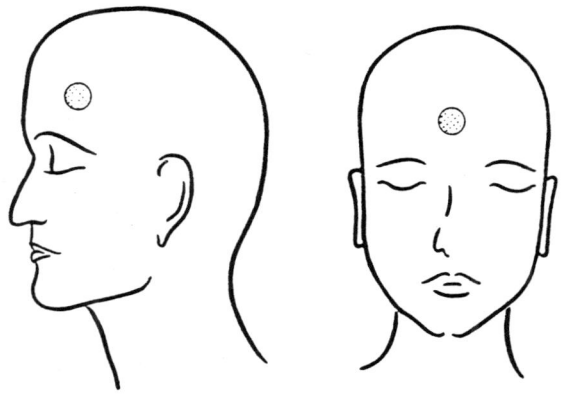

Point of Saraswati

It seems to be the egoistic period of Aurobindonians which may in due course be responsible for the downward curvature of a *sanstha*.

Dr. Radhakrishnan is an intellectual person and you will find him to be mostly honoured. An associate of mine, who was Pro-Vice Chancellor along with him at the Banaras Hindu University described him to be un-spiritual. A very great scholar Shri Jaideo Singh once told Dr. Radhakrishnan that at many places he had failed to convey the real spirit of Indian philosophy and Dr. Radhakrishnan replied that while writing his books he had been interpreting Indian philosophy to the West. If you study his system you will find inwardly dark and a kind of network in *sookshma sharir*. He is of course a learned person but with a limited scope of conception and is not really at the very top. He has no concern with the main source. I expect you also to study.

I take delight when you write anything about your progress, as you feel. There is no question, at all, of bothering me. About thoughts I have already written in one of my letters in detail. You are perplexed when you think those thoughts as yours. When you are mine, everything, good or bad, belongs to me, and you are free. I am dead certain that you are not forming samskaras as I had written to you.

(Your letter dated 18th September, 1958) — How much pleasure, excuse me, I feel when I see in your letter that it does not give you any satisfaction at all, because if a man is satisfied at any stage that means he has blocked the way for his further progress. I remained so restless for years together, but it had some taste. I remember I have spoken this thing before the gathering of my associates that the taste I found in *ashanti* state is not found in *shanti*, but then there came a time when I was thoroughly satisfied, since then I felt neither *shanti* nor *ashanti*.

Dr. Kuppuswami is decidedly improving and devotion has much developed. Since the prediction of Mr. Rodney was there in your letter I also thought of quoting an astronomer who had predicted about India recently, merely as an information for you. As for me I rely on what comes direct, because thinking may be incorrect, nature's work is of course going on, let us see what conditions it creates. In case I find anything worth mentioning I shall certainly write to you.

I am satisfied with your findings about Dinesh. My views about him are that he has been committing suicide all along for three *janmas* almost at the same age. In his previous birth he was a Kshatriya by caste. His family matters, though not very acute, were the cause of his suicide. His present *janma* had the suicidal tendency which was noticed at times by the members of the family, but I was told of these things when he ended his life. If you had talked with him, you would have felt that he is in a benumbed state which shows his internal absorption and carelessness to the body. When he was given any money he would usually refuse it saying that he does not need it. About his age my conception is that, had he not committed suicide he would have lived for some time more. I studied the case of Gandhiji and found that he was to survive because one of the saints had transferred his life when he kept fast unto death. All this shows that the effect of the stars is certain. Master had burnt all the samskaras, *punya*, and *paps* of Dinesh, hence the Liberation. He gave up his life in His thoughts first and thinking of myself when he shot himself.

I received a letter from Shri Manjanath Iyer that he will be going to you on the 2nd October, 1958. I have, however, asked him to fix up with you before going to Tirupati as you sometimes go out on official work.

With best wishes, and love to children. Respects to Appaji.

Yours,
Ram Chandra

Tirupati
30th Sept. 1958

My dear Revered Gurudev,

Please accept my sincerest and loving pranams. I am so very happy to receive your kind letter dated 25/26 inst. I am happy to learn that your health will get improved. I have been wondering sometimes whether your ill health is not on account of your system as such but a reaction to some cosmic and supracosmic events. I have several times felt very distressed when some far off events had happened. Being indeed that personality whose concern is the entire created world, it is just likely for me to infer that. I pray that thy health be restored fully as quickly as possible.

I am leaving for Trivandrum on the 2nd morning via Madras. I get down at Madurai for a few hours and then continue my journey reaching Trivandrum on the 4th morning. Starting back that night itself I shall get down at Trichy on the 5th Evening and if I can I will catch the Tuticorn express that night. If however associates press I may stay that day and start the next night and return via Madras on the

7th night. With your blessings and grace I hope that everything will go on well and my work for Thee will be successful.

The following new abhyasis took sitting from me freshly:

1, C. Sivaramayya Narayanavanam (Chittoor Dt. A.P.)

2, C.P. Krishnamurthy, Lecturer P.B.N. College, Nidubrolu (Guntur Dt.)

3, T.A.P. Anantachari, Clerk T.T. Devasthanams, Tirupati.

First and third are above forty or forty-five, the other is a young man.

I have been particularly happy about thy readings of Dr. S.R. It confirmed my perceiving just a blackness that would not yield. Thanks to thy grace I have been able to break through darkness of the abhyasis. Thanks to thy grace also am I able to conjecture the state of the abhyasis. Thanks to thy grace again I find that though the intervening thoughts come constantly I am just becoming indifferent. I also found that the Master has been pleased to clean up all that I had prayed for in respect of this place and temple and my father and children too. All belong to Thee and it is thy will that works. I am praying to Thee to experience that Real. Regarding the awakening of the point *sarasvati* it is yet too early to say how that divine force will work in me.

I am however very restless in a sense though I am seeing that the transmissions produce peace in the abhyasis.

I am looking forward to the reading that may be made in due course regarding the events to come in 1962.

Sometimes I have felt it impossible to do anything, no inclination to anything at all. My thoughts move only towards thee and the ideal for I feel that not until I am able to experience, attain and enter in that I would be competent at all to speak or write about any of the truths of being or reality or work, or speak about the same.

I have been attempting to find out what some (Aurobindo for example) means by the Logic of the Infinite. It has been rather difficult to make any real sense out of that term. I yet hope that with the help of *sarasvati* I would do it in the near future and submit it to thee.

All children are keeping fit. As you know Chiranjeevis Aravinda Rajagopal, Srivatsa, Narayana, Chitra and Bhagavan Vijaya sree are going for their final examinations and are working hard. By thy grace I feel that they will pass through them unscathed and well.

I am in all likelihood going to Ahmedabad for the Philosophy Congress in the Xmas vacation i.e., 17th to 28th December.

I trust all my sisters and brothers at home are keeping well. My regards to Capt. Srivastava.

With loving pranams,

Yours as body,
KCV

Tirupati
8th October 1958

Dear Revered and beloved Gurudev,

Please accept my humble pranams. As soon as I arrived last night at 12:30 p.m. I saw your telegram about the collapse of a portion of your house owing to high floods and that all are safe. This is one more of the incidents which casts a gloom over all of us. I can only pray that the Master should not be visited by the calamities that men ordinarily are having. However there is a deep reflection within me that this testing of us has to stop. Thou hast no samskaras of any kind and yet why these. Lacking as I say the sight and vision and knowledge we are open to serious doubts. This is about normal. I can only pray that the Master should not permit himself to appear to be a victim of ordinary events. Not that I seek miracles but I seek that poise of peace that passeth understanding. This is my prayer. What repercussions this will have, even as the other incident of Shri Dinesh on the Mission I cannot say. I can only pray that the Master keep us free from dejection and doubt and let the Mission grow from more to more.

I got down at Madurai but only Mazusekharan met me for the second time and got a sitting in the train, whereas Karuppanna swami met me on the 3rd evening and did not come on the 5th. He is yet undecided or experimenting.

I got down on the 5th evening at Tiruchi and stayed for the 6th also. That evening I met the abhyasis Thyagarajan, Krishnamurthy, Shri R.

Varadarajan and others and indeed gave a general sitting and individual sittings to those that did not have any sittings so far. I next morning gave to all abhyasis new and old a sitting and also in the evening. At 6:00 p.m. I addressed the Rotary Club on 'Raja Yoga' — however in a general way introducing them to the subject.

I was confronted with a problem regarding one who sought a sitting and wanted to follow this path. He is one Shri Ramanathan. I was told he met you during your last visit and Mr. Thyagarajan told me that you did not even pay attention to him. He seems to be very interested and indeed the sittings etc., took place in his house whilst I personally resided with Shri R. Varadarajan, Srirangam. His case is: he is suffering from leucoderma. He is otherwise all right. He had an operation for vasectomy and was afraid of yoga lest it should rouse Kundalini and so on and that this operation might unfit him for yoga. I was diffident also to take up but prayed for guidance from Thee and gave two sittings. I however made him understand that the Master's special permission will be sought. I found nothing seriously inwardly wrong — my impression may be wrong. I pray that the Master grant me guidance. Though I did transmission continuously for 2 1/2 hrs on Monday 6th I did not feel very tired. All this is due to thee. But since coming over I have been having quite blank mind and I do not know when the invading thoughts that have not stopped will stop.

Abhyasis:

1. R. Varadarajan Ranga Sramam, 140 Ammamandapam Road, Srirangam

2. V. Natarajan, Keelakalkandar Kottai Alatur Post.

3. K.S. Krishnamurthy, Keelakalkandar Kottai Alatur Post.

4. S. Ramanathan, 2 Andar St. Tiruchirappalli 2, (the gentlemen mentioned in the letter)

5. D. Radhakrishnan Hindi Pankit, National college high school.

6. C.V. Krishnamurthy, Electrical Servant 65 Chinnakadai St. Teppakulam

7. C.V. Subramaniam dispatching head S.M.E.S.C. Ltd. 67 Chinnakadai St. Teppakulam

8. K. Subramaniam, Cotton Press Bhimnagar Tiruchi 1.

9. Krishnamurthy, Vanapattarai St. Tiruchi 2

10. Masi, Vanapattarai St. Tiruchi 2

11. L.K. Krishnamurthi, 7 Butterworth Road. Tiruchi 2

12. M. Sundaram, 1 Narasupillai Lane Andar St. Tiruchi 2

I am sure Sri Thyagarajan will be writing to me in detail.

I am hoping that by the Grace of God and Master, Master will be soon free from all the worries that are of our condition. I dare not discuss more on that just now. I am awaiting a detailed letter about the disaster there in the meanwhile I am praying for all welfare. All are well at this end.

With loving pranams.

Yours,
KCV

Tirupati
19th October 1958

My dear revered and Beloved Gurudev,

Please accept my loving pranams. Since receiving Shri Ishwar Sahaiji's letter about the conditions at Thy place and how the Master had quite a trouble with the floods and how it was impossible to save everybody except with mere cloths worn at the time, and how everybody at home is forced to stay in the front portion of the building, I have been feeling very dejected. When I think of Thee in such a condition, my first reaction was what I wrote to thee in my first letter. But since then I have been constantly thinking of thee. Is it for constant remembrance of thee that thou has done this O Supreme Master.

Again Thou hast blessed me with the vision of Thy state — of perfect state of Blue-colourless state also, and I had felt since then thy occupying me fully though not yet constantly. Yet I am blessed by thy supreme condition in me when thou art in me.

On the very day thou hast sent me the telegram I was thinking of Thee as thou has directed me when I felt myself to be in a confused condition.

I had prayed and again and again I pray to thee O Master that thou shouldst not leave us as orphans in spiritual life. The trials that have visited thee these few months in almost quick succession and the letters of Brother Ishwar Sahaiji leave me in a state of mind that is far from jubilant. Indeed I have been feeling that I have not been blessed with the opportunity to go to Thee and be with Thee. Yet Thou hast in thy great love for me come to me and have poured thyself in me, a person who is almost nothing and unfit for thy residence. I know thou wouldst go on pouring thyself into me till I reach the place that I can by thy Grace.

Master when will I go over there?

I do not know how I can be of help to Thee and what thou directest I shall do as thy body and instrument.

I pray to Thee to let me know what happened at 8:25 A.M. there? At 11:30 I was overcome with a kind of dizziness and at 8:30 A.M. my wife also went through a severe attack of vertigo and palpitation of the heart. I believe that the Master is feeling better.

I had another feeling at the satsangh this morning, Thy presence. Secondly I asked all to pray for the Master. Thirdly I felt that the Master had the old building collapsed as it was reminding others at home of the sad incident of 20th June. The reconstruction of the building is of course urgent. I believe the conditions — after floods — are coming to normal. Please ask Shri Sahaiji to write to me. I learnt that Brother Raghavendra Rao is there. He is such a great soul and I consider him to be more fortunate than my humble self as He is having Thy grace of being with thee in the vacations. As I wrote earlier please do not fail to tell me what I should do.

Mr. Manunath Iyer wrote to me to say that he would be going over to Shahjahanpur after the 17th after reaching Delhi.

MASTER forgive me and us. Be with us and lead us to the Ultimate for that is thy great wish for all of us. Unworthy though we are Thou hast taught us to look within and see thee.

Thou art the only god and power to lead us to that ultimate state.

With love and devotion and surrender,

I remain yours,

KCV

No. C 531/SRCM Shahjahanpur, U.P.
Dated 24th October, 1958

My dear Varadachari,

Received all your letters, which I shall reply one by one after about a week. For your consolation I may say that I do not feel the least disturbed by the collapse of the house which was only 28 years old. On the other hand I feel rather happier in a way. The current of the river, after washing away the Railway line, close by, had diverted its course direct towards my house, striking the rear wall with full force and it was but the Divine grace that saved the portion of the house which survived. Regarding your query as to how you can help me, I think the best way would be to pray that I may remain as happy as I am today, even though the sky falls upon my head.

Shri Raghavendra Rao arrived here on 19th morning and I was very happy to have him with me. Perhaps that was the only happening of the day, I can recollect, about which you made a reference in your letter. He went back on 23rd evening. Shri Manjanatha Iyer also came here on 22nd afternoon and left for Delhi the next day at 11:30 A.M. I could give him only two sittings. I have given over the charge of reconstruction of house to Shri I. Sahai who has enough experience of the work. The reconstruction is going on since 10th October. The winter season has now begun.

With best wishes to you and love to children and respects to Appaji.

Yours,
Ram Chandra

Tirupati
2nd November 1958

My dear Revered Gurudev,

Please accept my affectionate pranams. I believe that all of you are keeping fit and have got over the effects of the floods. I am indeed thankful to get a letter both from Thyself and Shri Raghavendra Rao of Gulbarga about all that has taken place during last month. It is a matter for great gratification that by God's grace all things have happened after all not worse. I have been expecting Thy detailed letter which I am sure will be coming in a few days. In the meanwhile I am writing.

Shri Balasubramaniam told me that he had written to Thee about his proposal to apply for aid to the Andhra Govt. from the G. fund for promotion of spiritual and religious institutions. It is for the purpose of building the Branch Buildings at the site recently acquired. If it has thy approval we will proceed. We might be asking them for Rs. 20,000, and may be able to get a good amount. We have to install an electric motor pump and a main building. By Master's grace if we get the grant it will be good.

I have been going through a very peculiar period. Dryness and even a kind of invasion of all sorts of personal thoughts during meditation and sittings. Yet the abhyasis to whom I was giving sittings had been very much profitted and reached somewhat the states of samadhi both in the satsangh and individual sittings. I have been praying to the Master to absorb me more and more so that I could go beyond to the condition of beyond-mind and recover the memory that goes beyond this life. I do not know at what stage I am. I dare not think that I am just staying at one place. I pray for the Ultimate progress and end. A kind of intense longing has come to me to be able to reach the state of utter negation about which thou hast written. I do not know when it would be possible.

I learn that thy health is not as good as desirable, and thou art becoming weaker — is it a case of sacrificing thyself for us? Master I do not know why I love thee so much so much so I am almost all the time thinking of thee. Thou hast poured thyself into me and yet I have not risen to the heights of spiritual being or fit for the permanent indwelling of the All in me.

Master I have a few points to refer to thee. I have referred to thee the case of Shri Ramanathan of Trichy. Perhaps Shri Raghavendra Rao will be able to do the needful.

I found that last satsangh (dated 26th) when I concentrated on point 2 *pindapradesh* I saw Shri Meher Baba there. Today when in satsangh I saw Shri Mataramdas Omkarnath present. Are these two illusions of my consciousness? Of course thou hast written to me about Shri Omkarnath. Is there any relationship of these personalities to the points or why is there appearance? I am sorry to give trouble. I believe that the point *sarasvati* is now fully active in me. Yet I am very loath to speak or write nowadays.

I am praying for the Master's health and glory and my satsangh here also joins me in the Prayer.

All children are keeping fit as also my father.

I do not know whether the Master would be in a position to undertake a tour in December this year in view of the several things that have happened especially the house.

My regards to Brother Ishwar Sahai and love to all children,

with love,
Yours
KCV

No. C 537/SRCM   **Shahjahanpur, U.P.**
Dated 12th November, 1958

My dear Varadachari,

Received your affectionate letters dated 8th October, 1958, 19th October, 1958 and 2nd November, 1958. I have already given you the brief details of the flood disaster here. I had wired you simply because I felt you might be anxious after reading the accounts published in the papers. The small rivulet, Khanaut, which is only half a furlong from my house had high floods in 1842, 1894, 1905 and 1936 of which 1842 flood was the highest. But the present one has beaten the records by 6 feet. Out of thirty rooms in all, seven have completely collapsed besides minor damages to other portions. The lower walls are yet soaked with water. I am eager to have construction finished by 15th December but that seems to be almost infeasible. Under the circumstances I may not be able to undertake the South Indian tour. I may however go on tour in April although I am over eager to see you at the earliest.

I mark a peculiar thing in me that sometimes when I say "I will do a thing if God offers me an opportunity for it," I always fail to do it. For example this time I have informed all South Indian associates that I shall be there in December 1958 if God offers me an opportunity for the same. But I find I am failing to do it. But when I fix time and date I never fail to abide by it. I thought over it and philosophically I arrived at the conclusion that when I doubt I seek the will of God. The doubt itself brings the contrary result. I shall, therefore, advise my friends and associates not to let doubt come to their mind in any form because the inner force makes it stronger. Swami Vivekanand has somewhere said, irreligious though it might be, that the, "Weak is not helped by God." So whatever we are to do we must make our will firm and corroborate it with His Will as far as we can.

Your opinion about my health being due to some cosmic or super-cosmic events, may be correct. I find that something does come to me inwardly and it is diverted to others. But some of it definitely remains within me in the form of samskaras for the purpose of keeping up my life. My inner voice once revealed to me that a saint is the target of world sorrow and misery.

I am glad to find that your perception of the abhyasis is mostly correct, and I assure you that it will always be so. The first impression which strikes with firmness is always correct. If you doubt about it that will lead you to wrong conclusions because it will create an adverse effect as you have power in you.

Your work at Trichy had been excellent and I must thank you for it. As far as I remember Shri Ramanathan was keen about hearing the experience of other abhyasis in order to draw his own inferences. One or two abhyasis did relate their experiences to him. If he is the same man, he is so very gross inwardly that it will take considerable time for him to grasp its effect. I had declined to give him sittings on the grounds that he was prompted by expectations of miracles and not by the real thirst. I however told him our method and asked him to practise if he liked.

Regarding Shri R. Vardarajan I may say that leucoderma is not a contagious disease. When I guessed about him I found him as you have related. There are some strings inside his system which bar his advancement. I devoted sometime to free him of it when he had assured me that he would take up the practice. Mr. S.K. Rajagopalan of Delhi had been for a week to his house in Srirangam after your return from the place. He also met Shri R. Varadarajan and other satsanghis. Karuppa Swami of Madura is not taking any interest but following his own ways as I had written to Shri A. Balasubramaniam sometime ago.

It is a fact that you have been favoured with a vision of my state and you have also felt that I am occupying you, though not constantly yet. In this respect I may say that 'Supreme' (as you say) has taken charge of you. That is one of the reasons that the associates are spiritually benefitted by your company. You do not feel it constantly but the thing is there. The reason why you do not feel it constantly is that sometimes you are diverted to other work but when you again return to your own condition you feel that. Your feeling that I am automatically with you when you remember me and very often during satsanghs, is correct.

I perfectly agree what Shri A. Balasubramaniam has written to me in connection with applying for government aid for the building of Ashram. You may proceed on with necessary process for the same.

Dryness which you feel is the foundation of the state that will lead to Negation. Regarding invasion of thoughts I want to know whether it happens at all times or at meditation hours or satsangh. I devoted a few minutes every day before flood incident, to clear the sphere of your individual mind and I am sure that I did it to a great extent. What I find is that they are only at the outer surface; the inner layer being quite clear. This process will help you in breaking *manomaya kosh* (mental sheath). However you will soon be feeling free of these surface thoughts as well by His grace.

Your progress is not stopped but I feel that at the point D there is some grossness which when cleared, you will be sure that you are progressing. It is not a new thing with you but is common with most of the abhyasis. Please write to me if you feel like moving in a more congenial atmosphere.

We are in no way concerned with Shri Meher Baba or Shri Sita Ram Onkar Das. About the latter I heard from Dr. P. Sen that he is a great scholar of Sanskrit and well versed in the Vedas so he is worthy of respect. But I do not hold a good opinion about Meher Baba. Thinking again over the inner conditions of both, I may say that the former was in touch with egoism while the latter with Soul.

You have rightly discovered that the point of *saraswati* is active in you, but it is not fully yet. It will be so when the super-consciousness of *trikuti* is awakened thoroughly. I want you to come to it in natural course.

Dr. Kuppuswami is of course, almost free from inner darkness and that is due to your labour. I regret I could not reply to the diaries of associates at Tirupati which I shall do next time.

During *pitra-paksh* I offered *jal-dan* to your mother and found unadulterated peace being reflected from her to me. I had received four letters in Tamil which I had sent for translation to Shri Rajagopalan but since he had left for Delhi for his home, his brother sent the translation to me very late. All of them were orders for the 'Tamil books'. But I have none with me. So I send to you their addresses. You may send the books per V.P.P.

Our Appaji has also improved and he must be feeling peace.

With best wishes, love to children and respects to Appaji.

Yours,
Ram Chandra

P.S.- Received Rs. 100/- sent by you per m.o. The sale money of Tamil books may better be kept by you as I had written to you previously, so please do not send the money to me next time. I want to keep it reserved with you for next publication.

Ram Chandra

Tirupati
16th November, 1958

My dear Revered Gurudev,

Please accept my humble pranams. I was delighted to get your letter dated 12th November, 1958. I am glad to learn that the house is getting reconstructed and will be completed as early as possible. Though we are all disappointed that you will not be coming now we are happy to learn that you will come in April 1959.

It is somewhat of a coincidence to think that I suspected that which you have written about "if God offers me an opportunity". I am heartened to learn that hereafter you will not be in any doubt. I shall also be able to develop confidence if I do not doubt or leave an iota of doubt. This is a psychological discovery which is invaluable as a guide in the future.

There is a slight mixing up of names as between Ramanathan and Varadarajan. It is the former who suffers from leucoderma not the latter.

I am happy to learn that I am in charge of the Supreme and that more and more I shall be able to get out of the invading ideas however superficial. They come at all times. Perhaps I am very sensitive to the pressing day-to-day affairs though I suspected that it is the last gasp of these to take hold of the inner being. By thy Grace I hope to be rid of them.

Surely I would like to go forward pressing further to the Centre, whether it is going to be more congenial or otherwise that is Nature's will. I should like to know whether the points mentioned now such as A,B,C,D ... are capable of being localised at all, even as the point *sarasvati*? If so where?

I did not mention about Meher and others but because they came to the satsangh for whatever reason. I am not interested in them as such.

I have sent the books by V.P.P. to the addresses given. I sent the amount of the books *Reality at Dawn* and *Efficacy of Raja Yoga* (dozen each) as well as for the few copies left last time with me here of the same. The amount of the *Satyodayam* is being kept here alone as advised previously. On the 14th I posted the letter to the H.R.E. commissioner asking for Rs. 20,000 for building of the Ashram, as grant out of the Common Good Fund.

All of us are keeping fit. My wife today has taken ill but I hope by the Master's grace she will be all right soon. I must pray to Thee... ...with gratitude for having contacted my Mother during *pitr paksa* and given her thy darshan. My father's health is fairly all right.

I am enclosing herewith some of the diaries of abhyasis. Dr. Kuppuswami is improving very much. Shri C.R. Krishnamurti has been having asthma for the past one month so much so he could not attend either the individual sittings or the satsangh for the past one month. We had been to his place last week and he is slowly improving.

I believe that all are keeping fit there. Please convey my affection to Shri Ishwar Sahaiji.

With loving pranams,

Yours,
KCV

No. C 554/SRCM **Shahjahanpur, U.P.**
Dated 11th December, 1958

My dear Varadachari,

Received your affectionate letters dated 16th November, 1958 and 2nd December, 1958. Since the winter season has started I have improved a little in my health. Shri Ishwar Sahai is supervising the construction work. I have given him the full charge just as a client entrusts his case to the lawyer. The southern portion, under construction, is now nearing completion. I have set it apart for the rental purpose. The western portion of the house too will be reserved for the same purpose.

Thanks for a copy of the review of *Satyodayam*. Shri A. Balasubramaniam has demanded from me 20 copies of *Reality at Dawn* or at least 12 only. I am therefore sending you 20 copies. You have done well to send Mr. Annaiah Naidu to Hyderabad for the Government grant. Shri Ramanathan has not written to me anything as yet. I received only one letter from Shri Manjunatha Iyer since he left Shahjahanpur. I am writing to him now. Shri Raghavendra Rao has been transferred to Bellary. His address is as under:-

'Head of the Mechanical Engineering Section,

Polytechnic, Bellary.'

He had recommended Shri S.A. Sarnad for conducting the satsangh at Gulbarga during his absence, so I am calling him here during Utsava. He is also earnestly devoted to the Mission.

I am grateful to Mr. Varadarajan of Srirangam for his kind intention to pay for the Mission's publications. The Hindi book *Anant-Ki-Or* has now been taken up by the manager of the Press and it will be out by the end of January, 1959. I have requested Shri Radhakrishnan, the Hindi pandit of Trichy to translate it in Tamil, as he can conveniently do it, being acquainted with Hindi and he has agreed to it too. When the time for publication comes, Shri Varadarajan will be reminded of it. The Urdu book which I had written has been translated into English by Shri Raghavendra Rao, but we could not yet scrutinise it. Now Shri Ishwar Sahai has retired from service from 15th November, 1958. He will do it here in my presence after the construction work is over.

I want that whatever you speak on Sahaj Marg may be taken down so that it may form a valuable asset to the Mission, that is why I had requested Shri Thyagarajan to arrange for it, but since unfortunately it could not be taken down in full I shall wait for the next opportunity.

Shri Ishwar Sahai had sent six copies of *Sahaj Marg* in two covers for the sake of economy in postal charges. They were all for the Branch to be utilised in any way you like. You can offer them to deserving persons, libraries or associations at your discretion. I also received an order from Avadi for *Satyodayam* which I am sending to you for compliance.

You have asked me to locate the points A, B, C, D... It can be done if I give you the measurement of their localisation. They are adjusted one after the other but the difference between them is only a millimetre or two. As for *sahasra dal kamal*, there may be a difference of opinion over my views. I feel it for certain that *sahasra dal kamal* lies within the frontal lobe of the brain and the point commences after it. I have taken these points one by one in case of Saint Kasturi and she has described the condition of each in her letters. She has crossed on from A to Z and after it again from A-1 to Q-1. I do not know when they will exhaust. Now you can yourself put many dots as you like beyond the frontal lobe of the brain with the difference of a millimetre or two. In your case as well as in case of Shri Raghavendra Rao I want to take up several points together but after when you may be able to create an almost thoughtless state which will come automatically as you advance. I do not want to put a check in the thoughts. It should come automatically resulting from your devotion. I always proceed from the root and the same I am doing in all cases. As you advance your training becomes easier because the helping factor of God also develops. Doctor I tell you for your experience that when you feel confused or monotonous for days together or the presence of subtle grossness in you, think that you want to go up to another point for which a push is essential. The reason is that as you advance the subtle divine current becomes stronger and you have to go up the stream.

I am writing to you a recent example of Real Faith. Shri Kashi Ramji of Tinsukia underwent operation for appendicitis, and was in the course discharged from the hospital. After he came back the wound began to give out pus and blood. He ran to the doctor at Baraberi but the doctor was not present. The next time when he went to him he was again disappointed as the doctor was out again. In despair he returned to his house entrusting himself to the Divine care with the Master's thought in his heart. When he got up the next morning to his great surprise he found the wound totally healed up so that no bandage was required and there was no pain at all. Since then he is now all right. I envy his Faith. Doctor I do not know what has become of me. I neither feel devotion nor faith nor anything. I do not know whether I have been born or I am dead. At the same time I do not feel myself weak because that is the first lesson taught by my Master when he entrusted his work to me. He said to me that my will was working in matured state so if I thought myself weak I shall actually become weak. It is due to his grace that the thought of weakness never crosses my mind. When doubt totally vanishes the Will becomes unfailing and this is one of the characteristic features of *brahmagati*.

I often think of my sister. Please write to me how is she doing now. If you give her a very light sort of transmission in her heart thinking that her heart is gaining strength as much as is required for the body, it will be greatly beneficial to her. For the heart the transmission should be soothing. How to know that the transmission is soothing or not. When starting this sort of transmission if you feel yourself soothing it will work out the same effect on her. May Mr. C.R. Krishnamurti be relieved of asthma. Your reading about Dr. Kuppuswami is entirely correct. Due to his devotion he is developing a tendency towards absorbency. I am nowadays late in replying the letters due to my habit of procrastination which has developed on the pretext of displacement and unadjustment of things on account of dampness caused by the flood. Shri Ishwar Sahai offers his sincere apology for not writing to you since long. He conveys his *pranams* to you.

With best wishes to you, love to children and respects to Appaji. I often long for his *darshan*.

Yours,
Ram Chandra

I send herewith 50 Invitation cards of the Basant function and 15 copies of Mission's commandments in Kannada printed by Shri Raghavendra Rao.

Ram Chandra

No. C 566/SRCM **Shahjahanpur, U.P.**
Dated 24th December, 1958

My dear Varadachari,

Received your loving letters of 12th December, 1958 and 19th December, 1958. I regret I have to apologise again, this time for neglecting comments on diaries. I take up your letter only as it requires prompt reply. I had also sent *Efficacy of Raja Yoga* to some Professor in California, but the records not being in proper order yet, I cannot trace out his name. You can write to Patrin Sorokin for exchange of views. So far as I remember I too had once received their magazine and pamphlets long ago. It seems that he does not believe in yoga, which is the essential part of a spiritual life.

I have already taken up the work of developing your super-consciousness, which will help you a good deal when you begin writing on Sahaj Marg. I never took more than 21 hours for writing any of the books, childish though they might seem to be, for I pushed on with my own thoughts neglecting those of others collected in books. But you are gifted with spirituality and knowledge both so you can write very well. The help from the Master, I believe, you will be getting all through, every moment. What that help may be, you will feel yourself — easy approach to right type of thinking as you desire. I shall be grateful to you for your proposed introduction of the Mission's thought at the Madras Psychological conference. The Mission is yet poor in literature and I require the help of able men like yourself to make up for this deficiency. I shall be beside you when you shall be speaking on the Mission's thought at the conference. During this period I have been specially attending to you for the task ahead. There is a limitation between the spiritual and the material and if it is broken, both become one. In your case I thought of breaking it down but on second thought found it proper to let you come to it in the natural course and circumstances and factors for it will be created by His Grace soon. Your *anubhava* about your self as stated in your letter is entirely correct. You will please write to me if you feel more enlightened when you speak at Madras. I also congratulate you for the dryness which you have been feeling, though on the other hand people generally congratulate for richness. As you proceed the dryness which is a sure sign of higher development will be dwindling to take up the next higher approach towards Negation.

Recently a college professor of English came to me to learn hypnotism saying that it was of greatest utility so far as human welfare is concerned, whereas spirituality lacks in this respect. I told him that I know nothing of it so I am unable to help him in any way. He knew palmistry too. The next morning he offered to study my palm. Looking at it he was plunged in a sea of wonder saying that he never came across such a palm all his life. He had only read of such signs in books but had never found them out in any case. He told me that I had got the line of intuition and the Solomon ring and a few other things I do not remember. This made him convinced of what I do not know but soon after he promised to give up the idea of hypnotism and take up the practice on the Mission's lines. Since then he has been following with faith.

I am glad that my sister is quite well now. I hope to have her *darshan* soon. I also received a letter from Shri Balasubramaniam Iyer, after I had posted to him one along with your letter.

The construction work is not yet over. It may take about a month more. I remember Ch. Gayatri along with other children, very often these days.

With best wishes to you, love to children and respects to Appaji.

Yours,
Ram Chandra

1959

Tirupati
January 5th 1959

My dear beloved and revered Gurudev,

Please accept my humble pranams. I returned from Madras last night. I am reporting to thee about events at Madras. I had hardly any good opportunity of speaking about the subject dear to both of us. I do not know why I felt myself in a peculiar surrounding not propitious for the work. So that is the result of my Madras trip. But I was somewhat happy that a gentleman, Shri Ranga Rao, Chairman Railway Services Commission, was anxious to meet me. I met him yesterday and was with him for a couple of hours. He showed interest in the sadhana and I am sending him *Reality at Dawn* and *Efficacy of Raja Yoga*. I found that Shri Vedantam was improving and feeling it.

As for myself I do not know the reason why I was not feeling quite happy and indeed though I do not wish to work myself into depression for I would very much like to be free from it, the feeling of not progressing as fast as I may like it, and the transcendence over the mental state (*manomayakosa*) which somehow continues to dominate, though the high state has been reached, continues. I can only pray sincerely for the crossing over of this hurdle of mental disturbances.

All of us are keeping fit, though my wife's health continues to give anxiety. Other sundry troubles are cropping up but by the constant presence of the Master I trust they will pass without any serious repercussions.

I believe Master is keeping free from asthma and other allied ailments.

All that I can now say is that I am restless and looking forward to that realisation of peace and presence of the Master and absorption in the Ultimate and the Master.

Please convey my sincere regards to Shri Ishwar Sahai,

With loving pranams,

Yours,

KCV

undated

My Work as a Preceptor for a Year (1957-58)

My dear Gurudev:

A report of myself for the year is due to the Master. Of course the Master has always been with me during the work and it has not been difficult at all.

It was on the 22nd December '57 that the Gurudev charged me with this work of being a preceptor. It was however only on the next day that I did it at the Master's wish and in it I felt almost nothing. I was advised to do it in a particular way, that is, to feel that the power of the Master was descending into my heart and from thence it moved to the heart of the abhyasi who was asked to meditate on his heart. To observe my heart and see what is reflected of the abhyasi in it, was the second direction. Thirdly I was also advised not to concentrate or meditate on my own for my own sake for that would arrest the flow towards the abhyasi for whose sake alone the transmission takes place.

Indeed I found that in every case, whether I concentrated or meditated on my own and was seeking descent of the Master's grace and super-consciousness into myself or into the abhyasi the Master's grace was steadily moving into the heart of the abhyasi. So far as my experience goes I felt more as transmitting not when I wished to transmit Master's power, but when I was receiving the Master's power which automatically went to the heart of the abhyasi.

I felt throughout that Master was intent on my training myself as it was one way of keeping me inwardly connected with Himself. I was a channel of His power and got purified by it. It was a kind of self-offering to the Master for His purposes — which has been to lift me to the highest state or the Ultimate.

There were times when I felt extremely exalted during the transmission.

i) I felt sometimes actively willing the transmission.

ii) Sometimes I was merely passively looking on inwardly without making any effort after saying the prayer. Yet the transmission was taking place according to the abhyasi.

iii) Sometimes I was able to see the condition of the abhyasi clearly and was cleaning the system. Sometimes I was able only to intuit or I was somehow suggested the condition of the abhyasi. Sometimes I somehow hazarded the description of the abhyasi's condition, which the abhyasis confirmed.

iv) Master's power works even without my noticing the action.

v) I was able to clean the dark spots and places of the inner being of the abhyasi or even remove some peculiar features appearing to me when looking at them inwardly, of which they were not conscious, thanks to conscious use of the Master's power.

vi) I observed myself having series of thoughts of my own — which the Master has told me come from my *manomayakosa* (letter of the Master) but they did not affect the abhyasi going through transmission. Thus Master's Power is perfectly free from the imperfections of my consciousness. It is PURE.

vii) I however am finding that I rely on the Master more and more and though I feel sometimes utterly depressed yet because of the Master's grace I am growing in constant thoughts of him.

viii) I feel that I am merging in the body of God and Master is making me lose myself in him and is beginning to make me 'eat or live', breathe or move and Be in Him alone.

Regarding the sadhaks or abhyasis

At the beginning at the centre about 30 persons were admitted to this method even during the period the Master was at Tirupati.

After that a few persons have been admitted to it. Many of them were out of Tirupati. It is a pity some persons gave up the abhyas for what reasons one does not know. Some others have been transferred to other places and live elsewhere.

Some have not come again.

Regular members or abhyasis there have been who have attended satsanghs every Sunday and some of them have been taking individual sittings once a week.

The regular members whose reports have been sent to the Master are:

1. Dhond Rao,	2. A. Balasubramaniam,
3. C. Annaih Naidu,	4. G. Kuppuswamy,
5. S. Someswara Sarma,	6. Sitaramaih,
7. C.S. Raghavan,	8. C.R. Krishnamurti,
9. Gauri Sankar,	10. M. Srinivasulu,
11. K. Laksmanan.	

Shri A. Velu Mudaliar being very busy with the press has not been attending the satsangh or the individual sitting, though he has been very helpful for the purposes of the Mission. Shri Chalapathi had a disaster when he lost his brother in a bus accident a couple of months ago. Further he is in the same condition of one who has double loyalties — worship of Shri Venkataswara seems to interfere with the meditation of the Heart and the Master.

Shri D. Subramanyam, engineer, has not come except once and is usually carrying on his own at his house. Venkatesam, Shri Venkatapathi, Shri V. Krishnamurti (Railway Accts), Shri T.A.P. Anantachari, Kuppaih Chetty, Sundaram Iyer, have not been coming for the sittings or satsangh for the past four months.

C.R. Ramamurthy, engineer Cuddapah, has been in communication with me and is doing practice. He has also written to the Master. Shri C.S. Raghavan and C.R. Krishnamurti have not been keeping fit for the past one month and four months owing to cough and asthma and therefore they could not come. Y.K. Saksmanan has been transferred to or appointed at Madras and is carrying on with his meditation. So also Y.K. Srinivasan. Their father Y.K.V. Narasimhachari has retired and is regularly attending the satsangh. Dhond Rao has been transferred to Kuppam and is practising continuously. Shri T. Manjunath Iyer is also very regular about his meditation. Bathi Reddi attends satsanghs only.

GENERAL CONDITION: Of the regular persons I am almost certain that their inner condition is being cleared slowly. Their heart is illuminated and the outer and inner ideas are being checked by the Master's power. I also felt that almost all of them or indeed all of them have reached *ajapa* and have started their *pind pradesh yatra*. I wish to be corrected.

Shri S. Vedantam seems to be speedily improving at Madras. Nothing to report about others, specially.

I feel that almost all the abhyasis feel more and more happy.

Children at home are slowly feeling thy power and influence as well as my father.

Myself and my wife have begun to swim in Thee and seem to be illuminated by thee both inwardly and outside.

No. D 15/SRCM

Shahjahanpur, U.P.
Dated 27th January, 1959

My dear Varadachari,

Received all your loving letters. Basant Utsava comes off on 11th to 13th February, 1959. Meditation as usual from 6:30 to 7:30 both morning and evening on 11th and 12th and in the morning alone on the 13th. Havan on the 12th at 9 A.M. Those who are unable to participate here, may sit at the appointed time at their own homes or at yours. But since you propose to celebrate the utsava at your place, they must meet at yours. Shri Manjunatha of Mysore and Shri Ramulu and others of Hyderabad may also be invited to participate. Owing to snowfall on hills and hailstorm in the neighbouring districts, it was so cold here last week that the temperature came down to 39 degrees Fahrenheit. Now it is again rising towards normal. Shri Ishwar Sahai fell ill but recovered after three days.

For your information I regret to say that the saint of Ceylon, who had transferred his life to me left his body on the 5th January, 1959 at 6:15 P.M., which would otherwise have been the time of my death. He reserved for himself as much as I had in store for me, after transferring my life. He has attained liberation. Such examples are very rare in the spiritual history. Thus henceforth I shall be pulling on with the transferred part of his life — I do not know how much. Soon after I received two letters from two of my female associates stating in one or the other way that they felt I had left the body and then had come back to life again. The same night I had been with my Master in a dream for about four hours and found Him very happy. Since then I feel a bit irritated on trifling matters. I pondered over it and found that this thing was due to the transfer as the saint had it (while writing my Master wanted to convey to you on his behalf, congratulations for the security of your Guru's life). For the verification of my statement regarding irritation I recall to my mind the incident when I had transferred to the girl. I was afterwards told that since that she has become very calm, moderate and carefree. When she got up from the sickbed she did not think her children to be her own. It took some time to give her that sort of understanding.

Now I come to the topic of perennial interest as stated in your letters, as I was waiting to get hints of approach from yourself, though now I have every facility to write in time, everything having been arranged in proper order, except the library books. Much of the construction work is not complete though the work continues still.

On the night of December 25, while I was transmitting to you on the point E, I found you to be moving in the central region. I, of course went with you to ensure your safe arrival. This was due to your unconscious devotion and the thorough cleaning of your system. In your letter of 20th January, 1959 you have acknowledged that, "In a sense I feel utterly reduced to Nothingness." How exceedingly happy I am to write to you, in a funny language indeed, that now you are the tame animal of God and that is the sainthood. My duty as a teacher is now over but as a servant I may yet have a lot to do. I now feel that your bondages are speedily melting away. What I am busy with nowadays is to take out the weight of past samskaras from your *sookshma sharir*, in order to create harmony with nature. As a result you must now be feeling lighter and lighter. God is now Himself working for it and like a dutiful servant I only act as a wheel in the machine. I have yet to do much work on the points for your acquirement of the command. But I have not yet decided how to start with it. It may however be done gradually, just as fever must not be allowed to go down all of a sudden.

Miracles you have got but there is no awareness. I wanted to offer *prasadam* but the difficulty is how to send it to you. The time is now coming for the awakening of *kundalini*, which will create right thinking, though you have a good deal of it already. I will not follow the injunction of Ouspensky regarding *kundalini*, if its tendency for awakening develops.

As for your going to Calcutta on the invitation of the Aurobindonians, I leave it to your discretion, since the problem of leave is really a delicate one. Besides if greatest good to the greatest number in the best possible way may in any way be ensured, the job may be undertaken for the benefit of the people.

Shri Annaih Naidu is decidedly improving. Your *anubhava* regarding Shri T.B. Gopalachari of Madras is correct. Dr. Kuppuswamy may turn to be a useful member of the Mission. Mr. Manjunatha Iyer has now developed thirst for realisation. I am glad that Mr. Donde Rao has got promotion. I often feel anxious for my sister's health. Shri Ishwar Sahai is now quite well, he offers his profound *pranam* to you.

With best wishes to you, love to children and respects to Appaji.

Yours,
Ram Chandra

P.S.- After closing the above letter, I received your letter of 23rd January, 1959 along with your paper on 'Being and Becoming'. I read it with appreciation and have sent it up for the magazine. The above letter replies many of the points raised in your recent letter. The feeling that I have taken you over in all functions may be a reality in view of your silent and conscious devotion. Thirst for merging is a sign to show that you are being merged. When it is complete (to the last possible limit) there will be no thought of 'Me in Thee' or 'Thee in Me'. As for your idea about transformation I assure you that it has already begun. There is such a slight difference between one and the other state that it is neither describable nor discernible. Regarding thoughts, you complained of, they are merely like flakes of foam on the surface of the ocean. I do not reply the diaries this time also as I am very busy with Utsava arrangements as well. You may please reply on chief points if they require.

I have had no attack of asthma since January 1958, though the disease is still there. Mr. Manjunatha was kind enough to send me the medicine for it but it is only to be used when there is attack. I just received your article on Indian Philosophy and modern Psychology.

Ram Chandra

2nd February 1959

My dear Revered and beloved Gurudev,

Please accept my humble pranams. It gave me the greatest pleasure to learn that Master has passed the critical period and I am deeply grateful to Mahatma Gurudev of Fatehgarh for the loving congratulations passed on to me by thee.

I am also moved by the Grace of the Guru for leading me to the central region. On 25-12-58 I felt myself absorbed in the Divine. When I referred to my diary I found that I was increasing my irritability and felt almost a kind of so called deterioration from shanti. This I observed on the 28th December. On January 5th, I did not note anything in my diary. I was absorbed in the events that transpired from 1st to 4th about which I wrote to you. On 17th January, I felt that the blood of the Master began flowing through me and bringing up new energy. It was centred at the heart. I was led to speculate about the Master's constant statement that he would give his very blood if the need came up. I was wondering also about the words of Christ that a disciple would begin to live on His Master, symbolised externally as bread and wine which are in mystic consciousness but flesh and blood. The experience of this led as I observed to irritability of the 18th January about trifling things. I had almost come to feel that all events are as a matter of fact not referable to the immediate events around me but to some spiritual activity going on elsewhere. So I was feeling that something is going on elsewhere, right or wrong.

On 22nd January at 8:30 P.M. I was badly struck by a chair in darkness and I fell down with terrific pain but very soon I got up and took medicine, arnica, which reduced the pain.

On 25th January 1959 during satsangh (6:30 - 7:20 A.M.) I observed that certain figures (rather greyish) left the bodies of the abhyasis. It was rather funny I thought that they were the samskaras of the abhyasis leaving their systems even like Kalipurusa who left Nala.

On 27th January 1959 I felt that I was being shot to the Centre like an arrow by the Gurudev — I recalled the Mundaka Upanishad passage that speaks of Pranava being the bow, the soul as the arrow and the target being Brahman. Surely the archer is the Gurudev.

I have written to the Master in detail about the main events in the diary. I shall be so very happy to receive Master's remarks on the above.

I have written to Aurobindonians that I would be able to go over there only for a couple of days and if they so wish I could be there on the 26th and 27th; that means I would have to leave this place on the 25th and return on the 28th or 1st March. Please be with me all through the period.

I yet pray that I may be able to feel the whole thing. I prayed for the entry into the Divine — and merging which thou writest is taking place. I am hopeful that it will be soon, for I have a thirst for such experience in a radical and continuous manner.

I pray for the Master's long life and presence amongst us. You have written about *prasadam* to be given to me. I know it could be done by thee.

My wife's health is indeed causing anxiety and I pray to the Master for her recovery and health. Thy watch on her is constant and I have no doubt she will get all right soon. All children are keeping fit.

You can surely take your own time for the diaries.

I am glad to learn that Shri Ishwar Sahaiji is much improved in health. Shri Balasubramaniam has gone to Tirumangalam for his son's marriage.

We will celebrate the Utsav as directed.

With loving pranams, Yours,
KCV

No. D 60A/SRCM   **Shahjahanpur, U.P.**
Dated 9/18th February, 1959

My dear Varadachari,

Received your affectionate letters of 22nd January, 1959 and 2nd February, 1959. I have gone through your introduction on 'Indian Philosophy and Modern Psychology', which has nicely been dealt with. It inspires me with hope that now the Mission will not remain poor in literature, and the Sahaj Marg philosophy will come to light more and more.

I have also gone through your annual report, and am quite satisfied with your work. I hope it will be more efficacious, onwards, since the calibre of the preceptors, too, counts much. I tell you one of the most striking features of Sahaj Marg. Under the system, the very first sitting sows the seed of liberation within the abhyasi. Every preceptor of our Mission does the same, though unknowingly. To tell you confidentially, if an abhyasi has unflinching faith and practises, even a little if not much, with devotion, he will ultimately gain liberation, because the seed which has already been sown, develops by faith and devotion. My Varadachari, to tell you frankly, all that I got for my spiritual state, whatever it might be, was got very cheap, so I want to distribute it for no price at all. You will laugh at me if I say that I used to meditate only for 4 or 5 minutes every day, but there was one thing, by His grace I remained absorbed all the while in the sacred thought of the Master. He is the only God to me. I attach no importance to liberation. Rather I am one who can even sacrifice it at the altar of love for the Master.

With reference to your sentence, "so far as my experience goes... to the abhyasi", I may say that I feel I must see the day when you are not able to know even who transmits — you or the Master. Nor even you feel giving suggestions for the flow of Divine Current tended towards the required moulding of the abhyasi.

Your readings about all the abhyasis is correct. Shri Vedantam is indeed improving speedily and devotion is developing in him unconsciously. Persons who are attending your satsangh and have attended regularly for some time at least get a start of *ajapa*. It is often the case with certain people that they leave off after practising for some time. It is not a new thing with you but it has also been with me as well as with my Rev. Master. There can be several reasons for that. Firstly, they have no real thirst but start the practice merely for the satisfaction of their curiosity. Secondly, sometimes the force of *samskara* becomes so strong that they get entangled in it. But this happens with a bit advanced abhyasis of a few years standing. There may sometimes be a few who join satsangh with a desire to secure help for the fulfillment of their desired purpose. A man having real thirst cannot leave the real method, when he has access to it once. Sometimes it also happens that if a man is overdosed, he avoids satsangh till the thing gets digested.

Regarding your view about Shri A. Balasubramaniam I also felt the same when he joined satsangh but by way of respect for Shri Ramana, I did not disclose it to him or to anybody else. Whatever you observed in the image of Ramanaji is the true picture of his condition. Shri Ramana, about whom I had written to you a short while ago, proceeded in a peculiar way, not straight to but on the right and left side of the main point. I tell you one very important thing, that the image of a saint can be taken to heart only if his *indriyas* have come to their original state, and the saint is completely merged (*laya*) in Brahm. If he is short of the mark, the disciple, taking up his image will also be short of the mark.

Regarding Mr. Someshwar Sharma, your reading is quite correct. Now, Doctor! What do you say now about your reading of which you complained so often. I do not find even 1% error in your reading. Your reading of yourself, on about 17th January, is also correct so far as blood is concerned. During the period, I was trying to give your *indriyas* a fresh energy of the original form, which I had stated in my last letter as taking out weight of *samskara*. At 8:30 P.M. on 22nd January I noted down on my writing pad that at 8:20 P.M. I felt unsettled and confused.

My thought at once ran to you and convinced me that you were in trouble at the time. This condition lasted for about 10 minutes after which I was naturally diverted to the depth of my condition. Will you please inform me if you are alright now. The removing of the weight of *samskara*, in which I was a good deal successful, resulted in *bhoga*, though its intensity was greatly reduced so that as one might say that in place of a dagger you might have had only a needle to face with. January 25 (satsangh) — they were no doubt the *samskaras* of abhyasis which had left their system. January 27 — That which happened on December 25, led you to believe at different times that you had been shot to the centre by the benign hand of the Master.

About a week ago I thought of starting a training centre at Mysore, connected with your branch, under Shri Manjunatha Iyer. When I was at Mysore in 1945, I formed an impression that there was a good field there, provided one tackles the situation rightly. But Shri Manjunatha is very weak and advanced in age. I cannot say for certain whether he will get enough time for the work. I therefore leave this matter to your discretion. If perchance you go to Calcutta please inform Mr. P.N. Medayil (opp. Express Dairy Co. Ltd., Bhupenroy Road, Behala, Calcutta-34) the date and time of your arrival and the place of your stay. Sister's health is causing me anxiety. I shall pray for some energy to her to recoup her health.

With best wishes to you, love to children and respects to Appaji.

Yours,
Ram Chandra

No. D 60/B/SCRM   Shahjahanpur, U.P.
                         Dated 18th February, 1959

My dear Varadachari,

By His Grace the Utsava is successfully over. Of the participants from far off places two were from Assam and Shri Sripati Sarnad from Gulbarga and Shri Ramchandra Rao from Sedam. My Tamilian brother Shri S.K. Rajagopalan of New Delhi also joined. A new training centre has now been opened under Shri S.K. Rajagopalan as its prefect. The centre will be directly connected with the Headquarters. On Raghavendra Rao's recommendations, Shri Sarnadji has also been made the prefect and he is permitted to carry on the work of satsangh at Gulbarga, under the instructions of the preceptor of the branch.

I forgot to write to you previously that in the first week of January, I saw in a dream that I was at Tirupati and was dining with you in separate dishes. There were a few toys placed near your dish. As the dream was seen soon after your entry into the Central region so it must have some meaning. For this reason I write it to you. As far as I remember you were taking sweet rice at that time. That means you had got the real food, but taking into account the infiniteness of God, you may well be presumed to be yet playing with the toys like a child. That is a good lesson for us all.

I hope your celebrations at Tirupati on the Basant day must have been very successful, supplemented with the Divine Grace — Calm and Quiet.

The construction work is almost over except for some minor details which might take a day or two more. I have now taken up the repairs of another house which was in a run-down condition even before floods.

Shri Sarnadji and Shri R.C. Rao offer you their profound *pranam*.

With best wishes to you, love to children and respects to Appaji.

Yours,
Ram Chandra

P.S.- Mr. C.R. Ramamurti writes that he can not sit with his eyes closed. Please tell him to write to me about it now. Moreover, if you exercise yourself a little, imagining that the cause which give rise to it is removed, it shall be cured. When closing of eyes is inconvenient to him, he can meditate with open eyes.

Ram Chandra

4th March 1959

My dear Revered Gurudev,

Please accept my humble pranams. I believe all of you there are keeping well. I am glad to inform you that we are all well, and my wife's health I believe will improve hereafter thanks to Thy grace.

I wrote to you about my not being permitted to go to Nawadwip by the University. It was undoubtedly my inner wish and it has come to pass. However I must confess to a deep regard for the scholarship and versatility of Shri Aurobindo.

I am so very happy that I have the blessings and appreciation and approval of my Master for the work so far done and being done here.

I am happy to learn that Master is thinking of a centre for Mysore. I shall sound Shri Manjunath Iyer and let me have his response.

Shri Venkatanarasimhacharya (postmaster uncle of mine) celebrated the Gayatri Upadesa — *uppanayana* of his four sons, two of whom are already abhyasis, Y.K. Vedantam, and K. Lakshmanan. I officiated for *brahmopadesa* for one of his sons — Y.K. Kasturirangan. I believe thy blessings are with them.

I am free from all the ill effects of the event on 22nd January. Some small things are however always happening but I have not been able to pay heed to them.

The dream you have written about on February 18, is really suggestive. I was constantly thinking that God and Master ought to be my food and by that food alone I must grow. No wonder that Master saw me taking sweet rice. However Master, let me inform you nowadays I am unable to sit up as such but bow down to Thee all the time and praying for absorption and experience of my state free from the mental fluctuations.

We all are anxious to know when Thy tour to the South will be undertaken. I shall be glad to know the same.

Master this year Thou wilt be completing Thy 60th year on 30th April 1959 or 27th April (Indian calendar). By Thy grace I should like to start the construction of the Ashram Building in a modest way on that date. We do not yet know from where we will be getting our resources but I have a feeling that it will be possible. I felt it so in my yesterday's (2nd) meditation. As thou hast stated everything is done by prayer.

I believe the University will extend my services year after year till I am completing 60, at least. I believe by thy grace it will be so.

I feel the central region in action as shewn in the diagram. The general manifestation of that superconsciousness is yet to be full and all time. It is by thy Grace that can happen.

I felt that Grand Master has thrown his glance of grace on me on the 2nd. May it be stronger and stronger absorbing me in Thee more and more till the Ultimate is reached.

All the abhyasis are keeping well. I am enclosing a few diaries which may be commented as and when you feel doing so.

All children are preparing for their examinations which will come off this month. I pray to the Master to shed his grace on all of them.

My father's health is fairly all right.

My father cousin K. Gopalaswami Iyengar, whom you may remember as the person who proposed that I look after a Retiring Home about a couple of years ago on the recommendation of a discarnate Spirit Shri Ram Ram, had taken thy two books to read. He is now at Delhi, and may go over to have thy darshan. He is aged 78. But is a very active man with a practical mind.

I do not know whether *Anant Ki Or* has been released?

With prayerfulness and love for thee,

                      I am yours,

                      KCV

No. D 74/SRCM   **Shahjahanpur, U.P.**
                                  Dated 10th March, 1959

My dear Varadachari,

    I am again late in replying your letter of 16th February, 1959. I am very anxious to the welfare of you all. Please expedite in intimating your welfare. I believe you must have received my letters Nos. D 60/a/SRCM and D 60/b/SRCM dated 18th February, 1959. You correctly replied the question of the gentleman, who put forth his master's view regarding *ajna* and *sahasra* as the centres of all such experiences. *Ajna* is the distributor of power which we receive from above. Those who meditate on *ajna* feel the wavering condition and not the settled one. I have no experience of that sort of meditation but I think it to be so. Meditation on *sahasra* is better than that on *ajna*. Our last approach is when structure falls off and we feel ourself nowhere, while in the state of perfect Negation. An Urdu poet refers to the same condition in the following verse:

    "Ham wahan hain jahan se ham ko bhi kuch hamari khabar nahi ati" (We are wherefrom we do not get any tidings of our own self even.)

    When we slide down a little for the purpose of work, we feel our own fragrance (the Divine one) in every particle. Unless a momentary glimpse of that stage is witnessed it is very difficult to understand the condition. Think a little over it — whether it is so or not?

I intended to go to Kukra (Lakhimpur District) on the 10th, to join the Tilak (engagement) ceremony of one of our associate's daughter, as I shall not be able to attend her marriage owing to my South Indian tour. But I could not as one associate from Rajasthan came here along with his whole family only to see me.

The examination of my son Umesh Chandra comes off from 18th March, 1959 to 14th April, 1959. His preparation is satisfactory but there is one great defect in him. He reads the question very carelessly and so is often misled. Shri Ishwar Sahai tried to correct it but he has not given up this habit altogether. My second daughter will also sit for the B.A. final this year. Her examination ends on the 22nd April. She is reading in Y.D. College, Lakhimpur. I can leave for South India only when she comes back. For this reason my visit to Tirupati may not be possible before 10th or 12th May. I shall let you know the programme as soon as I receive the new railway time-table commencing from 1st April. When will your vacations begin?

With best wishes to you, love to children and respects to Appaji.

After dictating the above letter I received yours of 4th instant which I will reply later on.

Yours,
Ram Chandra

No. D 84/SRCM **Shahjahanpur, U.P.**
Dated 23rd March, 1959

My dear Varadachari,

I believe you must have received my letter dt. 10th March. This time I have such a great attraction for South India that I feel impatient to proceed the earliest. It is a new thing this time. It shows that our associates there are obliging me by their affection. I am very glad to know that you have given *brahmopdesh* to Shri Y.K. Kasturirangam. For this pious work I do not find a better hand than yourself.

At your present stage of progress it is not essential for an abhyasi to practise meditation, but since I want that the Central region may remain continually active for some time, I recommend meditation still, though as you have yourself written that the Central region is in action.

I remember what you had written about Mr. K. Gopalaswami Aiyangar. If he comes to see me in the last week of April, I fear he may not find me present here, for I propose to leave for South India by the last week of April. The exact date and programme will be fixed when the new timetable is received.

Shri Aurobindoji was really a personality to be respected. His sacrifices and services are marvellous.

I have gone through the diaries of Shri C.S. Raghavan and Shri Dhond Rao. There was nothing new to comment upon. But I have thereby concluded that the internal depth of Shri Dhond Rao is slowly developing and Shri C.S. Raghavan is gradually developing the tendency for realisation.

The book *Anant Ki Or* would have been printed by this time but for the urgent engagement of the press in some other important work. I have now requested him to complete it by the first week of April.

I feel anxious to know about Shri A. Balasubramaniam's welfare. I hope my sister must be feeling well now. I shall be very glad if all my children pass in the coming examinations.

With best wishes to you, love to children and respects to Appaji.

Yours,
Ram Chandra

P.S.- Cold has been subsided but the place is colder than Tirupati in winter.

23rd March 1959

My dear Revered Gurudev,

Please accept my humble pranams. I received thy affectionate letter. I awaited to reply to that as thou hast said that you would be replying to the latest.

By thy grace I learnt only a couple of days ago that they have extended my service at the University for one more year. The University closes for the vacation on the 8th April. I have however some work but I asked that all that may be over before the 10th May.

All children are in the heat of the examinations. Chi. Narayana is doing distinctly well and by the Grace of the Master he may take a First class. Chi. Aravinda Raja is going to the examination from today. Chi. Bhagavan has completed his S.S.L.C. examination on Saturday as also Chi. Padmini. Chi. Chitra will have her examination from the 30th instant.

You will be pained to hear the shocking news that Shri Manjunatha Iyer suffered terrible loss of roughly 30,000 rupees and an additional Rs40,000 for repairing the damage when his coffee estate at Chickmagalur was burnt with the entire produce and plants. I received the letter from him this morning and he prays for Master's blessings. I assured him that I shall be writing to thee today itself. I also add my prayer to his. His body was admitted a few days ago at the Mysore Medical College.

I have been passing through a peculiar indescribable condition, not of bliss surely. I found myself being constantly withdrawn into myself. I realised that I had reached a deep state which was neither bliss nor not-bliss. I suddenly a few days ago, precisely on the 21st morning at 6:40 A.M. when I was giving a sitting to Srinivasulu, two events, (i) his melting into me, and (ii) myself being dissolved into nothingness. It was a peculiar experience during meditation or granting sitting. Could thou explain the same to me? The satsangh on 22nd morning of 43 minutes duration was exhilirating and I found myself dissolving into nothingness. Of course it meant that I could not perform meditations as such during the past two days.

I pray that I may enter into this state more fully, and the manas that interposes even now will cease its activity more and more, and I shall be super-consciously with the Master without break and with awareness of the Ultimate or Godhead and Master.

I am enclosing the usual diaries of the usual abhyasis who have been regular about them. It shows the gradual development of devotion. As I wrote in the earlier paragraph I was surprised about the dissolving or merging activity of Shri Srinivasulu on the 21st. Shri C. Annaih Naidu seems to have grown more devotional as some of the obstructions were broken down by the Master last Wednesday. He came with tears of love to me on Wednesday morning and is now very moved. I told him of the Master's grace. Shri C. Ramamurthy of Cuddapah came this morning for a sitting. He is able to meditate with his eyes closed.

My wife's health is much better now. We are all looking forward to the Master's Visit.

My father's health is also fairly all right. The summer weather has come in full swing. Days are becoming hot and hotter. This of course causes him more distress.

I believe that Thy health is all right as also that of Brother Ishwar Sahaiji's.

With loving pranams,

I am yours,
KCV

No. D 105/SRCM   Shahjahanpur, U.P.
   Dated 10th April, 1959

My dear Varadachari,

Received your affectionate letter of 23rd March, 1959. I was greatly pained to hear of the terrible loss which Shri Manjunatha had suffered. I have written to him a sympathising letter in order to offer him some consolation.

How eagerly I wish that all my children at Tirupati may rise up to follow your footprints. I have a mind to take up the case of Ch. Narayan, not for spiritual benefit but for the intellectual purpose and for character building. It does not mean that I feel no obligation for other children. All my labour will ultimately result into a spiritual life, when they are settled in life. But since they are engaged in educational pursuit, I do not want to disturb them for the spiritual benefit purely. But I shall decide this thing when they are before me when I am at Tirupati, for I always find it easier to make vivid observation when the case is before me.

I am thankful to God for granting you extension for a year more. These are very hard times and your responsibilities too are very heavy.

Your observation of yourself is correct but you sometimes come to blissful state as well, which can be scrutinised if studied deeply. This will continue for some time till the region is free and the subtle particles are all dissolved. That means the greatest power. Generally abhyasis having read about bliss in the scriptures, begin to look upon it with admiration taking it alone into account. It is no doubt very soothing but by no means the end. What I want for all abhyasis is that they may be free from both 'bliss' and 'not bliss' and I pray for the same.

In this connection I may relate to you an incident that once, in reference to my spiritual state at the time, I asked my Master, "Is this the state of bliss so highly talked about and for which you have graciously exerted yourself so long?" He smilingly replied, "But if the state you are in at present though tasteless, is withdrawn from you?" Quick was my reply that I would prefer death if I got away from the state. Before acquiring this present state I sometimes returned, whenever I liked, to the state of bliss I had crossed over, but now from this state of 'not bliss' — the tasteless — I do not for a moment like to get down to that of bliss.

Doctor, my version will be accepted by those only who are well versed in *dharmic* literature or by those who are already in that state of 'not bliss'. But if one likes to reason it out he will come to the conclusion that this is the higher state of *manas*, which always likes to have its own course in a refined way. In *atman* there is no question of like or dislike. It is just as it is. In the highest state of advancement the individual mind becomes an instrument for higher work. If it remains attached with its soothing effect, that means it is playing its own game in its own way. All *siddhis* and miracles are performed through this instrument. So long as one is its instrument, he always finds himself wrapped in it. The orders and commands from the Divine always come to those who are not under the spell of *manas*.

If one observes closely the effect of my transmission, he will find but a little only of the charming effect of bliss, because I want to insert the very essence of God-realisation, not minding whether it is pleasing to them or not. Sometimes, of course, I do give a little dose of light bliss so that an abhyasi may not feel boring.

Doctor, I feel I am intellectually poor. I shall be grateful if you, please, guide me in this respect.

With best wishes to you, love to children and respects to Appaji.

Yours,
Ram Chandra

Commentary on Diary
of Shri C.S. Raghavan 1/3/59 to 15/3/59

Jerks and dozing are the signs of *samadhi*. Different colours which are sometimes noticed by abhyasis, are due to the effect of different *chakras*. About the blue light the Doctor will explain to you the best. When love takes seat in the subconscious mind, the eye witnesses it through the medium of tears. Please try to develop constant remembrance. The best way to do that is to remain mostly in His thought, just like a man who inwardly feels anxious all through about the illness of some of his dear ones. There are other ways too which I shall tell you when I am there.

	Arrival	Departure
1. Shahjahanpur		28-4-59
2. Hathras	27-4-59	28-4-59
3. Madura	28-4-59	29-4-59
4. Agra	29-4-59	1-5-59
5. Hyderabad	3-5-59	6-5-59
6. Tandure	6-5-59	6-5-59
7. Chincholi	6-5-59	7-5-59
8. Sedam	7-5-59	9-5-59
9. Gulbarga	9-5-59	12-5-59
10. Bellary	12-5-59	22-5-59
11. Tirupati	22-5-59	

The rest of the dates to be changed accordingly.

No. D 117/SRCM   Shahjahanpur, U.P.
Dated 15th April, 1959

My dear Varadachari,

Received your affectionate letter of 1st April, 1959. As per programme enclosed herewith, I expected to reach Tirupati on the 18th of May. But since you are to be out from 17th to 21st of May, presumably though you did not mention the month, I make an alteration in the programme. I shall now start two days later and stay two days more with Shri R. Rao, thus reaching Tirupati on the 22nd of May. The exact time and train will be intimated later on.

Shri Vedantam also has invited me to stay with him. I too was thinking of it but I did not write to him for it thinking lest my habit of smoking hookah might be annoying to him. Now in response to his call I shall stay with him during my second trip to Madras, on my way back from Trichy. During my first trip, while going to Trichy, I shall stay with Mr. Mudaliar, who is my old friend and associate.

I also received an affectionate letter from Shri Manjunatha in response to mine. It shows his faith. As for your feeling of flood of His Grace at times while detachment from it at other times, I may say that as your present state warrants detachment at time means that you are absorbed in Him. For myself I can say that I do not feel the grace at all, though It is always there. I feel it only when I take up duality for some good reason and that is mostly when I feel something tending to descend from the

Divine. It is a peculiar state for which I do not find words to express.

Dr. Kuppuswamy is a man of devotion. He has improved decidedly. His letter was full of affection. Mr. Gopalswami has written to me that he will be coming to me long before I leave for South India. But he has not fixed the date and time as yet.

I received a letter from one of my associates at Tibet. He writes that there is a war between the Tibetans and the Chinese and they hear the roar of machine guns constantly.

I hope my children must have done their papers nicely.

With best wishes to you, love to children and respect to Appaji,

Yours,

I. Sahai

for Ram Chandra

After dictating the above letter the Master immediately left for Bareilly in response to the telegraphic information of the serious illness of one of the associates, who had an attack of paralysis. He has directed me to sign the letter for him. He is expected to return in the evening.

No. D 166/SRCM   **Shahjahanpur, U.P.**
Dated 15th May, 1959

My dear Varadachari,

Received your affectionate letter of 9th May, 1959 with enclosure. I arrived here yesterday along with Shri I. Sahai. Owing to heavy rush in trains we could get in at Gulbarga with great difficulty. The same problem may arise at Guntakal for our journey to Renigunta, but with God's help we shall try to manage somehow or other.

How eagerly I wish to be with you the earliest. I want to teach you practically the proper use of power for all things. It took me 2 years to pick it up, though the Master's hints were there in almost all cases. I know your inner difficulties, which you often think of and wish there should be an end to it now. I also received a letter from Shri A. Balasubramaniam asking me to inform Shri Balarama Reddy of my Madras address which I shall do.

With best wishes to you, love to children and respects to Appaji. *Pranam* from Shri I. Sahai and R. Rao.

Yours,
Ram Chandra

No. D 219/SRCM **Vijayawada Camp.**
Dated 15th June, 1959

My dear Varadachari,

We reached here safely and comfortably. Mr. Kumaraswami along with his family and two other associates received us at the station. He lives in a house at a short distance from the river Krishna which presents a very nice view. There are only six satsanghis here. Three of them are gents and the three ladies. Mrs. K. Swami usually deals with the ladies. Some people here, maybe about 50 or 60 in number, know about the Mission.

I had asked you to conduct mass transmission for some time which you are doing. Due to this effect, the intensity inside has subsided, as I see it now. But something still remains at the surface and a little adjacent to it.

The work relating to yourself, which I had started at Tirupati is now being done by the Divine Itself and you must be feeling it if you study closely. It is indeed something very great and which when completed may entitle me to my *dakshina* according to our ancient culture.

I am happy to inform you that Shri Raghavendra Rao of Bellary arrived here this morning and shall stay till my departure. I shall leave on the 17th positively.

Now for the sake of amusement I may relate a few funny incidents that have come to my knowledge. When Shri K. Swami occupied this house, the bug menace there was great that all drugs and medicines applied for the purpose failed to stop their heavy raids. For some time he was greatly worried not knowing what else to do. At last finding no other alternative he resorted to prayer and meditation. As a result today we find not a single bug troubling us here.

Another incident equally funny relates thus. Once he was staying with some of his friends in the same room. One of them, being in the habit of snoring heavily was a source of great trouble to all of them. Finding no other solution he again sat down for meditation. For a time the snoring increased abnormally but afterwards it subsided and he was quite calm for some time, during which time they all went into sound sleep. Anyhow there was the least disturbance that night and all of them had a good sleep.

Has Mr. Muthia Datta gone back to his place? I feel his son has now recovered and he will know of it after studying it for sometime. There is still a little heaviness in the parts just above the temples, though it is not related to the original complaint. However, I shall see to it later on.

The weather here nowadays is not very hot and people generally say that this year the intensity of heat was exceptionally low. Thus we may think ourselves fortunate in this respect.

Shri R. Rao, K. Swami and I. Sahai offer you pranams. I remember Gayathri very much since she is the youngest of all my children.

With best wishes, love to children, and respects to Appaji,

Yours,
Ram Chandra

No. D 236/SRCM   **Shahjahanpur, U.P.**
Dated 24th June, 1959

My dear Varadachari,

Your affectionate letters of 16th and 17th were waiting our arrival here. We reached here on the 21st evening. My departure from Vijayawada was due on the 17th. But on the earnest request of Shri Raghavendra Rao, S.P. of Hyderabad I had to extend my stay for a day more. He proposed to see me at Vijayawada on the 18th along with Shri Ramullu Ji. But on account of I.G.'s visit to Hyderabad on the date he could not leave the station. However

Shri Ramullu Ji alone came to me for a day. I now feel that he will continue the practice, in spite of the sarcastic remarks of his friends who say that it is not meant for a young man like himself and even that he seemed to be going mad by the effect. This is the mentality of the cultured society of our sacred country.

All my children here have passed their examinations, Km. Chhaya, her B.A. Final, Km. Maya, her Inter Exam. and Chi. Umesh, his H.S. Exam and the youngest, Chi. Sarvesh, his V Class Exam. The question of Chhaya's and Padmani's marriage is now causing me some anxiety. I shall now pray for a suitable match for each of them. Sister's selection of the saris has been much approved by my daughters.

Since Chi. Narayan is a promising boy I like him to sit up for the competitions of P.C.S. and I.A.S. or any other such Exams. I shall write for him to Shri S.K. Rajagopalan of New Delhi who will advise me on the matter, after consulting Capt. L.N. Srivastava and Shri Rohan Lal, M.P.

I have also written to Shri Vedantam enquiring about the movement in his chest. This is all due to my nature of speediness in dealing with the abhyasis with a view to save their time as far as possible. I had awakened his Heart, though much before time, and I assure you that there can be no harm by it. But since he feels so, I now make it a little milder. Look here, Doctor, these are the handicaps which I often come across when I try to touch the higher centres at a premature state and though I do it with the greatest care still something or other often comes in in almost all such cases, which I mend and adjust as far as possible without retracing back from the step arrived at.

Your feeling of frustration might be due to the effect of old habit, which may not likely linger long. The intensity I found in you when I was at Madras has now subsided except say for 2% only. So mass transmission is now not essential for you, though you can be on with it if you like taking up any place you choose. When I peep into you I am filled with inexpressible rapture and the soothing effect thereof begins to reflect upon me too. For a hint I may say that if you study well you will find yourself becoming a 'dead man'. This is the state which I have expressed as that of a living dead, and that is in fact the beginning of *turiyatita*. The particles of the body have for the most part been transformed into energy and the process is going on still, which in due course will result into the Ultimate.

As a worldly man I do feel when I depart from my dear associates and I try to utilise the moments at my disposal for looking on them as much as I can. It may probably be that, which you mean to refer to in letters.

I am happy to hear of the *Upanayanam* celebrations of Chi. Narayan and Chi. Bhagwan. May they be bestowed with all the Master's blessings. The remembrance of respected Appaji is extraordinarily keen this time since I returned from South India.

Ishwar Sahai is leaving for Lakhimpur Kheri today in the afternoon.

With best wishes to you, love to children and respects to Appaji,

Yours,
Ram Chandra

On 17th June, night 1:30, time Shri Annaiah Naidu stepped into the *ajna chakra*, of his own accord and its yatra is commenced.

Sending herewith 10 copies of the *Reality at Dawn*.

No. 256/SRCM **Shahjahanpur, U.P.**
Dated 4th July, 1959

My dear Varadachari,

Received your affectionate letter dated 29th June. I had already replied your previous letter under this office No. D 236/SRCM.

I am deeply interested with Chi. Narayan and equally so with other children. But since the problem of Chi. Narayan arises itself I am also of opinion that he should be sent to some other University for a year to take research work. He will do well as a lecturer and will find the job peaceful. Shri Venkateswara University is not fit for such a conscientious boy where merit is not weighed. After securing such a job if circumstances favour us we will attempt for competitive exams.

I am very glad to know that *Upanayanams* of Chi. Narayana and Bhagavan is going to take place on 13th July. May the blessings of the Master be pouring in every fibre of their beings. I would have attended the function personally had the place would have been 3 or 4 hundred miles off. Still if I remember I will be there in some other way to take part in this sacred occasion.

I meditated on your form for about 3 or 4 days and I felt soothing. I tell you reason for doing so. The silent force was marking within you with enormous speed and I wanted to reduce it. Since I cannot catch the Divine Hand I took part in it with the result that the velocity decreased and the benefit remained the same. I am happy to note that you are greatly interested in the work of the Master and the Mission, please be sure that you will enrich the Mission with teachings, writings and speeches. I have strong hope that by His grace you will not suffer any obstruction. I expect that God will give you more than what you can conceive of. A few days ago I examined your kundalini and I found that it is taking turn towards its awakening and the work started which you already felt, but there is some heavier light still which when removed it will come to its full awakening.

Both the bones of the right wrist of my youngest son Chi. Survesh got fractured on 3rd July. Bones are adjusted rightly as the screening revealed and there is no matter of anxiety.

Love to children. Respect to Appaji.

With best wishes,

Yours,
Ram Chandra

9th July 1959

My dear revered and beloved Gurudev,

Please accept my humble pranams. I wrote to you yesterday immediately after receipt of yours dated 4th instant. I forgot to write certain other things.

I am enclosing my re-draft of page 29 of the translation of *Commentary on the Ten Commandments*. I rearranged the material a little in order to give continuity. I do not know whether it is right. I shall be glad to know whether the typescript has been perused by Brother Ishwarji. On hearing from you I shall begin to write my foreword and send the same to you.

Regarding my own experiences during the past one month, they have been marvellous in some senses and I believe I have yet to realise the fullest meaning of the Divine Flow into me. I believe sometimes that the whole being is vibrant with the energy and appears even so light and the experience is somewhat peculiar and indescribable. As thou hast stated, I believe the process of transformation of all the particles into divine energy is what has led to these sensations. However as I wrote earlier I pray to the Master that the lower centres are purified in such a way that they will not interfere with the Highest movement and indeed will transform their functions so as to be purest instruments of the Divine Master. I pray the duality that I witness may be removed and I experience perfect Oneness with the Master. It is a kind of restlessness, I believe it is healthy and divine.

I am fully convinced Master that the Divine will lead me to the work and that by His grace I shall have no kind of obstruction from whichever quarter. I am also convinced that I cannot measure the glory of God and the Master and cannot conceive of what they can grant to me in this work.

As I wrote to you, I am keeping Chi. Narayana here itself for a year more for advanced work and then make him get into a College as Lecturer. Maybe the forces here may be changed by Thy Grace for it is one of my desires and ambitions that Shri Venkatesvara University and Tirupati itself and the shrine have to be thoroughly cleaned and purified so that the Centre may be the finest in South India. I am even here sure that my humble wish will find approval from the Master and it will be done soon. More and more it has become clear to me that cleaning of the Indian soul from within is absolutely necessary and urgent and that Master's method of transmission will bring out quick and immediate results in the souls of the people.

Master I shall do all that the Master wants me to do for the cause of transformation of the minds of the people everywhere and primarily now in India.

Arrangements for the *Upanayanam* are proceeding and I am supremely happy that Master will be here in his celestial way on that date and make the intelligence of the boys grow to their real and fullest stature and make the Grace of the Master flow through every fibre of their beings so that they may really become transformed and divinised. Such a grace has been unheard of and blessed indeed are these children of thine.

My father is quite all right. Yesterday I had a close and intimate talk with my uncle and disabused him of many of his notions and tried to put him in the Sahaj Marg way, more closely.

Regarding Shri Annaih Naidu I am happy to find that he is responding very nicely. Regarding Shri Hanumantha Rao (82 year old gentleman) I find that his intellectual curiosity and comparative assessment overshoots its mark and I believe that will be rectified soon. Dr. G. Kuppuswamy is progressing satisfactorily, so also C.S. Raghavan and C.R. Krishnamurti and Somesvara Sarma. Shri S. Subramaniam has become regular. Shri Gauri Sankar is getting transferred to Bezwada from Bangalore and I shall ask him to get into touch with Shri Kumaraswami. I am keeping the diaries with me after study and shall send them whenever I think it to need getting instructions from Thee.

I believe all children there and Shri Suresh are well and the latter getting better. With loving pranams,

yours as body,
KCV

No. D 285/SRCM   **Shahjahanpur, U.P.**
Dated 16/18th July, 1959

My dear brother,

Received your affectionate letters dated 2nd, 8th, 9th July. Chi. Survesh does not feel pain and bones seem to be set up rightly as the finding of screening revealed. His leg slipped in the mud near the well while he was playing. I fully agree with your opinion about Chi. Narayan. He is very thoughtful boy. I studied the case of Chi. Arvind, Raja and found that he is mentally quite good and physically dull. He studies his course much but does not pay attention thoroughly or in other words does not concentrate over it. Hence the power he has in his brain does not get free scope towards learning. He exercises his brain abruptly and does not try to grasp the sense of the words contained in the book. I have noted to these points for your knowledge so that these things may not retard his further progress. Will you please verify it? If my reading is correct and the boy does not mend himself then the fault is ours. There is no use of having power when we cannot set right our own blood. When we know the disease we must cure it. Chi. Bhagwan is alright. Shri Ishwar Sahai's son has taken seriously ill as I come to know through his letter received yesterday. Before it I had written to him to go through the book. A few days after I will send to him your translation of Commandment No. 6. I shall write to you for foreword when the book is perused by Ishwar Sahai.

I want that the diaries should remain with you and you may refer to me any point if it is not clear to you. I have made the same arrangement in Gulbarga also. Shri Raghavendra Rao sometimes refers to me the important points. You have done well to put your uncle in Sahaj Marg closely. He was closely attached to his own way of worship and Sahaj Marg was a passing thing to him. It is good that Shri Gauri Shankar has been transferred to Bejwada than to any other place because there he will be getting benefit of Shri Kumaraswami's satsangh.

No doubt my life has been shortened by accident which you know already. I was expecting to leave this world at about eighty years. It cannot be said how far I have to live because I am living on borrowed life. But it is of course certain that I am not going back within the next few years. I like to see Chi. Narayan to his full glory before I go. It is not impossible by His grace.

Your sentence that the Mission will come to height in a couple of years time encouraged me and I pray for the same. You have also started the work of the Mission already and the guidance will come from Him. How I eagerly wish that your reasoning be merged in intuition and the signs are there. You make *sankalpa* and the guidances will come automatically. Kabir has said that the *sankalpa* of the saint cannot go without result.

When the energy deepens it gives a fine blue colour. Your feeling that you are charged with power is correct and the Supreme has really taken charge of you. I feel that one of the courses of nature is over and another has started. Before the second process was started you must have felt the state of poise. This time the work started from the lower region near about *kundalini*. I am simply watching and doing nothing. Your lower centres are mostly cleaned, if there is anything it is very little which will be seen after. I also want that Tirupati may rise to spread spiritually throughout. For that you should try when power is given to you by God. To tell you the truth the mentality can be changed over a night. If I say that it can be changed in a second's time then that will be an egoistic version. When God gives authority for a certain work

He does not meddle with the affairs and that is the authority enjoyed by the special personality. Now the question arises as to why he does not complete the work instantly when it is so badly needed. It is a mystery which can be verbally told. There is a general law that when God sends out such a personality for the change he departs as soon as his work is over. It is quite possible that he may be having some other spiritual work for which his presence in material form may be essential. I am sure that he has finished his work just as Lord Krishna did before the actual incident of Mahabharat took place. But it has not been brought in full swing owing to certain reasons. The things are coming slowly down. In every heart you will find his will working for the spiritual awakening.

Doctor, I appreciate the abhyasis of the Mission for their desire to progress soon and I also want the same. But the difficulty is that I cannot touch the higher centres unless they are needed. When Shri Raghavendra Rao came to Bellary I was so happy to see him that I could not check myself to give him still higher approach. I gave him a sitting and made him cross six points with all their *yatras*. When I wanted to proceed further my Master stopped me. The result is that he has high pressure and tension. Now I am busy in removing the tension and the pressure and the further work is stopped. By His grace I succeeded in reducing it but it is still there. I am thinking and thinking how to save the abhyasis from such pressure while giving high approaches in the shortest time but I could not arrive at a proper result. When I was at Tirupati you observed my mental lake (*chit*) and you found it dotted with ruby like things. That was your unique observation and a new thing to me. Please observe whether these dots are like ruby in other abhyasis also or something blackish. Saint Kasturi and Shri Ishwara Sahai have already given their observations. I shall wait for your observation to study it further. You will also write to me whether these dots are in hundreds or in thousands or in millions.

After dictating the above I received your loving letter dated 13th July. On such occasion God's grace generally prevails. There is no doubt about it that I was present specially on this sacred ceremony. Since you felt a deep state of absorption at the time of giving the *gayathri updesh* I must feel sure that it was I who did it. I heartily congratulate you.

Respect to Appaji and love to children.

With best wishes,

Yours,

Ram Chandra

Just now received a letter from Shri Ishwar Sahai that his son is better now. He has also been giving diet.

Ram Chandra

July 17th 1959

My dear revered and beloved Gurudev,

Please accept my humble pranams. All well here. I believe the same of you all. I believe Chi. Suresh is now very much better and the plaster of paris has been removed. The bones must have set by now and he would be in a position to use his wrists freely.

As I wrote to you the function went off by Thy grace very well; there was perfect calm except for slight interruptions. I remembered Shri Krishna and with a praise for him thy present was given to thy children.

I have to present a few points on which I shall require your approval and guidance.

Shri Manjunath Iyer was here on the 13th afternoon and stayed here till Wednesday morning. He sent me a draft for 1,000 Rs. which reached me on Saturday the 11th. I took it that he sent me the money for the Mission building about which I had already spoken to you when you were here. I had entered it in the receipts of the Mission. But on Tuesday he told me that it was not to be unconditionally used for the Mission building programme. It is to be used only when the total cost of the proposed building has been secured i.e. 4,000 Rs. In the meanwhile he asked me to cancel the receipt and the entries in the books of the Mission, which I did. So he wants me to keep the money in my personal name and if the amount is found for the building I could use this also or else to be returned to him. I am in a predicament. I have now got it in my personal account. In fact I have not opened an account in the name of the Mission as it was necessary to use the entire money for putting up the well and the huts, and now for daily running. As I wrote a cycle was purchased for the use of the Mission (used by Shri A. Balasubramaniam). I request now thy advice as to whether I should return the amount to Shri Manjunath Iyer — he had asked me to keep it with me as he wishes it to be used at my discretion for the Mission building programme. This is to set myself right in respect of such delicate financial propositions without getting into misunderstandings. I pray for Thy guidance and help as I am unable to decide.

Many abhyasis feel that to sink money at the site without proper plan for looking after the buildings would only mean waste. This is what makes them reticent to subscribe and further they feel it may be used for one individual or two alone, the rest would like me to have the training done in my own house. This is a point of diffidence that has entered the minds of some of them. This is also to be thought over in coming to any decision.

I think that the suspicions are reasonable and so am prepared to wait till our finances come to a sizable amount. Please advise and guide me for all this is Thine alone.

The above matter was oppressing my mind till this moment and now I have placed it before thee it is thine.

I have been feeling the duality very oppressive and I can only sincerely pray for the extinguishment of duality, between Thy consciousness and mine, and a complete absorption of myself in Thee. This is possible even as thou hast pierced through the *anandamaya kosa*, and split the atomic particles within me. The maya yet persists as me and thee, let it be Thee alone.

As I wrote to thee Chi. Narayana is here alone and may do either a year's higher work for a degree or do research, for 3 years. Shri S.K. Rajagopalan wrote to me asking for particulars about Chi. Narayana. There are no particulars except that he has taken the B.A. (Honours degree) equivalent to M.A.

of other universities for he will be awarded the M.A. degree in Philosophy with a High Second Class (57.25%). He is the first in the university in rank. He is just 20 years of age.

I have distributed the magazines sent to me by Shri Iswar Sahaiji and the arrangement will be quite all right. Mr. Moothadath's address is: Shri M.P. Moothadath, Railway Contractor, Shoranur (Kerala State).

I shall be remitting the subscription of Shri Dhond Rao separately to you, along with the cost of the 10 copies of the *Reality at Dawn* recently sent by you.

I am forwarding also the diaries of the abhyasis so that thou mayest peruse them and instruct me.

I pray again that I may break through the duality at a very early date and arrive at the heart of Reality-consciousness or Reality, simply so that this restlessness and doubt and so on may vanish at once and once for all. Let the Master take me into Himself utterly so that my problems will be solved once for all.

I am at present in a very peculiar state of restlessness, and old things arise to disturb me. I thought that all these would pass and never recur again. Why do they recur if I have indeed passed all these circles and the world has been left far behind? This is a crucial problem.

Regarding the journal *Sahaj Marg*. I pray that there should be a strict watch over the topics selected for publication at least on the English side. Proofreading leaves much to be desired. I am willing to assist in this piece of work if given the chance.

We must care for real contribution to spiritual knowledge and throw light on them rather than make it a mere machine for spreading the views of some abhyasis alone. The latest issue could be improved.

Regarding the manuscript of the translation of the *Commentary on the Ten Commandments* I believe Shri Sahaiji is looking it over again.

As I wrote to thee in the University what I had written has come to pass, but I have been told that something will be done soon to set right the anomalous condition. This is one more of the gifts that I have been chosen to enjoy by the Divine during the past forty years of my life. The trouble is I have not become immune to these and have not taken them as pleasant gifts, in other words it has not been possible yet to achieve the fulfillment of the commandment. But I have great faith and the colleague is a very good young man who has enoumous reverence and love for me. This is a great gain to me, thanks to thy blessings. May our relationship be good and prosperous.

I am yours with all loving pranams,

KCV

24th July 1959

My dear Revered and Beloved Gurudev,

Please accept my humble pranams. I received your affectionate letter dated 18th instant. I am glad the child is progressing satisfactorily. I am glad you have approved the course chalked out for Chi. Narayan. With your blessings I believe he will get out of his present feelings of frustration and opposition.

As instructed by thee I have begun to work on Chi. Aravindraja for the past two days, I am trying to remove the dullness of the physical and trying to link it with the mind. All this detailed process is what I do not know well but by thy guidance I hope to do it.

I shall do as desired and directed regarding the diaries.

I am deeply grateful to thee for assuring me that the Master will be with us for at least 15 years and till Chi. Narayan reaches a good stage. Yes. By thy divine *sankalpa* all things are being done through me. Where is my *sankalpa* at all? Further the effort to reach beyond *trikuti* is thine alone and I am wondering whether this *kundalini* and *trikuti* etc. are not precisely those that make for physical power or manifestation of the spiritual power? My attaining the central region and the *yatra* in it towards the points A to Z what have they to do with this yatra or awakening of the *kundalini* and *trikuti*? Is it for perfection and if so of what kind? As I wrote I am praying for non-duality.

I am also wondering what is the new course that Nature has taken now in me and what I may expect to realise? I do not know at what point I am.

Now regarding the *manasa-lake* or *cit-lake* or *manasarovar* in Thee and the observation you asked me to make, I have to report I tried to observe it in the case of A.B.S. and my son Aravind and my wife:

The area in all at the beginning appeared to be just a wave-filled area. It was without any dots or specks though the whole thing was light and shade. That was on the 22nd. On the 23rd again in a sitting I began to observe by transmitting firmly at the region. (Of course ABS did not experience anything peculiar and particular.) But I saw that the lake had reddish lines. But it was all in a state of vibratory movement. I slowed down the process and found that it may be considered that these lines are but the points in continuous rotation giving the impression of lines. I believe the points in thy case were brilliant rubies rather than dark or black specks. And obviously the *chit* was in such a placid condition that it was possible for me to see them to be an enumerable number rather than an innumerable one. Anyhow I should very much like to have thy reading. I shall try again with others. I could not succeed in the case of Shri Somesvara Sarma. Obviously they have to be cleaned before the observation can take place.

Shri Raghavendra Rao of Hyderabad wrote to me a letter that he is continuing his practice and wished that I also help his father at Waltair.

I received an invitation today to preside over Shri Aurobindo Birthday Celebrations at Calcutta on the 15th August. I have accepted to do so and pray that I have thy permission as they have been rather insistent and I did not go in February this year. I pray for thy guidance in this also.

In the meanwhile please lead me to the state of Non-duality which alone I believe will make me altogether with Thee always and in every sense.

All satsanghis are well except Dr. G. Kuppuswamy who had a slight fall and injured his metatarsal bones and has got them dressed with an osteopath.

I believe Shri Sahaiji's son is now much better.

With loving pranams,

Yours as body,
KCV

P.S. I observed today the *chit-lake* of the two other abhyasis Shri Dhond Rao and Shri R. Annaih Naidu. But I could hardly arrive at that clear condition in them though I transmitted to it for more than 20 minutes. This confirms my view that it is at this point that the descent to the inversion happens to the lower plane of existence or the *pind pradesh* which is in latency here. I do not know whether it is an index of a highly purified condition to have the dots of ruby colour in it revealing the *mani padma* of the Buddhist chant. The head decoration of Buddha containing petals of the lotus or more correctly the *manis* (gems) is the high seat of Boddhi, perhaps. But I am conjecturing here and would certainly be illuminated by Thy Grace.

I pray most intensely to Thee for the change of the consciousness. I was reading the Yoga Sutras of Patanjali with the commentary of Vyasa and also of Vacaspati. I read that it is the samadhi or trance state that reveals the nature of the particulars (atoms as individual objects and *purusas* (souls) which are distinct from one another or *visesas*. This is a very revealing thing and they hold that neither *pratyaksa* nor *anumana* nor *sabda pramanas* can reveal the particular for they are concerned with the general alone. Thus they seem to accept the Vaisesika theory as acceptable at the highest level of *samadhi-pramana*, the real *anubhava* according to Thee; in the Sahaja way, it is *sahaj samadhi* which is higher than the usual trance condition. This is also a fact for Thy clarification, for it reveals that one can know the entire ray of each individual soul in that condition. Whether it is revealed to oneself or not again is for the Master to let me know. I am praying that such a condition may be possible for me by Thy illimitable grace.

No. D 288/SRCM Shahjahanpur, U.P.
Dated 25th July, 1959

My dear Varadachari,

Received your affectionate letter of 17th July, 1959. Regarding Shri Munjanath Iyer's contribution I think, since the money has been handed over to you, you keep it in your account for a reasonable period. If during the time you are able to collect the remaining amount you may refer the matter again to him for his instruction. In case you do not succeed by that time consult him again whether the amount should be returned to him or should be detained further awaiting another chance.

The ashram shall not be for the use of one or two individuals but for the good of the people in general. It will be the centre of all activities of the Mission's branch. It will be a fit place for all functions celebrated locally. The associates coming to you from other places can stay there so long as they like and wishing so may settle permanently for spiritual pursuit. It is not necessary to have weekly satsangh there, as it might be very inconvenient to most of the satsanghis. You can have it at your own house as usual. Besides this, since the place has been charged, its very environment will fill those who visit the place with Divine impulse leading to their spiritual advancement by constant association. This may not be believed at my words alone, but may be practically experienced by anyone who is sensitive enough to realise it. We have been inspired for the work by the pious *sankalpa* (building the ashram) for no selfish purpose of our own hence the final success is but absolutely certain.

As for quality of articles published in the magazine the editors have already been instructed by me to keep a close watch over the matter to be printed but there is one great handicap. The articles for the magazine are not coming up in sufficient number so their selection is out of question. Sometimes we are compelled to take in such articles in order to cover the number of pages. Often the publication is delayed for that very reason. Your help and co-operation in work is greatly welcomed or rather earnestly craved for. I believe you will suggest to us means to get out of these difficulties.

I think you must have received my previous letter in which I had written that this time the Divine work had started from the lower region near about the *kundalini*. It is quite possible you might be feeling a slight aggravation of the lower *vrittis*. Let this, the Nature's second course, be over after which I shall think over again. Duality is not in you but the thought of it is persistent. When you think of me externally the continuity of thought is broken and subsequently it is dissolved in you. Is it a fact?

As for the diaries I am satisfied with their progress. They require no comments. All are on the way to improvement. Shri Someshwar Sharma's experience of perspiration all over the body is not quite unusual. It sometimes happens though rarely that transmission produces heat in the nerves with the result that the abhyasi begins to perspire. The perspiration helps cleaning as it carries with it some of the grossness. Mr. C.S. Raghavan writes that his wife also sits in meditation. The ladies can devote only the noon time for satsangh so they can attend to sister and have sitting from her as you will be at the University during that time.

I received a letter from Shri C. Raghavendra Rao, the S.P. of Hyderabad that he felt extremely happy during your satsangh. He has also rightly expressed his opinion that you are a devout soul doing wonderful work in the Mission.

With best wishes to you and love to children and respects to Appaji.

Yours,
Ram Chandra

Tirupati
2nd August 1959

My dear Revered and Beloved Gurudev,

Please accept my humble pranams. I received your kind and affectionate letter last week. I am watching the progress of the work on *kundalini* which you have stated has been started.

I took up the cleaning up of Chi. Aravindarajagopal, and continued individual sittings every day till Friday. He told me that he had begun to see the light in his heart. I pray for further guidance.

Shri Raghavendra Rao's wife and children and Shri Narayana of Bellary another abhyasi of the same place with his wife and mother came last week and left today for Bellary. They asked for individual sitting last week and I gave it. I also gave medicine to Mrs. Raghavendra Rao and Shri Narayana.

Yesterday two gentlemen from Madanapalle came to be initiated. They learnt about our mission from Shri D. Ramamurti of Chittoor. I gave them two sittings, yesterday and today. They are: #1. V.M. Kalyanaraman, 10/8 Reading Room Street, Madanapalli (Chittoor Dt. Andhra); #2. Donthi Krishnaih Chetty, General Merchant, Madanapalli.

Shri Dhond Rao is now Deputy Nazir Dt. Munsif's court Kuppam. He is going to be there only for a short time.

Shri C.S. Raghavan lives at Renigunta. He is an assistant in the Mission High School Renigunta (near Mission Hospital). Mr. Moothadath's journal copy can be sent to him: Contractor, Shoranur (Kerala). This information has been asked by Shri Ishwar Sahaiji.

I am glad to know that Shri Ishwar Sahaiji's son has recovered and it is so very gratifying to learn that Master had gone there with Shri Kashiram. Please convey my affection to Shri Kashiram. I believe Chi. Survesh is improving and the plaster has been removed.

As I wrote to you I am leaving for Calcutta on the 13th morning enplaning at Madras on the 14th evening about 5 P.M. and reaching Calcutta at 8:30 P.M. I return on the 16th morning. The meeting is to be held on the 15th between 9:30 and 11:30 A.M.

I am feeling sometimes that I have reached Master's grace fully. At other times there is a slight separation from thee. However it is clear that Master has been pleased with my humble self and will grant me fuller union in all planes of existence here and elsewhere.

Today satsangh was magnificent with thy supreme presence. I am also finding that the heart centre (central heart chest region) was peculiarly illuminated with a flower-like golden shape and linked up with the lower centres in the line of the *sat* chakras which had become luminous with many threads of inter-connection, below and above too. My head region has been experiencing tension. But as advised by you at Madras I have proceeded to transmit to all Tirupati and Tirumalai.

My father is much concerned with his eyesight. I pray that he may lose interest in what is incurable and turn towards Thee. So too Srivatsa. My wife's health has not been good.

I wrote to Shri Manjunath Iyer thy counsel about the money he had given to me to keep for the construction of the Ashram. I only pray to the Supreme Master to hasten the same and without dependence on any other person than Himself. He too can grant all if He wills and plentifully too to make this an ideal centre for our Mission's work.

Now Master can I feel that I am not separated from thee even for a minute? May this be my permanent condition and luminously too.

With profound loving pranams and self-offering,

I am yours,
KCV

No. D 322/SRCM   Shahjahanpur, U.P.
                  Dated 4th August, 1959
My dear Varadachari,

Received your affectionate letter of 24th July, 1959. I believe you must have received my letter No. 288 dated 25th July, 1959. For about a week I am having low blood pressure which causes heaviness in the brain and giddiness. For this reason I do not reply to your thoughtful questions at present but I shall do it later on. I find Chi. Arvinda (Raja) improving. His right and left portions of the chest are heavy which may be the cause of his heaviness. But by your labour I find it greatly reduced now.

Regarding my period of life I again refer you to my letter No. 285 dated 16th July, 1959 page 2 para 2. The sense you have taken to understand is not there.

I was invited at Jangaon to participate in the annual function of the Gita-Ashram and to address the audience. But I have declined on the grounds of ill health. I feel somewhat ashamed to express my inability to speak from platforms, but when people insist for it I have to acknowledge my deficiency.

Some new satsanghis are coming in at Bidar. Shri Sarnad shall be going there soon, for the purpose.

Since you have been invited, you may go to Calcutta to join the birthday celebrations of Shri Aurobindo. The people may be benefitted by your views. But please manage to find out time to the sittings to Mr. Medayil whom you met last year. I am writing to him to contact you. You may please write to him your address, where you propose to stay at Calcutta, immediately as there is not much time.

Shri Raghavendra Rao's father demanded from me practices which I have sent. I also advised him to contact you often, assuring him of your help.

The physical injury to Dr. Kuppuswamy is causing me anxiety. May he recover soon.

With best wishes to you, love to children and respects to Appaji.

Address:
Shri P.M. Medayil,
Opp. Express Dairy Co. Ltd.,
Bhupenray Road,
Behala,
Calcutta-34.

Yours,
Ram Chandra

August 10th/11th 1959

My dear revered Gurudev,

Please accept my humble pranams. I received your affectionate letter. I believe I wanted to understand your sentence in the way as I have done, of course your sentence does not bear my meaning. May it be my prayer if you will.

I got a peculiar experience which I did not communicate. It took place exactly on the morning (23rd July) of my receiving the letter from Shri Aurobindo Pathamandir Calcutta requesting me to preside over the Birthday celebrations on the 15th August. I was giving a sitting to Shri A.B.S. when suddenly I felt that the Mother of the Shri Aurobindo Ashram offered that I should take over the Ashram. I felt a little confused and dismissed it as an interference. But when after the sitting I was sitting in the Hall, I received this letter and it surprised me very much, for it came immediately after the experience.

I am going to Calcutta leaving Tirupati on the 13th morning and I hope to return to Tirupati on the 16th night or 17th morning.

I shall try to contact the gentleman at Calcutta. I do not know with whom I am going to stay nor do I know exactly how the programme would turn out.

I am also going to Trivandrum on the 20th instant for a meeting there on the 22nd. I do not know whether it would be possible for me to break journey at Trichy for a few hours on Sunday the 23rd.

I believe your low blood pressure has gone and you are feeling much better.

I am praying for more improvement and progress towards Non-duality of the finest sort.

I had another dream on the 8th morning of a European scientist who said that he would show me the soul. He showed a test tube like thing whose colour was greenish liquid. I observed and saw a greyish light passing and it looked precisely as what thou hast described as the near-about the Centre area. This European I could not recognize — but I am wondering whether he and his associate are by any means Gurdieff and P.D. Ouspensky. It was a very vivid experience.

I pray again and again that I may be constantly in Thee and Thou in me in the super-conscious condition and ordinary condition. Several times I am saying that I am in the *sahaja* condition, but feel a little concerned after I make that statement. Is it not funny?

I learn from Shri Raghavendra Rao of Bellary that you will be going over South again 3 1/2 months later, that is in November-December. It is bound to be a very nice period. I am also looking forward to thy visit.

I believe Chi. Survesh is all right as also Shri Ishwar Sahaiji's son. Please convey my best regards to Shri Ishwar Sahaiji.

With humble loving pranams,

Yours,

KCV

No. D 386/SRCM Shahjahanpur, U.P.
Dated 30th August, 1959

My dear Varadachari,

Received your affectionate letters. I am a bit relieved from headache and heaviness of the brain. Shri Ishwar Sahai has gone to Lucknow to see his son who fell seriously ill there. He reads in the Lucknow University and is a student of B.A.(Final). He is suffering from the same disease of mumps and tonsil which his younger brother suffered a fortnight ago. I just received a letter from him that he is improving and there is no cause of anxiety. I received a letter from Mysore, the copy of which along with my reply to it is being sent to you for your perusal. It will give you chance to study the condition of such a devotional man. You will also know thereby that how far he has advanced in spite of so much labour.

You must have read in *Efficacy of Raja Yoga* the wonderful research by my guru that a man can reach the central region having body. When a man reaches central region a bondage is kept so that he may have connection with the lower regions also. If bondage be not kept the soul will jump into eternal peace and the life will be gone. It is therefore certain that one must feel the air of the lower regions at times. This can be the condition of even the highest saint of the world if he somehow reaches the central region. In your case non-duality is reigning but at times, you get the fit of lower region; of course, at the highest pitch of negation the shock is very slightly felt. One always finds room for advancement at every stage. When everything is all right and one is charged fully with 'Divine power', swimming in the central region commences but after crossing the rings of light. To start the swimming, the help of very high power is needed; as my Guru is living permanently so you will not be wanting in such power which may move you to swimming. Tirupati is undoubtedly charged but to the extent that children and babies may not feel it unbearable. But certainly it is a pious place. The hall of your house as you feel is charged better than Tirupati. Regarding the work of Nature in you I can only feel but it is difficult to express in words. I hope that you will feel the result of this processes soon. You will find evenness in your system though it is disturbed sometime at the surface. There is no disturbance at the root. There is a bit of pressure of power in your *kundalini*. I want that it may come to a subtle state automatically. If I find delay in the matter I will do it myself. You asked me at what point you are now. There is no question of point now when you already got into the central region but I have yet to wait when these points evolve their full energy. You will be astonished if I write to you the great teachings of my 'Guru'. Every pore of the body has its own centre of energy and is itself a continent. Whatever is in the universe with its planetary systems is found there in it. They all must come in their full awakening state. I sincerely pray that all my associates may come to that stage and God may give me chance to render such service. It is the momentary work for my Master alone but who is prepared to grasp such power at a glance; so I am trying and trying that my associates may have the capacity to bear this 'Divine power', so we adhere to the gradual process of advancement.

Regarding your *anubhava* about *chit* I agree with you, Shri Ishwar Sahai and saint Kasturi hold the same opinion but I myself am unable to visualize it correctly. Let the heaviness of the mind be over, then I will study the subject and verify it with my Master afterwards. Your conclusion is right regarding the points looking like brilliant rubies about this poor being but why they look like that is the mystery yet to be solved. Your view regarding the descent through this point for the lower plane of existence is entirely correct. A man asked me as to why I do not take *agya chakra* as the point of meditation. I replied that the power for *pinda pradesh* comes in it and it distributes to the lower region. If one meditates on this point he will feel something flickering disturbing the meditation. I shall be praising myself if I say that to have dots like ruby colour is the very signal of the highly purified condition, but the truth must be expressed. I do not know whether Mahatma Buddha meant the same thing or something else. The Tibetan Buddhists chant 'OM MANI PADMA HUM'. There is a miracle of Mahatma Buddha shown to Jains that he sat decorated at one place with the petals of lotus and Buddhas one after the other was seen flying to sky. I hold that the purity of Buddha has been shown in this way. Precious stones are also kept in puja and often the idol is decorated with diamonds and so on. The chit lake was the only medium for him to see the light. We pray for something higher for the abhyasis. If you transmit through *agya chakra* or a little above it the abhyasi will feel light. In case you transmit with the points far above the *chit* lake one will not feel the light but pressure if they are unable to bear the power. We are the sons of the land where Sun never shines — where darkness has no place and the light bids farewell. Our yogis do not infer fire from smoke. They directly hit the substance. When a man comes to the real *sahaj avastha* he can read the real ray of each individual soul and the tendency of the Nature. A little concentration will reveal all this thing. With the help of that power you came to know the condition of my *chit* lake. You also read the abhyasis' conditions with its help. Now I want to enter into self-praise which only my Master deserves, in saying that one of the ablest eye-specialist, being my associate said that there is a point on which if a research is done, the operation will always be successful. I told him by the diagram that this is the point. He tried and said to Shri Kashi Ram that since I told him of my research of that point the eyes did not fail to recover light. I do not remember what it was but he makes use of it.

My dear Dr. trust in yourself as you have got that power and it is developing day by day.

I received your letter sent by you after return from Calcutta along with Mr. Vedantam's note. I also received his letter dated 18th August, 1959 intimating to me about his illness and also that he feels all right while sitting in meditation, that is, no movement in the chest as he felt sometime before. He is a man of very devotional mind and he is free to utilize my services in any way he likes. I have prayed for his early recovery. I am also asking him his condition to conclude if my prayers are answered.

I also received a letter from Mr. Mediyal from Calcutta that he sat in meditation at the time fixed by you and he felt the effect of transmission. He has formed a good faith in you. I will, therefore, request you to give him transmission once or twice a week as you think proper. There is one more way of transmission — that is, when you give the group sitting to the abhyasis think of him or anybody whom you want to transmit sitting before you.

One of my associates who was the Investigating Officer of Veterinary College, Mathura, has gone to America, to take up research work on bacteria, by air on 23rd August, 1959. He demanded a few books from me for America and I sent them. He will remain in America for five years. He is a Sindhi gentleman named N.K. Chandramani.

Mr. Rajagopalachari arrived here on 25th August and left for Delhi on 28th. He will stay there for

3 days and then go back to Tirupati. I enjoyed his company well and had the proud privilege of listening to his philosophical discourses on *Gayatri Mantram*; but unfortunately I couldn't follow him as it was beyond my intellect. He told me to write to you and Shri A. Balasubramaniam that he went over to Shahjahanpur as you and he ordered him.

I received a letter from Mr. Vedantam that he is feeling better, but he writes that when he sits in meditation he finds his forehead centre active instead of chest. I could not make out the cause of it. I will ask him whether he ever meditated upon *agya chakra*. You will please also think over it and inform me if it is due to some spiritual force or to some other cause.

My son Chi. Prakash Chandra has a daughter born on 10th August, 1959 just at 11:30 in the night. Both mother and baby are quite well.

Please inform me about the health of my sister. You can also transmit her a little energy for health.

My best respects to Appaji and love to children.

With best wishes,

Yours,

Ram Chandra

P.S.- Shri Ishwar Sahai arrived this night from Lucknow. His son is feeling well but the weakness persists. Shahjahanpur is very hot nowadays as we have had only a few light showers of rain. Crop is suffering and the paddy is not yet sown except where there are irrigation canals.

Ram Chandra

September 7th 1959

My dear Revered and beloved Gurudev,

Please accept my humble pranams. Your affectionate letter gave me great confidence and I am praying for futher definite and clear approach to the Ultimate. Indeed I am looking forward to swimming in the Central Region. Yet there are times when I feel that nothing has basically taken place; it may be due to the fact mentioned by you that the connection with the lower levels influences this mental state.

I shall certainly do the needed for Shri Medayil of Calcutta as advised. Regarding the gentleman from Chickmagalur, Shri Siddappa, it is a very interesting document. Shri Aurobindo had indeed written in the same way but without the desire for meeting Shri Krishna in person or reality as he seems to have enjoyed that too (his letters first series). In any case there is necessity for a clear vindication of spiritual life, a basic experience that will not be sublimated or cancelled later on. Mind or *manas* is capable of great illusions and steady illusification.

I am indeed very grateful for being confirmed about the ruby-studded experience regarding thee of the *cit-lake* or *manasarovar*. Somehow it happens that I am not always able to study the inner condition unless a little time elapses. I am praying for the full evolution of the energy in each point so that I may be swimming in the *anant*.

It will indeed be of greatest help if doctors are able to take thy guidance in respect of what centres or points have to be treated or taken care of for getting cures. I congratulate Thee for Thy help in the cause of obliterating human suffering and ignorance.

Shri Vedantam continues to be an ardent admirer of J. Krishnamurti and has studied vastly on Zen Buddhistic literature. I do not know whether it is due to their influence that he is experiencing the forehead. But as a matter of fact all abhyasis went through this period of concentration on the forehead centre or between the eyebrows as the Gita also puts it. They get this activity of the forehead and consider that to be a great advance.

I am enclosing the horoscope that I cast for Miss Ch. Prakash Chandra. I am praying for blessings for the child, and her parents.

My wife's health has improved. My father also feels better.

I am happy to learn that Shri Ishwar Sahai's son at Lucknow also is better and recovering from his illness.

I am returning the letter of Shri Siddappa.

I am sorry that the rains are short of the normal, and the place is very hot.

I am happy to note that your low blood pressure is yielding and you feel better.

With loving pranams,

Yours,
KCV

No. D 414/SRCM **Shahjahanpur, U.P.**
Dated 10th September, 1959

My dear Varadachari,

Received both of your affectionate letters. I am exceedingly happy to note that the restlessness to realise the Ultimate in its full aspect, is there. This is an admirable quality in an abhyasi without which there can be no real good. I eagerly desire rather I am compelled to do in your and Raghavendra Rao's case the highest that is in my power. I do not mean that I am a miser towards other abhyasis. All are equal in my sight but where I am naturally attracted to, there the thought compels me to do the most. I am paving the way for all that you want. These are very high things and for that I have to take into account everything connected with it. If I touch even the smallest point of the higher regions without preparing field for its working, which takes time, it may cause extreme tension on nerves. So I have to be very cautious at each step. Of course, I feel greatly interested in taking up higher-most centres, as in your case.

The problems of Mr. S. Vedantam requires deep thinking. It will be solved best when I actually go there and see him. Meanwhile I will do some thing.

I received Rs. 51/- from Mr. Mootha Dutta of Shoranur as donation to the Mission in connection with Gruha Pravesh ceremony in his newly built house on 16th September. He has also invited me to visit his place but there are so many difficulties in taking up the long distance journey, the chief factor being my health. Even then I would not have minded it had there been a number of satsanghis.

I also received a letter from uncle Mr. Gopalaswami stating that his visit to Delhi is doubtful. He assures me that he will see me when I am with you. I am writing to Mr. Medayil that you will also remain attentive to him at times. He wants to come to Shahjahanpur but his financial position stands in the way. After my South Indian tour I shall see what help I can offer him out of my poor purse, in response to his earnest desire to see me. I am a bit relieved of my low pressure. It constantly remains 85 in place of the normal 130. Further fall causes giddiness.

I also received the horoscope of my newly born granddaughter for which I am grateful to you. Has Chi. Narayan taken up the research work; if so on what subject?

Shri Kumaraswami had asked me some questions which I had answered in brief. I send a copy to you, as such questions are generally asked by the abhyasis. Shri Mootha Dutt writes to me that his son's condition is not much better. This is very surprising to me since I feel even now that he is quite cured. The only thing that remains is slight heaviness below the temples which does not at all relate to the brain. I understand that it may be lack of proper intelligence that he might be feeling in his son. But I think since the obstruction is removed, the growth of intelligence now depends upon exercising it more and more. I have written to him accordingly.

Mr. Justice Chaturvedi, now retired since July 1959, has come here last evening from Lakhimpur along with saint Kasturi and her mother and is expected to stay for few days. Mr. Chaturvedi is now devoting most of his time to puja practices since his retirement and is making a good progress.

My respects to Appaji and love to children.

With best wishes.

Yours,
Ram Chandra

Copy of letter to Mr. N. Kumaraswami
No. D 398/SRCM   **Shahjahanpur, U.P.**
Dated 5th September, 1959

My dear brother,

I believe you must have received my previous card in response to your card about the improper handling of receipt. Please offer prayer for it and inform me about it so far. I am rather anxious about it.

Now, I come to your letter dated nil in which you have put in queries.

You are right in saying that lot of propaganda is required everywhere and specially at Madras. We have got only two hands in the body and they do all what is required for it. It does not require the additional hands for its service. They do all the work for self and others. Nobody has ever prayed that God may add a few hands more for the work. You will generally say that two hands are sufficient to serve the body because you have no idea of the addition of more hands. Similarly you know that you have to do a certain work yourself so you utilise them for the work. A man should be more courageous when he knows that only he is the help for himself. If you are not getting any man for the work at Madras you should do yourself believing in God. Never mind if success does not attend in the first step. Work and work for a good cause, should be your motto. The result is in your hand.

It is a pity that Shri Radhakrishnan cannot do even what his health allows. He had promised me to do this work when I was at Madras. The people compel me to fulfill the promise but they do not care to abide by their own, even when they are reminded. It means they have no regard for my services which cannot be bought even by any amount of money. I and you both consume our blood for their making and growth but we cannot expect a better thing from them even though it may be for the good of others and ultimately for themselves.

The writing of good articles depends upon practice. You attempt for it and you will succeed. There is no deficiency in your knowledge, you simply lack practice and not the capacity. When you begin a thing with the idea that you won't be able to complete it you will never do it. The success of the work always lies in one's own will and confidence. You have got ample opportunity for the work. I never allow despondency to creep in me. So please learn this small thing from me, if you feel the examples of the past are not sufficiently convincing. I remember the words of General Hindenberg when at the time of the first world war he was called to attend the Kaiser of Germany for the discussion about the starting of war. He said that he, as a general, had no concern with anything but 'war and war'. How keen spirited he was towards his own duty which alone was in his view, though he was not religious minded at all yet how he had grasped unknowingly the teachings of Gita. We boast of belonging to a great religion but we do not rely upon the teachings of the sages of the past.

Now I come to your queries:

Queries of Shri N. Kumaraswami:

1. Do senses function when one is in a super-conscious state?

2. Is there a stage in which one forgets the body and body idea (i.e., even injuries to the body) as in the state of *jada samadhi* in the course of one's progress towards *sahaj samadhi*?

3. Are there cases in which one reached the highest stage without any experience other than peace (i.e., without any psychic or other experiences) in the course of his progress?

4. How is one to recognise a super-conscious state (i.e., how to distinguish a super-conscious state from that of ordinary consciousness).

Babuji's Responses:

1. Senses always work at every stage of spiritual development. Stopping the functions of the senses means to bring them to a balanced state which was before the creation. The latent motion is always there, in its absence the life will depart. We have only to learn the right use of senses and thus to create the balanced state in their own sphere.

2. We forget the body idea and the soul idea as well in the long course of spiritual development. As an example one often forgets to do what he is told to by anyone, but when he is reminded, the memory of

it revives in him. Why is it so? The impressions caused by it are implanted there, though in dim form. *Jada samadhi* is the state borrowed from the effect of some special process for a certain period. One cannot even feel the injuries to the body unless he comes back to the wakeful state. We are all trying for the *sahaj samadhi* state in which having everything we remain in oblivious state.

3. In support of my view I quote my Master's words. There have been a number of people of higher attainments who had no *anubhava* of any kind throughout their spiritual career. The criterion of sainthood depends not upon the feeling only but on having it. I give an example of my Master's *satsangh*. He often put my diaries before the associates to read my condition in it and the way of its expression. So that they may learn how the conditions are expressed. To tell you the truth I was the only example in his satsangh as he often said, to feel every slightest thing. I brought this thing from my past life and also developed it to the best of my ability. In my boyhood I was so sensitive that even I could feel the movement of the air waves. I was able to know the character of a man by simply smelling his perspiration. Now the question arises how I developed these instincts. I was always in thought of my Master having in view the condition prevailing in the region of my approach at the time, simultaneously. The other thing I did side by side was to create inwardly the state of *laya avastha* akin to that of my Master which fortunately I had a glimpse of. If you or anybody else does the same thing there is no reason why you do not progress towards *anubhavas*.

4. You have asked me a peculiar question that how a man can distinguish between super-conscious state and the ordinary one. Please tell me how you know that your hunger is appeased. There is something in you which makes you aware of the appeasement. Super-consciousness means to rise above yourself. You know the difference between cleanliness and uncleanliness. The former is a soothing state while the later unsoothing.

The dreams are the making of your own standard of living inwardly or outwardly. There are also the impressions of the past taking the passive form. We also clear our impressions in dreams.

You have not written about the health of Bhuvaneswari. Sometime I anxiously think of her.

Love to children.

With best wishes,

Yours affectionately,
Ram Chandra

11th Sept. 1959

My dear Revered and Beloved Gurudev,

Please accept my humble pranams. I believe that your health has considerably improved. It is our anxiety that thy health should remain unimpaired. I am myself having a slight trouble with my throat and I do not know whether I am bleeding in the throat or from the gums or both. I am trying to take medicine and get rid of it. By Thy grace I am sure I will be all right soon.

I believe you have received my previous letter. I am deeply aware of thy grace to me in lifting me to the central region and now to the swimming in it towards the Centre. I am sure I shall presently have the vision of that Master Cell in true nature, by thy blessing.

I have a very confidential matter to communicate. Please excuse my troubling thee. Shri A. Balasubramaniam came this morning to me and said that he wants to have his position clearly stated. He wants authority to do what he wants about the Ashram affairs, to take loans and so on for the Ashram, and feels rightly that I do not encourage all these as I feel the Ashram will get compromised with extra-ashram forces like a Government. He feels we are not working for the improvement of the Ashram. In fact he is finding that he is not having some 'position' in the Ashram or Mission as such, though he stoutly disclaims any such ambition. You know that Mr. Annaih Naidu and others have felt that he wishes to boss over all of them as if he knows more about spirituality than they and so on. They of course have not been feeling very well with this enthusiasm of Shri A.B.S. and have resented this unofficial pretension to authority. When therefore I took away the collection work of money from him they were glad and he was offended very deeply. Now the work at the Ashram grounds has to go on and somehow I have been finding with the help of Shri C.R. Krishnamurti and C.S. Raghavan some money for day to day running of it and paying the gardner and etc. They do not agree with Shri A.B.S. but they are not yet in a position to look after the ashram work. They may be able to do it a few months later. In the meantime last week Shri A.B.S. came and said that he has not any work at

Tirupati and will go away to his sons unless some work can be done at the Ashram which means expending non-existent money, or finding it. Shri Manunath Iyer has written again disapproving any expenditure on temporary constructions or developments of buildings. I am going to Mysore on the 27th September and may talk to him again. In the meanwhile this 'threat', though this is a harsh word. I told him that my main assignment from the Master was spiritual work and I am really not interested in this expenditure of all energy on the Ashram, though as in duty bound I have to care for it within the limits of my ability. I do not think I can be a party to borrowing and spending and trying experiments on 'self-sufficency of the Ashram'. Though it is wrong to say that Shri A.B.S. is interested in anything but the Mission and its work, which is very worthy and laudable, yet the main work I said that was before us was to grow to full spirituality. He showed me yesterday your letter asking him to take work from me. But I must confess that he is seriously more interested in this outer aspect of the work rather than the inner, for he considers rightly perhaps that Master will certainly help him if he improves the Ashram and its premises. But the deep psychological problem is his seeking authority and control over the Ashram land for doing improvements independent of any one of us. It is for the Master to judge and do the needful. As I have said my work for the mission is mainly on the spiritual side and unless I am able to make the mission really and basically a spiritual force in the South I am not prepared to be diverted to this building up of a place for residence and providing amenities. It should grow from within and not by the methods suggested by Shri A.B.S. A few days ago he brought up a proposal to enact a drama or benefit performance for the Ashram and I said that I am not willing to raise any amount for the spiritual work from such sources. I have faith that Shri will bless the Mission soon with infinite resources but it will be not till I am blessed by the Master further in that direction. I find that this is a problem: he may not relish it being put bluntly, for he is sufficiently sensitive, and above all trying to lift up himself to a good level of usefulness for the Ashram. He feels without authority to act on behalf of you directly for the purposes of the Ashram work and independently of me and others he is not able to do work at all. I told him of course that he need not think that he is not having a full free hand for his work subject to the limitations of money. I pointed out that the Mission has already sunk Rs.550/- for his book hoping that they would be sold out but we have not been able to sell more than 60 books and about 100 copies in several stages of sale or present and so on. That we cannot think that money will pour towards us, that all things take time, and that patience is needed. I do not think that he is convinced. The psychological feeling of being subordinate to me or any others is working in him and this others see more clearly than himself. One has to cultivate the sense of what others think of us, which Ouspensky calls 'others considering', which is more important and the giving up of 'self-considering' which is the bane of spiritual development. Anyway without money to work he thinks he is wasting himself here: I do not know how to set right the matter but I believe the truth is what I have said.

Of course this is my reading from outside. The psychic reading is also not quite clear.

This is purely a personal correspondence and confidential and he may also write to you as I have already asked him to do since we differ so much.

I believe Shri Ishwar Sahaiji's son has completely recovered and your son is walking about. I believe the child and mother (your grandchild and daughter-in-law) are progressing well and had bath.

With loving pranams,

Yours,
KCV

No. D 419/SRCM   Shahjahanpur, U.P.
Dated 14th September, 1959

My dear Varadachari,

I believe you have received my letter sent along with registered parcel of the manuscript. After dispatching the parcel I observed that there is some change in your inner condition which is almost inexpressible but somehow it can be translated as 'inner silence'. Please observe it and write to me in your next letter.

Love to children and respects to Appaji,
With best wishes.

Yours,
Ram Chandra

No. D 429/SRCM   Shahjahanpur, U.P.
Dated 17th September, 1959

My dear Varadachari,

Received your affectionate letter dated 11th September, 1959. Such things were not quite unexpected from Shri A. Balasubramaniam specially, in view of what you told me about during my last visit. For this very purpose I had previously written to him to win you over by affection and thus to try to compel you for his higher approaches. These words were very meaningful if he had given due consideration to them.

His recent card-copy enclosed herewith reflects his indifferent attitude towards your views. This is not at all proper. I have replied his letter clearing all the points (a copy enclosed). For the stability of the Mission's organisation it is absolutely necessary that preceptors should be treated with due regard and co-operation from the associates, and their views in respect of the Mission's work be duly respected. He is the responsible head in charge of all the inner and outer activities of the Mission and associates are his helpers in the work.

Shri A. Balasubramaniam's suggestion to raise funds by dramatic performance is really very awkward and quite against the rules of spiritual discipline and even against the constitution of the Mission. He is, I believe, under a false impression that he can be raised to a higher spiritual level by means of his such self-willed work, even though it might be against your views or the general policy of the Mission. No loan should on any account be raised for the construction work.

Two days before the receipt of your letter I had posted to you one, depicting in it your condition as I felt it. I presume it must have reached you in due course.

Shri Ishwar Sahai's son is now quite well and attends the University as usual. My newly born grand-daughter and her mother are also quite well. I am a bit relieved of the low blood pressure and I can now work for an hour or so at a stretch.

I am worried to hear about your throat trouble. Once in my young age I began to spit blood and the cause being laryngitis. A homeo-doctor prescribed Spigelia and I was cured with only three or four doses.

My respects to Appaji and love to children.

With best wishes.

Yours,
Ram Chandra

No. D 428/SRCM **Shahjahanpur, U.P.**
Dated 16th September, 1959

My dear Subramaniam,

Received your letter of the 11th September, 1959, I am very happy to note that you are so keenly interested in your progress. The interest should be such that all interests should be merged in it and may spring forth as one needed for your spiritual progress as well as of the others. But for this, one should not assume himself as the deciding factor on all points connected with it. There must be a guiding principle, governing all its activities, so as to ensure its smooth running. In this respect it is but essential to take a correct view of things and try to adjust himself to it, avoiding unnecessary pros and cons. Best minds are always required for a work, may it be spiritual or temporal. Even for a work associated with spirituality, though outwardly leaning towards the worldly side, one must look to its spiritual base. For this purpose the guiding support of such a spiritual master, who has made his own base for the Divine directions, is quite necessary in all cases. In this respect the responsibilities of one who is put in charge of the spiritual work in a particular sector should not be under-rated, as locally he represents that superior power for all practical purposes. It is thus quite proper for all concerned to follow his directions and try to co-operate with him just as they would, with the Master himself. Such a course of action will relieve the man of weight of the impressions related with it. A deviation from the rule happens when mind takes up an egoistic trend.

This is my conscientious view which I put before you, since I am convinced of your true love and nobleness of heart. I fully respect your feelings and highly appreciate your enthusiasm for the Mission's activities. But unrestrained enthusiasm, in disagreement with the existing circumstances, often leads to serious complications and in that case the real spirit is lost.

I therefore wish and request you to pursue on with your noble work for the interest of the Mission, as you have been doing so far, with due regard to my feelings and in active co-operation with Dr. K.C. Varadachari. You have written to me that he has his own views which are also correct. This goes to show that you agree with him. But that any slight difference, if it may be there as I smell it, must definitely have been not on the work but upon minor details of the ways of conducting it. That is but a very small matter and can be adjusted by yourselves like two brothers who disagree only for mutual agreement. Still if there is anything on which there is a difference of opinion, that may be referred to me. But I believe nothing at all of the type will be found there. Love to children.

With best wishes,

Yours affectionately,
Ram Chandra

20th September 1959

My dear revered and beloved Gurudev,

Please accept my humble pranams. I am in receipt of all your letters and the packet containing the revised translation of the *Commentary*. I shall carefully go through the same and get into correspondence about its publication with my uncle. He was here on the 14th instant and told me about your letter to him.

I also received the letter about the answers to questions and am benifitted by the same. Surely the questions asked are important and it is really good of Shri Kumaraswami to have put them to you.

The work here is keeping pace though no new abhyasis have come forward to take up this training. The reasons may be twofold: that the change wrought in our abhyasis has not been radical enough or the preceptor is not yet up to the mark capable of attracting more to the system or mission. I am conscious of this responsibility and that makes me many times restless to realise fully in the hope that it may be such an irresistible attraction to others — the spiritual force being magnetic in the highest degree. Of course there is the third point that the men should deserve to reach the highest or aspire for it seriously. This is God's work and His work alone.

Regarding Shri Balasubramaniam's case I shall go on as if nothing has transpired, and do what is within my capacity to do. His latest is a proposal to put up a cottage for residence which is better than the one now, and is based on the promises of some gentlemen. I shall try to do the needful within the resources. He believes in spending all that we have and waiting for resources to pour on that day, somehow to meet the further expenditures. It really shows his profound faith in things turning up by chance or grace. I love it myself but things in this world do not turn out as such. Anyhow his faith in the Master I do really like to copy.

I was waiting to give you some news about myself in the affairs of the University. There have been some proposals to increase my status and so on. I have so far not heard about their being implemented. Whatever happens it is Master's grace. I have been praying that the days of my being deceived are really over. I can only pray again and again till I am heard and my problems and my children's are solved.

Regarding the particular question about my present condition which you describe as 'inner silence' which you wished me to write to you about, I have tried to catch myself in that condition and discovered that it is a very deep state. I seemed to hear some supreme sound pervading the whole region of the brain and especially the back. It is a colourless state, nor is it blissful in the sense of being pleasant. It almost appears to be a state of nothingness and pushing me into nothingness but there is no fear. The anxiety that has been in respect of my throat trouble I connected with this and now this environmental trouble about my status in the University since in a sense they have not yet rectified the mistake of placing me on a par with a rank junior. But then now I am thinking that I am beyond the dualities and am trying to experience the same though supremely tried.

My wife's health has been rather bad. She has developed arthritis and in left hand and backache, it may be due to the climactic changes. By Master's grace I am sure she will soon regain her health. My father's health is improving. All children are keeping well. Chi. Narayan is now studying M.A. (Hons) in Psychology and will think of research next year, which will be a 3 year course.

Master, I am really in deep anxiety about the Ultimate realisation and I pray that I may be blessed in full measure. I feel myself thoroughly charged sometimes and then I am able to do all the transmission, sometimes the other condition of being nothing prevails and all my superficial thoughts scamper in.

Shri Vedantam wrote to me that he is yet suffering from his ailment about 20%, and hopes to be better. He is undergoing Malabar treatment.

With pranams and love,

Yours,
KCV

No. D 450/SRCM   Shahjahanpur, U.P.
                         Dated 4th October, 1959
My dear Varadachari,

Received your affectionate letter dated 20th September, 1959. I received a letter from Shri A. Balasubramaniam in response to my own. It shows that he has come to compromising attitude apparently. The copy of his letter together with my reply to it is sent herewith for your perusal. I do not understand why he wants another hut for his abode at the Ashram when there exists already a hut which can accommodate him very well. The money should be saved for the permanent building. The existing cottage may not be according to his liking but he should yield to the situation. You are the sole authority for the Ashram and the satsangh. You should do whatever you think right. If Shri Balasubramaniam does not yield to it he may refer the point to me and I will always feel wise to work according to your suggestions.

I am faced with a puzzling problem which I refer to you for your advice. I am writing to Shri Raghavendra Rao also. A harijan, of Chincholi district, Gulbarga, has written to me that he wants admission to Shri Ram Chandra Mission along with ten others. Shri Bhimsen Raoji of the same place has recommended their cases in a way that they should sit in separate group in a corner but all this arrested my deep thinking towards this matter. In Northern India we are forced to yield to the circumstances as there are so many harijans entering into the offices and demanding equal status in the society, and the law also favours them.

Those who are hungry for spiritual food we are bound to satisfy them but the difficulty is that *supatras* are rarely found among the harijans. Naturally every saint will be moved if there is need for spiritual food. My fellow disciple late Shri Rameshwar Prasad Misra was eager to give all his spiritual earnings to a harijan if one could be found. By this he wanted the uplift of the degraded ones. This problem requires deep thinking since the prevailing social laws cannot be altogether ignored.

I came to know through the letter of Shri Manjunath Iyer that you have been to Mysore and your speech on Sahaj Marg was appealing to the gathering. The main cause that the Mission is not widely spreading is that the people even do not know that there exists a Mission which can satisfy their spiritual need. When they will know the teachings of the Mission they will naturally be drifted towards it. The training of the Mission as you know brings about subtle changes, so they are not noticed easily. We are really proceeding from grossness to subtle states. It is wrong to think that you are weak because then, I will have to admit my weakness. Your restlessness for the work will pave the way for others to join the Mission. India is bound to come to an awakening state sooner or later and if you study it you will find that some sort of such activity is rolling into the mind of others.

Regarding your third point you have yourself beautifully replied but how the grace of God will move towards the irresistible attraction of our fellow beings is the question. Your very thought in the depth of the being will work to bring His grace, because it is the pious thought corroborative to the will of the Almighty.

Now I come to you wherefrom I never depart. If you study yourself you will feel in you the subtlest changes every day and it is very difficult to convert them into words. You want to cross the rings of light which so I sincerely wish to have the ultimate realisation. Really speaking I have not transmitted you since I left you at Madras but my watchful eye is always there. You have got such a tremendous force within you that if bondages are removed nobody can bear the power if it is transmitted for a second only. What I want is the dried up force, i.e., forceless force as I feel in myself. As you will proceed on towards negation you will feel yourself liquidated so to say. At times you come in that state to a greater degree but in every case the condition is there growing.

The Divinity is itself working to take you to the Ultimate Reality which comes after crossing the rings of light. This conception of realisation is in the Mission only, or it has been in the minds of the past sages. Before this condition is achieved even the bigger saints of our land will call it realisation.

My feeling is that the Divine is itself pulling you towards the Ultimate and the capacity is being developed. If I exercise myself for the sake of crossing the rings it will not be proper at this stage. What I do is that my thought is always there for the uplift. This will help you greatly in your pursuit and will create the favourable circumstances. If I take you by the force of the Master instantly brain nerves may shatter but I assure you that you will get at them. My prayer is always with you.

I am also sending a copy of the list of satsanghis attached to Mysore Centre. There must remain a list in the branch under which the Centre is working. I shall inform Shri Manjunath Iyer to intimate to you further additions. I am greatly worried to hear about the ill health of the sister. Homeopathic medicines cure diabetes soon. I am now improving in health when I began to take an Indian medicine, Jawahar Mohra, which even works in collapse cases. A few days back my blood pressure was very low. Then with the consultation of a physician I began to take it. I could not yet make the tour programme but I think it will be possible for me to reach Tirupati in the beginning of the second week of December visiting several other centres.

My associates Messrs. Anniah Naidu, Shri Raghavan, and Dhondhe Rao of Renigunta are attracting me much nowadays the former is the most. Mr. Anniah Naidu is developing inner power very much. The love in Dr. Kuppuswamy is also developing. Lastly I think often of Shri Krishna Murti, Jeweler of Renigunta. My respects to Appaji and love to children.

Yours,

Ram Chandra

P.S.- Chaturvediji has gone to Nainital along with his friends for a pleasant trip. Shri Kashi Ram has started business of pure desi ghee on small scale at present. He conveys *pranams* to you.

Ram Chandra

P.S. Dr. P. Sen of Calcutta has taken *sanyas* as I came to know through Chaturvediji. His yoga pat (christened name) is something plus *atmanand*.

**Tirupati
October 8th 1959**

My dear revered Gurudev,

Please accept my humble pranams. I received your affectionate letter dated 4th October today. My own letter of the 25th along with enclosure viz. the foreword to the translation of the *Commentary on the Ten Commandments* must have reached you by now. I had mentioned there about my visit to Mysore and my talk. Shri Manjunath Iyer had supplied me with the list of abhyasis there (copy) a couple of months ago when he came here.

Regarding the admission of the Sahaj Marg to admit the harijans or for the matter of that any one who seeks spiritual help there can be no difference of opinion. The whole question would arise only if we did not admit. The trouble is that they have to grow and the transmission must be capable of changing them. If it has no effect on them which they will notice sooner or later, they will themselves drop off. It must be left to the preceptor there whether he will be able to transform them or not but any preceptor must be prepared for hard work, of course the Divine Master must decide. I believe I came across no instance in which the Master said he will not help, but if the others do not find immediate effect they do not come again. The harijans who are aspiring for real spirituality will go along with us slowly but so far as they are concerned satisfied with their bliss experiences or peace. Others who come for some other ulterior motive will drop away if they do not get it from us. This point however must be made clear: the goal of the individual must be utter liberation not any lesser ideal. Any encouragement in other directions can work harm to the mission and lead to disappointment. Further it must also be clear that no one can say that as advancement happened to one faster than another, a caste man must faster than the harijan or otherwise, that it is due to the partiality of the Master or the preceptor.

I have known that I hardly do anything and indeed many times I have been not able to witness even the condition of the abhyasi until the very end of the meditation. Therefore partiality cannot be consciously practised by the preceptor and the abhyasis should be warned against thinking so. Yet this communal virus and caste-virus will be there. Indeed it was to that that I referred in my previous letter regarding an article in the Sahaj Marga latest number accusing brahmins as not accepting Gurudev. We have to set a very high standard in our own lives and lectures and articles and never accuse anybody, or set of persons, of things that we do not like to practice for it will only breed difficulties. I can now understand why the problem has arisen. Leaving out the legal nature of the demand for admittance into this Sahaj Marg, it seems to me that we must permit every opportunity for everybody if he uses it. Anyhow it is necessary not to get into any unnecessary trouble, though it is indeed one of the most important things in spiritual life to test the fitness of an individual for higher approaches. As a matter of fact the Master in the letter received today almost expresses concern about the misuse of the transmissional power in me by me as it may be very powerful.

It is however within the Master's power to change the mind of the abhyasa or the harijan if fit or unfit.

Thanks very many for the letters from Balasubramaniam and your reply thereto. I have asked Mr. Krishnamurti and Annaih Naidu to go over to the site and do the needful to help Shri Balasubramaniam. I believe after some time by thy Grace he will see others' points of view. He even now suggested that a hut for whomsoever to stay there is necessary. I gently hinted that whoever wants to stay there might construct for himself a hut or house (of course which will become the property of the Mission in case he leaves). But I am not sure he caught my point. Anyhow the work will go on slowly. I am not anxious for power or control but for the most important thing: namely improvement of the spiritual condition of the abhyasis so that our Mission will have some persons to speak with experience about the method we are following.

My own condition has been very peculiar. I must confess that I felt even that no progress has been made at all and this made me feel very much but that I am constantly thinking of the Master for the highest approach. Without it I feel wretched. I do not know what will happen with it — death? Death? Nothingness? Any way I have surrendered to the Master and He knows.

I am awaiting thy reply to my previous letter. All are well.

Yours with loving pranams.
KCV

No. D 468/SRCM   **Shahjahanpur, U.P.**
Dated 13th October, 1959

My dear Varadachari,

Received both of your affectionate letters. I will reply them later on.

I am proposing to be at Tirupati from 19th December to 24th December, 1959. I shall be glad to know if these dates will suit you. On hearing from you I will fix up my programme.

Love to children and respects to Appaji.

With best wishes,

Yours affectionately,
Ram Chandra

October 19th 1959

My dear revered and beloved Gurudev,

Please accept my humble pranams. I received your kind letter today. I am happy that you have been able to allot 8 days for Tirupati. It shows your great love for me.

I am equally grateful for the kind remarks you have made about my views. I have only done that out of a sense of duty. I am unaffected by whatever is said about me.

Things have been taking a turn for the worse in respect of our good friend Shri A.B.S. but I do not wish to trouble you, for I am by thy grace trying to convert him inwardly. He has gone out of Tirupati for a few days and I think he will have time to think. I am deeply touched by your accepting my view that we have to improve the spiritual quality of the abhyasis rather than try to make a show of bringing up an ashram, though I am also trying to do so with the help of good friends. Shri R. Annaih Naidu and C.R. Krishnamurti are looking after the developments at the Ashram.

I thank you for the clarification of the points made in my previous letter. I think the first can become a note in the book.

I do not know whether the printing of the book can be taken up now. Tirupati cannot as there is no good press. I am just thinking of the offer made by Shri R. Varadarajan of Trichy who may be able to get the same printed at Trichy where there are some good presses.

I think that the Sahaj Marg must be able to improve real intelligence. Indeed I am hoping that the real divine consciousness that is capable of surpassing the scientific ability and knowledge of the Russian scientists who have mastered space-travel etc., will be the possession of the abhyasis. I do not know whether it will be so.

Shri C.R. Ramaurti will be here tomorow. He is now an engineer at Kakinada. Shri Gourisankar who is now at Bangalore will also be here on the 31st and 1st. I shall let him know about your programme.

Regarding myself, I have nothing to present or report. It is truly dreary and indeed I am losing all hope and all bliss. It may be called an act of ingratitude to say that this is a very unsatisfactory state. As you have said in the Commandments one has to take all as His gift. In the outer world I have been treated most badly, superseded and so on, though I have earned applause elsewhere. I feel that God has selected me specially for ill-treatment and so on, which of course you wish me to take as gifts from my beloved Godhead. In the inner world I have now come across a state that is verily like a T.B. patient, helpless — my throat yet shews signs of bleeding at 11 O'clock everyday, but I do not know whether it is not mixed with teeth or gum bleeding. I have been losing a few teeth also during the past three months. Therefore I do not feel quite happy though I am out of a sense of duty and love for the Ultimate which is testing me and trying me putting up, since there is no other way. Again recently a temptation or something like that was placed as if I was going to be made the professor of the Department but all that has calmed down to nothing. I do not know whether this will never happen, though it should have happened a few years ago. I am unhappy about this matter however much I try to forget the same.

I do not know what work I have to do and the magnitude of it. In any case I am happy that the abhyasis feel that my transmission is giving them feelings of joy and bliss and improvement. Shri Kuppuswamy, Annaih Naidu, C.R. Krishnamurti, C.S. Raghavan and others feel very happy and from October 5th they feel that a new development has taken place. Did anything happen on that date?

Master I do not know what I shall be. I have left myself in the hands of the Master. Whether I should be absolutely incapable of slightest movement without the will of the Master or anything else, is to be decided by the Master.

Here Chi. Gayatri was down with typhoid from 22nd. Today the morning temperature reached normal. All others are keeping fit. My wife is happy that you will be staying here for 8 days in December.

I do not know whether I can be with you at Madras on the 3rd and 4th January as the College here reopens on the 4th January.

I do not know whether you will be able to write before you start on the 15th November. Anyhow if there is anything that you would like please write.

With loving pranams,

Yours as body,
KCV

No. D 482/SRCM **Shahjahanpur, U.P.**
Dated 25th October, 1959

My dear Varadachari,

Received your affectionate letters. I entirely agree with your opinion about the admission of harijans in the satsangh. You will hardly find a harijan who may have the capacity for *brahm vidya* to grasp yogic teachings. If however any of them having that capacity well developed in him does come to us, we will naturally be attracted towards him and will be compelled to help him in the pursuit. I, therefore, replied to him neither as denial nor as affirmation.

The English translation of his Hindi letter is enclosed for your perusal.

When I saw in the Magazine the article referred to in your letter, I asked the editor and Shri Ishwar Sahai as to why such an article was published in Patrika. They said that the fellow being our satsanghi had insisted upon its publication. On meeting the gentleman I also asked him why such an objectionable article was pressed upon for publication. He apologised saying that he had not written it in that light.

The problem, as stated to me, is that when any change or curtailment in any of the articles is made the writer takes it ill perhaps as personal insult. There have been several cases like this and the one in connection with one of the associates at your place is already in your knowledge. But since now I find it essential, due strictness, at all costs will be observed in this respect as I had already written to you previously. I am grateful to you for your kind and useful suggestion.

You have written in your letter dated 8th October, 1959 that "as a matter of fact the Master in the letter received today almost expresses concern about the misuse of the transmission power in me by me as it may be very powerful." I think it refers to para II page 3 of letter No. D 450/SRCM dated 4th October, 1959. I believe you have misunderstood me. There is no question of misuse and it is not in any way possible in your case. I meant that you have got such a strong connection with the real power and such a tremendous force that if the bondage is removed you will not be able to transmit according to the capacity of the abhyasi. Since there will be no check the abhyasi will become the target of the entire power rushing out full-fledged and you will not be in a position to control it according to necessity. In your present state, if you were exercising your will it will run like a stream. This limitation is not however a check to realisation. I had been in this position and my Master also had put a check over it as I did in your case but if I form a will the whole force will be directed towards the abhyasi. I think I have cleared this point sufficiently. If there remains anything still I shall clear it further. In all your letters I feel that you are despondent over your present condition. While on the other hand I felt exceedingly happy over it. I think since you love me as your own the condition which offers me happiness, though it may be unpleasant to you, must also be a source of happiness to you.

Now I come to the main point. I had also written in my letter referred to above that what I want is the dried up force, i.e. forceless force as I feel it in myself. In my case my Master while commenting upon this state had written to me in a Persian verse meaning,

"Such rare an attainment is not the outcome of human effort but it is a Divine Gift."

Now see how highly did he appreciate this condition. I also complained to my Master when I had the similar condition. In reply he asked me to remove this idea as it amounted to ingratitude towards the Lord. So my dear Varadachari, be happy to have this as a blessing for which I must congratulate you. This is the first chapter of your present condition. Whatever you might be saying about it I would not mind the least nor attend to it in any way, and I would not rest a while till I have brought you to the dreary state like that of a T.B. patient who having lost heart feels himself incapable of slightest movement of limbs. I feel impatient to know if this has been satisfying to you.

I perfectly agree with your opinion that spiritual training is more important than the construction of Ashram which is only for the convenience of others and a source of publicity.

I have gone through the foreword and like it much. You have also asked me that you will add further if I desire anything more. Your work is always complete so you alone can decide if any addition is to be made or not. I have given my views over the points raised by you (enclosed herewith).

The cold season has now set in and my health has begun to improve. I received a letter from Mr. S. Vedantam stating that he is being benefitted by the medicine and that Mr. J. Krishnamurthi is to visit Madras on the 20th November and will be staying with him for about a month at his residence there. I also received a letter from Shri C.R. Ramamurti who is very happy with his spiritual condition. The address as given by him is incomplete yet I will reply to him by it. My sister must be very happy to know that I am coming again. The tour programme is enclosed herewith. Shri Bhimsen Rao of Gulbarga had visited this place during Dasehra holidays and went back on the 17th October.

Love to children and respects to Appaji.

With best wishes.

Yours,
Ram Chandra

English translation of my Hindi letter addressed to Harijan.

Ram Chandra

My dear brother,

I was glad to receive your two letters. I feel greatly overjoyed to find you eager for Divine pursuit. When the resolve is made with earnestness, the success is sure, and nature provides for all the necessary requisites. It is only the want of earnestness that causes deficiency in the way to success. The impulse which brings an abhyasi to the point leading to fulfillment comes from God. Not only this but when God's will tends towards fulfillment, he brings the Master to the very doors of the aspirant and then everything settles by itself. Evidently thus, the only essential requisite for the divine pursuit is intense longing. When it is there, it is beyond the power of the Shri Ram Chandra Mission or any other Master to deny imparting training. A Mahatma in true sense, is he and he alone who is all over bound by the Divine Will.

I forgot to answer one of your points which I do now. The Sahaj Marg system of training is of a very high standard. It hits at the very root and proceeds from the centre to circumference. It is a centrifugal process and produces deep-rooted and lasting effect. There are however teachers of the type who follow the otherwise course, touching the surface layers of grosser consciousness, in order to paralyse the senses of the abhyasi and to create the state of coma. The effect thus produced, though pleasing to the abhyasi at the time, finally results in dullness of mind and the loss of intelligence. Under the Sahaj

Marg system you will find the intelligence of the abhyasi growing wonderfully till it transforms into Divine Intelligence. One may however feel the gradual transformation in his being if he is sufficiently sensitive.

No. D 505/SRCM   **Shahjahanpur, U.P.**
Dated 6th November, 1959

My dear Varadachari,

    Received your affectionate letters. I hope you must have received a money order for Rs 100/- by this time. Nowadays the stomach ache has begun to trouble me very much. I used to feel dull pain but now it is rather acute. I have begun to take homeopathic medicine prescribed by my associate but this will not hamper my movement to South. I hope I will feel better within a few days. Your throat trouble is creating anxiety. Please get yourself examined by a competent Doctor and have screening done, failing which I will take you to Madras for the purpose.

    I also received letters from Shri Balasubramanian. I have replied his letter a copy of which I am enclosing herewith. The purpose of this letter is only to pacify the situation and I hope you will agree with my views and try to adjust accordingly as much as possible.

    My first station is Hyderabad and I shall put up with a brother of Shri Raghavendra Rao. I give below his address so that if you want to write me anything you can conveniently do so.

    There is no doubt that your merits were not considered by the University authorities. In this way, they have done wrong to themselves and to the others as well because if the ability is not valued the man naturally will not be able to work freely and willfully. Such a type of consciousness is yet to develop among us, and for that we should pray.

I have sent you a copy of letter addressed to a Harijan. It was very guarded letter still it has produced a good effect on them and satisfied them. My associate Shri Bhemsen Rao informed me that they were prepared to oppose the mission. Another Harijan, who is graduate, has written to me to join the Mission saying that he was practising something for realisation but he could not see the light. I also wrote to him a similar letter a copy which I am sending to you for perusal. I always send such copies of letters to all the preceptors of the Mission so that all of us follow the same policy.

As I am coming to you we will discuss about the printing of the book. I want this book to be printed at Madras where are good presses and the proof-reading be arranged by you. I do not know whether the Sadhu Press who printed Satyodayam will undertake this book.

I am happy to note that you are speedily coming to the state which I so eagerly wish. I have also started my work from this week to bring you soon to the state where one feels himself liquidated. Shri Annaiah Naidu is attracting me very much and all the abhyasis are going leaps and bounds towards advancement under your able guidance.

I believe Chi. Gayathri must be feeling better. I am very anxious about her health. May she become all right soon so that she may be able to take sweets which I will bring for her. If you want to meet me at

Madras also we will manage to change the programme to suit your convenience.

I have been to Sitapur to an eye specialist to get my eyes tested for correct spectacles. I talked about the eye trouble of Appaji. He asked me for a history of eye trouble to enable him to give his opinion which I hope you will keep ready when I come. He is an efficient doctor and my associate.

Love to children, respect to Appaji.

With best wishes,

Yours,
Ram Chandra

address
c/o
Shri Madhava Raoji M.Sc.
52/4 R.T.L.I.G.H.
Barkatpura
Hyderabad (Deccan)
A.P.

No. D 504/SRCM **Shahjahanpur, U.P.**
Dated 6th November, 1959

My dear Subramaniam,

Received your kind letters, the two dated 5th October and 24th October, 1959 in one cover and two post cards dated 26th October and 29th October, 1959. I was really taken by surprise to see such letters from you. That may in fact, be my own draw back for as I think I have failed to create in you a sense of tolerance necessary for spiritual pursuit. I admit my fault in this respect. On receiving your letters I tried to look into myself. One of my hands was placed over the head and the other was turned round towards the back. When I pondered over it I found that both my hands were distinctly apart from each other. When I awoke to consciousness I deduced that both hands should set to work to maintain the body and not to stop the channels of the life blood. The consciousness grew deeper till I lost myself. What I saw in that state was the real scene along with the suggestions for work promoted by the consciousness. I was almost sunken in the idea presented by the suggestions. Then the consciousness took a centrifugal trend and the hands set again to work. They had lost the suggestions which had previously entered in and the work began to run smoothly. They set to work only that which was proper and genuine and directly connected with the sense of duty. I learnt a nice lesson, 'better one's own duty though destitute of merits'. If some one, there might be, who takes objection to this type of work, I find no reason to turn against what the suggestion offers. Fighting for *dharma* remain only till that state is not developed, and this is in fact below the stratum of true *dharma* which includes the pangs of sufferings that are commonly ignored as having no value at all. Selfless service never brings one to the torturous dilemma of heart. Since you treat me as one fit for your service I feel it my privilege to put forth the "real" which is to be followed. Such a work is almost Divine and we are trustees of it. If some one suggests something, may it be right or wrong it must not be a cause of annoyance since all of you have the tendency of doing good. If perchance, due to the unknowingly defective suggestion good result does not follow, it will serve as an instructor to enable us to mend ourselves. When we feel ourselves to be the doer we are in annoying difficulties. For a clearer definition of insult I may say that to follow the dictates of individual mind is in itself an unspeakable insult to the supremacy of the soul. One who corrects it and begins to follow the dictates of the purified soul, he shines forth.

Love to children.

With best wishes,

Yours affectionately,
Ram Chandra

Letter to :
Shri Sangappa Mandoli Chincholi (Gulbarga)
No. D 506/SRCM   **Shahjahanpur, U.P.**
Dated 6th November, 1959

Dear brother,

Received your letter. I am happy to note that all the arteries of India are coming to the awakened state, but the question arises how to control the work for the smooth running of the blood. We must devise means for it. No doubt you are one of us and the educated one. You should help us and your fellow beings who require strong hand for their uplift. The ways and means are common but how to adopt them is the question. The first thing we have to do is that the environments must be changed and a new life is to be created. If we are brought up in a family having its own tale of ancestors, we will have to slide a little from them to adopt the ways which bring us to the level of spirituality. If any of us takes up this work, time is not far off when we will be able to plunge into the sea of morals and spirituality coming up from the sea of ignorance.

How to begin is the question, because it has become the tendency in general that nobody wants to come out of his own environment and conservatism. The civilization of the world beyond India is being brought to India, which is neither cultural nor ethical. The wretched things of the west are being pushed into India with the result that we are leaving our high morals adopting their own. We do not want to work on these lines but on the lines laid down by our antiquities. I want men of that nature among you, to work on the real basis on which the temple of knowledge and spirituality is to grow. If you are prepared for it and take some other men like you, I will not hesitate to start the work among you on moral basis at first, awakening them to their real duty. Your letter of course was very nice and showed craving for the reality. What I want is that you should create the same thing in others as well, following the path of the ancients.

The training under "Sahaj Marg" is very high and it requires a bigger heart and devotion to grasp it. Even the high class people and the well educated find it difficult to understand it and a few of them will not wait for the results and forsake it. For that teaching one must be content upon himself leaving the responsibility on God and adhering to his own. Now I take up your case. The tendency, of course, is towards Realisation but the means adopted by you are not sound to lead you to the goal. You have created, as the case is in general, the grossness in the body, marring the way to progress which, if not removed, you will not be able to grasp the yogic teachings of the Mission, backed by transmission. So please try to remove it by giving up the methods of worship which are not suited to the spiritual growth. Recite 'Ram' and 'Ram', meditating on its meaning. Thus you will proceed from quality to substance. I must tell you the meaning of 'Ram'. One who is all pervading, the quality which only Ram has. We must remember Him who has this quality. In this way your thought will directly come to the work. You wish to see the light which is only possible when the field for its working is clear.

With best wishes,

Yours sincerely,
Ram Chandra

8th November 1959

My beloved and revered Gurudev,

Please accept my humble pranams. I believe you would have received my two previous letters. Shri Manjunath Iyer's letter would have reached you most probably along with mine. He requests change of dates.

May I suggest that you could come over here from Bellary and then leave for Mysore from this place and go from there to Trichy keeping to the dates at Trichy and the second visit to Madras. I do not mind if you come here earlier and stay till the 20th or 22nd preferably, thus giving us the usual ten days. Of course I leave that to you. This would mean minimum change in the programme given.

As I wrote to you Shri A.B.S. has stopped completely from coming to me and I learn he is at

Tirupati. I also learn that he had been going about saying that there is a split in the Mission here; as far as I know of the members not one is of his opinion. All of them hold that it was his own doing. In fact I was not a little worried about the matter as Thou knowest. All of the abhyasis began to suspect the motives of Shri A.B.S. in respect of erecting huts. The latest outburst was because I definitely told him that the Mission will not put up a new hut or permanent building for his stay (calling it of course as the Guest house). He in fact made the servant occupy the hut in which Master sat and which he said was his own residence there. This of course upset us who visited the place. I am afraid that during the past few months after Master's visit here he has been feeling exceedingly dissatisfied about himself, and the Mission as it did not give him a status. Manjunatha Iyer's being made the preceptor and thy commendation of Shri Annaih Naidu seem to have obsessed him much. That is why he wanted to **know** his place in the Mission and wanted **power** to do certain things. I am sorry that he has begun to say that there is a split. I requested him on the last day he saw me that he will continue to look after the garden etc. of course with the help of Shri C.R. Krishnamurti and R. Annaih Naidu. This he did not like and dropped out without any notice to me.

This morning I got another information. That there has been no improvement for the past two years of an abhyasi; this information I got from Shri Hanumantha Rao the old gentleman of 80 yrs. I said that if an abhyasi is not earnest about reaching the highest and has not faith how could such a one ever rise. When he said that he was feeling that the atmosphere of my room is not so very intense as previously, I told him that it is likely he has lost his sensitivity or it is due to the higher tension of the room which he could not discern, or still that the Master for the purpose of soothening the transmission of my humble self has produced softness rather than intensity, which is higher and more potent as transmissive power than before being forceless force. Anyhow this is a step that I have anticipated. I pray to the Master to guide me and lead me out of this new crisis about which I was worried from the day that Shri ABS was anxious to set himself up for building the Ashram independently if possible, nearly 2 years ago.

Other abhyasis are feeling the present day transmissions very very elevating. One and all feel that they are improving and I find their love for the Master is growing by leaps and bounds. I myself Master, felt that Thou hast poured thyself in me all the time and without interruption. What more can I say except that I do not know what I can do except to lose myself in thee. I pray that thy visit here will remove all doubts about me and others. I feel this is a new phase and I almost have felt of weeping to thee.

Anyhow when anybody feels that the Master's judgement is wrong and wishes to increase his own ego, there is hardly any ground for cure. I have felt that Shri ABS was all the time thinking of the Ashram rather than his own sadhana or inner improvement, perhaps thinking that karma yoga is better than dhyana or raja yoga. Anyhow I also of late have been experiencing sometimes the feelings of the abhyasis and then realised that they were just other's not mine.

This makes Master's visit something of a painful thing but I believe Master's grace will get rid of all unpleasantness and give us unalloyed joy.

I am herewith sending the Audit Report Of Accounts from 27-3-58 up to 31-10-59.

I received today the four copies of Sahaj Marga. I shall read through the same. My article to the Psychology conference could be published if you think it fit for publication in the next issue. Perhaps it is too long.

Shri Manjunath Iyer wants advance pamphlets etc. for giving it to the interested men.

Your love for me is so much that you say that whatever I write is good. However it is with thy blessings alone that I have been enabled to write.

There is a gentleman at Hyderabad, Professor Shivmohan Lal (Philosophy department, retired gentleman) 2/16 Tarnaka. Osmania University P.O. Hyderabad, who is a soul of devotion and I had met him at the Shri Aurobindo Ashram in 1947 or so. He came here yesterday for a meeting and expressed a sincere desire to meet you and pay his respects to you. Kindly drop a line to him to show where you would be residing at Hyderabad. I learn that Shri Raghavendra Rao of Hyderabad will be bringing a few abhyasis.

Shri C.S. Raghavan's son-in-law, K. Ramachari, will probably meet you at Hyderabad for being initiated. His son C. Rajagopalachari is laid down with a peculiar sycotic disease for the past 15 days owing to Barber's itch. His body swelled and now he is undergoing treatment at an Allopaths here. It has been causing anxiety since he is boy who was married recently in September 1959. I pray for Master's grace.

All well. We are all anxiously awaiting thy stay with us.

My pranams and love to Shri Iswara Sahaiji and others.

Yours as body,
KCV

No. D 526/SRCM **Shahjahanpur, U.P.**
Dated 14th November, 1959

My dear Varadachari,

Your kind letter of 5th November, 1959 to hand. I was a bit reluctant to admit any change in the programme since it meant a good deal of botheration and unnecessary correspondence. But as it was earnestly desired by Shri Manjunatha Iyer and recommended by you I have altered it as per slip attached herewith. I think now it will be more agreeable to him. Please inform all concerned individually of the changes.

I also received a letter, just now, from Shri Vedantam but I regret that due to over engagement in tour preparations I am not able to write to him. Please inform him of the changes.

With reference to Shri A.B.S. I may say that none, especially a responsible head, can ever please everybody. I shall, however, talk to you about it when I am there.

Love to children and respect to Appaji.

With best wishes,

Yours,
Ram Chandra

No. D 544/SRCM **Hyderabad camp**
Dated 25th November, 1959

My dear Varadachari,

Received your affectionate letters. I along with I. Sahai reached here on the 21st and will leave here for Sedam on the 27th. I also received a letter from Shri T. Manjunatha Iyer, acknowledging receipt of the revised programme. I believe you must have by now received the money order of Rs. 200/ sent by me from Agra. Shri R. Rao also met me here on arrival and will accompany me up to Bellary. Shri Shiv Mohan Lal had had a few sittings. Shri C.S. Raghavan's daughter & son-in-law also came here to see me and stayed here for two days, having sittings from me.

If you observe minutely you will find day to day changes, subtle they may however be. What you eagerly wish for, is my earnest desire too, and you are having it step by step. You like to be freed from the endless circle of rebirth. I assure you that you are **destined to be so.** Not only this but you shall also be able to liberate others by His grace. The method may be dangerous but you have power and courage to break the limitations instantly.

As for Shri A.B.S. my policy has so far been very conciliatory but that seems to have produced no effect at all. Constitutionally a preceptor is a controlling authority at a place and everybody must in duty bound to obey him. His inner condition as you already know showed that he was not receptive to Divine influence. It was you who made him receptacle but he seems to have no sense of obligation for it. That is nothing but sheer ingratitude on his part. I am of course sorry for him when I take into consideration his age which warrants devoted adherence to his spiritual pursuit at all moments. The incident reminds me of the golden words of my Master that 'one can be successful only when God wishes him so.'

Please accept *pranam* from I. Sahai and R. Rao. My respects to Appaji and love to children.

With best wishes,

Yours,
Ram Chandra

No. D 571/SRCM   **Bellary**
Dated 2nd December, 1959

My dear Varadachari,

Received your affectionate letter dated 30th November, 1959. It is better if you inform Shri A.B.S. of my arrival and stay at Tirupati, though I myself am writing to him about it. I think it will cause some ill feelings if you remain silent and do not inform him. In fact he requires not a doctor for his spiritual purposes but a surgeon.

I went through the review of the *Anant Ki Or* in *The Hindu* dated 29th November, 1959. It was indeed well written.

I also received a letter from Mr. N. Kumaraswamy stating that his wife burst into tears when she heard that I had cancelled my visit to Vijayawada. She had previously proposed to see me at Hyderabad also, along with Kumaraswamy. But due to her sudden illness she could not go there and Kumaraswamy met me alone there. Now she feels greatly mortified to have missed the chance. She however proposed to come to Tirupati or Madras to see me there. She also insists on break of journey at Vijayawada for a day or two, though it may not be possible for me to do so.

My respects to Appaji and love to children,

With best wishes,

Yours,

Ram Chandra

I shall be reaching Renigunta by the No. 11 Bombay Madras Express at 16:05 on Sunday, the 6th December, 1959 as stated in the previous programme.

With *pranam* from I. Sahai & Shri R. Rao

No. D 604/SRCM   **Shoranur**

Dated 16th December, 1959

My dear Varadachari,

Received your loving letter of 12th December 1959 just when I was anxiously waiting for it. All of you deserve more than what I have been able to do. The affection of my sister, children, Appaji and yours is highly commendable. The associates too are playing their part well. I hope and pray for Shri A.B.S. to be up again and progressing.

I came here on 14th morning. Shri Moothadatta along with a number of his friends received us cordially at the station. His newly constructed house is a very nice one and we were very comfortable there. I saw his factory which is being set up. A number of persons are coming to see us both morning and evening but none has so far offered to take up practise, though they seem to be convinced. They want public lectures which I am incapable of. Mr. H. Jacobs also came to see me and stayed here for a day. He has been greatly confused by the numerous practices of *asan* and *pranayam* advised to him by various saints whom he has met so far. His attention seems to be located on the Tantric ways of *sadhanas*. I find him going on without any definite object in view, following this and that and without any idea of the final goal. He also seems to be confused by the different shastric views. He was all the while seeking my opinion on numerous topics for the verification of his views. I told him plainly that every system can do you some good if you proceed with some definite object in view connecting yourself with the divine thought. Finally he seemed to be somewhat convinced and sought for some time to consider over it. He is a German and much inclined towards miracles.

I have given the manuscript to Mr. Vedantam telling him that you would see him during Xmas holidays probably on the 20th or 21st in the same connection.

I shall leave for Madras this evening and then I shall proceed to Vijayawada on the 18th by G.T. I shall leave for Shahjahanpur on the 20th via Allahabad and Lucknow and hope to reach home on the 26th or 27th. This route is taken up in connection with my own case work at Allahabad.

Mr. Vedantam devoted a good deal of time with me. Two of his friends have taken up our practice. All the while he himself was speculating and writing some thing. I put a slight check over it and now when I go again to Madras tomorrow I shall see whether it is necessary to increase it or not. Mr. Thyagarajan and Mr. Subramanian of Trichy came to see me at Madras. Mr. Moothadatta had a slight car accident while returning from Madras. Fortunately none were injured, though the car was very slightly damaged. Thanks to God.

My love to children and respects to Appaji,

With best wishes,

Yours,

Ram Chandra

I am anxious to know of Appaji's health since I have done something great for him, though I believe he must be going on normally.

No. D 626/SRCM **Shahjahanpur U.P.**
Dated 29th December, 1959

My dear Varadachari,

Received your affectionate letter of 19th December, 1959 at Allahabad. We reached here a day earlier, on hearing of the arrival of one of our associates with his family from Assam. They were eagerly waiting for my return. The biting cold here is felt all the more distressing since we dropped in suddenly from a warmer climate. I am now satisfied that my spiritual service to Appaji did not meddle with his health. I am really so much captured by the high devotion of all the members of your family that I feel myself mortgaged. I am glad to say that I feel you to be in a peculiar state, as if everything has been taken away from you and I am sure that in about a month's time you will realise that it has brought you to something still deeper.

Two new persons have started practice at Shoranur and a few more may likely begin soon. I find that there is a good field for the work of the Mission. Shri Moothadatta has immensely developed devotion and burst into tears several times. Most of those who came to see us off, were in tears at the thought of separation. A peculiar thing which I noticed in his son was that he has brought dim light in his chest, from previous birth, though the inner layer of the left part of his chest is dark. The 80 years old mother of Shri Moothadatta was praying to me for her liberation, though she was full of darkness all over (to tell you confidentially). I am however thinking of transforming all the darkness into light, instead of taking it out which is an awfully tedious task. I have, however advised her to take her as one of her sons, as she is too old and weak to practise meditation. Mr. Moothadatta wanted peace for his father also. I have advised him to offer daily a short prayer, prescribed specially for the purpose. Mr. Vedantam devoted much of his time with me at Madras. Your friends Shri Krishnaswami and Shri Subramanian also came to me. The former was boastful of his spiritual attainments based upon his self-avowed findings. He presumed to have his link with Queen Elizabeth of England and that some celestial being comes to him and reveals things to him. Such instances may also be helpful to you in having an experience of things. Mr. Thyagarajan, a newly admitted abhyasi offered me a surprise when I found him proceeding along the Sahaj Marg system of spiritual training. On asking him about it I learnt that he had read the *Reality at Dawn* and since then he has been thinking of me all the time. Mr. Mudaliar has now somehow been prevailed upon to conduct *satsangh*, but the enterprising spirit seems to be sadly lacking in him.

My respects to Appaji and love to children.

With best wishes,

Yours,

Ram Chandra

I send under registered book post 12 copies of *Anant Ki Or*. You must keep the spare copies with you. Shri I. Sahai has gone to Lakhimpur-Kheri.

Glossary

Abhyas: Practice.

Abhyasi: Aspirant; one who practices yoga in order to achieve union with God.

Advaita (or Adwaita): State of unity (Non-duality).

Agya chakra: See Ajna chakra.

Ahankar: Egotism.

Ajapa: Meditation without utterance of any mantra.

Ajna Chakra (or Agya Chakra): The point located between the eyebrows. Trikuti.

Anahat (or Anahata): Sound which cannot be heard.

Anand (or Ananda, or Anandam): Bliss.

Anandamaya kosha: Sheath of bliss.

Anant: Infinity or endlessness.

Anant Ki Or: Towards Infinity

Anasuya: One who has no jealousy.

Anansuyatmaka buddhi: Mind free of jealousy.

Anubhava: Intuitional perception or personal experience in the realm of Nature or God.

Anubhava shakti: Intuitive capacity, capacity acquired by experience.

Anumana: Hypothesis; hypothetical.

Apaan: One of the five pranas.

Asan (or Asana): Posture.

Ashanti: Disquiet; peacelessness.

Asuya: Jealousy.

Atman: Soul

Atmanand: Bliss of the soul.

Avasthas: Conditions; states.

Avyakta gati: Inexpressible condition.

Bhajan: Chanted prayer.

Bhamuk: Illusion.

Bhog (or Bhoga, or Bhogam): Process of undergoing effects, impressions, experience, enjoyment.

Bhrumadhya: Between the eyebrows.

Brahm: Center; God; Ultimate.

Brahm vidya: Spiritual knowledge.

Brahmagati: Divine state, State of Brahman.

Brahman (or Brahm): Creator, God.

Brahmanda (or Brahmand): Astral world. Cosmos.

Brahmanda mandal (or Brahmanda desh): Mental sphere, supra-material sphere, cosmic region; sphere where everything manifests under a subtle shape before taking place in the material world.

Brahmandi sur: Celestial vibrations.

Brahmopadesa (or Brahmopadesh): Initiation; or teaching of higher knowledge about Brahman.

Buddhi: Intellect.

Chakra: Center of super-vital forces located in different parts of the body; figuratively called lotus.

Glossary

Chaultry: A free rest house for pilgrims or travellers.

Chit (or Chitta): Consciousness.

Chit-lake (or Cit-lake): Another name for Brahmanda Mandal.

Dakshina: South; also offering by disciple to Guru for training received.

Darshan: Vision of someone's inner Reality.

Dharma: Righteousness; that which upholds.

Dharmic: Of Dharma.

Durga chakra: Durga plexus.

Dvaita: Duality.

Gayatri upadesa (or Gayathri updesh): Teaching of the Gayathri mantra.

Gayatri mantram: A Vedic chant or mantra.

Granthi: Knot.

Gunas: Tendencies.

Guru: Master, who transmits light, knowledge; a spiritual teacher.

Harijan: Children of God; the fifth caste.

Indriyas: Ten senses/organs of Indian philosophy, subdivided as jnana and karma indriyas. The former are five senses pertaining to perception, knowledge or wisdom, while the latter are five senses pertaining mainly to action.

Jada samadhi: Lower level of samadhi.

Jal-dan: Prayerful offering of water.

Janma: Birth.

Japa: Repetition of a mantra.

Jiva (or Jivatma): Individual incarnated soul. Life.

Jivan moksha: Liberation while alive in the physical body.

Kantha chakra: The throat plexus.

Karana sharir: Causal body.

Karma: Action.

Karma indriyas: Organs, or senses, of action.

Kundalini: The power which is coiled like a serpent at the base of the spine.

Kuredan: Scratching deeply.

Laya: Dissolution.

Layavastha (or Laya avastha): The state of merging.

Mahapralaya: State of complete dissolution when everything in existence merges with the Center. The complete dissolution of the whole universe.

Mahasamadhi: The final samadhi when a saint renounces his body and enters the brighter world.

Manas: Psyche, mind.

Manasa-lake (or Manasarovar): Another name for Brahmanda Mandal.

Mani padma: The jewel in the Lotus.

Manomaya kosha: Mind sheath.

Mantra (or Mantram): A sound repeated over and over again.

Maya: Phenomenal appearance. It is really a power of God. All manifestation or expansion which seems illusory is the play of Maya. Illusion.

Mayavic: Illusory.

Glossary

Moksha: Liberation or Salvation. But in Sahaj Marg, both are not the same. "Freedom from bondage is *Liberation*. It is different from *Salvation* which is not the end of the process of rebirth." (*Reality at Dawn*, pg. 22, *Complete Works of Ram Chandra, Vol. I*).

Musabbar: A herbal medicine.

Namaskaram: Greeting; bowing.

Narayana: Lord Narayana.

Nyasa: Something entrusted to another; put in trust.

Panch agni (or Pancha agni): The five fires, or powers, of the five points of the *pind desh*. (see footnote in *Towards Infinity*, discussion on Fifth Knot).

Paps: Sins.

Para Brahman (or Par Brahma): Indeterminate Absolute — God as the Ultimate Cause of Existence (see *Reality at Dawn*).

Para brahmanda: Supra-cosmic consciousness.

Para brahmanda mandal: Supra-cosmic region of the mind.

Pind: Material or gross existence, that which exists in the gross or material state.

Pind desh (or Pinda desh, or Pind pradesh, or Pinda pradesh): Material sphere; the heart region.

Pitra-paksh: A special fast night of offering to departed ancestors.

Praan (or Prana): Life; also breath.

Pradeshas: Conditions; states.

Prakriti: Nature.

Pralaya: State of dissolution, applied not to the whole universe but only to a part of it.

Pranam: Respectful salutation; obeisance.

Pranahuti: Process of yogic transmission; derived from *prana* meaning life and *ahuti* meaning offering. Offering of the life force by the Guru into the disciple's heart.

Pranayama (or Pranayam): Derived from *prana* (life, vital force) and from *ayama* (to restrain). The regulation of Prana.

Prasadam (or Prasad): Divinized food, usually sweet; an offering to Master or God.

Pratyaksa: Present before one's vision or eyes.

Puja: Religious traditional practice (in Sahaj Marg the meditation practice).

Punya: Righteous, or meritorious, actions.

Purusas: Male person.

Raja yoga (or Raj yoga): Ancient system or science followed by the great rishis and saints which helped them to realise the Self or God. Usually used for meditative practices, as distinguished from hatha yoga.

Rig Veda: One of the *Vedas*. The others are Yajur Veda, Sama Veda and Artharvana Veda.

Saguna: With gunas or tendencies or qualities or attributes.

Sahaj Marg: Literally: natural path, simple path.

Sahasra dal kamal: Lotus of a thousand petals.

Sahasrara: The Chakra of the thousand petalled Lotus at the crown of the head.

Sakha: Friend.

Sakhaya: Friendship.

Salokya: In the same world as another.

Samaan: Similar.

Samadhi: State in which we stay attached to Reality. In Sahaj Marg the return to the original condition, which reigned in the beginning.

Samarth guru (or Samartha guru): A perfect guru, who possesses all the qualities. A perfectly balanced guru.

Samipya: Near-ness.

Samskaras (or Sanskars): Impressions; grossness.

Sankalpa (or Sankalp): An act of will.

Sanskrit: Culture; also name of the ancient language of India.

Sanstha: Spiritual tradition; organisation; group.

Saraswati: The goddess of learning.

Sarupya: Similarity, become one with; having similar form or appearance.

Satyodayam: The dawn of reality.

Satsangh (or Satsang): Spiritual assembly; be with.

Satsanghi: Member of a spiritual organisation.

Sattva (or Satva): One of the three *gunas*.

Sayujyata (or Sayujya): Close conformity; something identical; become one with.

Sensorium: The area of the brain recieving and integrating sensations from the outside world.

Shakti: Power.

Shanti: Peace.

Shikhar (or Sikhar): Crown, top, summit.

Shirsasan (or Shish asan): Standing on one's head; a yogasana.

Shraddha: Faith; devotion with faith.

Shrap: Curse.

Siddhis: Capacity to do miracles; powers.

Simooms: A desert wind.

Sooksma sharir (or Sukshma sharir, or Sookshma sharir, or Suksham sharir, or Sukshama sharir): Astral body, subtle body.

Sruti: The basis of each musical note. Also the Vedas, or revealed scripture.

Supatras: Well deserving persons.

Swadhishtan chakra (or Swadhisthana chakra): The chakra situated at the level of the genital organs.

Swadhyaya: Reading holy scriptures.

Tam: The actual state we were in when the world was born. Real state of being.

Thas: Condition of total grossness.

Trikuti: The point above the nose between the two eyebrows; one of the points of concentration.

Turiya: Fourth state; the other three being: Jagrat— waking state; Swapna— dream state; Sushupti— deep sleep state.

Turiya avastha: Fourth state of the soul, when it becomes one with God.

Turiyatita: Beyond the turiya condition.

Udaan: One of the five pranas.

Glossary

Upanayanam (or Uppanayana): Opening of the higher eye.

Utsav: Religious celebration.

Vedas: Ancient Indian scriptures, in which a superior knowledge is revealed.

Vian (or Vyana): One of the five pranas.

Virat: Cosmic.

Visesas: Specific objects or qualities.

Vishudha chakra (or Vishuddha chakra): One of the six chakras or plexuses; situated at the throat.

Vyana: (see Vian)

Yatra: Voyage, spiritual pilgrimage.

Yoga: A system of Hindu philosophy showing means of emancipation of the soul from further migration, mainly subdivided as raja yoga and hatha yoga.

Yogi: One who practices yoga; one who achieves union with the Absolute.

Yuj (or Yuja, or Yujya): To join; to yoke.

Debbie Laheis

Letters
of the
Master

Volume II

Shri Ram Chandraji

Letters

of the
Master

Volume II

Letters between Shri Ram Chandraji
and Dr. K.C. Varadachari — 1960 to 1971

Edited by
Mr. Thomas J. Whitlam

First Edition   1992 : 1,000 Copies

All rights reserved

© Shri Ram Chandra Mission
North American Publishing Committee
Pacific Grove, CA, USA, 1992

No part of this book may be reproduced in any form or by any means without permission in writing from Shri Ram Chandra Mission.

Printed in U.S.A.

ISBN 0-945242-21-2 (Vol. II)
ISBN 0-945242-19-0 (Set)

Table of Contents

Publishers' Notes vii

1960 1

1961 103

1962 207

1963 235

1964 265

1965 297

1966 319

1967 339

1968 357

1969 387

1970 407

1971 427

Glossary 431

Dr. K.C. Varadachari

Publishers' Notes

Volume II of *Letters of the Master* is the second of two volumes containing all the existing correspondence between the divine Master, Shri Ram Chandra Maharaj of Shahjahanpur, U.P., Founder-President of Shri Ram Chandra Mission, and one of his foremost disciples from South India, Dr. K.C. Varadachari of Tirupati, Andhra Pradesh.

Dr. K.C. Varadachari was a renowned scholar and philosopher, an expert especially in the Visishtadvaita philosophy. He was a reputed academician and the last post he held was as Professor of the Vivekananda Chair of Philosophy at Madras University. Apart from being one of the first abhyasis of the Mission in South India, he was also one of the first preceptors, and brought the lustre of his intellectual acumen and devotion to the Mission's work, ever since he came to the feet of the Master in 1954. He passed away in 1971 after a brief illness. He rendered signal service to Babuji Maharaj in furthering the aims and objectives of the Mission.

The publishers hope to release in due course further volumes of the Master's correspondence with other preceptors and abhyasis.

Please note that the photos in these two volumes are not in any chronological order.

This correspondence was kindly made available to us by the family of the late Dr. K.C. Varadachari and to them we shall be ever grateful.

1960

5th January 1960

My dear Revered and beloved Gurudev,

Please accept my humble pranams. I am in receipt of your kind letter dated 29th December. I had been to Madras from 30th to 3rd instant in order to make arrangements for the printing. Paper is scarce. I believe my friend Rajam will manage to get things done. I am not able to place my friends Krishnaswami and Subramaniam. I am not able to know who they are who posed as my friends. No abhyasi met me at Madras. I was myself sick with chest pains (right side) on the 31st and 1st and 2nd. Even Shri Vedantam did not meet me. My Thyagarajan phoned but did not come. Most probably they do not feel well in health.

I believe your matters at Allahabad got settled satisfactorily. It is true that I feel that all things have gone away from me — I felt it very much at Madras. Indeed there is a peculiar feeling of helplessness though I am also saying that I have reached a very high state as you have so stated it, so as to convine myself that it is true. Further on the least occasion of transmission there is in the head region all over especially from the 'central' region and in the two sides a peculiar feeling of strain and sensation, sometimes comfortable, sometimes uncomfortable. I am praying that as you have written a month hence I will know about the deeper condition.

All of us are well. Father's health is good; my wife's health which was not good continues to be the same though slightly improved.

Seshadri had been not traced for a few days but he has returned to Tirupati a couple of days ago. He is causing anxiety to his father-in-law and all of us Master's grace. Shri C.S. Raghavan is progressing well. Shri A.B.S. is regular but he is yet not interested in the meditational aspect, though he does not speak about the garden etc. affairs. Shri Subba Rao of Gudivada has been here and is very devoted and comes every day for meditation.

All others are coming regularly and having abhyas. I am very sorry that Shri C.T. Mudaliar is not keen on the satsangh. The real trouble is that whether one likes it or not the improvement in material matters and the lack of space etc. at his place makes him desist from this abhyas or its spreading. After all what is the charm in this abhyas except if it takes one really above the bondage to material limitations, at least in respect of basic service that one wishes to do. I do not know how to put it but it is clear that unless one is clearly aware of his growth and development internally and from that developed point of view is able to change and modify or shape the outer circumstances according to the Divine Will (which is not purely a will for *nivritti* as such) one will not be able to keep up the faith. Though all say that they seek the Highest, it is clear to me almost all seek something more than that, if not other than that, in addition to that. This I found to be the true reason for not making up. Others offer all these though how far they do get them or realise them is not clear. I found that in respect of the Sai Baba worship.

I do not know how far all these things can be transformed. I even now think about my humble prayer on the 11th December morning for a definite and radical power to change or transform all those who come to see that the Highest includes, in a very subtle way, all that men seek and is greater than any and all of them. This is to evolve into the superman I believe.

Please convey my pranams to all and to Shri Ishwar Sahaiji,

With loving pranams,

Yours,
KCV

I believe you would have received by now my registered post with the articles I sent to you for perusal and publication in the *Sahaj Marg*. I shall be deeply grateful if you would please let me know your comments on my talks on the Commandments.* It will help me to go ahead.

No. E 42/SRCM   **Shahjahanpur, U.P.**
Dated 14th January, 1960

My dear Varadachari,

Received your affectionate letter dt. 5th January, 1960. Your health is a great blessing to us and I get worried when I hear that you are indisposed. Chi. Chhaya wants to attend the convocation so I am going tomorrow along with her to Lakhimpur. I shall come back on 18th January, 1960 and will again go to join the marriage ceremony of one of my associate's daughter at Kukra on 20th January,

---

* Editor's Note: "Commandments" or "Ten Commandments" refers to the "Ten Maxims" of Sahaj Marg.

1960. I am expected to return on 25th January, 1960. I will be, then, in a position to reply to your letter.

I received the articles for Patrika under Regd. cover. They will ultimately form a book. They are well written. You deserve the reward and I prayed for it.

Love to children and respect to Appaji.

With best wishes,

Yours,

Ram Chandra

P.S.- Those who are unable to join the Utsava may sit at the fixed hours at their own places but I prefer your place for it.

No. E 47/SRCM   **Shahjahanpur, U.P.**
Dated 30th January, 1960

Dear Varadachari,

Received your affectionate letter together with the articles for Patrika. I arrived from Bankey Ganj on 26th instant. I participated in the same marriage for which invitations for yourself and other preceptors of the Mission were issued. The marriage was peacefully over, the father of the girl spent about Rs. forty thousand. I am writing to the father of the married daughter your good wishes for the happy couple. Since my return I became extremely busy with the celebrations of the birthday of our Master hence I could not reply your previous letters. I shall reply every point of your letters after the function is over.

Please write to me if you feel a change in your condition from 27th or 28th January. There will be decidedly a change although not so sharp because you have acquired mostly the changeless state. After the receipt of your letter I shall write clearly the change occurred. It is of course inexpressible, but from the hints I receive from you I will be able to express something.

This year six persons are coming from South including Shri Raghavendra Rao from Bellary and Shri Shiv Mohan Lal with his wife and his son from Hyderabad. The boy is said to be mentally deranged but as his father has written to me he is greatly improved by the good treatment in the mental hospital. This is also one of the cases of *shish asan*. You have done well to take up the case of Chi. Srivatsa. In such cases after clearing the complexities soothing transmission works wonder; but that sort of transmission is a very higher one so not more than five or ten minutes be devoted at one stretch. It is for those who have not taken up abhyas regularly.

Love to children. Respects to Appaji.

With best wishes,

Yours,
Ram Chandra

P.S.- Please write to me if your depression is subsided.

Ram Chandra

3rd February 1960

My dear and beloved Gurudev,

Please accept my humble pranams. I am thankful to you for your affectionate letter dated the 30th instant.

We are celebrating the auspicious function with solemnity and meditation as instructed by you.

I am sure by the time this letter reaches you all the functions would have been over. I am glad that Shri Raghavendra Rao and Shri Shivmohanlal and family are attending the Utsav.

Regarding the question which you have put to me about my condition as from 27th or 28th January — I have to write the following. In addition to being rather agitated about certain things I noted in my dairy, "I am becoming aware of my nothingness — but ecstasy of it is not there. I am not doing any work — it seems that I am not even interested in it. I am in a funny mental condition — I have no evidence of sheer peace and absorption in the Infinite — life has become meaningless whether as child or boy or youth or adult or old man. ... The body is getting shattered.

I am condemned to live among men who seek self-advancement in all fields of life, though I am not also condemned to their thoughts and hopes. Indeed God has seen to it that I am denied all of them.

On the 28th night at 8:30 P.M. there was an earthquake with thunderlike sound and with tremour beneath.

On the 30th dejection continues and I have noted that

1. The transmission is not as well as it should be.

2. There seems to be a withdrawal of all power from the Master.

3. Things about me also at University do not seem to go well.

I am wondering how all things are going to be set right.

I am sorry all this certainly is not quite up to the expectations. That changeless state about which you have written has not been fully experienced and I am yet feeling dejected over all things. I am sorry however that I am yet unable to move up to your expectations.

I am eagerly awaiting thy letter.

With loving pranams,   Yours,

KCV

No. E 67/SRCM   **Shahjahanpur, U.P.**
Dated 12th February, 1960

My dear Varadachari,

Received all your affectionate letters. Utsava is over in full divine grace. Shri Shiv Mohan Lal had joined the function along with his family. He was very grateful to you for leading him to the right path. He also remarked that he found you completely transformed and the same thing I heard about from other quarters too. The opinion of all these laymen offers sufficient proof of your transformation and you can thereby infer your true state. Shri Raghavendra Rao and his father also participated and also Shri Ram Chandra Rao with his wife and cousin.

It is surprising to note that you feel dejection even in your present state. I pondered over it a good deal but I could not arrive at a definite conclusion. Then on peeping within you I discovered a pool like within, which was widening. There was no condition in it. Now I am definite over the conclusion. The negation is started and is developing. You say that there is no evidence of peace and absorption in the Infinite and life has become meaningless. I think, Doctor you are relating about my own state. I am trying to make you and all others like me. The transmission as you say is not as good as it ought to be. For this I may say that its consciousness has taken a deeper turn beyond mental aspect. For an experiment take some well advanced abhyasi and transmit to him for not more than 2 or 3 minutes from your own level of the present state and let him relate his condition. But take due precaution so that it is not intense.

You say that the condition is not up to my expectations. That is right but thank God that it is coming.

Feeling of the withdrawal of power means something akin to nothingness. I had already told you when I was there that I do not want to have in you even power but only its ultimate state. In that condition the power when it is required is there. As a test concentrate a little forcing yourself to it you will feel the power within.

I am sorry that your merits are not rewarded by the University although you are spoken of so highly by the learned men all over the country. Personally I am of opinion that if we are deprived of all things necessary for the upkeep of worldly life and in its place the inner life which is worth having is given to us we are in no way the loser.

In the letter dated 15th January you write that you experienced a flow of light power which filled your whole being. I think this experience must be over all convincing that some superior power is at work for your good and all that is happening is right.

Your reflections about Mr. Mudaliar are just to the point. Before his departure from this Province he had come to me for a few hours only. During this time I did for him all that was necessary to bring him up to the standard required for a trainer. In order to convince him of it I asked him to transmit to a few persons which he did. The conditions they related offered sufficient proof to convince him of his developed capacity. But he persisted in being almost incredulous in spite of all these clear indications. Since then he never tried to exercise his power on any one not even upon his wife and daughter who had also started practice. Whenever I wrote to him about it he offered some excuse. Several times he even said that he did not feel any power. It was for this very reason that I had to appoint Shri N. Kumaraswami for the work at Madras. However I kept him goading on, but he seemed to be inwardly adamant. This time, again I insisted upon him to carry on satsangh taking in his wife, daughter, and son-in-law and a few others who lived close by and whom I had induced to attend regularly. But he takes no interest. I am not the least satisfied with his work.

On this Path, I think the question of changing the outer circumstances does not fit in aptly. It is rather that the abhyasi has to adapt himself to circumstances in order to practise submission to the Divine Will. The Divine Will is predominant and the circumstances are the results thereof. We have to learn to take them as divine gift. Of course, I agree with you that it is not an easy job for a common man to get up to it, so the natural limitations appear to be most distressing to him. But instead of worrying over the circumstances which are often beyond his control, it is better to apply his effort for the mending of his own grosser self.

But the difficulty is that most of those who come to you for spiritual pursuit as they profess, are inwardly actuated by material purposes which they wish to have adjusted according to their liking and taste. If they do not have it they break off and even if they have it they will not stick to it because their purpose is served. There have been several cases like that. My Master's ways of spiritual training are absolutely free from material touch. I know that certain saints do offer such material allurements and they are often successful to some extent, but it is definite that for this they have to deviate from the right path and resort to unspiritual ways which for me would be the bitterest pill to swallow. I strictly abide by the directions laid down by Master and shall not like to adopt unspiritual ways at any cost.

No doubt I try to transform everybody who comes to me, to whatever extent it may be possible at the time, for I think it to be my duty. But then something rests on the man as well. It is for him to let the transformation work its way. Where this is lacking, the man though he may at the time be induced to follow the practice, will definitely break off after some time.

My difficulties are manyfold. I have to take everything upon myself, i.e., to discuss and convince, to create craving and constancy, to mould and transform and finally to keep him firm upon the path. But I do not grudge it provided full co-operation is coming forth from the other side. It is however, a matter of pity that in certain cases even co-operation is wanting. What do you, my dear Doctor, think of such cases? By this time you too must have experienced that quite a good number comes in without having the real craving. All that they seek for is external or material. Our system is meant exclusively for the attainment of liberation and beyond, hence far far away from baser ideals. The same I impart to every one even from my very first contact but this takes time to mature into fullness if he is eager for it. Those coming to me without the real craving often lack patience to wait for the transformation to take deeper roots and to work out its results. I am at a loss to understand what to do in such cases, unless I induce myself to force everything into them. But that may be a risky process.

There is an organisation in this part of the country, which professes to impart spirituality. It commands a pretty large following and people who join it, seldom break off even though some of them, to my personal knowledge, are greatly disgusted and averse. The thing as I find it is that they have adopted to unspiritual ways to keep them bound fast not only by inducements and allurements but even by frights and threats. But when I study their inner condition, I find not one of them having any spiritual achievement but only caught up by some material force. You will find hardly one amongst them who is nearer the Mark in any way. Whereas, in your *sanstha*, you will be happy to note that none of the preceptors including yourself has ever the slightest touch of maya in all his transmissions. It is only the pure wave that runs through from him to the abhyasi. In my opinion such pious methods must at all cost be adhered to in order to promote piety and righteousness all over. I pray for the making of such noble personalities to work for the enlightenment of the world and time alone shall bring the results to light. We must try heart and soul to prepare such worthy souls as may be useful and helpful to the future world. It matters little if a few break off from us, because what they have gained during their brief contact will develop in the subsequent life, if not in this one. Thus our labour is by no means wasted or lost.

I had received a letter from Mr. Jacobs a few days ago in which he has put me certain questions. I send you a copy of my reply. I have dealt with him in frank and outspoken terms somewhat against my usual conciliatory ways. During my contact with him at Shoranur I had made references about you and had advised him to contact you if possible. He may likely happen to see you sometime. With this view I would like to keep you informed of everything in this connection.

My respects to Appaji and love to children.

With best wishes, Yours,

Ram Chandra

P.S.- After closing the letter, I received another dt. 9th February, 1960 from you along with your comments on the book. The typed letter contains the reply of your present letter too. I do not mind if the printing is delayed a little. Mr. Vedantam will naturally be eager to have it done soon.

The opinion of your friends about yourself, is not correct. Even a developed soul cannot understand the real condition of a man like you, because it is not very easy to guess the highly subtle states. Mr. A.B. talked to you of the establishment of the R.K. Ashram near your place. Let others grow externally but we are to come out from the inner to the outer. Sooner or later your Ashram shall too be constructed definitely because it has turned into one of our objects. A poor hut, which is available and accessible is more valued than a big palace which is inaccessible to us.

Shri Shiva Mohan Lal had reminded me again to apply for financial help to the Nizam's Trust Fund. Probably he has some influence there and may be of some help in it. So please do apply, as a preceptor, and inform him of it. If their conditions are not favourable to us we can refuse it then.

I have appointed Shri Ram Das, a very good man, as the preceptor of the Tinsukia Branch (Assam) in place of Shri Kashi Ram.

Address:
The Secretary,
Nizam's Trust Fund
Hyderabad (Deccan)

Ram Chandra

No. E 55/SRCM
To Mr. H. Jacobs   Dated 8th February, 1960
My dear Brother,

I was very happy to go through your kind letter, seeking for the real values needed for a *sadhak*. Individual tendencies always differ. For that Hinduism alone offers solutions according to their particular capacities, since it is but certain that one and only one method can never suit the purpose of all the varying mentalities, though finally they have all to come round to the very Path near-most to God. They learn swimming, gathering strength by every different means and ultimately they begin to flow with the current. Their intensity becomes greater if they have taken up the goal. Suppose a man not fit for ascent by the direct path approaches me, I shall definitely advise him to take up the path suited to him, for I do not like to devote myself to lower aspects of realisation which might in course of time develop into the real aspect. Help, of course, I can, if he is really earnest about the Truth. But if I find that the methods applied by him are not rightly directed and are based on his own sweet will, I will give up the case. I believe that if the right process can do him good, the wrong process can do him immense harm as well, by enhancing obstructions. Though I do not profess to be a Ram Krishna Paramhamsa in any way, it is also not every *sadhaka*, that come to me, as a Vivekananda. I am therefore bound to the ways and means prescribed by my Master alone, the efficacy of which stands undisputed and unchallenged. I had also written to you previously that the earnest cry of a real aspirant brings the Master to his doors. If any of you has the real craving, he will set up a wave in the Main Source, which will begin to descend through some great personality to seek for the real aspirant. If I relate to you experiences of great saints of the past you will be astonished to know that they were often ordered to train persons whom they neither knew nor had any contact with. It has therefore been rightly held that to get a true disciple is equally as difficult as to get a true guru.

As for yourself I may, with due apology, be frank enough to say for the sake of your own good, that though you profess to be in India for learning the yogic science, which pertains directly to the realisation of the One Absolute, perhaps you might be having some other purpose besides, since I do not find your whole-hearted attention and energy devoted to it. For the realisation of God it is but essential to treat it as the primary-most thing and remember Him all through, putting every thing else as secondary. That amounts to real liquidation which is indispensable. But if that is not possible for one at his present stage, he must pray rather meditate for a capable guide to lead him up to it. I myself had done so, and also a few others and none ever happened to miss the mark by this means.

Miracle is an attainment of a very low grade and is also cheaply earned, but it is by no means the criterion of a saint, though he may at times be working it out in accordance with the Nature's demand. The display of miracles for the sake of amusement or demonstration is the grossest abuse of power.

As for myself I am always ready to help any and everybody in need of my help, and guide him through but only in a way I have myself experienced. The perpendicular line is the shortest and there can be only one perpendicular from a point to the base. All other lines, though finally meeting the base, must necessarily be oblique and longer. The wave of spirituality is flowing abundantly through every nook and corner of India but one has to prepare himself to grasp it. Seekers of things other than Reality keep themselves confined to their own self-planned tests for purposes best known to themselves, but it does not hold true in the case of a real devotee who rests his entire responsibility of right conduct and proper care upon the Divine.

With best wishes,

Yours affectionately,
Ram Chandra

22nd February 1960

My dear Revered Gurudev,

Please accept my pranams. I was happy to receive your kind letter dated 12th instant. I am grateful for all the good things that others have said about my humble self. Despite your writing to me that you are not able to understand my dejection and offer no solution for it, I did experiment on that matter — i.e. transmitted for a couple of minutes from 'my own level', whatever that is, to Shri Annaih Naidu and Shri Somesvara Sarma and also to C.S. Raghavan. The first two described that condition exactly as their experience of 'deepening pool within which was widening — of dawn colour'. Shri

C.S.R. said that he saw full light bathing him. Of course I did not exceed this Shri Annaih Naidu was of course feeling this the whole day. Shri Somesvara Sarma requested that I should lead him to the highest state. But I am not satisfied and indeed feel yet great difficulties. I have today enclosed my talks on the 14th and 21st instants. It has been very difficult for me to get over the sense of deep dejection over outer events in my case — with all my attempts to get over the whole thing — even Master has not been able to turn away my mind over the matter or to see the righteousness at the source of things. Something of this thought has pervaded my talk on the fifth commandment. Indeed one gentleman proposed that one should change the minds of men in power who do the wrong thinking it to be right, and are unwilling to do the right because they think it is wrong; I had only to quote to him the dangers lurking in the 7th *granthi* — a very unwise course. Thus one becomes helpless — but thou hast written that I am in no way a loser in losing position, honour and place and even the freedom to do work, because I am gaining the spiritual. A superior power, if it is working for my good, is quite an assurance and I can only pray that I may be more aware of it and fully. Anyway Master must be correct and I am yet in the imperfection.

I have read with regret about the work of Shri Mudaliar. But what can we do. This fact you also spoke of in respect of Shri Kumaraswami, who is of course much younger and can do good work. We must find somebody who might do well at Madras.

I thank you for the comments on the Ramakrishna Mutt at Tirupati. Yes. We shall do the best and hope for the best, and use spirituality for all our work despite the recalcitrance of matter and material methods. I thank you for the kind compliments for our transmissions, but it is all thy work as again and again I had to say and write to you.

All the children are well. They are all preparing for their examinations which are due next month.

I have been greatly distressed over so many things of the world and about me, but you have warned me that our work being for liberation, anything that leads to diversion of thought even is wrong. However I have to place before you my condition in all its aspects and I have done it. There are so many things I am unable to speak or put on paper and God alone can help me and Thee.

With profound pranams,

Yours loving,
KCV

No. E 126/SRCM   **Shahjahanpur, U.P.**
Dated 6th March, 1960

My dear Varadachari,

Received your affectionate letter dated 25th February, 1960. My health is so much improved in this season that it was never so for the last 5 years. It seems to me the miracle of your prayer and good wishes. Mr. M.L. Chaturvedi the former Judge of the Allahabad High Court has been given a job by the Govt. as the member of the Union Public Service Commission on a salary of Rs. 3000/- p.m. at Delhi. He has taken charge on 3rd March, 1960. I had opened a school for spiritual training under him under the instigation of Dr. Hafiz Syed but the man is now at Delhi where a centre is already functioning under Shri S.K. Rajagopalan.

Regarding the employment of your first son please write to me if I may be of some help to him. I shall be very happy if my daughter Chi. Padmini be married. The boy you have selected for her is well behaved and good but as I told you when I was at Tirupati that we will have to change a little the secluded mentality of the daughter. The time itself will do it moreover we are also meant for it to speed up the change. My blessings are always with our children. In case of Shri Y.K. Srinivasan the stars are quite good and the sun is *Uccha* which shows that the boy will shine out. That is merely my imaginative view as I am not an astrologer.

I am worried about your health and I think you are more fitted to live a longer life in this world than myself so will you please do me a favour to write in details the chest troubles and also whether you have got the troubles in the right chest or in the left. For the health of the sister I like to suggest to transmit her once or twice a week with the suggestion of the improvement of her health. The transmission should be very light and not fully concentrated. For removing the disease the process is the same that it is going out in the form of vapour or smoke. Both of you can do this process at your leisure hours.

Shri (Vineet) Ram Chandraji of Dharwar, the editor of a Canarese monthly magazine named 'Pradeepa' has taken up the practice of the Mission in right earnest along with his wife. He sent the first letter saying "I humbly dedicate myself at your sacred feet." This is how it happened. He seems to be a man of capability and it is quite possible that people may get light from him. I also received the letter of his wife Prabhudass Nivedita likewise. Shri Sarnadji of Gulbarga used to contribute articles in his journal which attracted him deeply.

Somehow he got our books *Efficacy of Raja Yoga* and *Reality at Dawn* from one of my associates who is at Dharwar, where he lives. The books thoroughly satisfied him and he concluded that this poor self will be able to satisfy his thirst for realisation. Now he has written to me to allow him to quote in his editorial the passages from the books or the books themselves be translated in Canarese to appear in 'Pradeepa' so that they may eventually form books in Canarese language. He also wants my life to be published in the magazine for which Shri Sarnadji has requested me to send him in brief. I have done it but I did not disclose the facts which only people will believe after me.

My version about your condition has now stood test and it made me sure that I was right in my judgement. Shri R. Annaiah Naidu is praying for higher approaches and also Shri Someshwar Sharma and Sita Ramaiya. Among these three associates Shri Annaiah Naidu is one who is prepared to go to *brahmand mandal*. There is one new experience about him that he went up to mind lake (Chit) and the working and expansion is there. I was observing this peculiar thing and waiting for its effects. I assure you that he will himself very soon reach *brahmand mandal*. You should also study his case which is a new case for experience. Someshwar Sharma is also quite good but I find a little grossness in the right chest connecting with *kantha chakra* or the 5th point of *pind pradesh*. It is, no doubt, becoming thinner and thinner and the space is growing lighter day by day. Sita Ramaiah is of course interested but I find something in the system which requires time although your power is working quite all right. If you want to hurry in this matter or in any other case remove all those obstructions.

The abhyasis are getting calm by your transmission while you feel irritated, restless and so on. The reason is simple that Divinity itself works through you and you play the part of humanity which is essential for the man having bodies. A saint at his highest approach cannot wash off the humanity because the life in that case will be extinct. This limitation will always remain and it will play one part or the other, that is the secret of Nature. My dear Varadachari, have you ever observed, at the time when you get irritated, the constant incursion of ideas and feelings of the external worlds? If you study deeply you will find yourself just like a man on the top of the hills looking towards the man walking on the base. Shri Raghavendra Rao very recently has written to me, but in a peculiar way, that he observes perfect peace while thoughts come and go but he does not feel as they are. If any of us takes the idea deeply and concentrates on it he will find the intensity greater.

I had written to you in one of my postcards that I prayed to God to give you remuneration for the writings with which you have now begun to enrich the Mission. I am delighted that my prayer is granted and am seeing its effect now after a month or so. You will laugh at me if I disclose it and everybody will do so. It shall be adding godliness to God.

You are so highly intellectual that I am proud of having you in our midst as our associate, but at that time it was to me a shadow of the real intellect. Now I find that it has been transformed mostly into its real aspect. More than 3/4 work is over. I will now write when the work is complete. Your mood of writing is now changed and purity is there. Please observe.

I am transmitting to you almost daily for the last 10 or 12 days. What I am doing I will not tell you unless the work is complete or I may get some hints from yourself. I like to inform you that you have crossed the first ring about 20 or 25 days ago and that was the order of my Master for doing so. The system must have grown lighter. You must not be feeling even the weight of the body or of the soul just a little.

Love to children. Respect to Appaji.

With kind regards,

Yours affectionately,
Ram Chandra

6th March 1960

My dear revered and beloved Gurudev,

Please accept my humble pranams. I am enclosing herewith my two talks on the 28th February and 6th March on the Commentary. I do not know how you like them. If it is considered to be not all right I shall be glad to know about the same.

I believe you received my previous letter, and enclosures. I am leaving for Mysore on Tuesday 8th instant, and leaving my wife at Bangalore. I proceed to Mysore on the 9th and stay there for the 9th and 10th. I am returning to Bangalore mostly on the 10th night and leave for Tirupati on the 11th. Shri Manjunatha Iyer wrote to me that he was not keeping quite well. He is extremely troubled about the litigation that his sister seems to be intent on starting. I do not know what comfort I can give him.

My own condition is very peculiar and I do not know when I shall be aware of the divine state at all. I shall very much like you to enlighten me about the meaning of the experience called — *adityavarnam tamasah parastat.* So too I have found that the word *annam* has to be conceived as being the primary: *an*, pra-*an*, apa-*an*, vi-*an* (vyana), sama-*an*, uda-*an*, and *an-na* it is the breath or power of life in all and which comes from plants *osadhih* — not from *pasus* or animals: animals are those which move and grow — anima.

In two weeks time the talks will be over and the final pages will reach you.

I have nothing more to do but to surrender to Master.

With loving pranams,

Yours,
KCV

13th March 1960

My dear and revered Gurudev,

Please accept my humble pranams. I returned from Mysore yesterday. I was with Shri Manunath Iyer. I gave two sittings to him and his son, and a sitting to Shri Puttagawda and to the yoga teacher.

I found Shri Manjunath Iyer very good. He is physically weak, but he told me that he is now very much better. Shri Puttagawda is also clear and aspiring.

I am indeed very happy that by the blessings of the Master Shri Chaturvedi has become member of the Union Public Service Commission. Please convey my sincere thanks and congratulations to him.

I am very hopeful that by Master's supreme grace Chi. Padmini will get all right and I pray for it most earnestly.

Regarding Chi. Aravindarajagopal: He has passed his B.A. in Philosophy in the Second division. He is completing his 25 years on 7th August. I have been trying to put him in the Indian Express at Chittoor.

Master I do not know why I should suffer at Tirupati so much and get set back again and again. It is all my *purva karma* perhaps. I do not know whether anything can be done there. But Master can do wonders and miracles. He is a mild sort of chap and more interiorised. He is a very timid boy also. A quiet job which will help him to go on with his real spiritual nature will be good and as far as possible at Tirupati. Regarding Chi. Narayana it is different, he can go anywhere and can look after himself very well.

I thoroughly agree with you about Shri Srinivasan. But from what I can read you suggest that they may not be made for each other? I do not know Master's will in the matter. My wife is indeed most anxious.

I do not know about my future. Frankly let me confess that I am tired of this kind of life and I do not know how I can indeed be useful to God or the Master.

I do not nowadays even think of what I am and where I am in the higher stages. Surely Shri Raghavendra Rao has a higher approach than my humble self for I have more karma about me which is flowing into me. The plains have been too much with me though I may be at the top of the Hill. Regarding my physical condition, I do see that Master is really worried about me — ever since I believe Master mentioned that my condition is like a tubercular patient unable to do anything by oneself I have been having the spitting of blood, between 11 A.M. and 12 noon, and the chest, both right and left have been tense, the throat has been sore and obstructive causing uneasiness when swallowing, causing suffocation too sometimes. The chest has been tense and chest has also been similar to what happened in May last at Madras — then I transmitted to the whole place and it came down. For the past two days it is not as severe as before. I have been taking medicine. My gums have been bleeding also and I thought it might be both but what with the throat irritation and venous blood in very small quantities when spitting phlegm I did become anxious. But I now know that Master will remove the defect and am hoping that it will be nothing at all.

I do feel quite all right otherwise; I do feel light and not heavy. Sometimes some sensations are about the chest region both near the heart and about the sternum to the left as well as to the right alternately.

I am enclosing the talk on the 9th commandment and the 10th alone is now to be delivered next week.

I am indeed happy that the gentleman Shri Vineet Ramachandraji of Dharwar has taken deep interest in Master's works. I am sure it will enlarge that sccpe of the work of the Mission.

My father's health is quite all right otherwise. My uncle Y.K. Narasimhacharya is regularly attending. His condition also is improving. I agree with your reading of Shri Anaiah Naidu as also as of others.

KCV

15th March 1960

My dear beloved Gurudev,

Please accept my humble pranams. I returned from Mysore on the 12th. I stayed with Shri Manjunath Iyer. I gave two sittings to him and his son Gopal, and one each to Shri Puttagawda and another abhyasi who is teaching yoga to students in the local institution there.

I found the trip pleasant thanks to Master's grace.

Please convey my hearty congratulations to Shri Chaturvedi on his being appointed member of the Union Public Service Commission. It is all due to thy grace.

I am sure with the grace of the Master Chi. Padmini will become normal and all will be well. Shri Srinivasan passed his first test which is very difficult and very soon he will pass his second test which entitles him to an officer's post. He will be here on the 28th and he will continue his abhyas which he has been carrying on steadily.

Chi. Aravinda Rajagopal is likely to get fixed up in the Indian Express as a probationer proof reader. He is a B.A. with Philosophy and Sanskrit as his subjects which he passed on the 2nd division. If he can get employed in a State Bank (at Tirupati) it will be good. But I have to state that he is mild and rarely moves with others but he is getting more confidence of late thanks to Master. He is completing his 25th year on 7th August, 1960.

Regarding my condition, what can I say which the Master does not know? My physical condition did cause me anxiety due to the strain in both right and left chest, but alternating sometimes and together at others. The bleeding from gums and throat used to take place between 11 and 12 noon and sometimes in the nights also. For the past three days there is no bleeding worth speaking. But the throat has the sensation of something like a hair or something like that. It causes suffocation sometimes when drinking or when saliva slips into the bronchial tubes.

There is no feverishness though sometimes I felt heated in the evening.

Regarding my spiritual condition, I do feel light. But other things continue to be what they have been. I can only pray that by the Grace of the Master I shall always be in that state to which He has taken me. Sometimes I wonder why I should yet not know the full essence of the Ultimate Reality and act always in that awareness. I do find that all things have lost meaning for me or rather that I am helpless to do anything around me. I am of course dead and it is Master perhaps who restrains me from passing out.

May I express my utter gratitude for the blessing of the Grand Master Samartha Gurudev in taking me to the second ring of Splendour. I only pray that all irritation, all love for the worldly prosperity (which does not come) be given up by me and I may more and more fully enjoy that work of the Master even as my brother Raghavendra Rao is enjoying the peace. I do not know whether my abhyasis are with much more karma than his. But I am quite a laggard I believe.

I am enclosing the letter of Shri C.S. Raghavan about his condition. I pray to the Master for his betterment and peace. He is a very regular *sadhaka*.

I am enclosing the talk on the 9th commandment for thy kind scrutiny.

My father's health is fair as also my wife's. But I shall do the needful. My uncle Narasimhachari's health is somewhat indifferent. He is now regularly coming for the satsangh also as also his son Kasturi.

I now surrender to Thee for everything. My life is at thy service. I pray for the highest approach and highest efficiency in service.

Yours with loving pranams,

K.C. Varadachari

No. E 186/SRCM   Shahjahanpur, U.P.
Dated 4th April, 1960

My dear Varadachari,

Received your affectionate letters dated 6th and 15th March, 1960. I had been to Allahabad in connection with the cases pending there. The appeals are admitted and I have handed over the case to the advocate. Chaturvediji also arrived there to fetch his car during that period. I offered your message of congratulation to him directly and he thanked you in return.

You have written in the letter dated 6th March, 1960 that you do not know when you should be aware of the Divine State at all. May I ask you whether you feel restlessness still to gain the divine state? The other thing you will please also intimate to me whether you feel the mood of thoughts quite distilled. Now I express the meaning of *adityavarnam tamasah parastat* according to my poor ability. In chapter 8 sloka 9 of *Bhagavad Gita* the Lord has described the effulgent form of ultimate Reality, which is the object of all *upasana*. This is also the point of all beginning as the word *adi* in *adityavarnam* suggests. But beyond it lies the still finer region of Reality which the Lord has described in slokas 20 and 21 of the same chapter 15. This is the region beyond all beginning, where even *upasana*, in the ordinarily comprehensible sense of the term has come to an end. As it may be dangerous to speak of the end of *upasana* before those who have not yet tasted the condition in a natural way, the *adityavarnam* may advantageously be described as the ultimate condition to them. You have stepped into the finer region of Reality. So please note and compare your experiences recalling your previous conditions through which you have already passed.

He is beyond everything that can be imagined, seen or heard. We reach Him after crossing the splendour and so on created by Him.

You have made a very fine point in attempting to derive the word *anna* from the root *an* (breath) instead of *ad* (to eat). The grammarians sometimes have failed to grasp the real significance of words from the point of view of the nature and development of Reality due to their over emphasis on symbols and preoccupation with language.

I saw a peculiar dream in the night of 30th March. What I remember I lay before you which may explain your meaning of *anna*. Somehow I got the wound of a dagger in the neck and died. I was thrown in the river. There was no breath and no beating in the heart but I was conscious of what has happened. A man knowing that I was assassinated by somebody wanted to report to the police of the incident so he examined me thoroughly. He examined the pulse which was stopped and he also found the beating of the heart ceased but I was aware of all this although there was no breath. The life began to creep again, the beatings of the pulse commenced and the heart resumed its function. Afterwards I got up from sleep and began to muse over it. I came to the conclusion that consciousness was there although the breath and other things were not there and the body was lying lifeless. It goes to show that consciousness is the root cause of life. I think this was the vision shown to me to solve the mystery of breath. How far am I correct in my judgement I leave it to you.

Regarding your spiritual state I like to deal with it after some time but I will not hesitate to say that I must give thanks to God that you have such an excellent state. The experience of the ultimate begins when every experience dies out. Those who have acquired *laya avastha* in Brahman as much as is possible for the human being remain in it sometimes with the full depth and sometimes a little shallow. A man fully absorbed in Brahman all the time cannot do any work but will look like a statue. The condition which you enjoy at present can be called a little above the ignorance. Do you feel as if you have lost something? You have yourself written in your letter that all things have lost meaning and you feel yourself as dead. Is it an ordinary state? If you translate the condition as living dead it will explain your condition better. You are not laggard, your abhyasis feel very good condition which is due to your own state.

I liked the idea that Shri Raghavan sent his letter through you. I pray that he may feel calmness and sublimity.

I am writing to you a few peculiar things for your information. One of my associates read in an American magazine that some ten or twelve years ago the Russian submarine found an air-tight container with papers in it at the shore of Madagascar. The papers were written probably in Pali language dealing with rocketry at the time of Ravana. It shows that India was also advanced in the material science. Lord Curzon, when he visited Ajanta cave in 1906, found a railway map on the wall of the cave. When I visited the cave I asked the guide to show me the place where the railway map was engraved. He at once reminded me of Lord Curzon's visit and said that the paint has fallen off. The other peculiar thing which appeared in several papers is that a young boy aged 16 died at Meerut, a place about two hundred miles from Shahjahanpur. When the dead body was prepared to be taken to the pyre it came to life and said that he died by a fall from some conveyance that very time. He entered the body lying lifeless. This accident occurred a few miles away from that place. The parents of the boy were called and the boy narrated the whole story.

I shall be very happy if my boy Chi. Aravinda be employed somewhere in good service. I pray for his success.

I wish that you may be free from the marriages of the children and their education within four or five years and the boys may become the earning members of the family. When the responsibility is over, you will be left free to devote yourself exclusively to the work of the Mission. To tell you the truth I live for the sake of the Mission. The charms of life and the world are totally lost and I feel no interest in this world.

I feel that Chi. Narayan is unconsciously improving in spirituality.

A few persons are coming from Gulbarga between 10th and 15th April. Summer season commenced but the mornings and the nights are still as cold as Tirupati in winter.

Love to children and respect to Appaji.

Yours,
Ram Chandra

9th April 1960

My dear revered and beloved Gurudev,

Please accept my humble pranams. I received your most affectionate letter dated 4th April. Only on the morning of the 6th instant did it strike me that the unusual cause of the delay in receiving any letters from you should be due to your being away at Allahabad.

Regarding my state I am yet unable to state anything. Yet I want to achieve that final rest which is eluding me. Therefore restlessness persists.

Regarding the other matter whether I feel the mood of thoughts quite distilled, I am yet in the very thick of their being, though I again and again try to think of thy words and hope they would pass away. I find however that the abhyasis are not affected by my invading thoughts. That is the only thing that makes me feel assured about thy pregnant words.

I thank you most sincerely regarding thy interpretation of the passage beginning with *Adityavarnam*. Of course I do not know whether we could derive *adi* from *aditya*. But it appears to need careful understanding in the light of your comment.

Regarding the derivation of *anna* from *an* and not from *ad*, and the experience of 30th March which verified the point, I am indeed most grateful. I am however not able to see the further meaning of that dream of thine.

I only pray that the full light of the Divine experience be granted to me and I am impatient and even worried when the Master tells me or writes to me that I am having an excellent state. I again and again ask myself as what I am in — living dead — and so on. The world thoughts and day-to-day affairs crowd into me and there is lot of feeling of frustration etc., though sometimes I do say that I am in the state of a buddha and so on which appears rather ludicrous, to me afterwards.

I tried to merge in the Supreme Master and some abhyasis especially C.S. Raghavan was telling me that he experienced the presence of Samartha Gurudeva along with thee with me. Thou givest intimations to me through the abhyasis.

I went to Shri Annaih Naidu's house last Monday and gave him a sitting in his own house and room of meditation. Incidentally I thought I removed the place of some of its shortcomings.

I went to Chittoor with Chi. Raja (my first son) on the 7th morning only as my neighbour has begun to give trouble again in the litigation going on between us. Unfortunately Shri Dorapati (our abhyasi) is the District Munsif and he is not quite happy over this litigation. I do not know what would turn out. Chi. Raja was appointed in the Indian Express office as a proof reader probationer. He wanted to join or rather get into some service and he has been given an opportunity. By the grace of the Master for which I pray fully — since let me confess I find that I am attached to him very much because of his early defeats in education — let him gain confidence and push and please his officers so that he may become a great journalist — sub-editor soon.

I returned on the 7th evening itself for the sake of finalising the affairs of the litigation. All these do indeed invade my thoughts. I pray that even these may be liquidated in a new way by their causes being destroyed.

I just explained to Shri Annaih Naidu about my theory that the cleaning activity or the removing activity of the samskaras by the Master is by a simple act of thought by the Master when he perceives in any abhyasi or in... sky of inner perception of vision. The speck of darkness or samskara will represent any trouble for the abhyasi and will get removed in a miraculous way. I yet do not know how the Master knows what the trouble is though he removes it automatically. Could the Master be pleased to explain whether it is as I have described or is it different and could I be told about it or shown it?

I handed over thy letter to Shri C.S. Raghavan after reading through it. As he says we do feel the truth of the thing but again and again our lower thoughts get disturbed and we feel for our children and others and over our other troubles — just as in my case. But by the Grace of the Master and by arriving at the highest state alone can one master these emotions and sentiments regarding children, nation and so on.

I am deeply appreciative of the several incidents which you have narrated. But not until I can verify them am I willing to accept them. It is one of the perfections of the spirit to be aware of all that from a personal point of view of experience of past lives etc. Indeed some say that without a knowledge of one's own past lives — not to speak of future — one is not fully realised.

My father and wife and children are all keeping fit. The summer has seriously started.

I got a letter from Shri K. Lakshmanan from Madras that he is getting along very well. He is finding himself to be lighter than before and rightly thinks that it is due to the Master's grace.

I have not heard from you regarding the talks on the Commentary by me to the abhyasis. I believe you would have received the last of them last week.

I shall continue to deliver the talks on the *Efficacy of Yoga* but I am putting down the summary of them yet.

With loving pranams, I am yours,
KCV

No. E 217/SRCM   **Shahjahanpur, U.P.**
Dated 16th April, 1960

My dear Varadachari,

Received your affectionate letters dated 1st and 9th April, 1960. I also received talk on Ten Commandments. They will all be published as I had written to you in some letters. I am glad that you have started talk on *Efficacy of Raja Yoga*. I want your comment on it as elaborate as possible.

There was a heavy storm at Shahjahanpur on 5th April. The wind was blowing at the speed of 50 miles per hour. About seventy villages caught fire and hundreds of lives were lost and many have received burn injuries. The materials of the house including granary were burnt. Arrangements for food and clothing for victims are being made by the Government.

I shall be very happy if my boy Chi. Narayan get first class first. He is a brilliant student, he can easily get it provided the authorities conscientiously deal with the answer copies. I am happy that Shri

Arvinda (Raja) was appointed as a proofreader. I like the post of journalist very much and handsome pay is also given to him.

In the perfection of the spirit Divine attributes are developed. If it has the bearing of something it is not on the point of full realisation. It has the awareness having of no awareness for the past, and a little moulding will enable it to know the abstract. Humanity remains even if one be at the top of realisation as I had written to you in one or two letters. My submission is that *anubhava* and everything should go into one channel. I shall write to you further on this point after some time.

Shri Bhimsen Rao with his wife and Shri Madhukar Rao arrived here yesterday from Gulbarga.

I have called Shri Ishwar Sahai from Lakhimpur Kheri to pass two months with me as I have to do lot of work of the Mission. He will come here on 20th of or 21st April, 1960.

Love to children.

Respect to Appaji.   Yours,

                                Ram Chandra

P.S. Have you applied for Nizam's Fund for Ashram, if so please inform Shri Shiv Mohan Lal at Hyderabad.

                                Ram Chandra

May 1st 1960

My dear and revered Gurudev,

Please accept my humble pranams. All of us are keeping well. The examinations of all children are practically over. The results are expected in due course. It appears that Chi. Narayana will get a first class in his latest examinations. He has applied for a lecturer's post at the University, but I have been asking him to prepare for the I.A.S.

In consultation with Shri R. Annaih Naidu I have only on Friday sent in an application for grant to the Nizam's trust fund and have also sent a copy of the same to Professor Shivmohan Lal and Shri M. Sreeramulu at Hyderabad.

I have been getting on quite without any change. However I found that last week on Thursday I had the feeling that Shri Krishna was transmitting about the evening and I immediately asked Shri R. Annaih Naidu, C.S. Raghavan and my uncle Venkatanarasimhachari and Shri A.B.S. to sit up in receptive meditation. It was a fine experience and I was anticipating it from the morning.

Today at satsangh I had a peculiar feeling that the whole room or hall was being transformed into a rich spirituality unknown before. Shri Annaih Naidu also felt so. The talks on *Efficacy of Raja Yoga* are found to be very helpful to the abhyasis. I must confess I have not been able to put down those talks. Another experience on Friday was when transmitting to Annaih Naidu I thought of transmitting my own state. I observed a white background with blue dots even similar to what you had last year shown me with yellow dots, but these blue dots began to expand and fill the whole field and it was of course very soothing. Shri Annaih Naidu confirmed this by himself.

Master yet the lower hinders though it is much less strong than before. I am of course losing myself in the Master and seeking to arrive at that total transformation which will make me experience or be one with the Ultimate Master which art thou in human form.

I found that Chi. Raja at Chittoor peculiarly developing illumination in his left region of the chest. This happened when I transmitted to him last Sunday and again today. I believe he is growing sensitive to thee and soon he will get rid of his fear and slowness.

Of course I am much concerned with Chi. Padmini and am praying that she will be changed sufficiently soon so that we could proceed to celebrate her marriage. Thy blessings alone can help the transformation and yield happiness.

We recently got into a futher lease of litigation with our neighbour who is a born litigant and what not. Our District Munsif Shri Dorapathi our abhyasi has been indeed accused of being my friend and as such he claims for a transfer of the suit to some other court. I do not know why poor Dorapathi has become a target of attack. He was so very regular for personal sittings every Wednesday. I am doing my bit for him and told him to continue the abhyas and that he will get the benefit spontaneously from the Master.

All of course is God's Will.

I have to review a book on Meher Baba, who calls himself God. He claims to synthesize the Sufic doctrines with Hindu Philosophy. It has been interesting to read it and there are many parallel opinions and views. However one finds that when I tried to look into Him I found merely a dark sky with lightning flashes — what it denotes I am at present unable to say except to say that it is much lower than what he claims for himself — in identity with the Ultimate. There is perhaps a truth of recurrence of about the same experiences in inversion at different levels. I shall be very happy to know from yourself. It is likely that the book will be out in about a fortnight's time. I believe Shri Ishwar Sahaiji has come over there to help you. Please convey my sincerest affection and love for him.

With pranams to all and to Thee who art my self,

KCV

No. E 260/SRCM Shahjahanpur, U.P.
Dated 8/9th May, 1960

My dear Varadachari,

Received your affectionate letter. I pray that all my children may come out successful in the examinations. Chiranjiv Narayan is a fit candidate for I.A.S. Chi. Raja is decidedly advancing towards spirituality. I have mentioned in *Efficacy of Raja Yoga* bisecting the heart that it contains two regions upper and lower. The lower one is the dark but it can be made use of. If you transmit two or three seconds not more than that, that the will is developing, you will see its marvellous effect. For developing material will, it is the best method. This region is for material benefit.

I came to know through Thyagarajan at Trichy that a heap of books *Satyodayam* is lying in the bookseller's shop for sale. He is selling them at six annas per copy. On enquiry Shri Thyagayajan found out that he got them at Madras in auction sale. He also inquired if they may be repurchased. If I correctly remember you left a number of books with Mr. Rajam at Madras. I doubt very much if the same were auctioned by some mistake. Shri Thyagarajan will also write to you.

Your reading about Meher Baba's condition is totally correct. I gave the same opinion to Shri Ishwar Sahai only when his admirers in south were saying something very high of him. He has not crossed even one region and there is light on the first and the second point like an arc but how he could perform the miracles is yet a mystery to me. I find one more thing that there is a slight pressure over his *indriyas* but darkness side by side. If somehow the pressure be removed of such person *indriyas* will take the bad turn again. We pray and try to bring everything in original form so that we may be able to use them rightly.

Shri Krishnaji Maharaj often transmits us and your feeling about it is correct. He named as it *ganga yamuni* transmission.

Your room is no doubt being transformed into a rich spirituality. I want that what you say must be put down in writing about Sahaj Marg.

Chi. Padmini is sufficiently changed. You may celebrate her marriage. I am sending 14 copies of *Reality at Dawn* by reg. parcel.

Shri Ishwar Sahai came here for three days only as he is busy in searching match for his daughter.

Respect to Appaji.

Love to children.

Yours,
Ram Chandra

No. E 279/SRCM   Shahjahanpur, U.P.
Dated 31st May, 1960

My dear Varadachari,

Recd. your affectionate letters dated 10th May and 26th May, 1960. I am suffering from dry cough and strong headache so I am not in a position to reply the details of your letters at this instance. I shall take up all those points of the letters when the headache is subsided. Since the reply of the letter dated 26th May, 1960, is urgently wanted, I am replying a part of it.

Shri Shiv Mohan Lal of Hyderabad informed me that Nizam's Trust Fund is not for religious purpose but for the general welfare. I am writing my views over it but I leave upon you as well to consider it thoroughly before giving any undertaking. Money you will get if not from them, from some other corner. Please look to article 2 of the constitution and byelaws of the Mission. We may give assurance to the authorities of the Nizam's Trust Fund only to that extent. The spiritual training is imparted freely without any distinction of caste and creed and everybody is welcome provided he is fit to have spiritual training. It is not safe to give assurance to the authorities that 'yoga ashram' is non-denominational, we are not prepared for it. Please think twice before you do a thing. We do not want, that in any way the interest of the Mission be jeopardized by the touch of the Nizam's fund.

We are governed by our own constitution and byelaws of the Mission which are for the general benefit without any distinction.

Love to children. Respect to Appaji.

With kind regards,

Yours,
Ram Chandra

E 281/SRCM **Shahjahanpur, U.P.**
Dated 2nd June, 1960

My dear Varadachari,

Received your affectionate letter dt. 30th May, 1960. I presume you have received my letter No. E 279/SRCM dated 31st May, 1960. My headache and dry cough is not yet subsided. With that I developed giddiness also in the brain due to lower blood pressure and I am physically unfit at this time to write a letter or to do any brain work. Still I am trying. Before dealing with the subject of the interest of the Mission, I am taking up the case of Shri Subramanyachari. He dared to write me to pray for his marriage with a girl who belongs to his own community as he said. I did not reply his letters but he continued with the letters to the same effect. Lastly I sent his letters to Mr. Kumaraswamy to inform his father to do the needful. I also wrote to Shri Subramanyachari that he should approach his father through some elderly relation or directly himself. That is what happened up to this time. I do not know what sort of man he is that he approached you with the letters and Shri Raghavendra Rao as well. His lewdness made him shameless.

It is a nice idea to send two dozen copies to Shri Muttadatt. You should keep with you at least 300 books besides what you sent at Bellary or other places for which they have paid.

The Mission stands for the common good of the world. Any man belonging to any caste, creed or religion can take up the spiritual training from the preceptors of the Mission. When the Mission welcomes all the religions and societies there remains no question of sectarianism. That much assurance can be given if it serves the purpose of the authorities of the Mission. The copy of constitution and byelaws of the Mission may also be sent there. I think I have expressed my views in my previous letter sufficiently. Shri Ishwar Sahai is out of his Station. He must have given the work of sending the Patrikas to somebody. It seems due to his negligence that the Patrika did not reach Tirupati. The question of payment or non-payment of the subscription is not involved. I am writing letter to some important person at Lakhimpur.

Love to children. Respect to Appaji.

Yours,
Ram Chandra

June 4th 1960

My dear beloved and revered Gurudev,

Please accept my loving pranams. Your kind letters were received by me both yesterday and today.

I fully appreciate the standpoint taken regarding the aims and methods and the mode of admission for spiritual training. I have today sent through Mrs.

Sriramulu of Hyderabad the byelaws of the Mission along with your endorsement in the latest letter.

I fully concur with the standpoint taken regarding Balsubramaniachari though I would like to pass the final verdict only after the facts of his father's behaviour towards him are proved. His father is not above board and may be cunning. Therefore I wrote that Shri Kumaraswami may know better; I am happy you have asked Shri Kumaraswami to look into this matter.

I shall ask Shri Rajam to send me three hundred copies and send you 500 copies. That I think will be all right.

I am happy to write to you that owing to Thy blessings Chi. Narayana secured a decent First Class in his M.A.(Hons) and Chi. Bhagavan has secured his pass in the IInd division. Other results are being awaited. Chi. Bhagavan wishes to take up Engineering Course and is applying for the same college for a seat.

Our litigation has begun seriously. I only pray it may be short torture.

I have written down about 20 pages (typescript) on the *Efficacy of Raja Yoga* lectures on Sundays. I shall send you the same as soon as it is completed.

I am only praying that Master's health must be quite all right very soon and he will be free from all cough and headache. Is it due to extreme heat?

With loving pranams,

Yours
KCV

P.S. I have been thinking of writing about my experiences as a preceptor. This thought came to me this morning as I was transmitting to Shri Srinivasulu. I found that I was withdrawing him into myself, a thing which I experienced was being done by Thee in regard to me. Indeed I felt that I was drawing in all the abhyasis into me and then lifting them up to the higher levels. Is it correct? Again I was experiencing the process of central purification as a complement of the circumferential purification or centripetal and centrifugal corresponding to the *pilu-paka* and *pithara paka* theories of the Vaisesika philosophers?

Yours loving,
KCV

No. E 292/SRCM　　　　　Shahjahanpur, U.P.
　　　　　　　　　　　Dated 13th June, 1960

My dear Varadachari,

Received your all the affectionate letters. It is intolerably hot at Shahjahanpur. The temperature ranges from 107F to 115F. I am now quite well but the weakness persists. I am really very grateful to Mr. Rajan for his service to the Mission. I love him very much and pray for his long life and prosperity. If he is in spiritual need you may do it on my behalf. I am also ready for that kind of service, if he so requires.

I am exceedingly happy that Chi. Narayana secured a decent first class. He should try to sit in the competitive tests of I.A.S. or some other competitions. I am also happy to note that Chi. Bhagvan has also passed, I heartly congratulate you. Now about my children here. Chi. Chaya passed M.A.(Pre) in Hindi and has secured second class marks. Chi. Umesh passed Intermediate (first year) and Chi. Survesh passed VI class in the Ist Dn. My elder daughter appeared this year in the B.A.(Pre) and we are awaiting results. She is at Bombay with her husband's brother who is doing atom research there and is now going to Canada on 18th June. She will return in the end of July along with his family.

Both of us are entangled in litigation. Let us wait for His grace and hope for the better. The appeals in the High Court are fixed for hearing on 8th July but they will not be taken on that day as I was informed by Mr. Chaturvedi. But I will have to go on 4th July. Litigation is, of course, very torturous for a man like you and myself.

The case of Meher Baba is yet a mystery to me. I am of course definite that he has not attained liberation. I meditated on his early life and found the image of Lord Krishna in his heart then a form of some goddess appeared. Afterwards I went to sleep and saw a peculiar dream that I am walking on the street like a vagabond, on the way found my father praying with Hanuman in the Temple for my reformation. Hearing these words from my father I went straight to my mother and began to think that my father must be aggrieved. I do not know whether it has any relation with my meditation on Meher Baba. But I think it throws some light in the early part of Meher Baba's life. After the meditation on his boyhood, he was all along dark and I felt it a trouble to meditate further. He acquired power, no doubt, but how I could not solve it yet. I shall consider his case further for the sake of interest and give you my views, privately. But if you meditate on his mature age you will yourself come to the conclusion, as your super-conscious state of higher type has been awakened.

Before writing anything further I will request you that all your talks should be written for publication, because I do not see anybody to give such a good writing. May you live long!

Pl. send your talks on the mind region and every thing in its connection, when it is complete you have already given. It will help me to consider further. Your views written in the letter seem to be correct. The inactivity is related to that pious being, who is free from all He does. We want to have similar condition, which we have by nearness to Him and thus acquiring *laya avastha*. You have written that you feel a kind of idleness and sleep which shows that you are greatly charged with the real atmosphere of "Braham". There is no doubt about it, that you remain in that condition and you never part with it, of course absorbency is further needed and you are having it gradually. Your condition remains almost changeless no doubt, you are disturbed by the worldly environment which is due to the fact that the bondage of humanity must remain of course in mild form to prevent a man from jumping thoroughly to the Eternity. There is one thing, which often occurs with the man of higher calibre. Whenever a thought comes he begins to think it with full force, with the result that its intensity becomes greater. Really we should apply our thinking as much as needed for the work. Anxieties creep in, because the burden of family lies on our shoulders.

But whenever we feel that they have gone out of bounds, we should drop it for the time being.

As you want me to write about my work, I tell you that I am still working on the atoms and the particles of the body and I do not know how much time it will take. It is easy to do it at once, but it is strictly forbidden. It was also the call of Shri Raghavendra Rao's condition and I have begun it. I see that you are not feeling my work like a child who does not feel his growth. I do not only do this work, but also look to the region whereto you are proceeding.

I often remove the pressure of power on that part of the region where you are. I am very happy that few more have joined the Mission.

A few abhyasis at Tirupati are showing hopeful signs for the work.

I will be very glad if you write your experiences as a preceptor, they will be beneficial to others. The method you have done with the abhyasis is quite correct. I have also written the method of training in Urdu as I had told you when I was at Tirupati. It has been translated in English and it will be sent to the preceptors only. I have a mind to supplement it with IInd part. But that is only an idea at the present stage. Shri Ishwar Sahai has translated it and he will bring with him when he comes.

I have asked Shri Ishwar Sahai the reason of the delay in sending the Patrika to you. He said that he was out of the station and he sent the Patrika as many as he could get from press after stitching. He is very sorry for that. On his return he has dispatched the Patrikas and I hope you have received them.

Love to children. Respect to Appaji.

With kind regards,

Yours,

Ram Chandra

P.S.- I just now received a letter from Shri Shivamohan Lal of Hyderabad requesting you to file a fresh application for Nizam's Fund. He along with Shri Ramuluji is trying his level best for fund.

Ram Chandra

June 17th 1960

My dear Revered and beloved Gurudev,

Please accept my humble pranams. I received your affectionate letters and also that of Shri Ishwar Sahaiji. I shall be applying with a fresh application in the course of the next few days. I have sent by registered post the manuscript on *Efficacy of Raja Yoga* till the mind region. I have stopped speaking on the Central region as I am not so confident. I have also sent you my work as preceptor and report for the year 1959-60. I am exceedingly grateful that Master sees among some here fit for our future work. I am eagerly looking forward to your remarks.

I shall also observe my father as instructed by Shri Ishwar Sahaiji and write to you.

My wife is now down with fever (typhoid symptoms) and boil in the back and I find she has sugar in the urine. It is now five days since and she is undergoing terrible pains. By the Master's grace I am sure she will pull through this illness. She was thinking of you and indeed dreamt of you and of course she has argued vehemently with you she says in the dream, and about you. Well I am sure she is in your thoughts and you may be able to understand her condition.

I am very happy all children there have done creditably and my sincere compliments to them. I am told by Shri Rajam that the culprits were arrested and convicted but only 122 copies of *Satyodaya* were recovered and they are yet with the Police. He has offered to bear the expenses of paper etc. himself in lieu of the books lost by him. I am so very happy Master has turned to shower his grace on Shri Rajam. He verily deserves Thy grace.

I received the two bundles of copies of the *Sahaj Marg* sent by Shri Sahaiji. Thanks for the same. I shall be remitting some of the subscriptions during the course of the next week.

I am praying for further approaches and finer state of perceptions.

As at present there is the invasion of dejection and also a kind of inability to see the future of the boys and girls here. As I wrote to you Chi. Raja is at Chittoor but he is also feeling that the present place may not help him to go far. Chi. Narayana is of course having many ideas and he is nebulous. Other children are making slow progress and the idea of marriage is slowly to take shape. When is the marriage to be celebrated there?

I sincerely pray that we attain the thing here and uniquely so that we all can speak for the Mission with full confidence. Shri R. Annaih Naidu is very diligent so also Shri G. Kuppuswamy and Sri. C.R. Krishnamurti and C.S. Raghavan. I am very happy when I am transmitting to these abhyasis. I pray for their speedier advance.

Please bless me with fuller powers of perception of the central region and the mind region so that I can speak and write about them fully and more adequately.

With sincerest pranams and loving salutations,

Yours,

KCV

No. E 309/SRCM   **Shahjahanpur, U.P.**
Dated 20th June, 1960

My dear Varadachari,

Received your affectionate letter just today. I am greatly worried to hear about sister's illness. Please get the boil examined soon lest it be of the carbuncle type for there is sugar in the urine. Sugar must be stopped immediately by any of the medicines. If you exercise your will in a mild way, but not with deep force, it can stop overnight. Also please take out the disease from the body and the boil just as you do in satsangh.

I also received your *Talks on Efficacy of Raja Yoga*. I shall write about it later, along with my reply to your letter. Here I write these few lines only in view of the urgency in connection with sister's illness.

Respects to Appaji and love to children.

Yours,

Ram Chandra

P.S.- Please do not accept anything for the cost of paper or anything else from Shri Rajam on account of books stolen from his place.

Ram Chandra

1st July, 1960

My dear Revered Gurudev,

Please accept my humble pranams. I received your reply prepaid telegram inquiring about my wife's condition. I replied at once saying that she was better. However since Tuesday she has not much improved. The abscess yet persists though there is no pain, it is yet full of bloody pus. She has developed further troubles. Her feet, especially the soles are very painful, pricking and stinging, so much so she is not able to walk or place her feet on the ground. However all this is her purification I believe and the fifth maxim has to be observed in spirit as well as letter. I can only pray for her speedy recovery.

I sent 6 copies of the publication by registered post. The 500 copies will be sent by Railway parcel at an early date. You would have received the 6 copies by now. I have also dispatched to most the copies and have advised Rajam to send 100 copies to Shri Raghavendra Rao. I believe it will be done in a few days.

Shri Annaih Naidu has gone to Hyderabad and perhaps will do the needful about getting sanction of amount from NTF.

I am enclosing postal order for Rs.6/- being the subscription for the Sahaj Marga: 1. C.R. Krishnamurti, 2. Somesvara Sarma. (Tirupati).

I am awaiting your letter about the points raised. I should very much value your guidance and correction regarding the talks I have delivered.

Personally my condition is not quite to my inner satisfaction. So long as there is dissatisfaction there is need for progress to the Ultimate. Nothing has been satisfying. I do not know really why it is so. I am not easily pleased with all that has happened. Master, canst you not grant me that which is totally transforming and satisfying till...? It appears that I am in a peculiar state of non-knowing whilst I am yet performing the work of the preceptor to the satisfaction of the abhyasis.

Dr. G. Kuppuswamy is attending on my wife and giving allopathic treatment. I am now almost looking on.

I believe you wrote to me that you will be proceeding to Allahabad on the 4th July. I do not know whether this will reach you before that date.

All children and my father are keeping fit.

With pranams and love,

Yours,
KCV

4th July, 1960

My Revered and beloved Gurudev,

Please accept my humble pranams. I believe you would have received my previous letter dated 1st July by now. My wife is maintaining improvement thanks to Thy Grace.

I cannot adequately express my humble thanks for thy extreme kindness to me. In a sense I feel all too unworthy to deserve all this grace to my humble self. Whilst I rejoice at the steady improvement kept up, I have been extremely distressed over the occurences at the official level. It has been simply difficult to believe that human nature could be so very dubious and deceitful. As you know full well I am at the mercy of elements and I am unable to understand how the spiritual progress on the one side can be kept up along with the physical regress and these two have to be set off against one another. I have prayed to Thee again and again and have found that my miseries are not at an end and do not appear to come to an end. Things expected to turn out good turn out to be either contrary or else disappointing. Of course I am continued for one more year and it may be that they continue me for another year also, according to the 60 year rule. Anyhow it is all very trying.

I have been again and again asking myself as to the clear knowledge when I can be able to say that I know the *brahmananda* and the *parabrahmanda* in clear detail, and also as to the status of the several seers of the present as also the past. How can I say that our system grants real knowledge of the Ultimate or attainment of the Ultimate as contrasted with that presented by Shri Aurobindo. Though Master has stated that I have crossed the regions of the heart and the mind and am in the central regions rings of splendour, yet why is it that I am unable to make clear and decisive headway.

In my satsangh yesterday (3rd), I felt that I was instructed by Thee to take every day some abhyasis for cleaning especially their centres. I shall of course obey this command.

Shri V.K. Narasimhan (Hindu Madras) came here yesterday and showed willingness to follow the meditations again. I asked him to meditate on Thee and offer prayers prescribed by our Mission. I also presented him a copy of the *Commentary on the Ten Commandments*.

Shri Manjunatha Iyer wrote to me that his sister has filed a suit against him for 4/5 his property. His daughter was operated upon last week and he is anxious. But he is feeling much better.

I pray to thee to lead me to that point from whence all my problems will be solved. I am feeling utterly dejected sometimes but that soon I feel that I have thy guidance and grace. The problem of my present seems to me to be why do not men seek for the Ultimate and Philosophy and young men are being corrupted by elder men. The halls of the universities contain men who are materialists and hedonists rather than brave and worthy men of India and her culture.

I am really troubled by the future for Chi. Narayana and pray that I may be guided by thee as well as he by thy grace. So too the other boys and girls.

I shall be deeply thankful if you could give me a detailed instruction as to how further to progress myself and how best to transform the abhyasis and the entire environment. Could it be done at all?

With loving pranams to Thee and all respects to Shri Ishwar Sahaiji.

Yours as body,
KCV

No. E 342/SRCM Shahjahanpur, U.P.
Dated 6th July, 1960

My dear Varadachari,

Received your affectionate letters and six copies of the book *Ten Commandments*. The print and get up of the book is very nice and I am thankful to Mr. Rajam for it. On Mr. Chaturvedi's advice I postponed my visit to Allahabad. Instead he wished me to have a trip to New Delhi. I am therefore leaving for Delhi along with Shri Ishwar Sahai on the 7th and shall be back by the 14th.

Your *Talk on the Efficacy of Raja Yoga* is very nice, though I have not yet gone through it completely. I pray for and hope you to be able to comment on the central region too in the same way. But that may be after some time when I write to you about it. I also went through your report on work as a preceptor. I am quite satisfied with it and appreciate your sincerity and zeal.

I feel much worried to hear that sister is not improving since Tuesday last. I have prayed for her speedy recovery and feel a sort of satisfaction within. Your batch of satsanghis is very nice. It is all due to your hard labour and their own faith. I received a letter from Mr. Sriramulu stating that he is trying all with Shri Shiva Mohan Lal, for the sanction of the grant and he is hopeful of success.

Your feeling of dissatisfaction over your present state is in fact due to the reaction of my thought, since in your case I have been proceeding with an idea of farthest approach into the Infinite and I am on with it and shall not be satisfied till then and it is unlimited. Dejection in this respect is of course a human weakness and must be overcome. Can you say what you mean by the state of 'non-knowing' as you say? Does it not correspond to some extent with the state of ignorance as discussed in the *Anant Ki Or*?

I could not yet find a suitable match for Chhaya. I am trying hard for it. Shri Ishwar Sahai is also involved in similar anxiety for his own daughter. Regarding my children at Tirupati I may say that we are only the trustees. I pray that all of them be nicely placed in life. Amen. But that does not mean that we may be indifferent or in any way negligent towards their proper interests and best advantage.

I received a letter from Shri V. Mohan Rao of Rajampet stating as follows:- (While sitting in satsangh with you) "I saw Dr. Varadachari disappear and appear in turns. I found an aura of light. He changed and in his place I saw your (Ram Chandra's) figure. I was calm — no thoughts — no questions — and no necessity for mental sphere to dominate in the peace of calmness. I sat thus for half and hour. I came out as fresh as the morning dew."

He could not express correctly. But it was an indication for him to think you and me alike. Now you can yourself infer to what extent you are absorbed in me.

Just now I received a telegram from Shri Raghavendra Rao stating that his brother Shri Madho Rao at Hyderabad is suffering from a severe attack of insomnia. This has caused me great worry.

My love to children and respects to Appaji.

With best wishes,

Yours,
Ram Chandra

July 21st 1960

My dear and revered Gurudev,

Please accept my humble pranams. I am happy to write to you that by thy grace my wife has recovered from the boil carbuncle and is able to move about. Her fever has subsided. Her condition is very much better. The urine however continues to contain sugar. But I am hopeful that it will also get reduced by the use of homeopathic drugs. Dr. Kuppuswamy's devotion to the Master is fully worthy of admiration. He has also been moving up in his ability for *anubhava* of the higher states. I am enclosing his letter.

I believe your trip to Delhi was a success. I must report to you that I experienced (i) that you had asked me to clean the entire series of planets from Pluto, Uranus, Saturn, Neptune and Jupiter on 5th July (between 2 and 3:50 A.M.). Indeed I was forced to get up and sit up for this task. I felt that all that showed to me that the Master is the Master of all the worlds and secondly that Master has a great work before him which requires a complete overhauling of the machinery of the universe. Some very radical change is imminent for the world as a whole and the cosmic powers are being got ready. The regions I was moving in were of transcendent grey and streaked with lightning hues. Am I right in my guess? I believe I saw Master's work, not my being bidden to do this work.

Shri Naik of Madras (chief engineer) came here on the 5th afternoon and after half an hour he left for Madras.

I have been delivering lectures on the mind region alone. Last week I did not speak at all and I felt that the descent of Master's grace can be left to be experienced.

I shall pray to the Master to lead me further on and on as He has stated till the ultimate is reached and one goes beyond all ignorance.

I am sending by separate money order Rs.24/- (21 for 14 copies of the *Reality at Dawn* and Rs.3 annual subscription of Shri Dhond Rao.)

Shri Raghavendra Rao wrote to me today about his brother P. Madhava Rao's condition. It is indeed pitiable. I am really worried about this "One day's sannyasa" of Chinmayananda, and the extraordinary fascination these swamis have on the youthful minds. I am really sorry that though Shri Madhava Rao came under thy divine influence his fate drew him to that swami, who lectures and instructs and leads men to madness and women too.

Master, some things constantly lead me to depression — this is one of them. I see it nearer home also at universities and temples. Is there any hope at all for India? Is the cleaning of the forces of the celestial world and planets a preliminary to purification of the world? I pray that the Divine Master may help the world to get out of its darkness and in the correct way without falling into the pit of pseudo swamijis and by psuedo methods.

Chi. Raja is getting on at Chittoor. Chi. Narayana has registered for Ph.D. but is also working for his I.A.S. Chi. Bhagavan has joined Engineering course. Srivasan is in Murrays.

I am of course looking forward eagerly for detailed criticisms of my talks. I believe Shri Ishwar Sahaiji has gone through them. I welcome guidance and greater approaches to the central region, which will solve all problems.

My father's health is better. The satsangh is getting on very well. I did not receive any letters from Shri Venkatapathi. I do not know whether you have thought about the 2nd edition of *Efficacy of Raja Yoga*.

With loving pranams,

Yours as body,
KCV

Tirupati
28th July 1960

My dear revered Gurudev,

Please accept my humble pranams. I am glad to write to you that my wife's health is much better in the sense that her old boil (carbuncle) has healed but the sugar continues and I am trying to see that it gets reduced. It is of course a hard process. As I wrote to you I cannot adequately thank my brother Kuppuswamy for what he has done and is doing. I feel indebted to him. My wife just now tells me that a small boil has begun to appear in her left arm. I trust it is not serious. In the meanwhile about the 9th July a cousin of my father (a man of large family and poor) who was suffering from typhoid was asked by my father to come over for treatment. I was seriously worried about taking this additional burden with the burden of my wife's concern, however he came and is with us. He was progressing favourably till four days ago and on Monday 25th, he developed trembling owing to extreme weakness says Dr Kuppuswamy, and has been giving lot of anxiety. I pray to the Master to help in this very deserving matter. This anxiety for this person is pervading the whole atmosphere. It has been a great strain imposed by fate. In the meanwhile Chi. Padmini and Gayatri got the fevers and are lying in the house with fever for the past two days. I think that all this is proving quite a strain on everyone and most on my wife. MAY I pray to thee O Master to help me out of this quandry. Of course I did try to remove the disease with a prayer to Thee and I pray that it may be so done.

Shri Thyagarajan was here last week for a couple of days and had 3 sittings. He would have written to thee.

All others are keeping fit.

I believe that all of you there are keeping well. I was awaiting Thy letter after thy return from Delhi, so I did not write earlier. I wished to save Master the tale of these sufferings here, but I could not resist the same and therefore I am placing before thee everything. Without Thy grace nothing can be done by me.

I am continuing the abhyasa for the abhyasis regularly and I am told by one and all that they feel extremely happy. The satsangh is being regularly held and I talked last week on the fact brought to my notice by Shri Thyagarajan. I have not reduced to the form of a note. I shall do so.

Forgive me Master and make me thine own.

Yours as body,
KCV

No. E 373/SRCM   **Shahjahanpur, U.P.**
Dated 30th July, 1960

My dear Varadachari,

Received your letters dated 4th and 21st July. I am happy to note that my sister has almost recovered. She has so much work that she does not get sufficient rest. Anyhow it must be given to her now. There is a fruit called here as *jamun* and in Tamil as *navapazham*. It is a sure cure for diabetes. The pulp if available may be used, otherwise its stone to be dried, roasted and then powdered. The powder is to be used with milk, coffee or honey. Here the doctors prescribe it generally to the patients of diabetes. It is out of season here now but if the stone is not available there I can send it from this place. It can be had in plenty here.

I hope and pray that all my children will do well and that Ch. Narayan did what I wanted. In the I.A.S., I may perhaps be of some help to him when he is called for interview at Delhi. The study of books of knowledge shall be helpful to him. The books can be had from New Delhi if it is not available there.

I also received Dr. Kuppuswamy's letter along with yours. His *anubhav* is quite correct and that is the only reply to his letter. It also speaks the transcendental state reigning in him at that time.

Reward he will get because he treated my sister very carefully, and most probably he may be having it.

When I was at Delhi some persons came to me and two of them have taken up the practice too. One of them is Shri Suryanarain, Asst. Secretary to Govt. at Port Blair in Andaman Islands. He also came here and passed three days with me. He is very good man and will come to Tirupati on 2nd or 3rd August as he told me. He will attend your satsangh and his wife too will start meditation under your guidance. He has to go to Tirupati for *chura karan* ceremony of his son.

Now I come to your letter. You pray for the full experience of the Ultimate and you write in your letter dated 21st July 1960, that the regions you were moving in, were of transcendental, grey with lightning hue. Your *anubhav* is entirely correct and this is one of the experiences of the Ultimate.

But I pray that lightning should also give way. To speak the truth, hardly there may be one or two persons having such a state throughout India, and they may be only in this Mission. The saints no doubt there are in India, but this marvellous condition will be found nowhere else. This is also a fact that sometimes you are led away towards despondency by the torturous touch of the world. The reason is that you are sensitive like myself and my temper in the early age coincides with yours. It is now refined by the grace of God, and you will too find the same in yourself. But as I have written to you, that the bondage of humanity cannot be removed lest the soul may jump out in its ultimate state. But I tell you that it is by your own force of will that the trouble develops so much. So we should always take the medium course. If it is necessary to take up any problem we should think its pros and cons and after coming to any definite decision, we should stick to it.

There is every hope for the betterment of India and the world at large. The personality working for the change of the world has almost finished his work, and it is coming very slowly to the earth in material form because if it is brought into full swing, the personality will have to depart immediately as his work will be over. I think I have mentioned it in my previous letter also. You have done well to exert yourself in cleaning the planets just like our world, they also have become charged with heaviness and grossness. The cleaning of the celestial worlds too is essential since the overhauling of the entire Universe is imminent and destined.

You are slowly moving towards the work of Nature which becomes automatic at your level of approach. You might have observed that when the oil of the *deepak* has exhausted it gives out a flash before it is extinguished, the same thing is going on here.

Shri Raghavendra Rao is coming to me on 10th or 11th August, 1960. I am so sorry about Shri P. Madho Rao having fallen in the mire of Swami Chinmayanand and he has been so soiled with his writings that he spent 8 days and nights to read his writings and speculating over them. This resulted into insomnia causing mental disturbance. I gave an express reply wire to Shri Shiv Mohan Lal asking about Shri Madho Rao's condition, but due to strike I got the reply after 6 days stating that he was sent to the mental hospital. I am not getting the correct diagnosis because I have not seen the man, still I have prayed for him. To tell you the fact he has not firm faith in me, and when I was there during my last tour, he was highly speaking of Swami Chinmayanand and his captivating ways. Our case is that we generally take in people who are wanting in capacity; most of them do not wait till the capacity for the inrush of grace is developed. That is why some of them walk off after doing it for sometime.

In such cases I admit my weakness. I do not know whether Swami Chinmayanand is doing service or disservice to the country. If during my South Indian tour I may be at the station where his lecture is going on, I will surely attend it in order to come to a definite result. I have heard several complaints of this sort from other quarters too. Mr. S.K. Rajagopalan was also complaining that a girl in the South who passed the M.B.B.S., attended his lectures and joined his Ashram, severing all connections with her relations.

Shri Ishwar Sahai had gone to his house for a week now he has come back again. He is all along busy with the Mission's work. He is completing a booklet on Methods for training of Abhaysis under Sahaj Marg system. He will send it to Shri S.K. Rajagopalan who will have copies of it cyclostyled. He shall also go through your notes, 'Talks on....' after he has finished this work. I think there may be little room for the criticism since they have come out from the super-conscious level of your state. If you recall your condition at time of giving it out, you will find that you were almost in a benumbed state.

I am glad that Appaji's health is better. I too am very anxious to know about Shri Venkatapathi. Will you please do me a favour of asking for his address from Shri Krishna Murti to enable me to ask him directly about his health. I have not yet received the copies of the English translation of the *Commentary on Ten Commandments of Sahaj Marg*. Here all children are well. The question of marriage of Ch. Padmini and Chhaya often comes to my mind simultaneously.

As for the printing of the second edition of *Efficacy of Raja Yoga*, I do eagerly wish to have it done the earliest. You know our difficulties, we have to wait for the funds.

Shri Ishwar Sahai offers you pranams.

Respect to Appaji and love to children,

Yours,
Ram Chandra

6th August 1960

My dear Revered Gurudev,

Please accept my humble pranams. I received your affectionate letter on the 2nd instant. The patient who was in my house under my treatment after a gallant fight of eight days finally succumbed on the 3rd afternoon. He leaves behind him a young wife with four sons all below 13 years and two daughters through his first wife, one of whom is married and the other yet to be married and absolutely destitute. The whole thing has affected me deeply in a sense and it would be wrong on my part if I did not confess to a feeling of extreme dejection. But God knows what is best for each. I feel utterly tired and weak after the whole business.

My wife has recovered from the second boil also and indeed she and I had hardly any time to think of her at all during the past fortnight. Chi. Padmini is yet in the second week of her typhoid and Chi. Narayana has taken ill on Thursday the 4th. He is having temperature of 103 and 102 today. Chi. Gayatri is now all right. It is now nearly two months of incessant medical attention to all at home and myself.

Shri Suryanarain has not come yet. Of course if he comes I shall do the needful.

The transcendental experience is however not yet continuous and steady. The waves of depression are always there and indeed I am made oblivious of my condition again and again. The constant tendency to withdraw myself into myself is there, and the feeling of extreme tiredness also supervenes both to me and my wife.

I am yet unable to understand how my 'desire' for truth or excellence to prevail could cause so much torture to 'me'. However I leave so many things to be answered in due course of time as the *anubhava* will develop. Shri Venkatapathi's address is: Shri Venkatapathi, Poonimangadu, Tiruttani (Taluk), Madras State.

I am yet in the very dark about the future. It is all Thy will and I believe that what thou said on the first visit will yet prove true. I have of course moved very much since then and hope that I will be able to say that I have crossed the rings of splendour and have attained the central Being which is perfection.

The coexistence of all is undoubtedly the most difficult to reconcile. Shri Venkatapathi wishes to finance the second edition of *Efficacy*. Shall I make any enquiries about its publication?

I shall be deeply thankful to Shri Ishwar Sahaiji if he would go through what I have written and talked and give his invaluable suggestions.

All of us offer our loving pranams on the auspicious day today when we celebrate the *Upakarma* ceremony.

With loving pranams,

Yours,
KCV

Tirupati
23rd August 1960

My Dear Revered and Beloved Gurudev,

I received the affectionate letter from Shri Ishwar Sahaiji conveying to me thy message. Please accept my humble pranams and love.

Thanks to the grace of the Master and prayers of my dear spiritual brothers, Shri Ishwar Sahaiji and Shri Raghavendra Rao, the children are progressing steadily. Chi. Padmini is now fairly all right and will go to the College tomorrow. Chi. Narayana has touched the normal and will have his bath preliminary today. It is all due to Dr. G. Kuppuswamy's careful attention, as I had almost completely got exhausted. My wife's health is of course not quite all right.

I had to go to Trivandrum on the 20th. I left Tirupati on the 19th and flew to and fro Trivandrum on the 20th after finishing my work at Trivandrum. I could not break journey at Trichy as I thought at first. But I hope to go there about the end of next month for a couple of days.

I am really concerned with the Master's physical condition of weakness and exhaustion and low blood pressure. I am sure he will very soon be all right. I am also told to have low blood pressure when recently I was trying the blood pressure instrument in the university laboratory.

I believe you have by now received the books from Murrays. Shri S. Rajam wanted me to give the *Efficacy of Raja Yoga* for reprinting immediately and said he will get it out in a few days. He thinks it can be done in the same size and format as the *Commentary on the Ten Commandments*. If you approve I shall give it to him on the 3rd Sept 1960 when I go over to Madras. If any alterations and additions are thought of, kindly do send me instructions. He is absolutely convinced that he must bring out the book soon. Of course he refused to accept payment for the cost of paper etc. for the previous book.

As I wrote to you Shri Venkatapathi is anxious to pay for the publication of the *Efficacy of Raja Yoga* (second edition).

My own condition has been very peculiar. Whilst on the one hand I am not devoting even a second to meditation, I am almost always (especially during last week) in the peculiar condition of being absorbed in the Centre — with very cool calm feeling pervading me from above. Shri Dr. G.K. had the same feeling last week when I was transmitting him last Wednesday — and told me that it was something that he never previously experienced.

The satsangh is going on regularly and in spite of all the anxiety at home about the children's health etc.

Of course I am sure that by Master's grace I am having the strength and faith to carry on with the day-to-day work. However trying the circumstances I am sure the constant presence of the Master in me is being felt.

Shri Vendantam is finding improvement and he has such a fine admiration for the spiritual greatness of Shri Ishwar Sahaiji.

Shri V.K. Narasimhan, who had a nervous breakdown last month or the month before, had been to me then and I advised him to prayer. He told a couple of days ago that he is feeling a new life and force working in him. I told him it is all due to the Master's grace.

I am hoping that all will be all right by the Grace of the Master.

I am praying that Master's health be restored at a very early date.

With loving pranams to You and Shri Ishwar Sahaiji.

Yours,
KCV

No. E 306/SRCM   Shahjahanpur, U.P.
Dated 2nd September, 1960

My dear Varadachari,

Received your affectionate letters dated 23rd and 27th August, 1960. Shri Ishwar Sahai has gone to Lucknow and he will also go to certain other places in search of the match for his daughter, he may come again after two weeks. Method of Training, Part Ist has been sent to Mr. S.K. Rajagopalan Ayangar for cyclostyle, as he wanted. May God help me to add the IInd part.

Two copies of *Efficacy of Raja Yoga* are being sent to you along with blocks of diagrams. As far as I remember I have sent you the block of diagram no.5 for the book *Sathyodayam* with a block given in *Reality at Dawn*. If diagram no. 5 is not traceable another may be prepared in place of it. I am also sending a new block of emblem. I know, you have got a block with you, if it is unserviceable you can use the new block. The blocks of photographs of myself and my Master you have got with you which may be used in this book also. If possible the photos may be printed on art paper.

In *Efficacy of Raja Yoga* footnotes have been added and at certain places English has been improved. You may please go through it and can add anything you like. I leave upon Shri Rajam and yourself regarding paper, print and get up. Mr. Rajam is so kind to us that he helped us much in our work. I often think that how I will be able to repay it. I am sure he has affectionate heart for me. May God bless him.

I am glad that my children are now well. But my worry is not yet over owing to the indifferent health of my sister. You will please write to me in the next letter whether her weakness is subsided. I was extremely weak but when I received your post card dated 26th August, I found marvellous improvement and so I have taken up the work of Mission again.

You have written to me that you are waiting for the reply to the questions. I do not know, is there any other letter containing the questions which might have been misplaced. You do not require any meditation but I am awaiting the orders from my Master for it. Your *anubhav* about your condition that you feel absorbed in the centre with the calm feeling, is correct. I feel that you are being absorbed in it day by day. Your condition is really inexpressible because the words are wanting. When I meditate on your condition I feel that the refined or pure grace of God is pouring on you or in other words you are inhaling what is there in a way that your system is being divinised. You are correct in your judgement that I am always with you and do not leave you even for a moment, if you think of me within, the flow is there.

I recall the *anubhav* of Dr. Kuppuswamy about myself when he saw me infusing divine influence in the Universe. May I ask you if you feel the same thing in cleaning the atmosphere, which has grown poisonous. The work is automatic. If you do not feel please lie down on the cot quietly and see that the work is carried on. I want to open this condition a little more.

Shri R. Seshadri is a devotional man and feels keenly interested in meditation. I hope he will be a better man for the Mission.

I am really very grateful to Dr. Kuppuswamy for his kindness bestowed upon my children and sister. This obligation is so great on me that I can only serve him till I am alive. May the blessings of my Master be pouring on him and he may reach the destination he is longing for.

Shri Raghavendra Rao's brother is now better. He reached Bellary safely visiting certain places where our associates reside.

Love to children,

Respect to Appaji,

Yours affly,
Ram Chandra

P.S. No. of copies to be printed — 1000.

Tirupati
September 4th 1960

My dear Revered Gurudev,

Please accept my humble pranams. I believe your health has become better and blood pressure has decreased. Your weakness should also have abated.

I did not go to Madras as I was awaiting your letter and the manuscripts of the *Efficacy of Raja Yoga* to be handed over to the press. Shri Raghavendra Rao wrote to me that Shri Ishwar Sahaiji has completed his translation of *Anant Ki Or* into English. He also wrote that he went through my scripts of the Talks. I am glad to hear that his brother Madhava Rao is better.

I am writing this letter with a definite purpose of having your advice.

i. I have been asked to visit the Shri Aurobindo Ashram for a few days to help the University or Academy with my suggestions about their post graduate Courses. Incidentally to deliver a talk or two to their students and Staff. This is to be at the end of September about the 28th to 30th or 4th. What would you advise me to do? On hearing from you I have to write to them within a week's time. Kindly do advise me. What should I do when I am there?

ii. Shri A.B.S. came to me on Thursday 1st September. Of course he has been very irregular and was saying that he was not in town and so on. On that day as he came at meditation time I asked him whether he wanted special sitting and gave special sitting.

He came after an hour and wanted to speak to me about matters impersonal. I asked him to come in the evening as I was going to College. He came in the evening and had a talk with me. The gist of the talk is this:

1. He is not pleased with the manner the *sanstha* is working. He avows faith in the Master but not in the *sanstha*. He further stated that he finds that all those who entered the *sanstha* have begun to suffer from all sorts of things: quarrels and disagreements with others, ill health, humiliation etc. Whereas he found relief from all these when he was with Ramana he found that all these have revived when he

came to this *sanstha*. He had been some person of importance in building up this *sanstha* at Tirupati and therefore he is very unhappy that he is not going properly. He spoke about Manjunatha Aiyer's losses etc. But I told him that it is true that all of us are suffering but not due to entering into the *sanstha* and that our woes were being borne cheerfully as the gifts of God rather than as results of joining the *sanstha*. The crow-apple falling analogy will not be satisfactory (*kakatalika-nyaya*). Secondly Shri Manjunatha Aiyer did not complain about this and connect it with his becoming a member of this *sanstha*. I also told him that I do not think any abhyasi agrees with his reading of the working of the *sanstha*. On the contrary all the abhaysis are steady and are having blissful experiences. (This deep experience of the cool fragrant power of the Divine light and not heavy bluish is being experienced by all. I called it the grace of Shri Krishna.) I told him that as such I am not at all agreeing with his view. I told him the *sanstha* is of the Master and indeed it will be steady in one individual at least and that is enough. People who have other aims and goals can go and achieve them elsewhere and not in this *sanstha*. I also reminded him that he should have known all this when he translated the *Reality at Dawn*. I told him without abhyas there is no *sanstha*.

As I knew that abhyas was not his idea and that meditation was not to his liking he said he will consider. He did not come for the satsangh today. I also told him that there is no compulsion for any one to stay in the *sanstha* if he felt that he can gain his ends elsewhere.

I spoke to the satsangh today about this accusation against and insinuation about our *sanstha*. The danger is not so much from our abhyasis but by this false propaganda that he wishes to make to frighten everybody. I told that it is a welcome thing. It makes two things clear: God saves His devotees (*na me bhaktah pranasyati*) and secondly that God removes all heavy things from one whom He has decided to save (*yad anugraham icchami tasya vittam harami*). One who is near the Ocean must be eager to be swallowed up by the Ocean — the bhakta is near the Ocean of Bliss and must be prepared to be drowned in it or be flooded by it and attain beatitude. This is the nudity that God grants the nakedness that is to be practised by those who are fit (*arhats*).

Shri A.B.S. was reminded also about his own specific statements that Master has been blessing him and though he accepted them and stated that Master even now blessed him and answered his prayers the *sanstha* is going wrong — obviously because I am in charge of it and he has no place in it of importance as preceptor or superior or something such.

He has borrowed a Rs.100/- from me in January saying that he would return it in a month. Of course I did not ask except at the beginning. Well it may be that he may offset it for his work for the Mission. I do not read his mind however.

No one in the *sanstha* has regard for him and he has complicated his personal affairs very badly and wants to throw all the blame on the ill will of others and now the Master too!

I believe that he is straying away and away. I am so sorry about it all. I am exceedingly sorry to disturb you with this story but nothing more can be done and Shri Annaih Naidu requested me to write to you. I have indeed asked Shri A.B.S. to write to you himself about his views. He may or may not.

All of us are well. My wife's condition is better but sugar continues to be present in the urine. The boils are subsiding. Chi. Padmini and Narayana are moving about and the former is going to the College. Chi. Chitra has recovered from measles and had her bath.

I shall be most happy if the Master will write to me in detail about the several things and myself and condition. I pray for fuller experience. My major difficulties are yet there (i) the encroachment of my thoughts during transmission, they come again and again. I pray that the mind be under the restraint; even when I think they are thine, they do not cease. Others or the abhyasis get the freedom from the mental but not I. Why? This when I am said to have reached the central region's circles of splendour.

Anyhow Master I pray to thee with all my heart to lead me to perfection in the yoga, fullest experience of the Centre, and also to be able to do my precepteral task adequately and efficiently leading all to thy State.

With loving pranams,

Yours affectionately
as body,
KCV

A new abhyasi, Shri Swaminatha Iyer, Tirupati Cotton Mills, Renigunta, initiated on 2nd Sept.

No. E 314/SRCM Shahjahanpur, U.P.
Dated 9th September, 1960

My dear Varadachari,

Received your affectionate letter dated 4th September, 1960. I am glad to know that my children are now quite well. The diabetic condition of my sister is causing anxiety but I am sure it will subside soon. I have already dispatched two copies of *Efficacy of Raja Yoga* adding footnotes to it together with the emblem and blocks which I hope you might have received by now.

If Aurobindonians want your help you may render it. You have asked me as to what you should do when you are there. You will do what is best for them and you will display what is BEST in you. I pray that they may have natural awareness that they are being benefitted rather spiritually by the dynamo charged by your spiritual alma mater.

I am very sorry to hear such talk from Mr. A.B.S. You have rightly replied them. If he writes to me anything about *sanstha*, I shall reply to it satisfactorily. You already know that he was not receptive. It is you who has made him such. It is very sad and that Shri Maharishi Raman is not physically present in this material world, but in his absence if anybody renders spiritual service, howsoever insignificant it may be, we should welcome it. I personally do not feel anything wrong with the *sanstha*. If Shri A.B.S. feels any defect, he should refer it to me. It is merely his hallucination to judge that I have told him that *sanstha* is going wrong and I doubt very much in his truthfulness.

Regarding borrowing of Rs. 100/- from you, I tell you a living story -

'Shri N. Kumaraswami lent Rs. 10/- to one of his associates, the outcome of which was that he did not turn up even for satsangh to him, so that he may not tap him for the refund. When I was to reach Vijayawada Mr. Kumaraswami sent message to him that he should come to see me and have satsangh with me and he forego the money — only then he came to me.'

Regarding troubles of the world, nobody is free having material forms. Even our avatars were not free from troubles. We must make the end of the troubles we get from birth to birth. If we compare ourselves with those in trouble, I am sure we will find our pangs in lesser degree, because there is something reigning inside which does not give rise to the seriousness of it.

I have already written to you about your condition in the letter sent with the Registered Parcel. If you want to ask me in that matter, you may write it to me. You are praying for fuller experience and so the experiences are forsaking you to have experienceless experience. That is the matter of study.

Now you complain about the encroachment of thoughts during meditation, for that I would earnestly say that during transmission, as my Master says in one of his writings, that the *sookshma sharir* of the teacher enters the body of the abhyasis knowingly or unknowingly, which brings the wavy thoughts which the abhyasis have. Of course, they may be translated in a way that you think them as yours. Happily you have got very good abhyasis, so the bad and vicious thoughts get no chance to attack you. I unfortunately found a few men whom when I transmitted, I was feeling the squalid sensation within me. I then refused to accept them as members of the Mission. There is one case in which I found when I transmitted to him that the pictures of naked fair sex were coming to me as he was a perfect debauch. So I did not take him into the Mission. My Master too had met with similar observations in two cases. If you want to minimise such thoughts occurring in you, you may give suggestions to your individual mind to stop such working during transmission and it will be helpful. But this process should not be done very frequently because you know many things of the abhyasis by the help of the individual mind.

You are doing your preceptorial work adequately and efficiently and you have got power to bring anybody at a glance in your condition, but this should not be tried.

I am now better in health and have increased the milk diet.

Love to children and respect to Appaji.

With best wishes,

Yours,
Ram Chandra

6th October 1960

My dear Revered Gurudev,

Please accept my humble pranams. I returned last evening from Pondicherry via Madras.

I handed over the blocks and printed book to Shri Rajam and he will be taking up the work in a few days. It will be in the same form as the *Ten Commandments*. I trust that it will be all right unless you would like it to be different. The price also will be Rs.1-25 not 1-50 as it has been put in.

I received the copy of the *Sahaj Marg* latest number containing my talks. I did not receive the additional copies. I believe they have taken additional reprints of the article so that they could be later stitched together and be issued as a separate book. If not, do you not think it will be better to have it done?

Here all of us are keeping fit. During my absence nothing has transpired here to give worry to my wife.

At the beginning I felt very much why I should be going over to Pondicherry. But on later thoughts and feeling that I owe very much to Shri Aurobindo and the Mother of the Ashram I went. It was all very nice. I must say that they are trying to do a lot of work and try very much to act in the spiritual way. However there are some who feel that it should be much better.

One intimate and old associate of Shri Aurobindo and the Mother told me that he felt that in my recent writings that I had the real spiritual grace. Another felt very much that I could not go over there and do something which the Mother really wanted to do as there are lack of real men there with the deep spiritual nature and equipment that I have. They showed me round every one of their educational activities, and they were really good. I had a separate conference with all the heads of the Centre of Education, a selfless European, a Bengali Professor, a Gujarathi Registrar, a Kannada Scholar and so on and spoke about the importance of spiritual education and Sanskrit education in true Veda knowledge and gave them a programme which they said they would consider, and were eager to implement.

I attended the darshans given by the Mother on the 30th, and 1st Oct. and though I did not have a talk with her yet I could see that she was deeply aware of me. As I wrote to you a year ago in July 1959 when I was invited to preside over the Calcutta celebration of the Birthday of Shri Aurobindo (15th August), it appeared that they want my help in the spiritualization of the work. Master knows what will happen.

I have also met two or three there who had come to know of my present association with Master and asked more information about the Mission. I gave the same. Not that I think much but it showed that some of them were deeply interested in making a further movement upward to true spirituality.

On the whole I felt that there was the atmosphere that helped the movement towards spirituality, but unfortunately there was not the sufficient power to transform the material vital and mental levels towards the super-consciousness. It was distinctly different from the theosophical and other places and the Maths of Shankara and Ramanujaites, insofar as there was real dedicated search and aspiration all the time.

One more phenomenon was that though there were lot of boys and girls of both the sexes in the

Centre and co-education was the rule, and sadhaks, there was the absence of sex awareness all through. This is rather rare in other ashramas. Quite the contrary. I observed this in 1947 when last I had been there and now also. I complimented the *de facto* secretary of the ashram Shri M.P. Pandit, a close collaborator of that very good Sanskrit scholar Kapali Sastri who wrote a commentary on *Rig Veda* according to Shri Aurobindo.

So I have submitted my report of the work. I was very happy about the reception that I had. At the end of my talk there was such a quiet which nobody dared to disturb and everyone felt that here was something very different. Such a silence they experienced. I knew that it was all thy grace.

Shri Vedantam is progressing nicely at Madras. He met me yesterday morning. Shri Rajam requires thy blessings as also his wife.

I found that my condition however remains same and the upward movement has not taken place. However now I have come to the conclusion that I should not worry myself. A friend yesterday spoke to me and said that though all have been profitting from my advice and predictions I myself continue to remain in the same place without improvement and recognition in my profession. I told him that I could do for others but nothing at all for myself. God alone could anything and he knows what is good for me. I said this remembering thy words: I can ask for others but I cannot ask for myself.

I am awaiting your letter.

With loving pranams,   Yours,
                                                     KCV

As I went through Shri Aurobindo's room I meditated and found that there was deep calm but the vibrations were at the region of the feet and passing upward in a serpentine way. Again I meditated at another place before an old bronze statue bust of his and felt a deep black with golden lights.

Regarding the Mother when I meditated I found that she had developed much and we looked straight at each other but thrice I felt being pulled towards her. She has a very developed *atma*-centre and not the blue which of course is the colour that she has chosen for her flag. She has very deep love centre in action.

I do not know what you yourself feel. However I have written as I have felt.

One difficulty is that she has been admitting whoever came as she wanted to help all. This was not so before 1938 when the selection was strict. Even then there were some mistakes and now too there are mistakes made and men come for all sorts of things and goals even as they come to Tirupati. But being very sensitive some of the advanced souls and *sadhaks* there they are worried. A few self-seeking gentlemen come but sooner or later they also leave.

No. E 363/SRCM   **Shahjahanpur, U.P.**
Dated 15th October, 1960

My dear Varadachari,

Received your affectionate letter dated 6th October, 1960, when I was anxiously awaiting for it. No doubt I was under the impression that you were out of the station. This year several Districts faced terrible flood. My house was also surrounded by water twice in a month and the water entered the gate of my house up to the certain length in the open space only. The current was not as strong as it was in 1958, because my son along with the other gentlemen succeeded in building a wall to check the flow of water through it. Lucknow is in very bad condition. The boys of the college have been sitting on the roof for three days without food. The boats were not sufficient to meet the emergency. We all pray that this untimely catastrophe may come soon to an end.

I have again intended to start for South in the second week of November, but the difficulty is that my associate Shri Ishwar Sahai had been taken seriously ill due to lower blood pressure and irregular pulse. He, no doubt is improving and has completed the course of injections. He has been removed to a forest area, and he is being treated there. He is living there with one of my associates with comfort. He has asked me in the letter just received, that when we are intended for south. Shri Manjunath Iyer, having come to know about my visit to South, has written to me that the practical examination of his son will begin from the 2nd Dec. and end on 31st Dec. It means he wants me after this date. This time, I want to start from Madras direct to Shahjahanpur taking Vijayawada in the beginning of the journey. If Mysore be my last station it will be very troublesome journey from that place to Shahjahanpur. I want to come back in the 1st week of January or utmost in the middle of January. I believe Basant Panchami Utsav will fall this year in last week of January. I could not see the calender as yet.

Since the *Sahaj Marg Patrikas* were sent from Shahjahanpur to the subscribers, so the oversight occurred in not sending you the additional copies, they have been sent now per book post. We have not taken the additional reprints of the articles, because so many mistakes occur in print. This book will be printed in Madras under the care of my brother Shri Rajam. I owe much to him and often feel that how should I be of some help to him. Will you please suggest me any service for him.

You have done very well in Shri 'Aurobindo Ashram'. Frankly speaking, you can spiritualise the ashram better than mother. Our would be Ashram is also waiting for your help; and it is you, who will do it. How I wish that the light be spread from south to north and Tirupati be the centre of it.

You have meditated in Aurobindo's room and found the calmness prevailing. With all the apology to the saint, may I ask you whether you have observed the heaviness or the frozen calmness, please observe in comparison to your room, where you sit for satsangh.

Your *anubhav* about the mother is correct. She seems to be attached with the outer layer of superconsciousness, but according to my old habit I would submit that she requires cleaning of the inner system. I have written all this so that you may ponder over it and may have better knowledge.

The selection, of course, may be fairly well done. But if our ideal is not sacrificed, we selected rubies from stone. I appreciate your sentence, "However now I have come to the conclusion that I should not worry myself." A baby having no care of, mother takes its care.

Will you please intimate to me if the sugar in the urine of my sister is stopped. How is she enjoying her health?

Respect to Appaji.

Love to children.

Yours,
Ram Chandra

19th October 1960

My revered Gurudev,

Please accept my humble pranams. I received your affectionate letter dated 15th and am deeply grateful for the same. I am sorry that Shri Ishwar Sahaiji is not keeping good health, but I am sure he will be able to go with you to the South. You have said that you will be starting about the middle of November and will do Vijayawada first. As I do not know how you will arrange the itinerary I expect you will be here about the 1st week of December. Or would you like to be here in the third or fourth week of December when my College will be closed. Obviously, you will have to spend some time at Vijayawada, Bellary, Tirupati, Hyderabad, Gulbarga, Madras, Trichy, Bangalore and Mysore.

If you will have Mysore in the first week of January, then you could go to Bangalore and then to Madras and catch the G.T. Express at Madras and return to Shahjahanpur straight. Shri R. Seshadri told me that he has requested you to grace his house at Bangalore. Shri Vedantam will also arrange to receive you at Madras Tambaram. Anyway there is no difficulty for going straight to Shahjahanpur if you finish Vijayawada earlier on your forward journey.

2. My wife is much better and though there may be sugar she is feeling all right. I believe Master is curing her fully. Shri Thyagarajan writes to me that his wife is now much better and that he intends coming over here when you are here so that he could take you to Trichy. Well I do not know the programme and I shall wait.

3. Regarding my capacities Master alone is the judge. I am sometimes feeling diffident but somehow am going on with the work. How can I judge my room myself, I am always there and perhaps its condition and mine are identical? As Shri Aurobindo did not seek emancipation but sought only to change the earth-consciousness here I believe the heaviness is there and the sensation was about my feet when I meditated in the room of Shri Aurobindo. As for my capacities to purify that ashram I can only say that I have not done it at Tirupati yet — its gods and men are a perpetual anxiety to me. I believe that what the Master says about me will happen and I may do the service demanded by the Master. When will the South flow northwards and repay the debt that it has contracted? That is for the Master to decide.

I have begun to talk about the sphere beyond the *brahmanda*. I am enclosing the gist of my talk. Please let me know whether I have done the right thing.

I am writing to Shri Rajam to bring out the book before your arrival. I received the extra copies of the *Sahaj Marg*. I thank you for the same.

I am awaiting your letter fixing up the programme.

A few persons, including Balaram Reddie of the Ramana Ashram, came here and one of them was Mrs. Talyarkhan (the parsi lady). They wished to know whether you would be willing to visit their ashram at Tiruvannamalai. I said I cannot say but shall enquire. I do not know whether it is not mere curiosity that impels them. You know Balaram Reddi who wishes to show off himself. Of course he does not forget my severe remarks but could not help visiting me because Mrs. Talyarkhan wished to meet me. Anyway I have communicated the matter. No useful purpose will be served by going there either for their good or for our mission.

As for building up the Ashram here which is to be as good as that of Shri Aurobindo, that is yet a long way. One confronts opposition, contradiction and persecution, humiliation and all everywhere, and how it can happen should be by the miracle of God's and Master's grace. As I wrote I come back to the feeling, I should not worry but leave everything to the Will of the Master and place implicit trust in the Master-Mother. May I be steady in this faith: this is my prayer.

We are all eagerly expecting your Southern trip and hope to receive you and Shri Ishwar Sahaiji with all our hearts and souls.

My father is progressing well. I believe your own health is all right and will not give any trouble during your tour. I believe all the affairs are settled satisfactorily,

with humble and loving pranams,

Yours as body,
KCV

No. E 401/SRCM　　　　Shahjahanpur, U.P.
　　　　　　　　　Dated 31st October, 1960
My dear Varadachari,

Received your affectionate letter dated 19th October, 1960. I am happy to note that my sister is all right now. No useful purpose will be solved by going to Tiruvannamalai. There will be discussions and criticism whether heart lies on the right side or on the left. I only go to my associates who love me and I take delight in serving them. I therefore will not go there.

Shri Ishwar Sahai is now much better. Only he will have to take three injections before he starts with me. I found great difficulty in chalking out the programme for the journey.

Shri Shiva Mohan Lal wanted me from 27th to 29th Nov. as his son's marriage is going to be performed on those days, and Shri Manjunath Iyer wanted me in January. I have accommodated all what was possible for me although I was put to some inconvenience. Programme is enclosed herewith. I will stay with Shri R. Seshadri at Bangalore. I am also informing him.

Will you please let me know if you feel some openness in mind since you started writing further talk on the *Efficacy of Raja Yoga*. I am sorry I could not give much time at Tirupati because I have to travel a long way off and have to come back before 21st January 1961, the date of Basant Panchami Utsava, still I will be too late in reaching this place.

These days I remember my sister very much. Since I added "my" before the word sister the affection is greatly developed.

Love to children. Respect to Appaji.

Yours,
Ram Chandra

No. E 440/SRCM   **Shahjahanpur, U.P.**
Dated 7th November, 1960

My dear Varadachari,

Received your loving letter dated 1st November, 1960. Shri Ishwar Sahai is now quite well. I am coming along with him reaching Tirupati on 19th Dec. 1960 at 17.25. I have already sent the programme under this office No. E-401/SRCM dated 31st October, 1960. I believe you have received it.

I am happy to learn that Chi. Narayan has done well in the competitive examination. I pray that my sister may become all right before I start for south. I received all your talks but since I was busy to finish sowing before I start, I could not get time to go through them. I will do so after three or four days.

Shri R. Krishnamurthi, R. Annaih Naidu and Dr. G. Kuppuswamy are really very sensitive and they are progressing well. I believe Dr. Kuppuswamy has got the reward prayed for. He is becoming internally subtler day by day. Some times the abhyasis feel the very high states because the grace comes from above through the teacher. It also happens that the teacher even unknowingly transmits from a very high state and the sensitive abhyasis feel that effect. Vacuumised state you have got but they have felt the refuse of it. If you study yourself you will find that you are no more in you.

During the period of my abhyas I devoted myself fully to become *laya* in my Master because I, by His Grace, got such a Master. If I write to you its result that may be thought to be an egoistic version. In one of your last letters you wrote to me that your further movement seems to be stopped. Your feeling was right but it is not the case now. There was some resistance which would have been over by your own force but I did not wait for it. Now you are going on smoothly.

I received a letter from Shri N. Kumaraswami that Swami Chinmayananda is blazing Vijayawada by his speeches on *Gita*. Thousands of men and women assemble there to hear him.

Appaji will be very happy and all my children and sister too, to learn that I will be again in their midst shortly.

Respect to Appaji and love to children.

Yours,
Ram Chandra

No. E 458/SRCM **Viajayawada**
Dated 19th November, 1960

My dear Varadachari,

Received your affectionate letter dated 15th November, 1960. I pray for God's Grace in fixing your son up in life suitably.

I feel worried about your ill-health and wish you speedy recovery.

I reached here in the morning of the 19th as per programme, and shall stay till 23rd morning.

With best wishes.

Love to children and respects to Appaji,

Yours affectionately,

Ram Chandra

Sedam
Dated 29th November, 1960

My dear Varadachari,

I hope you must have received the amended programme. I heard nothing from you about your and my sister's welfare. I feel anxious for it. Will you do me the favour of replying by Bellary address. Shri R. Rao met me at Hyderabad and he is and shall be with me up to Bangalore. Mr. Seshadri also came to see me at Hyderabad and stayed for 2 days. He shall meet me at Bellary again. I saw Mr. Madho Rao in the mental hospital. He began to weep when he saw me. It seems to me that now he has almost recovered. I have heard some 2 or 3 other such cases at Hyderabad where people were excited to madness after hearing Swami Chinmayananda's lecture. It seems something quite strange to me.

We are leaving for Bhutpur tomorrow by jeep. Several associates of the place and of near about place will also accompany us. My love to children and respects to Appaji.

With best wishes,

Yours,

Ram Chandra

November 29th 1960

My revered and beloved Gurudev,

Please accept my humble pranams. I was happy to receive your kind post card as also the letter from Shri Ishwar Sahaiji intimating the change of programme. I have just a suggestion to offer: you could take the Bangalore Tirupati Bus at 9:00 or 9:30 at Bangalore on the 18th and be here by 4:30 P.M. It is an express bus and arrangements can be made by Shri Seshadri at Bangalore. You could get down at the house itself if the conductor is intimated about the same. Otherwise you would have to go to Arkonam and catch the train and reach Tirupati at 6:30 P.M. You have to change at 2 places.

I have been passing through a lot of introspection and heart searching. Again of late I am utterly transmitting in darkness as it were, though the abhyasis feel entirely happy and elevated. Of course I feel myself dissolving and merging and so on. On the 20th satsangh I found myself transmitting from a centre lower down in the abdomen though I never knew of its existence previously. All that I felt was that the physical system was being attended to.

On the 27th satsangh I found myself in the middle of the transmission a great personality — white all through, coming and asking for initiation. It was of course not visible to others, but I found myself talking to her and finally gave her the prayer. After that she departed. Though she was all luminous yet I felt that it was rather heavy atmosphere. Shri R. Annaih Naidu confirmed that he found a flow of light from overhead and pressing down his own chest region. But he did not see anything more. I felt again that it was the Mother of the Shri Aurobindo Ashram, but I am not competent to say more.

I am unable to explain these things. In many cases I am entirely in the dark.

My wife's health is of course not all right: nor is my health quite all right. Chi. Chitra has developed again a new trouble: her face is completely swollen, her eyelids are also swollen. I do not know whether it is an attack of eczema which she got over about a couple of months ago. I am praying to the Master to help cure her.

Other children are keeping good health.

Shri Srivastava has sent me the original typescript of the talks on the 3rd and 4th commandments given by me so as to be handed over to you when you come over here.

I believe all of you there are keeping fit. Please convey my best regards to Shri Raghavendra Rao, Shri Ishwar Sahaiji and others.

With loving pranams.

Yours,
KCV

No. E 497/SRCM   **Bellary**
Dated 8th December, 1960

My dear Varadachari,

I am rather worried to know about Chi. Chitra's condition and have prayed for her recovery. It is also a matter of great anxiety that you and sister too are not free from ailments. How I wish you to be happy and free from miseries.

Your transmission is free from matter and it has grown so subtle that it is not easily perceptible. Moreover, you transmit from high region. If you come down to heart and transmit you will feel its force. When the particles of the body are charged every point becomes good for transmission. If one having this condition transmits even from his toe it will have due effect upon the abhyasi.

It is often the case with every preceptor that sometimes the hungry souls come to him for having transmission. Your case is of similar nature. During my recent tour I had such experiences at Hyderabad, Bhootpur and Sedam. It sometimes happens even with advanced *sadhakas* that souls appear in order to partake of the effect coming to them from the Master. This happened to me several times during my abhyas period. Souls from even other worlds sometimes come down for this purpose. I had one such case of Chandra Lok and one of Surya Lok. Besides, I am sometimes drawn to other worlds for the purpose. I am sure the soul appearing to you was one from Chandra Lok. I now like to say that you should in your leisure hours transmit to her after due cleaning.

I know about the bus service between Bangalore and Tirupati but I was reluctant to avail it since it causes me giddiness. Now Mr. S. Seshadri who is here has offered to take us to Tirupati by car dispatching the luggage by bus shortly before. We expect to be there at about 4:30 P.M. on 18th as per the programme.

With *pranam* from Shri Ishwar Sahaiji, Mr. and Mrs. Narayan Rao and Mr. and Mrs. Raghavendra Rao.

My respects to Appaji and love to children.

Yours,
Ram Chandra

30th December 1960

My dear Revered and beloved Gurudev,

Please accept my humble pranams. I believe your journey to Trichy was comfortable and your stay at that place satisfactory. So too your journey to Shoranur will I hope be satisfactory. Please convey my best wishes to Mr. Moothadath.

Of course the ten days you spent with us here has been most happy. I believe you were pleased. By your blessings and continuous fostering care I am hopeful of further progress at this centre.

I am yet suffering from cold that I contracted when you were here. My wife and children are all keeping fit. So too my father. The routine will start again on the 2nd January.

I only pray that I will be able to do the work much more efficiently, by being able to exercise more attention on some abhyasis' conditions. I am sending you enclosed my short note on Triple bodies (*karana, sooksma* and *sthoola*). Please write to me whether you agree with it. It is of course a tentative statement.

I do not see any direct result of the arousal or awakening and up going of *kundalini*. Of course all the vibrations have completely seized.

I only pray that I may be able to discharge my obligations to all my daughters and sons without much suffering. I have been thinking of how best to write on the topics you have asked me. Yet I am not sure of the 7th school as to what it is. But all will be meaningless if it cannot clearly give a real account rather than an imaginative account like Swedenberg of Sweden.

I am indeed grateful to you for blessing my present writing. Yet the world is not ready for this new direction and I have not yet fully changed. I am myself feeling diffident of many things what with the past with me. Anyhow I am hoping that the things will change and change quickly for the ushering of the New message.

My deep regards to Bro. Ishwar Sahai.

How is your asthma? I believe it has come down.

I wanted to know many things when you were here but somehow I am unable to ask or tell them. I know you do avoid telling many things and rightly perhaps from the cosmic point of view. I have not been able to understand many things clearly though I am accepting them since they come from you. To be able to write authoritatively and for the entire world one has to arrive at the stature of a world figure or cosmic figure, or else the works will simply be written off. I pray for many things but I am waiting for the Divine response. However I know that if all that thou hast done for me is to be taken it is sheer Grace itself, and Divine Grace in all its glory. How little I deserve the same I am aware of knowing only, so too my associates feel verily grateful to thee.

Shri Venkatapathi will be able to pay for the publication. He will be meeting you at Madras on the 5th or 6th at Tambaram.

With loving pranams,

Yours,
KCV

1961

No. F 22/SRCM　　　　　　　　　　Shoranur
　　　　　　　　　　　Dated 4th January, 1961

My dear Varadachari,

Received your affectionate letter of 30th December, 1960. The lumbago pain has greatly diminished but asthma persists still though somewhat reduced. I am often reminded of the kind hospitality offered by my sister and of the love and affection of the associates there. I pray for their well being. In Shoranur there is practically no work for me and I think I have wasted my time. Of course, I have been of some help to Mr. Moothadath's late father but no one does realise it. His mother is so weak that her case cannot be taken up in any way. After thinking deeply over it for two days I discovered a method for her. I put into her heart a divine spark so that it may develop when it finds a congenial atmosphere. But though by my Master's Grace I undertake such tremendous tasks for others, still none is going to believe it, and I am regarded merely as a chip of wood added to the furnace to stimulate fire. My Master is of opinion that no value at all or even any importance is attached to all such super-normal services. I may therefore be frank, though with some hesitation, to say that nobody has yet been able to understand me properly. I am reminded of Lord Krishna's predictions intercommuned to me some time ago, that the time has not yet come for the people to have a full understanding of your existence though it shall definitely come but only when you have given up the material form.

I hope you must have recovered from the attack of cold and be better now. I received and went through your article on 'Triple bodies'. I shall write to you about it afterwards, because here I am all the time busy doing something for south India.

Your *kundalini* has, without doubt been aroused and you feel signs of it at the time. Even now you are having subtle changes which require deeper study of the condition in comparison with the previous one. But that may not tally with the depositions of modern commentators on *kundalini* who had not their own *kundalini* awakened at all. The vibrations have ceased and that is the result of my doing since they were a bit troublesome to you and I told you about it there. Yet they exist in a latent form and can be roused at any moment when needed.

You failed to ask me questions when I was there. You can do so now. I think you do not understand what you actually are, because the doubt is there, though I am perfectly satisfied. I though apparently take a mass of stone, with no learning, never doubt what I say or write about. It is only because of my faith in my Master.

Regarding the book *Sahaj Marg and Modern Psychology* you may start with it after a month. It is possible that you may not at present feel convinced of its being a seventh school but ultimately it shall for sure come out to be so. All that we have to look to is that there should be **no clash of ideas** put forth in this connection. We must therefore rely on God and begin contributing our share to it. Thinking will always be correct if the idea **that Dr. K.C. Varadachari is writing, is removed** therefrom. For your query about the special personality I had told you the method as given in the book. If you do it please inform me of the results. I shall discuss with Shri Venkatapathi and Rajam at Madras.

Respects to Appaji and love to children.

Yours,
Ram Chandra

Tirupati
4th January 1961

My dear revered and beloved Gurudev,

Please accept my humble pranams. I believe you received my previous letter to Shoranur. I was eagerly awaiting your letter about your journeys to Trichy and Shoranur. Anyhow your trip should have proved spiritually useful to all the abhyasis.

I have been having a boil in my knee for the past five days. On the 1st Dr. Kuppuswamy gave me an injection also. I am feeling better today. My wife has been again complaining of pain in the region of the right back. Obviously her strain was great during past fortnight. By your grace I think that she will get all right soon.

Have you been able to fix up anybody at Trichy for work? I have now begun to devote more time for the abhyasis study, as I find that I have not done as well so far. This seems to be necessitated by the fact that I have to write the work on the subject. I pray that I may be able to study the astral conditions better. Of course it was all casually done so far but now after our discussions on the three kinds of bodies (I sent the article to you to the Shoranur address), it becomes imperative that I should have your grace to be able to have this sight of the astral body more clearly. Is there any connection with the astral body as theosophists claim as that which is the *lingasarira*?

Please convey my best wishes to Shri Vedantam, Rajam and Shri Ishwar Sahaiji.

With loving pranams,

Yours as body,
KCV

9th January 1961

My dear revered and beloved Gurudev,

Please accept the humble pranams by thy body. I have no separate existence from Thee and I am living in Thee wholly. Master this is the latest development. I had prayed to thee to grant me that approach by which I shall go beyond the seeing as object and seeing as subject. Thou hast indeed taken me into Thee. So I believe I know not what is my condition apart from Thee. Such a deep love is welling within me for thee so much so I am unable to feel the separation. Therefore Master I pray to Thee to keep me always within Thee and enfold me both within and without.

Now I constantly wish to be absorbed in Thee without any intermission for to be separate means almost disintegration for me. That may be the cause of fear and so on. Therefore I have nothing more to do than to **have** Thee as my Self and existence always without any break. Let my *laya* in Thee be complete and total. I wish to contemplate on Thy Divine form (astral form) and physical presence always and I pray that Thou wilt grant me this humble prayer.

I believe your stay at Madras has been more fruitful than previously. My health has not been quite all right. That is the reason for my not going over to Madras.

I am very anxious to have thy presence always with me and this longing is growing. Somehow Master I do not know when it will be my privilege to do personal service to Thee as a servant and instrument and body more intimately than at present.

Master Divine! I was speaking on Shri Krishna as a philosopher on Saturday 7th January. Though I was to have read my paper as the light failed I had to speak *ex tempore*. I spoke something other than what I wrote. I spoke that Shri Krishna was the founder of the Seventh Darsana — being the founder of the Pancaratra School of Philosophy in India. It then passed my mind about the correctness of the Master's statement that the Sahaj Marga will be the seventh darsana. Master though Thou sayest that Thou canst speak Thou makest us speak out eloquently. Though Thou sayest that Thou hast not read vastly, Thy knowledge and presentation of Reality goes far beyond anyone who has lived. May I humbly say that Thou art verily of the stature of Shri Krishna Himself. This is what I have been discovering these days and this makes me feel that I am not always with Thee.

I remember Thou wert telling me when thou wert here that it is making delay for transforming me fully as I am at a distance and not nearby so that changes can be undertaken immediately. I now feel the excruciatingness of this delay in transformation and divinisation. I do not know how this can be changed and overcome. I pray to Thee fervently to lead me onwards to that state of inseperation and *laya* in Thee so that neither distance nor time will delay the attainment.

I believe you will be very busy as soon as you have returned with the Grand Master's Birthday celebrations. We will celebrate the days with devotion. May Thy Centre at Tirupati grow and become Thine fully.

All of us are keeping fit, fairly well. All abhyasis look with gratefulness to Thee and our loving Brother Ishwar Sahaiji.

Please convey our humble pranams to all the abhyasis there and we pray that Thou will draw us closer and closer to Thee day by day.

My loving pranams and Surrender are to Thee,

Yours,

KCV

No. F 45/SRCM **Shahjahanpur, U.P.**
Dated 14th January, 1961

My dear Varadachari,

Received your affectionate letters, one at Tambaram, the other at Madras, and a third dated 9th January, 1961, here, but for want of privacy I could not reply any of them earlier.

I have appointed none as preceptor at Trichy, because there everyone is anxious for himself being so. If one is appointed others will be jealous of him. I therefore think of appointing one not at Trichy proper but at some neighbouring place like Madurai or so but that too only when I am convinced that it will serve some useful purpose. I have not yet decided anything finally.

Shri Rajagopalan of Delhi wanted me to move his brother Shri Ramaswamy to remind Shri Varadarajan of his promise to have our books printed. Ramaswamy said he shall do it and get at least one book printed by him. He also showed his inclination to contribute his own help to it. When I receive the final reply I shall consult Rajagopalan again when he comes to me in Utsava.

Madras was not of course so unresponsive this time and this is due to you. Your friend Shri Rajagopal took up the practice along with his wife and both felt much peace. His friend Major Lingam also joined the Mission with faith. Mr. Nayak also attended along with some of his friends. One of them seemed very much satisfied with my talks and has started studying my books with interest. Mr. Seshadri also came to Madras. His brothers and your sister along with other ladies of the house have taken up this practice. Your sister reflects signs of high spiritual improvement. She is a very pious lady.

I have brought about 150 copies of *Efficacy of Raja Yoga* with me and the rest I have left for Mr. Seshadri to bring along with him when he comes here in Utsava. He himself offered for it saying that he will be travelling I class and shall not have to pay any extra charge for the weight. I left 300 copies for you which must have been sent to you by this time.

Mr. Mudaliar conducts satsangh on Sundays, but very feebly though with a little interest of course. He does not try to develop confidence in himself and so he is always complaining of having no power in him. Last year he told me that he was not having any improvement. I told him that the spiritual lift he had got was for the Mission's work for which he would have otherwise taken at least 15 years to acquire. Since he is not taking up the Mission's work he has to wait till the expiry of that period. He was very much displeased at this answer but he however took up the satsangh work though very reluctantly. Now I feel that the period is about to expire and the vibrations for improvement have begun to grow in him.

On my way back I met Mr. and Mrs. Kumaraswami at the station. They had come to see me. I was overjoyed to find them a good deal transformed.

Your letter of 9th January, 1961, is a source of satisfaction to me. It is so lovely that I want to read it again and again. It speaks of a high type of devotion. You crave for that approach where you may be beyond 'seeing as object and seeing as subject'. I am reminded of a Hindi couplet which means, 'My Beloved let me hide you within the lids of my eyes so that neither I may see nor let you see any other.' It took me at least seven years to acquire this state and 22 years for its complete fullness. But I do not want my associates to take so much time. Please study and write to me how it goes on and advances further.

Lord Krishna is of course very kind to us and I am always confident that his power is always at work at my request. It is He who has named this *sanstha*. It is He who had sent me to south India in 1945, entrusting me with some important duties there. He was quite satisfied with my work and I was amply rewarded.

Of course I can have better reading of the condition and the changes caused by my working, if the man is before me. But that applies only to cases of high-level states. Still when such a chance is not available, I then form a will to the effect that the power is working according to the capacity which too is increasing. Sometimes love induces me to do more than required but then the Master who is always alert offers me hints for its regulation. Moreover, if I be with you for a year I may hardly be able to transmit to you for more than 3 or 4 times. I am however in search of a way for it. For your consolation I may say that for most of the time I remain thinking of you except when I am deeply in touch with the state where even consciousness has no place.

My love to children and respects to Appaji.

With best wishes.

Yours,
Ram Chandra

P.S.- Shri S. Vedantam is suffering from nervous debility and his veins have become thicker so he feels such kind of vibrations. Now the system has improved and the vibrations are felt very mild. Only in forehead or very slight in occipital prominence. Shri Ishwar Sahai has gone back to his place.

No. F 50/SRCM Shahjahanpur, U.P.
Dated 24th January, 1961

My dear Varadachari,

Before this I had dropped you a letter on the 14th January. One point of your previous letter remained unreplied which I now reply herein. You had written to me that you saw fearful dreams some times ago. The cause is not spiritual. During sleep if the hand comes over the chest one has fearful dreams. If it comes over the heart then horrible dreams are there. This is a matter of experience. When I was at Tirupati this time I saw a frightful dream. When I awoke I found my hand at the heart. Sufis also say that sometimes an abhyasi feels fear for no cause. That means divine fear has developed in him which will cause no wrong. It seems to be right and I have had that condition. One or two sensitive abhyasis also wrote to me the same. But I differ from Sufis in one respect. One of the Sufis says that this is the last stage of development. According to my experience it comes in the beginning after some advancement and it may come after stepping into a bit higher region. I felt this thing after two years of abhyas. The sensitive abhyasis who experience this are those who had practised for two or three years. This I write to you merely for the sake of your knowledge.

Utsava is gracefully over. Mr. Seshadri is also here. He will leave for Delhi on 25th via Hardwar. He will stay at Hardwar for a few hours in order to have a dip in the Ganga. Four persons from Gulbarga including a lady also joined the Utsava.

I tried to see Mr. Rajam and he also promised to see me at Tambaram but none of us was successful. Mr. Venkatapathi, could not come to Madras to see me. If you find any difficulty in paying up the bills of the press please write to me. I shall try to manage for it somehow though it may be a difficult task.

I hope I shall, somehow, be able to give your talk on 'Ten Commandments' to the press. So the book is being scrutinised as you wanted and the suggestions will be sent to you. This book and the *Efficacy of Raja Yoga* will help us in having it as the 7th Darshan. Of course other books will also be helpful. When you begin writing *Sahaj Marg and Modern Psychology* I shall suggest that if a correct thought does not agree with the modern psychology you may write it as my original thought. There is a note to this effect, which is a thought from the above. It says that, 'You will depict a new line of philosophy.'

For the present world, vast reading of books is essential which I do not know why I do not do. It may be due to nothing but my laziness. Regarding practical knowledge, as my Master says, he has transferred all to me and any question regarding the practicality, I trust, I can answer by His Grace. He showed me everything practically and what I have written in *Efficacy of Raja Yoga*, I have seen all these things. But nobody values the spirit but only the handsome body.

A few days back before Utsava I transmitted to you for three days devoting two minutes each day. On the third day, my Master stopped me because it seemed to him more than required. Please write to me your feelings or condition so that I may proceed further in my work. The higher sort of training is very easy. A few minutes are sufficient but good deal of thinking and also the capacity and reading are necessary. For your guidance I may say that when you are not able to decide as to what or how much is needed for the capacity then think that what is in accordance with his capacity or as much as the Master wants him to have, is going to him. There is some reference to it in the book on the methods of training also.

Since you want me to tell you what I am doing in your case I say that I want to convert all your knowledge into divine and that is why I asked you to attempt writing the book after a month. My Master has controlled what I did in three days. I only want the reply of it by return of post if possible. I am thinking of some means to be with you for this work though I remain there in the room all the time. I think you remember that I wrote to you some time ago that you do not require any meditation now, though then I was waiting for my Master's orders in this connection. Now my Master also is of the same opinion and says that you need not meditate as you used to do, but devote that part of the time also to the work of the Mission.

Please write to me about sister's health. I am glad that she is better than all of us. But tell her again that she should transmit to the ladies if they come to her for that purpose. I entrust her with this work only because ladies are more free with ladies. Besides when they have time to come to you for the purpose, you will be at the university at that time.

Mr. Seshadri, Saint Kasturi and Shri Ishwar Sahai offer pranam to you.

With love to children and respects to Appaji,

Yours,
Ram Chandra

P.S.- As regards the use of the word 'ignorance' for 'Agnanta' what do you think of substituting 'Agnostic' or 'Agnosis' for it.

Ram Chandra

Tirupati
26th January, 1961

My dear and revered Gurudev,

Please accept my humble pranams. We are all keeping well. You would have by now received my previous letter enclosing an article for consideration and correction.

The following gentlemen had taken to our abhyas.

1. A. Deenadayalu, C. Kanaka Durga Mining Syndicate, Rajampet
2. Rajagopalachari, B.E., Asst. Electrical Engineer Construction, Renigunta
3. V. Srinivasan, B.A. (Hons.), G.M. Street, Tirupati
4. Rangarajan, B.Sc., G. Sannidhi Street, Tirupati
5. Ramanarao, Clerk, State Bank of India, Tirupati
6. Dr. V. Parthasarathi, 26/114 A Dasaravari Street, Suryaraopet, Vijayawada 2 (this gentleman is the brother of Shri V. Pandurangarao of the Veterinary College here who is already our abhyasi

along with his wife who comes every Sunday for sitting.)

I am enclosing a copy of what Dr. G. Kuppuswamy wrote and gave me last night for your consideration.

20th January, 1961 — Morning satsangh. Pleasant quick grace could be felt flowing down the crown of the head down to the chest and permeating all through the body. Every cell and fibre was felt as if bathed in His grace. Later the flow was impinging on the heart region transmission coming from the preceptor.

Evening: Disturbing though transmission was felt intensely.

21st January, 1961 — Morning. Transmission was very intense. Grace was felt in every cell of the body, descending from above and from the front. The place where the preceptor was seated was one mass of light. Not even the form or outlines of the preceptor was discernible, even after the wanton imagination of his form. The transmission was flowing from this mass of light towards me covering me entirely. This unforgettable phenomenon lasted right through the whole hour almost.

Evening. A little disturbing. The transmission was felt as vibratory in character and the whole body was tingling and warm right from start to finish. A big grey whitish fleecy cloud appeared hovering in the room and from it small bits of separated and was seen entering into everyone in the room.

22nd January, 1961 — Morning. Began feeling the transmission even from 6 am at home. At the sitting transmission was producing the tingle and warmth in the body but not so strong as in the previous evening session. A little disturbing. I have not got the other reports of the Basant Panchami transmission of the Master.

I am awaiting Master's instructions and advice regarding Chi. Narayana.

Shri Manjunatha Aiyar has written to me that his son failed in the examination ù that is what I anticipated. His sister also seems to have again started trouble. He writes that he has started the regular satsangh at his place.

With loving pranams,

Yours,
KCV

No. F 58/SRCM. **Shahjahanpur, U.P.**
Dated 27th January, 1961

My dear Varadachari,

Received your affectionate letter dated 23rd January, 1961. I presume you received my letter F 50/SRCM dated 24th January, 1961. I only wanted its reply for my proper adjustment to the work I have undertaken. The family members of Shri R. Seshadri are quite good. Shri R. Seshadri was telling me that they have joined the Mission because they have observed that he has been transformed. Since I saw your sister in Madras, I remember her very often because she is very pious, but am sorry she is asthmatic.

I am happy that Chi. Narayan has got the job. I am of the opinion that he will shine better in the officer line than as a professor in the university. But as there was no good service at hand I wanted that he may take doctorate. It was also my selfish motive that he may acquire knowledge like you, rather better than yourself. Practical knowledge he can have easily but for theoretical knowledge he will have to depend on himself. I pray he may rise and rise. Amen.

The book *Reality at Dawn* is now exhausted and there are only thirty-one copies left but the demand is still there. An American Mr. Robert Lester has gone through the book *Efficacy of Raja Yoga* and the *Commentary on Ten Commandments of Sahaj Marg* and feels interested as I was informed by Mr. Rajagopal of Salem. He also wrote to me to send the books of the Mission to Mr. T.S. Krishnaswamy Iyer of Madras for sending them to Professor Smith of Syracuse University, U.S.A. and I have done it.

I have already given my finding about Mr. S. Vedantam. It is his wrong impression that transmission could do him harm. It sometimes cures the disease. What I am trying that he may be free from the disease at least to the extent that he may go on well with his abhyas. Really I did not transmit him except a little in the end of each sitting to soothe the heart and invigorate the nerves only while I was at Madras. Now please advise me if I proceed with the work. I think his consultation will also be necessary in this respect. I assure you that I get guidance in all my work according to the capacity and the condition of the taught. So there can be no danger. Of course, I developed a habit that sometimes in a few cases I give a little more than their capacities but in that case my Master keeps guard over them. I am not taking time in your case as I have taken in my own one. The same is the case with all others who are following you with faith. Regarding your complaint I would say that it is not due to the awakening of the *kundalini*. It has taken its right course. You have said something about it. Please recall. I relaxed the check a little. You will become all right. Think a little that it is going out of the body in the form of vapour or smoke as you do in the evening meditation. A day before the Utsava I became all right. Sister's ill health of course worries me and I shall pray for her recovery.

Mr. Seshadri has gone back on 25th Jan. and will reach Madras on 30th Jan. staying two days in Hardwar and Delhi. I also received your article about the 'astral body'. I feel that *karana sharir* is at the head of the astral body discharging its effect to the astral body. If one wants to end their *bhogam* very soon he can draw the impressions from it to the astral one. In this way time for *bhogam* will be reduced and the intensity will develop. What we do, we try to fry the impressions as much as possible. Further study in this matter reveals that it is the field for the play of that centre (*karana sharir*). So it is something separate but connected with it.

Love to children and respect to Appaji.

Yours,
Ram Chandra

Tirupati
27th January, 1961

My dear beloved Gurudev,

Please accept my humble pranams. I received your affectionate letter today. You have asked me to let you know the effects of the transmissions you have made before the 20th instant. I find that I have not recorded anything special. I tried to write down my attempts to study the astral conditions of the abhyasis. During the Utsav I found myself deeply moving near and nearer the centre. I had entered into your body so to speak, and was being led on to the centre beyond the rings of splendour. I sent a letter yesterday to you in which Dr. Kuppuswamy's reaction is given. He also told me that he saw me moving farther and farther away into the central region so to speak.

I note with great joy that I am going to be divinised in all my works hereafter. It is all due to the grace of the Master. Yes I shall try to devote more time to the work of the Mission. My wife in fact started giving transmission to ladies. Mrs. V.P. Rao got it last Sunday. I was sitting by my wife's side.

I have no doubt that the fears and so on in dream conditions are of the superficial level, but having got it now I felt bound to communicate the same to you. In fact during the Utsav some dark figure came into the satsangh. But I was able to send them out after burning their dross.

Yes I shall try to write the book on Sahaj Marg and Modern Psychology.

I am so sorry that Shri Rajam had not met you. I am equally sorry that Shri Vedantam has somehow got a feeling of the kind he got after this visit of yours this time. Well Master knows all and each one's evolution is determined by his fate.

I am expecting your advice about Chi. Narayana. We are all keeping fairly well.

My devout pranams to you,

Yours,
KCV

No. F 70/SRCM Shahjahanpur, U.P.
Dated 3rd February, 1961

My dear Varadachari,

Received your affectionate letters dated 26th January and 27th January, 1961. Your *anubhava* about the central region is so far correct that you are going nearer to the centre. You are being pushed towards the third ring of light by your own effort, that is devotion but you require a push from this poor being. What I want that you may not remain dependent on me for your approach. If I find that you are taking unnecessary time I will push you on. So please leave this work on me. I have taken up your case again for the work which I have recently started. Since it is a new type of work which you so kindly have given it to me, I want that whenever you feel anything worth communicating please write to me. I am sure everything will go well because I do things very mildly and cautiously. How I eagerly wish that I may get the people who may encourage me to give them my humble services after a very high approach. May I ask you if you are feeling the subtle changes in your body.

Dr. Kuppuswamy observed correctly that the grace was felt flowing down the crown of the head. On this occasion the power of the Master becomes active to give us direct satsangh also. The feeling of 21st Jan. 1961 that he observed the mass of light instead of the preceptor is correct. He is really very sensitive and he observed rightly. As far as I remember, though not correctly, that I left something accidentally to be entered in all of you in the form of grey cloud.

I have already expressed my views about Chi. Narayan under this office letter F 58/SRCM dated 27th January, 1961. I again pray for his betterment in every fibre of his being.

Shri Raghavendra Rao and saint Kasturi wrote to me in their letters simultaneously that when I am before them even then they long for my *darshan*. This is a peculiar state, of course admirable.

So sunk am I in quest of Thee,

I be in Thine, yet search for Thee.

I am sending you twelve books of *Reality at Dawn*. Fifteen copies have been demanded by Mr. Manjunatha Iyer that will exhaust the whole stock leaving four or five with me. I am for the time being detaining the order of Shri Manjunath Iyer or I will send to him a few.

I received a letter from Robert Koch from Berlin to allow him to translate the book *Reality at Dawn* in German. I am sending to you a copy of the letter for your opinion and a copy to Shri Raghavendra Rao. I hope both of you will like this idea.

Love to children. Respect to Appaji.

With best wishes.

Yours,

Ram Chandra

Letter to Robert Koch of Germany
No. F 72/SRCM   Shahjahanpur, U.P.
                           Dated 6th February, 1961

Dear brother,

Your kind letter dated 28th January, 1961 to hand. The Mission is really grateful to you for your kind appreciation of the book *Reality at Dawn*. Since you are interested in yogic science — a short cut to realisation, I have the pleasure to forward under separate cover my earlier publications — *The Efficacy of Raja Yoga in the Light of Sahaj Marg* and *Commentary on the Ten Commandments of Sahaj Marg*, for your kind perusal. My latest work *Anant Ki Or* (Unto infinite) which I had to write in Hindi due to the pressing demand of the Hindi speaking people of India can be sent to you if it be possible for you to read. The book contains the actual experiences of an abhyasi (one who practices) from beginning to realisation.

I am very happy to learn that regularly you do the meditation. If it is aided by 'transmission' it brings easy success. If you so desire to utilize my humble services towards the divine pursuit, I shall be able to do it from this place — the distance is no bar to transmission.

I have noted with pleasure that our German brethren are inclined to catch the true spirit of the religion. To me the world is one unit. Hence my services are equally available to the aspirants.

As for the authorisation for translating *Reality at Dawn* in the German, the matter is under the consideration of the publication department of the Mission and it is hoped that shortly you will find favourable reply.

With kind regards,

Yours affectionately,

Ram Chandra

Tirupati
9th February 1961

My dear and revered Gurudev,

Please accept my humble pranams. My wife's health has been causing me anxiety. Her right leg, ankles, heel and soles are very painful. She has varicose veins which have tended to increase and she is unable to walk.

My own health has been not quite all right but it is tolerable. Chi. Narayana will follow your advice and take up the job, though it is not attractive at present. He may yet try for the I.A.S. next year. Of course I am left without any help here at home. But one cannot but sacrifice one's own comforts and interests in the interests of the children.

My major anxiety was caused by a recent event and that is concerning my daughter Chi. Padmini. I do not know how to put it up to you. You have rightly gauged that perhaps her mind is not turned towards the boy Y.K. Srinivasan whom I had thought of and even think of as the fit and proper husband for her. I pray that her mind be now turned towards accepting the alliance as being in her interest finally. I find that her mind is likely to stray and make her miserble. I do not wish to canvass in my mind or to you the various possibilities and the shocks that myself and my wife have to go through. I pray that Thou wilt guard her from any lapse and lead her to a happy alliance. It is necessary that the marriage must be completed by the end of May 1961. Her final B.Sc examinations are expected to be over by the end of April. I am having sleepless nights over this matter. I am always thinking of your holy mantle as protecting like a sheath Chi. Padmini. May your blessings be with us all and her specially.

I have tried to write the first pages but have not been able to proceed. I shall try again and again.

I learnt from Shri Ishwar Sahaiji that you may be going to Lakhimpur about the 12th or so, and would be staying there for the marriage of his daughter. My best wishes for the couple's long life and prosperity.

I have nothing more to add. With loving pranams,

Yours as body to whom I am dedicated and confide all.

KCV

No. F 89/SRCM Shahjahanpur, U.P.
Dated 10th February, 1961

My dear Varadachari,

I presume you have received my letter sent along with the parcel of books. Please inform me where Chi. Narayan has been posted?

I am going to Lakhimpur Kheri tomorrow to participate in the marriage ceremony of Shri Ishwar Sahai's daughter and will return on 20th or 21st February.

My health has been greatly improved due to massaging of the body with mustard oil. How is sister going on with her health?

Love to children. Respect to Appaji.

With best wishes.

Yours,
Ram Chandra

12th February 1961

My dear revered and beloved Gurudev,

Please accept my humble pranams. I received your kind letter dated 3rd February. I also received the copies of the *Reality at Dawn*. We have to think of issuing a second edition of the book. I shall see what can be done about it after I go and meet Shri Rajam at Madras sometime in April.

I think you would have received my confidential letter. I have no sort of doubt that the divine Master will look after me in every way as also the children. Chi. Narayana will do as you have advised; he is expecting the final orders. I shall be writing to you as soon as he gets it. He has to go to Delhi for training. With Master's blessings he may be able to complete the training satisfactorily. He will be happy to have Master's directions and help in Delhi. My wife's health continues to be unsatisfactory.

Regarding my own *anubhava* which you have asked me to write. I find quite a dry region, and it is inexpressible in a sense. But as I have left myself at your hands for any transformation, I am even insensible of what is happening. As I wrote I am not able to go ahead with the writing, perhaps it is arrested to have a greater purity and perfection from the Centre itself — Thy grace is all that I am aiming at. I am eager to go beyond the 7th ring also as Thou determinest. I am indeed supremely blest that I have been able to get a Master who will take me to the highest Divine condition open to man. The divinisation of my entire being is my goal and thou alone canst do the same for me. May I be worthy of Thy love and grow as part and parcel of Thy being — the central Being the Ultimate. I feel several times that I am nothing at all. When can I write divinely superior to Shri Aurobindo and lesser men like those we meet in universities?

I spoke to Dr. Kuppuswamy about his experiences as you have stated. He is about the most sensitive as even Shri Annaih Naidu did not mention this.

As for the experience of Shri Raghavendra Rao and Saint Kasturi all that I can say is that the many statuses of the Divine require to be simultaneously experienced. I have always prayed that I may behold the five statuses of God or the Deity at the same time as in the *visvarupa* of Shri Arjuna in the battlefield — the transcendent, the creator-sustainer-destroyer, the *avatara*, the *antaryami* and the loving wonderful form of nearness and light — *arca*.

I am praying for the darshan and company of the Master, within me, without me and all about me, I pray for the Master keeping me within him and myself within feeling it as if he is within me. All these are what the *Upanishads* tell but I want it to be real and not merely imaginary. When can I feel and know and enter into the Divine Master all these and more. For the Master has given and can give more than all that the *Vedas* also have stated. Shri Aurobindo claimed that he had gone beyond the *Veda* and the *Gita*. But I now know that thou hast and the Samartha Guru has also gone far beyond all. The divinisation of man is of course the greatest occult secret and I pray that it may be the true principle and method of transformation and divine birth of man that will save mankind.

It is very nice to read the letter of Robert Koch from Berlin. Yes the *Reality at Dawn* can be translated into German on the terms proposed by him, provided in some sense you are assured that the translation is accurate. Master, with thy supramental knowledge thou must be keeping him inspired to translate properly. It will be good to have this work in German.

He can also be sent the *Efficacy of Raja Yoga* and the *Ten Commandments* also to correct his understanding.

I do not know whether there are any other commitments.

Anyhow it is good that the work will get a wider publicity and the West may be better fitted to receive the message of the Master than the East.

Today I wrote to Shri Y.K. Srinivasan asking him to give his consent for the marriage. If he agrees then May end may be the time for the celebration.

My father is all right in health. So also all other children. Nothing more to add about the other things.

With loving pranams.

Yours as body,
KCV

No. F 106/SRCM **Shahjahanpur, U.P.**
Dated 26th February, 1961

My dear Varadachari,

I am replying your letter dated 12th February, 1961. When Chi. Narayan goes to Delhi for training I must be informed so that I may write to Mr. Rajagopalan to take him to a few persons who know you by name and respect you. Mr. Rajagopalan will most probably come to see you at Tirupati from Srirangam on his way back to Delhi. If need arises I will myself proceed to Delhi. I wish him every success.

Sister's health is causing me anxiety. I am praying for her recovery and wish to see her healthy again.

I have already sent *Efficacy of Raja Yoga* and *Commentary on Ten Commandments of Sahaj Marg* to Mr. Robert Koch and later on 22nd February the authority for the translation of the book and its publication has been given. If he informs me that he is going to translate the book I will pray my Master to keep him inspired so that he may be able to translate the book properly. The letter which I sent in reply is also enclosed for your perusal.

I must speak to you plainly that it is the mere delusion of Shri Aurobindo to claim that he had gone beyond the Veda and the Gita. His system was not at all divinised. I can only boast by the grace of the Master in the present time that a few associates have come to the standard that their system may be divinised. He, of course, was an intellectual giant only touching the spiritual plane and he is now hungry for spiritual food. Do you not believe if I say that your whole system is being divinised but there is one difficulty with me for this sort of training, which my Master knows, only that I have to make the capacity to grasp this highest teachings that is why the delay. To tell you the truth I have devoted nearly forty hours in a month in your making for one and half year, and still I give you some time. I have devoted so much time not because you were lacking in any way in spiritual capacity but I wanted to finish your work soon for my work. At the higher stages it becomes almost impossible to express the condition, still you have done, saying, "I find quite a dry region." This hint is sufficient for me. If I translate your condition I will find you like a man in an arid desert where life is extinct, squall of winds have been ceased and heat of the sun is not intolerable. I assure you that you can divinise the system of others in a second provided you are absorbed in me at that time, but the practice will be dangerous for the abhyasi if the power behind you are in conjunction with you as I see. The divinisation is not at all difficult, but to bring a man to that standard is a difficult job, so it takes time. When I am at Tirupati I am charmed with your affection and I forget many things which I want to do, so please make a note somewhere to remind me when I am there, to apprise you of the condition of Gita and Veda so that you may feel yourself how far you have travelled to that direction. Will you please try to see whether I am not with and within you as you want and this is my work to study whether I am not keeping you within me.

You feel that you are nothing at all. It was the condition of Hanumanji; but please try to gather yourself at one point and see, if the force is there. I myself feel the same.

I got prepared 'Amla Hair Oil' which I will send it in a few days by postal parcel. Let us see if it reaches safely.

I shall write further when both of us are relieved from worries as mentioned in the letter annexed hereto.

Love to children. Respect to Appaji.

Yours,
Ram Chandra

5th March 1961

My dear revered Gurudev,

Please accept my humble pranams. I received your letter dated 25th and 26th. I am profoundly grateful for the same. I am sure my prayers will be answered.

I am glad you have decided to grant permission to Herr Koch of Berlin to translate the book. Chi. Narayana has not yet received any orders. He will certainly avail of all the help that Shri S.K. Rajagopalan will be pleased to give him. Shri S.K. Rajagopalan was here yesterday afternoon for a couple of hours. I am glad to say that he is a lovable person with deep faith in the Master.

My wife's health has been giving me anxiety. It is one of those things that makes me hesitate to send away Chi. Narayana who is of great help to us here. She is in fact confined to bed. I can only pray that she will be getting strength to stand the strain of the next three months. I am going ahead with the preparations for the marriage of Chi. Padmini which is tentatively dated for 26th May. It will be a very simple family affair. I can only pray that she will be able to do all the work that will fall on her. We have hardly any help.

You will be glad to learn that they have extended my service for one more year.

I am rather diffident about the whole. I cannot explain my condition. Except for the fact that the Master states that I am in a very good state I find that the period is really marked by nothing. As the daily weather report runs: Mainly dry — no change.

Of course I felt in one satsangh that I had reached a changeless state. There is hardly any desire to write or do anything. I am even unaware of my transmitting condition. Shri Annaih Naidu is forging ahead. So too Dr. Kuppuswamy. Dr. V.P. Rao (Panduranga Rao) is also finding good experience. Shri C.R. Krishnamurti and C.S. Raghavan are feeling much better. I pray for their betterment in both directions.

I can only say that our *sanstha* is so very unlike any other that it is difficult to explain even to others. I can only pray for the change. Shri Rajagopalan was telling me that there is not one abhyasi whom he is getting to train at New Delhi. May I pray that we will be able to get more persons to take interest in this real yoga.

Once again praying for the speedy recovery of my wife and blessings for the happy marriage of Chi. Padmini I remain,

Yours,

KCV

Shri Ranga Rao who had taken to abhyas under you at Bangalore, wrote to me from Calcutta. Among other things he asked why I had accepted you as my guru giving up Shri Aurobindo and Shri Ramanuja. I replied that they did not accept me as their disciple. It was you alone who came asking me to take to this practice. Therefore the response.

Shri Mohan Rao of Rajampet wrote to me about his invitation to you to go over to his place next time you visit South. Yes he is earnest. Shri A.B. Subramaniam has practically severed all connections with our work. I have not heard from Shri Manunatha

Iyer of late. His sister is giving him lot of headache. He has prayed for his son's passing the examination in the ensuing April.

I have not heard from Shri Venkatapathi after he left on the 23rd January. I believe your health is all right.

I should like to have a short note from you about what divinisation means and how it can be recognised.

Yours affectionately,
KCV

No. F 146/SRCM **Shahjahanpur, U.P.**
Dated 19th March, 1961

My dear Varadachari,

Received both of your affectionate letters. I am greatly worried to hear the illness of my sister. May she recover soon. Since the receipt of your letter I have begun to pray for her speedy recovery. I have strong hope that our prayers will be answered. I am observing her from a long distance so I am not sure of my diagnosis, but as thinking goes on I find that it is not the case of typhoid. Please assure her that she will perform the marriage of Chiranjivi Padmini happily. Please also inform me about her leg trouble. Herr Robert Koch demanded help in his meditation. He also says that he felt some power in the heart after the receipt of my letter, and the meditation was quite good.

I want to write to you many things about your condition as I feel but I shall do so after the recovery of my sister. You wrote about your condition that you feel diffident. I wrote the same word to my Master and he was glad to hear that.

Shri Raghavendra Rao's wife was taken seriously ill and she has been taken to hospital for treatment. I presume that she will be now better but I am waiting for Shri Raghavendra Rao's letter. Love to children. Respect to Appaji.

Yours,
Ram Chandra

Tirupati
23rd March, 1961

My dear revered Gurudev,

Please accept my humble pranams. I am happy to write to you that thanks to thy grace my wife is slowly recovering and will be completing the third week of typhoid satisfactorily in a couple of days. Chi. Narayana is not yet in receipt of his orders but it is expected in a few days time. As I wrote to you I am preparing to have the marriage on the 26th May. I believe by thy grace all will run smooth.

The college will be closing for the vacation sometime about the 9th April. So I hope to get busy afterwards. Of course my wife is very much worried about her health and her inability. She wishes to thank Thee for all that thou hast been doing to her.

There is nothing that I can write beyond saying that I am praying for highest approach to the Ultimate. Let me be free from all that prevent the same.

With humblest and loving pranams,

Yours as body,
KCV

undated

My revered Gurudev,

Please accept my humble pranams. My wife is better but very weak. We are indeed most thankful to you for thy blessings. I am sure we will be able to perform the marriage without much worry and difficulty by thy grace. Her leg has varicose veins and there is gouty condition. The doctor thinks that she has also blood pressure. But it is all due to disappear soon.

I am unable to write anything about myself. But I have been receiving good reports from Shri Annaih Naidu, Dr. G. Kuppuswamy and other abhysis.

KCV

No. F 162/SRCM **Shahjahanpur, U.P.**
Dated 6th April, 1961

My dear Varadachari,

Received your affectionate letters dated 23rd March and 27th March. Thanks to God that my sister has recovered from fever. I believe she must have come to normal diet. If so please inform me. During the marriage of Chi. Padmini, I shall pray to God that she may feel herself energetic to do the management of marriage. I am sure that by His grace she will not feel so much fatigue of the work. If doctor allows, please give her the juice of the boiled vegetables. In this case the vegetables are boiled without water and then squeezed to obtain the juice. Of course there should be a fixed quantity so that it may be easily digested. Please also inform me, what kind of job is being given to Chi. Narayan. Shahjahanpur is still cooler than Tirupati in winter, but in two weeks time it will grow hot. Really the summer at Tirupati is very troublesome. Mrs. Raghavendra Rao is now improving. Mr. Robert Koch has started the practices of our Mission and he has given in his letter the report of the condition he felt during meditation. He also wrote to me that he is searching for some editor in Germany for the publication of the book. In case he does not find any of such editors, he will see to it how to make the publication possible. He also wants to write a book of philosophy with my footnote given at page 4 of 'Efficacy of Raja Yoga' as motto. I could not yet understand why he is asking my permission for it when everybody is free to quote the passage of any author. It is very surprising that doubts and diffidences are still dominating. I do not know whether you recall them or they themselves enter into you. It is of course certain at your stage that if you create doubt and contemplate over it, it will surely get power. Please make it as a habit at such circumstances to divert your attention towards the Real Being. I am also praying that you may get over your difficulties. If I say that in such a case my vision is wrong then I will have to admit that I am abusing my inner condition. I find life in every word you write to me. You wrote to Shri Ishwar Sahai during the marriage of his daughter a few sentences of prayer which I read thrice, because they were discharging a kind of spiritual force. The same thing I find in your letter sent to me. I find you quite changed. Now allow me to throw light on your inner condition as I observe. The life is dead and the death is meeting, its own death. I do not find better words than these to express your condition. As you advance, you will feel yourself quite barren and liquidated. The power will work when you intend to do a certain thing.

You are in the second ring of light of the central region. I wanted that you may cross it by your own effort. When I find that your effort fails it becomes my duty to push you further. So by the time the letter reaches you you will have glad tidings to enter into the third ring.

I despatched Amla hair oil about one seer by parcel, but it met the same fate. I was informed by the Presidency Post Master at Madras that it is in leaky condition and connot be sent further. The tin case was very thick and strong and these tins are used by Shri Kashi Ram in sending ghee and oil to Assam. I, therefore, did not put it into a wooden case. I wrote to you in my previous letter that "I will send the oil in a few days and let us see if it reaches safely." As the doubt was there, it came to pass. I have kept one bottle reserved to bring it with me for you in the next tour.

A few days after you will become busy in the arrangement of the marriage. So I will not hurry to compel you to reply my letters promptly.

Love to children and respect to Appaji.

With best wishes,

Yours affectionately,
Ram Chandra

7th April 1961

My dear Revered Gurudev,

Please accept my humble pranams. I trust that all of you are keeping well.

My wife had a relapse of fever last week. It was clear also that she had developed a state of delirium so to speak having hallucinations but all of them were centred around you and the Grand Master. She was constantly speaking about you and arguing with you as she said to me. Thanks to thy grace she was restored to normalcy by some drugs used by me. Dr. Kuppuswamy was of course attending on her case all through and with great diligence. Now which is roughly the fifth week or sixth she has touched normal but not steadily. I hope that in a few days she would be able to take normal diet.

My college closes from tomorrow for the vacation. But the work regarding the preparations for the marriage have to take place and here too thy constant grace is my guide. Chi. Narayana has not yet got the orders to proceed and take charge. He is posted to Vishakhapatnam (Waltair). However as you know he has to forego one year of research work for the Ph.D. Secondly he has to forego also the U.G.C. scholarship for the period already undergone also perhaps. Thirdly of course we will have no assistance during the next month. These have been worrying me internally and externally. I am wondering as to how all these are helpful. I pray that I may become more and more aware of that high state that I am said to have attained and be more and more resigned to Nature or Thee, trusting thee like a child.

My father is doing well. Children are in the full swing of the examinations. Chi. Chitra's examination comes to a close today. Chi. Padmini's examination starts on Monday and goes on till the end of the month. Chi. Bhagavan's examination is in the first week of May.

My son Chi. Aravind completed yesterday one year of probation. Of course he is dispirited as he has to go through another strenuous year of probation. He prays that he may be confirmed earlier.

All the abhyasis are regular. Shri Annaih Naidu and Dr. Kuppuswamy and C.S. Raghavan and Krishnamurti as also Dhond Rao are progressing satisfactorily. I pray for their progress as well as those of others.

I pray that I may have more light and knowledge about the higher conditions and attain the perfect state. May the Master be pleased with me and lead me to perfect state.

I pray that all the arrangments for the marriage go on smoothly and above all I pray that the couple be affectionate to each other and have long life of union and happiness. Nothing but thy grace can lead them to real bliss and conjugal happiness.

Thou art the Absolute Truth and Being for me. May I be dissolved in thee and be supported by thee alone for ever and ever.

Yours as body, with loving pranams,
   divinised by thee in every cell and atom,
                                        KCV

10th April 1961

My dear revered Gurudev,

Please accept my humble pranams. I received your affectionate letter today. My wife has been having steadily 97.6 during the last week. It has risen to 97.8 today. I am told this might be due to Chloromycitin that was administered earlier. She has not yet begun to take the normal diet. I shall advise her to take the diet you have written. I have communicated your message to her so that she may have her mind at rest. Thy Grace is all. Chi. Padmini's examinations began today. I believe she will do them well. More than all I pray that she may be a loving and devoted wife to Chi. Y.K. Srinivasan. Srinivasan was here for a day on Saturday and Sunday. He has passed his second examination last week which entitles him to promotion as superintendent A.G.'s Office in the course of a few months. Both of us are praying for the satisfactory and happy ending of the marriage next month. I am sure my wife will be relieved of the greatest anxiety and her health will get better.

I am glad to learn that Mrs. Raghavendra Rao is getting better in health. May she become all right soon.

It is usual for foreign authors always to take permission to quote an author. So Dr. Koch should have followed that etiquete.

I am greatly happy to receive the Master's admonition about my doubts and diffidence. I do not know whether it is not due to the long lasting habits of dependence on the sense and sensate reasoning that are too much with me as a teacher of philosophy. Further it is also due to my being absorbed in the experience of my images and memories and anxieties. I pray that they may all be withdrawn. I shall follow the advice to divert my attention to The Real Being — the Master.

I am writing off and on and shall send them to Thee who art in fact making me write. I pray that Thy will lead me to the Real and the Absolute condition. I am grateful to Thee for having admitted me to the second ring of splendour and that I will be admitted to the third. Thy love knows no limits.

I am sorry that the hair oil again failed to reach me. I find that Swami Sivananda makes a particular kind of packing which is absolutely good. I shall show how he sends the oil month after month to me and without any damage. I however realise the force of 'doubt'. I pray that doubt may never cross my mind when I am doing thy work.

I am thinking of going to Madras with my wife after the 1st May as there is no possibility of her undertaking a journey now or for a fortnight more. All things have to be got from Madras and then alone it will be possible to go on. I can do all that within the 20 days before me then. Of course I am facing lot of funny situations and difficulties from all sides. But I am relying entirely on the Master for the successful completion of this and performance and welfare, so that I can avoid all sorts of criticisms. This is not out of vanity but good will to the children God has entrusted to my humble care.

Your letter has been a balm to me and threw me into calm and quiet state of love. Therefore I pray to the Master to write to me almost every week so that both of us will feel more and more with Thee all through these weeks of anxiety and work. I do not know Master whether all this throws such a burden on thee of the earthly work. But I beg pardon and pray for thy grace so that I may be more and more part and parcel of thy Divine Nature and Being.

Chi. Narayana has not yet got his orders but is expecting the same. Though it has been gazetted he has not received the individual order from his State Director. Chi. Chitra's examination was over last Friday.

My health is fair and I am hoping nothing will upset the same.

With loving pranams,

Yours as body,

KCV

No. F 173/SRCM   **Shahjahanpur, U.P.**
Dated 11th April, 1961

My dear Varadachari,

Received your affectionate letter dated 7th April, 1961. I believe you have received my previous letter by now. The package containing Amla hair oil which was lying in Madras Presidency Post Office in leaky condition was taken by Mr. C.M.T. Mudaliar, as I authorised him to take it. There was only four oz. left in the tin case.

I was under the impression that sister has recovered but I am worried to read your letter about her condition. May she recover soon. I am greatly interested in the case of Chi. Narayana, hence I think my intuition is not working properly. I am in puzzle what will be the best course for him. About a week ago I saw him in dream sitting as an officer in his office. It may be due to the fact that I was contemplating the same thing.

You have requested me to have awareness of your condition. Please meditate going at the depth of your condition to know what you are this day. Do you feel any sort of satisfaction in the heart? What is the condition of your thoughts? Are they minimised? Really speaking I do not know myself if I am aware of my condition, although there is no restlessness; and contentment and satisfaction are there. How earnestly I wish that the marriage ceremony of Chi. Padmini be gracefully performed. A few satsanghis from Gulbarga side have written to me that they are coming on 25th April. I am happy to note that the satsanghis are progressing well. I am entirely satisfied with your work which is excellent.

The M.A. final examination of Chi. Chaya is over now. Chi. Umesh appeared in Intermediate and his examination is also over.

Respect to Appaji.

Love to children.

Yours,
Ram Chandra

Tirupati
17th April 1961

My dear revered Gurudev,

Please accept my humble pranams. My wife has taken her bath and has begun to take small quantities of normal diet. All this is due to thy grace.

Chi. Narayana got the orders to proceed to Vizagpatam as Assistant Employment Officer. He is starting on the 19th and will join duty on the 21st inst. I am so sorry that I have given Thee cause for the reflections you have made in thy letter — regarding thy readings about his future. It is a great test for me — my doubt and my condition of anxiety and helplessness. This is my problem and my condition of anxiety and helplessness. This is my problem and not the problem for my wife or Chi. Narayana. He wants a job in which his intellect will be able to develop unhampered and wishes to give this a chance. As I wrote to you this job is the lowest in the Gazetted scale and at the present moment the lecturer's job if it could be had is more attractive. Anyway I have completely discovered that I have lot of doubt in me which requires to be overcome. May I pray to the Master that this incubus of doubt be once and for all removed root and branch? I am almost certain that that must be the cause of my slow progress in the crossing of the rings. My mental condition is in the present condition of restlessness even now — maybe the old samskaras and memories are crowding on me. It will be clear that my present worries will begin to haunt but I am trying to transcend them by not contemplating them. In any case

I am afraid that I am giving thee lot of work: I pray for thy blessings to Chi. Narayana and improvement of his inner being and intellectual attainment and material welfare.

I have written down some portions of whatever came to me during the few weeks before. I do not know whether you will find time to go through them.

I received a copy of a journal published by Prof. Srivastava of the Y.D. College Lakhimpur Kheri in which there is an interesting article on the yoga techniques and western psychological methods. It is well written.

After my wife's health gets regularised I intend going to Madras and return with all purchases for the marriage. I am deeply grateful that it has pleased God to attend upon my needs though I hardly know why I deserve all this kindness. But I am thy body and thou are my self — Let thy infinite realisation flow into me purifying me and divinising me as a perfect instrument of God for ever and ever.

All are going well. I pray for the pass of all children there.

With loving pranams,

Yours,
KCV

No. F 194/SRCM   Shahjahanpur, U.P.
Dated 22nd April, 1961

My dear Varadachari,

Received your affectionate letters dated 10th April, 1961 and 17th April, 1961. I am glad to know that my sister has now recovered. I am sure she will regain health very soon. I am glad that Chi. Narayana got a job. Lecturer's job is no doubt attractive to dear Narayan because there is ample scope for intellectual development but he is already intellectual. Thinking develops when a man gathers himself at one point and becomes used to it. I have enough time, you can send me whatever you have written during last few weeks.

You are not on the second ring of splendour, as you have written to me in your letter, but on the third ring. I mean to say that you have already crossed two rings of splendour. For your experience and information I write to you that there is no question of *yatras* (journey) when a man enters the central region. What I feel, is that there is potency in every ring but of a peculiar type. I am trying to find out words for its expression but I am not getting. There is no question of matter there so we cannot call it a material force, if we call it as spiritual force it will be only touching the meaning. This is pure force resulted by His existence. As far as I think nobody can cross these rings out of his own efforts so the guide here is always necessary. It is not your fault if you cannot step further out of your own effort.

I am quite sure that you will succeed in removing the doubts and I shall also pray for it. It is not very difficult for you to be free from doubts. Come toward certainty and you will see that the doubts are dispelled. It is only a habit with no foundation which can easily be shaken off.

The correspondence between myself and Robert Koch is going on and he is being profitted by the practices of the Mission.

I have sent to you a copy of photograph taken during Utsava. I hope you must have got it by now. I pray that all my children may get through. I think Chi. Gayatri must be doing her papers very satisfactorily.

Love to children.

Respect to Appaji.

Yours,
Ram Chandra

P.S.- I have been suffering from acute pain in the stomach for the last ten days. I am now on the way to recovery.

Ram Chandra

April 27th 1961

My dear Revered Gurudev,

Please accept my humble pranams. I received thy letter and the photo. The photo got crumbled in transit. But it gave me an idea of the grand celebrations on the occasion of the birthday of Shri Samartha Guru.

Chi. Narayana has joined at Vishakhapatnam. I received the letter after his joining that place. He is new to this type of life and finds the work not yet congenial. But it is only after his training at Delhi from next month onwards that he will find it interesting or otherwise. I have asked him to write to you. I believe he will do so.

I am proceeding on with the arrangements. Under the circumstances you know I am or rather both my wife and I are entirely depending on Thee for the change of mind on the part of Chi. Padmini and the easy and happy conclusion of the marriage next month. It is exactly one month ahead. I pray to Thee for thy guidance and help and inspiration at every step.

I was wondering as to what divinising meant. It came to my thought that it was possible in two ways: (i) by substituting the divine organs left by those who have gone beyond the need for using them, in the place of the human and other organs including the mind, *manas* etc. or (ii) changing the very nature of the organs themselves as they are by infusion or breaking up their components and rearranging them or by inverting them. The ancient *Upanishads* and later thinkers have entertained the first view which perhaps is a kind of spiritual surgery, whereas the other view is that of persons who have the gradual theory, and who want to be nearer man. Whatever it is I believe at one stage the spiritual surgery may be necessary for it is very much the distinct break away from any human element. I shall be very happy to know what you think about this.

My paper may have reached you by now. I shall be most happy to have your comments on the same. Somehow I find myself feeling dead and mostly seeking absorption in thee.

Mrs. Panduranga Rao (wife of Dr. V.P. Rao) has been having special sittings for the past three months and more along with her husband. I found that she has developed a fine clarity in her heart centre. It appeared to be clear ocean as it were. She is also feeling unusually happy.

I am now working at the *Chit-lake* for most of the advanced abhyasis. Transmitting on that point I am trying to study the condition of it in each. I found that in Somesvara Sarma it was beautiful but not that which I saw in thee. The greyish points were arranged in a tier and there was also movement from the lower tier to higher tier.

My wife's health is improving every day. I pray once again for thy grace which is omnipotent and omnibeneficient and incomparable.

With pranams,

yours loving
body,
KCV

No. F 207/SRCM　　　　**Shahjahanpur, U.P.**
　　　　　　　　　　　　　　Dated 4th May, 1961

My dear Varadachari,

Received your affectionate letter dated 27th April, 1961. I am happy that sister is regaining health day by day. The responsibility of the marriage really lies on her shoulders. I am meant for the service of the children too because I have a tie of relationship as much with the world as with God. They both go together parallel. That alone can result in perfection. I remember Chi. Narayana very often. When he goes to Delhi he should inform me. You can also write to Mr. Rajagopalan about his arrival there so that he may have no inconvenience. I shall also do so if I get timely information. I can guess that you are proceeding with marriage arrangements in almost a benumbed state, so to say.

In other words, inner absorbency is there while the limbs are doing their work. It means that God is connected with everything that you do. When such is the case everything must go all right. We can and should pray wherever we are in some difficulty.

I am very happy to note the excellent work at your centre. The associates are progressing well and a few of them have come up to the level where they can be entrusted with the work.

Really I learnt the word Divinisation from you and since it carries full sense I too have adopted it. I have expressed my views about it and also about *manas*.

I have gone through your article on 'Sahaj Marg and Modern Psychology'. It is very nice. I shall go through it again when it is complete and will give you my views and suggestions if any. For the present I only give you my opinion about the last sentence on page 13. Here you may please proceed with the following view — that the seven rings of splendour have no connection with the eight kinds of thought. The conception of rings is quite original and is based upon my personal experience.

I remember that once while commenting on Sai Baba you had correctly remarked that he was not at all spiritual still the miracles were there. I now give you a living example of one of my own associates, Shivalingappa, who came to me only last year. He can perform miracles perhaps better than Sai Baba himself. It is intimated to me by the South Indian associates who are now here. He had learnt these from a Mohammedan guide who had once come to see me also. At first Shivalingappa was very reluctant to have sittings from Shri Raghavendra Rao. But when he had two or three sittings he appreciated the condition like that of *samadhi* which he experienced practically. He acknowledged that he had wasted eight years of his life labouring for eight hours a day, on the things which were not the least spiritual. My respects to Appaji and love to children.

With best wishes,

Yours,
Ram Chandra

9th May 1961

Dear Revered Gurudev,

Please accept my humble pranams. I received thy two letters and the enclosed note on the mind (*manas*). I am fully illuminated and clear that far.

Both my wife and myself had been to Madras on the 3rd and returned to Tirupati on the 6th after making necessary purchases and preparations. All went off well with thy constant grace. In fact I almost replied to one who asked as to what I was doing as the work was going on of purchase etc. that I was indeed active whilst absolutely inactive.

I will be more and more busy as the day of the marriage 26th May draws near. My uncle is of course very much distressed that his daughter has not been fixed up in marriage as she is older than the bridegroom. I learnt that some boy had come to see her day before yesterday. I pray that that will fructify so that he will not have that worry hereafter, nor his son who is equally worried that his elder sister is not yet married.

My wife's health is of course slowly bettering but it is all due to her intense anxiety to go through these functions without hitch and worry and difficulty. She was telling me that she is constantly thinking of your divine self and the Grand Master always.

Chi. Narayana will be coming over here on or about the 21st and I will write to you about the date when he is likely to leave for Delhi.

My father's health is good as also of all children.

I believe all there are keeping fit as also at Lakhimpur. Shri Manjunath Iyer seems to be yet going through lot of worry. So too Shri Thyagarajan at Trichy. Shri Seshadri was at Mysore it seems. I have not received any news from him. Shri Mohan Rao of Rajampet was anxious to hear from you. I have had no information from Shri Venkatapati of Punimangadu. But I believe all are progressing.

With loving pranams,

Yours as body,
KCV

13th May 1961

My dear and revered Gurudev,

Please accept my humble pranams. I received thy affectionate letter with the note on *manas* and divinisation as also today Thy present of Rs. 101 for the marriage of Chi. Padmini. I do not know how to express our feelings to the Divine who has taken up all as His own. The body rejoices in its Self.

My wife's health is of course improving though new pains develop here and there in the organism.

The strength and force and determination are all of thine nature and they are working in perfect harmony. Only what is hers is the temper that comes out of human weakness.

Chi. Narayana wrote to me that he feels awe to write to thee. But he will overcome that in due time. He is expected here on or about the 22nd instant.

The first function in connection with the marriage took place yesterday viz. *nischitartham*. The marriage will take place on the 26th May at 6 A.M. and it is expected will be completed by 7 A.M. Chi. Srinivasan will arrive here from Karwar where he has gone on camp on the 23rd instant. Chi. Padmini has been given thy note and the amount and that worked wonder in her mind — she was indeed grateful. I trust this will be an abiding change. Of course the usual invitations are getting printed with the compliments of the Master. They will reach you. My whole being is in that peculiar benumbed state mentioned by thee and now it is also experiencing off and on a superb calm, that is of the Divine Master's presence.

I read thy note with profit. The *manas* here is comparable to *dhi* rather than the *manas* that has become the sensorium-cum-object-consciousness. I shall continue the writing as and when there is found time and inspirational urgency.

I am indeed grateful for thy reference to the *chit-lake* which has begun to attract my attention during both abhyas and training of the others. I am also now clear about the direct path and the peculiar invention of Master in respect of ascent to the point five (5) from the heart or point (1). I am also glad to hear about the distinction between the seven rings which again is the discovery of the Master.

Please accept our supremest surrender and love, with loving pranams,

Yours as body,
KCV

No. F 230/SRCM Shahjahanpur, U.P.
Dated 16th May, 1961

My dear Varadachari,

Received your affectionate letter dated 9th May, 1961. As the date for marriage comes nearer I feel happy. I therefore infer that the marriage ceremony will be performed by His grace gracefully and smoothly. The anxiety naturally grows on such occasions, because we have to think of all corners. Sister will feel better and progress will not remain so slow. I wish to join this marriage but I am sorry I will not be able to be there physically.

Mr. Manjunath Iyer has written to me that he has decreased in weight and has come down to 82 1/2 lbs. He can only walk slowly for two furlongs and digestion is weak. May he recover his health.

I shall try my best to be at Delhi when Chi. Narayan goes there. I will also call him at Shahjahanpur, rather I will bring him with me when he is there. I have replied Mohan Rao what he wanted from me in his letter. I shall write to Shri V. Venkatapathi saying that you are very anxious to know about him.

How I eagerly wish that your cousin be married. It will be better if it is settled before 26th May, 1961.

Let us abide by will of God, who will do what is better.

I do not want to disturb you for replying my letters during marriage time. I have also drafted such a letter for which no reply is necessary.

Love to children and respects to Appaji,

Yours,
Ram Chandra

No. F 238/SRCM   Shahjahanpur, U.P.
Dated 21st May, 1961
(Sunday)

My dear Varadachari,

Received your telegram and the letter dated 15th May, 1961. The letter reached me after five days of the date of dispatch. I at once sent an express telegram to Shri Ishwar Sahai calling him to accompany me to Tirupati. I am expecting him today. If he comes I will start on 22nd night, reaching Tirupati on 25th evening (via Gudur). You will be telegraphically informed when we leave.

Talk of Chaya's marriage is going on and they are expected to come to see the girl during this week. Besides there are other important things to attend to during these days. But in spite of all these I will leave for Tirupati if Shri Ishwar Sahai comes in time. I would have even taken up the journey alone but for fear of heart attack which I generally have in long journeys on account of dryness of lungs. At that time I need the help of someone.

Since I received your telegram I am much upset like my sister. When a thing is deeply taken to heart, such results do follow. There are certain things which as a duty we have to take up seriously. In that case every man, whether you or I will surely feel upset. I have been praying since I received your telegram and will continue it till the marriage is over.

What I wrote to sister was to console her during her illness, and we must still hope for the best. God is Great and the most Bountiful and we must trust upon Him.

I enclose herewith a letter for Chi. Padmini. If you think it can serve any useful purpose, you may give it to her.

Love to children and respects to Appaji.

Yours,
Ram Chandra

P.S.- I hope you received my telegram in reply to yours.

Ram Chandra

No. F 239/SRCM   **Shahjahanpur, U.P.**
                            Dated 22nd May, 1961

My dear Varadachari,

Received your telegram and the letter dated 18th May, 1961. Thank God for His bountiful grace.

In response to my express telegram Shri Ishwar Sahai came here yesterday. He told me about his present difficulties. His wife is in a serious anemic condition, due to attack of bleeding piles which lasted for over a month. His daughter-in-law also who had had abortion several times before was passing through the same stage of pregnancy. Both are confined to bed. They require careful attention and nursing. But in spite of all these he got ready to accompany me in the journey. But these circumstances put me in a fix and I was not able to decide anything. I was thinking over the situation, when to my greatest relief your telegram and the letter were delivered to me. Thanks to the Great, Good Master. I think by His kind grace the problem is now solved, though I shall still be busy with prayer till the marriage.

In view of the above circumstances I now change my resolve to attend the function in person, though I shall actually be with you all the time.

With love to children and respects to Appaji,

Yours,

Ram Chandra

Shahjahanpur, U.P.

My dear Varadachari,

I am very happy to learn from your telegram that the marriage function went off grandly. Thanks to the Master. I also gave an express telegram on 26th morning offering blessings to couple. I received your invitation and the invitation from the father of Shri Shrinivasan. I could not reply him for want of address.

My revered Master remained at Tirupati with you for several days together and this I could observe on 24th. He left your house on 26th May at 10.55 A.M. I am so happy with this marriage that I offer again the prayers for the long life and the prosperity of the couple.

Love to children. Respect to Appaji.

With best wishes,

Yours,
Ram Chandra

29th May 1961

My dear Revered Gurudev,

Please accept our heartfelt pranams. By Thy Divine Grace the function went off most pleasantly. Of course the inward fear was finally overcome when the *muhurtam* went off at 6:15 A.M. and all present felt happy. It was all so mechanical in one sense and in another sense Divine. Nature Herself worked the thing. There were all abhyasis with their prayers and other relatives too who observed the function go off so smoothly. Chi. Padmini also began co-operating well and in the night the function culminated with the consummation of the marriage. All this was seen through the 'almost' divine force that seemed to animate my wife all through. She recognized her own benumbed condition and thy supreme force that was seeing all things through. Of course I did not stint any money to make the function a success but there was hardly any extravagance. All things only brought out the significant realisation of Thy presence.

We only pray that the Master's glory increase day after day. The marriage of my cousin is fixed for the 5th June and by thy grace that too will be gone through.

Though the hurdle has been crossed yet there is much that requires for a total change. We were worried about certain undesirable consequences that might arise from the fact of the 'letters' etc. I pray that they may be of no consequence.

I am so sorry to learn that Shri Ishwar Sahaiji is not well and that his wife is not doing well also. I pray that she may have relief. In any case I am sure that Shri Ishwar Sahaiji will be all right soon. You have written that Chi. Chaya's marriage will be fixed during this week. I do not know whether it has been fixed. I pray that that might take place soon.

I am not in a position to express my feelings but pray that The Master's great work be carried out to success and more success through my humble self who is thy Body.

Chi. Narayana has left for Vizag on Saturday (27th) and is scheduled to be at Delhi on the 4th of June. I have asked him to telegraph Shri Rajagopalan. I also shall telegraph to him as soon as I learn about the precise date and train and time he will be reaching Delhi. He is thy child and thou alone knowest the destiny. He wished to resign seeing the terrible corruption in departments. But I prevailed upon him to continue and look for guidance from Thee.

The guests yet are here and will leave in the course of this week.

I received the fine present from Ishwar Sahaiji for Chi. Padmini and she likes it very much. I also liked it well. I am also grateful for the contribution made towards the marriage expenses from him. It is a new life that thou hast given to all here.

I shall be writing to you more about the affairs here which have been temporarily buried. I can only pray that the past be buried entirely so that the new future will manifest for the young couple.

As thou hast stated the DIVINE WORK IS WHAT WE TWO BEHELD and it is something that is incomparable.

We have had the same peace (*shanti*) and happiness throughout though some of us were otherwise worried out of deep disbelief, and doubt.

The doubt has been thoroughly dispelled and with loving pranams I remain,

Thine as Body,
KCV

3rd June 1961

My dear revered and beloved Gurudev,

Please accept my heartfelt pranams. I received thy wonderful letter dated 29th. It was really so very divine of the Samartha Guru to have personally looked after the marriage by staying at my humble place. I do not know how I deserved it all. Nor my wife. Anyhow the Supreme Master has blessed us and linked up Himself with us all here in eternal bonds of love. Chi. Srinivasan's sister's marriage will take place tomorrow (4th) and not on the 5th as originally fixed. He will be staying here till next Sunday.

Chi. Narayana telegraphed and also wrote to me that he will be reaching Delhi on the 4th. I have written and telegraphed to Shri S.K. Rajagopalan I trust he will be taken care of at Delhi. Of course he may have occasion to go over to you and will probably explain his position. Master knows all. I also sent a telegraph (express) to you on the 2nd. I believe it would have reached you.

Shri Sahaiji has written that both his wife and daughter-in-law are better but that you were suffering from pain in the waist when he was with you. I believe that would have passed away by now.

My college reopens on the 15th instant. I hope that I will be free from all worries to concentrate on the work thereafter. I pray that I may be able to go ahead with the work. Both of us, that is, my wife and I, are entirely filled by thy energy and being and of the Samartha Guru and hope that it means that our work will be of the highest order.

I pray that thy illimitable grace will take me onward to the crossing of all rings which will mean that I shall be in full possession of that Vision Divine which will reveal the Reality in all its fullest potentiality — the Centre itself. Thy Grace alone can grant me that condition. We pray for it.

I do not know at what stage the marriage prospects of Sow. Chi. Chaya are. I pray that it may also take place at an early date relieving Thee of all anxiety. My loving pranams to thee,

Thine,
KCV

21st June 1961

My dear revered Gurudev,

Please accept our humble pranams. After my last letter I have been very much in a condition of exhaustion or blankness or both. I have been of course in no mood for doing anything but the bare minimum. Owing to a symbolic dream that my wife had when Chi. Padmini was born and also just prior to the marriage of Hannman she wished to visit the very famous shrine at Sholinghur (about sixty miles from Tirupati near Arkonam) along with Chi. Srinivasan and Chi. Padmini. This was done just a fortnight after the marriage and on the 17th day after the marriage Chi. Srinivasan joined duty at Bangalore. He proposes to take his wife (Chi. Padmini) about the middle of August or first week of September. As I had written to you his sister also got married on the 4th thanks to thy grace.

Today my sister's son Chi. Chakravarti got married to his own cousin and I was told that Master was pleased to bless the couple. The function went off without any difficulty gracefully. I was happy to find that my brother-in-law was very much aware of the Master's grace, thanks to Shri Seshadri. Shri Seshadri came here on Sunday night and his own son's *upanayanam* is to be held on the 23rd. Shri Seshadri demanded from me a meditation but I gave him only a transmission. He is earnest and enthusiastic and is craving for higher approaches. He proposes to go over to Shahjahanpur next week.

Shri G. Kuppuswamy's son's *upanayanam* went off very well. Master's grace was evident in all things.

Our Narayana wrote to me from Delhi that he had been to you and that you had given him some sittings. He writes that Master did not agree with anything that he spoke about. But his faith is good. May Master's blessings be with him always. Chi. Aravind has come down for the marriage here, and of course he is dejected. Only the grace of the Supreme can take him out of it.

I have not been able to write anything at all. The benumbed condition continues and I am wondering when and how I shall be able to fulfil my work for the Mission. I am to say the least utterly thine and even that sometimes I am unconscious of.

My wife's condition is fair though weak. She has thanks to these ordeals much purified. Of course she has developed a formidable confidence that Master will help her to overcome all obstacles. I am supremely aware of the grace of the Samartha Gurudeva in cleaning me thoroughly and I trust that it will help in the crossing of all the rings of splendour at an early date and that I would be in a position to do all that is asked me in the supreme spirit of utter identity.

My father's health is much better though he occasionally suffers from prolapsis of the anus, owing to piles. I am giving medicine now and again.

I believe Master is free from all pains in the waist. I shall attend the marriage function of Shri S.K. Rajagopalan's son's marriage on the 3rd July at Madras.

The satsangh has been functioning normally since a fortnight. Though I am dissatisfied with the progress made here, yet I am praying that higher approaches are made possible for the abhyasis here.

With loving pranams,

Thine,
KCV

29th June 1961

My dear Revered and Beloved Gurudev,

Please accept my humble pranams. I trust thy health is excellent. The children are all keeping well. My wife's health also has been slowly improving. Chi. Seshadri would have by now reached the place and he may give an account of all things. I am going to Madras on the 2nd October and stay there for the son's marriage of Shri Rajagopalan. I believe you are in receipt of my last letter.

I have been trying to write further on but somehow or other I am not doing so. I pray for greater flow of divine inspiration and thought. Things here are going on at the College as usual, unsatisfactory for me. The case is dragging on since Mr. Dorapti did not wish to deal with it and he has since been transferred. Men in this world are 'willing to do the wrong but afraid to do the right'. Strange but altogether true. The case is posted for the 6th July for my examination!

Since I have become so much one with thyself as body and all and of the Divine Master I am more and more resigning myself to nothingness. Shri C.R. Krishnamurti returned to Tirupati after a month's stay at Coconada and Vizag. His health has not been good at all. Asthma, numbness of the legs and general weakness even in speaking. I pray for his recovery. He has been consulting doctors at those places.

Chi. Rajagopalan, last son of my uncle Y.K. Venkatanarasimhacharya, passed out in his M.Sc in the 1st class with 1st rank. He is now working at Bangalore A.I.R.

With humble and loving pranams,

Yours as Body,

KCV

No. F 314/SRCM

Shahjahanpur, U.P.
Dated 8th July, 1961

My dear Varadachari,

I received all your affectionate letters. They are so lovely and charged with life that I like to read them again and again. You are displaying piety, chasteness in all your writings and I am very happy to see all these things. I pray further that your writings and words may become the 'voice of God', the foundation of which is already laid by your own devotion. To tell you the truth I myself too remain restless in giving you further approach. You are, no doubt in the third ring of splendour and how I wish that you may go beyond it but these are very powerful regions and cannot be taken till one gains the power of going further. I can take up just as I have done in case of Appaji but that I do not want in your case because you must have lot of experience and power for the work.

I wrote to you in my previous letter that you are in benumbed state. Now a few days ago, I have got noted the time, you have begun to rise. I want to explain but the expression fails. Even then if I try I can say that the state of negation is pregnant with freshness. This is not *mayavic* freshness but something very superior.

I am very happy that Chi. Narayana came here and he expressed his liking to take up job where there is possibility of intellectual food and that can be the university area. I can allow him to do it if he so really wishes, but I am really a worldly man than spiritualist because if food is not there nobody can remember God. So I wish that he may have good earnings and alongside the spiritual development. He is a man who can successfully compete in examination like I.A.S. but he does not like the post of District Magistrate, as he said. I think it is better to rule in hell than to serve in paradise, as someone has said. I pray for his long life and prosperity.

Mr. R. Seshadri arrived here in the morning of 2nd July, 1961. He will go to Delhi in the night of 17th July, 1961 and leave that place for Madras on 19th July, 1961 because he has to rejoin duty on 24th July, 1961.

Shri Ishwar Sahai will come here after three or four days to see Shri Seshadri. His wife is now better but sometimes her temperature shoots to 100°F when there is irregularity. I am now better in all respect except that stomach ache has become my constant companion, although it is not very painful this time but to the extent which I am able to bear. Sister does not get sufficient rest to recoup her health. Somehow, she should be given rest. I felt very happy to take the marriage sweets of the marriage of Sowbhagyavati Padmini brought by Mr. Seshadri.

Love to children. Respect to Appaji.

With best wishes,   Yours,

Ram Chandra

P.S.- I want to know the definition of *sayujyata* and the equivalent word for it. Shri P.N. Sreenivasachari gives the English word for it 'intimate union or communion'.

Ram Chandra

16th July 1961

My dear Revered Gurudev,

Please accept my humble pranams. I am in receipt of your divine letters. I am thankful indeed that I am assured I am proceeding to the highest state. I can rest assured of it because Thou hast stated it. On all matters it is my duty to abide by thy decision and however much I may not see its significance at present. Devotion I believe means the acceptance of God and Master under all and every circumstance. Both the outrages of fortune and life and the rejoicings proceed from the One Ultimate Divine, good as well as evil so-called being but mental reactions to the Natural Activity.

We have been keeping indifferent health and however we are carrying on. The satsangh is going on as usual. I am only again and again confronted with the lower mind but I think that it is all Thy will and leave it at that.

Chi. Narayana wrote to me about himself and his problems. By thy grace I pray that they will be satisfactorily solved. I do not of course see any solution at any rate at present.

You have asked me about what is meant by *sayujya*: which has been translated by Prof. Srinivasacharya as intimate Union. Yuj means to connect: yoke is the English word similar to it.

The word *yuja* is used in the Mund.Up. 3.1.1 & Svet.Up. 4.6 in the context of being with one another of the two birds on the same tree, *dva suparna sayuja*... : Thus the being with God is the meaning of *sayujya*. How intimate that is the question of experience. Some think that the being together is as intimate as husband and wife or lovers or friends. Shri Aurobindo translates the Mundaka Passage: Two birds beautiful of wing, close companions, cling to one common tree. But in the context of liberation they speak of *sarupya* (having the same form as that of God), *salokya* (dwelling in the same world as of God), *samipya* (dwelling near God) and *sayujya* (enjoying the same unity with God). The mystic union is said to be so much that one almost becomes one with the Divine developing identity. *Aikya bhava* or *aikya* simply is the result. However the word *yuj* or *yujya* does not lead up to that meaning at all. Both the individual soul and the Divine Lord who looks on the individual soul's enjoyment of the world fruits remain on the same tree. The word *sakhaya* of course suggests that they are on the same *sakha* (branch) but one eats and the other does not eat of the tree's fruits. In realisation both do not eat of the tree's fruits. Perhaps the eating of the Divine being quite different the soul reaches up to that level and kind of eating appropriate to the Divine. The state of *sayujya* is one that comes only after the others if it is the ultimate state. But if it is the first stage then the *sarupya* state will be the last, only the word *rupa* seems to have misled many into thinking that it is lower because of its *saguna* implications. However one must link oneself with God and enjoy the tree of God — then one becomes nearer and nearer to God (*samipya*) and begins to see the world of God as God sees it (*sub specie eternitatis*) and this is *salokya* and lastly reaches the stage of having the nature (*rupa*) of God. Since the writers and translators of the ancient texts hardly had these experiences their speculations have led them astray. I do not complain about them but just pass them by.

I do not know whether I have explained this correctly. However the word *sayujya* is not intimate union, but really a term that intimates the practice of union or yoga connection with God through mind (thought) which leads to spatial, and spiritual nearness and vision and identification of the entire structures of being continuous with God in all His Universal and individual creation.

However Master knows all and I have but put down all that seems to appeal to me alone.

With loving pranams, I remain yours as body,

KCV

22nd July 1961

My dear revered Gurudev,

Please accept my humble pranams. We are keeping fit as things go. I have been praying for the expansion of our Mission's activities. There seems to be quite a halt in the progress of the Mission. Though we are steady in our practice we have not been able to attract really more liberation-loving souls, obviously they are fewer in number. The clouds of materialism are gathering and the atmosphere is becoming darkened in every way. At Tirupati itself I am feeling the gathering of these clouds in all walks of life and the Mission is to work in and through only a truly few. I am also feeling the weight of this. How long is this to last? Though the Master has stated the work of the Supreme Personality is over and He may well depart there is nothing that I can perceive today in the dynamic reorganization of the world or earth consciousness that even signs the trends towards truer spirituality. The persecution of the good goes on merrily and the adulation of the wicked makes it much worse. Humiliation of course may be the greatest glory — to whom? I am tempted to ask. All are gifts of the Divine revealing the love of God in truest sense and love may be the glory of God and His grace.

Please forgive me these thoughts but they are perhaps thine alone. My son Aravinda is thoroughly dissatisfied with his lot, so much so he wrote to me that he will be giving up his present job at Chittoor as he is not able to stand the partial treatment meted out to him. My second son Srivatsan of course is not at all sure what is to be his future, he is at Murray as auctioner officer's manager (one of three there). My third son Narayana whom you have selected is anxious to settle down as a householder and has sought my permission to ahead with his idea.

You have of course all information about my daughter whose marriage came off recently. Her change has yet to get full effect and that is when she may be setting up her family at Bangalore next month. My father's mental condition is agitated over so many things and I am wondering as to his intentions. All these have been agitating both me and my wife during the past few months and they are of course coming to a head. The marriages of the boys is being talked about but I am unable to make a decision. These of course are personal matters with which I am acquainting you who art my self. I pray that in these too thy will and grace come to my rescue. It may be a consolation to feel that as things are in this state alone are we both remembering thee always and praying for constant presence of thee. I am praying for the speedier progress of the abhyasis and to be able to enthuse them so that we may be able to do more work of transformation. When will our Mission grow to its fullest stature and perfection? I am praying that we may not shrink to a few individuals alone. May I take this liberty of praying for the fullest development of our Mission all over India and the world in the shortest possible time?

With loving pranams,

Yours as body,
KCV

No. F 344/SRCM   Shahjahanpur, U.P.
                        Dated 25th July, 1961

My dear Varadachari,

Received both of your affectionate letters. Nowadays I am badly suffering from lower blood pressure. Hence I suspended correspondence work with the intention of taking rest for about 10 days. There is nothing to be worried about. I shall be quite all right within a week.

You have mentioned your difficulties in the letter dated 22nd July, 1961, for which I will pray and you should also join hand with me in this respect.

Mr. Rajagopalan on his way to Delhi broke his journey at Shahjahanpur on 23rd instant and went back the other day. He suggests English word alikeness for *sayujyata*. I will discuss all this a week after when I am free from giddiness due to lower blood pressure. I will also throw light on your present condition, which I am destined to see in my lifetime.

Mr. M.L. Chaturvedi of Delhi has dispatched a book for me written by M.P. Pandit of Pondicherry, saying that the author quoted *Anant Ki Or* in his book under the heading 'Unto Infinity'. He has highly praised this book covering four pages. He is the man who reviewed this book.

Mr. Seshadri has gone back to Bangalore on 17th July spending a day at Delhi.

Love to children. Respect to Appaji. I hope and pray that you will see him better.

With best wishes,

Yours,
Ram Chandra

No. F 389/SRCM   Shahjahanpur, U.P.
Dated 16th August, 1961

My dear Varadachari,

Received all your affectionate letters. I am now a bit better. The Indian medicine did me no good. Chi. Chaya took good care in giving me almond, milk and boiled vegetable soup at times, which proved beneficial to me. Chi. Narayana came here in the morning of 12th Aug. and went back to Delhi on 15th Aug. afternoon. He is keeping good health. He

1961

explained to me what you have referred to in your letter. He is already praying but he wants that necessary precautions should also be taken as a duty. He will write to you about the present job of Chi. Aravinda (Raja). I have myself started praying on the basis of the information given by him. I pray that all may go well and our boys rise higher and higher, earn much and be prosperous.

Shri Ishwar Sahai was suffering from influenza. Now he has recovered. Shri Raghavendra Rao with his wife and children is doing well. He is coming to me on 30th Aug. for a week.

Now I am coming to the real topic but before doing it I must admit that there is a good deal of heaviness in my brain. So I cannot say if I will be able to give correct expression of my feelings and thoughts. Still I am trying. Your spiritual condition is extraordinarily good, and you might be feeling as if you have been robbed off. In your case there is a discovery of a new point at which I was astonished (diagram given) but I have yet to consider over it. I will be able to say effectively when your present condition is complete. I could observe how far you have proceeded so far. To tell you the truth this is my first experience and the first observation of this type. May God bless you. A new condition revealed in you by the direct touch of Almighty. I cannot even touch that point. In this way my task is over. In your case I am only guided to take you to a fresh ring when the former is complete. No transmission is necessary and no cleaning is required except to keep you guarded by the forces of the thoughts swimming in the atmosphere to avoid disturbance in your present condition, which is developing. May I call it the state of *sayujya*? I think I will be able to say definitely when it reaches its fullness.

I agree with your definition given for the different types of liberation. I give my own view. *Salokya*, when it comes he begins to feel that he is born in some higher world and the phase is altogether changed. The air becomes different and he begins to breathe in some different higher region. *Sarupya* is the condition when an abhyasi begins to develop the attributes of God and he feels at that stage that he is Rama and Krishna if a man talks about them. In other words, if there is any talk about Rama and Krishna going on he will feel that he is being talked of.

Samipya — when an abhyasi enters into this condition he feels in him utterly destitute of everything, and develops the nature of Brahma and feels his expansion everywhere. Extreme subtleness is there and one does not feel even the weight of the body.

Sayujya — It is yet to study and I am sure you will transmit the knowledge of it but at present I am thinking it is the last stage. A man of higher approach should be very cautious because if any thought or idea is taken deeply that will be troublesome by one's own force. If so happens as has been with me many a times that one must pray to his Master to diminish its intensity.

I am very happy to hear from you that you want to pray for the fullest development of our Mission all over India and the world in the shortest possible time. At times this flashed across my brain to give this duty to you and when finally I wanted to write it to you, you yourself volunteered for that. Please do it. I have given this duty to my brother disciple also. Your *anubhava* is correct that the atmosphere is growing darkened everywhere. I am also feeling the weight of it as you feel. A year or two back I observed the same thing but it cleared off. This condition is prevailing everywhere. The effect of the change of the world is percolating slowly. In *viratdesh* it is almost over. It can be brought down immediately on the earth by the Special Personality but we will lose him if his work is over. It is really a boon that it is percolating slowly to keep up his life and that must be my Master's work. Please give me the details of your father's mental condition and what are the common things which cause irritation.

Shri Ishwar Sahai gives English word as 'close conformity' for *sayujya*. But Mr. Seshadri did not agree to it. What is your opinion about it? I agree with the English word given by you i.e., 'Being with God'.

Love to children. Respect to Appaji,

Yours,
Ram Chandra

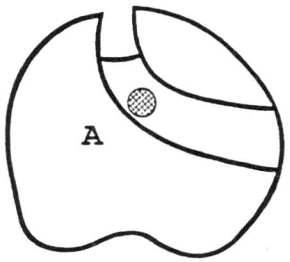

Diagram A

In the middle of the heart the point denoted as A is a playground of God as I feel in your case.

22nd August 1961

My dear Revered and beloved Gurudev,

Please accept my humble pranams. I received your affectionate letter (16th instant). I am happy to learn that you are feeling better in health though not yet free from the heaviness of the head.

I am sure Shri Narayana profitted by his stay with you in every sense. He wrote to me about his stay with you but not any details. He is much concerned about his sister and brother and of course he is also having his share of knocks. Thy blessing can take him to the highest condition.

The word *sayujya* is definitely in meaning 'to be linked up or yoked to' God. It does not mean conformity which is perhaps the meaning of *sarupya*. I thank you very much for the enlightening exposition of the four terms. My note on *sayujya* would show that all the states lead up to total or integral being with God. Of course without the same linkage from the very beginning the others cannot be realised. For in yoga the Master links up Himself with the abhyasi and makes it grow into the other conditions of *salokya, sarupya* and *samipya*. This very close proximity to God is verily culminated in the union inseparable or linkage inseparable.

I do not know precisely how I could explain my condition. I also am waiting for this *sayujya* experience in its fullest nature. To me the others do not appeal which are because they are more like *siddhis* than Being that is perfect in God.

I am placing myself in Thee and I know that I shall be absorbed in Thee sooner or later.

I pray for the entire emancipation of the world from the forces of Darkness and deceit.

My wife's health is not quite all right but we are pulling on by thy grace. My father's condition is peculiar. During the past few months owing to the marriage and the incident complications and his peculiar views about the property and its disposal after him, I had to celebrate the whole marriage out of my own earnings and I did not get or take a pie from my father. Obviously he is feeling for this and the attitude he had for my wife throughout has not been quite happy. We have been strictly disinterested and acted strictly correctly throughout. He complains about his eyesight and wishes to be taken to Madras — though the doctors do not have any hope of restoring his eyesight. He is now 80. Anyway I am praying that he may be well disposed to all of us. This is all that I can say about the details you have asked for.

I shall try to study the point Thou hast pointed out as the playground of God in my heart which Thou sayest is the point of *sayujya* developing in me. I offer my humblest love and offering to Thee for this unexampled grace.

Praying for Thy health and speedy recovery to the Lord and for the glory of the supreme personality.

With loving pranams,

yours loving body,
KCV

3rd September 1961

My dear revered and beloved Gurudev,

Please accept my humble pranams. We all hope to hear that your health has improved considerably and the blood pressure has become normal and your head condition is better. We are keeping fairly well as things go.

We had the Shri Jayanti satsangh on Friday evening. Yesterday Shri R. Viraraghavan came from Madras and consulted me on many points of personal clarification. He also showed me your letter to him directing him to meet me. I gave a sitting last evening and he attended the satsangh this morning.

I believe Shri Raghavendra Rao had been with you for the Janmashtami. I learnt from Mysore that Shri Manjunath Iyer is confined to bed owing to arthritis. I pray for his recovery.

Chi. Narayana has I believe by today returned to his work at Vizag. He wrote to me that he has been completely changed by his stay with you and I am sure he will have done so. He is extremely grateful to Shri S.K. Rajagopalan to have taken him into his household as it were. This is all owing to Thy grace.

Thy/my daughter's examination (Chi. Padmini) comes off on the 18th instant and goes on till the end of the month. As perhaps you know she failed in her examination and I found myself in an irksome position and gave permission for her to appear for this September exam. Her husband also granted permission. So she is appearing and next month they will set up the family at Bangalore. I pray for the best guidance during this period. I do not know whether

I would be at Tirupati during this period as there is an invitation to Jaipur Rajasthan. If I do go to Jaipur I hope to spend a day or two with you and offer my humblest pranams and get Thy Blessings. For all these Thy will is my guide and support. My wife is offering her pranams to Thee for the welfare of her children and their future. I wrote to Chi. Narayana that terrible shocks are given so that the individual may awake to his real nature. Of course I am aware that if the shocks are either too violent or too frequent one becomes entirely helpless or cynical or pessimistic which may lead to the worst — suicide. May God grant that such a thing does not come to our abhyasis anywhere or the Master is always with one both within and without.

I found during my recent meditations after I received your last letter intimating to me about the centre in the mid-point of the heart, the new point, which incidentally you have also hinted might mean the sayujya in process, that I have been taken into a bright cave in the heart region with a dark interior that began to open up itself and became also bright. 2) I found that the *chit-lake* developed the rubies or ruby-like points but not as I saw in thee: I persisted in seeing the central point shewn by you in the diagram which is the point for the 'play of God' in my heart and this morning I began to see the point expanding — it verily became a *sahasrara* circle but not the lotus: it was of diamonds and with platinum (whiteish or greyish background). It was not golden. I found that gold refers to *rajas* whereas silver refers to *satva* though I cannot say when the inversion took place. *Suvarna* would be *satvarna* which is white (*suklavarnam*). These inversions have happened in many instances I think this has been done purposefully by some ancients for their own reasons. This small circle-point began expanding till it covered me from head to foot as it were. I then found that I was transmitting from point 5 — throat point — green and cool and the satsanghis felt so cool and calm and happy.

I have communicated this as the results seem to be somewhat significant. Shri Viraraghavan also experienced this downpour of cool water as if a bath.

Shri Viraraghavan also told me that he experienced the descent of force from the *brahmarandhra* point. I told him that it is usual to have it when the Master has taken up the person for quick development. The fact that his case has been taken up by the Master is now clear. He told me that in the sitting yesterday and at the satsangh he experienced the similar fact. I told him that it shows the Master's transmission is clear and confirmed.

I invited him to come as often as he can for the sittings and satsangh.

On 20-8-61 one S. Venkataramana B.A. B.L., clerk in the District Court, 18-7-15 Ponniammal Kovil Street, Chittoor, sought our abhyasa and I put him in the way. He appears to be promising. He was brought here by Shri D. Ramanurthi who is now back again at Chittoor. Shri Dhond Rao is at Madanapalle. He came last week. He is showing great earnestness. So also Shri Sitaramaih. Shri Annaih Naidu asked me permission to come spend his evenings in the Hall every day. He is now coming regularly and stays on for meditation in the evenings. He is feeling happy and changed. The two boys: V. Srinivasan and Rangarajan both M.Sc.s are now regularly coming in the evenings for meditation. Our doctor is feeling progress. Shri C.R. Krishnamurti is slowly improving in health. Shri C.S. Raghavan has been also regular and I feel is improving very well. Great absorption is also revealed by Shri Somesvara Sarma.

I believe Shri Ishwar Sahaiji is now very much better in health. I shall send the subscriptions of others as soon as I receive them.

I pray for the glory of the Mission and the welfare of yoga in this age.

I got a certain advertisement on the occasion of the Rakshabandhan which promises the advent of Brahma Himself incarnate very soon. It was issued by a Brahma Kumaris Ishwariya Vishwa Vidyalaya Pandav Bhavan Mount Abu.

With profound pranams of love, Thine,

KCV

No. F 436/SRCM **Shahjahanpur, U.P.**
Dated 11th September, 1961

My dear Brother,

Received your affectionate letters dated 22nd August, 1961 and 3rd September, 1961. Shri Raghavendra Rao spent a week with me, along with four other associates and went back on the 5th September Mr. M.L. Chaturvedi of Delhi will soon be going to Calcutta, Bombay and Madras on Government business. His visit to Madras will be from Oct. 3 to 5, about which time he also proposes to see you at Tirupati. He has told Chi. Narayan also about it.

His address at Madras will be, "c/o. Shri R.K. Chaudhari, Adyar House, Madras". I shall write to some of the associates at Madras to see him and have satsangh with him as he is one of the Prefects of the Mission. His stay at Calcutta will be from September 18 to 22. I am informing Mr. P.N. Medayil also. I have called Shri Ishwar Sahai and his wife here. She is suffering from high blood pressure and anaemia due to excessive bleeding of piles. I want her to be treated here on Ayurvedic lines. Regarding Appaji I hope he will change his attitude when he gives due consideration to his views. When I was at Tirupati he was speaking highly of yourself and sister. I am praying continually for the good of Sow. Padmini.

Shri V. Raghavan is a very good man and his case was recommended by Shri Seshadri who assured me of his valuable services when brought to that level. Since then I feel purity developing in him and his heart exhibiting light akin to purity and simplicity. I am very happy to know that you shall be coming to my humble cottage while on your way to Jaipur. I hope you will please write to me the date and time of your arrival so that I may be able to see you at the station. I may also give you my house address. It is as follows:- Rai Bahadur Buildings, Diwanjograj, — Near Carew-Ganj.

Your life is now considerably transformed. Even in your writings I find the clarity of thought and purity and innocence of expression. Every sentence you write has life in it. I agree with what you have written about your condition. You are now really under the charge of the Divine and It is doing Its work. I cannot even meddle with it; I am only an observer, though as a servant I have sometimes to do some duty. For example I found in you that the diffusion of a certain state was being checked by something like heaviness in the left part of your chest. I removed that heaviness and now the action thereon is going on in the usual way. I really want that all *chakras* and points of your body may acquire a uniform state but it is the work of the Divine which is going on.

Your *anubhava* about the point is correct. You have written that you have been taken into a bright cave with a dark interior that began to open up by itself and became bright. The darkness does change into brightness and then brightness into grayish or the dawn colour. The point is no doubt expanding. The effect which it is shedding might have come to your vision as the *sahasra* circle, like the sphere of light when it has travelled to its extreme limit. I agree with your interpretation of the term *sayujya* and I shall put the same in the English translation. There is one difficulty with me that sometimes it so happens that I have to dive deep into the depth of my being and there the thing comes like *richa*. I have a very poor knowledge and vocabulary, so expression becomes difficult.

All the sadhakas at Tirupati are nicely improving. It is all due to your labour and their faith. If the number of satsanghis increase sufficiently at Chittor then you may have one as a Prefect there under you. Please write to me as early as possible what disease Shri C.R. Krishnamurti is suffering from and in which part of the body he feels pain or trouble.

Shri Ishwar Sahai's health is all right now. He conveys his pranam to you. I may call myself a little better in health, though weakness persists still to a great extent. I may be all right when colder season sets in.

My profound pranam to sister, love to children and respects to Appaji.

With best wishes,

Yours,
Ram Chandra

No. F 470/SRCM Shahjahanpur, U.P.
Dated 23rd September, 1961

My dear Varadachari,

Received your affectionate letter dated nil on 22nd September, 1961. I was so anxious to know about your health that I wanted to write to Mr. A. Naidu to intimate to me about your health. I have prayed for your speedy recovery and shall continue to be so till you are restored to complete health.

Do not fear the cool flow of Grace. What is done is done. But take it from me that you should think twice before you do. I have developed a habit of finding out ways for doing such things and it is not very difficult. I shall tell you the method when we meet next, provided you remind me of it.

I shall be very grateful if you request Mr. A. Naidu on my behalf to report to me your condition at the time when this letter reaches you, in case you find any difficulty in writing yourself.

Love to children and respects to Appaji.

With best wishes, Yours,
Ram Chandra

No. F 527/SRCM **Shahjahanpur, U.P.**
Dated 10th October, 1961

My dear Varadachari,

Received your affectionate letter dated nil dispatched from Madras. It is happy to know that the disease is not glaucoma as you have yourself written in your letter from Tirupati. I am feeling your trouble very much. May you soon regain normal health.

You may not for the present transmit to abhyasis till your headache is completely cured. I do not mean of course to forbid you for it but only for the purpose of avoiding strain lest it might aggravate your trouble. Satsanghis can however sit for group meditation in your room and they will experience as good a condition as they do when you transmit.

You must not be worried about the barrier. It will melt away very easily. Even having it in a small degree, it will in a way check your progress onwards. I shall write to you all about it and about yourself when you recover completely. I was observing all these things even when you were ill. Divinity was doing its work even during your illness but in a way so as not to aggravate your troubles. Nature's work when once started cannot be stopped till it is complete.

It is good that you got a chance of meeting Mr. M.L. Chaturvedi. He was eager to see you and for that he wanted to go to Tirupati.

I shall be able to write to you about my tour programme after the Dasehra because by that time I expect to get a final reply over the question of

Chaya's marriage. If it is favourable so far so good, otherwise I shall have to seek for another match.

As for your piles, you can use any of the tried medicines. Shri I. Sahai tells me of a very simple way of curing piles. It is thus -

When you wash the private parts after evacuation, take care that the ring-finger of your left hand touches the pile-pimples. Do this regularly. He has been doing it for more than a year and says that during all this period he had no trouble at all and there is a considerable shrinking of the pimples too. He now feels himself relieved of the trouble. But he had dry piles. The man who had told him this method had said that this will be equally useful in bleeding piles also.

Love to children and respects to Appaji.

With best wishes,

Yours,
Ram Chandra

No. F 536/SRCM **Shahjahanpur, U.P.**
Dated 14th October, 1961

My dear Varadachari,

Received your affectionate letter dated 10th October, 1961. I hope that you have received by now my letter written on the same date. Four of my associates have arrived from Gulbarga and two or three more are expected in a day. They will pass their Dasehra holidays with me. I also wrote to Capt. V. Mohan Rao, that you will be waiting for his next visit.

I believe you had no idea of diabetes before it was detected for the first time. Shri Kashi Ram who was at Assam 2 years back, is now doing business here. He is a good naturopath and cured diabetes simply by regulation of diet. After your recovery from headache I will write to you about it. Shri M.L. Chaturvedi has recently discovered sugar in the urine. I will also prescribe the same thing to him. If you meditate that you are being cured of diabetes you will feel that it is gone.

It is good that Sow. Padmini will go to Bangalore to live with her husband. She will learn there the household work and management. The *grihastha* life is the school for learning things necessary for the upkeep of the family. Sister might have been reduced on account of her anxiety about your illness. I hope and pray that you may recover soon and regain health. All will go well; God is great.

I sent a bottle of Amla Hair Oil through Mr. R. Seshadri to Madras requesting him to send it to you through somebody who might be going to Tirupati. I do not know whether you have received it or not.

Love to children and respects to Appaji.

With best wishes,

Yours,
Ram Chandra

Tirupati
26th October 1961

My dear Revered Gurudev,

Please accept my humble pranams. I received your affectionate letter on the 19th. As I developed trembling in the fingers I did not go to Bangalore. I am yet very weak. Though I have been taking insulin injections the sugar has not completely eliminated in the urine. You wrote to me that if I meditate I can get rid of the diabetes. But I should like to know how to do the meditation. As you know nowadays I am not meditating at all. Except for the satsangh on Sunday mornings I am not doing anything at all. There is aggravation in the nights of headache and pain in the right eye. Though I am attending the College from the 23rd instant, yet it is quite a strain on me. I do not know how much longer this condition will last.

I am proposing to send with my wife Chi. Padmini on Saturday 28th but I do not know. Anyway I pray that thy blessings for their happy conjugal life. My wife also is taking treatment for extreme exhaustion owing to diabetes.

As my right eyelid has not completely relaxed and is slightly dropping the Doctor feels that some more time is needed for doing refraction. So Dr. Mohan Rao has not come but I shall write to him as to when he can come and do the refraction.

Shri Seshadri has not handed over the hair oil you sent till now or sent it through somebody. Mr. Viraraghavan wrote to me that Seshadri is keeping the same with him and would deliver it when he goes over to Tirupati. Well that is so.

I believe you are now completely free from low blood pressure.

I also think that Shri Ishwar Sahaiji is with you and is in good health. I think that under the new treatment Mrs. Sahaiji is getting better.

All of us here are otherwise well.

With loving pranams.

>Yours,
>KCV

No. F 559/SRCM **Shahjahanpur, U.P.**
Dated 8th November, 1961

My dear Varadachari,

Received your affectionate letter. I hope you are well on the way of recovery. I have been suffering from stomach-ache, acute in nature, for the last about 10 days. So I am unable to attend to correspondence at present. I shall reply your letter shortly when I am in a position to do so. You need not worry about it. Capt. V. Mohan Rao has informed me that he would be going to Tirupati for refraction when you call him for the purpose.

Love to children. Respect to Appaji.

With best wishes,

>Yours,
>Ram Chandra

No. F 591/SRCM **Shahjahanpur, U.P.**
Dated 21st November, 1961

My dear Varadachari,

Received your letters. I hope that the marriage of Chi. Chaya will be settled soon. The father of the boy has not yet given the words but he seems to be inclined to finalise the marriage. He is coming to finalise the marriage proposal on 3rd December,

1961. Shri R. Seshadri has been transferred to Madura and he will reach Madras on 22nd November and will remain there till the building is got for the office at Madura. Has Sow. Padmini gone to Bangalore?

I also received the post card of Shri Thyagarajan sent by you in the envelope. He sent a post card to Shri Raghavendra Rao to the same effect. One of his friends at Trichy also informed me that he is telling the same thing to his friends about myself. I was requested by his friends to write him a letter that he should not be strict on his family and should not break the household things. I reluctantly did it. This is all due to the state of lunacy for which I am very sorry. I take pity upon his children but he does not deserve our sympathies. If I pray today for his recovery, I do not remember the other day. Moreover, I work on my own diagnosis which is only possible when I myself see the patient. Last year when I was with you at Tirupati you said something about Thyagarajan which I remembered when I came over here. Your finding was totally correct. When I saw him at Trichy, I told him that you have lost all what you have gained and I asked him, "What it is due to?" He replied that he was greatly worried due to the illness of his wife. I wanted to say something but I declined. The cause was very bad and filthy which he admitted in the letter so sent to me on my arrival here. All his letters were showing that he was creeping into madness. I wanted to write to you but I did not disturb you. Still I love him. May he recover soon. But after his recovery it will be very hard job for me at least to reinstate his former condition.

I wrote to you that you can get rid of diabetes by meditation. The process is the same what we do in our daily meditation. Disease is going out of the body in the form of vapour or smoke and auto-suggestions to cure the disease. Of course, there are some other methods also for instance drawing energy from *brahmanda mandal* for the sun to cure the disease. You wrote to me that you have been feeling that you are absolutely doing nothing at all. It reminded me of *nishkam karma* given in *Gita*. This is the stage where this thing is possible. You do not require any meditation now; that has been withdrawn already (vide my previous letters) so you should spend that time in some other work of the Mission (Master's words in the same letter). I am exceedingly happy that you enjoy the excellent state. After crossing all the rings of splendour abhyasi enters into the state (words fail to express it) of Godly ungodliness so to say. I do not find a better word for the expression of this stateless state. At present you enjoy the state as I wrote to you in one of the letters that the death is meeting its own death. Really I am very lucky to see such condition and I pray that all my associates may be drawn to this state. Probably I wrote to you for your experience that when a man enters the ring of splendour the journey is altogether over. Only one begins to absorb potency, which the ring contains of.

I am very sorry to inform you that one of my satsanghis Shri S.R. Mukerjee died of heart failure on 12th September, 1961. I did not inform you so far because you yourself were in trouble. He was the only Bengali in our *sanstha* and very enthusiastic in all his work. He joined the Homeopathic college at

Calcutta and obtained the degree. Shri Raghavendra Rao was suffering from appendicitis, when he met me for the first time. He cured him in one dose. My son Sarvesh was suffering from heart disease due to typhoid. He also cured him in one year. He took Railway service and recently he was transferred from Fatehgarh to Muzaffarpur (West Bengal). His family is staying with me and I have to make arrangements for the education of his two elderly sons aged 12 years and 9 years. There is nobody to support them. Mrs. Mukerjee's brother has passed Matriculation who can help him much if he is employed. I am trying my level best to get him employed. I hope I will succeed. There were some other work regarding G.P. Fund and so on that we have done.

I have got my own observation about Mukerjee's soul and Kasturi has also given her findings with which I partly agree. I want to work on him. I also invite your observation about the soul to ensure the correctness of my reading. I shall also let you know my finding afterwards. In his case the difficulty is that I could not yet enter into the depth of his being.

I am now better and have now begun to improve in health. The pain is normal that is which I can easily bear. I hope and pray that you and the sister may develop bodily energy very soon. I shall pray for the recovery of Shri C.R. Krishnamurti. I am sorry to hear the sad demise of the gardener of the ashram. May his soul rest in peace.

Love to children. Respect to Appaji.

With best wishes,   Yours,

Ram Chandra

No. F 595/SRCM   **Shahjahanpur, U.P.**
Dated 27th November, 1961

My dear Varadachari,

I had been to Lucknow for three days. I returned on 26th November, 1961 and got your telegram. I am extremely sorry for the sad demise of dear Padmini. May her soul rest in peace. May God give patience to all of you. Loss is really irrepairable.

Was it the sudden death or she has been ill for sometime? I have no words to express my deep sorrow. How to console my sister in such a state of agony.

I also sent a condolence telegram today.

Yours,
Ram Chandra

No. F 606/SRCM   **Shahjahanpur, U.P.**
Dated 30th November, 1961

My dear Varadachari,

Received your letter dated 24th November, 1961. I believe you have received my postcard and the telegram. The untimely and accidental demise of Padmini is shocking to all of us. As soon as I saw your telegram, I was overclouded with deep melancholy.

I devoted a greater part of the night in prayers that you may all be free from the shock of her death. In the morning when I got up I found that I am a bit relieved. I should believe that you might have also by now reciprocated the same.

It is our duty to pray for her emancipation and I will start this work no sooner the saddest and melancholic weight of the mind will be lessened with the passage of time.

Again praying for peace to the departed soul.

Yours,
Ram Chandra

Tirupati
6th December 1961

My dear Revered Gurudev,

Please accept my humble pranams. I am deeply thankful to thee for thy kind letter, telegram and postcard. I am sure that it is owing to thy blessings that we were able to go through this ordeal unscathed, for it was all an ordeal. For the past eight months it was the most engaging worry. Somehow the event has lifted a burden off our shoulders and indeed I felt myself light. I am not weighted down by sorrow nor my wife, but for the fact that nothing could be done to make my son-in-law's and uncle's life happy nor could that child have a change of mind and being that would have made for happiness here in this plane of life. I have no doubt that though there were whispers and so on, the thing is over — at huge cost and sorrow to all. Yes: God's ways are inscrutable and I had not even the inkling of this kind to come. I have had disgrace in profession, disasters in personal life but this threat to honour and now death I never thought would be my portion. Indeed this has been a shock to faith on the part of the onlookers and perhaps even of abhyasis. So the Mission's work is somewhat slowed up. I can only pray that the last of these has been over and my *prarabdha* as well as that of my wife has been exhausted. My wife's health is continuing to be bad — and now this shock. So too my father, children are all shocked. Most probably Chi. Narayana would have written to you his reactions to this — he thinks that all my knowledge, yoga and Master's grace are just nonsense. May the Master be pleased to grant him peace of mind.

Master has asked me as to whether I found relief even as thou hast had after a night's prayer. Yes. In a sense the event has become remote and one feels that one is not connected with it.

However I feel again and again for that poor soul that was my daughter for 20 years and so misguided and deceptive. But all these I forgive and pray that she may be granted a solace and development that will take her to brighter worlds.

I received letters from Shri Ishwar Sahai and Raghavendra Rao of condolences.

I have tried to see the astral condition of Shri Mukerjee: it was not clear. Perhaps my present condition is not quite suitable to see it. I shall try again later. Somehow I do not know how to express my condition at all — and so absorbed am I in what I cannot say — You have written that death is destroying itself — in my state. I am unable to grasp the significance of all that. You have also stated that godly ungodliness prevails in me or would when the rings of splendour are passed or crossed and one swims in the centre. Of course is it not an ungodliness to question the wisdom of God when one goes through the tragedies such as these.

I can only pray that I may realise and experience all the splendour of realisation and be able to have the vision of the Ultimate, and so also the abhyasis who have taken refuge at thy godly feet.

With loving pranams,

Yours,
KCV

No. F 622/SRCM **Shahjahanpur, U.P.**
Dated 15th December, 1961

My dear Varadachari,

Received your affectionate letter dated 6th December, 1961. My son Chi. Narayana is also greatly shocked by the sad demise of daughter Padmini. He wrote to me a letter which is now replied. I prayed for Chi. Narayana that he may get peace of mind and forget the shock. He will become all right, I am sure. I am sending you a copy of his letter with its reply so that if you want to write to him anything you may also do so.

The shock is not an ordinary one and every conscious man should feel it. The abhyasis too have felt it naturally but it is their sympathising attitude towards you that they have shown a shock to faith.

It is our duty to give peace to Padmini's soul and we should all pray for it. I transmitted her several times and with great difficulty I succeeded in turning her attention towards myself. Now I could not properly guess how to take up her problem further I believe some solution for the work will come. Generally I do not give trouble to my Master unless I am exhausted. Moreover, I have to abide by his will for which the direction itself comes before taking up the work. I request you and the sister as well to pray for the peace of the soul for about 10 minutes and this is our last office.

I did not disclose to you so far that a few hours before her death I was at Lucknow in a marriage party and doing some spiritual work, during that interval my attention was naturally drawn towards Padmini and automatically I began to draw out poison from her body. Twice or thrice I did afterwards when I came to senses I stopped work without pondering over it taking it to be the work of the individual mind. But even those jerks could not give her any benefit because the span of life was over.

There is another example in my experience that a daughter of one of my associates was bitten by a dog and I informed her father, of course very late, that she should at once be moved to some expert doctor. During that time I drew out poison and it was drawn out but there remained a dot which created the poison again. These things show that nobody even the highest saint of the world can meddle with God's affairs, what to say of this poor being. For the rest of your letter I shall write to you sometime after. Needless to say that you are as dear to me as anybody can be, so I will perform my duty for your highest approach though the case is in God's hand.

Shri Raghavendra Rao wrote to me that he will undergo the operation of squint on 13th or 14th December.

Love to children. Respects to Appaji.

With best wishes, Yours,

Ram Chandra

19th December 1961

My dear revered and beloved Gurudev,

Please accept my humble pranams. Your affectionate letter dated 15th instant to hand. I read the same as also your letter to Chi. Narayana with deep gratitude. I am sure he will understand. He was so worried about me and Chi. Srinivasan that he wished to take a month's leave on loss of pay and go over here to stay with me. I firmly told him that he would have to stick on at Vizag, even though he was posted back as A.E.O. Sub regional Employment exchange from the University, which he did not like. I think he is reconciling himself.

I have no doubt nor my wife about the altogether terrible calamity, but Padmini had to go through this and it is good that her life was short. I have no doubt that her good luck amidst all wrong things and turns was her getting Master's blessings thanks to her being my daughter in this life. May God's grace be on her for her future. Both of us are remote hereafter. Her horoscope pointed to this unhappy end and I did not know it for I was carried away by the readings of another eminent person. This too is a blindness. Only I am sorry that we could not train the mind to accept God's and Master's words. I feel utterly guilty insofar as I have failed to be of any inspiration and guidance to the children.

I received kind and affectionate condolence letters from Saint Kasturi, Raghavendra Rao, Mohan Rao and others. It is with a shock that I learnt from my eminent brother Ishwar Sahaiji about the passing away of his wife. Shri Srivasthava wrote to me and Saint Kasturi wrote that it was due to heart failure. This again shows the inscrutable workings of the Master. I take heart that the Master's assurance is all to me. I believe in the Master and Master alone. I pray that I will have a *shraddha* that is unshakeable and so too all of us. Though everything seemed to be crumbling at one stage everything is restored to me in the form of greater love of Master. May my love increase till it is totally giving up itself to Him, without remainder. May I and my wife be dedicated to Thee integrally. Her nobility came out clearly during the month that has gone. My father also has been standing up to this wonderfully.

Chi. Chitra today left for a week's study tour to Rameshvaram and prayed that I should write to thee about this so that she may have your blessings and refuge all through.

We have started our regular work of individual transmissions and satsanghs. Last Sunday I felt the presence of Master sahib's wife in the satsangh and perhaps also Padmini. Shri Dr. Kuppuswamy substantiated this. Dr. Kuppuswamy told me that on the 23rd November morning satsangh he saw two nude young women in bath. He brushed this aside as an interference of an evil sort. But when the event of death took place of Padmini that night he felt that it was a premonition. He did all with thy name to save her. But I felt when I meditated for a few minutes (one minute to be exact) that she was gone out of the body.

The meditations are of intensest kind. Sheer Blankness is what Shri Annaih Naidu experienced during sittings here.

I am much better. I believe the diabetes is subsiding.

I believe Master's health is much better and the stomach trouble has subsided.

I am enclosing a letter of reply to Saint Kasturi. As she did not give me her address but wrote from Bareilly, I request that it may be sent to her. I am grateful and indeed honoured to be linked up with affection to all our brothers and sisters and daughters.

With loving pranams,

Yours as ever and integrally,

KCV

No. F 646/SRCM **Shahjahanpur, U.P.**
Dated 26th December, 1961

My dear Varadachari,

Received your affectionate letter dated 19th December, 1961. The letter addressed to Saint Kasturi was sent by me to Bareilly the same day I received it. There is extreme cold in U.P. and Punjab. The temperature has gone down to 3.9°C. There is a radio news that the chill will increase. The weather remains cloudy and so many deaths have occurred on its account. Kanpur and Delhi are under cold blast. If I would have been in south these days I would have been saved from the trouble but it is a pleasure to me that I am sharing chill along with others.

I was informed by Shri Raghavendra Rao that one of my southern brothers is travelling in North India along with his students and he may come here also along with them. He is newly admitted satsanghi and has not seen me as yet. I remember him daily and I am worried as to how they will be able to withstand the cold climatic condition. Schools are being closed and Government has sanctioned Rs. 1500/- per city for the blankets to the poor and the firewood are being kindled at main crossings of the towns.

The shock of Padmini's death is really very great, but there is no help except to invite blessings of God on her. My idea is that she is peaceful now and waiting for the transmission which she is getting. It seems to me the Master's work. I rely much on you in astrology. Since it was going to be happened you yourself did not care to see horoscope yourself and work accordingly. Do you remember the case of Dinesh that I knew a year before that he will commit suicide by gun. When he returned after seeing the result the same idea came to my mind, but I forgot it at each step. Everybody is powerless here and God has taken much in his hand.

I think of you and the sister very much since this unhappy occurrence. May you all enjoy unbroken peace. Amen.

It is really praiseworthy that even during serious troubles you thought of your spiritual approach. May you live long. I think it will not be out of place if I write to you something about your spiritual condition. During this period of troubles the work of God was going on in your system but slow. Now in this week this work is in full swing according to your capacity which He Himself makes. Please observe.

I wish happy tour of Chi. Chitra.

Love to children. Respects to Appaji.

With best wishes,

Yours,
Ram Chandra

1962

No. G 6/SRCM   **Shahjahanpur, U.P.**
Dated 4th January, 1962

My dear Varadachari,

Received your affectionate letter dated 1st January, 1962. The severity of cold has, no doubt, subsided but U.P. is still very cold. During this period the temperature at Kanpur, Allahabad and elsewhere had gone down below freezing point. It does not seem advisable to travel to Jaipur in January. The place will be colder than other districts in U.P. The proper days for travelling in this part of the country are the end of March and onward. If you are compelled to do it have sufficient clothings and two thick blankets. In case you travel, please inform me the date and time of your arrival at Shahjahanpur so that I may receive you at the station.

You have written to me that it is beyond you to see the Beyond. It is not the case. If you get any such abhyasi, you will be able to know all about it. In my case I do not understand what is there in me but I can, by my Master's grace, read the others. I am observing your condition but up till now I do not find the words for expression. The condition no doubt, is almost changeless. I use the word almost because subtle changes are taking place and it is not easily discernible.

I am glad to inform you that the marriage of Chi. Chaya is settled at Lucknow but the date has not yet been fixed. Probably it will fall in the end of May or June because in March the examination of children will begin. I shall let you know when it is fixed.

Love to children. Respects to Appaji.
With best wishes,

Yours,
Ram Chandra

No. G 103/SRCM **Shahjahanpur, U.P.**
Dated 24th January, 1962

My dear Varadachari,

Received your affectionate letter dated 15th January, 1962. You will be pleased to know that the date for Chi. Chaya's marriage is fixed for 8th March, 1962. We will be busy in the marriage work just after the Utsava is over. Please pray that marriage may be gracefully performed. Invitations will be sent in due course. I shall be mostly free after performing the marriage of my second daughter.

You have done well to satisfy my boy Chi. Narayana. I myself could not satisfy him. He also wrote to me the letter to the same effect. I pray that he may rise spiritually and worldly and he may take up any job in any department where he finds chance of rise.

I have gone through your article appeared in the 'Divine Life' magazine. It was very nicely written. Clarity of thought was there. Every sentence was giving out a new life. I can take upon myself to say that hardly any one can write such an article. Moreover you have corrected the views of Swamiji also. I have not yet seen such a good article anywhere written by yourself. In the whole of the article there was simplicity to the core. It was really your part to show that the scientific researches cannot bring peace to humanity. When I was reading that article

I felt that divine influence was gushing out from the letters in ample measure.

For your knowledge and experience I must inform you that the divinity is working peculiarly in your system. Sometimes its working goes in full swing and sometimes slow as I see in this week. But the influence it leaves in your system is working all over in bringing a peculiar condition, which all of us should aspire. I am studying it so that I may also work like that but it seems to me difficult to work like that because only God has the perfect wisdom.

I believe you have received the invitation cards for Utsava. I have already sent invitation to Shri V. Mohan Rao and Dindayalu of Rajampet, Shri S. Vedantam, Shri Viraraghavan, Shri Krishnamachari, Shri Rajagopal and Major Lingham of Madras but I am sorry that I am very late in informing you. For Mr. Naik and other associates I have directed Mr. Mudaliar to issue invitations.

Respects to Appaji and love to children.

With best wishes,

Yours,
Ram Chandra

No. G 152/SRCM **Shahjahanpur, U.P.**
Dated 20th March, 1962

My dear Varadachari,

Received your affectionate letter dated 13th March. By Master's blessings and good wishes marriage function went off gracefully. Shri Ayal Reddy of Sedam and Shri Gopal Rao of Bidar participated in the marriage. Shri S.K. Rajagopalan also attended it. They have helped us much in the work.

I am happy that you will grace my house in the second week of April. In the second week of April there will be moderate climate and is good for journey to this part of the country. So when the date for going to Jaipur is fixed you will please inform me the date and the time of your arrival here to enable me to reach the station at that time. My house is situated in Mohalla Dewanjograj, near Carewganj and Rang-Mahila.

I see that you are getting some trouble or other for a year. I do not know whether these be His lovely embraces. Sister's health is creating anxiety. I think she remains over-burdened with the household works and gets no rest which is necessary. May I request you to send me the details of Shri C.R. Krishnamurthi's illness. I pray that Chi. Aravinda may be employed on some good post.

I am very happy to note that on 18th November at 5:58 P.M. you stepped into the fourth ring of splendour. Before it I was feeling a complete purifying state in you. When I peep into you, I feel solace.

Whenever there is an anxiety I look into you and the anxiety is over but on the contrary you wrote to me that you have been much troubled for your progress and feel it very distressing.

Now by my Master's blessings both my daughters are married and this anxiety is over. I want to devote myself more and more to the work of the Mission but there is one difficulty with me that I have grown sluggish and waste my time sitting idle.

Please help me that this habit may be changed and I may become active and smart.

Respect to Appaji and love to children,

Yours,
Ram Chandra

No. G 210/SRCM   **Shahjahanpur, U.P.**
Dated 3rd May, 1962

My dear Varadachari,

Received your affectionate letters dated 23rd April, 1962. I also received the copy of horoscope of my grandson. Thanks for it. I have already replied the letter sent by Dr. Kuppaswamy under this office No. G 200/SRCM dated 18th April, 1962. I believe that he has received it by now. Sister's health is creating anxiety. For the treatment of boil homeopathic medicines are quite good and also the allopathic injections. My Master was deadly against the allopathic injections and was in favour of homeopathic medicines.

I read with pleasure what you have stated in your letter about your present condition. We proceed from grossness to subtleness, that too in the long run gives way. It happens when we begin to arrive at the reality, so simple. The material force widely differs from spiritual force. The very essence of power lies when we go even beyond its limit, afterwards we reach the spot when the feelings of both these things are gone. A man reaching such a height can display force when he forms the will like that and at other times he seems to be inactive and that is the powerless force. May God bless you all with that. You yourself stated in the letter that bliss seems to be absent and even knowledge seems to be left behind. Does it not clearly show that you have gone beyond both and are acquiring nearness to God? If this condition at its ripening state falls in the share even in one of my associates I will be compelled to presume that my Mission is complete, although I am sure, and I pray for it, that I will get a few men who may give tidings to come to that state. My dear Varadachari, please remove dissatisfaction and thank God for it. I also complained to my Master once or twice when I had only a glimpse of this condition which you are enjoying at present. He asserted strongly to remove this idea altogether otherwise it would be ungratefulness to God.

Now there are no centres or sub-centres to pass through. When you enter any ring and begin to live in it you become the part and parcel of the power which it contains of. So *yatra* is not there at all. In your letter you wrote the same words which I had written to my Master.

When the next meeting is fixed, please inform me. When I was writing this letter I was remembering Dr. Kuppaswamy very much. Chaya is going to her father-in-law's place tomorrow. Respect to Appaji and love to children.

With best wishes,

Yours affectionately,
Ram Chandra

No. G 259/SRCM　　　　　　Shahjahanpur, U.P.
　　　　　　　　　　　　　Dated 7th June, 1962

My dear Varadachari,

Received both your affectionate letters. How eagerly I wish for a successful career for Chi. Narayan. As a student he has been brilliant all through and such alone are the fittest candidates for competitions like I.A.S. This was why I had suggested it to him. Moreover, as I find it, the south Indians generally fare better in competitions than the north Indians, for the higher standard of education there. You write that the time for admission is now over. But Mr. Chaturvedi's view that he may get permission to appear in the exam, if he applies after resigning his job, shows that there may be chance for him yet.

As I could gather from my talks with Chi. Narayan, I think that he prefers educational department to the administrative one. It was only after some discussion that he at last accepted my views, somewhat reluctantly. I think if one has entered the administrative service he has better chances of helping his relations in securing good posts. For myself I find it very difficult to say anything definite on the point, since my intuition seldom offers a correct clue in cases where I am personally interested. However, I advise Chi. Narayana to think twice before doing a thing. It may also be better to consult someone else who has experience in such matters. There seem to be chances for him no doubt (in I.A.S.) but nothing definite can be said about it.

I believe Shri Kuppuswamy must now be better. On observing him a few days ago, I found in him strong vibrations in the *brahmanda mandal*. I waited to watch the tendency of their movement. But after four days I saw that they had subsided though at times they rose up again a little. I wanted him to proceed by it in the natural way, though I may do what may be demanded at the time. I shall then inform you about it. For your experience I may tell you that perplexity, confusion and impatience, often felt by an abhyasi on such occasions, are symptoms to show that he wants to go up to the next region but he cannot by his own power. Then is the Master's helping hand needed to put him on into the next. Regarding your condition it is all clear to me by the one sentence you wrote in this connection.

Sow. Maya is quite well and Sow. Chhaya has shifted to Allahabad on account of the transfer of her father-in-law. Ratanam remembers you often for your toffee.

My respects to Appaji and love to children.

With best wishes,

Yours,
Ram Chandra

No. G 310/SRCM   **Shahjahanpur, U.P.**
Dated 18th July, 1962

My dear Varadachari,

Received your affectionate letter dated 18th June, 1962. My reply to it is much delayed owing to my bad health. For about three weeks I had been suffering from dysentery and diarrhoea successively. Now I am better. But the blood pressure is much gone down. For this reason I cannot do mental work even for an hour without having headache. But in spite of all that I cannot give up transmitting to my brothers at night though I do it only for about ten minutes almost daily. Under the present situation I have therefore to give strong suggestions, keeping in mind the capacity of the abhyasi. I am now taking due precautions to restore my health and I believe it shall be normal in about ten days.

The sufferings and ailments are indispensable for the body and they help much in the purification process. A great benefit which we derive from them is that in that case the watchful eye of the Master remains on the devotee and that means closer contact and nearness. Nature is the greatest healer, so they say. It is a clear proof to show that the sympathies of the Master are turned more towards an ailing brother. The world is full of sorrow and misery. To undergo them is like undergoing an operation by the Highest for setting us in proper order. That means an affectionate motherly treatment. A man may have reached the highest summit in spirituality but that does not imply that he has gone beyond physical afflictions, unpleasant to his senses. The power of endurance, no doubt, also develops with it. These things do not touch the deeper layers of being. They only float like straw on the surface of water. One of the commandments of our Mission directs us to be thankful to God for all the miseries and troubles. There are reasons for it. When we are in a thankful mood we touch the inner core of the being coming in closer contact with it. As a result every nerve of our body gets charged with that pious influence effecting all the uniform state all over. In this way man so cleverly turns hell into heaven for himself.

Your letter to Shri Ishwar Sahai provides me hints for further thinking and I have preserved the letter for that purpose. The translation of *Reality at Dawn* in Kannada has been printed and you must have received a few copies of it by this time. You might have got back the photograph of the Master from Sarnadji.

You will be happy to learn that Dr. Kuppuswamy has out of his own effort stepped into *parabrahma mandal* on 28-6-62 at 9:28 P.M. Now Shri Annaih Naidu is also slowly developing a tendency of going into that region. I received a letter (copy enclosed) from a newly admitted satsanghi named Shri Parthasarathi of Vijayawada. I am glad that he has moulded his mind in a way to allot to me some services for which I am grateful to him. I also received a lovely letter from Shri Kuppuswamy. I am replying to it.

I received the preface written by you. It is very nice. I shall send the book itself after about ten days along with the preface, so that you may go through all that once more to see if anything is not wanting yet.

How is sister doing now? Love to children.

My respects to Appaji,

With best wishes,

Yours,
Ram Chandra

No. G 356/SRCM Shahjahanpur, U.P.
Dated 4th August, 1962

My dear Varadachari,

Received both of your affectionate letters. I have gone through your foreword. It is quite illusive and to the point. I shall soon send the manuscript along with the foreword to you for your final opinion after which it shall be sent to the press. A quotation from Swami Vivekananda's speech is to be added in it but the book could not be available yet, hence the delay.

I received the marriage invitations from Annaih Naidu and Shri Srinivasulu. I have replied to them. The letter of Dr. Kuppuswamy is pending reply. I am glad to find in him signs of higher improvement. It is due to his love and devotion and also to his service to you. Other abhyasis too are doing well with their abhyas. I am glad that Chi. Aravinda has joined M.A. in Philosophy and Chi. Chitra M.A. in Zoology.

I do not think you have been even for a while, in the state of disintegration. As a rule you feel yourself integrated when you are concentrated but when loose you feel like disintegrated. As a matter of fact there is only a slight difference of degrees, due to the touch of external things around you.

You say that you are unaware of all and live as if nothing has happened in the shape of experience. There are three things, Ignorance, Knowledge and Beyond Knowledge. Beyond Knowledge is in itself a state of ignorance. The difference between these two states of ignorance is that the former is far heavier than the latter because it is associated with *tamas*. When this ignorance has been refined it converts into knowledge. That means that in knowledge the ignorance is there in the essence form. When one transcends to the higher state, described as 'Beyond Knowledge' both of them are gone.

Experience you want and everyone tries for it but when differentiation is over, wherefrom shall the experience come. In my view it is a higher state and I pray for you to rise up to it. Since the commencement of Manifestation, there have been two forces at work in Nature, the differentiating and the unifying. Both must co-exist in order to keep up the creation. If either of them is gone, that means the end of existence. For understanding's sake you may call unification as a state of the inner being while differentiation as a state of outer being. Even at higher spiritual stages, this differentiation remains though to a nominal extent only. For instance, the presence of different colours may be taken as differentiation but when they are all unified, they lose their distinctive feature and are merged into one — the colourlessness. To an abhyasi, affected with unification, the differentiation seems to be a far distant view, hence troubles and afflictions, though they are there even then, are much less effective. But when he is inclined towards differentiation, the force of the feeling faculty increases, because he himself makes it powerful by his concentrated thought-force. The demarcation line between them can never be non-existent till the very time of the Final Dissolution.

I am better now, though weakness persists still, which usually goes away with the advent of the winter season. Kasturi must have written to you about my health upon the basis of her intuition as she often does. Usually I do not inform her about it till I am quite recovered, lest it might be painful to her.

Shri Raghavendra Rao along with a few other associates is reaching this place on the 20th, for a few days' stay at the time of Shri Krishna Janmashtami (21st August).

Chi. Umesh had passed the I.Com. in the second div. But there being no B.Com. here he had to be got admitted in the University at Lucknow. I am going this afternoon for a short trip to Lucknow and Kanpur. I shall be back in about a week.

I shall also be having a tour of Assam in the coming month. Love to children and respects to Appaji.

With best wishes,

Yours,
Ram Chandra

No. G 370/SRCM   **Shahjahanpur, U.P.**
Dated 14th August, 1962

My dear Varadachari,

Received your affectionate letter dated 11th August, 1962. The word 'illusive' in my last letter is a type mistake. It was really 'lucid' in place of illusive. So please correct it accordingly. I have made the correction in the office copy. I am sorry for the mistake. The rest of the letter will be replied later on.

With best wishes,   Yours,
Ram Chandra

No. G 378/SRCM Shahjahanpur, U.P.
Dated 15th August, 1962

My dear Varadachari,

Received your affectionate letter dated 11th August, 1962. My last postcard No. G 370 dated 14th August, 1962 explains to you the mistake in my letter No. G 356 dated 4th August, 1962. The word 'illusive' is to be replaced by 'lucid'. I believe you must have noted it. The preface is indeed very nice. I have sent the manuscript with the preface too to you for a cursory revision to see that nothing more is necessary for it now. You will please sign the preface in your own hand.

I am writing this letter on 15th August, the day on which we achieved freedom, but the more I think of freedom, the more I feel in bondage. To my mind the only difference between the two is that freedom covers a wider space while bondage the narrower. Thus freedom itself is a bondage. When we are away from the idea of both, the freedom and the bondage, then we are free in the real sense. In that case, the feeling of bondage or freedom is altogether swept away. I believe the word liberation also carries a similar sense. I have replied Dr. Kuppuswamy's letter also.

A few days back while thinking of Shri Raghavan of Renigunta I discovered that his condition warrants further lift to the *ajna chakra*, but there is something in the centres of the *pind* which tends to keep him down where he is. It appears like a sort of heaviness clutching hard at the points. But since I am watching it from a distance, my reading may not be exactly to the point. Will you please look to it to trace it out and correct if needed.

I am so happy to note that you have developed the inner vision to the extent that you have felt my working. I had directed your mind to take up the direct course to the farthest extent of human approach which has appeared to you in a 'tunnel-like' form. That was a sort of help or push to impel further movement.

Your feeling that you are occupied by the Master is a correct one. It is a kind of *laya avastha* of a high order. When it gets settled down it is a further step onwards. When the feeling of the body, *buddhi* or soul is all gone and you are not able to know whether it is yours or mine, even though you meditate to understand it, then that is a very high state. The last phase of *laya avastha* comes when, while speaking the word, 'I' refers to none, neither to self nor Master nor God, even though you force yourself to know it. Having gone so far, when that which comes next, is also dissolved and negativated then that is the state of Realisation in the true sense.

The transfer of Shri Tulsi Das has been postponed for the present. I have written to Kasturi to write to you about her condition. She expects to be here on the 21st.

I have received with great pleasure your offering of Rs. 60/- for your 60th birthday present. I wish to expect a double one after the next 60 years.

You should be more attentive towards the inner cleaning of Chi. Narayana and his brothers and sisters so that they may be feeling lightness and peace.

It is better if you devote about 15 minutes for it once a week.

I returned from Lucknow on the 10th. I got my last surviving tooth pulled out at the medical college there. A student doctor, one of our associates, has insisted upon me to have a set of teeth prepared under his care. I shall order for it after my return from Assam.

Chi. Umesh had come here in a three days' holiday. He has now gone back. Shri Raghavendra Rao with his brother and three other associates is arriving on the 20th.

Shri Ishwar Sahai conveys to you his *pranams*.

Love to children and respects to Appaji.

With best wishes,

Yours,
Ram Chandra

No. G 427/SRCM   **Shahjahanpur, U.P.**
Dated 15th September, 1962

My dear Varadachari,

Received your affectionate letter of 8th September, 1962.

Before we started, the Brahmaputra was in high flood, about 6 ft. above danger line, and the rains over the region were also excessive. But since my purpose of the tour was purely divine, I felt sure that the rains and the flood will come down to normal, offering no hindrance and it turned out exactly to be so.

Tinsukia is a beautiful place with smiling fields and tea gardens all round. It is an industrial centre too. But the living here is very costly. Every eatable is abnormally dear — especially the vegetables.

Shri I. Sahai, Kashi Ram and Professor Hardutta Singh are here with me. We had several gatherings at different places and message of the Mission was conveyed to the people by Shri H. Singh and others. I also had to speak sometimes.

I am staying here with Shri Bhagwandass who is a big magnate. He entertains feelings of deep love for me and the Mission. He had been to Shahjahanpur with his family about two years ago.

We shall leave for Calcutta on the 18th arriving there on the 21st where we shall stay till 24th. Then we shall go back and staying for two days at Lucknow, reach Shahjahanpur on the 28th.

The journey to Calcutta is very tedious, but I undertake it with a view to have personal contact with Mr. Medayil whom I have never seen so far. It is rather touching to be faced with taunts and rebukes in place of sympathy and consolation for the sad demise of Padmini. Anyhow you have to put up with them under such cases, though in the end they will finally prove to be to their own disadvantage and worry. Your tolerance will surely count much in this respect. I had also received Mr. Srinivasan's marriage invitation, but the thought of Padmini aggrieved me all the more. So I did not reply to it.

Previously I had written to you about the heaviness in the *pind* centres of Shri G.S. Raghavan. I find it reduced now, though it is there to some extent yet.

I feel worried over the condition of Shri Seshadri's father. I have learnt from one of our associates that Shri Seshadri is transferred to Trichy. I enquired from him about it by his Madras address, but received no reply. I propose to have my South India tour from third week of November and during my visit to Trichy I wish to stay with him there. But if I do not receive his reply by the time I fix up the programme I shall have to arrange for my lodging at Shri S.K. Ramaswami's house.

Please return the manuscript with your preface signed and fixed at the proper place, and also your suggestions, if any. I shall return it to you afterwards for having it printed.

Love to children and respects to Appaji.

With best wishes,

Yours,
Ram Chandra

No. G 422/SRCM **Shahjahanpur, U.P.**
Dated 30th September, 1962

My dear Varadachari,

I believe you got my previous letter from Tinsukia. After brief halts at Calcutta and Lucknow, I arrived here on the 28th. At Calcutta I had visited Dakshineshwar and the Belur Math. They presented a beautiful sight. I also went to the *samadhi* of Swami Rama Krishna and meditated there for about two minutes. I found a good effect on the heart. This shows that his heart-centre was exciting, and it is not with him alone but also with most of the other saints that the *chakra* prominent in him displays its effect strongly. My Master's technique in this respect is but unique in so much as at the last pitch the Master's help unifies all the *chakras*, I mean everything being charged with divine influence becomes equalised.

At Belur Math I found the effect to be very pleasant. This was the place he (Swami Vivekanand) lived in. We sat in meditation by the side of his *samadhi* for about five minutes. The effect caused on us all was very nice. We had no thoughts and a moderate state prevailed all through.

At Tinsukia there was a great demand for the *Reality at Dawn*. They pressed me for the immediate reprinting of it. In view of my financial difficulties in the matter they offered me contribution of Rs. 800/- for the purpose. I left the money with Shri Ram Das, the preceptor at Tinsukia, to be sent to you under insured cover, which he must have done by this time. Please keep the amount with you for the expenses of printing of Ishwar Sahai's book. The money I had for that purpose will be utilised for the printing of *Reality at Dawn*, which I shall look to when I am there during my tour.

I talked to you several times about the impending rebirth of Shri Aurobindo, stating that he is gathering *paramanus* for his physical existence and that he will soon be reborn near about Madras. During our last meeting at Shahjahanpur I had further told you that the time of his rebirth is now approaching fast and that I shall inform you when he is reborn. He is now reborn on 20th September, 1962 at 8:32 A.M. at about 100 miles south of Madras along the coast (may be near about Pondicherry). The time may likely be a minute earlier because having known of it

I asked for the time and was told that it was 8:32. The process might have taken a minute. For a proof of his rebirth I may say that his soul being in body now, does not come at call. The vision does not speak precisely of the exact location but only reveals the view of that place, which may be taken into understanding by the help of a map. I am sorry to say that the *sanstha* of Shri Aurobindo is now going down fast and the light is gradually disappearing from the Ashram.

Mr. Robert Koch has informed me that he may be coming to me early in 1963.

I believe you must have by this time dispatched the manuscript along with your signed preface to me for finalisation.

Shri Iswar Sahai is going to Lakhimpur for about ten days in connection with the death anniversary of his wife.

Love to children and respects to Appaji.

With best wishes,

Yours,
Ram Chandra

No. G 478/SRCM   **Shahjahanpur, U.P.**
Dated 31st October, 1962

My dear Varadachari,

Received your affectionate letters. I had been to Lucknow for denture-making. It took me a fortnight. I returned on the 29th. But I am now going to Allahabad in connection with my cases in the High Court which are expected to come up for hearing on the 7th or later, according to the weekly list issued by the court. The advocate I had engaged is now a judge of the High Court. So I have to look for another. So for this reason and for certain other reasons also I think that my tour to South may not be possible in the coming November and December, though I shall finally decide it after my return from Allahabad. But the fact about the case should not be given out to the associates for the cause of postponement. However, if postponed at present, it may be taken up after the annual Utsava (on the Basant Panchami day).

I am sending herewith two copies of the manuscript along with 50 invitation cards. One copy is for you and the other for the Press.

As for the Mother and for her Ashram, I can say much but only when we meet. But if you like you may read and have your own views about her inner condition. I am sure you will find some awkward changes rapidly taking place in her, and to tell you in confidence, some external influences are touching her inner being and have begun to overshadow her. It is just a hint for you to think upon and that may add to your experience in the work of training. She is growing arrogant of her power. Her work in connection with the Chinese problem does not seem to be effective since her power does not go beyond herself, though she may be exerting herself to work for the victory of our mother country as is the duty of every saint.

I am glad that Shri A. Naidu has taken over the management of the *matha* but he feels pinched for it which is only the reaction of his thought. Please tell him that it cannot meddle with his abhyas if he thinks that he is doing the duty. Every work is divine if one remains connected deeply with God while doing his duty.

I feel you have amply moved towards Negation. The monotony you feel will go away after some time. Please take care of your health. Either start morning walk before breakfast or for an alternative practice some *asanas* but I do not recommend *shirsasan*. I do not agree with your views regarding the reading of others condition. The fallacy which sometimes comes in is due to the fact that when one exerts one's self with the force of will to read the condition of others he leaves no room for the feelings and conditions of the other to enter in him. In other words you block the way for its in-coming. The proper method would be exercise yourself very mildly (but with concentration of course) to read the condition of others. In this way his thoughts and feelings will be entering your super-consciousness. My respects to Appaji and love to children.

With best wishes,

Yours,
Ram Chandra

No. G 548/SRCM **Shahjahanpur, U.P.**
Dated 10th December, 1962

My dear Varadachari,

Received all your letters. Since I have been using the new set of teeth, I have developed ulcer in the jaw for which the doctor wants me to be there for three or four days. Consequently I am going to Lucknow on 11th December and thence to Allahabad for a day or two. I hope to return by the 20th. The appeals in the High Court are expected to come up for hearing in January 1963, and I fear lest it may be during the Utsava days. The Basant falls on 30th January, 1963, so the Utsava comes off from 29th (6:30 A.M.) to 31st (7:30 A.M.) 1963. The *havan* will be performed on 30th at 9:00 A.M.

I feel grateful to Mr. Rajam for the interest he is taking in the publication of our books. May he have a long and prosperous life. Shri Krishnamurti's illness is a worry to me. May God grant him speedy recovery.

Your affairs at the University and your colleague's behaviour is no doubt a matter of deep concern to me. Some people are often used to taking delight in teasing and torturing others not realising that the same is finally for them too. I have prayed and will pray more for it.

Your letter of 12th November, 1962 was a bit disappointing to me. The thoughts you complain about are never so serious as you take them to be unless you yourself make them so by giving your attention to them. It is only on account of your undue attention to them that they become strong and forceful. Your dissatisfaction about the correct reading of the abhyasi's condition also seems to have no reasonable basis. Some time ago I made it sufficiently clear to you that your reading of the abhyasis' condition was cent per cent correct and this was verified by the statements of the abhyasis also. Now I again quote below a passage from Mr. Viraraghavan's recent letter:-

"When Dr. Varadachari visited us last Sunday in connection with the death of my father-in-law, I was able to spend with him nearly two days and had a feeling that I had regained my lost treasure. I found that a good amount of transmission had taken place in me at my mental level."

The fact is that the power possessed by a man can be utilised both ways i.e., for his advantage and for his disadvantage. In the spiritual field it is absolutely essential that this power must not be allowed to be overshadowed by feelings of doubt or despondency about one's own capabilities. Because of my own responsibility towards my associate, I must frankly say that if you persist and get accustomed to it, you will thereby be supplying nourishment to 'thoughts' making them stronger still. I shall thereby be pulled into serious difficulties for removing the effect thereof. It may not be so difficult for me in case of a man of ordinary approach but for one of your standing who is possessed of immense power, I too may have to apply my will to that higher most extent. So please do your best to save me this unnecessary hard labour. Once during my course of *abhyas* I had written to my Master that my present condition I like to weep, and for this he had seriously admonished me.

You know and feel that you are rendering excellent service to the abhyasis which each of them fully acknowledges and appreciates. Now compare it with your own reaction to it. As a matter of fact when one attains a highly subtle state, he passes on the same subtlest force to others which is most often undiscernable to himself. My condition is almost similar when I transmit to others. In a way I am thus trying to bring you closer to my own, whereas you (may I not conclude so) seem to be trying to get more distant away.

I have written all this to bring home to your mind that with due regard to your present condition, your responsibility towards self, the Mission and the humanity in general is very great, though I am definitely sure that you are up to it with spirit, enthusiasm and devotion. I wish you to be blessed with power and capacity for the accomplishment of the great task entrusted to you. May your efforts be crowned with success. Amen.

My respects to Appaji and love to children.

With best wishes,

Yours,
Ram Chandra

P.S.- The financial year of the Mission closes on the 31st December. All Branches and Centres are therefore expected to send in a statement of their accounts during the year 1962 in the prescribed form enclosed herewith.

The statement should reach the Headquarters as early as possible to facilitate the completion of accounts in time (i.e., before the Utsava function).

Blank columns in the form are meant for additional item if any.

Ram Chandra

No. G 577/SRCM Shahjahanpur, U.P.
Dated 29th December, 1962

My dear Varadachari,

I felt extremely sorry to hear the sad demise of Mr. S. Vedantam, whom I loved. We all must pray for the peace of the departed soul. I have already prayed for it. I also wrote a condolence letter to his wife because the address of Mr. Rajam was not with me.

Yours,
Ram Chandra

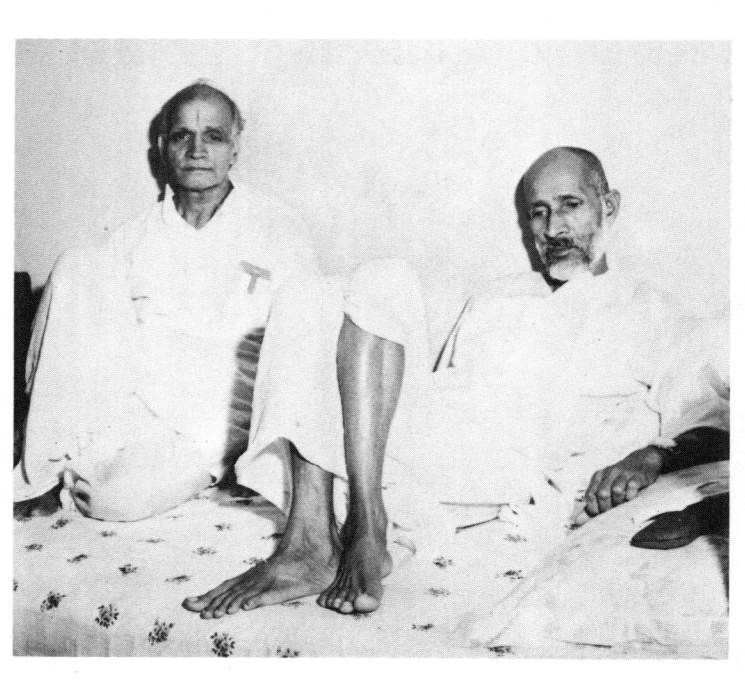

1963

No. H 101/SRCM Shahjahanpur, U.P.
Dated 23rd February, 1963

My dear Varadachari,

Received all your affectionate letters and all of 16th February. I regret that their reply has long been overdue, though I was feeling all along that you must have been very anxious to know of my welfare. For a period of about a month from the last of December 1962 to the third week of January 1963 I had to devote all my time awaiting for the hearing of the cases, at Allahabad. Fortunately now by the Master's grace I have got a man there, a retired advocate of the High Court, who has taken over the full responsibility of the cases upon himself saving me thus all the unnecessary botheration. He is looking after the cases with due attention and care, just as I would have done myself. We expect the cases to come up for hearing either on the 25th or in the beginning of March. The cases have so far been put up a number of times before the court but were adjourned sometimes on the application of the Applicant and sometimes due to the engagement of the Court. Let us see when they come up now. For this reason it does not seem possible now to take up the South Indian tour in the month of February as previously proposed. I therefore postpone it till the middle of May.

I have received no letter from Shri Manjunatha Iyer. I am writing to him now. During my last two visits to South India I had included Mysore in my programme, but had to give it up on some of the excuses offered by him, though I was eager to have a personal contact with the associates there, whom I have never seen as yet. This time now I feel inclined to give up the idea and avoid including Mysore in my programme. How do you advise me now! I shall like to have your frank opinion in this matter. Moreover after this present tour (in May and June) the next tour shall be in November and December 1963, that is only after six months.

I am glad to hear that you are to deliver a number of speeches at Behrampur. I am also grateful to you for having taken the subject you intimated to me, for your discourse on the last day. I shall like to have a copy of it if possible.

In reference to the proposal for having you as the Hon. President of the Aurobindo Society at Tirupati I may be frank to say that it can never be in the interest of the Mission you are attached to. I am therefore positively of opinion that you must not accept it on any account. You can however, if you like impart to them the spiritual training on the Mission's lines, at your own place, if any of them is desirous to have it. This practical service shall obviously be of greater advantage to them as well as to the cause of the Mission for the glory of which you have prayed in your letter.

At Allahabad I had an attack of hyper-acidity which developed seriously. I had therefore to leave Allahabad immediately. It took me a number of days to recover from it. Later on I developed diarrhoea which persisted with intensity for several days. Now, though I am much better, still I often have loose motions at times. I have now started taking buttermilk once in a day. I think it shall improve my digestion. But in my case these are the things of daily occurrence hence should not be a cause of anxiety.

I have now received back the German preface and the German poem, translated into English by one of the friends of Mr. Viraraghavan. The preface is very nice indeed and so is the poem also. Mr. Koch has written to me that he would like to send to me his philosophical thoughts in the German language as they are, if I find anyone among our associates able to translate them into English. Mr. Rajagopalan knows German but he is out of practice. Besides he is over-busy these days due to national Emergency. If you know of one of our associates who is able to do that, please intimate to me.

I believe you could not have got time to proceed on with your book *Sahaj Marg and the Modern Psychology*.

Your spiritual condition as described by you in the letter offered me a kind of solace. After a good deal of thinking, I had started on with a new type of work in your case when I was at Allahabad, and I was waiting for its results. But I could not carry on with the work beyond three or four days on account of my illness. Now since you have offered me an encouragement I am taking it up again. I shall write to you or tell you when we meet, when it is finished.

I am aggrieved to hear of the illness of Shri Y.K. Srinivasan. Will you please write to me the details of his troubles.

The Basant Utsava went off well. Only three persons from Gulbarga side had joined. Others stayed away for reason of my coming visit. Mr. Rajagopalan could not participate owing to office emergency. Mr. M.L. Chaturvedi was at the time in the hospital laid up with fever and liver troubles. He has now come back from the hospital. The fever has subsided but the liver trouble is not yet completely over. The doctor will test him again. I am glad that Shri Narayan is better now.

The last batch of satsanghis (those from Assam) who had come for participation in the Utsava is now leaving on the 25th.

Respects to Appaji and love to children.

With best wishes,

Yours,
Ram Chandra

No. H 198/SRCM **Shahjahanpur, U.P.**
Dated 21st May, 1963

My dear Varadachari,

I regret I have been very slack in replying your letters received during this period. The appeals in the High Court have been compromised, as I ever wished for, by the pressure of the court upon the other party. I now feel considerably relieved.

I am having bad health due to frequent attacks of diarrhoea and dysentry for nearly the last four months. In spite of that I have now decided to proceed on tour to South India. I have therefore tried to avoid some of the stations which I would otherwise have taken up but I could not however avoid certain other new stations and Rajampet is one of them for which you had recommended to me in one of your previous letters. For that very reason, I have to curtail the period of stay at stations.

I have received from Shri Viraraghavan the English translation of the prologue to the German translation of the *Reality at Dawn* by Mr. Robert Koch, a copy of which is enclosed herewith.

I am grateful to you for your speech on Sahaj Marg at Gulbarga which was so nicely impressive. I have received high appreciations of it from our associates.

As per your condition, to my view, it is beyond doubt highly appreciable but it is a wonder to me why you do not feel it as such. Saint Kasturi had also expressed her surprise about it? In your letter of March 3, you write that you have nothing special to report except thorough dryness with a spirit of resignation. Is it an ordinary thing. I believe such a high state cannot be bestowed so easily to anyone. As a result of my previous working a few months ago, I find you now filled up with immense power all through, which is now subsiding slowly. When it has completely subsided I may take it up again after making a close observation of it.

The tour programme is enclosed herewith. Chi. Umesh has passed B.Com. Pre. with good marks and Chi. Survesh the IX Class examination. He has come to the X class and shall appear in the High School Examination at the end of the year.

Love to children and respects to Appaji.

With best wishes,

Yours,

Ram Chandra

P.S.- Shri S.P. Srivastava of Lakhimpur Kheri is here with me. He is going to submit his thesis in about a month. It is quite probable that you will be requested to be his examiner as there are many references to Sahaj Marg in his thesis, hence you are the competent person to judge the same.

Ram Chandra

No. H 235/SRCM   **Shahjahanpur, U.P.**
Dated 28th May, 1963

My dear Varadachari,

Received your affectionate letter of 3rd May, 1963. I believe you have received my letter along with the tour programme. I have yesterday sent a m.o. of Rs. 100/- to you to keep the money for me.

I had already read the bibliography but I forgot to mention about it in my letter. I am happy to note the wonderful work you have done for the benefit of man — may you live long to serve humanity.

I had previously written to Shri Rajam for hastening printing of the book and I am glad he has acceded to my request. He has thus served the Mission and may he be rewarded for it.

I do not want the books to reach here during my absence. I will take them when I reach Madras. Please keep 250 books with you.

I wish fullest success to my children who are yet studying. Amen. May God take care of them. Today I received Shri Raghavendra Rao's letter stating that he has been transferred to Hassan. But the tour programme will be maintained as it is.

Love to children and respects to Appaji.

With best wishes,   Yours,

Ram Chandra

No. H 248/SRCM　　　　　　　　　　**New Delhi**
　　　　　　　　　　　　　　　　　　5th June, 1963

My dear Varadachari,

Received your affectionate letters of 31st May and 2nd June.

I feel worried over the illness of Dr. Kuppuswamy's mother. I implore for God's grace for his spiritual well-being.

Mr. M.L. Chaturvedi has left by air for Hyderabad today on Govt. business. He shall be back on 8th. I shall proceed on according to programme.

Love to children and respects to Appaji.

With best wishes,

　　　　　　　　　　　　　　　　　　Yours,
　　　　　　　　　　　　　　　　　　Ram Chandra

No. H 268/SRCM　　　　　　　　　**Camp: Bellary**
　　　　　　　　　　　　　　　　　　26th June, 1963

My dear Varadachari,

Received your affectionate letter and a copy of *A Peep into Sahaj Marg*. The printing is of course good but not as good as that of *Efficacy of Raja Yoga*. I regret to find that the instructions to the press were not followed strictly. Passages quoted from other places were to be printed in a smaller type, but it is not so. The most serious omission is that of the emblem. I cannot understand how this could have been omitted. Without the Mission's emblem the book, in my opinion cannot and should not be issued to the public. I therefore advise you to detain the copies with you, till we find out some way of putting in the emblem, there. We might have to remove the cover and replace it by another with the emblem on it, not minding the increase in the cost. Another alternative may be to change the front page of book by another with the emblem. Any how that is a problem and must seriously be thought over.

Since I left Hyderabad I have been suffering badly from cold, cough and fever. Today I am much better and hope to be well by tomorrow. On account of this illness I feel considerably weak.

By the time you must have received the insured cover with notes valued Rs. 1000/- One thousand only. Please keep the amount with you. We shall talk about it when I am there. I have asked Mr. Mudaliar of Madras to arrange for our reservation for return journey and sent to him the money for the purpose, but no reply has been received from him.

Respects to Appaji, and love to children.

With best wishes,

Yours,

Ram Chandra

P.S.- Shri Viraraghavan is coming to Tirupati to see me on 6th July, 1963.

Ram Chandra

Shahjahanpur, U.P.

My dear Varadachari,

Received your letter of 27th June, 1963. I prefer your suggestion to paste a wrapper with the emblem printed on it. The contents of the wrapper will be the same as on the title page with the addition of the emblem marked below the author's name.

You should not mind the omission as 'to err is human'.

As for the suggested change in the programme, I think it may not be possible since I have already asked Mr. Seshadri to get the reservation of seats for the 10th July, so that would mean reduction of stay at Trichy by a day. But there is a lot of work at Trichy, while at Tirupati I do not feel any necessity of mere stay, because of your good and laborious work.

Shri Ishwar Sahai has already written to you today that we shall leave Rajampet by Express as scheduled arriving Tirupati at about 4 P.M. We might travel II Class from Rajampet to Renigunta.

I have written to Mr. Mudaliar for having two seats reserved on the 15th and have also informed Mr. Veeraraghavan accordingly and requested him to contact Mr. Mudaliar in this connection through letter.

Love to children and respect to Appaji.

Yours,

Ram Chandra

P.S.- Shri Raghavendra Rao will receive Chi. Narayana at the station on 29th. A telegram is already sent to you.

No. H 317/SRCM Shahjahanpur, U.P.
23rd July, 1963

My dear Varadachari,

I reached Shahjahanpur on 21st July afternoon.

I got Shri Ishwar Sahai's eyes examined by one of our satsanghis, an eye-specialist. His finding is that formation of cataract in left eye has begun. He gave some medicine to stop its progress. My son Chi. Umesh who is reading in B.Com. II Year had been under his treatment for two years. He said that the sight in right eye is dying out and the eye does not co-operate with the left one. Please pray for his recovery. The very day I arrived here Chi. Survesh got a crack in his left arm due to fall from cycle. Three years ago he had this right arm bone broken.

I enjoyed well the company of my associates at Tirupati and other places. I long to have it again. I am much impressed by the affectionate treatment of sister by way of hospitality. Regarding Kuppuswamy, as I told you, the vibrations are rising for the entry into the next region. But his self efforts seem to fail him. I wanted him to go up by himself. I believe him to be there within a week. The process I generally do is to increase the capacity for it.

On 21st July night I saw in dream that I am dictating the medicine for tonsils to Shri Ishwar Sahai and after that I began to ponder as to how a man can live an immortal life. The thought was there but I could not come to the proper solution. In the morning when I awoke I was having the same thought. I came straight away to Shri Ishwar Sahai spoke to him about it and again pondered over it. By Master's grace I came to know the point but how to do it? and who can do it? are questions to be solved. Please recall the talk I had with you when I drew the diagram of heart at Madras. I have chalked out four points in the heart (diagram given). The middle one is the point, which if worked on, will make a man immortal. If a man used to live for a hundred years, another hundred can thus be added to it and so on. The middle point which I marked as V is the nucleus and around it are the spring-like things (like that of a clock). As a man grows old they begin loosening. Please recollect the episode of Allahabad. At that time I had found these springs loosened almost completely. But when other's life was brought in they were tight again. I am now definitely correct about this discovery.

Mrs. Seshadri has been given permission to carry on the training work as a prefect. She will work during the absence of her husband. The copy of the letter of authority (which Shri Ishwar Sahai forgot to give you at Madras) is enclosed herewith. Ratnam was very happy to receive the toffee boxes sent by you.

The scanty rains here are causing damage to crops.

My respect to Appaji and love to children.

With best wishes,

Yours,
Ram Chandra

No. H 359/SRCM   **Shahjahanpur, U.P.**
Dated 19th August, 1963

My dear Varadachari,

Received all your affectionate letters. During our talks at Tirupati I had told you that the trustees of Shri Venkateshwara University were contemplating that they had lost a very good professor. Thereby I did not mean that they meant to re-employ you. I had also remarked that if you get employed somewhere at least for four years, most of your family problems will be solved.

It is astonishing to find that Chi. Umesh's eye has greatly improved. One of the eye-specialists at the Lucknow Medical College has declared no defect in his eye except weakness and for that he has recommended change of glasses. It is, I think due to your prayer alone, and seems nothing short of a miracle. I shall again consult the doctor who has been treating him. I shall also consult Dr. Kuppuswamy if need arises.

I received the plan of the Ashram, a copy of which is sent to Shri Hari Gopal of Madras.

I do not understand what you mean to refer to my writing in your letter dated 22nd July 1963, 'I am sure you would have taken stock of the situation of the Mission.'

As for the points of the heart I have yet to consider over it. I shall let you know later on whether there are corresponding centres in the mind and the central regions too. The heart region extends up to *sikhar* (top). After that there is the mind region which extends up to the occipital point. There is also one super-consciousness in it as I have hinted at in *Efficacy of Raja Yoga*, but it is not very active.

I shall suggest to you a few things in connection with your writings which are next to be given to Press.

I have written to Shri Viraraghavan to get the following blocks prepared soon:-

1. One block of emblem 3" by 3" (to be inserted in the *Reality at Dawn* for its explanation.)

2. Six blocks of emblem 1.5" by 1.5" for outer covers of books and magazines.

3. One block of circle diagram as shown in *Reality at Dawn* on page 25.

4. One block of rising sun as on outer cover of the book.

I have also asked him to request Mr. Rajan on my behalf to complete the book *Peep into Sahaj Marg* as early as possible.

Thank God, Dr. Kuppuswamy has stepped into *parabrahma mandal* on July 31 at about 11.30 P.M. But there is some confusion there which you will please look to and remove. Mr. Annaih Naidu's condition now is very good and the impressions are removed by your effort. My respects to Appaji and love to children.

With best wishes,

Yours,
Ram Chandra

No. H 385/SRCM Shahjahanpur, U.P.
Dated 29th August, 1963

My dear Varadachari,

Received your affectionate letter dated 21st August, 1963. I believe you have received mine No. H 359 dated 19th August, 1963.

I have already dispatched copies of plan and estimate, one to Shri Hari Gopal and another to Shri Ayal Reddy, who seems to be very enthusiastic about it.

I feel worried about Shri Krishnamachari's illness. He has not recovered yet. I have prayed for his recovery and shall continue it. You may also join with me in prayer. It appears to me that his disease though tending towards cure is proceeding on that way very slowly, maintaining its persistent nature at the same time. Great care must be taken in the matter so as to avoid risk of any serious development although there are no such symptoms at present.

I have gone through your *Talks on Efficacy of Raja Yoga* very minutely of course since it comes from a responsible member of the Mission and is now going to be published. I have put in certain suggestion which may please be noted. I think of including in it your two speeches also. What do you think about it and of its title then? As for *Talks on Ten Commandments* I shall take some time to go through it. So, that may be published later on, separately.

I have made some minor corrections and additions in the *Reality at Dawn*, a copy of which is sent herewith for your proofreading. An appendix giving an explanation of the emblem together with a full page print of it is added at the end. (Copy of instructions to press at Vijayawada also enclosed.)

I shall send another copy of it to the press at Vijayawada together with necessary instructions. You may please send the photo blocks of mine and the Master's to the Press when required.

You had given to me your article on Dhi and Buddhi (at Madras) — copy enclosed. Please see and intimate to me if it is the same. The copy need not be returned.

Shri Viraraghavan has intimated to me that he is expediting the dispatch of books in the press.

It is good that you have sent the books to Mrs. Wendy Sorensen. Let us wait for its reaction.

My respects to Appaji and love to children.

With good wishes, Yours,

Ram Chandra

P.S.- The invitation cards for the coming Utsava (50 only) are sent herewith. Please keep them with you. I shall inform you the dates later on at the time.

No. H 418/SRCM   **Shahjahanpur, U.P.**
Dated 16th September, 1963

My dear Varadachari,

Received your affectionate letter dated 7th September, 1963. I did not receive books from Madras as yet. I have written again to Mr. Viraraghavan for it. Have you got erratum printed? If so please send 550 to me and 200 to Shri Ayal Reddy, Bijai Store, Sedam, Gulbarga. I shall very soon send the English translation of *Anant Ki Or* to Trichy for print. I have already prepared the diagram of knots. I shall reply your letter after about a week.

I have a mind to go to Assam, Calcutta, Patna and Buxar in the 3rd week of October. I shall let you know the date when it is fixed. My blood pressure often goes very low and in that condition sometimes it becomes difficult to work continually for an hour even because giddiness prevails.

I remembered Chi. Narayan very much in the last week. Please send me his address.

Love to children and respect to Appaji.

With best wishes,

Yours affectionately,
Ram Chandra

For the Press to note

It is requested that utmost care should be taken to maintain the efficiency of work and avoid mistakes and omissions.

The printing should be in almost the same size letters with similar space between the lines.

The outer cover must have the print of the 'Rising Sun' and the front page that of the emblem.

Proof reading shall be done by the press or any of the local members there, but the final proof shall in every case be sent to Dr. K.C. Varadachari, M.A., Ph.D., 'Shri Rajagruha', 8, G. Car Street, Tirupati, Chittoor Dist.

The two photographs and the full page emblem blocks (at the end) should be printed on art paper.

Ram Chandra
President

No. H 424/SRCM Shahjahanpur, U.P.
Dated 18th September, 1963

My dear Varadachari,

I believe you have received my card No. H 418/SRCM dated 16th September, 1963. I received the consignment of books from Mr. Veera Raghavan yesterday. The books will be reaching here within 7 or 8 days. Love to children and respect to Appaji.

With best wishes,

Yours,
Ram Chandra

No. H 455/SRCM Shahjahanpur, U.P.
Dated 30th September, 1963

My dear Varadachari,

The sad news of the untimely demise of Shri Krishnamachari came as a deep shock to me. When I was at Madras, I felt that he was devoted to me greatly that made me feel much about him. Sometimes I look to Appaji getting this blow at the old age, and sometimes I think of sister who is soft hearted to bear this loss.

Now it is our solemn duty to pray for the peace of the soul, and the patience for the bereaved family.

Yours,
Ram Chandra

No. H 501/SRCM   Shahjahanpur, U.P.
                 Dated 12/14th October, 1963

My dear Varadachari,

Received your letter dated 1st October, 1963. The sad death of Shri Krishnamachari touched me deeply and filled my heart with grief. I wished for his cure, trying for it through prayer and will, without allowing any idea of the reverse to enter in my heart. That is my usual course in all such cases, it is in accordance with the explicit directions of my Master, who had warned me of it. To be more clear I may say that even if one's condition be very serious I am warned against taking in an idea that it is his end. If however at any time such an idea trickles down in my heart by itself, sometimes even years before, I do not let it get fixed in my mind.

In the case of Shri Krishnamachari, when I prayed for him I found that it offered him only a little relief but the disease remained as it was. Then I tried to pull it out and I did, but again after a minute or two it was there as before. That is in brief the whole story of my helplessness in the matter. But in spite of all this I feel I had discharged my duty as a human being, just like a doctor, who tries and tries to save the patient, till the very last moment of his life.

Now a question arises in my mind as to why I was, in this particular case so deeply touched, which may obviously be against the declared rules of spiritual discipline. In this connection I may relate an old incident of my life. About thirty years ago, my eldest son — the only son at that time — died in his ninth year. My feeling about it was not even as much as one might have felt at the death of a pet parrot. I had expressed it like that, at that time, to one of our trainers then. This was during the 8th or 9th year of my abhyas. But now after forty years of abhyas I feel so deeply touched by a similar incident. Why this strange contrast, let my wise and learned associates discover and solve. Can it not be presumed that my condition at the time was higher and superior to what it is today? To my view I am far advanced and better accomplished now that I was at that time. I reserve, at present, my solution of the mystery, though for a mere hint I may say that Humanity and Divinity must both go along side by side and that is my view of 'Completion'.

I can't say whether my associates are in the know of the fact that I have surrendered with deep love to all and every one of them in place of the otherwise. The result therefore is that I usually feel overburdened with works, materially related with them. However, now I am grateful to you for having brought to my knowledge my shortcoming in this respect, which is in my full view now, and I feel induced to avoid it in future. It may no doubt be reasonable not to pray, since God does not listen to one's prayer sometimes. I hope you will also help me in this respect in order to enable me to reconcile myself not to take such jobs. Instead of this it would be better to devote that much time to the spiritual service of my associates, in whatever poor way I may be able to do.

I am going to Assam on 21.10.63 and shall also visit Calcutta and certain other places on the way. I shall be back on 10th November. I have gone through the revised manuscript. It is quite good now. I shall send it to you shortly.

My respects to Appaji and love to children.

With best wishes,

Yours,
Ram Chandra

No. H 561/SRCM **Shahjahanpur, U.P.**
Dated 23rd November, 1963

My dear Varadachari,

Received all your affectionate letters. I returned from tour on 11th November, 1963 afternoon. A day before leaving for Assam I got a mild attack of asthma which persisted all through during the tour and continues even today. Somehow I did not allow it to meddle with my work there. By the time I returned the trouble had grown all the more intense but now it is subsiding and I hope to be all right in four or five days.

This time there was a greater response in Assam and Calcutta as well, and people seemed to be more impressed and favourably inclined towards it. A number of persons have started the practice also. Signs of the Mission's progress there are more hopeful now. But frequent touring is required for which there are serious handicaps.

Mr. Krishnamurti met me at Calcutta twice and he feels sufficiently impressed and also benefitted. He might have written to you about it.

I am sending back your *Talks on Efficacy of Raja Yoga*. It is very nice and worth publishing along with your two addresses at Gulbarga and Madras included with it. Your further writings (Talks on Satsangh and *Sahaj Marg — a New Darshan*) are with me and I shall go through them when I have recovered of my present illness. I think the latter should better form another work of yours so it should not be included with the *Talks on Efficacy of Raja Yoga*.

Now about your present condition as I observe it, I feel that power and strength have altogether left you off. I am waiting for what comes next after it i.e., becoming Divine-like, or complete smoothness which is the Divine's. Onward stages are governed on the same level. It carries a sense of nothingness. The idea of 'having' is not there and to put it in words, the word 'nothingness' shall also be a bit heavier. What may it come up to when one cannot distinguish between 'having' and 'not having'? The complete state of Divinity cannot however come to a human being because that would mean another God, which I believe you will agree with. That is my recent experience. I had tried to work in others, as God is doing in your case, but I could not, since that final smoothness remained lacking in my working. I am trying still and when I am not able to do it, I shall consult my Master.

As for your question about *brahmanda* I may say that *brahmanda* begins from *ajna chakra* where one comes to after crossing over the *pind pradesh*. Thus the *chit-lake* lies in the *brahmanda* and so also the point of *saraswati*. I have stated in the *Efficacy of Raja Yoga* (II Edition, page 25) that the heart region is extended from head to foot and the entire creation lies within this circle i.e., up to *shikhar*.

My experience reveals to me that after the *parbrahma mandal* there are three more regions for which I have put down the name in Persian, in accordance with the condition of each. After that there are innumerable points each having its own specific condition. I usually take up these points one by one. As for saint Kasturi, she has crossed fifty-four of them and I do not know how many more are there still. She has also described to a great extent their particular conditions. All these points end in the *brahmanda (shikhar)*. After *shikhar* the heart region ends and then we come to the mind region. There is also a kind of super-conscious state which I have not taken up in the *Efficacy of Raja Yoga*, because it serves as an instrument for the Divine to work with. All other super-conscious states appearing normally in a bud-like state, turn into full bloomed flower, when opened. But this super-conscious state has inverted position with its petals pointing downwards. An abhyasi when having passed through it, reaches the central region, this super-conscious state helps him to gain Divine powers. But depends entirely upon God to bestow it. It is quite beyond the abhyasi to extract it. When an abhyasi enters the central region with complete devotion and faith in the Master, it begins to open automatically. But that is only a matter of experience.

I believe you have gone through pages 47 to 50 of the *Efficacy of Raja Yoga*, II Edition. Centre is God itself. The Master cell and all other cells are its creation. If anybody tries to meditate upon the Centre, his efforts will not be successful, though in his imagination he may however take the Centre in view to meditate upon. The only way for that would be the one I have hinted at in the *Anant Ki Or*, but I forbid you and every body to attempt it. I had attempted it twice (with prayers to the Master) only for two or three seconds each time, because of the immense power there on the border ring. I had myself put a strong check over my heart and at the same time the Master's powerful hand was also there. Even then I could only peep into it but not meditate upon, at all, because the pressure on the heart was unbearably great. Moreover, it is very difficult even to approach the ring because of a strong backward push from it. The Master had however admonished me for it and warned me against repetition.

I have received the 'Hindu' containing the review of the book, which you sent to me. Mr. Pandit had also sent a typed copy of it for which he deserves our thanks.

I have examined the account submitted by you. Please keep Rs. 108.40 with you in reserve.

The photo blocks of my Master and mine are with you. Please send them by the following address:-

Shri V. Parthasarathi, Regd. Medical Practitioner, Suryapet, Vijayawada-2.

They are required for the new edition of the *Reality at Dawn*, the printing of which is nearing completion. The final proof was to be sent to you for approval. But as that would mean an extra delay of about a week for every 8 pages of the book, Doctor Parthasarathi objected to this proposal, assuring me of his due care and vigilance in the matter. I therefore left the matter to his charge.

I am very sorry to inform you that the youngest son of Shri Raghavendra Rao who was about a month and a half old has recently passed away. May God rest his soul in peace.

Love to children and respects to Appaji.

With best wishes,

Yours,

Ram Chandra

P.S.- I have already sent the English translation of *Anant Ki Or* to Mr. Seshadri for print. He might have handed over to Mr. Varadarajan for it. At page 17 of the manuscript I wrote Towards Infinity instead of Towards Eternity because the English translation has been named as Towards Infinity. The reasonable price of the book should be fixed. Please go through it once more to correct the type slips if any.

Ram Chandra

No. H 615/SRCM   **Shahjahanpur, U.P.**
Dated 12th December, 1963

My dear Varadachari,

Received your affectionate letters and telegram. I am grateful for it. I am better now, except for slight attacks at times which I can well tolerate. I have taken up the work now and am going through your discourses during satsanghs. Since you are developing the philosophy of Sahaj Marg in the form of a new *darshan*, I shall soon write to you some of my recent researches in this connection, in order to give you a further insight into it. But I shall require about ten days time for that.

I had previously requested you to send the book to the press under the name *Talks on Efficacy of Raja Yoga in the Light of Sahaj Marg*.

Your speeches at Gulbarga and Madras, which are so good, may not be included in it if they do not seem to fit in. In that case they may be taken up separately or along with any of your other works. Please do not forget to put in the emblem on the front page. A bigger size emblem (1 1/4") is already under preparation at Madras and shall be had from Shri Viraraghavan.

In view of the growing number of satsanghis at Vijayawada the necessity of a preceptor there seems to be urgent now. Mr. Kumaraswamy has requested me for it twice. I have consequently started preparing Dr. Parthasarathi for it. But that will take about a year's time, so for the meanwhile I have given him provisional permission to work in that capacity.

The Basant Panchami falls on 19th January, 1964. So the Utsava comes off from 18th to 20th morning, with general satsangh from 6:30 to 7:30 morning and evening as usual. During that time every abhyasi must sit in meditation at his own place but preferably at yours (all together).

I remain internally in touch with Chi. Narayan wishing him every success.

Love to children and respects to Appaji.

With best wishes,

Yours,
Ram Chandra

P.S.- Thanks to God that you have stepped into the 5th Ring of Splendour on 11th December, 1963 at 7.55 P.M.

No. H 649/SRCM **Shahjahanpur, U.P.**
Dated 19th December, 1963

My dear Varadachari,

Received your affectionate letter just today. I shall reply it later on. The work *Reality at Dawn* has almost reached completion. You may write to Dr. Parthasarathi direct for the number of books you require to have for your branch.

Love to children and respects to Appaji.

With best wishes,

Yours,
Ram Chandra

Letter to Shri H.B. Siddappa

My dear brother,

Received your kind letter, which gave me much pleasure. There are various ways for realisation, and one is free to choose any which suits his inclination and temperament. There have been rare personalities who have directly realised God without the medium of Guru. Devotion is of course essential for the spiritual growth. Nobody can deny the authority and power of Lord Krishna. Every *sanstha* of the past had itself connected with the last avatar and same is the case with the Sahaj Marg but it requires, of course, sufficient power to strengthen the bond of union.

There are men who presume to have real direct connections with Lord Krishna, but the accuracy of the mark remains to be decided still, because the individual mind (*manas*) too plays its own part. The fire of devotion, no doubt works for setting right the *manas* but before time comes for its proper setting, the individual mind often tends towards misguidance. This is generally the case and I have got instances where a man taking any of the *devatas* for his guru, has been led into hallucination. If you jump into the plane of the individual mind you may have glaring *anubhavas* and intuitions which may wrongly be connected with spiritual. If you take in its atomic energy you may have tremendous power, enough to shake the world even. But can you call it a spiritual force when it works in its own plane? The force of *manas* though extraordinarily great is contrary to spiritual force, which can develop only when existence loses its existing value.

Silence of course counts much in developing the power of speech but it is better to try for the inner silence so that the words and actions may become charged with the silent force, and that is the spiritual stage which comes in the long run. When this spiritual stage comes in, the impressions of the past almost die and the divine impressions take their place. For this purpose cleaning of every nerve centre is essential, which I hope you will please take note of.

Regarding your views about myself I may say that when a man meditating upon me feels my existence, he witnesses sparks coming out. When he does not feel so the sparks do not appear. In other words when I exist in me the sparks appear, but when I am non-existent, the sparks vanish.

With apology I beg to reserve my comments upon *om* and *atman* as it will be a voluminous subject. Besides these points have already been dealt with elaborately in the scriptures. In fact there is nothing in it to understand but only to realise. You may be able to see Lord Krishna when you become real yourself and that is the only solution.

Our method of yoga is explained in our books which can be had from Shri T. Manjunatha Iyer. A quarterly magazine is also issued which deals with spiritual subject connected with our system of Sahaj Marg.

With kind regards,

Yours affectionately,
Ram Chandra

H.B. Siddappa
Thunderi Extension,
Chickmagalur, P.O.,
Mysore State.

1964

No. I 23/SRCM **Shahjahanpur, U.P.**
Dated 2nd January, 1964

My dear Varadachari,

Received your affectionate letters. I believe you have received my postcard requesting to write to Dr. Parthasarathi for the copies of *Reality At Dawn* you require for your branch. We are sorry for a few spelling mistakes in it. The required foreword by Shri Ishwar Sahai will be sent to you after Basant Utsava. For the last ten days nearly we had been in the grip of the cold wave. Now it is coming to normal. A few of the south Indian brothers are reaching here on the 13th and others afterwards. I believe by the time of Utsava the weather might lose its intensity.

I have gone through your Sunday speeches. They are quite good. If it may not be inconvenient to you the time may be extended to 15 minutes for these discourses, so that we may get more matter for the next book. Since you are dealing with the subject in the light of a new *darshan*, I am sending herewith one of my articles which might be of value to you in this respect.

I believe Mr. Raghavan and Dr. Kuppuswamy's daughter must be better now.

Regarding Mr. Kuppuswamy's condition I do not exactly remember what I actually saw and said about a year before and after, but as far as I can imagine proper clarification must have remained wanting in my expressions. It is quite possible that previously though he might have crossed in, he might have remained adhering closely to the border line of it but subsequently a little onwards presenting a full view of his position there. However I cannot say anything definite about it since I do not remember, but this much I am quite definite about that at present he is in the *parabrahmanda mandal* for sure.

Regarding your condition I may say that I might have viewed it in another way and that too can never be wrong in any way. In this connection I give you my Master's view. He had said that the condition attained by an abhyasi at a particular point or region is sometimes reflected on higher regions too by the Master's Grace, with the result that they begin to seem like awakened to a certain extent. In that case the abhyasi's approach up to it can be presumed for understanding. Thus there are two ways of approach, the one (to use the Master's Urdu terms) is *aksi* or reflected and the other is *Kasbi* or acquired. In your case I may say that you are in touch with the Centre in the *aksi* way. But that too is appreciable and of value also, whereas you are otherwise in the fifth ring as regards the *kasbi* way. The *aksi* method can as well be applied all through even up to the level of trainership, but I do not follow it except in rare cases only. For example Mr. Dhonde Rao is at present on the 2nd point and is slowly doing the *yatra*, but the reflection of it has extended up to the fifth point and a little on the *ajna chakra* also.

I sent the manuscript direct to Mr. Seshadri under the impression that you had already gone through it and had discussed with some of its points.

Now in reply to one of the points in your letter of 15/12 I may not be egoistic to say that I cannot live without Him (Master) and He cannot display without me, because so is His will. Wherever I am, He is also there. But since I am after all a human being His watchful eye is every moment essential to regulate the quantity and efficacy of the dose. Sometimes he comes when any of the preceptors is transmitting, especially in higher regions. If anything there is not clear still please refer again.

I may now tell you of a recent experience establishing the Master's greatness and my own insignificance. I had written to you sometime ago that there is a super-consciousness, lying between the *shikhar* and the occipital prominence which I had left untouched in the *Efficacy of Raja Yoga* because that was meant only for God's working. I tested it on you but with the Master's permission of course and keeping one eye upon the Master for directions and the other upon you. I did it but for half a minute, with as much subtleness as possible. The effect was there and it flowed on to the central region. Two days after, while in the bathroom I discovered that subtleness as needed was lacking still. I tried my level best to make it subtler to the required extent but I could not. Then I prayed to my Master and He did it all right.

It has also come to my experience that God takes over some of the responsibility upon Himself even before entry into central region. But when He takes over the full charge of the abhyasi, the Master's work is practically over, though he has yet to go on with cleaning if needed, in order to smoothen the Nature's work. My super-consciousness reveals to me that when an abhyasi has entered the central region, the Divine takes over charge of him and this applies to all cases. Your reference to my previous writing expressed in your letter stating, "Thou hast stated----- as God is doing" is not clear to me. Please quote the full text related with the point to enable me to reply.

Thank God Umesh has improved his eyesight a little. I expect improvement by His kind Grace. How is sister doing now? My respects to Appaji and love to children.

With best wishes, Yours,

Ram Chandra

After completing the letter I received yours dated 30th December, 1963 with accounts statement. The book *Talks on Efficacy of Raja Yoga* must be sent to the press after getting the foreword from Shri Ishwar Sahai as you desired.

No. I 126/SRCM **Shahjahanpur, U.P.**
Dated 3rd March, 1964

My dear Varadachari,

Received your affectionate letters. I expect sister and yourself to be in better health. For about two weeks I have been suffering badly from lumbago but now I am recovering slowly.

By the Master's Grace the Utsava went on well. Sixteen persons from the South, including a lady had joined. Shri Venkatapathi, along with his nephew was also here.

You have done well in giving the book for printing at Vijayawada. Your visit there was badly needed and has been a source of satisfaction to several satsanghis who did not feel quite convinced at first. Shri Ayal Reddi has been ill for about two months so he could not look to collection of funds for the Ashram building. He has recovered now and is coming here in the 2nd week of March. The sum of Rs 1000/- is with me and shall be delivered to you when you like. Capt. Mohan Rao wrote to me that he is satisfied with your answers.

You have grasped well my views on parallelism in Nature. Your presumption that human line includes the whole creation up to the human level is quite correct. Here I may add further that humanity, though charged with Divinity, is not however altogether lost, but exists still, though on a nominal level only. So even when one secures closest nearness to God, the human instinct remains in him still.

I have received your discourses up till 5th January, 1964. I am waiting for more. The theory of parallelism offers a clue to a new way of spiritual training, but while proceeding along with it we have to be very cautious to make a correct observation to decide how much of humanity is to be retained and to what extent should it be charged.

I remember Chi. Narayana very often and about ten days ago I saw him in a dream and transmitted to him for an hour. You and sister were also there. I asked her about her health and she replied something which I have forgotten. She gave me a cup of coffee. There was another lady there cleaning the utensils in one corner. Chi. Survesh's H.S. Exam begins from the 17th and that of Umesh from the 20th (at Lucknow).

My respects to Appaji and love to children.

With best wishes, Yours,

Ram Chandra

No. I 185/SRCM Shahjahanpur, U.P.
Dated 3rd April, 1964

My dear Varadachari,

Received both the affectionate letters of yours. For over a month I had been suffering from acute lumbago pain, which later on developed and spread all over the legs. It was so intense that I could walk even a few steps with greatest difficulty. Every movement of the body was very painful to me. But at the same I must frankly confess that I have grown lazy too during all this period. That was the cause of my not replying to you so soon and for this I owe my apologies to you. But though I did not reply you are in my heart all the while. So if the reply is somehow delayed that must not cause you any distraction. I am at a loss to understand what to say in reply to your letter dated 31st March, 1964, though I always wish you to be happy.

It is but right that you cannot look to every work all alone but what I mean is that the construction work must proceed under your guidance and instructions.

In compliance with the Master's wish, I have laid the foundation of the Mission and now it is my earnest wish, which I believe you will not reject, that you may lay the foundation of the ashram yourself. Owing to my present weak state of health I feel myself incapable of undertaking such a long journey for that purpose. I expect to be there only in the next winter, and it will not be wise to postpone the construction till then.

I wish all my children success at examinations.

I have received a letter from Shri Viraraghavan stating about his heart attack, on account of which I am very much worried. May he recover soon and be free from the disease altogether.

Copy of Constitution and Bye-laws of the Mission is sent per book post.

Love to children and respects to Appaji.

With best wishes,

Yours,
Ram Chandra

P.S. I have already written to Mr. Annaiah to take up the construction work.

No. I 217/SRCM **Shahjahanpur, U.P.**
Dated 23rd April, 1964

My dear Varadachari,

I am happy to note that Shri Viraraghavan is on the way to recovery. May he soon be healthy. The pain in the loins continues still along with cough and hyper-acidity besides, which seriously disturbs my sleep in the night. I have therefore grown very weak now and a little mental work causes me great exhaustion. Since your letter was long waiting reply, I do it somehow now.

1. The ashram site is no doubt at a distance from the town, but that must not matter much since ashrams are usually, and preferably too, established in suburb areas, away from the busy part of the city. Besides a distance of about two miles is not too great.

2. A caretaker is of course to be put in there and he shall be a paid servant in the capacity of a gar-

dener or a watchman. He will look after every thing there and maintain the garden as well. There shall be one of our associates to direct and supervise the work of the servant. This arrangement, I think will not be very difficult.

3. Shri Annaiah Naidu has already accepted to look after the construction work and shall therefore be in charge of the work.

4. The money, of course shall be in your charge and you will advance money to Mr. A. Naidu in lump sums, who will disburse it according to need and maintain its account.

5. As already intimated to you there is no need to delay the construction. You will lay the foundation stone on my behalf and start construction. I wish the construction may be finished by the time I am there, and the opening ceremony may be done at the time.

6&7. As for your condition you have guessed my answer as well and it may be correct to some extent. You are being treated unjustly by God (identified by you as Venkateshwar). Why don't you then entrust yourself to the Higher-most, who is in no case expected to be unjust. If you take Venketeshwar to be the Highest there can possibly be no justification for taking him as unjust. But if you take him as a subordinate functionary, then there is a higher authority to appeal against. Just decide for yourself and try to be clear on the point.

A gift is of avail only when fairly utilised in an appreciable way. The complexities are due more to the mental un-adjustment than to external circumstances.

You say you have no peace ----- etc. This is obviously in contradiction with your previous statements even at lower stages of advancement. That means your advance has carried you farther away from peace, hence no advancement in the true sense. But this is very surprising since you acknowledge that your associates are getting peace and calmness through you in spite of your irritability. You have tried to reconcile the two views on the basis of my theory of parallelism. But then you seem to be ignoring your part of the work (getting humanity merged in the Divine).

The root cause of all this, in my opinion, is the uncalled for brooding over sorrowful reflections, taking into view their darker aspect. This indirectly amounts to meditation on miseries and sorrows. Hence the inevitable result must naturally be the growth of adverse effect. This we have therefore to be very particular about and try to avoid at all cost. But how can that be done? It can be only through resignation, dedication and submission to His will. Prayer does not imply dictation or enforcement of our will upon God, but submission to his will, laying down our sorrows and ills before Him.

Your view of the zero as full with your sorrows is somewhat strange. If it is so, it cannot be zero then. What do you think of it? I am a bit frank in my above expression, because you wanted answers based on Divine consciousness.

My respects to Appaji and love to children.

With best wishes,

Yours,
Ram Chandra

Shahjahanpur, U.P.

My dear Varadachari,

Received your affectionate letter of 27th April, 1964. I am happy that my previous letter has relieved you much. I pray for your happiness and peace. As for the question of employment I like to say that there is no harm in it if necessity arises. It shall not meddle at all with the spiritual work.

The marriage of children is the prime responsibility of parents. So one must try for that in full dependence upon God.

The next and the last daughter of Shri I. Sahai is to be got married. June 26th is fixed for the date of marriage. He shall soon leave for Lakhimpur to make necessary arrangements. The boy is very good. He and his parents are devoted satsanghis.

Regarding your experience while transmitting I may say that it is really the great Master's power that works through the preceptor. We are all only instruments for his work. This impression often comes to view in different shades. Such types of experience are usual in other cases as well. You have absorbency (a little or more) in me and I in Him, so it follows that often the Grand Master is there in your place and abhyasis sometimes feel it.

My heart is about the same with no difference practically.

A few satsanghis from Gulbarga side had been here for a few days. A marahthi professor of Bidar is now here to pass the vacations.

Sitapur associates have decided to hold a large function of the Mission there on 23rd and 24th May and have called associates from neighbouring part to participate. We shall also be there on dates. I am glad to inform you that Shri Manjanath is gaining health now. His case shall come up for argument soon. My respects to Appaji and love to children.

With best wishes

Yours,
Ram Chandra

No. I 257/SRCM   **Shahjahanpur, U.P.**
Dated 20th May, 1964

My dear Varadachari,

Received your affectionate letter. I hope you must have returned from Madras and Shri Viraraghavan must be doing well now. I presume you must have received my previous letter. In that letter I forgot to write my view about Shri A. Naidu's condition. Your finding that he is not improving is quite correct. It may be due to his over-all attention to the work he has taken up. If a man maintains constant consciousness of God along side with his usual routine of work, such a situation would never arise. I believe when he takes up the construction work of the ashram, his condition will mend and he will again begin to improve spiritually, because he shall thereby be in continued consciousness of the Mission's service.

The blueprint is returned herewith. I approve it but for a suggestion that the design to be carved at the entrance should be of the type shown in the enclosed diagram. The emblem may be of about 1

1/2' (one and a half ft. size). The bottom line with the name of the Mission in it should be a little wider so as to hold bold letters of sufficiently big size. The word 'Shahjahanpur' should be omitted. Below it should be the word 'Branch'. If you like you may put in the word 'Tirupati' as well. This design shall be common for all ashram buildings of the Mission at any place. The drawing may be got prepared by an artist.

Upon the initiative of associates at Sitapur (fifty-two miles from this place) a Mission's function has been arranged there for 23rd and 24th May. I am going there with a few satsanghis. The people there are much interested in Sahaj Marg.

Shri Varadarajan of Trichy had of his own accord offered to have one of our books printed at his own cost. But when upon his repeated requests the manuscript was delivered to him he kept it for several months, after which he returned it to Mr. Seshadri, expressing his inability to do the work, since he could not find anyone who could offer free paper for it. This was somewhat surprising to me. But however soon after that, thank God, we got one who came forward to offer a *gupthdan* (secret gift) to cover the entire printing charges of the book. So the book is now in the press.

I am worried about sister's health. You may pray for her speedy recovery. Love to children and respects to Appaji.

With best wishes,

Yours,
Ram Chandra

No. I 288/SRCM   **Shahjahanpur, U.P.**
Dated 12th June, 1964

My dear Varadachari,

Received your affectionate letter dated 6th June. I am happy that the construction work of ashram has started. I am also grateful to Mr. Pullaiya Chetti, who is helping a good deal in the construction work. In my previous letter I wrote to you about my ailments which I am having for 3 months. Now I have developed a sort of quivering sensation probably (Thimari-Telugu) which makes difficult for me to walk on. I fear lest I may develop numbness. The doctor's diagnosis is beri-beri and have prescribed Berin. If it continues I shall devote some time, at Tirupati, for the treatment of Dr. Kuppuswamy, whose medicines do me much good.

My son Chi. Umesh has passed B.Com. but is placed in IIIrd Dn. He was expecting IInd Dn. In the Part 1st there was distinction in Accountancy. He wants to take up the Chartered Accountancy Course, which is very expensive and beyond my capacity yet I have applied to Government for loan. Chi. Survesh has appeared in the High School Exam. and is waiting for his result. Umesh has gone to Delhi to see his sister Sow. Chaya. When is the result of my children expected there? I am going to Lakhimpur Kheri on the 22nd or 24th June to participate in the marriage of Shri Ishwar Sahai's daughter, coming on 26th June.

I pray that your anxieties may be over. May God bless you.

The printing of English translation of *Anant Ki Or* is nearing completion. Please write to Shri Seshadri for your requirements.

Love to children. Respects to Appaji.

Yours,
Ram Chandra

P.S. While dictating this letter Ratnam is with me and she tells me to write you to come here again. She conveys you *pranam*.

Yours,
Ram Chandra

No. I 326/SRCM **Shahjahanpur, U.P.**
Dated 8th July, 1964

My dear Varadachari,

Received your affectionate letter dated 1st July. Nowadays I am under the treatment of an Unani physician. There is no marked difference in the condition, yet the tendency of improvement is noticed.

I have noted down your homeopathic medicines prescribed for me. Please take care of your health, for you are to do a lot for Mission. I shall also pray for your health. Really I want to give you five minutes in every week, it will at least give you some strength. I shall try my best not to forget it.

Your book *Sahaj Marg a New Darshan* I hope will be taken up again by you. This book is more needed than the *Talks on the Ten Commandments of Sahaj Marg* at present. Your talks need rewriting and revision by you. I will very much like the completion of the book *Sahaj Marg a New Darshan*. You want the inspiration for writing it further. The inspiration which inspired you to write is already there. Plunge into it the completion will take no time.

I am very happy that my children here and at Tirupati have come out successful in exams. I pray that they may all flourish. Amen.

I am acquainted with the boy Chi. Srinivasan; when I saw him for the first time, the idea struck both of us simultaneously for the marriage with Chi. Chitra. I like the match very much and I agree to your proposal. It is good that you have decided to marry your sons, who have attained marriageable age.

Shri Ishwar Sahai has not yet come from Lakhimpur, he is expected to come here within a week or so.

Respect to Appaji and love to children.

Yours,
Ram Chandra

No. I 393/SRCM **Shahjahanpur, U.P.**
Dated 28th August, 1964.

My dear Varadachari,

Thanks for your kind invitation.

Please accept my heart felt congratulations with my best wishes to the happy couple. May the couple enjoy a long and prosperous life.

Yours,
Ram Chandra

No. I 398/SRCM Shahjahanpur, U.P.
Dated 9th September, 1964

My dear Varadachari,

Received your affectionate letters. I am on the way to recovery, though slowly. The pain has not yet subsided completely. Recently I suffered from intense giddiness about four days ago which lasted for the whole night. The orange juice gave me much relief. You may have your blood pressure examined. Sufficient rest will be useful and orange juice several times will also do you good. I am glad that Chi. Narayana has been transferred to Tirupati. It will be more convenient to him now.

My coming tour to south India shall commence from about 20th November. I shall be at Tirupati early in January '65. So you may keep up your programme of Gulbarga and Gauhati. Please inform me the dates of arrival and departure there so that I may inform the satsanghis near about the place.

During my last trip to Benares I had lost my handbag which contained my glasses and denture. Consequently I am going to Sitapur on the 17th for having new glasses and thence to Lucknow for having a new set of denture on 19th. I do not know how long shall I have to stay at Lucknow for the purpose. Last time the doctor took about 25 days for it.

I had been to Delhi in the month of July. There on 22nd July at 7:01 A.M. while I was transmitting to Mr. Rajagopalan, I found you moving from the navel point to *swadhishtan*. Perhaps you remember that during my last visit to Tirupati I had remarked that the work on the navel point had already started.

For your knowledge I may tell you that in our system of sadhana the three *chakras*, the *nabhi*, the *swadhishtan* and the *muladhar* are taken at the very end, in quite a natural course. Rather I may say that Nature herself takes them up then. The Master's work is only to prepare the ground for Nature's working so as to speed up the work. Again on 22nd Aug at 8:50 A.M. I looked to it and found that the flow from the navel to *swadhishtan* was growing stronger. I am now observing it and am waiting to see how Nature works. Afterwards I shall see what part I have to play therein.

Your book *Sahaj Marg A New Darshan* shall be a wonderful book. You have requested me to inspire you further for that purpose. You had previously been inspired for the work. Your request now reminds me of the word 'Vedic Consciousness', used by me on previous occasions. The very word inspired me to further thinking and the solution also came. In your case I simply prayed to my Master and I witnessed something chord-like in you which had been serving as an impediment. It is being dissolved and by now almost 10 percent of it only remains. The process is still going on, with speed. The result as I observe it, is that your understanding is now becoming Divine.

Please send to me the gist of your speeches at Gulbarga and Gauhati for publication in the magazine if they are on Sahaj Marg.

I may now relate to you a sad event which I had avoided to write to you so far because of the marriage festivities at yours. In the middle of August my sister's daughter at Lucknow, aged 16 and reading in B.A. was burnt by the stove and she expired within a few hours. Unluckily there was none in the house at that time and she was all alone. On raising an alarm the neighbours came up and helped her to the medical college. My sister, having lost many of her children had now only a son and this one daughter. Her death is now a heavy shock to her. I had sent Prakash and his wife there to console her. I could not go owing to my illness. I later sent there my maidservant to stay with her for a few days.

I also have received several letters from Mr. Thyagarajan. He has already resigned from the Mission. I have also written to him that since he has no connection with the Mission it is useless to talk of it further.

Love to children and respects to Appaji,

With best wishes,

Yours,
Ram Chandra

No. I 450/SRCM   **Shahjahanpur, U.P.**
Dated 13th October, 1964

My dear Varadachari,

Received your affectionate letter of 1st October, 1964. May God grant you speedy cure. I am glad to know that Chi. Baghwan is appearing in the final examination and I wish him brilliant success.

In your last letter you referred to a certain dream. The dreams are often had when during sleep the hand accidentally happens to rest upon the chest. Sometimes when it is just upon the heart the dream is much frightening. I had sometimes ago talked about it in one of my letters. There seems to be no other cause of it. You cancelled your Gulbarga visit and that was but proper in view of your bad health. I think it shall be better to avoid the Gauhati visit as well, because the long journey will be much taxing to you.

Under such a weak condition of health you should also avoid giving individual sittings and for the weekly satsangh too, you may just ask them to sit in group and meditate by themselves. The Master shall, in your place, look to it himself.

If you feel the necessity of having someone else to conduct satsanghs, please write to me, so that I may fill up Dr. Kuppuswamy with the necessary force to enable him to conduct the satsangh for the time being. The Doctor being a kind and devoted soul deserves my gratitude for the sympathetic services to you and my children there. He needs be rewarded for that and the reward must be of the nature as to be of advantage to him as a doctor.

Your article from the book was given for publication in the magazine long before the book was out. But the publication being delayed it was out after seven months, during which period the book was out.

I had my eyes examined for having new glasses. The doctor discovered then, cataract in both my eyes which is just in a very elementary stage. Besides it is outside the sphere of pupil hence can be treated successfully through medicine. Lo! the Nature's helping hand in these affairs. Had I not lost my spectacles, the discovery would never have been made. I shall relate to you later on the strange story of the loss of my glasses and denture.

I propose to begin my south India tour from November 20th or near about. It will be finalised after I receive the new timetables.

My health is not good as yet, though the physical troubles are now tolerable. Anyhow I will definitely undertake the tour not minding what the condition of health might be.

You need not send the manuscript of the book *Sahaj Marg A New Darshan* until it is complete. I shall then go through it. My love to children and respects to Appaji.

With best wishes,

Yours,

Ram Chandra

P.S.- Chi. Umesh has secured admission in the chartered accountancy course, through the efforts of Shri Hari Haran of Mysore, who had come here in May and has since then taken up the practice of meditation.

Dated 24th October, 1964

My dear Varadachari,

Received your affectionate letter. Your illness causes me much worry. You are no doubt improving definitely, but I wish you to be quite healthy soon so as to carry on well with the weight of the work.

I had no mind to appoint anyone else as preceptor or prefect. My only purpose was to provide for a helper, who might serve you as a relief at times when needed. This was the basis of the suggestion, I made in my last letter. We shall, however discuss the matter when we meet.

New timetables having been received, the programme is being prepared and will be intimated to you when ready.

I am feeling very weak nowadays and sometimes my thought goes towards the strain I would be having during the coming tour. I may not mind the strain of the journey but the strain of the heavy work of satsangh is too great in view of the present condition of my health, though I do not mind that even. At every place I try to complete the work during the period of my stay there, which if too short (say only a day) taxes me much.

I am going today to Bareilly for a couple of days. Km. Kesar is also there. She had been transferred to Bareilly. Your money order has been received (Rs 9/- only). I wish Chi. Arobindo success. Love to children and respects to Appaji.

With best wishes,

Yours,
Ram Chandra

P.S.- <u>Part programme</u>

Tirupati: arrive on 31 Dec at 3:32 A.M. (by Tirupati Exp from Trichy)

Trip to Rajempet from 3/1 (15:06) to 5/1(12:45)

Depart on 6 Jan at 9:04 ......(for Madras)

Thyagarajan's letters need no reply.

No. I 497/SRCM   **Shahjahanpur, U.P.**
Dated 28th October, 1964.

My dear Varadachari,

Received your affectionate letter with manuscripts of both books. I shall go through them minutely and shall make suggestions where needed.

I hope you must be feeling better day by day. I sincerely wish that I may see you healthy, and I pray for my sister's complete recovery. May God bless you all.

I have sent the copy of Programme to the following

Shri ViraRaghavan	Madras
Shri V. Mohan Rao	Rajampet
Shri S. Raju	Tiruvannamalai (a new station)
Shri R. Seshadri	Trichy
Shri Dr. Parthasarathi	Vijayawada
Shri. C.M.T. Mudaliar	

Love to children and respects to Appaji,

With best wishes,

                         Yours,
                         Ram Chandra

TOUR PROGRAMME

Station	Arrival Date	Time	Departure Date	Time	Address
Delhi	21/11	05:45	22/11	17:35	Shri S.K. Rajagopalan, A-20/25 Lodhi Colony, New Delhi.
Vijayawada	24/11	04:55	26/11	22:25	Shri V. Parthasarthy, Regd. Med. Practitioner, Suryaraopet, Vijayawada-2.
Hyderabad	27/11	09:45	30/11	Bus	Shri P. Madho Rao, 52/4, Barkatpura, Hyderabad A.P.
Sangareddy	30/11	Bus	02/12	Bus	Shri C. Raghavendra Rao, Supdt. Police, Sangareddy, Medak Dist. (S.I.)
Bidar	02/12	Bus	05/12	05:15	Shri Narayan Rao Phabba Dattaiya Gali, Pansal Taleem, M. Bidar (S.I)
Seram	05/12	12:55	08/12	12:55	Shri Ayal Reddi, Vijay Stores, Seram Gulbarga Dist.
Gulbarga	08/12	15:36	10/12	07:16	Shri S.A. Sarnad, IIA/3-1 Govt. Quarters Jiwarji Road, Gulbarga (S.I.)
Bijapur	10/12	13:08	13/12	06:41	Shri Narayan Rao, Manager, Govt. Polytechnic, Bijapur (S.I.)

Station	Arrival		Departure		Address
	Date	Time	Date	Time	
Hassan	14/12	09:25	18/12	09:33	Shri Raghavendra Rao, 3374, K. R. Puram, Hassan Mysore State (S.I.)
Mysore	18/12	14:30	21/12	11:45	Shri T. Manjunatha Iyer, Coffee Planter, 882, Vanivilas, Mysore-4.
Channapatna	21/12	14:39	22/12	14:39	Shri M.D. Jahagirdar, Police Training Centre Channapatna Bangalore Dist. (S.I.)
Bangalore	22/12	16:35	24/12	11:10	Shri Doreswamy Iyer, 191, I Block, Jayanagar, Bangalore-11.
Tiruvannamalai	24/12	19:59	27/12	09:47	Shri S. Raju, Dy. Coop. Registrar, Tiruvannamalai, North Arcot Dt. South India.
Trichinopoly	27/12	20:32	30/12	08:40	Shri R. Seshadri, C-29, Rajaji Street, Ramnagar, Srirangam, Trichinopoly-6.
Tirupati	31/12	03:32	03/01	15:06	Dr. K.C. Varadachari, 'Shri Rajagraha', 8, G-Car Street, Tirupati, Chittoor Dist. (S.I.)

Station	Arrival		Departure		Address
	Date	Time	Date	Time	
Rajampet	03/01	19:05	05/01	08:30	Shri V. Mohan Rao, Eye Specialist, Rajampet Cuddapah Dist (S.I.)
Tirupati	05/01	12:45	06/01	09:04	Dr. K.C. Varadachari, 'Shri Rajagraha', 8, G-Car Street, Tirupati, Chittoor Dist. (S.I.)
Madras	06/01	14:25	11/01	12:00	Shri R. Viraraghavan, 39, First Main Road, Rajaannamalaipuram, Madras-28.
Bhupal	12/01	20:23	13/01	20:23	Shri Mukund Murari Gupta, Astt. Surgeon, Hospital, H.E.(1) L, Bhupal.
Orai	14/01	06:22	16/01	15:41	Shri P.K. Bisaria, C/O B.B. Shri Kanta- -Prasad Saxena, Advocate, Ramnagar, Orai, Jalaun Dist.
Lucknow	16/01	18:20	17/01	09:15	Shri Nasib Chand, II-13 A, Baraha Railway Colony, Lucknow.

No. I 556/ SRCM	Shahjahanpur, U.P.
Dated 7th December, 1964

My dear Varadachari,

I did not receive any letters from you since I started my tour to south. I am very anxious to know about your health as well as of sister. It will be very kind of you, if you inform me about the health and welfare of children.

The number of satsanghis is increasing everywhere and by His grace we are getting good persons.

Respect to Appaji and love to children,

Yours,

Ram Chandra

P.S. The amended programme sent to you, indicates that we are reaching Tirupati by train at 10:00 in the night. But it is likely that instead of the train journey I may take up the bus journey from Bangalore to Tirupati, if at the time I find myself able to stand the strain of the road journey of 150 miles. I shall however wire to you from Bangalore if the change is effected.

No. I 568/SRCM	Hassan Camp
Dated 19th December, 1964

My dear Varadachari,

Received your letter dated 11th December, 1964. I am very sorry that Chi. Baghwan got plucked in one paper. He should take courage to proceed with the Examination. There is nothing to fear. May God help him!

The illness of the children, your's and the sister's is worrying me much. I have started prayer for their health.

Mrs. Manjunath Iyer came to see me here yesterday and invited me to Mysore. Shri Manjunath could not come on account of pain in his legs. There is no work at Hassan for Shri Raghavendra Rao. Two persons here have now started meditation. Shri Raghavendra Rao has been with me from Hyderabad till now. I am to leave for Mysore day after tomorrow and he will be there also after a day. Nearly a dozen members of the Mission have accompanied me up to this place. They are going back now except Shri Gunde Rao who will accompany me up to Bangalore.

I have an idea to have a trainer in each town or district for the good of the associates. With this view I have permitted the following persons for the work.

1. Shri Narayan Rao, Bijapur
2. Shri Gunde Rao, Kappal
3. Shri C. Raghavendra Rao S.P., Sangareddy

Shri Raghavendra Rao and Shri Seshadri have recommended one more case at Bangalore. He is Shri Doreswamy Iyer. They are also of opinion that the case of Shri Raju of Tiruvannamalai should also be considered. I have decided to give provisional permission for work to Shri Doreswamy Iyer. For Shri Raju I have yet to decide. No centres are maintained at these places since they are on transferable posts.

Owing to hard pressure of work I am often passing sleepless nights. Yesterday I had a rest and a good sleep at night. I have given up taking tea and coffee because they promote sleeplessness.

My respects to Appaji and love to children.

With compliments from Shri I. Sahai and Shri Raghavendra Rao,

Yours,
Ram Chandra

Mysore Camp
Dated 19th December, 1964

My dear Varadachari,

Received your affectionate letter. I am happy to know that the opening ceremony of the Ashram building has been duly performed according to Vedic rites. The Ashram shall decidedly grow and signs of it are there. But we have to work on and on for it.

I am grateful to Mr. Annaiah Naidu and Mr. Pulliyya Chetty for the pains they have been taking for the Ashram building. I believed that for this they will be growing on spiritually even without least touch. This has now turned out to be true and I find them immensely benefitted by the effect in quite a natural way.

We arrived this place after a comfortable journey from Hassan. I had some stomach disorder yesterday which has subsided now.

There is a vast field here, but one like you is required to push on with the work, one who can, like you, speak authoritatively on the subject. A few of them have started practice after having their doubts cleared.

Mr. Doreswamy Iyer of Bangalore shall also be coming to Tirupati along with us. He shall stay there on the 25th. He is a friend of Mr. Seshadri and very devotional too. Mr. Seshadri has recommended him for the work of training-ship. I could not yet decide whether I should give him the provisional or the full permission. My heart feels inclined towards giving him full permission but Mr. Mudaliar's experience is before me which induces me to take at least a year's time to give him full fledged permission on the level of prefect-ship, though I have already prepared people for prefect-ship while in train during the course of my journey.

Regarding Mr. Raju's case I do not think of going beyond provisional limit since he has much of grossness in him yet, though he is so much devoted and greatly transformed in only a month's time by Mr. Seshadri's efforts. Mr. Seshadri recommends his case. I want your help in the matter. Please think over it well and give me your opinion about it.

We have now decided to reach Tirupati by bus which leaves Bangalore at 9:30 A.M. It reaches Tirupati at about 4 P.M. Mr. Doreswamy Iyer has informed me that he will do every possible thing for my convenience during journey.

I believe all of you must now be better in health. Mr. Manjunath has now recovered from pain in legs. He feels strength of vibrations in his legs, thanks to God.

Mr. C. Raghavendra Rao S.P. may likely come to Tirupati for a day.

Respects to Appaji and love to children.

With best wishes,

Yours,
Ram Chandra

P.S. Extreme cold wave with hailstorm is reported from Shahjahanpur.

1965

No. J 47/SRCM Shahjahanpur, U.P.
Dated 23rd January, 1965

My dear Varadachari,

Your loving letter dated 18th of January '65 to hand. It was, really, the grace of my Master that kept me in health during the tour of South India. Sometimes, now on return, I feel giddiness and it is due to the pressure of work I have brought from South. Still I have to do it as much as possible. Moreover, I love this kind of work which naturally moves me to it.

I am indebted to you for the love you have for this poor being and I think of how I will be able to repay it. Your love for me is developing which in no way I can repay excepting prayers for the prosperity of yourself and children. I also eagerly wish and pray that the torch of spirituality may remain alight in your family from generation to generation ever and after.

At Tirupati I told you that I want to take two more persons for special training. I selected as you know Chi. Seshadri and Sarnad of Gulbarga. I am going on well with Seshadri but in case of Sarnad I am feeling unconscious resistance on his part. I have not found out the reason for this. Will you please help in finding out the cause with him. I am in a way restrained in his case. Man proposes but God disposes.

I have heard about the existence of Dhyan Yoga Mandir at Chandigarh. I don't know the gentleman — Dr. Mohan Singh. It is absolutely wrong that he has realised *kapila*. I have contacted the great sage

(Kapila) and found that he has no connection with this gentleman. It is all his figment of imagination which is nearer to hallucination than spirituality. Grosser type of man he is but his egoism has made worse of him. Some time after he will feel himself webbed and it will be impossible for him to come out from the meshes. The grossness has its own excitement which the abhyasis think as spiritual advancement. Take it as a sure sign of degeneration. One thing in reference to Dr. Mohan Singh, I have to say that it is generally a case with the abhyasi who proceeds on his own dictates of *antha-karan* which is made of *manas, buddhi, chit* and *ahankar*. They are marred and soiled. Everything goes topsy-turvy. In short their vehicle is running in back-gear.

After receiving your letter, on 22nd instant I prayed at night through my Master to God for giving you strength and power to write the reply of that letter with 'Uniqueness and Universality'. My prayer is well answered and I have noted the required power coming unto you from God direct. So I am sure you will reply the letter with authority — the way you wish. I will very much like to have a copy of your reply to him.

You have written that you feel yourself dried up. That is a very good state and I wish that all of my associates may have it. But all depends upon the grace of God. In your case I am waiting for its advancement. What will be the last pitch of this state? When you will not be able to feel its consciousness. In the fullness of this state man loses the idea of existence. He feels that neither he is born nor he will die. He does not feel any power but when he concentrates himself everything is there. This is purely a Divine state. I would like to assure you once more that except one which is reserved for the incarnation of Deity all your super-conscious states are awakened.

I am concerned about your health as well as of sister. May all of you be restored to health. Shri Ishwar Sahai has gone to Lakhimpur Kheri for a week.

Love to children and respects to Appaji,

Yours,

Ram Chandra

No. J 129/SRCM **Shahjahanpur, U.P.**
Dated 10th March, 1965

My dear Varadachari,

Received your affectionate letter. The continuity of stomach pain is now stopped though occasionally it shoots up again. I am happy that about 25 abhyasis from South India had this year participated in the function and took keen interest in all the activities which offered an additional grace to the occasion. But they could not stay longer since many of them had come only on casual leave. Mr. Seshadri however stayed till 17th Feb.

Your finding about Shri Sarnad was correct. I have written to Shri Raghavendra Rao to try for the removal of the unconscious resistance in him. Let us wait and see. Seshadri's is however a good case and I have taken it up. His wife too is very devotional and bears signs of higher improvement. Both are in the same region. I think Mr. Seshadri will leave the region sooner than his wife.

I had once told you that being unaware of the Sanskrit language I had put in Persian names for the three regions after *parabrahmada mandal*. On Mr. Seshadri's suggestion I have now substituted the Sanskrit names for them and they are:- for the first *prapanna*, for the second, *prabhu*, for the third, *prabhu-prapanna*. Henceforth I shall use the same names.

I am confident that while in sleep, you work somewhere else and when you are quiet you do some Divine work. I am happy to inform you that God has now begun to work in the system of Appaji or in your words has taken over the charge of him from 16th February, 1965 at 5 P.M. This has now come into effect after probably 5 years of his advancement.

I consulted my Master over the question of the individual creation. He agrees with your view and with the method you suggested. He says, "This point will automatically be entered into while proceeding point by point beyond *prapanna-prabhu* region. If it comes in the chain there is no danger. Just after that **there is a point** and that is the last one. If one works with it the individual point of creation will open by itself. It cannot be precisely determined how many points are there after *prapanna-prabhu*. St. Kasturi has so far crossed 54 of them. Now another thing comes to my mind and that is the point of God's creation. If the force of that point be exercised mildly on the individual point it shall be effective in restoring proper order in its working. But Master says that this method is also correct but we have to be very cautious in touching the individual points. But to bring in the Divine glow from the God's creation point to the individual's is not the work of every preceptor but of a specially favoured one because in case of ordinary one's their will shall quickly slip down. In the old incident of my transferring of my life to one whom you know, I had done it from the point of God's creation and the result was that if I lost a year of my life she got even more than that. I did not know the actual method of it so I did it that way. Once I had asked my Master for the way to do it. But he declined to tell me because as he said he did not trust me in that respect. I have hinted about it may be able to get even more for help in our work by thinking over it. I often think about how to use it in the early stages of abhyas. You should also think over it. If we succeed in this, it will be a great work. But I must warn everybody not to touch God's point of creation. As far as I know it is meant only for changing the character of the world. Nothing there is drawn out. It is a secret. One who is bestowed with special powers can only concentrate on it with a suggestion for what be required to be done. I have hinted over it somewhere else also, which I may tell you afterwards. I think, but I am not quite definite yet, that there is some power at the Base. We have yet to think how to utilise it. When I have done it I shall give you a diagram of it.

The Sitapur associates want to have your speech there, when you visit Shahjahanpur at the time of your trip to Delhi. It is only 55 miles from this place and only 3 hours journey by bus. We shall arrange for a car if possible and go in the afternoon and return the next morning. I hope you will adjust it in your programme and find time for it. The date may please be intimated well in time. Respects to Appaji and love to children.

With best wishes,   Yours,

Ram Chandra

No. J 207/SRCM   **Shahjahanpur, U.P.**
Dated 21st April, 1965

My dear Varadachari,

Received your affectionate letter along with enclosures — the Railway Receipt, the gist of your speeches and the inland envelope addressed to Shri G. Venkataraman. The letter is quite nice and I have posted it.

Really I want to have your speeches printed in book form in volumes each covering about a hundred pages or more. For this purpose I want your full speeches. I therefore send to you the shorthand written notes of your speech at Sitapur to be completed and corrected. The speech at Shahjahanpur could not be taken down, so please try to reproduce it if possible. Since you did not seem to agree with the terms suggested by Shri Seshadri, I give below the actual condition of each, after studying it by going down into it myself. You may thereby judge the terms or suggest their alternatives.:-

1. *Prapanna* — In this state the abhyasi feels unmeasurable greatness of God, imagining himself to be like an ant on the surface of an ocean. If he ponders over he falls in wonder. This is also one of the stages, above several other lower ones, where there is the danger of one being turned into an *avadhuta*.

2. *Prabhu* — Here the abhyasi feels that it is his own lustre that appears in the sun, the moon and the stars. He feels that it was he who sent Shri Krishna and Rama for the adjustment of his work. It was he who revealed the Vedas to the *rishis*. Everybody passes through it, as my Master has written somewhere, but only the sensitive ones feel it by His Grace, and I was fortunate enough to visualise it. For this, the only method, I think, is that of constant remembrance.

3. *Prabhu-prapanna* — At this stage an abhyasi feels that devotionary state and *prabhu-gati* have all faded away and nearness develops to such a state that he feels himself all the time in Brahma, in and out, and charged himself with Divine Force.

I received a telegram from Mrs. Rajeshwari, intimating that her husband having a heart attack, was admitted in the Gandhi hospital, Secunderabad. I had wired to her enquiring his condition. Yesterday I received Sriramulu's letter stating that his condition which was alarming in the beginning is now better.

I was not informed of any sad events which stopped the birthday celebrations of Mr. Rajagopalachari. I have enquired about it from Mr. Viraraghavan. I am happy to know about your appointment at Madras. You have already made arrangement for satsangh at Tirupati and it will continue during your absence. I believe your Madras stay will be of much help to the Mission's cause. May God help you.

My health is deteriorating on account of stomach troubles but I believe I shall soon be better. My son-in-law has gone to his father's place on two month's leave. The temperature ranges from 90 to 90.5. I hope he must be better by now. How is sister doing now?

My respects to Appaji and love to children.

With best wishes,   Yours,

Ishwar Sahai
for Shri Ram Chandraji
President.

P.S. The Master having left for Bareilly after dictating the above has directed me to sign for him.

No. J 244/SRCM   **Shahjahanpur, U.P.**
Dated 14th May, 1965

My dear Varadachari,

Received the script of the three talks. They are very nice. I have gone through *Sahaj Marg and Modern Psychology* and *Sahaj Marg — A New Darshan*. Both of them should form one book as you suggested at Madras. *Sahaj Marg — A New Darshan* is a wonderful chapter of the book. Regarding other part *Sahaj Marg and Modern Psychology* I am finding difficulty at several places to grasp the sense thoroughly. At some places you will have to give the clear expression of thought. Very soon I shall return the manuscripts with a little suggestion if any.

My son Chiranjiv Umesh has suffered from high fever and now the temperature has come down to 98.6 degree and it rises up to 99.6 degree, this is persisting. Blood report shows deficiency of E.S.R. He is alone at Delhi as Chhaya has gone to Kanpur to her father-in-law. He has to attend his office work also because of the number of days work required for examinations. I could not leave Shahjahanpur because my South Indian associates are coming and going these days, therefore I have sent Shri Ishwar Sahai and Chi. Survesh to Delhi a week ago for his help. Umesh will be going to Kanpur for his work so Shri Ishwar Sahai will be coming to Shahjahanpur within a few days. My associates at Sitapur have arranged a function of the Mission there from the 29th to 31st of May 65.

I believe Appaji is better by now. I am happy that the marriages of my children — Chi. Narayana and Chi. Chitra — are going to be celebrated soon. My heart naturally blesses them.

I have received the Sanskrit version of the prayer.

Respect to Appaji and love to children,

Yours,
Ram Chandra

No. J 268/SRCM **Shahjahanpur, U.P.**
Dated 2nd June, 1965

My dear Varadachari,

Received your affectionate letter. I am sure you will give account of yourself in the new assignment. There is nothing unusual about it, you deserved this position most long before.

You will be happy that Shri S.P. Srivastava has been awarded Doctorate about ten days ago. He is suffering from colic pain nowadays, although he is a bit better.

Shri C. Raghavendra Rao is still in the hospital although he is better. I am in receipt of his letter today. Of course, this is not proper time to write him. For Ashram I have got already one thousand. It can be sent at any time you want it. I am thinking for the ways to find money for the Ashram. Shri Ishwar Sahai has gone to Lakhimpur Kheri for a month to attend certain marriages. Chi. Umesh is almost in the same condition. He has come here for two days. My son-in-law has recovered. I have received the invitation of marriages of Chi. Sow. Chitra and Chi. Narayana. I am sending a sari and a piece for blouse for Chi. Sow. Chitra and Rs. twenty-five as *neota*. I hope that sister will be better now.

Respects to Appaji and love to children.

With best wishes,

Yours,
Ram Chandra

No. J 278/SRCM **Shahjahanpur, U.P.**
Dated 7th June, 1965

My dear Varadachari,

It is really a matter of happiness that our children Chi. Sow. Chitra and Chi. Narayana are going to be married on June 10, 1965 with Chi. V. Srinivasan and Chi. Sow. Santha respectively.

My heart naturally blesses them. Let these marriages bring happiness and prosperity to both sides.

May God grant long, happy and prosperous life to the couples.

Yours,
Ram Chandra

No. J 343/SRCM   Shahjahanpur, U.P.
Dated 21st July, 1965

My dear Varadachari,

Received your affectionate letter despatched from Madras. I believe you are going on well with your work. For several months I had been in constant worry. Now I am almost relieved of them but only to get into another new one which is pending still.

Shri Ishwar Sahai had gone to Delhi to attend Chi. Umesh during his illness. He had been suffering from slow fever for about two months. Now the fever is down but collities remains to some extent still. My son-in-law, Chi. Rajendra Kumar is better now but he is still very weak. He continues on leave. During his stay at Delhi Shri Ishwar Sahai himself got collities. He is now better. But his left eye is now almost mature for cataract operation which will be undergone after return from S.I. tour. His right eye too has cataract under formation and the sight is much reduced. Now another worry again. My younger sister's husband is suspected of having developed cancer. He is under observation in the medical College at Lucknow since July 1.

Krishna Janma Ashtami falls on Aug. 20. Shri Raghavendra Rao and a few other satsanghis from the south are expected to be here during the period.

I have arrived at a solution (avoiding risk or danger altogether) about the dynamo of individual creation and I have experimented it on advanced abhyasis and noticed changes. The cases are yet under observation. The inner action seems to tend towards some thing better in the form of a change. But what it is can be known only when actual change comes into effect. One thing I have to study yet is whether we should transmit only once or repeatedly at intervals. This I shall be able to ascertain only when the actual changes have come into effect. This is really a sort of nuclear weapon and I shall require combined efforts for it and I hope I shall be able to tell you about it within a month, when some perceptible results have come to light.

Love to children,

Yours,
Ram Chandra

No. J 354/SRCM **Shahjahanpur, U.P.**
Dated 25th July, 1965

My dear Varadachari,

Received your letter dated 19th July, 1965 after the despatch of my letter No. J 343/SRCM dt. 21st July 1965. These are the days of the worries and anxieties for us. I am worried to hear the condition of sister and Appaji but I hope they must have been progressing under the care of Dr. Kuppuswamy. I have already written to Mr. Annaiah Naidu to enquire of his condition. I hope and pray for their speedy recovery.

About a week before I was looking to the heart of Shri C. Raghavendra Rao and found wonderful improvement. The reason now I came to know that it was due to your sittings. In such cases the patient of heart is amply benefitted by mild sittings. He requires a little more strength in the heart and he will be all right soon if he gets a few more such sittings. I am writing to Chi. Narayana to inform me of the condition of sister and Appaji.

Love to children.

Yours,
Ram Chandra

No. J 558/SRCM **Shahjahanpur, U.P.**
Dated 14th October, 1965

My dear Varadachari,

Received your affectionate letter. I am worried to learn that sister is still in bed. Regarding Appaji the vibrations as he feels seem to be due to nervous exhaustion. Some nervous tonic may do him good.

I received letter from Dr. Kuppuswamy. I find in him some darkness in the *parabrahmanda mandal* and onwards. But since I am reading from a distance, it is possible that it may have been exaggerated to my view. The darkness is there, that is definite, but how much exactly, is for you to find out and remove.

I am sending you a copy of "Tour Programme" and another to Chi. Raja at Tirupathi and one to Dr. Kuppuswamy. I have also sent to Shri Kuppuswamy Rs 1000/- through bank draft for the Ashram. You may have it and utilise for the purpose.

Yours,
Ram Chandra

No. J 595/SRCM Shahjahanpur, U.P.
Dated 24th October, 1965

My dear Varadachari,

I am sending you back the *Sahaj Marg a New Darshan* after much delay for which I apologise. Both the articles *Sahaj Marg a New Darshan* and *Modern Psychology* should form one book, as you had suggested at Madras. I could not help you much in these writings. But I have put in notes on the left page for your consideration. I hope you will go through it minutely to see that every thought is well cleared.

Typing mistake may also be looked to. Shri S.A. Sarnad of Gulbarga has gone to Delhi for some training for two months. He is coming here on 23rd for two days. I believe you have received "Tour Programme". Shri Subramaniam of Rajamandri, the brother-in-law of Dr. Swami, is here along with his wife.

Love to children,

Yours,
Ram Chandra

No. J 651/SRCM Delhi
Dated 14th November, 1965

My dear Varadachari,

Received your letter. I am worried to learn that sister is not yet wholly recovered. When you come to Delhi, please stay with Shri S.K. Rajagopalan. He will feel happy if you stay there. The satsanghis are very eager to see you at Delhi. While you come, intimate to Shri Rajagopalan the date of your arrival at Delhi. He has gone to Villupuram to attend the marriage ceremony of his sister-in-law's daughter. He will return by the 21st November, 1965. If he finds time, he will meet you at Madras.

I shall try to write out a few words for the opening ceremony and anybody will read it.

We should try our best that Chi. Baghwan may get a befitting post. You please tell Shri Seshadri to inform Shri D. Malusekaran of Madura of my arrival at Trichy.

Maya is still in the hospital and is slowly recovering.

Sripathi Sarnad is here for two months (till 4th February, 1965) for a short term training course in examination reform. He conveys his pranams to you.

With best wishes,   Yours,
Ram Chandra

No. J 673/SRCM   **Shahjahanpur, U.P.**
Dated 24th November, 1965

My dear Varadachari,

I am extremely sorry to hear of the demise of dear sister who has given me the awareness of her affection even after leaving her mortal coil. May she rest in Eternal Peace.

I pray for consolation to the bereaved members of her family.

Yours,
Ram Chandra

No. J 692/SRCM **Camp Sindanoor**
Dated 2nd December, 1965

My dear Varadachari,

Received your letter. Since I left Delhi I am having one or the other trouble but I am somehow pulling on with my work. I am having no rest not even for an hour often, since so many new persons are coming in to join everywhere and there are long discussions and queries, but I am happy for all this.

Here I have got a separate room in which I am alone with Shri Ishwar Sahai of course. This is actually what I desire, since I did not like to dictate this letter in the presence of anyone else. It is about 11 P.M. and all have gone to sleep.

The effect of the sad incident as displayed in your letter is no doubt shocking and so long as one is in the world in human form, one cannot escape from miseries. This thought of miseries sometimes promotes in one's heart a craving for freedom from the circle of birth and death. Under the circumstances there remains no other course open but to submit patiently to the will of God. Feeling of the pangs is but the human nature and even saints and prophets have to undergo it. In my Master's words a perfect man is he who has in him the feelings of both — the humanity and the Divinity, duly adjusted together, both going side by side. If one is deficient in either of them he is not perfect in the real sense. At a higher approach the effect of miseries remains at the surface level and does not go deeper to effect the formation of samskara.

Negation means having given up every thing of one's own, but the effect of the surroundings one happens to be placed in is there round about him which must cast forth its shadow. In other words if such a one happens to be in the company of those afflicted with sorrow he must have at the time similar feelings of sorrow and condolence by way of fellow feeling and sympathy. That is a human etiquette and must be abided by in the sense of duty.

About two months before the incident I had once a hint of it, when I got no response coming forth for all my prayers for her. But it slipped away instantly from my mind just as it happened in the case of Dinesh which you know about. On receiving the sad news the recollection of the previous idea suddenly flashed across my mind and its awareness was revived. Had it touched my consciousness previously she might have, rather decidedly, lived for a year or two if not more. But my Master seemed to be specially watchful in this respect as he has to take much work from me still. In sister's case the Master has been very kind to grant what I had promised for her during her life time. She is now free from the circle of rebirth and we shall meet her again after we give up our material form.

I must also relate to you a peculiar experience which I had soon after her sad demise. An hour after I felt she was covering my entire body. After about twenty hours I felt that she was entering into my body. The process continues still. Now I feel my body as hers. She is in the brighter world with no thought of either husband or children. She seems to be merging into me having her set up in the brighter world. In this respect, I am now the mother for the children. Her affection was too great to measure even now, and it was motherly. For instance I may say that when she felt I remained half starved she kept on feeding me with liquid diet several times a day with coffee, cocoa, milk etc. I cannot repay her affection. Just as you cannot repay her services.

Your responsibility has now become greater. You have now to play the part of a mother as well, along with that of the father.

I pray to God to bestow patience to the children and to Appaji. May God bless you all.

Yours,
Ram Chandra

P.S. Shri Ayyal Reddy has informed Dr. Kuppuswamy that readymade carpets of the size are not available at Adoni.

No. J 712/SRCM   Hassan
Dated 11th December, 1965

My dear Varadachari,

Received your letter. It is but sad that I cannot get back the sister in embodied form. Whenever I think of her either intentionally or accidentally the feeling that separation is not there flashes across my mind and I do not feel her separation at any time even for a moment. But how to pacify the children is the question, though I have prayed for consolation to them and I find that they are mostly relieved. Appaji, of course, does sometimes begin brooding, but he is also better and you too.

I and Raghavendra Rao have both received the invitation but he will not be able to attend since he will exhaust his casual leave by the time.

I am remembering you very much these days.

Love to children,

Yours,
Ram Chandra

1966

No. K 53/SRCM   **Shahjahanpur, U.P.**
Dated 1st February, 1966

My dear Varadachari,

Received your affectionate letter dated 14th January, 1966. As I was busy in the celebration of the birthday of my Master I couldn't reply earlier. The function went off well. We were all charged with the Grace of the Master. About 300 people attended the function and all were happy. I am happy that my children are doing meditation in the Ashram and hope that other satsanghis will also be going there. I remember Chi. Gayathri very much. According to my instructions she has begun to think of me as her mother. The process of merging in case of sister is almost complete. Only the hylem shadow remains to be covered.

I do not remember the method of transmission and meditation carried on by you this time, so please write to me a little so that I may be able to explain it. As well as the points of criticism, which have been made by the abhyasis. By your transmission abhyasis are immensely benefitted, so it cannot be wrong in any way. For the purpose of training, an intelligent man will be more accurate in the work, and that is the God's gift to you.

I perfectly believe that your intelligent works and wisdom help in getting you the direction properly. I tell you one thing in general. When thinking is in the right direction the petals of the heart-plexus begins to open and it is the case not in the transmission but in all the worldly and Godly affairs.

It has become a difficulty to know your spiritual condition, because the conditions have bidden farewell for good. When I try to peep into the expansion the thought jumps out and the heart begins to beat a bit fast. But whatever I must know, I know it. On 31st January, 1966 at 8:45 A.M. vision of the Absolute commenced. Reaction is there but I feel it difficult to express the nature of it. In other words it is so colourless and original. Can you know and feel and express your present state?

I believe Mr. Seshadri must have reached there safely.

Love to children.

Yours,
Ram Chandra

No. K 141/SRCM   **Shahjahanpur, U.P.**
Date 18th March, 1966

My dear Varadachari,

Received your affectionate letter. My son-in-law is improving and Doctor is surprised to find such an improvement in a very short time. It is due to prayers of my associates. I am going this time to Bareilly for three days. I shall reply your letter after coming back. You want to put in my life in the book. I shall send it in about ten days. Somebody has given the life sketch in 'National Herald' long ago. I do not know what it was.

I am very happy that Chi. Narayana has a son born. I pray for his long life and prosperity.

Shri Ishwar Sahai has gone to Sitapur. His cataract operation is successfully over.

Love to children and respect to Appaji.

Yours,
Ram Chandra

No. K 150/SRCM   **Shahjahanpur, U.P.**
Dated 28th March, 1966

My dear Varadachari,

Received your affectionate letter. My son-in-law, Rajendra, has wonderfully improved in the beginning but now the progress is very slow. Dr. Mittra at Delhi has advised him to go to Sitapur for electric treatment. He is now at Kanpur with his father. I will have to go to Sitapur when Rajendra goes there. In the left eye there is retinal detachment. Let us all pray for his recovery.

I am sending you a few facts of my life story. If you want family history or any other matter directly connected with me please let me know. I am sending you a few more facts.

Mr. M.L. Chaturvedi has sent me a copy of the foreword for the book. I believe Mr. Vira Raghavan has received a copy of the same.

I am happy that Chi. Narayana is taking interest in abhyas. I believe he is half prepared for provisional permission. How earnestly I wish that Chi. Baghwan may get a suitable job. May God help him.

I hope newly born baby in the family is having favourable stars.

Love to children and respect to Appaji.

Yours,

Ram Chandra

P.S. A brief data of outer life is also enclosed herewith. Please correct the English where necessary.

Just now I received a letter from Shri M.L. Chaturvedi intimating to me your arrival at Allahabad on 13th April, 1966.

I shall surely be there. He will invite the High Court Judges, professors and the gentry of the city to hear your talk.

RC

In all we are four children to our parents — two brothers and two sisters. The eldest child is my sister named Radha Piari, who has been married to Shri Raghubir Sahai Raizada, an advocate at Mainpuri. I am the second child. I was married at Mathura. My wife left this world in 1949. The third child is another sister named Kutumb Piari, who was married to late Shri Laxmi Shankar of a Taluquedar family at Lucknow. She is a creative genius. She has written several novels and plays in Hindi. Unfortunately she has recently lost her husband. The youngest of all is my brother, Dr. Harish Chandra, who left for England on 29th August 1935 for higher studies after obtaining the M.B.B.S. degree from the University of Lucknow. He is almost settled there practising as a physician at Lancashire.

RC

No. K 158/SRCM **Shahjahanpur, U.P.**
Dated 1st April, 1966

My dear Varadachari,

I have already sent on 28th March, 1966 No. K 150 a few facts about my life. I doubt very much whether you have received it as the address written by me in the envelope was incomplete. If you have not received it please write to me so that I may send its copy. A brief account of my outer life was also there. I shall meet you at Allahabad. I remember Chi. Raja very much. Love to children and respects to Appaji.

With best wishes,

Yours affectionately,
Ram Chandra

No. K 174/SRCM **Shahjahanpur, U.P.**
Dated 15th April, 1966

My dear Varadachari,

Received your affectionate letter. I am sending you a few necessary details about my life as desired by you. You may utilise the information as per your requirements.

Now you have reached Tirupati. Mr. Kuppuswamy will make up the deficiency. To me Chi. Raja appears to have improved a bit better than Chi. Narayan. Whatever instructions I have given him at Madras he is following them. I hope both of them will improve. I am anxious to know that Chi. Baghwan has not yet got any job in spite of so many efforts. We should pray for it.

A few South Indians are staying here with me. They are all going back except Shri Kumaraswamy. I am going to Sitapur tomorrow morning along with him to see my son-in-law Chi. Rajendra. He has been admitted to Sitapur eye hospital for electric treatment. I shall stay for a few days there.

Respects to Appaji and love to children,

Yours,

Ram Chandra

No. K 223/SRCM   **Shahjahanpur, U.P.**
Dated 7th June, 1966

My dear Varadachari,

Received your affectionate letter. I am happy that the marriage of my boy has been settled. May it be performed gracefully and successfully. My son Umesh appeared in the 1st exam. of the Chartered course and he did his papers in Typhoid. The examination is very difficult and there is only 1st division. After the examination was over, he came here almost in fever. Fever, of course, left him ten days ago, but he has developed rheumatic pain in the left arm. We have changed three physicians since then. He had acute pain last night. He feels a little relief now.

I was going to Sitapur to attend the function on the 29th of May 1966. When I was half a mile away from the city, the bus in which we were travelling, collided with another bus. As it was on a turning point of a crossing, I could not see the other bus. The result was that I got a cut injury on the left eyebrow and I am very happy that I was the only man to get hurt. In front of my seat, there was a glass of the size of about 3' X 2'. Somehow, by chance, I got up from my seat and just a few seconds after, the collision took place and my head dashed against the upper plank in which the glass was fitted. Had I not stood up, my both the eyes would have gone and that is the God's Grace. Now, I am better and there is a little swelling left in the bone.

I have got Rs 17,500/- this time for the press. So, I am arranging for it. After it, only the maintenance will be the problem, which will be looked into later.

I have not heard for about 3 weeks last, about the condition of my son-in-law Rajendra. I am writing today to his father. Although I feel that he is better, but to which extent — that is to be ascertained.

Love to children.

Respect to Appaji.

Yours,
Ram Chandra

No. K 302/SRCM

Dated 9th July, 1966

My dear Varadachari,

Received your letter yesterday, intimating your arrival at Allahabad on 21st July. For sure I shall also be there on 21st morning but I shall come back to Shahjahanpur on the 25th at the latest, because I have to prepare for a case which comes up for hearing in the civil court on 30th July. If you like to come with me to Shahjahanpur, you are welcome.

I have now recovered from the injury caused by the bus accident. Umesh is also quite well now and so is Chi. Rajendra Kumar. His vision has come up to normal. It is really a miracle of the prayers of you all and I am thankful for it. I believe you have received my letter of greetings at Madras and also that of Shri I. Sahai.

The press equipments and machine have all been purchased at Delhi and some of it has already been booked but owing to transport strike it has not been delivered to me yet.

Now my reply to your letter of 11th June, 1966. Really there should be a tape recorder at your disposal and we will see to it. Everything gives way at the stage of Realisation. There is neither inclination, nor inspiration nor even *anubhava*. They all become *laya* but when the intention is there the thing comes in again. You have referred to the flight of thoughts of the lower region. That is a secret of Nature. In this I translate my Master's words, "Higher a man ascends, lower down his vision goes to." If a man comes to know of the actual state of Realisation, he will never like to attempt for it while a realised man will never like to part with it, tasteless though it may be. You say that you find your transmission not to be so effective as before. I like to convince you that it is definitely, as before, rather more than that. You do not feel it so, because a purely Divine state runs through your thought, and this being of Highest potency can change the very life of man. At this stage ego does not function at all so one is not able to mark its effectiveness.

Love to children and respects to Appaji.

With best wishes,

Yours,
Ram Chandra

No. K 356/SRCM **Shahjahanpur, U.P.**
Dated 6th August, 1966

My dear Varadachari,

Received your affectionate letter. Since meetings had already been arranged at Allahabad during the dates of your visit, Shri Raizada and Kasturi addressed the meetings. The people were impressed. Kasturi stayed there for some time with her uncle.

Chi. Umesh failed in the Chartered Accounts examination. During his examination days he suffered from typhoid and had done some of his papers in high fever. Chi. Sarvesh also failed in the intermediate examination. I received a letter from Chi. Baghwan from Roorkee. He intends coming to me in the first week of September.

Press machines with all equipments have been received. A man has been engaged to fill up the cages with type. We are waiting for the firm engineer to come to set up the machine in the working order. The work is expected to be started in about a week or so.

I am intending to go to Assam in the month of October, but it has not yet been finally settled. I had learnt at Allahabad that the appointment of the Professors was to be made in your presence. So it is possible they may call you again soon.

You will be happy to note that I am blessed with a second grandson, born on 16th July at 12:30 P.M.

I want to consult you whether I should allow Parthasarathi, son of Shri Rajagopalachari of Madras, permission to transmit, since he is mostly on tour and may come in contact with people there. Secondly, should Chi. Narayana be also allowed similar permission. You want to experience both God within and without. The stage has long gone by. It is only a condition of the heart, which gets rarefied as one proceeds on further. I had an idea of giving you transmission from the swimming point, though it is not necessary since Nature's work is already going on. I was waiting for the Master's permission for it. After about a week he said that I could not be so subtle as the work demanded. This means I should not do.

I hope, yourself, Appaji and children are all doing well.

With best wishes,

Yours,
Ram Chandra

No. K 392/SRCM   **Shahjahanpur, U.P.**
Dated 7th June, 1966

My dear Varadachari,

Received your affectionate letter. I am very sorry to hear from you that you have lost the case. I believe you must have filed appeal against the order of the Munsif. I do not know much about the facts of the case and the judgement but appeal should be preferred consulting your advocate.

Please take regard of your health. Your health is precious to all of us. My blood pressure is very low as it is always the case in summers and the pressure of work is also increasing and I am happy with it.

About your indifference towards Swami Vivekananda as you feel these days, it will not last long. I believe Appaji will now be better in health. I had consulted you about the Provisional Permission of Chi. Narayan and Shri Parthasarathi of Madras. I do not know whether the letter has reached you. For Shri Parthasarathi I only want to give provisional permission because he visits certain places where the people want to adopt this method. For Madras it is not necessary to give him provisional permission.

Love to children and respect to Appaji.

With Blessings,

Yours,
Ram Chandra

No. K 430/SRCM

Dated 26th September, 1966

My dear Varadachari,

When I saw you at Allahabad my weakness had totally gone. On 17th I left for Bareilly and returned to Shahjahanpur two days after, weakness again returned. I found here a bundle of letters to be replied. After reading 5 or 6 of them my brain gets puzzled. If I continue I begin to feel giddiness. I have attacks of stomach pain almost daily. I have been avoiding substantial diet mostly and it will help me to recover very soon.

I have gone through your paper for 'Sahaj Marg Research Institute'. I appreciate the idea and am entirely in favour of it. May God help you in the work. You will act as a Director or the chief head of the institution. Dr. S.P. Srivastava met me at Bareilly and he is also strongly in favour of it. He may prove helpful in the work.

I would have sent the manuscript of the book but I want to add something in the chapter of 'Concentration' which I will do when I am relieved a bit from my ailment.

Love to children and respects to Appaji.

Yours,
Ram Chandra

No. K 462/SRCM   **Shahjahanpur, U.P.**
Dated 22nd October, 1966

My dear Varadachari,

I am very happy to learn of the birth of daughter to Sow. Chitra. I pray for the long life, good health and prosperity of both the child and its mother. I wish and pray that my boy may soon get a good employment.

The tour programme is enclosed herewith. I could have drawn it earlier but I was waiting for the marriage date of Shri Ayal Reddi's son, which as he now informed me, has been postponed till March. I have, this time, left out a few places in order to avoid as much strain as possible. My health has not yet improved. The pain persists still and at times it is severe, besides frequent attacks of diarrhoea and excessive weakness. I am taking nothing but fruit juice, butter milk and a little *pongal*. If my health does not improve, I fear I might have to cancel the tour programme. But I hope I shall recover by the time. I have now started Homeopathic treatment because Allopathy has proved to be not much effective. But the difficulty is that the doctor under whose treatment I am, at present, lives at Bareilly. I am therefore thinking of going there for a few days. Mr. Seshadri and his wife were here. They have gone back yesterday.

With respects to Appaji and love to children.

Yours,
Ram Chandra

P.S. Please see that the programme is not inconvenient to you. Otherwise it may be amended. It will be finalised after your approval to it is received.

Shahjahanpur, U.P.
Dated 25th November, 1966

My dear Varadachari,

The manuscript of the book *Voice Real* is sent herewith. Please go through it minutely and note down corrections or modifications if any.

Also please look to the classification of the sections, the titles of the articles and to all other things necessary for the purpose.

It shall be given to the press only after you approve everything about it.

I am somewhat better now, though the pain repeats itself often but it is not so intense as before. My respects to Appaji.

With love to children,

Yours,
Ram Chandra

P.S.- My son-in-law Shri Rajendra Kumar has again hemorrhage in both his eyes. He is admitted in the Sitapur hospital for the electric operation. Sow. Chaaya is attending him. Please pray for his complete recovery.

In reference to the enclosed letter I shall request you to find out some way to offer the required proof.

------------ Enclosure ------------

News Item Published in the National Herald, Lucknow Dated 28th October, 1966 (covered by Associated Press).

James Kidd who died in 1951 left $2,00,000. His will said that his estate would go to any person or group furnishing some scientific proof of a soul of human body which leaves at death.

Lawyers believe that the money could be awarded also to anyone who is merely researching the existence of soul.

The Judges announced that hearing lasting 18 days would begin in March.

The following are expected to contest:

1. California Parapsychology Foundation Inc.
2. Arizona Board of Regents.
3. Arizona Foundation for Neurology and Psychiatry.
4. Parapsychology Foundation Inc.
5. University of Life Church Incorporation.
6. Neurological Science Foundation.
7. Psychical Research Foundation.
8. Aquarian Foundation.

The above news has been furnished to the Master by Shri B.D. Mahajan of Delhi. (No. 9653 Islam Ganj, Azad Market, Delhi- 6) Copy forwarded to K.C. Varadachari.

No. K 546/SRCM   **Shahjahanpur, U.P.**
Dated 10th December, 1966

My dear Varadachari,

Received your affectionate letter. I believe you have received the manuscript by this time. You need not send it back till you get the foreword from Dr. S. P. Srivastava of Lakhimpur Kheri. I am sending the office copy to him for foreword.

The stomach ache has come to normal and at times I do not feel it at all. But the diarrhoea persists and sometimes it turns into dysentry. Homeopathic treatment is going on. My brain is so weak that if I take up the case of any satsanghi for ten minutes I begin to feel giddy. So I am not taking up the cases of the satsanghis nowadays except those who come from far off distance. But that too once or twice utmost.

I was very adamant for the South India tour but Master asked me to cancel the programme as the pressure of the work will be very high and I will not be able to withstand it. Hence it was postponed for March or April '67. I am very happy to inform you that Master took up the work of the satsanghis of the South, because I was unable to do it owing to the extreme weakness and they are being amply benefitted. If any of my satsanghis observes his condition, he will find the unadulterated *shanti* in him. Dr. Parthasarthi, of Vijayawada, without knowing the fact, has written to me that the abhyasis of that place are feeling *shanti* a good deal.

I was expecting, no doubt, the transfer of Chi. Narayana but I wanted that if it may be essential he may be transferred near about Tirupati. All right I shall now give him the Provisional Permission for the work, meanwhile you will please clean him of grossness to make my task easier as I am very weak. I may take about two weeks more to resume my work.

I am very grateful to you that you have taken up my case for recovery. Your reading about the ball of fire is correct. My whole chest and a part of abdomen was burning and that was the additional trouble. Since you have taken it out the burning sensation has totally gone and I felt the signs of recovery, about which I also spoke to my Homeopath doctor.

When I was at Tirupati about four years ago, you proposed for the certificate to be printed for the preceptors instead of giving them the typed ones. Now the circumstances have favoured me and I got them printed at Calcutta on a very nice paper costing Rs. 175/- per hundred.

I want to give them each personally, hence I have kept them with me.

I came to know through the letter of Shri Parthasarthi of Madras that Chi. Narayana's son is ill. Please inform me about his condition, I am anxious to know about his health.

Respect to Appaji and love to children.

Yours,
Ram Chandra

No K 562/SRCM   **Shahjahanpur, U.P.**
Dated 26th December, 1966

My dear Varadachari,

Received your affectionate letter. I am sorry I could not reply earlier. I appreciate your suggestions about the book *Voice Real* and I agree with them. So please do accordingly.

I am having frequent attacks of intense pain continuously. I am therefore compelled to give up the Homeopathic treatment and to try Allopathy again.

Shri C. Raghavendra Rao of Hyderabad came here along with his wife, son, mother-in-law and one abhyasi and stayed for two days. They have left for Allahabad yesterday. They will go to Varanasi and Gaya also and shall return to Hyderabad on 1st January, 1967.

With love to children and respects to Appaji,

Yours,
Ram Chandra

1967

Shahjahanpur, U.P.
Dated 5th January, 1967

My dear Varadachari,

I am extremely sorry to inform you that Shri Ishwar Sahai breathed his last on 2nd January, 1967 at 8:50 p.m. after a short illness of 4 days. He served the Mission for about twenty years selflessly. He also served me well which I cannot repay. His death was a saintly one.

Yours,
Ram Chandra

No. 96 SRCM Shahjahanpur, U.P.
Dated 2nd February, 1967

My dear Varadachari,

Received your affectionate letter. I am not wholly recovered but I find relief sometimes for a few days in a week. I wanted to travel for South in March or April, but there seems to be no possibility of going in South in the aforesaid months because the man who will accompany me belongs to the education department and he will be free from the 20th May. This time I will have to finish my journey in a month's time and I will visit principle stations. I shall let you know in the month of April.

For Sahaj Marg Research Institute, I am sending you my suggestions. You may add, if necessary. Please start the work on Basant Panchami, a very auspicious day for all of us.

Chi. Narayana will start the work of training on the basis of Sahaj Marg from Basant Panchami. I shall give him provisional permission on the eve of Basant Panchami. He is allowed to work every where, but he will not start the work in Tirupati unless you allow him to do it.

Respects to Appaji and love to children.

Yours,
Ram Chandra

Further Suggestions

1. Add at the end of the Note to Objective no. (ii)

"Pertinent cases falling away from the general trend may be referred to the Master for his comments; and the explanation provided by him be utilised to develop an objective picture of various stages."

2. Add at the end of the Note to Objective no. (iii).

"In cases of significant divergences Master's ratings about particular preceptor's limitations and capacities may be taken into consideration to arrive at comprehensive results."

3. Add at the end of Objective no. (iv) after a comma (,)

"subject finally to verification by the Master."

4. Add a new item in form B- for preceptors, after item (3) joined Mission as follows-

5. Minor spelling and language mistakes may be corrected before the plan and objectives of the Institute of Sahaj Marg Research, is published in the final form.

Ram Chandra

No. C 193/SRCM   Shahjahanpur, U.P.
Dated 28th February, 1967

My Dear Varadachari,

Received your affectionate letter. I am happy that Chi. Narayana is blessed with a son. I heartily congratulate you.

I feel that I am physically improving now but the brain is very weak. Even after a little work I feel tension in the brain. It may be due to the fact that I fell seriously ill at Raichur. Hopes for recovery were given up by the doctors. Beating of heart was very mild and the pulse was very feeble and life cell had become dimmer. Then Kasturi and Jahagirdar started weeping. Doctor said only prayer can save the life and not the medicine. Then Jahagirdar and Kasturi started prayer and 10 or 15 minutes after I began to come to the normal condition. My temperature at that time was 96.2. Thanks to the Master that I am alive today to serve the humanity. I had an impression in the mind as to why the people cannot resist the death. The same idea came to my mind at that time for the sake of experiment. I succeeded a bit to bring the life cell to normal; now my experiment is over thanks to the Master. This is the law of nature that nobody can resist death and automatically the things move. I am not very sure of it but I think that there is no self in the soul so we cannot resist or work on it.

Mr. Ram Chandra Reddy has gone to Cuddapah on 23rd February. It is good that he passed so much time with me. There was some unevenness in the *brahmanda mandal* which was hampering his further progress. I made it correct which took me ten days to put him in *parabrahmanda mandal*. Saku Bai is here and is staying with me and probably she will remain here for about two months, because she has started naturopathy treatment available in 'Shri Ram Chandra Mission' for filaria and she is being benefitted.

I was observing that some time the preceptors take the hopeless persons in the satsangh. Hence I issued the instructions a copy of which is being sent to you for the Prefects of Chittur and Tirupati. Shri Ram Chandra Reddy who is coming in the month of March will bring with him the copies and hand over to you. Shri Ram Chandra Reddy will also go to Madras so I have given him a few copies to fulfill the requirement of Madras. I am successfully doing the work allotted by the Master.

Love to children and respects to Appaji.

Yours,
Ram Chandra

No. 278/SRCM **Shahjahanpur, U.P.**
Dated 25th March, 1967

My dear Varadachari,

Received all your affectionate letters. I am sorry I could not reply. I gave a telegram yesterday intimating to you that I am doing well so that you may not be anxious about my health. Since the death of Shri Ishwar Sahai the work has not yet come in our grip although we are trying for it. Shri Ishwar Sahai was very diligent and hard working. He used to see himself all the work of the Mission including correspondence, press, translation work and so forth. I am not getting such a man nor do I hope to get here. It is of course God's grace that a fortnight before his death a man offered his services to the Mission and he is now here all the time. It was Ishwar Sahai's labour that he produced the book *Voice Real* out of my writings. It seems difficult to produce any other volume now but I hope God will help me. I have grown so lethargic that I do not attend to the work except the work I have especially taken, which is very laborious, and my attention to that work remains constant.

I have given permission to Chi. Parthasarathi also on Basant Panchami day with instructions that he would do the work outside Madras unless and until Shri R. Viraraghavan refers any case and he would not take up any case in Madras of his own accord. Similar is the condition with Chi. Narayana at Tirupati. Chi. Narayana has been transferred to Chitoor. The satsanghis if any at that place be directed to attend him and he should give the individual sittings as well as sittings in group. Chi. Narayana's presence at Tirupati was a great help to you but being a Government servant he may be transferred to any place. We should pray that he should remain happy wherever he goes. I remember Chi. Raja very much and do not want to neglect his case in any way. He is following the instructions given by me at Madras. He is very affectionate. I wish that he may get some job at Tirupati so that he may be of help to you in the worldly work and help us in Mission's work.

I believe you established Sahaj Marg Research Institute on Basant Panchami day. May God help us all.

Dr. Kuppuswamy wants his entry in the central region which if it may be possible will not be liked by him. It is the condition which one feels as tasteless taste. Personally I am afraid to take him immediately into Central Region. If it can in any way be done it will be just as I did in case of Appaji.

I am worried to know about your health and I hope and pray for your health. As long as we remain under his shelter, we are fortunate. I received a cheque for Rs 1000/- to purchase Ashram land. Thanks for it. The matter of building an Ashram at Shahjahanpur was taken up by my associates so many times in the past but I declined. This time I had to agree with their proposal reluctantly.

Love to children, respect to Appaji,

Yours,

Ram Chandra

P.S. Herewith enclosing the certificate for Chi. K.C. Narayana.

RC

No. C 300/SRCM **Shahjahanpur, U.P.**
Dated 20th April, 1967

My dear Varadachari,

Received your affectionate letters dated 3rd and 10th April 1967. The papers for copyright should be from the publisher. Shri Viraraghavan has sent the papers to the department intimating to me that he has done so. No doubt I am better in health but I suffer from diarrhoea or dysentery very frequently. I shall travel to south under all the conditions of health. I am sending you a copy of the programme to see if the dates of my arrival at Tirupati suit you. You need not send back the copy of programme but only the amendments if needed.

Shri V.P. Rao has sent me a letter with full details about the marriage of his daughter, and he was really very sorry for it and I also felt it very much. He wanted the reply of his letter but his letter was itself the reply of his own. We are compelled to go with the time.

In the state of realisation the man generally becomes lazy. The breath becomes very slow and so he requires either long walk or some exercise for the sake of getting more oxygen. I remember my Master once said that I do not at all breathe sometimes. There is no doubt about it that you have proceeded a long way off towards negation and this condition is developing.

On sixth April at 12:20 P.M. I found that the *yatra* of the heart region of Chi. Raja has started and that was the step he has taken himself. But to my surprise now the further movement has been stopped although the tendency for *yatra* is there.

I feel some impediment in the heart which you please see and remove it.

Love to children and respects to Appaji.

Yours,
Ram Chandra

No. C 344/SRCM Shahjahanpur, U.P.
Dated 9th May, 1967

My dear Varadachari,

Received your very affectionate letter dated 24th August, 1967. I have grown weak again owing to lower blood pressure and diarrhoea. Formerly I had no such attacks so frequently. That is the new development. During weakness the hard labour and continuous transmission create fatigue, but I will have to do it as I have given very little time to the centres. I must finish my work during the period of my stay at different stations. The weakness you feel in transmission is due to the physical weakness. The inner making of a man is a very laborious job. I have sent a money order of Rs. 200/- to you and I will take that money when I come to you. Same amount I have sent to Shri R. Viraraghavan for the tickets. Reservation these days for long journey is done one month in advance. This time two persons are coming along with me. One Shri J. R. K. Raizada, a lecturer in History and the other Shri Uma Shanker the preceptor of Sitapur Centre. If you feel the shortage of accommodation in your house you may arrange in *chaultry*. To my mind my room where I stay will somehow accommodate all the three persons.

In case of Dr. Kuppuswamy I would like to say that if it is your desire the Master may fulfill it. My reading about him is that his further regions are abnormally gross and so it seems to me that a good deal of labour is required to make way to Central Region. Every preceptor has the power to send him or anybody immediately to the Central Region but it is a very dangerous task. I have already written the second part of the Method of the Training, but I have not disclosed in it the method of giving highest approach at a glance without harming a man. I am afraid that the preceptor may try it. This is my research work for which a proper moulding is necessary at that time. If preceptor fails accidentally to mould himself accordingly, the man is gone. I am sure you can mould it but still I do not trust unless you do one or two cases before me.

About your sister I will try to do as much as is possible. Yesterday at noon I saw Chi. Chittra and her daughter in dream. The dream as you mentioned in the letter has a meaning. Lord Krishna appeared before you in dream and has given you a very mild transmission also. He is interested in Sahaj Marg and he has given the name to the *sanstha*. Our *sanstha* is connected with him through the Master. When you asked for the mergence He disappeared. I feel shy to interpret it but I feel if I do not relate it to you, you will be anxious to know it hence I am writing to you. Shri Krishna disappeared because He felt that you have got the difference between Him and the Master so you are asking this boon.

Shri V.S.R. Murthy of Tirupati has asked me a few questions which I want to reply verbally when I am there.

Love to children and respect to Appaji.

Yours,
Ram Chandra
President

No. G 425/SRCM Shahjahanpur, U.P.
Dated 7th July, 1967

My dear Varadachari,

Received your affectionate letter dated 20th July, 1967. I feel weakness generally in the morning when I get up. When I take a little milk, I feel relief. You should not be very anxious about my health. I will be better after the summer subsides. Shri Raghavendra Rao of Raichur has arrived here today for two weeks. A colleague of Shri Raghavendra Rao, Deputy Commissioner of Hyderabad has arrived here along with his wife and mother. He is the follower of Meher Baba, but he has started our meditation also.

The management of Ashram is entirely in your hands. You may appoint anybody to your satisfaction. There is nothing wrong to appoint a Harijan as a watchman.

I have dropped a separate letter to you to enable you to work on its strength and you may show it to Mr. Annaiah Naidu or to anybody you like.

I consulted my Master about Shri Viraraghavan of Madras. He said if he promises to do the work he may be appointed. It will be better if you intimate him that I want to take the work from him provided he promises to do it regularly and ask him to write to me directly so that I may start preparing him for the work. To such persons sometimes constructive and destructive works are also allotted by Nature.

I must tell you what work you have done so far unconsciously and what you are doing at present. You worked for about a year in Afghanistan and now you are working in Asian Russia near the Chinese border. The result of your work in Afghanistan is that they are calm and pacified. They are not much attracted towards the luxuries of modern life. I have received the introduction so well written by you.

I am confident that the prayer will do much in case of my son-in-law Chi. Rajendra. This is what we can do.

Respect to Appaji and love to children.

Yours,
Ram Chandra

No. G 409/SRCM   **Shahjahanpur, U.P.**
Dated 15th July, 1967

My dear Varadachari,

I am sorry to learn that Chi. Gayathri got plucked this year. May God pacify her and give strength to pass meritoriously next year. These are hard days for us. My son Sarvesh has failed in Physics this year and he has not been admitted in the college. I have, therefore, sent him to Sitapur. My son-in-law, Chi. Rajendra, has developed the eye trouble again and his left eye has indifferent vision. Some times he sees man of a few inches long and sometimes without head. His right eye also has got hemorrhage. He is the only source of livelihood for my daughter Chhaya.

How much I wish Chi. Raja be employed in Tirupati, I cannot express. If not at Tirupati he may be employed anywhere else on good salary. I do not know if Chi. Parthasarathi of Madras can be of any help to him.

I have grown so weak that only by walking hundred paces I felt very much tired as if I had walked a mile's distance. I have taken Decca Duraboline injection, which has improved me a bit. I am taking medicines and diet according to instructions of my physician. Pain, sometimes, I do feel but very little.

I have gone through the diagrams brought from Tirupati and found that late Shri Ishwar Sahai had not given the correct diagrams. I told him once in a general way that the centres on the trunk of human body corroborate with, to a certain degree, the centres of the spinal cord even the centres above it also seem to corroborate with centres of the backbone of the head. I only gave him the hints and he made the diagrams and he left the centres of the spinal cord. If I could not reproduce them again my labour of fourteen years is wasted. I depend solely upon my Master's Grace, in this respect, because a revelation comes to me only once. Please advise me what I should do to bring those things back to my memory.

It is about a week I am having an idea that the atmosphere, polluted due to evil thoughts of the people, be purged out of poisonous effect thoroughly. There is one person somewhere in India doing the work. Still I need one more man. Can you suggest one? I have chosen Seshadri for some other work. He can be given this work also but it will be boring for him. Raghavendra Rao (Raichur) has already been given a duty of some other work. But I have not brought them up to the Divine post. For the work of cleaning of atmosphere one must be at *dhruvagati*. Generally the experienced hands are chosen for the purpose but I want young man from South India. I did this duty some time in early days of my present state afterwards the higher one and now the most important one I am doing. I can also take this work upon myself but the work of the higher nature will suffer. Suppose I propose Viraraghavan, would you like this idea? If I select you for the purpose it would not be fitting because you can be entrusted with some higher work, which unconsciously you do. I will take a year to prepare Viraraghavan, provided my Master agrees to it.

Why I want a man in South India? Because they are very dutiful and know what obedience is.

Respect to Appaji and love to children.

Yours affectionately,
Ram Chandra

P.S.- The theft was committed at the residence of Sushi (Bareilly) when her parents were at Shahjahanpur. She has suffered the loss of Rs. 10,000/-. She is the same girl who met you at Allahabad.

No. G 424/SRCM   **Shahjahanpur, U.P.**
Dated 27th July, 1967

My dear Varadachari,

I feel that the work of the Ashram at Tirupati is not going on properly. I feel some type of mismanagement there. Please find out the cause and if you find that the change of persons necessary for the improvement you may do it without consulting me.

Yours,
Ram Chandra

No. C 444/SRCM   Shahjahanpur, U.P.
                     Dated 12th August, 1967

My dear Varadachari,

Received your affectionate letter dated 13th August, 1967. You will be glad to hear that Shri Raghavendra Rao has been posted as Principal of Raichur Polytechnic. He is required to take over the charge on 18th of August. He is leaving this place on 14th August.

I have received the letter from Viraraghavan promising me to do the work. I shall take up his case after a few days. I shall send him your introduction also. Shri Raghavendra Rao has also liked it very much. You want your complete divinisation and I wish it more than what you do. It is going on day by day. In my opinion about 3/4ths of the work is complete. I am sorry that you are regularly troubled by the world condition. But I am happy to see all these things, because when the conditions are at its climax the real *shakti* descends and the people are benefitted. *Bhaktas* in one way and the vicious in the opposite way.

When a man acquires nearness to God and his own expansion is there the man begins to do his work automatically.

Respect to Appaji and love to children.

                                   Yours,
                                   Ram Chandra

P.S. Umesh (my son) again failed this year. This is the third time. I received just now a very disappointing letter. He can appear only once more in the exam. He is very sensitive like my other children.

No. C 593/SRCM   **Shahjahanpur, U.P.**
Dated 20th November, 1967

My dear Varadachari,

    I have been to Sitapur for two days. The medical attendant of my son-in-law Chi. Rajendra Kumar, has kept him for observation for a few days. He will see if electric treatment will benefit him. In case electric treatment does not benefit him he will do retinal operation. He has very little vision in the left eye and occasionally the hemorrhage occurs in the right eye also. The vision of right eye is quite all right but the left eye has got very little vision. The treatment seems to be very long one. May God cure him.

    I am enclosing herewith the tour programme which has been now finalised. I am working here alone, seeing the press and other things and will have to do for a week more. So I request you to send the dates of my arrival and stay at Tirupati to Chi. Narayana. Mr. Doreswami of Pondicherry may kindly be informed as I do not know his address. I believe you have received my previous letter.

    Love to children and respect to Appaji.

    With best wishes,

                                      Yours,
                                  Ram Chandra

No. C 638/A/SRCM   Shahjahanpur, U.P.
Dated 3rd December, 1967

My dear Varadachari,

Received your affectionate letter. About ten days ago I felt that the progress of Chi. Narayana had been slowed down. The cause seems to be some worldly anxieties. Now he has begun to improve by the grace of my Master. I believe you are carrying on the instructions given by me in his case. Although at present it is not very much essential still it will help me a good deal in giving him higher approaches. He is now on the third point and the *yatra* has commenced.

I have received from Railway Ministry four first class passes on 29th November. So there is a bit of change in the timings. I am sending you the amended copy of the programme.

Raizada and Narayan Sahai and St. Kasturi are coming along with me. St. Kasturi will be the guest of Chi. Gayathri and for Raizada and Narayana you will please arrange in lodging house.

The people of Hyderabad eagerly wish to see you. I will be very happy to meet you at Hyderabad and I am requesting to Appaji to allow you.

Love to children.

Yours affectionately,
Ram Chandra

P.S. I believe you have received a m.o. of Rs. 200/-.

1968

No. C 4/SRCM　　　　　　**Shahjahanpur, U.P.**
　　　　　　　　　　　　　Dated 4th January, 1968

My dear Varadachari,

Received your affectionate letter. I am glad that the daughter is doing well. I received a letter from my son Chi. Umesh from Delhi, who has taken up Chartered Accountancy course, that his result will be out on 25th January 1968 and this is his last chance. So he is a bit perplexed. May God help him.

I have to consult with you on a few things. For that I have not yet consulted my Master because I give him trouble only when my efforts fail. Whether we should work in throwing out the idea of subtle existence in the beginning and, if so, in what way? As an example, in your case, I feel an imaginary cord from *kantha chakra* to *nabhi*. In it God's work is there. But it is throwing out something and that is being removed by one. My eyes are so trained that I do not want to see anything awkward in our abhyasis and with that idea I am working. Suppose I do not work, where will it go from the system? At this stage cleaning is not very necessary because actually there is no grossness but only a reflection of it which requires attention.

When an abhyasi proceeds rightly and reaches at least *brahmanda mandal* at that stage I take up in some cases and not in all cases, the work of awakening the *hridya chakra* and then *atma chakra*. Even then, I do not awaken the *chakras* fully because I fear very much. To touch the further *chakras* my heart does not allow, rather it checks one to take up the 3rd and 4th points and so on. In your case I have taken up two points 1st and 2nd only. Now divinity has taken this task to awaken the other *chakras* but not in full state. In other words the *chakras* which have been touched by me are in awakened state and hence God is not touching them.

Why does the heart not give signal to proceed further? Finally I will consult my Master after discussing with you when we meet in Madras. To save time it will be better if you write out your opinion and bring it to Madras so that I may start thinking on it just on your arrival there.

Respects to Appaji and love to children.

Yours,
Ram Chandra

No. C 21/SRCM   Shahjahanpur, U.P.
Dated 21st January, 1968

My dear Varadachari,

Received your affectionate letter. Shri Viraraghavan has sent me a letter asking me the mistakes he has made, apologising at the same time. Everybody commits mistakes and it is our duty to correct him, anyhow. So we have done. Regarding the atmosphere at his house, I could not study much about it, still I would do something. Vira Raghavan is a very good man and we must all help him in every way. I am sending you a copy of my reply to his letter. Regarding my daughter at Tirupati, I have to do a lot of work to wash away the impressions which cause her trouble. She said to St. Kasturi that from the age of 8 she used to have fear. I will surely be attentive to Raja devoting a few minutes every day or on alternate days. When my sister was alive, I cleaned him, as far as possible, at that time. There is some layer in the brain as it looks, which I will be able to remove by Master's Grace. Rest assured.

We arrived here safely on 15th evening. Kasturi went to Bareilly on the 16th. I also followed her and remained there for two days. She will go back to her place today or tomorrow. On 23rd I have to go to Lucknow to help my younger sister in the work of the marriage of her son, as she wants me there for two days. The marriage comes off on 15th February, 1968. On the pressure of my associates there, I have to give them about two days. Lucknow centre is developing fast.

I am so lucky to observe the very higher condition prevailing among our satsanghis. Really speaking you have given me much experience and gave me food to think upon. On the night of the 18th instant at 9:45 P.M. when I was taking food, I found that your *laya avastha* in the Brahman commenced. I was taking food and at the same time observing your condition. After an hour i.e. about 11 o'clock, I found that the work of nature as started was being done vigorously which I did not want. I was rather puzzled how to bring in the moderation. As I cannot touch His work, I, at last, prayed the Master and in a minute, the Master brought the condition to normalcy. Now I am satisfied that it is going on as I want it. God has taken up your work but I feel my responsibility is still there. I have to watch so many things at higher levels. This is now your experience and it comes out of it that when the subtle idea of existence in subconscious mind goes out, absorbency in Brahman follows. Dr! how difficult it is to train systematically. I do not know how the others do specially when immediate help is necessary to the taught. I must say that hardly anyone will be so fated to get such cases of very high level. Congratulations!

Since my return from South, I am not getting rest because I have to go out and at the same time satsanghis are coming and I have to do the work. I received a very lovely letter from Mr. C. Rajagopalachari of Madras. I appreciated his affection admiring the satsanghis of Madras but added, "among abhyasis there are a few who want to purchase Spanish gram from the merchant dealing in cloth."

Love to children and respects to Appaji.

Yours,
Ram Chandra

No. C 62/SRCM **Shahjahanpur, U.P.**
Dated 15th February, 1968

My dear Varadachari,

Received your affectionate letter dated 26 Jan 68. I am happy that Chiranjiv Baghwan has passed the examination. May he get employment soon.

About your *laya avastha* in Brahma it is established to a great extent but I am hoping that rotation will commence again when what you have gained is complete. It is the first case for me at this time for observation and experience. There will be coming other cases also but after some time although, I am working on that line to speed up the progress of the satsanghis.

I believe the people at Madurai and Trichy must have been benefitted by your talk. There were about five hundred people who participated on Basant Panchami Utsava and it is now gracefully over.

About Chi. Narayana my instructions are the same that is you should devote a few minutes twice or thrice a week in cleaning the system and the rest I will see.

I am very sorry to write you that Umesh again got plucked this time by three marks in 'Mercantile Law' and this has been happening all the time when he attempted for the examination. He got one chance more to sit for the examination by applying to the Directors. He was highly dejected so I sent his brother Chi. Prakash to Delhi for a couple of days. I called him in Utsav and I found the dejection still there.

In his dejection he went to the Registrar and he said to him confidentially that in Delhi sixty percent student passed the examination and out of them they take seven to ten percent only so he should sit in Patna centre where so many students fail. Now he is taking Patna as centre.

Really speaking I am the cause of spoiling his career. From the time he joined the Chartered course, accidentally, I imbibed the idea of his failure so deep in the subconscious mind which is working against him. It is so deep rooted that in spite of my best effort I could not remove it. It now requires a strong hand to remove it wholly for which I request you to do so. Please do not leave it till it is wholly removed.

Kasturi also prayed for it but did not succeed. I take regard that any type of such thing may not enter into subconscious mind but here I failed. It now requires your immediate attention.

Kasturi participated in Utsav and she has gone to Bareilly for two or three days and I have also accompanied her. Kasturi will come in the next tour also.

Regarding Gayathri there is now a very little work. I shall leave her case when I am thoroughly satisfied. Raja is improving but I am taking his case bit by bit, not resting unless the complaint is over.

I have obtained the exemption certificate from Income Tax. Few copies of the letter I have sent through Parthasarathi. You might have got one, if not, then please write to me.

Love to children and respect to Appaji.

Yours,

Ram Chandra

All right I am sending one copy of the exemption certificate.

No. C 88/SRCM **Shahjahanpur, U.P.**
Dated 29th February, 1968

My dear Varadachari,

Received your affectionate letter. The complex as I have expressed in my previous letter is almost over. But when I think deeply I find two or three percent still there. It should be uprooted wholly, and you can do it well. Since Patna is not the centre this year and I came to know of it afterwards I kept Vijayawada as centre. He will stay there with Dr. Parthasarathy. The examination dates are from 1st

May to 7th May. He will come to you after examination is over and from Tirupati he will also go to Madras. I shall write to you finally later on.

When my daughter passed B.A. examination I started negotiation for her marriage and when she appeared in final M.A. I got the match and married. Similarly I want for Gayathri that negotiation should be started. Meanwhile she may join M.A. I think she wants her marriage after she passes M.A. We should have regard for her feeling also. While consulting her my view may be known to her. We should try to free ourselves from our responsibility as soon as it may be applicable.

You have asked me about the nature of soul. Nowadays I am suffering from headache badly and there seems to be much tension on the nerves of brain. I will therefore take it up a few days after. There is a footnote at page two in *Efficacy of Raja Yoga* about the origin of human mind. Regarding your condition I have no words to express it. You have expressed your condition as paradoxical. Would you please elucidate a little to enable me to write on it. About the rotation as you felt below the navel I cannot explain it at present. I feel some power centred there. Since I cannot touch your case I often meditate on it from the highest point of my approach. The nature has begun to change but it is yet to be revealed. I will write you when it comes to the standard in my view. You have complained about your transmission to others. Really it is not the complaint but the actual condition which goes deeper in the heart of abhyasi. I also feel like that transmission becomes so natural that sometimes it becomes difficult to feel it, so the preceptors feel that I have not transmitted. When Kasturi is available I sometimes asked her the nature and effectiveness of my transmission. I give you an example. When I was working in the Judges Court I gave a sitting to a Mohammedan friend of mine in the office itself. Now twenty years after he met with my fellow disciple and said that a sufi met him and said that somebody has transmitted you so well that its effect is still there. About a week ago my fellow disciple related this story to me.

Love to children and respect to Appaji.

Yours,

Ram Chandra

P.S. I have sent the books *Efficacy of Raja Yoga in the Light of Sahaj Marg* and *Commentary on 10 Commandments of Sahaj Marg* for printing at Madras as here it would have taken much time. *Reality at Dawn* is being printed here.

RC

No. C 156/SRCM **Shahjahanpur, U.P.**
Dated 26th March, 1968

My dear Varadachari,

Received your affectionate letters. I am grateful to you that the complex has been removed. There is something very little at the edge of the right part of the heart which is very nominal. I hope I will be totally free when I reach Allahabad on 8th April to see you. I have received the articles in connection with your 'New Darshan'. I am sorry I could not see it yet because I was indisposed and feeling the weakness of brain. I shall be better in a day or two and will take up my normal work shortly.

I believe Chi. Gayathri will be better now. Your cataract is a matter of great anxiety to me. You may engage any of the abhyasis for the part-time work of the Mission on salary if he so desires. The Mission will pay for it.

I have taken up the case of Chi. Narayana as I had told you when I was at Tirupati or Madras. I was under the impression that I will take one year's time in his case but I feel that one year is not the sufficient even for heart region. We will see to it. I presume that my Master has adopted the same course after giving me a certain amount of approach necessary for the purpose.

Mr. S. Sarnad of Gulbarga, and Mr. Gujarati from Bidar, and Shastri from Hyderabad arrived here today. Mr. Vira Raghavan of Madras is in hospital for checkup.

Love to children and respect to Appaji.

Yours,
Ram Chandra

No. C 202/SRCM   **Shahjahanpur, U.P.**
Dated 22nd April, 1968

My dear Varadachari,

Received your affectionate letters. Thanks to God that he has saved you from the electric shock. I appreciate the intellect of Chi. Gayathri, who remained in proper senses at the spur of the moment in switching off the current. I have sent Rs. 125/- by money order to Sri Doreswamy Iyer to purchase a

Sujata wrist watch and send it to you directly for Chi. Gayathri. St. Kasturi and Vimla, daughter of Shri M. L. Chaturvedi, have preferred the silver tint but I preferred the golden one.

You were lucky to have a sitting from the Master at Allahabad. It was wholesome and elevating. I do not transmit to you because now there is no need for it. I simply regulate and adjust the condition you are in. When the process is complete, I will inform you. I only guess what will be coming after this process is complete. But if I tell you further that will be a great temptation for you. I am waiting for that condition to come. I believe when the present process is complete you will be able to know the secret of nature which I have not yet revealed to anyone. I feel the signs of that by your writings and studying your condition.

I have previously told you that I am preparing Chi. Narayana and Chi. Parthasarathi of Madras for the work because they should be very strong men and I am happy that I am getting co-operation from both of them.

I have left your articles at Allahabad with Mr. M.L. Chaturvedi to write the introduction as you wished. I have received a letter from Shri C. Raghavendra Rao of Secunderabad that he would be starting for Delhi on 23rd for some government work and he would be here on 29th instant.

Respect to Appaji and love to children.

Yours,
Ram Chandra

No. C 209/SRCM   **Shahjahanpur, U.P.**
Dated 26th April, 1968

My dear Varadachari,

I believe you have received the wrist watch for Chi. Gayathri. Is it just the same as you have directed me at Allahabad? I had written to Shri Doreswamy for golden polish watch. These days I was put to loss for about one thousand rupees. It so happened that the bullock cart loaded with tuaram (Spanish gram) caught fire and whole of the cart with the tuaram caught fire and reduced to ashes in the field. It is due to the smoking that it caught fire and it was the mistake of my ploughman. Yesterday my tamed dog bit my grandson Sharad on the face. Injections will be necessary in that case because it is facial bite.

Now I am coming to your case. The process of *laya avastha* is complete in a way. The thing started below the navel and completed its course on April 23rd, 1968 at 7 P.M. reaching into the central region. On April 24th, 1968 at 9:34 A.M. the volume has begun to increase. I am studying very deeply. There is no transmission on my part. Only my thought is there so really speaking I do not do any work. I simply wish that it may be regulated in this way and the force of the wish regularise it. Please write to me whether you feel some tension in the brain. If it is so whether it is mild or strong. Many a time in the day I have to watch its course. It is the Grace of my Master that the difficult task becomes so easy. When this process is complete I shall add this thing also in the second part of the Method of

Training by your consultation so that nothing may be left there. I wish that all the preceptors of the Mission may write their experiences which they have while training others and how they have removed the defect which they have complained of. You have got so many cases and you have done wonders. Thanks to the Master.

Very recently I came to know the way of doing prayers for others but I have still to think much over it. One thing I write for which I am sure. One who has reached central region he must not pray by entering into it. One who can work in universal dynamo he must not work on any account by putting himself into it. But such personalities are very rare so I am writing this for the sake of knowledge. For the spiritual benefit a man can pray from the central region but not for worldly things. Why we should not pray from the central region that is yet to be studied. I shall write to you when it is studied. I am happy that Chi. Parthasarathi has purchased a tape recorder known as Crown corder CTR 5400 model with two speeds and two tracks and capable of recording up to three hours. You will get it after a fortnight when Chi. Parthasarathi returns from tour. I presume Chi. Gayathri and all other children will be very happy to see it. It is the thing mostly needed and now you will feel convenient while doing your job.

I am going to Lucknow on 4th May by night train to participate in the marriage ceremony of my sister's son and will return on 10th May. Shri S. A. Sarnad of Gulbarga, Shri Ayal Reddy of Sedam, Shri Gujrati and Ram Shastry of Bidar have gone back on 18th after staying with me for about 20 days. Shri

C. Raghavendra Rao of Hyderabad is coming to me on 29th from Delhi.

Love to children and respect to Appaji.

Yours,

Ram Chandra

P.S. Chi. Umesh reached Vijayawada on 20th April. His examination will begin from 1st of May and will continue up to 7th May 68. Please take care that the complex which you have removed may not come again. Although it will not yet care should be taken.

RC

No. C 223/SRCM   Shahjahanpur, U.P.
Dated 18th May, 1968

My dear Varadachari,

Received your affectionate letter. I came to know through Shri C.A. Rajagopalachari that you have sprained your ankle and are limping. I believe you must have recovered now. I received a letter from Vira Raghavan that he is getting recovery. I have told you at Allahabad that there is some blackish thing on the heart which can be called as disease. It is mostly removed. Only 3 or 4 percent is there. He should take rest for some time more. On 11th May, 1968 at 1:35 P.M. I found your condition coming to normalcy. It has now mostly come to normal. But I want that this state may be so settled that I may find it almost unreadable and it is going to be such. At this stage I deserve *dakshina* that you should try to prepare at least a dozen like yourself and continue to help others spiritually.

I am worried to hear from you that the cataract in the right eye is developed to such an extent that you cannot read with the help of that eye. Please get your eye examined to see if it is matured for operation. There is of course one difficulty in your case that you are suffering from diabetes. Somehow or other it should be stopped before the operation if needed either by injection, oral medicine, or both.

Now I have intended to go to Assam in the second week of June. I will take only eleven or twelve days. Mr. S.K. Rajagopalan of Delhi is here with me and Mr. Chetty of Hyderabad is also here. Mr. Rajagopalan will have to stay at Mattur for five months with his daughter-in-law as his son is going to foreign countries for that period.

Mr. M.L. Chaturvedi has sent me a copy of foreword of your pamphlet without his previous designation. I presume the book has been sent to you together with foreword. It should be sent to me for print as has already been decided.

Love to children. Respect to Appaji.

Yours,
Ram Chandra

No. C 257/SRCM   Shahjahanpur, U.P.
Dated 9th June, 1968

My dear Varadachari,

Received your kind and affectionate letter. I was not feeling well during these days, but hoping to get energy I am starting for Assam on 10th of June and will return on 22nd of June. Saint Kasturi went back after staying with me for two weeks. She stressed to write to you to forego the idea of cataract operation for some time and also to get your urine and blood examined and inform her the result. About a month ago I wrote to Seshadri that the moving force (impetus) has been diminished. He should find out what is wrong in him. I know its cause but I am waiting for his letter to touch him. After coming back from Assam I shall again remind him.

I am writing to you a case of my experience in connection with Saint Kasturi. She is in the first ring of Splendour, but I feel that there is some shadowy thing in it which hampers her progress. I am now writing its cause which I have already told her. I felt and she had admitted it that she has undue attachment (mamata) with her brothers, sisters and mother. She has now begun removing it. While working in the central region the preceptor, in order to correct it, should be as subtle as the state of the region is. It becomes a difficulty to the preceptor.

I am sending you a piece of paper to be attached in the end of the supplement already cyclostyled in the II part of 'The Method of Training', and also a paper to be pasted in the end of the said book. It contains the directions for prayer. I shall reply the rest of your previous letter after coming back from Assam. Dr. Swami of Tirupati wants to come to me and so Chi. Narayana. They should come to me after 22nd of June. I have obtained complimentary passes from the Railway Ministry.

Love to children and respect to Appaji.

Yours,
Ram Chandra

No. C 329/SRCM Shahjahanpur, U.P.
Dated 26th July, 1968

My dear Varadachari,

Received your affectionate letters. Chi. Umesh has got very good marks in Accounts work but failed in Mercantile Law and Commercial Law by two and three marks respectively and this has been the case throughout his student career in chartered course. He was disheartened and wanted to avoid last chance. He also went to St. Kasturi and she gave the same advice. It is nothing but his fate. Let him try once again. God is great. Dr. Kuppuswamy gave me sufficient time and he remained very happy here. I am very happy to know that you are coming to Shahjahanpur. I am not having here any programme of your speech only to give you rest. My son-in-law Chi. Rajendra has arranged your speech in Cultural Institute and important persons will assemble there. I believe you have got the tape recorder. If it is the case please keep it with you when you start your journey. I do not want to miss any of your speeches. I am collecting all your speeches to have volume and a few months later I shall arrange for their publication. These days I was compelled to take the election work in the press because the compositors would have worked in some other press and I would have fallen in difficulty.

Observance of fast during Shri Krishna Janmashtami is the order of my Master. The instructions were issued accordingly. Almost all the satsanghis in India used to observe fast on that specific day. Now this year by the permission of my

Master I have withdrawn this order for North India alone. Our South Indian brothers will observe the fast as they used to do. The reason is that in spite of my continuously explaining to the North Indians that it is not the Utsava but religious rite, they have begun to think it to be Utsava. If it is also taken as Utsava then the importance of Basant Panchami Utsava will be lost. A few people of North India sometimes said that since they could not attend Basant Panchami Utsava they will attend the Shri Krishna Janmashtami Utsava. I am writing you privately that Shri S.K. Rajagopalan, when he came to me and stayed for a week I took up his case vigorously. When I pulled him to *prapannagati* I found that his one foot was on *parabrahmanda mandal* and the other at *prapannagati* and grossness was quite condensed. I wanted to select him for the special training but I could not do it. He is so very devotional and a very good man all round still such a type of grossness I found in the upper region. Since then I often cleaned the grossness but still there is no end to it. So this is the difficulty before me. I also frankly express today that I have been transmitting South India every time for the last ten years. The results are good but not according to my labour. The case may be that they are mostly dogmatic instead of Godmatic. To be more plain I should say that they have in mind the value of the grosser type of worship and one link is attached to God and the other to the devil. Thus they take milk but also take pickle after it. We have to give time to think over these dificulties. I do not know how long I will live to serve all of you but as long as I live I want to render best services causing excellent results. If I and you both succeed in making two dozens of people like yourself appointed in different corners of India then in twenty years the face of India will be changed and spirituality will reign throughout.

Love to children and respect to Appaji.

Yours affectionately,
Ram Chandra

No. C 362/SRCM **Shahjahanpur, U.P.**
Dated 8th September, 1968

My dear Varadachari,

I feel that you might have felt exhausted after strenuous journey. Now after taking rest you will be feeling better. Whenever I remember I will devote a few minutes for your health as well. I had taken charge of your soul and that work is over. Now comes the body and health for which, as you said, Swami Shivanand had taken charge. He might have done something good regarding your health. Since he is dead I like to look to it. Kasturi is already doing something for your health. You can also draw energy from *brahmanda mandal* for your health.

I had been to Delhi for two days as the case of Shri C. Raghavendra Rao has taken the serious turn. May God help him. He was also there with his wife. His wife came to Shahjahanpur along with me for two days and Shri Raghavendra Rao has gone to Dehra Doon in some meeting. He will come back to Delhi on 11th morning. I received the letter from Chi. Narayana and I am satisfied with my work. I am trying to send him gradually to the subtler state and he has given an account of it in his letter.

Three persons have come from Bidar and they will stay for some time more. Out of them there is one Shri Lingoji Rao. He has been following this practice for the last four years. He is very gross and not receptacle. I do not know what the preceptor does. It is very easy to know this state of abhyasi. Now for your experience I am telling some thing about him. Self is predominant in a way that you will hardly find this thing in any other case. When he comes before me I feel as if I am afraid of him. This shows that his heart has some cruel tendency. Now about his way of life. Whenever any controversy occured in Bidar he was its ring leader. For instance he said to the abhyasis once that they should receive training from a man who belongs to Bidar. In other words they should have their own preceptor. I requested Shri Ayal Reddy to go to Bidar at least once in two or three months but he was not welcomed. Then I told him not to go to Bidar at all. When I came to know about it I told them plainly that they should prepare some preceptor for themselves at Bidar itself and I am not at all responsible for their spiritual improvement. Afterwards I wrote so many letters to the satsanghis to the same effect. Then they bent on their knees and realised their mistake. I then said to them when they came to the proper senses not to give place to Lingoji Rao in the satsangh. He was not turned out but has been given time to mend himself. I feel that he has now come to his proper senses and so he is here. Forgetting everything I am attending to him but not vigorously. The chief remedy for such persons is to convert the self into Divinity but I have not yet studied its consequences. So I am not doing it. We will see further on if it can be done slowly.

Shri Raghavendra Rao, Principal of Polytechnic, Raichur, is reaching here along with Mr. M. D. Jahagirdar of Chennapatna, Abhaya Kumar from Bangalore and Ayal Reddy from Selam, on 10th September.

I want to know how many copies of *Reality At Dawn* you require. We got 2500 copies printed. The programme drawn up by Shri Rajagopalachari for South India to start tour on 26th November may be three or four days earlier because our Delhi satsanghis want me on Sunday the 23rd November at Delhi. I am sorry to write to you that Raizada got his bone of the back side broken by motorcycle accident on seventh September. We have very few showers at Shahjahanpur and other districts of U.P. The standing crops are being damaged already and the wheat and paddy crops will not have good results. I had been to Modinagar also and brought Kasturi to Delhi for two days. She has now recovered from typhoid. Only fever remains up to 99 degrees and that is her old complaint. Once you gave her a medicine which was so effective that she did not suffer from fever for several years.

Respect to Appaji and love to children.

With best wishes,

Yours,
Ram Chandra

No. C 463/SRCM   **Shahjahanpur, U.P.**
Dated 24th October, 1968

My dear Varadachari,

    Received your affectionate letters. I am sorry that I am replying them with much delay. The typist whom I partly engaged has not been doing well for the last two or three months. The main difficulty with me is that when I want to write, what I think, I forget the ideas. Your word 'fatalism' in the letter dated 19th September, 1968 worried me very much. At last I came to the conclusion that this restlessness is due to some physical disorder and it may be nervous weakness. I also suffer from restlessness, sometimes, due to nervous debility then I start taking B.G.Phos. When there is heavy pressure of work, I suffer from restlessness in the heart and in that case medicine is immediately needed because it becomes intolerable. I am sure now you will be free from this.

    But I think I may get rest in the Railway train while on tour. I try to be away from home for three days for the sake of rest. There is a tension in the brain and sometime I feel like the pangs of the boils as if they have come out in the brain itself. Work and work should be our principle because one cannot say when life will go. I am already engaged up to 31st October 68.

    I want to give you most important work but you are more busy than myself. That is one of the reasons that I could not yet study about the psychology which you want to incorporate in your book. Anyhow I will do it.

I want to entrust you with so many duties for which you will naturally require a helper in order to give you rest. In that case if you take work from Kuppuswamy, that will be all right. The man is prepared for the work. Even if I do not permit him legally, he can do the work. By permission broadness is developed. Now you will decide yourself whether provisional permission be given or full one. When I think these both things are present in my mind and my heart decides the latter.

I agree with your view that higher attainments need not be for preceptorship only, I loudly said almost in every centre the same thing. There are lot of abhyasis at Tirupati whom Provisional Permission can be given and that is due to your good work. What you have decided for P. Rao and his wife, will be done when I come to you.

I do not take any step unless I consult you. Last time when we were at Hyderabad, you gave me very nice suggestion and I abide by it, that each one may get an individual sitting once a week. For that preceptors are needed. One preceptor does this work then each abhyasi will get one individual sitting in one year, because numbers are enormously increasing everywhere and specially when I am there. I am following your beautiful advice everywhere in the North and South. Regarding Shri Ram Krishna of Madras, Shri Vira Raghavan was right not to recommend his case for the job. If he has got the heart on one side he has the heart on the other side also.

About appointing preceptor at Tirupati I might have said to somebody, that Doctor was not prepared to permit Chiranjiv Narayana for the work because the senior abhyasis might have thought that permission is given to Narayana as he is your son. That was of course your far sightedness and sense of justice. I wanted to do it and I did it. It was really highly appreciable and speaks of your rising above selflessness.

I have gone through the lines written in the light of Shri Ramanuja's method. I agree but a good deal of preparation is necessary on the part of the abhyasi. I have also written a method done by myself in the second part of the 'Method of Training', which if correctly done automatically hits the point. There are so many ills in the self which can be only experienced and so far I have taken the man reaching the central region. Before it, it is the work of the abhyasi and in a way it is a preparation for the last touch of the Master, very rarely such cases come to us. It requires deep study. You might have remembered that in your case it was in a very mild form yet it took me three years. The last touch I gave at Hyderabad. You know probably that at its last step there was an idea of only subtle existence which is removed altogether. Now you exist but you do not exist.

Now another topic starts. Really it is a new thing to me. You might have received the letter from Shri Lakshmi Narasimhan and you replied it wisely. Now I quote the sentence of Lakshmi Narasimhan as Shri Seshadri said to him, "Master has made a *sankalpa* to keep me tied in a knot (he found me enwrapped in a triangular barrier)." While Lakshmi Narasimhan was giving individual sitting to Tharkananda, he related his experience of the individual sitting to Seshadri. He gave his opinion, "Possibly, Master put up the triangular barrier to protect him."

Now in the previous sentence the word *sankalpa* is used, now he has asked me about my opinion. Keeping in view the respect of Shri Seshadri I will have to reply it. About two or three weeks ago, I was studying the 'self' of Mr. Seshadri. Now here is a clue to understand it. It shows that the idea of self-importance is also there. To bring the 'self' in the right form is a very difficult job. To turn it to Divinity at a glance is very easy. But it is not permissible because danger is there.

My typist being absent I could not send the programmes to the centres. Now I have got them typed somehow and am sending one to you. I have already sent one copy to Madras a few days ago because Chiranjiv Parthasarathi wanted it earlier in order to publish it, I am sending you a paper to add it in the end of the 'Method of Training.'

I presume Chi. Narayana will not be satisfied with this condition because the thing has been taken by me so early of which he had not a glimpse of experience before. I tell you, as I feel, that his heart is divinised and *atma chakra* is also divinised but there is a little tinge of roughness. Super-conscious state of the heart is also open. Now the Master does not allow me to move further in this way.

It is quite possible that after completing the *yatra* for the second time up to *brahmanda mandal*, I may take up the heart again. But I am not very definite to take it up. It is to be decided afterwards.

Dr. Kuppuswamy has written to me for the crossing of the rings. Now you may do it so that you may add to your experience in this higher state of things as well. I already brought the power to normalcy and the excitement is over. This was necessary before we start the working on rings I tell you the way which experience has taught me. Transmission is not needed to bring the power to normalcy in the central region. Only the thought that the power is coming to normalcy is a proper way.

Whenever I think of my late sister she says to give permission to Sow. Chitra for work. Now I will have to do it whether she gets the work or not. She is almost prepared for it and this is the work of the sister.

Chi. Umesh was here for about 6 weeks. His examination starts on 31st October, 1968 and will last up to 7th November, 1968. He has kept Delhi as centre. May all our prayer for his success be fruitful. My son-in-law Chi. Rajendra has again had hemorrage in his eye. He is coming to Sitapur for check-up. May God give him cure.

Raizada is now doing well. His bandage has been opened. Since he has already taken one month's leave and if he accompanies us he will have to take further leave for tour and the students will suffer. Therefore Dr. S.P. Srivastava would be coming with me. St. Kasturi and Satyapal will also accompany me. Pain in my stomach has again started because at the instruction of the doctor I began to take a little solid food at evening. Now I am obliged to leave it. I will be all right very soon. I have applied for complimentary passes on 4th October, 1968.

Love to children and respect to Appaji.

Yours affectionately,
Ram Chandra

P.S. Shri N.K.Krishna Murthy (Higginbotham's firm) of Madras passed 5 days with me. He is on pilgrimage. He will be at Madras on 24th October, 1968. I am sending you a paper to be added in the end of the Method of Training Part II. The review of *A Peep into Sahaj Marg* appeared in Bhavan's Journal of 22nd September, 1968. Since then there is a demand of books but it is out of stock. I have sent it to Allahabad for publication.

No. C 539/SRCM   **Shahjahanpur, U.P.**
Dated 10th November, 1968

My dear Varadachari,

Received your affectionate letter. I am worried to know about the ailment of Chi. Raja's wife. I pray that she may recover soon. Please tell me whether it is the right hip joint or the left one which is giving trouble. I also received the letter of Chi. Raja. I am replying that letter also.

Shri Parthasarthi of Madras was here for a day. This morning when I was transmitting to him I felt that he has got wonderful attraction, which is the sign that the people will join in the Mission in large number through him. It is natural and not created.

I am rather worried about one of my associates of district Kheri who had the second heart attack very serious in nature. Oxygen is given at least six to seven hours in a day, and oft times the pulse failed. I have been there for two days and I am going again tomorrow. He had the heart attack on 31st October, 1968.

There is a minor change in the programme which please note.

Change In Programme

Place	Day	Date	Time	Train No.
Bangalore	A. Sat.	14.12.68	13:00 Hrs.	
-do-	D. Wed.	18.12.68	18:10 Hrs.	Island Express
Salem	A. Thur.	19.12.68	00:45 Hrs.	(Through Carriage Trichanopalli)
Nagpur	A. Fri.	3.1.69	10:40 Hrs.	21Dakshin Express
-do-	D. Sat.	4.1.69	10:55 Hrs.	-do-
Shahjahanpur	A. Sun	5.1.69	18:36 Hrs.	5 Up Mail

Yours affectionately,
Ram Chandra

P.S. I have received the draft of Rs. 214.0. There was no hurry about it.

Camp Vijayawada
Dated 27th November, 1968

My dear Varadachari,

We reached here safely and the journey was very comfortable. Satyapal, St. Kasturi and Professor Suresh Chandra are accompanying me.

I have gone through the articles 'Psychology of the Mind' and 'Psychology of the Divine Experience'. They are very nicely written. In the end of the last para of 'Psychology of Divine Experience' I have given my view also.

Please observe your condition on the basis of last paragraph written by me and see where you are.

Love to children. Respect to Appaji.

With best wishes,
Yours,
Ram Chandra

P.S. I and St. Kasturi will stay with you. Satyapal and Prof. Suresh in hotel like previous years.

1969

No. C 6/SRCM **Shahjahanpur, U.P.**
Date 13th January, 1969

My Dear Varadachari,

Received your affectionate letter together with the article. Chi. Narayana has crossed *brahmanda mandal* on 11th January, 1969 at 10:42 P.M. and Chi. Parthasarathi also on the same date at 10:40 P.M. Thanks to the Master that both of them are in the *parabrahmanda mandal*. The progress of Chi. Parthasarathi is swift. Chi. Narayana should also be swift and he should try for it.

Chi. Umesh failed again and this was his last chance. Now my anxiety has become double — one of Chi. Raja's employment and the other of Chi. Umesh. May God help them. Love to children and respect to Appaji.

Yours,
Ram Chandra

No. C 152/SRCM/69 **Shahjahanpur, U.P.**
Dated 5th March, 1969

My dear Varadachari,

I received all your loving letters. I detained Shri C.A. Rajagopalachari for nineteen days during the cold season; but he felt quite happy. I put him into *prabhu gati* and I made his way clear for further approach. Last year when he was here along with you I did the same; but this time I felt that he needed again the way to be cleared. He has written in his letter that since he got my letter he is very restless and does not feel so congenial as before. He feels some confusion. I am hoping that by Master's Grace this complaint will be over. But I couldn't yet make out the cause of it. Would you help me in this respect? I am very happy to write to you that in the case of Shri Raghavendra Rao of Raichur absorbency in Brahma commenced. I want to prepare ten more such persons, if not more, to complete the dozen, as I said to my Master to do it in my life time.

I took up the work of Shri Seshadri of Madras; but he developed a sort of *ahamta* (egoism) which stopped my work. Unless that is corrected, further approach is not possible. I am surprised that at such higher state how the egoism creeps in. The answer, as I see, can be that egoism is not washed away totally. The form is changed. It means that any sister idea sometimes comes and the abhyasi deepens it by his constant thinking due to the power within him, which grows as he advances. I could remove about ninety percent of his defects, when he was here. The condition was that this *ahamta* was spread throughout his system. What I did I am writing to you for further experience. Instead of hitting at the root at that time I began to remove the extension of it in the system.

I am sorry to learn that the case of Shri C. Raghavendra Rao of Secunderabad has not been decided in his favour. I offered prayer but it was not answered. In the worldly matters I am mostly unsuccessful in prayers because the heart hardly co-operates. The reason as I think, seems to be the tendency of the mind is changed and the mind seems to be withdrawn from the world as its natural effect. I am doubting it might have disturbed his faith.

Chiranjiv Umesh has filed an appeal to the President of Chartered Accountancy to give him another chance to appear in the examination. It is allowed generally if the student obtains more than thirty five percent marks in the aggregate, and which he had always secured in every previous examination. He will get the chance. Meanwhile he is in search of an employment. He has come back from Delhi and is living here.

Love to children and respects to your father,

Yours,

Ram Chandra

P.S. Mrs. A. Balabriga will come to Tirupati to discuss spiritual matters. She got *Efficacy of Raja Yoga* from somebody, studied it and wrote a letter. I got it drafted and sent through the secretary of the Mission mentioning in it to see you. She is staying at Aurobindo Ashram Pondicherry. She follows some method and has experiences. Probably she is French.

No. C 175/SRCM   **Shahjahanpur, U.P.**
Dated 14th March, 1969

My dear Varadachari,

I received your kind letter. I agree with what you have written about Mr. C.A. Rajagopalachari of Madras. I wanted to make his present region a bit intense, so I did a little but the force of the will applied for was a bit strong and he could not absorb it, therefore the region has become a bit thicker. I am now setting it right.

Shri Seshadri is now better. The vibrations in the central region had become dull, now they have begun to rise again. He has also sent me a letter giving correctly his condition.

You have not enclosed the copy of the application of Chi. Baghwan with the letter, please send it by return post to enable me to write to the person concerned. I am hoping that Brig. Rao will do his best. He knows you with all your qualities. I shall write to Mr. Mathur also.

I am worried about Raja's wife. Chaya's husband, Rajendra, has again developed the eye trouble. I had asked him to take homeopathic medicines but he has not done so.

Love to children. Love to Appaji.

Yours affectionately,
Ram Chandra

P.S. Full name of Brig. Rao will be needed. I am also asking it from Shri C. Raghavendra Rao of Secunderabad.

No. C 192/SRCM   Shahjahanpur, U.P.
                     Dated 24th March, 1969

My dear Varadachari,

You will be glad to know that Seshadri is now almost free from the grossness he had accumulated by *ahamta* and the vibrations have now begun to rise in the central region. I had left him in the third ring. Now I will proceed further when I find that Seshadri feels restless to go above. I think you remember about Mr. Rajagopalan. A bit I have succeeded in one and a half year. You please study him. I want to send him to you for a few days after some time. When I do not want to transmit owing to the danger which I foresee, then simply I think it should be cleaned and intricacies may be removed. That is my last weapon.

The examination of Chi. Umesh will continue from 1st to 7th May 1969. He has chosen Vijayawada as centre. I did not hear anything from Chi. Bhaghwan. At least I should have the reference of the application with dates and the post for which he has applied at Ramachandrapuram and Delhi. I am remembering Narayana very much nowadays. I presume he is doing constant remembrance. Mr. Vasudevan, sub-editor of Nagpur Times is here with me. I had requested him to be with me for three days when I was at Nagpur for the purpose of starting a centre under him.

Love to children and respect to Appaji.

Yours,
Ram Chandra

No. C 430/SRCM   Shahjahanpur, U.P.
Dated 13th May, 1969

My dear Varadachari,

I hope boys must have reached safely. I shall be reaching Madras on the 17th May by G.T. and will stay there for a week. I wanted to give you telegram but it was not accepted by the post office as the telegraph wire went out of order on account of gale and thunder storm.

Love to children and respect to Appaji.

Yours,
Ram Chandra

No. C 545/SRCM Shahjahanpur, U.P.
Dated 24th June, 1969

My dear Varadachari,

I received your affectionate letter after coming back from Assam. The season was very good there. Assam is famous for the green grass all the year around. Assam is a really very troublesome journey specially for me who travels III class. When I reached Gauhati I felt so exhausted that I was unable to move further. After night's rest I started again for Tinsukia. Shri Dhayabhai Patel, who is very well interested, has made good arrangements for our stay and speeches. Now I am writing to you the mentality of the persons there. Most of them think me a little better than a fool and take me little better than other *sadhus* who wander in the street like the rolling stones not fit for the building. If you prescribe them our method, some of them will do it for some time but if they suffer any loss in the business they will attribute it to this method and will give it up. I told them plainly that business promises money and not realisation and yoga promises liberation and not money. It is one of the wealthiest places in Assam with a very little education.

I had the idea in mind that Chi. Raja may start some work at Tirupati and Chi. Narayan may remain near about Tirupati for your service. Now I am happy that Narayana is there at Tirupati. I am feeling the symptoms in Narayana that he will grow dynamic. I also feel a little openness in *parabrahmanda mandal* which is also a good symptom. I am simply observing his condition at *parabrahmanda mandal* to know how to work further in the best possible way. You have done well that you permitted D. Rama Murthi of Chittor for work.

I shall issue a certificate when I come next. Now about yourself. You have written that sometimes you feel absorbed seeking to move swiftly to the Centre. There is no change at all in your state. It is a changeless condition as I say. A little bit humanity is there as it ought to be and so you feel the difference. In the beginning your inclination was to reach the Centre, a tinge of it is still there so you feel seeking to move swiftly to the centre. Nothingness or negation is your state but I feel the weight of nothingness in your condition which will itself disappear. This is not the defect at all but as I am very weak so I admire weakness if I find like that in anybody. Now I am telling you the cause of weight. You started with keen inclination for realisation. Since that inclination came in contact with power so it became a bit stronger to help you in your spiritual pursuit and really it worked wonders. Now it has no place. It has done its work. A bit amount of keenness is still there and I shall speak to my Master for it because I cannot touch. If He allows me to do it, I will do it or He will Himself do if my request is just and proper.

Love to children. Respects to Appaji.

Yours,

Ram Chandra

P.S. I want 100 copies of the book *Thus Speaks* price Rs 1/- each. I have already received 99 copies which are all sold. I will send the price of 200 books after 1st July, 1969. I have also requested Shri R.

Vira Raghavan to send me 50 copies of *Efficacy of Raja Yoga* and 10 copies of *Lectures on Sahaj Marg*.

No. C 909/SRCM Shahjahanpur, U.P.
Dated 28th September, 1969

My dear Varadachari,

Received all your affectionate letters. I am very happy that Chi. Gayathri got the higher class. It is very surprising to me and I attribute it to the grace of God. I am going to Nepal on 17th October and other adjoining districts. This time I shall be able to visit only Nepalganj and not Khatmandu because the air service is stopped on account of rains for two months. If I take up the air route by Patna it shall be very costly. I will be coming back on 24th October.

I received a letter of Shri C.A. Rajagopalachari from Rome (Italy) that twenty-two persons started the meditation when he introduced Sahaj Marg in the meeting. He has a call from Sweden and Copenhagen (Denmark) that a few people want to start the meditation. He is not going to Sweden, but he will go to Copenhagen only. Mr. A. Lakshminarsimhan will be there before his arrival. West is hungry for spiritual food but I am sorry that our saints who go there cannot satisfy them because regarding spirituality they are themselves paupers.

For about four weeks I have been suffering very badly from stomach-ache. Medicines could not give me any relief but the milk advised to be taken every hour stopped the pain. I am now better. Chi. Narayana has completed about 3/4 *yatra* of *parabrahmanda mandal*. Thanks to the grace of my Master.

Sahaj Marg Philosophy has been released from press and they are ready for sale. I am sending a copy of it by Registered Book Post as a presentation to you.

Love to children and respect to Appaji.

Yours,
Ram Chandra

P.S. As Mr. Poray and Herr Robert Koch with his wife are coming in winter so it will not be possible for me to tour S. India in winter. It may be performed in summer if the building of the Ashram is not under construction, however I will try.

RC

Tirupati
21st October, 1969

My dear and revered Gurudev,

Please accept my humble pranams. I received your affectionate letter. I am glad that Chi. Narayana is progressing nearer and nearer the other border of the *parabrahmanda*. Here children are doing well. Chi. Bhagavan is at Bombay undergoing strenuous training — from 8 A.M. to 9 P.M. I believe your trip to Nepalganj has been useful. The Assam people have written that owing to agitation they have to postpone the trip. I am rather concerned about our country's affairs drifting immorally to chaos. That is one trouble in my lower mind. I hope to rise above it by thy Grace. Chi. Raja's wife has picked up 99 lbs. But her knees continue to give trouble.

I am herewith sending the Account from 1-1-69 to 30-9-69 as required by your office.

I am also sending the list of new abhyasis:

Mr. Seshadri, Radiologist, Ruia Hospital, Tirupati.

Dr. Easwara Marthanda Sastry, c/o Dr. E.N.B. Sarma, First Surgeon, Ruia Hospital, Triupati.

L. Lalitamma, w/o N. Laksminarayana M.Sc., Lecturer in Physics, Govindaraja College, Tirupati.

Mrs. G. Kantamma, w/o G. Satyanarayana M.A., Lecturer in History, Govindaraja College, Tirupati.

Mr. P.V. Subramaniam, c/o Shri P.V.S. Murthy, Room No. 206 Central Lodge M.G. Road, Indore.

R.V. Srinivasan, Ari Ranga Nivas, 18, 3 Temple Road - 5th Cross, Krishnappa Block.

KCV

No. C 1028/SRCM **Shahjahanpur, U.P.**
Dated 3rd November, 1969

My dear Varadachari,

Received your affectionate letter. I am thinking of Chi. Narayana these days very much and simultaneously the thought of Parthasarathi also comes. I certainly expressed my view about your giving talks on *Sahaj Marg Philosophy*. It will be a unique book then. May God Bless you.

You really require a good tape recorder for yourself. I felt it much when we missed your talk of Vijayawada and Rajmundry. Really I wish whatever you talk with the associates, may it be a joke, should be brought in writing datewise. And we should not miss any of your speeches delivered anywhere. Sometimes you also speak to the abhyasis during Sunday satsangh. That also should come in black and white. Now the Mission is in a position to spend money on your requirements. I am writing to Mr. Viraraghavan to transfer 1700/- to the account of the Mission at Tirupati for the tape recorder of your choice. If you have to give a little more, then that also be paid either by the Headquarter or the Madras centre.

This year my house was saved from flood. But another river named Garrah was in very heavy flood with the result that so many houses in that locality collapsed and the water in the Ashram land was 3 to 4 feet deep. Now the plans require a change and what we neglected before will have to be done now. The hall go on pillars and for the sake of economy we are reducing its area. We are trying to build the hall in one lakh. But the contractor says that we need Rs. One lakh sixty thousand. At present we have got Rs. 1,02,000/-. A man who has a dyeing factory at Bombay, being disgusted from the saints, wrote me a letter and I replied it. On getting my reply he came to me and was satisfied, by Master's Grace, in one sitting. Mr. Kamalanathan of Tirupati was also here at that time. He saw the Ashram land and the plan which was estimated at 1,11,000/-. He (the gentleman from Bombay) asked me the present position of the Ashram fund which was Rs. 48,000/- at that time. When he went back satisfied to his place, he sent Rs 50,000/- in two monthly installments. He also wrote to the Assam satsanghis to help us in this matter. He promised that within a year's time we will find the whole of Gujarat growing spiritually;

and he has started the work with the help of the newspapers.

You have written in your letter about five types of idols defining each of them. I am giving you one more kind of idolatry, pointed out by my Master. He said that if a man is a slave of his habits he is also an idolater. I go on so far to say that what we suppose even if it does not exist is also idolatry. If a man loves his family, children and so on he is also an idolater. Any attachment towards material things is idolatry. How can it be abolished altogether? When the thought does not take any such impression, if it comes it is thrown back automatically. But this is the case after a long reach. We should avoid the worship of concrete things so that we may rise above and catch it for the things better. There are men whom, anyhow practical hint for realisation be given, they will not leave the idolatry of the rocky type. There are a few examples with me whom I showed practically the state of realisation momentarily; and they felt it and appreciated very much but they are not prepared to leave their idols because they have become habituated to it. And their wisdom has become quite blunt. Discriminative power, they have already lost and that is the cause of our downfall. When the power of discrimination goes away then fear sets in. They will not leave it because their forefathers have been doing so all along. This is one thing. Another thing is, they think that if they leave it, some calamity will befall them. This is our tragical story.

You want me to give provisional permission to Mr. Dhonderao. This idea has struck me several times when I was at Tirupati. He is prepared for the work. Clean him thoroughly and fill his heart mildly for a few seconds and the man will be fully prepared for the work. Please note down his full name and the date on which you permit him. And I will issue certificate from this place. Please let me know the date of provisional permission of Mr. D.R. Moorthy of Chittoor for issuing certificate.

I am going to Delhi on 9th November, 1969 to finalise the building plan of the Ashram Hall with the help of an engineer. I will be returning on 16th morning.

Please arrange to send 200 copies of *Thus Speaks Shri Ram Chandra* by railway parcel. The cost of these books may be adjusted against the cost of *Sahaj Marg Philosophy* sent by you.

Shri C.A. Rajagopalachari has informed me that Mr. A. Poray will fly to India from Rome on 22nd November, 1969. But I have not received any communication from Mr. Poray in this regard. I have also written to him regarding this.

Love to children and respects to Appaji.

Yours,

Ram Chandra

P.S. Mr. Poray has sent me a cheque of $50 from Switzerland for the payment of the cost of books sent by you and Madras Centre. What remains after the payment of the cost of the books will be the donation for the Mission, says he. So please tell me how much you have spent in postage and books. The same I will ask Madras Centre. A very little amount of exchange was given to Shri Rajagopalachari for the way. So I gave him the same cheque endorsing his name which he encashed it in Rome.

RC

No. C 1133/SRCM **Shahjahanpur, U.P.**
Dated 15th December, 1969

My dear Varadachari,

Received your affectionate letter. I am very happy to inform you that Chi. Narayana and Chi. Parthasarathi have crossed *parabrahmanda mandal* and are in the *prapanna* region. Chi. Narayana requires cleaning very much. I feel there is some stiffness behind the *sookshma* body. I have removed about 70% of the grossness already. Since you are on the spot, you will please look into it.

Mr. Poray stayed with me for a week along with Parthasarathi and two other associates. He went back thoroughly satisfied. He said to me to come to Madras during his stay there. I agreed on condition that if our European associates agree to come to Madras instead of Shahjahanpur, then I will surely be there on 30th of December. Mr. Poray also wrote letters to them. One Englishman and his wife will surely come to Madras if Doctor allows him to go to India. Doctor's permission is required only because he has undergone cataract operation recently. Herr Robert Koch with his wife have postponed their voyage up to February 1970. Mr. Paulo of Rome wants to come to India on 10th of January as has been written by Shri C.A. Rajagopalachari. I have written to Mr. Paulo to confirm the date of his arrival requesting him to meet me at Madras. I shall wait for his letter. If these hurdles are over, I will surely be at Madras on 30th at 1 P.M. probably with St. Kasturi. This time I am obliged to take up journey by air from Delhi. In 1970 Basant Panchami falls on 10th of February, so I will have to be back 10 or 12 days before the Utsava. This time I will be able to take up only 2 or 3 stations spending a day or two at each station. Anyway you will get the information of my arrival at Madras.

Shri Rajagopalachari has done wonderful work in the West. They are hungry for spiritual food to bring peace in them, but the Indians, who go there, cannot satisfy them practically. Some have prescribed *asanas*, which did them harm, so they have begun to fear from yoga. Mrs. Birthe of Denmark wants to start a centre there and she is a very devotional lady. I have written to her by consulting Shri Lakshminarasimhan that she would be made preceptor within two months. At Rome Shri Rajagopalachari has already made arrangement. After discussing from Shri Rajagopalachari I shall appoint somebody as the prefect of the Mission.

Commentary on Ten Commandments of Sahaj Marg has been printed at Madras and I got some copies. I have given *Voice Real* to Parthasarathi for printing in Madras. Shri Ramchandra Reddy of Cuddapah has sent the book *Thus Speaks* by railway parcel from Vijayawada to Shahjahanpur, which is awaited.

Love to children and respects to Appaji.

Yours,
Ram Chandra

P.S. When I came back from Delhi in November '69 my associate, an architect of Gulbarga, joining me at Delhi came along with me to Shahjahanpur. He visited the Ashram plot and rejected on account of flood havoc. It was the grace of the Master that we got another plot the third day. It is a plot near about three acre in area. We have purchased it for 19370/- with registration inclusive. Now he has drafted the plan of the hall to be erected there.

RC

No. C 1145/SRCM   **Shahjahanpur, U.P.**
Dated 23rd December, 1969

My dear Varadachari,

Received your affectionate letter. Madras has now begun to realise its duty and it will improve further. When Chi. Narayana was here, I told you not to touch him for some time because I wanted to touch him myself. Afterwards, if I correctly remembered, I had written to you to take up his work. Now you can do the needful.

The thought of Gayathri's marriage often comes to me. I believe you are searching for a good match.

Saint Kasturi came here by car on Dec. 17th night. She is here and will go along with me to Delhi on Dec. 27th night and from there she will fly to Madras along with me on 30th morning, reaching there the same day at 1 o'clock in the afternoon. I am not going to prepare any programme for further journey from here because I will be waiting for a European associate. His arrival I will be able to know at Madras while Mr. Poray will be there. I want, if possible, to leave Madras to Tirupati on

January 7th for two days. I am expecting you at Madras soon after I reach there.

I agree with the view of Chi. Narayana that he should write a pamphlet *Life and Its Value* and you will please help him so that it may be the best. My health has now begun to improve slowly. I will stay with C.A. Rajagopalachari this time. Love to children, respect to Appaji.

Yours,
Ram Chandra

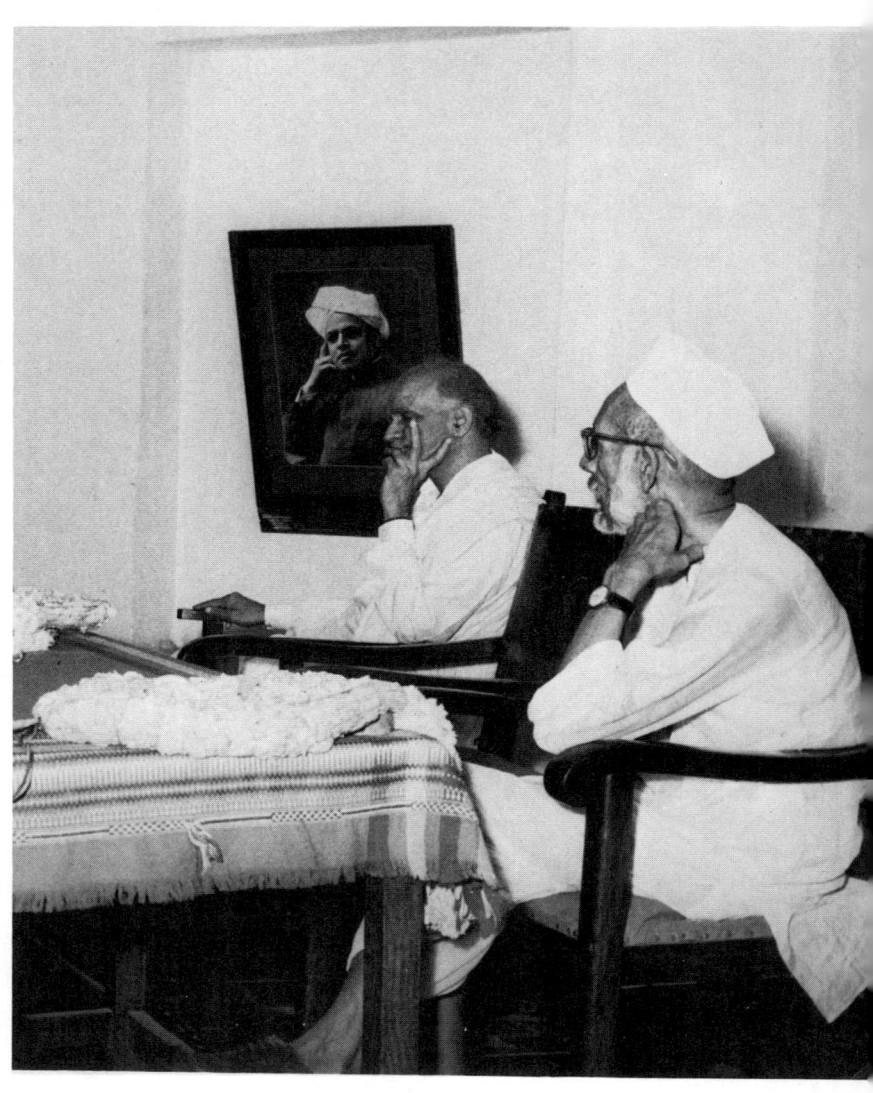

1970

No. C 384/7/SRCM/70   Shahjahanpur, U.P.
Dated 18th April, 1970

My dear Varadachari,

Received your affectionate letter. My health has been good during winter. I am better no doubt, but not as good as in winter. I am happy to inform you that the marriage of Chi. Umesh has been settled. The girl is M.A. in Psychology with good cut and fair complexion. The date for marriage will be either 23rd or 24th of May '70. I will let you know when it is finalised.

Chi. Narayana wants to go to America on Government scholarship for further course. The boy must rise but I do not know how much time will he take abroad.

Now I have engaged an able man for correspondence and other things of the Mission, so there will be no difficulty in replying to the letters.

I have promised to send Shri C.A. Rajagopalachari to West in 1971. Mrs. Birthe Haugaard of Denmark is taking great interest in the Mission and is a very devotional lady. She has cyclostyled your talk delivered at Vijayawada *Way of Life Under Sahaj Marg* and spoke several times there on Sahaj Marg. She is a good painter also and wrote to me that she is very good painter and 180 types of paintings are with her. If they may be sold in India and elsewhere, the sale proceeds will go to the Mission. I have given her provisional permission for the work of the Mission.

For your experience I am writing to you a case where grossness was due to his laziness. After 15 years I could know the cause of it. You know the man. He is Mr. N. Kumaraswamy. I tried my level best whenever I met him and removed his grossness with great difficulty, but it again relapsed. So this time after my illness at Raichur when I reached Hyderabad I could read out the cause of it. I told him that your laziness is the cause of all this grossness and I have prescribed walking and manual labour and also that his wife will not do the marketing any more and he will do all his housework except cooking in her stead. He has started the work and now grossness is being removed automatically. During Utsava when Shri Mahendrakar met me I sent words to Mr. Kumaraswamy through him that if he does not follow the instructions given by me, he would decidedly suffer from cancer, and I found its causes under formation. This is my strange experience that laziness can also breed cancer. I have come to the point that laziness is surrender to the self. In other words, a lazy man surrenders to the self which is suicidal for spiritual growth. I am also very lazy but in household work. Please pray that this habit of mine may be removed.

Love to children and respects to Appaji.

Yours,
Ram Chandra

No. C 463/SRCM Shahjahanpur, U.P.
Dated 30th May, 1970

My dear Varadachari,

The marriage went off well. Shri Seshadriji, Shri Rajagopalachari with his children, Jahagirdar and Abhaykumar participated in the marriage. Chi.

Umesh is going to Madras via Delhi on 10th June with his wife. He has taken a house on rent near Rajagopalachari's house. Mr. Kumaraswamy wants to go back with his children to Madras because his presence is essential there for the sake of realising the rent of his houses there. I am writing to him that he can go to Madras giving charge of the Ashram Mr. Joga Rao. Seshadri will leave for Madras on 10th June.

I received a letter from Sow. Chitra with the happy news that she wants to come to Shahjahanpur after 10th June, along with Srinivasan and Chi. Raja. She is welcome. I am not going to Assam and nowhere till end of June, because I have given time to other associates to be here in that month. I must know the exact date and time of her arrival here, so that I may receive them at the station.

I want to send Chi. Narayana to the next region. But the difficulty I am facing is that nowadays he seems to be less attentive towards spirituality, being engrossed in office or some other work, although I have cleaned him and am doing it as well.

Respects to Appaji and love to children,

Yours affectionately,
Ram Chandra

No. C 499/SRCM **Shahjahanpur, U.P.**
Dated 13th June, 1970

My dear Varadachari,

Received your letter just when I was ready to give a telegram to intimate to me the date and time of arrival of Sow. Chitra and Chi. Srinivasan.

If Chitra is so eager to be here she can come in 1st class with her husband and daughter. In that case I shall pay the expenses of the journey from Madras to Shahjahanpur.

I am very happy that Chi. Raja got the job. May he flourish.

Love to children and respect to Appaji.

Yours,
Ram Chandra

Tirupati
18th June, 1970

My dear and revered Gurudev,

Please accept my humble pranams. I received your kind post card. It is not want of money to travel by a higher class that made my daughter cancel her trip but the last minute railway declining to allot the reservation, though the tickets were purchased within the time requisite for getting reservation. I am sorry that you have misunderstood my letter.

I believe you would have received the manuscript I sent to you. I trust you will find it correct representation of your philosophy.

I declined to go to Assam in October owing to:

1) my operation which would require two to three months, secondly the absence at home of Chi. Raja and possibly Chi. Narayana. I requested Mr. C.A. Rajagopalachari to go if he feels inclined.

Owing to growing disability in many respects I would request you to permit me to divest myself of all organizational work of the Mission at this Centre, and to permit me to nominate either Dr. G. Kuppuswamy or Dr. V.P. Rao to carry on the correspondence etc. with your Secretary at Madras. I am unhappy over the growing developments and pray that I may have peace of mind — which is thoroughly gone. "You wrote about a year ago that I am in the changeless state and there is no movement at all." In January my sister St. Kasturi cast doubts on that statement and held that I had not after all reached the limit. In any case it is clear that my mental peace is very much shattered. I do not know the reason. It has of course grave consequences in our appraisal of the ultimate state possible under our system. Further I had asked the question why even in a very high state far above the circles or rings of splendour there is the growth of resistance to the Ultimate dissolution or absorption or mergence. You have not so far replied to me on that matter. That may also explain the reason why I am in this peaceless condition, though obviously granting peace or calm through transmission to others.

I fully realise that you require freedom from organisational work for the sake of spiritual work. I trust every one will cooperate with you. But I must utter a word of warning if I ought not to be misunderstood. Let us not commercialise our Mission in our haste to secure financial stability for the Mission, and in embarking upon works which are not immediately helpful to spiritual development of the abhyasis. We have to imbue the sense of Mission — spiritual, and not mix it up with other ends. If I am not to be misunderstood I believe some things can be thrashed out with other seekers who also know about the deviations that take place in spiritual work. I trust you will not misunderstand me.

I have today sent a cheque for 250 for life membership of the Sahaj Marg.

With loving pranams.

yours as ever,
KCV

No. C 567/SRCM **Shahjahanpur, U.P.**
Dated 21st June, 1970

My dear Varadachari,

Received your affectionate letter. I have not yet received the manuscript but I hope to receive it within two or three days. Regarding philosophy of our system whatever you have written will be the correct representation because you can better understand this subject. When I dictate any such thing I am not much aware of what I am dictating. Even afterwards I understand but a little what I have done. I feel that I have become blind to this world and have opened myself to the Divine. Whatever falls to my lot, I am happy. At present I do not know whether I am in Reality or I am with Reality. What I remember the most is the pain only in my stomach when it is unbearable.

I can say with certainty that you are in Absolute Reality without minding what Kasturi has said. Saint Kasturi also uttered the same thing at Madras. I told her plainly that she is absolutely wrong. She is after all a student under me and I am the student but under the Master whom the world will remember ever and after. I again emphasise that you have crossed the limit of approach and swimming in the Limitless. I know that the peace is disturbed on account of some such circumstances but it is in surface alone and it is the state of humanity, but if you think it deeply you will find inner calmness. You have written to me that there is the growth of resistance to the Ultimate dissolution or mergence. Mergence is there without doubt and it is not the resistance, but in such a state a man having absorbed in Reality, feels linked with other side also, i.e. the world. It is natural for the humanity because humanity cannot survive without it, and it is essential also because we have to exist as human being first till we close our eyes permenantly. It is the secret of Nature. I have just said that these anxieties remain at the surface. When one ponders over it they aggravate, because the power is there. If such things strike, take out that thought with mild and natural force. I wanted to write it very elaborately but I couldn't do it much. If you ask the questions about it I will try again.

I always appreciate your suggestions and to the best of my power allowed that to flow in. I also hold that Mission should not be commercialised in any way so it will not trade at all. I never misunderstand you and I will be grateful if you say all what you want for the good of the Mission. I did one thing that I admitted advertisements in the Magazine to compensate the loss we are incurring in the press. I also welcomed the suggestion for Life membership for the magazine but it is voluntary not compulsory.

You want to take work from Kuppuswamy or V.P.Rao in correspondence work in order to relieve you, you may do it with your valuable suggestions.

There is a custom in Northern India among Hindus that when daughters come they pay one side fare as it is thought auspicious. I not only treat your children as mine but I feel them as my own as such they have every right to demand my services as they can demand from their father. When reservation was not available in 3rd class probably I wrote to you that 1st class ticket may be purchased because I thought that it will be easy to have reservation. I had a mind to give one side fare beforehand so if Sow. Chitra would have come with 1st class ticket that should also have been paid by myself as a custom here.

You have advised Sow. Chitra to come here in the month of September. It is a very good season for travelling in this part of the country.

The people of Assam really want you to be there but since you cannot travel alone on account of old age and eye trouble I have written to them for two persons. In my opinion after operation when the doctor allows travelling then you can go. I will call you at Bombay also and Vallabhdassji is ready for that. I shall do so after when I am there. Shri Vallabhdassji wants me during Deepavali for the inauguration of his new building which is under construction.

Shri R. Seshadri had been with me for eighteen days. With good deal of my labour I could make him all right by Master's grace. You have rightly gauged about his condition. Your finding about him was that he has closed the door for grace. In rings there is no grossness at all but in his case I felt a peculiar sort of thing in the third ring. I do not find suitable words for its expression still I try. In third ring I found as if it has become very fatty and Grace of God did not cross it. Or in other words some unnaturalness was there. It took a good deal of my time in bringing it to its naturalness. After correcting it I found it necessary to put him in fourth ring.

With respect to Appaji and love to children,

Yours,
Ram Chandra

No. G 27/887/SRCM   **Shahjahanpur, U.P.**
Dated 2nd September, 1970

Personal

My dear Varadachari,

Received your affectionate letter and a telegram. When I received the telegram I prayed for the recovery of Dr. Kuppuswamy. Somehow the effect of the medicine he has taken in excess should be neutralised. All depends on God. You will be glad to know that Chi. Umesh passed the 1st group of Chartered Accountancy this year with 63% marks. He will appear in the 2nd group in May 1971. He and his wife were taken ill. His wife was running high temperature and myself has become so lazy that I have not even written to him inquiring about them. But I came to know this day from Moradabad that they are better.

My blood pressure has come to normalcy, but sometimes it is again lower. If I read half an hour my mind becomes puzzled and suffer from headache also. I remain lying almost throughout the day doing very little work. I have to do a lot of work besides the work of satsangh. I so eagerly wish that

I may be able to prepare the field for other saints after me, and I am expecting this work also very soon. I work during night as much as possible and suffer from exhaustion during day. This is one of the reason that I could not go through your manuscript from beginning to end. Still I have seen about one-third of it. Within 2 or 3 days I shall start reading the book.

Seth Vallabhdass of Bombay came here for the first time and he was thoroughly satisfied with my poor service. He had suggested out of his own accord that 4 rooms should be built for the guests in my residential quarters. I told him I shall try. Next time when he came during Basant Utsava he got the plan drafted and by an engineer who came along with him, and is my associate as well. In the month of May he sent the plan that I should construct the rooms according to it. In the beginning of July he has sent his engineer and his friend to supervise the work going to be done. They have started construction from 13th of July and it will be complete by the end of this month. He sent Rs. 25000/-for this work. Now they are all looking after the work and I have to do nothing. I have handed over the work of the account to his friend who is supervising the work. He wants to give us rooms well furnished. Only a little tension is there that the building is being built, although I do not even watch the work. Seth Vallabhdass is also constructing his house at Bombay spending 3 1/2 lakhs of rupees. He wants me to inaugurate it on 25th December, 1970. So I should be there two or three days before. He also wants that I should travel with him up to Ahmedabad in Gujarat. Mrs. Robert Koch of West Germany is coming in December here. So I shall write to her that she should come avoiding the days I shall be out. Sethji has got *Efficacy of Raja Yoga* translated in Gujarati, and got it printed. So we will not be called in October as I had written to you before.

I received the copies of symposium. I shall write to Chi. Parthasarathi to get volume II of your *Lectures on Sahaj Marg* printed and we will try our utmost to sell the remaining books of *Sahaj Marg — a New Darshan* after we exhaust them, because after the second edition the first one will not be sold.

I had already said to the preceptors of the Mission to write their experiences in Sahaj Marg method of training to have the third part of the Method of Training cyclostyled. You have put the said idea, which I was contemplating, for a seminar or symposium. I entirely agree with you. Please have it at Tirupati and inform all concerned. I want to let you know that the preceptors in Southern India are far better in condition and calibre than the Northern ones. So their experiences will be very valuable. I am sorry that I will not be able to come during this period. In this respect Seth Vallabhdass should also be invited and as far as I think he will surely attend the symposium.

I hope that you will be better in health and I will also pray.

I was thinking to have built at least two rooms for Tirupati Ashram. Now I am happy that you will be getting Rs 8000/- for this purpose.

Love to children and respects to Appaji.

Yours affectionately,
Ram Chandra

No. C 891/SRCM   Shahjahanpur, U.P.
Dated 24th September, 1970

My dear Varadachari,

Received a draft of Rs 900/- and the paper as well, which is nicely written. I had written you before that blood pressure is coming to normal, but it again went down on account of heavy pressure of work during extreme weakness. I began to take some medicine which is doing good. The other difficulty is that I developed a boil on the left leg near the hip joint at the injection seat. It is giving me trouble very much.

Since you want me there I shall be there in the 1st week of November 1970. Shri Vallabhdassji of Bombay was here for a few days. He will attend the seminar at Tirupati. So please inform him about the change of date as early as possible.

The construction of the building will be completed in a few days. I have already sent a telegram to you.

With love to children and respects to Appaji,

Yours affectionately,
Ram Chandra

Madras
Dated 18th November, 1970

My dear Varadachari,

Received your affectionate letter on 17th instant when Dr. Swamy and Shri Pullaiya Chetty have gone back. I am perfectly in agreement with your views about Dr. Kamalanathan. I shall be reaching Shahjahanpur on 20th morning starting for Delhi today. Within 10 days of my arrival at Shahjahanpur both of them will be prepared for work. Your health is the constant worry to me. May you be healthy very soon. These days please take sufficient rest and take work from Chi. Narayana.

I shall pray my Master further to do what is necessary or if He gives me your charge for a week I shall try to bring inner and out as one. Regarding your present condition there is no deficiency at all and immense power is there. There is a minor distance between inner and out and it is not the deficiency, if you view it with higher angles.

I told Umesh to search for a house but he is not getting. Moreover there is an agreement that he would live in this house and cannot leave it before one year. Anyhow he will have to live in this house. The house is very big. There is a hall and three rooms and verandah and rent is only Rs 200/- per month. It can accommodate 30 persons.

The protection we will have to give. A light thought of protection from you at times will be enough for both husband and wife and he will write to you when necessary. The spirits living here are terrified when I gave them the vision of my power bestowed upon by my Master. I do not want to harm them except what God wants although I am authorised to do it. I have to finish all this work till 11th May, 1971 for the good of the whole world.

Love to children and respect to Appaji.

Yours,
Ram Chandra

No. C 1192/SRCM   Shahjahanpur, U.P.
                          Dated 2nd December, 1970

My dear Varadachari,

Received your affectionate letter.

I reached Shahjahanpur on 23rd staying for 4 days at Delhi. Under the present state of your health you need not go to Delhi, but send somebody else who may read your paper there in the conference.

I received a letter from V. Shyamala from Varanasi that at her request the Vice Chancellor of the Hindu University wants you to speak on Sahaj Marg and will pay 1st class fare. I have written to her that it will not be possible for you to be there on account of ill health and weakness at present.

Within this week you will find by His Grace that Dr. Swamy and Pullaiya Chetty will be ready for work. I want the full names of both of them to write in the certificates.

I am worried to know that the sugar is not subsiding. So many of us have offered prayers and are doing it already for your recovery. I shall continue the prayer. Dr. Swamy is sending me your sugar report weekly. I have consulted Dr. Kashi Ram, a Naturopath. He prescribes for you vegetable of bitter gourd, curd and pumpkin (Shikakai probably is the Tamil word for Pumpkin). Chi. Narayana knows it, as I have told him also. You please take rest for 2 or 3 weeks and hand over charge of satsangh to Chi. Narayana and Kuppuswamy can also help, because I want to give you full rest for some time.

Umesh and his wife are well protected. Thanks.

Shri C.A. Rajagopalachari of Madras wants to send you the revised article read in seminar at Tirupati for print. I want that the flow should not be disturbed and words should not be changed, and also that thoughts given therein should not be left. There is no doubt that I cannot write good English, but what I write is naturally charged and effective.

Respects to Appaji and love to children.

Yours affectionately,
Ram Chandra

Tirupati
7th December, 1970

My dear and revered Gurudev,

Please accept my humble pranams. I received your affectionate letter. I do not know when your prayers will be answered. The condition continues to be about the same. The added feature is growing weakness, cough and etc. owing to cold weather.

I wrote to Mr. P. Rajagopalachari but he has written back saying that he will not be able to go to Delhi for the Congress. Therefore I request you to write to Dr. Srivastava to go to Delhi for the Congress. I am enclosing a letter which he will make him deputise for me and read and participate in the proceedings. My paper is scheduled to be read on the 20th Dec. evening 4 P.M. to 5 P.M.

I note your views about the revised paper sent by Mr. C.A. Rajagopalachari and believe that you do not want this substitution. The original paper alone will be printed in the Symposium, as it has been recorded in the tape-record.

I am glad that Master has prepared both Mr. E. Pullaiya Chetty and Dr. K. Satyalinga Swamy for being accorded provisional permission to do training work under the Master. I shall ask them to begin doing work during this week. The copy of my paper can be sent to Dr. Srivastava. I shall also be writing to the Congress about Dr. Srivastava on hearing. Chi. Gayatri is to-day applying for her final M.A. exam. May Master's blessings be with her.

With loving pranams.

Yours,
KCV

No. C 1228/SRCM Shahjahanpur, U.P.
Dated 10th December, 1970

My dear Varadachari,

Received your affectionate letter. Prayers are being offered for your recovery. May God give you speedy recovery.

Yesterday I sent you a telegram that the provisional permission has been given to Dr. Swamy and Shri Pullaiya Chetty. The permission was given on 9th December 1970. They should start work under your guidance. Certificates either I shall bring with me or will send through somebody in Utsava. Before that I should know their full names.

Mrs. Ruth Koch is coming to Bombay on 18th December, 1970 from Germany. After two days stay she will move to Madras. From there she will inform me the date and time of her arrival here at

Shahjahanpur. She will stay here for a fortnight. Mr. A. Poray of France and Mr. and Mrs. Davies of London will be reaching here on 19th January, 1971. The dates of Utsava are from 30th of January to 1st February, 1971 (morning). You can extend invitations to Tirupati abhyasis.

Mr. Poray has written to me that I should be at Madras from 15th to 20th January, 1971. Since I also wanted to see you in February at Tirupati, so this is the best opportunity. I shall inform you when it is finalised. I shall try to bring Kasturi with me if she is better in health. There is one more difficulty with her, that her sister's daughter is going to be married in January or in February, the dates are not yet finalised.

I have finally written to Mr. Rajagopalachari to search for a house for Umesh, so that we may be free from anxieties.

Love to children and respects to Appaji.

Yours,
Ram Chandra

1971

No. C 23/SRCM Shahjahanpur, U.P.
Dated 7th January, 1971

My dear Varadachari,

Received your letter. I am glad that your health is improving, but worry will be over when the percentage of sugar becomes nil. Liver action seems to be sluggish and that Dr. Kuppuswamy will decide and will give some medicine if necessary.

Mr. A. Poray of France together with Mr. and Mrs. Davies of London, are reaching here on 19th instant. Mr. Poray had written to me from France that he would be at Madras from 15th to 20th of February, 1971 and I may also be there for that period. I accepted the offer because I wanted to be at Tirupati. But finally it will be decided when he is here and you will be informed accordingly.

When I was at Tirupati last time Chi. Gayathri was remembering Kasturi very much. I had told her to bring Kasturi next time. I have therefore requested her mother again to send Kasturi along with me to Tirupati if she can be spared from attending the marriage of her sister's daughter. I feel she will be spared. She will come in Utsava with her mother and then it will be finally decided.

I am preparing Chi. Narayana and Chi. Parthasarathi for the access to the Central Region, as you wish but I shall finally decide it when I am on the spot.

Mrs. Ruth Koch is also coming from Germany round about 16th of January 71 after staying at Madras with Rajagopalachari. He will also accompany her.

I believe Dr. S.P. Srivastava must have written to you in detail about the conference at Delhi. It was really the child's dream. A very strong and spiritual man is needed for this work. Your article was appreciated and a few have taken the address also. Shri J.R.K. Raizada was also there and he was made observer.

It is very cold here nowadays on account of cold wave. My health is a bit better.

Love to children and respects to Appaji.

Yours affectionately,
Ram Chandra

Editor's Note: Dr. K.C. Varadachari passed away on 30th January, 1971 at Vellore Mission Hospital after a brief illness.

Glossary

Abhyas: Practice.

Abhyasi: Aspirant; one who practices yoga in order to achieve union with God.

Adi: Original.

Aditya: The sun.

Adityavarnam: Colour of the sun.

Ahamta: Egoism.

Aikya: Oneness or unity.

Aikya bhava: Feeling of oneness.

Ajna Chakra (or Agya Chakra): The point located between the eyebrows. Trikuti.

Aksi: Reflected condition.

Anant Ki Or: Towards Infinity

Annam: Food.

Antaryami: The God within; the in-dweller.

Anubhava: Intuitional perception or personal experience in the realm of Nature or God.

Apaan: One of the five pranas.

Arca: The idol to which puja is offered.

Arhats: One of the qualifications of Gautama the Buddha; one who is fit; one who deserves.

Asan (or Asana): Posture.

Ashanti: Disquiet; peacelessness.

Atma chakra: Heart chakra.

Atman: Soul

Atmanand: Bliss of the soul.

Avadhuta (or Avadhoota): Generally revered as elevated souls, but are really persons with spiritual aspirations who have become "fixed" at a certain level because their development has been arrested.

Avatar (or Avatara): Incarnation of a Divine soul.

Bhagavad Gita: Divine knowledge given to Arjuna by Lord Krishna in the *Mahabharata*.

Bhog (or Bhoga, or Bhogam): Process of undergoing effects, impressions, experience, enjoyment.

Brahman (or Brahm): Creator, God.

Brahmanda (or Brahmand): Astral world. Cosmos.

Brahmanda mandal (or Brahmanda desh): Mental sphere, supra-material sphere, cosmic region; sphere where everything manifests under a subtle shape before taking place in the material world.

Brahmarandhra (or Brahmarindhra): An opening in the crown of the head.

Buddhi: Intellect.

Chakra: Center of super-vital forces located in different parts of the body; figuratively called lotus.

Chit (or Chitta): Consciousness.

Chit-lake (or Cit-lake): Another name for Brahmanda Mandal.

Glossary

Dakshina: South; also offering by disciple to Guru for training received.

Darshan: Vision of someone's inner Reality.

Deepak: Lamp.

Devata: A god; Cosmic personality.

Dhi: Higher wisdom.

Dhruvagati: State of Dhruva.

Ganga yamuni: A level of transmission from Lord Krishna.

Gita: See "Bhagavad Gita".

Granthi: Knot.

Grihastha (or Grahasta): One who leads a worldly life, a householder.

Gunas: Tendencies.

Gupthdan: Secret offering.

Guru: Master, who transmits light, knowledge; a spiritual teacher.

Harijan: Children of God; the fifth caste.

Havan: Offering of sacrificial gifts for departed souls into fire.

Hridya chakra: Heart plexus.

Indriyas: Ten senses/organs of Indian philosophy, subdivided as jnana and karma indriyas. The former are five senses pertaining to perception, knowledge or wisdom, while the latter are five senses pertaining mainly to action.

Jal-dan: Prayerful offering of water.

Kantha chakra: The throat plexus.

Kapila: A sage, the founder of the Sankhya school of philosophy.

Karana sharir: Causal body.

Kasbi: Acquired condition.

Kundalini: The power which is coiled like a serpent at the base of the spine.

Laya: Dissolution.

Layavastha (or Laya avastha): The state of merging.

Manas: Psyche, mind.

Matha: Spiritual organization.

Maya: Phenomenal appearance. It is really a power of God. All manifestation or expansion which seems illusory is the play of Maya. Illusion.

Mayavic: Illusory.

Muhurtam: Auspicious moment.

Naabhi (or Nabhi): Navel.

Nischitartham: Fixation of an event to be celebrated.

Nishkam: Desireless.

Nishkam karma: Desireless action.

Nivritti: Retrogression; (destructive), returning, withdrawing.

Om santih : Invocation of peace.

Osadhih: Medicine.

Para Brahman (or Par Brahma): Indeterminate Absolute — God as the Ultimate Cause of Existence (see *Reality at Dawn*).

Para brahmanda: Supra-cosmic consciousness.

Para brahmanda mandal: Supra-cosmic region of the mind.

Glossary

Paramanus: Subtle particles, fine particles.

Pasus: Generally this refers to all living things; specifically, to animals; in very specific terms, to a cow.

Pind: Material or gross existence, that which exists in the gross or material state.

Pind desh (or Pinda desh, or Pind pradesh, or Pinda pradesh): Material sphere; the heart region.

Pithara paka: Sacrificial offering to departed ancestors.

Pongal: South Indian rice dish.

Praan (or Prana): Life; also breath.

Prabhu: Master; God.

Prabhu gati: State of, or condition experienced as, being the Master.

Prabhu-prapanna: Spiritual condition experienced as being both Master and one who has surrendered.

Prakriti: Nature.

Pranam: Respectful salutation; obeisance.

Pranahuti: Process of yogic transmission; derived from *prana* meaning life and *ahuti* meaning offering. Offering of the life force by the Guru into the disciple's heart.

Pranayama (or Pranayam): Derived from *prana* (life, vital force) and from *ayama* (to restrain). The regulation of Prana.

Prarabdha: Fate; destiny.

Purva karma: Past actions — their effect.

Raja yoga (or Raj yoga): Ancient system or science followed by the great rishis and saints which helped them to realise the Self or God. Usually used for meditative practices, as distinguished from hatha yoga.

Rajas: One of the three Gunas. Leads to activity, egoism and selfishness.

Richa: Cosmic recording of all thoughts and events.

Rig Veda: One of the *Vedas*. The others are Yajur Veda, Sama Veda and Artharvana Veda.

Rishi: Saint; seer; one who has realized Self.

Sadhak (or Sadhaka): Disciple who practices a *sadhana*.

Sadhana: Spiritual practice.

Sadhu: Religious or spiritual person.

Sahaj avastha: Natural state or condition.

Sahaj Marg: Literally: natural path, simple path.

Sahaj samadhi: Conscious state of total inner absorption.

Sahasra dal kamal: Lotus of a thousand petals.

Sahasrara: The Chakra of the thousand petalled Lotus at the crown of the head.

Samaan: Similar.

Samadhi: State in which we stay attached to Reality. In Sahaj Marg the return to the original condition, which reigned in the beginning.

Samadhi-pramana: That which is proved by going into samadhi.

Glossary

Samarth guru (or Samartha guru): A perfect guru, who possesses all the qualities. A perfectly balanced guru.

Samatva: Balanced condition.

Samskaras (or Sanskars): Impressions; grossness.

Sankalpa (or Sankalp): An act of will.

Sanskrit: Culture; also name of the ancient language of India.

Sanstha: Spiritual tradition; organisation; group.

Sanyas (or Sannyasa): Renunciation of the world, solitary life of celibacy and asceticism.

Saraswati: The goddess of learning.

Sarupyata: State in which we acquire the same form.

Sarvam khalvidam Brahma: "All this is but Brahman," a Vedic statement.

Sat: Being, Reality, Existence.

Satyodayam: The dawn of reality.

Satsangh (or Satsang): Spiritual assembly; be with.

Satsanghi: Member of a spiritual organisation.

Sensorium: The area of the brain recieving and integrating sensations from the outside world.

Shakti: Power.

Shanti: Peace.

Sheethali: One which endows with coolness.

Shraddha: Faith; devotion with faith.

Shrap: Curse.

Siddhis: Capacity to do miracles; powers.

Sikhar: Crown, top.

Sooksma sharir (or Sukshma sharir, or Sookshma sharir, or Suksham sharir, or Sukshama sharir): Astral body, subtle body.

Sthoola sharir (or Sthula sharir): Gross body.

Suklavarnam: White colour.

Suvarna: Golden.

Swadhishtan chakra (or Swadhisthana chakra): The chakra situated at the level of the genital organs.

Tamas: One of the three *gunas*. Inertness. It leads to inactivity, sloth or procrastination.

Udaan: One of the five pranas.

Upakarma: Name for 16 different religious ceremonies, one of which is the auspicious shaving of the head.

Upanayanam (or Uppanayana): Opening of the higher eye.

Upanishads: Vedantic part of the *Vedas* (*Jnana Kanda*).

Upasana (or Upasna): Devotional practice.

Utsav: Religious celebration.

Vedas: Ancient Indian scriptures, in which a superior knowledge is revealed.

Vian (or Vyana): One of the five pranas.

Virat: Cosmic.

Virat desh: See Brahmanda mandal.

Visvarupa: The cosmic form of the Lord.

Vyana: (see Vian)

Yatra: Voyage, spiritual pilgrimage.

Yoga: A system of Hindu philosophy showing means of emancipation of the soul from further migration, mainly subdivided as raja yoga and hatha yoga.

Yogi: One who practices yoga; one who achieves union with the Absolute.

Yuj (or Yuja, or Yujya): To join; to yoke.